ANNUAL REVIEW OF ANTHROPOLOGY

ANNUAL REVIEW OF
ANTHROPOLOGY

VOLUME 32, 2003

WILLIAM H. DURHAM, *Editor*
Stanford University

JEAN COMAROFF, *Associate Editor*
University of Chicago

JANE HILL, *Associate Editor*
University of Arizona

www.annualreviews.org   science@annualreviews.org   650-493-4400

ANNUAL REVIEWS
4139 El Camino Way • P.O. Box 10139 • Palo Alto, California 94303-0139

ⒶⓇ

ANNUAL REVIEWS
Palo Alto, California, USA

International Standard Serial Number: 0084-6570
International Standard Book Number: 0-8243-1932-X
Library of Congress Catalog Card Number: 72-821360

TYPESET BY TECHBOOKS, FAIRFAX, VA
PRINTED AND BOUND BY MALLOY INCORPORATED, ANN ARBOR, MI

PREFACE: Bring Back the Reading

Do you ever wonder how colleagues who take time each day for scholarly reading in a monograph or professional journal manage to pull this off? In the hurry-up world we live in, there always seem to be too many classes to teach, too many meetings to go to, too many papers to grade, and, indeed, way too many emails to answer for scholarly reading to make the daily "to do" list. And yet when you stop to think about it, we also like to think that anthropological knowledge is cumulative and selective, forever building on the best of what came before. The resulting paradox pops to the surface as fast as a cork: How can we achieve selectivity and accumulation unless we also read, and read a lot? The time has come to bring back the good ol' habit of daily scholarly reading. The time has come to rebel against the tyranny of overload to make space daily to read each other's works and discuss them. What a radical thought! We need to become more like those colleagues we all admire: For most, a small proportional drop in email will net a big percentage gain in scholarly reading.

At the *Annual Review of Anthropology*, we are committed to helping with this project to bring back reading. We endeavor to be a reader's ready resource—a scholarly oasis in the middle of a busy day, an intellectual hideout for busy people. We take seriously the charge of the Annual Reviews slogan of trying to provide an "intelligent synthesis of the scientific literature" within the field and are always eager to try new ways to better achieve that goal.

With this volume, we are pleased to announce a couple of new features that we believe provide significant resources for active readers. First, Annual Reviews has added an electronic back-volume collection to the *ARA* and indeed to all AR series. This means that anyone with an individual or institutional subscription to the *ARA* can now go online to quickly and easily access over 620 chapters from 31 previous volumes. Better still, one can also now do a "quick search" (and it *is* quick) of a particular topic in all volumes of the *ARA* series going back to 1972, or indeed in all volumes of all 29 Annual Reviews series. Either way, the result will be a list of chapters on the topic that are "just a click away"—the perfect oasis for a reader's afternoon. Indeed there is even a window where one can now "search within these results" for an ever-more-selective list of chapters (e.g., one can first search for "pastoralism," say; then "Maasai"; and on to "Ngorongoro" to be really specific). And one can have them arranged by date or by estimated relevancy. Now that is selective access! Whether one has an afternoon or only an hour, we offer just the right hideout. But there is more: Once a chapter of interest has been selected, with another click one can request a search for "citing articles" in the entire ISI Web of Science or request that *ARA* "alert me" when new chapters come out subsequently that match the same search criteria. Yes, we are trying to make it easy to be cumulative and selective.

Second, with this volume we also offer "Reviews in Advance" whereby readers can access our most recent reviews just as soon as they are accepted and edited. No longer does one have to wait until that unmistakable orange volume appears in the autumn mailbox: With an individual or institutional subscription, the latest is available online as soon as it is ready. We hope this feature will keep readers coming back to check for what is new and interesting. We also hope readers will check the *ARA* website for supplemental materials pertinent to each volume. The volume before you, for example, includes our first online supplemental video clip, so you can see for yourself some of the "Intergroup Relations in Chimpanzees" featured in Wilson and Wrangham's chapter. With all these additions and improvements—not to mention a record of six color plates—we hope that maybe, just maybe, we can lure more people away from more and more email. Bring back the healthy habit of reading!

The annual rotation of *ARA* committee membership has again this year brought a couple of changes to our roster. We gratefully bid farewell to Tim Earle (of Northwestern), who departs the Editorial Committee after five years of dedicated duty, and welcome Carla Sinopoli (of Michigan), who will help us in the general area of archaeology. Similarly, Andre Gingrich of the University of Vienna rotates off our roster of International Correspondents. Happily, one important player does not rotate off our list this year, despite abundant cause. All of us are delighted by the continuation of diligent editorial services by Production Editor Jennifer Mann, even as she expanded the family genealogy and increased her reproductive fitness. Please do not hesitate to let Jennifer, me, or any of us at the *ARA* know of your suggestions for making this publication an ever-more-seductive read.

William H. Durham
Editor

Ⓡ*Annual Review of Anthropology*
Volume 32, 2003

Contents

ERRATA

An online log of corrections to *Annual Review of Anthropology* chapters (if any, 1997 to the present) may be found at http://anthro.annualreviews.org/errata.shtml

RELATED ARTICLES

From the *Annual Review of Sociology*, Volume 29 (2003)

The Changing Picture of Max Weber's Sociology, Richard Swedberg

The Lopsided Continent: Inequality in Latin America, Kelly Hoffman and Miguel Angel Centeno

The Potential Relevances of Biology for Social Inquiry, Jeremy Freese, Jui-Chung Allen Li, and Lisa D. Wade

Population and African Society, Tukufu Zuberi, Amson Sibanda, Ayaga Bawah, and Amadou Noumbissi

ANNUAL REVIEWS is a nonprofit scientific publisher established to promote the advancement of the sciences. Beginning in 1932 with the *Annual Review of Biochemistry*, the Company has pursued as its principal function the publication of high-quality, reasonably priced *Annual Review* volumes. The volumes are organized by Editors and Editorial Committees who invite qualified authors to contribute critical articles reviewing significant developments within each major discipline. The Editor-in-Chief invites those interested in serving as future Editorial Committee members to communicate directly with him. Annual Reviews is administered by a Board of Directors, whose members serve without compensation.

Annu. Rev. Anthropol. 2003. 32:1–12
doi: 10.1146/annurev.anthro.32.061002.093257
Copyright © 2003 by Annual Reviews. All rights reserved
First published online as a Review in Advance on June 4, 2003

IN PURSUIT OF CULTURE

Ward H. Goodenough

*University Museum, University of Pennsylvania, 33rd and Spruce Streets, Philadelphia,
Pennsylvania 19104; email: whgooden@sas.upenn.edu*

Key Words   language, emics and etics, cultural change, evolution, genetic heritage

■ **Abstract**   In this brief, autobiographical account, I trace the development of my
intellectual and theoretical interests, especially as they relate to culture. How can
we account for culture's being learned by individuals and yet apparently shared by
members of a community? How do cultures as shared within communities change
and evolve? How does what we know about languages, themselves a kind of cultural
tradition, contribute to understanding culture and cultural evolution? Are processes
of cultural and linguistic evolution analogous to those in the evolution of biological
species and, if so, in what ways? How, also, do genetically based behavioral proclivities
manifest themselves in social arenas that are structured by language and culture?

The education that has informed much of my work as an anthropologist began in
my childhood, when, in the fourth grade, I had a teacher who excited me about ancient Egyptian civilization. Later grades exposed me to ancient Greece and Rome;
I was soon fascinated by the Scythian, Thracian, Celtic, and German "barbarians,"
wondering how I might learn more about them.

My secondary schooling involved six years of Latin, three years of Greek,
three years of French, and two years of German, as well as courses in European
history. In my junior year, I discovered Old Icelandic (Old Norse) literature, and I
decided that was what I wanted for my major subject in college. I opted for Cornell
University because I could take Beginning Old Icelandic there as a freshman and
not wait until my junior year for it, as at Yale or Harvard. I was more interested in
what I could learn about old Scandinavian culture, mythology, and history from
the Eddas and sagas than in the literature as literature. At Cornell I continued
Latin, Greek, and German and took courses in Middle High German, Old High
German, Gothic, and Swedish. I also had a good course in Indo-European historical
linguistics.

By the end of my junior year, it was obvious to me that there was no point in
going on for a doctorate degree in Scandinavian languages and literature. In the
late 1930s there were very few academic positions in that field, and most of them
were filled by native Scandinavians. When I talked over this situation with my
father, a professor of history at Yale, he asked me if I had thought of anthropology
as a possible field of study. I had never heard of it.

"Anthropology," I asked, "What's that?"

"Well," he said, "as I understand it, you can be interested in almost anything, and it's all right." I have repeated that to students many times since.

So, as a senior at Cornell, I took a course in cultural anthropology from Lauriston Sharp and, on my future wife's recommendation, a course in personality theory from Leonard S. Cottrell, Jr. While I was writing my term paper for the latter course, something became evident to me that has influenced my approach to cultural anthropology ever since.

I saw that psychologists had made considerable progress in developing a theory of instrumental (means-ends) learning; but they had no way to describe the cognitive content of what had been learned. They had no way to get at the contents of the "black box." Social psychologists had a good theory of the interactive process by which people acquired a sense of self; but they had no way of describing the cognitive content of that sense of self. Anthropologists were concerned with describing culture as a product of learning in social interaction. Some of that content informants could explain, but much of it they could not. Its content had to be inferred from observed behavior and from informants' applications of their cultural knowledge to specific situations. But the methods for doing this were poorly developed. How to objectify rigorously the content of what people have subjectively learned struck me as the major challenge to anthropological and behavioral science.

As a beginning graduate student at Yale, I was urged by my advisor, George Peter Murdock, to take a year-long course in phonetics and phonemics from George Trager. Edward Sapir had recently died, and Trager was a visiting lecturer in linguistics. It dawned on me halfway through this course that structural linguists had developed a rigorous method for describing the content of what speakers of a language must learn in order to speak in a manner that fellow speakers find acceptable, and this at the most basic level, namely phonology and morphology. The method was that of systematic contrastive analysis. Linguistics, classed as a humanity, was revealed to me as the most advanced of the behavioral sciences.

Basic to this method was making a transcribed record of speech that was fine-grained enough phonetically to catch all of the phonetic contrasts that made a significant difference to a language's speakers. The categories of sound that made such a significant difference were the language's phonemes. Phonetic differences that did not have contrastive value for speakers were allophonic variants of the same phoneme. An alphabetic system of writing required a symbol (a letter) for each phoneme. Morphology and syntax involved the ordering of phonemes into meaningful forms and of combinations of forms into words and words into phrases, clauses, and sentences. To describe all of this was to make what in current jargon would be called an emic description of a language.

This set me to thinking about social behavior. In every human society people must learn how to conduct themselves in ways that are acceptable to their fellows. People articulate what must be learned as rules of conduct and lists of "dos and don'ts." But much of what they learn remains subjective. They cannot explain to someone else the working principles for which they come to have a feel any more than they can explain to others the working principles of their language's grammar. They can apply their subjective knowledge to correct people in specific situations, but they cannot explain the underlying understanding by which they make their immediate judgments.

Learning how to behave, it seemed to me, must be much like learning how to speak. For culturally appropriate behavior to be readily learnable, its content had to be reducible to organizational principles analogous to those of a language's grammar. I presumed, therefore, that the methodological strategy of descriptive linguistics should be applicable to getting at those underlying principles. So I proposed as my doctoral dissertation project an exploration into the possibility of formulating a "grammar of social behavior" while doing ethnographic fieldwork.

While at Yale, I had the opportunity to study under Bronislaw Malinowski in 1940–1941 and, on my return to Yale after World War II, under Ralph Linton in 1946–1947. I took courses also from G.P. Murdock, Clellan Ford, John Dollard, and Cornelius Osgood and archaeology courses from Irving Rouse and Wendell Bennett. From November 1941 to December 1945, I served in the Army, where I had the good fortune to work for three years doing attitude and opinion research in the Research Branch of the Army's Information and Education Division, under the sociologists Samuel Stouffer and Leonard S. Cottrell, Jr. There I learned about sampling and questionnaire survey methods, and, most importantly for me, I learned Guttman scaling, which led to my first publication (Goodenough 1944).

My dissertation fieldwork was done in 1947 in Chuuk (formerly Truk) in Micronesia. I was part of a team that went there under the National Research Council program called the Coordinated Investigation of Micronesian Anthropology (CIMA), funded by the Office of Naval Research. Our team, led by Murdock, also included Isidore Dyen, as linguist, and fellow graduate students Thomas Gladwin and Frank LeBar. Under our division of labor, LeBar (1964) worked on the traditional material culture, Gladwin on the life cycle, life histories, and personality and culture (Gladwin & Sarason 1953), while I was assigned social behavior and religion. Murdock took on social organization, but he had me working with him because he was having trouble with the Chuukese language and I was making good progress in it. I learned a great deal about fieldwork from him in the process. After he left, I continued working on social organization as well as my other topics (Goodenough 1951).

In accordance with my linguistic (emic) methodological approach, I found that study of the traditional property system required learning what one needed to know to do a search of title in the system. This required knowing the different kinds of entitlements individuals and corporate groups could have, the transactions that could occur with these entitlements, and the new entitlements that could result from the different possible transactions. It also required knowing what were the rights and duties associated with each of these entitlements. As far as I know, the resulting ethnography stands almost alone as an account of how a property system is culturally constructed and actually works (Goodenough 1951). My emic approach led me also to try to learn what were the choices that the Chuukese saw available to them in making decisions about marital residence. These choices could be mapped into the standard anthropological (etic) categories, but these categories did not describe their choices. Similar experience in fieldwork in Kiribati and New Britain led me to formulate the need for emic description in doing ethnography and at the same time attend to how the emic formulations could be mapped into the etic concepts needed for comparative, cross-cultural research (Goodenough 1956a). Some years later these considerations led me to examine anthropology's etic concepts in relation to marriage, family, kin groups, and kinship terminology with the object of refining them for comparative purposes (Goodenough 1970a).

Writing my ethnographic account of Chuuk's social organization, I encountered a problem involving the order in which things were to be described. To describe kin groups seemed to require describing property first, but describing property seemed to require describing kin groups first. The problem resolved itself when I saw that both entitlements and kin groups depended on property transactions. Describing transaction first made it possible to treat entitlements and kin groups as emergent forms resulting from previous transactions. An orderly, linear rather than circular account of social organization thus became possible. From this I learned that customs and institutions were not only largely interconnected and to be understood in terms of one another, as Malinowski (1922) demonstrated long ago, but also that the understanding of some was dependent on the understanding of others. Finding the logical starting points for orderly description of interconnected cultural systems was something requiring attention for an emic ethnographic account (Goodenough 1951).

With an eye to my premise about underlying principles specific to a particular culture's ordering of social relationships, I was able to come up with two empirically based examples from my fieldwork in Truk in 1947. One of these examples involved the application of contrastive analysis to the sets of genealogical relationships that were designated by the same kinship terms to arrive at a set of cross-cutting criteria that allowed me to use every kinship term correctly by informants' standards in every relationship to which the term denotatively applied. Having the genealogical connections among all the community's members already recorded, I went through the roster of the community's members and listed for one informant what kinship term, if any, I predicted he would apply to every person in the community. Subsequently, I had him say what kin term he applied as I called the roll of the community's members. He called them just as I predicted, except for one sublineage whose members I had predicted as his kin but who he said were not kin. When I inquired why he classed them as not kin, he confided that they once were his kin, as I had predicted, but because he had been caught in a love affair with one of them, in violation of incest taboos, the community had decreed that henceforth he and that sublineage were no longer kin. The unexpected exceptions to how one thinks things work can be illuminating.

The other example involved the distribution of obligations and taboos in different social relationships. Through the application of Guttman scale analysis I found that distribution of some of these was a function of deference, marking different degrees of deference. Others were a function of sexual distance. There was, indeed, something akin to a grammatical ordering of the distributions of dos and don'ts in different social identity relationships according to a limited set of variables of which these distributions were functions.

Preliminary accounts of these findings appeared in my published dissertation (Goodenough 1951). Subsequently, I had the opportunity to present them more fully in articles. Presentation of my semantic analysis of Chuukese kinship terms under the title "Componential Analysis and the Study of Meaning" (1956b) led to adoption of the term componential analysis (a term I had borrowed from linguistics) by fellow anthropologists for this method of contrastive analysis of the complementary distribution of words over fields of denotata. In the same issue of *Language*, Floyd Lounsbury published a similar approach to the semantic analysis of kinship terms, also inspired by the linguistic method of contrastive analysis. I subsequently explored applying the method to the analysis of other kinships systems (1964, 1965a, 1967, 1968). Important work along these lines in regard to color categories and the cultural classifications of plants and animals was subsequently conducted by fellow anthropologists (Berlin & Kay 1969, Berlin et al. 1974, Witkowski & Brown 1977, MacLaury 1997). And Lounsbury (1964) went on to adapt Chomsky's (1957) method of transformational grammatical analysis to the semantics of kinship terms as well.

My early analysis of the distributions of dos and don'ts in different social identity relationships subsequently led me to reappraise the concepts of "status" and "role" (1965b) and to use my data from Chuuk (Truk) to suggest a method for systematically describing a cultural "grammar"of social behavior. I was able to illustrate how knowing such a grammar illuminated behaviors that were in violation of it, providing a way to measure the seriousness of breaches and even insight into what could be understood as incidents of what we call poetic justice. I then undertook to make a more systematic application of the method in a follow-up study in Chuuk in 1964–1965, when I collected a large inventory of identity relationships and recorded how one informant applied his understanding of how a large number of different kinds of behaviors should be distributed between different pairs of egos and alters in those relationships. The idea was then to sort the distributions into sets that were functions of the same variable and therefore conformed to a Guttman scale. As I gathered the data, it became evident that the distributions were not confined to different Guttman scales. There clearly were scale-like patterns, but they exhibited complexities that I had not anticipated. Unfortunately for me, there seemed to be no computer program that was designed to do what I wanted, so the data sat until this past year, when Kimball Romney indicated he would like to see what he could do with them.

In 1952, I was invited by Leonard S. Cottrell, Jr., of the Russell Sage Foundation, and Alexander Leighton to prepare a book of guidelines for people engaged in what was then called "community development" in cross-cultural settings. Russell Sage Foundation had already published two books of case studies (Spicer 1952, Paul 1955), and my book was to be a companion to them. The book, with my wife's valuable help, grew into a discussion of the nature of culture and the social psychological processes involved in cultural and social change, especially when such change was being engineered by outside change agents (Goodenough 1963a). Why on some occasions do people welcome change and on others resist it? Why, when people begin to take charge of their own change processes, do outside agents of change so often find themselves dismayed? Does what we know about the process of individual identity change provide any insight into the process of collective identity change? How can we use ethnography to forecast the ways in which an introduced change will set in motion ramifying effects and what those ramifying effects will be? What relation do programmatic efforts at change have to the cultural revitalization process described by Wallace (1956)? What did I as an anthropologist have to say about such questions? Trying to address such questions was challenging, indeed. The book took eleven years to write instead of the two initially projected.

In the course of writing it, I was able to refine my developing understanding of how to think about culture in the classic anthropological sense that it consists of what humans learn as members of societies, especially in regard to the expectations their fellow members have of them in the context of living and working together. Culture, in this sense, did not consist of patterns of recurring events in a community, though in practice it was often taken to be such and was argued by cultural materialists to be only such (e.g., Harris 1964). Rather, as something learned, culture was like a language, which is not what its speakers say but what they need to know to communicate acceptably with one another, including constructing utterances never made before yet immediately intelligible to others. Learned in the same way culture is learned, language was thus to be seen as one kind of cultural system (Goodenough 1957, 1981a).

This led me to a definition of culture that has guided me ever since, consisting of (*i*) criteria for categorizing phenomena as meaningful stimuli, (*ii*) criteria for deciding what can be, (*iii*) criteria for deciding how one feels about things (preferences and values), (*iv*) criteria for deciding what to do about things, (*v*) criteria for deciding how to go about doing things, and (*vi*) the skills needed to perform acceptably (Goodenough 1963a, pp. 258–59).

Because it consists of what each individual has made out of his or her experiences, what is learned must be located in people's individual minds and bodies. It follows that no two people have exactly the same criteria or exactly the same understanding of what they perceive to be the expectations (the criteria and standards) of those with whom they have dealings. As long as the variation in their individual knowledge and understandings does not interfere with their ability to interact readily with one another, they have the sense that they share their knowledge and understandings and therefore have a common culture. Just as no two people have exactly the same way of speaking what they perceive as their common language, so no two members of a community have exactly the same understanding of what they perceive to be their community's way of doing things, its culture. Thus people see communities as having languages and cultures, but, in fact, these are collections of individual understandings of what the languages and cultures consist of. As long as these differences do not get in the way of people living and working together (sometimes, indeed, they do), people ignore them and may be unaware of them. We can legitimately speak of a community's language and culture, just as we can legitimately speak of biological species or subspecies (Goodenogh 1981a). The collection of individual understandings comprising a community's culture are analogous to the collection of individual genotypes comprising a breeding group's or deme's gene pool. The cultural variance within a community and the genetic variance within a deme are considerably less than the variance across communities and across demes. Most individuals, moreover, are likely to have knowledge of more than one cultural or subcultural tradition as a result of interactions with different sets of others in his own and other societies (Goodenough 1976).

For any community, then, it is more precise to speak not of its culture but of its cultural makeup: the content of its culture pool and the distribution of that content, subject matter by subject matter, among the community's various subgroups as well as individuals (Goodenough 1981a, p. 112). An ethnographer seeks to develop his own understanding or version of that community's culture. If it enables him to grasp the meaning of events in the way the community's members grasp them, then his account of that culture is a valid one but not the only possible valid one. It is a model of what one needs to know to function acceptably as a member of that community in the same way that a grammar and dictionary of a language aim to provide a model of what one needs to know in order to speak the language acceptably.

This way of understanding culture opens up insights into cultural evolution and cultural change. Individuals' understandings of their society's culture change through time. They are different, moreover, with each new generation of learners. Thus there are constant small mutations in these understandings, each mutation making a small difference (and sometimes a big difference) in the content of a community's culture pool. As new generations come along, learning at first from parents and other seniors and then, very importantly, from peers, new mutations diffuse across the channels of communication and social interaction. In the course of ethnographic description we create portraits of communities' cultures, which are, indeed, informative and useful; but these portraits, like snapshots, do not reveal the ongoing processes that are constantly affecting the contents of these communities' culture pools.

These insights led me to become interested not only in cultural evolution as a process but also in cultural phylogeny and the methodological problem of recognizing cognate cultural traditions (Goodenough 1997a, 1999). It became evident to me that a community's cultural makeup as a whole, though changing through time in response to a number of different processes, was not the basic unit of cultural evolution. Discrete bundles of how to do things, such as build a house or celebrate a marriage, become relatively distinct traditions as they are passed down across generations. These traditions are the main units of cultural evolution and change. Thus the community meeting house, its organization, and protocol in Kiribati (Gilbert Islands) constitute a tradition that was introduced by Samoan immigrants several centuries ago (Maude 1963). As such it has been integrated into the makeup of Kiribati culture, but it is cognate phylogenetically with the tradition in Samoa relating to its community meeting house, the *fono*. The Kiribati and Samoan versions of what was once a common ancestral tradition have diverged over time, but they remain cognate traditions. Other traditions in Kiribati and Samoa have different evolutionary histories, though they too may be more distantly related phylogenetically.

Traditions are tied to activities. When I was trying to formulate a method for predicting the probable ramifying effects, if any, of an introduced cultural or technological change, activities were the key. I found that Malinowski's (1944) model of the structure of an institution, appropriately elaborated, was perfectly suited to the structure of an activity. By taking inventory of all a community's activities that involved more than one person and seeing how they were structurally interrelated (e.g., involving the same standing groups), it would be possible then to posit any change and game out its structural effects. Retrospective analyses of changes in the availability of traditional outrigger sailing canoes in Kiribati (the Gilbert Islands) (Goodenough 1963a, pp. 337–43; 1963b) and the introduction of outboard motors in Kapingamarangi in Micronesia (Lieber 1994) illustrated the utility of this approach. Looking at a community's cultural organization of activities proved very useful also, in describing the political organization of a stateless society (Chowning & Goodenough 1966). The social organization of that community's many activities followed one or another of a very few designs. Lines of authority were clearly revealed in these designs.

A long-standing concern of anthropologists has been the search for cultural universals. In thinking about what, in practice, we treated as cross-cultural categories for comparative purposes, I saw that these were not, in themselves, specific to any given culture as a part of its emic makeup. In emic terms the categories of one culture were not exactly the same as those of any other. For comparative purposes we map these emic categories into functional types. Thus we map particular emic categories of containers into bowls, jars, etc., or particular emic criteria for residence choices in marriage into patrilocal, matrilocal, etc. Then we say that containers are cultural universals, instead of saying that in all cultures there are things that people use as containers, recognizing that the universal is a functional category rather than an emic cultural one. The common denominator of cultures is thus to be seen as composed of functional categories, such as shelter, food quest, food preparation, socialization of children, treatment of illness, disposal of the dead, religion, and so on (Goodenough 1981b). The *Outline of Cultural Materials* gives a detailed list of categories that are largely of this kind (Murdock et al. 1967).

Seeing religion as a functional category struck me as having important theoretical implications. Definitions of religion have always centered on belief in supernatural or spirit beings. Atheists were presumably without religion, yet the great salvation-promising movement of the twentieth century was atheistic communism. People were converted to it as to other visionary religions. Salvation is, of course, the achievement of an ideal state of being, whether in life or after death, a transformation of self whether through individual endeavor or through collective effort to transform society. When we stop to look at what the concerns are that people are addressing through prayer, ritual, magic, etc., we find that they have to do with the state of their selves and the selves of others who matter to them, including the state of the groups with which people identify themselves. What is addressed is the maintenance of selves as people wish them to be, the repair of damage to selves (as from pollution and illness) and the enhancement of selves (as with rites of passage and rites to earn merit). These rites may be elaborate or they may be as simple as avoiding stepping on the cracks in the sidewalk or carrying a rabbit's foot. Our folk wisdom recognizes this when we speak of people doing their morning exercises religiously or making a religion of their business. A customary practice that is readily abandoned in favor of another lacks religious value for people. Their selves are not threatened by it. The greater the emotional distress, exhibited by the suggestion that a custom be abandoned, the greater the religious (i.e., self-maintaining) value it has for those who are distressed. The equivalent of children's security blankets are legion. Horace Minor recognized this years ago with his much-cited article "Body Ritual Among the Nacirema" (1956).

Looked at functionally in this way, the ethnographic description of a people's religious life requires examining all of their institutions and customary practices with an eye to how they function religiously, if at all, and for whom. This is no different from what we must do when describing a people's economic life or their political life. The same institution may function economically, politically, and religiously. I followed this approach to describing a people's religious life in my recent book on pre-Christian religious tradition in Chuuk (Goodenough 2002). I was able to do this because of the availability of psychological test materials that provided a profile of the major concerns that were generated by the way people experienced themselves in the framework of Chuuk's social culture (Gladwin & Sarason 1953).

In recent years I have become interested in looking at how genetically programmed behavioral tendencies from our animal heritage are manifested in the complex symbolic world stemming from language and culture in which we humans exist. A surprise to me in this regard was the realization that the bristling response we call moral outrage is the human equivalent of what ethologists refer to as the territorial response (Lorenz 1963; Ardrey 1966, p. 3). Among humans, the rights, privileges, and immunities they have in their various social identity relationships are symbolic territories. Trespass on these territories evokes the bristling umbrage of the animal territorial response (Goodenough 1997b). In this regard, it is evident in the ethnographic record that there is no human society whose culture of interpersonal relationships does not involve the definition of kinds of social identities and kinds of possible inter-identity relationships. These relationships are organized in terms of what are formalized in jural relationships as the complementary conceptual pairs, right versus duty, no right versus privilege, power versus liability, and no power versus immunity (Hohfeld 1919), as was observed years ago by Hoebel (1954). Of these, right and duty are fundamental, the other concepts being derivable from them.

Rights and duties are affected by what among the four universal interactive modes described by Fiske (1991) is appropriate to the context of a social interaction. These modes are communal sharing; authority ranking or priority ranking (the cultural ordering of dominance); equality matching (everyone getting or owing exactly the same); and market pricing (negotiation and contractual arrangement). All but equality matching appear to be present in rudimentary form in chimpanzee interactions (de Waal 1989, 1991, 1994). Although these modes are present in all human societies, the subject matters to which they apply and the relative valuation placed on them vary considerably cross-culturally, again illustrating the complicated ways in which behavioral proclivities already present in higher primates are elaborated and transformed by language and culture. People unconsciously shift from mode to mode in accordance with their cultural grammar of social interaction in the same way they compose grammatical sentences (Goodenough 1997b).

I have also had occasion to explore how other proclivities and cognitive capabilities present in other higher primates required only the addition of language and, with it, the ability to state propositions to produce the ability to formulate beliefs (Goodenough 1990).

In conclusion, I should say that my early interest in languages has remained with me over the years, especially in historical linguistics. The methods for reconstructing the ancestral vocabularies of languages ancestral to genetically related languages, like those in the Indo-European and Austronesian language phyla, produce insights into prehistoric cultures that complement the data from archaeology. This interest has led me to examine problems relating to proto-Indo-European culture (Goodenough 1970b) and Proto-Austronesian origins (Chang & Goodenough 1996). It has also led me to the reconstruction of the proto-languages of two subfamilies in the Oceanic group within the Austronesian phylum (Goodenough 1997c, Bender et al. 2003). This interest is what I expect to continue to pursue in the future.

The *Annual Review of Anthropology* is online at http://anthro.annualreviews.org

LITERATURE CITED

Ardrey R. 1966. *The Territorial Imperative.* New York: Atheneum

Bender B, Goodenough W, Hsu R, Jackson F, Marck J, et al. 2003. Proto-Micronesian reconstructions. *Ocean. Linguist.* 42:In press

Berlin B, Breedlove D, Raven P. 1974. *Principles of Tzeltal Plant Classification.* New York: Academic

Berlin B, Kay P. 1969. *Basic Color Categories.* Berkeley: Univ. Calif. Press

Chang K-C, Goodenough W. 1996. Archaeology of southeastern coastal China and its bearing on the Austronesian homeland. In *Prehistoric Settlement of the Pacific,* ed. W Goodenough, pp. 36–56. Philadelphia: Am. Philos. Soc.

Chomsky N. 1957. *Syntactic Structures.* Janua Linguarum, Ser. Minor No. 4. The Hague: Mouton

Chowning A, Goodenough W. 1966. Lakalai political organization. *Anthropol. Forum* 1:412–73

de Waal F. 1989. Food sharing and reciprocal

obligations among chimpanzees. *J. Hum. Evol.* 18:433–59

de Waal F. 1991. The chimpanzee's sense of social reciprocity and its relation to the human sense of justice. *Am. Behav. Sci.* 34:335–49

de Waal F. 1994. Sex differences in the formation of coalitions among chimpanzees. In *Primate Evolution*, ed. G Schubert, R Masters, pp. 128–40. Lanham, MD: Univ. Press Am.

Fiske A. 1991. *Structures of Social Life: the Four Elementary Forms of Human Relations* New York: Free Press

Gladwin T, Sarason S. 1953. *Truk: Man in Paradise.* Viking Fund Publ. Anthropol. No. 20. New York: Wenner-Gren Found. Anthropol. Res.

Goodenough W. 1944. A technique for scale analysis. *Educ. Psychol. Meas.* 4:179–90

Goodenough W. 1951. *Property, Kin and Community on Truk.* New Haven, CT: Yale Univ. Publ. Anthropol. No. 46

Goodenough W. 1956a. Residence rules. *Southwest. J. Anthropol.* 12:22–37

Goodenough W. 1956b. Componential analysis and the study of meaning. *Language* 32:195–216

Goodenough W. 1957. Cultural anthropology and linguistics. In *Report of the Seventh Annual Round Table Meeting on Linguistics and Language Study*, ed. P Garvin, pp. 167–73. Washington, DC: Georgetown Univ. Press

Goodenough W. 1963a. *Cooperation in Change: an Anthropological Approach to Community Development.* New York: Russell Sage Found.

Goodenough W. 1963b. Ecological and social change in the Gilbert Islands. *Proc. Ninth Pac. Sci. Congr.: Anthropol. Soc. Sci.* 3:167–69. Bangkok

Goodenough W. 1964. Componential analysis of Könkämä Lapp kinship terminology. In *Explorations in Cultural Anthropology*, ed. W Goodenough, pp. 221–38. New York: McGraw-Hill

Goodenough W. 1965a. Yankee kinship terminology: a problem in componential analysis. In *Formal Semantic Analysis*, ed. E Hammel,

pp. 259–87. Spec. issue of *Am. Anthropol.* 67(5, pt. 2)

Goodenough W. 1965b. Rethinking 'status' and 'role': toward a general model of the cultural organization of social relationships. In *The Relevance of Models for Social Anthropology*, ed. M Banton, pp. 1–24. ASA Monogr. 1. London: Tavistock

Goodenough W. 1967. Componential analysis. *Science* 156:1203–98

Goodenough W. 1968. Componential analysis. *Int. Encycl. Soc. Sci.* 3:186–92

Goodenough W. 1970a. *Description and Comparison in Cultural Anthropology.* Chicago: Aldine

Goodenough W. 1970b. The evolution of nomadism and Indo-European origins. In *Indo-European and Indo-Europeans*, ed. G Cardona, H Hoenigswald, A Senn, pp. 253–65. Philadelphia: Univ. Penn. Press

Goodenough W. 1976. Multiculturalism as the normal human experience. *Anthropol. Educ. Q.* 7(4):4–6

Goodenough W. 1981a. *Culture, Language, and Society.* Menlo Park, CA: Cummings. 2nd ed.

Goodenough W. 1981b. Some reflections on the common denominator of cultures. *Soc. Cross-Cult. Res. Newsl.* 8(1):10–18

Goodenough W. 1990. Evolution of the human capacity for beliefs. *Am. Anthropol.* 92:597–612

Goodenough W. 1997a. Phylogenetically related cultural traditions. *Cross-Cult. Res.* 31:16–26

Goodenough W. 1997b. Moral outrage: territoriality in human guise. *Zygon* 32:5–27

Goodenough W. 1997c. Proto-Kimbe: a new analysis. *Ocean. Lingist.* 36:247–311

Goodenough W. 1999. Outline of a framework for a theory of cultural evolution. *Cross-Cult. Res.* 33:84–107

Goodenough W. 2002. *Under Heaven's Brow: Pre-Christian Religious Tradition in Chuuk.* Philadelphia: Am. Philos. Soc.

Harris M. 1964. *The Nature of Cultural Things.* New York: Random House

Hoebel E. 1954. *The Law of Primitive Man.* Cambridge, MA: Harvard Univ. Press

Hohfeld W. 1919. *Fundamental Legal Concepts*. New Haven: Yale Univ. Press

LeBar F. 1964. *The Material Culture of Truk*. New Haven, CT: Yale Univ. Publ. Anthropol. No. 68

Lieber M. 1994. *More Than a Living: Fishing and the Social Order on a Polynesian Atoll*. Boulder, CO: Westview

Lorenz K. 1963. *On Aggression*. New York: Harcourt, Brace, and World

Lounsbury F. 1956. A semantic analysis of the Pawnee kinship usage. *Language* 32:158–94

Lounsbury F. 1964. A formal account of the Crow- and Omaha-type kinship terminologies. In *Explorations in Cultural Anthropology: Essays in Honor of George Peter Murdock*, ed. W Goodenough, pp. 351–93. New York: McGraw-Hill

MacLaury R. 1997. *Color and Cognition in Mesoamerica*. Austin: Univ. Tex. Press

Malinowski B. 1922. *Argonauts of the Western Pacific*. London: Routledge

Malinowski B. 1944. *A Scientific Theory of Culture*. Chapel Hill, NC: Univ. North Carol. Press

Maude H. 1963. *The Evolution of the Gilbertese boti: an Ethnohistorical Interpretation*. Memoir No. 35. Wellington, New Zealand: Polynesian Soc.

Minor H. 1956. Body ritual among the Nacirema. *Am. Anthropol.* 59:503–7

Murdock G, Ford C, Hudson A, Kennedy R, Simmons L, Whiting W. 1967. *Outline of Cultural Materials*. New Haven, CT: Hum. Relat. Area Files. 4th rev. ed.

Paul B, ed. 1955. *Health, Culture, and Community: Case Studies of Public Reactions to Health Programs*. New York: Russell Sage Found.

Spicer E, ed. 1952. *Human Problems in Technological Change: a Casebook*. New York: Russell Sage Found.

Wallace A. 1956. Revitalization movements. *Am. Anthropol.* 58:264–81

Witkowski S, Brown C. 1977. An explanation of color nomenclature universals. *Am. Anthropol.* 79:50–57

Annu. Rev. Anthropol. 2003. 32:13–40
doi: 10.1146/annurev.anthro.32.061002.093137

CONTEXT, CULTURE, AND STRUCTURATION IN THE LANGUAGES OF AUSTRALIA

Nicholas Evans

*Department of Linguistics and Applied Linguistics, University of Melbourne, Parkville,
Australia 3010; email: n.evans@linguistics.unimelb.edu.au*

Key Words   grammaticalization, semanticization, Australian languages, language
ideology, coevolution

■ **Abstract**   Using Australian languages as examples, cultural selection is shown to
shape linguistic structure through invisible hand processes that pattern the unintended
outcomes (structures in the system of shared linguistic norms) of intentional actions
(particular utterances by individual agents).
    Examples of the emergence of culturally patterned structure through use are drawn
from various levels: the semantics of the lexicon, grammaticalized kin-related categories, and culture-specific organizations of sociolinguistic diversity, such as moiety
lects, "mother-in-law" registers, and triangular kin terms. These phenomena result from
a complex of diachronic processes that adapt linguistic structures to culture-specific
concepts and practices, such as ritualization and phonetic reduction of frequently used
sequences, the input of shared cultural knowledge into pragmatic interpretation, semanticization of originally context-dependent inferences, and the input of linguistic
ideologies into the systematization of lectal variants. Some of these processes, such as
the emergence of subsection terminology and moiety lects, operate over speech communities that transcend any single language and can only be explained if the relevant
processes take the multilingual speech community as their domain of operation.
    Taken together, the cases considered here provide strong evidence against nativist
assumptions that see linguistic structures simply as instantiations of biologically given
"mentalese" concepts already present in the mind of every child and give evidence in
favor of a view that sees individual language structures as also conditioned by historical
processes, of which functional adaptation of various kinds is most important. They
also illustrate how, in the domain of language, stable socially shared structures can
emerge from the summed effects of many communicative micro-events by individual
agents.

INTRODUCTION

The nexus between language, culture, and thought has seen a revival of research
interest in the last decade. Most research efforts have concentrated on the influence
of language on habitual thought, mustering new evidence that language structure
can shape cognition (Lucy 1997, Levinson 2000).

0084-6570/03/1021-0013$14.00   **13**

This neo-Whorfian renaissance has not been accompanied by a body of work on the complementary question: By what mechanisms do cultural preoccupations find their way into linguistic structures?[1] After all, the language structures now being found to play a role in shaping thought have to come from somewhere. Whorf's predecessors had long assumed that "the form of the language will be moulded by the state of the culture" (Boas 1966, p. 63), but the processes that would achieve this are not being incorporated into new developments in linguistics, which are beginning to theorize how structure emerges from use.

The universalizing bias of this new body of approaches has obscured the way language and culture can be viewed as coevolving systems, with cultural practice selecting for particular patterns of structuration within the language system. That is, in addition to coevolution on the more widely discussed twin tracks of cultural and genetic transmission (Durham 1991, Tomasello 1999), there is coevolution at a second level, between the dual lines of cultural and linguistic transmission. For example, a cultural innovation, such as generational moieties within the kinship system, may end up feeding into a linguistic innovation, such as the grammatical-ization of a "different generational moiety" category within the system of pronouns, as discussed below.

This article reviews two strands of research in a way that illuminates these issues. I first draw on recent research within general linguistic theory on the emer-gence of linguistic structure. Then I review work on the indigenous languages of Australia, focusing on three levels that offer a particularly sharp challenge to universalizing approaches to the emergence of structure: lexical polysemy (see Semanticization and the Emergence of Lexical Polysemy), grammar (see Culture Selecting for Grammatical Structure), and lectal systematization (see Language Ideologies and Lectal Systematization). At each of these, cultural selection ap-plies in a rather different way. I conclude by touching on the broader implications of culture-specific structuration for currently dominant universalizing theories of human linguistic competence and ways in which language documentation needs to be extended before this approach can move beyond the programmatic.

STRUCTURATION AS AN INVISIBLE-HAND PROCESS

Evolution, Adaptation and the Emergence of Linguistic Structure

There is increasing convergence among linguists that evolutionary approaches are valuable in explaining not only the evolution of language and the human language faculty in early hominids but also the ongoing evolution of language structures from use. The question "Why are languages the way they are?" on such approaches translates into "How do languages become the way they are?,"

---

[1]An exception is Hill & Hill (1998), who discuss a case where culture, in the guise of Hopi matrilineal social organization, has reshaped the inherited structure of noun categorization.

refocusing explanation from structure itself to structure-generating process. There are two periodicities to this program.

The first underlies the original evolution of the language capacity and in its more plausible form sees a coevolutionary intertwining of biological evolution, in the form of increased neurological capacity to handle language, and cultural evolution, in the form of increased complexity in the language(s) used by early hominids. Both evolutionary tracks thus urge each other on by positive feedback, as upgraded neurological capacity allows more complex and diversified language systems to evolve, which in turn select for more sophisticated neurological platforms. A crucial goal of coevolutionary approaches, then, is to account both for the capacity of humans to learn a wide variety of language structures and for the possibility of many distinct language "softwares" evolving against the same neurological hardware. As Levinson (2000, p. 5) puts it, "we are built to handle the diversity: language is a bio-cultural hybrid. The way to naturalize this duality of traditions, genetic and cultural, is through the theory of coevolution."

The second periodicity concerns the patterned variation in modern tongues, now all spoken by groups assumed to have the same neurological capacity, and focuses on how the kaleidoscopic reshufflings of linguistic structure result from interactions between communicative, cognitive, and processing constraints, which, against the background of differing cultural emphases, reshape existing systems in the context of use.

In both, notions of evolutionary theory are applied to the emergence of linguistic structure from use. Following Keller (1994, 1998), language structure is seen to emerge as an unintentional product of intentional communicative acts, such as the wish to communicate or to sound (or not sound) like other speakers. The way language structures emerge, in other words, is analogous neither to structures in the natural world (such as eyes or wings), which arise without any intention at all, nor to products of intentional human design, such as cathedrals or symphonies. Rather, like other "objects of the third kind," such as shortcut paths across lawns, they arise as invisible hand processes operating on what speakers produce as they strive to achieve other goals: Speakers do not plan to create accusative cases, pluperfects, or ejective stops, but they do intend to communicate clearly, locate what they describe in time, or sound like (or unlike) particular target groups. Observed structures arise, through time, by summing the outcomes of many communicative acts by individuals (Haspelmath 1999).

Tomasello (1999, p. 527), discussing the ratchet-like way in which cultural transmission allows the gradual accumulation of cognitive complexity, emphasizes the way changes occur on two timescales: cultural/historical and individual/ontogenetic. A major preoccupation of functionalist approaches has been to map out the complex temporal subprocesses by which grammar emerges, as frequently used patterns sediment into conventionalized patterns (Bybee 2000). The terminology developed within functionalist approaches typically focuses on one or another level of linguistic structure, at which "a large number of micro-events give rise to a macro-structure in a surprising way" (Haspelmath 1999, p. 204): lexicalization, semanticization, grammaticalization, phonologization, etc. To abstract away from level-specific terminology, I use the general term structuration, originally coined by the sociologist Anthony Giddens (1984) in a somewhat different context.

Within linguistics, functionalists generally see themselves as ideologically opposed to the nativist position articulated by Fodor (1975) and Chomsky (1980), which assumes a hard-wired language of thought and a universal grammar that generates constrained diversity through a number of parameter settings against a background of fixed principles. Instead, functionalist approaches argue against the need for a universal grammar and see similarities across languages arising from general constraints on language use. The preoccupation with offering an alternative explanation for these "linguistic universals," however, has led to a focus on how the limits on surface diversity can be explained though the constraining effects on language change of universals of communicative architecture, shared constraints on our species-specific vocal apparatus, and shared human cognitive structures such as biases on metaphor-formation stemming from similar patterns of embodiment. But the cost of this focus has been the bracketing out of possible culture-specific effects on language structure.

There is nothing inherent in this emerging new paradigm, though, that requires cultural selection to be ignored in this way. In fact, by zooming from our first-level double track of genetic and cultural transmission to a second-level double track of culture (in general) and language (as part of culture, but transmitted to some extent independently), we can develop a more anthropologically satisfying coevolutionary approach better able to account for the true diversity of the world's linguistic structures.

Getting Cultural Selection into the Emergence of Structure

Two key mechanisms postulated by functionalists have the clear potential to show how culture can select for the emergence of structure.

The first mechanism concerns the impact of frequency of use on language structure: Grammars code best what speakers do most (Du Bois 1987), and

> repeated patterns become part of 'grammar' in terms of ritualization, showing that the effects that repeated stimuli or repeated action has on an organism—automatization, habituation [. . .]—are also operative in the process of grammaticalization or the creation of new grammar. (Bybee 2000)

Though Bybee doesn't exploit the possibility, this approach can be as readily adapted to culture-specific patterns as to those patterns that are universal. In cultures that talk frequently about kinship, for example, kin-based categories could be structured into the core grammar, as brute frequency of token appearance leads to phonetic erosion through Zipfian effects, resulting in the reduction of free words to grammatical morphemes.

A second mechanism for getting culture into language structure comes from work on pragmatic inferencing and grammaticalization. Since Grice's pioneering work on conversational implicature, we have known that utterance meaning is enriched by inferences in context: Besides the lexicogrammatical or semantic meaning of a given sign, inhering in linguistic items regardless of their particular context, there is the pragmatic meaning contributed by sign users in context, using inference procedures that draw on mutually shared knowledge—which may well be culture specific. And the last two decades have shown numerous cases where conversational implicatures become "semanticized," i.e., absorbed into the conventional meaning of the sign, and thus freed from particular contexts. Frequency of use plays a role here as well: "[F]or inferences to play a significant role in grammaticalization, they must be frequently occurring, since only standard inferences can plausibly be assumed to have a lasting impact on the meaning of an expression" (Hopper & Traugott 1993, p. 75). Semanticization may lead to the transfer of information from ellipsed material to that which remains, as frequent mention enhances the ability to presume recoverability from elliptical contexts. Alternatively, frequent discussion of particular topics may embolden a speaker to presume a desired figurative inference by the hearer, again owing to the presumption of shared knowledge. Both ellipsis and figurative language may thus lead to culture-specific patterns of polysemy.

The Boundaries of the System

Research on language change has increasingly looked beyond the boundaries of the one-language speech community for the sources of innovation, and there are several Australian examples where the phenomenon can only be explained with reference to communities of practice at broader regional levels. A good case is the emergence of subsection terms in Australia, which classify all members into one of eight sociocentric categories that schematically represent descent and marriage relations. The wide diffusion of a common system enables strangers to establish classificatory kin relations without the need for a common link relative. Because of its elegant algebraic characteristics, the subsection system can be represented in a number of ways. In Figure 1 it is shown as two four-generation matricycles linked by preferred marriages between pairs of subsections. Though different modern languages have different phonological variants of the terms, the original forms as reconstructed by McConvell (1985a) are used here.

Von Brandenstein (1982) had suggested that the subsection system was a deliberate invention by a single individual. However, McConvell (1985a,b) showed how this complex structure could arise, without intentional planning, through the interaction of two distinct linguistic systems within certain ethnographically well-attested assumptions regulating section transmission, the bestowal of spouses, and code choice in bilingual settings.

McConvell begins with two observations. First, groups to the west and north of the area using subsections employ systems of four sections, and the subsection system is the union of these two four-section systems. Second, the eight terms of the subsection system can be broken down into four patricouples—pairs of terms between which members of a male descent line oscillate generationally—and, of

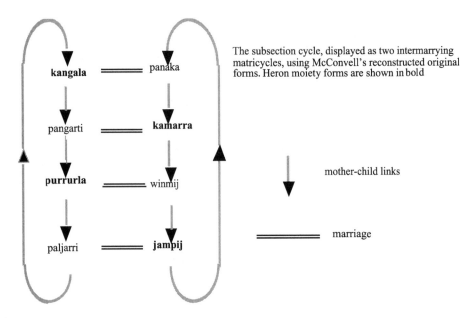

Figure 1   The subsection cycle.

these four patricouples, two contain pairs drawn from the same set (one patricouple draws from the northern set, another from the western set), whereas two mix pairs from both sets. He then shows how a subsection system with just these properties could have arisen in a socially integrated bilingual community, with intermarriage between adjoining groups possessing structurally equivalent but terminologically distinct systems of four sections.

Figure 2 gives the terms from the two-section systems (western and northern), made up of two intercycling endogamous generational moieties intersecting with marriage across two exogamous patrimoieties (we employ the patrimoiety names used in mythological accounts from the region). In fact, within the system we

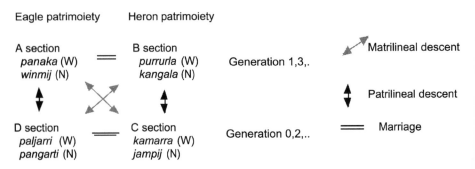

Figure 2   Structural parallels between the western and northern section systems.

can toggle between patrimoiety groupings, linking the pairs of sections joined in Figure 2 by vertical arrows, and matrimoiety groupings, joining the pairs of sections linked by diagonal arrows in the same figure. This means that descent rules can be phrased either patrilineally (*A* fathers beget *D* children) or matrilineally (*A* mothers conceive *C* children). Another way of viewing this system is as regulating the circulation of women among social groups: *A* women are given as wives to *B* men, giving birth to *C* daughters who are then given as wives to *D* men.

Now imagine a situation where speakers of languages employing the western and northern systems live side by side (Figure 3) and participate in a common system of spouse exchange based on a shared system of sections. Imagine further that wives are bestowed in a circulating fashion (as in Eastern Arnhem Land), such that women belonging to the two Eagle sections are bestowed within their respective language groups (the language boundary is shown in the figure by a double wavy line), whereas women belonging to the two Heron sections are bestowed to the other group. Assume further that residence is primarily patrilocal, with wives taking up residence in their husband's territory. The circulation of wives between social categories, arranged in lingual space, will then be as shown in Figure 3.

At this point we still have a four-section system, albeit bilingual: An individual from *A* section may be known as either *wirnmij* or *panaka*, according to the language used. McConvell's account of the transition to an eight-class (subsection) system relies on the following further assumption involving a codification of

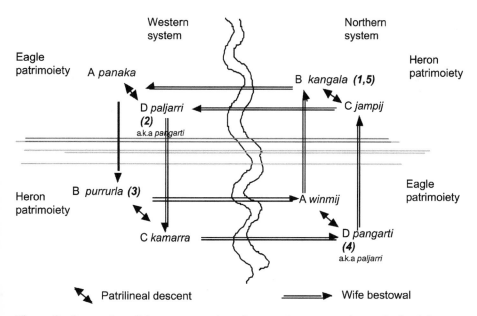

Figure 3   Integration of the western and northern section systems into a single eight-term system.

language choice in this bilingual community. In monolingual marriages, children will be known by the term from both parents' language. Thus the child of a western heron *B* (*purrurla*) man and a western eagle *A* (*panaka*) woman will be known by the appropriate term for a *C* child in the western language, *kamarra*. However, in bilingual marriages—which all comprise eagle men and heron women—practice is assumed to favor terms from the wife's mother tongue to denote the child, where a person's mother tongue is determined by place of birth. Thus, the daughter *D* of a *panaka* man (*A*, western) and a *kangala* woman [*B*, northern, shown as (*1*) in Figure 3] will be known by the northern term *pangarti*, even though she appears in the figure in the western half, on the basis of where her mother was born (*2*). She, as a western *D* woman, will now marry the western man *C*. Their daughter (*3*) will be *B* and known by the appropriate western term *purrurla* because both parents are western born. (*3*) will now marry a northern *A* man, and their daughter *D* (*4*) will be known as *paljarri* in the mother's (western) language. This northern-born *D* (*4*) will then marry a northern *C* man, and their daughter *B* (*5*) will be known by the northern term *kangala*, thus completing one matricycle. The genesis of the other four-term matricycle can be traced in a similar way.

All that remains is to elevate the ad hoc terminological choices made within each participating marriage to the status of a prescriptive norm, and we reach a single, integrated eight-class subsection system for reckoning marriage and descent, integrating four from each erstwhile section system.

Crucially, the emergence of this eight-class subsection system does not require intentional design; it arises as the unintentional collective outcome of other intentional acts (regulating descent in a four-section system, arranging a circulating system of spouse bestowal, and choosing language terms from one language rather than another in bilingual marriages).

Moreover, the structuration process cannot be explained by reference just to a monolingual speech community but requires reference to two interacting languages, as what begins as conventions of language choice in a bilingual community turns into an elaborated and systematized terminological system drawing on both contributing languages. In Language Ideologies and Lectal Systematization we return to other cases where an overarching multi-lectal community is the locus of sociolinguistic structuration.

SEMANTICIZATION AND THE EMERGENCE OF LEXICAL POLYSEMY

The meanings embodied in a language's vocabulary have long been seen as the most appropriate site for studying the impact of culture on language. Spitzer, studying the conceptual underpinnings of the Judeo-Christian world, wrote that "of all linguistic branches, it is in semantics that the changes due to cultural development can best be seen at work, for 'meaning' is the best barometer of cultural climate" (Spitzer 1947, p. 2).

During the Chomskyan turn, where the deep questions of language were held to concern grammar rather than lexicon, this often led to a quarantining of culture-specific elements to the vocabulary. Hale (1986, p. 233), writing on the relations between language and worldview in Warlpiri, first singled out a "World-View-1"—"the primary logical principles upon which a philosophy is based—the central propositions or postulates in a people's theory of how things are in the world"— going on to note that "its connection to language tends to be superficial, in the sense that it is reflected primarily in the elaboration of certain lexical domains. . . . It may or may not be shared by all speakers of a language, being something which is learned separately from the grammar of a language." (We return below to his "World-View-2," seen as more deeply embedded in grammar.)

However, recent developments have blurred this convenient boundary between grammar and lexicon. As the emergence of grammar(s) has come to be seen as an evolutionary process at the social-historical rather than the biological level, it has become clear that, since the same learning mechanisms apply right through the lexicon, including the functor words that turn into grammatical elements, these grammaticalizable notions display general properties of concept formation (Slobin 2001, p. 439). The issue of how broad principles of pragmatic inference interact with encyclopedic knowledge to generate particular interpretations in context, which may go on to become depragmaticized to yield conventionalized polysemy, then becomes potentially relevant to the study of grammar as well as the lexicon.

Creative speakers who first use novel figures of speech must be confident that the particular cultural knowledge needed to generate the appropriate implicatures is mutually manifest and is therefore part of the shared knowledge of the speech community[2]: Figurative language gives "access to an encyclopaedic schema with one or two dominant and highly accessible assumptions" (Sperber & Wilson 1986, p. 236). The need to characterize the culture-specific aspects of these encyclopedic schemas to understand Kwaio figurative language has been articulated by Keesing (1979, p. 27):

> By explicitly articulating semantic analysis to ethnography, and hence to per-vasive cultural assumptions about the cosmos, causality, time and being, we begin to capture not only the subtleties of meaning accessible to native speak-ers but the creative powers of language in metaphor and symbolism as well.

Consider the problem of explaining how a single word can mean both "hear" and "know" (Evans & Wilkins 2000). This is a problem of motivating lexical

---

[2]This is not to deny that particular tropes or semantic connections may also be used more esoterically. See Morphy (1991) and Keen (1994) for two interesting accounts of the Yolngu concept of *likan*, literally "elbow" but thence "joint, connection," and the way that "*likan* names" are used, in contexts of art and ceremony, to indicate more allusive readings to the culturally knowledgeable. On the issue of how far the same semantic connections underlie polysemy in everyday and other semiotic registers (ceremonial language, sand-paintings, hand-signs) see Evans (1992) and Wilkins (1997).

polysemy—why particular forms conventionally have two meanings, *p* and *q*, and are known not to be just chance homophones because of the recurrent pairing of these meanings, with different forms, in a good number of languages. A related problem is explaining inferred semantic shift historically between a cognate meaning *p* in one language and *q* in another—e.g., whether and how the Nyangumarta word *paja.rli* "fat, dripping" is related to the word *palya* "good" in Pitjantjatjara (O'Grady 1990, Evans 1997). A third problem is explaining how a word *p*, in particular individual contexts, is creatively endowed with special interpretation *q* by processes of inference—e.g., how the Yidiny word *binanga-L*, listed in Dixon's (1991) dictionary of Yidiny as meaning "hear, listen to," can be enriched, in context, by reading "remember and know," as in example (1), where Dixon's translation is reproduced exactly (material in square brackets supplies contextually inferred meanings). This is a problem of explaining the implicatural extension (symbolized +>) from *p* to *q* in a given context.

(1) *bamaan guwal jarral galiingal/garru **binangalna** bulmba wanyja galing*
   "People's names must be given to places all along the way.
   So that by-and-by [people] can **listen to** [and **remember** the sequence of place-names along a route and **know**] where the places are going to."

These three problems are all related, and Evans & Wilkins (2000) argue that they arise from implicature in particular "bridging contexts" by the following four-step process (Figure 4): A form *f* has an original meaning *p* (*1*), then extended, by implicature, to an additional contextual reading *q* (*2*), with *q* then becoming semanticized or released from contextual dependence, so that it becomes a regular part of other speakers' mental lexicons (*3*), possibly followed by the loss of original meaning (*4*).

For the crucial first transition, from *p* to {*p*, +>*q*}, we are dealing with the pragmatics of situated individual communicative acts: Which contexts, and which

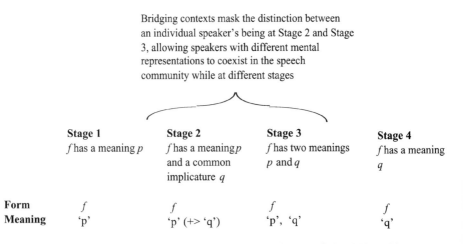

Bridging contexts mask the distinction between an individual speaker's being at Stage 2 and Stage 3, allowing speakers with different mental representations to coexist in the speech community while at different stages

Stage 1	**Stage 2**	**Stage 3**	**Stage 4**
f has a meaning *p*	*f* has a meaning *p* and a common implicature *q*	*f* has two meanings *p* and *q*	*f* has a meaning *q*

Form	*f*	*f*	*f*	*f*
Meaning	'p'	'p' (+> 'q')	'p', 'q'	'q'

Figure 4   Stages in semantic change (diagram adapted from Enfield 2003, p. 29).

cultural scripts, allow particular pragmatic extensions to occur. The fact that polysemy is generated by such implicatures links lexical polysemy to the problem of how to represent the culture-specific encyclopedic knowledge upon which pragmatic inference draws.

Extending from "hearing" to "knowing" or "remembering," for example, may be mediated by widespread cultural scripts in Aboriginal Australia in which travel routes are remembered and known through lists of place (names) in mnemonic stories or songlines, so that (mentally) replaying these enables one to "know" or "remember" the way. This common cultural practice may then engender frequent texts in which knowledge and memory are reported in terms of "hearing (+> names of) places," so that utterances like example (1) become frequent enough to serve as templates for semanticizing this extension: For new learners, the (originally implicated) meaning is now paired directly with the signifier without requiring pragmatic deduction. That this extension does not simply reflect universal principles of embodiment is clear from the fact that it is culturally and areally patterned. Sweetser (1990), for example, in an influential study based only on Indo-European languages, found only "see," never "hear," as the source of verbs for "knowing" and "understanding."

From the point of view of pragmatics, which examines the contribution of context to the interpretation of meaning by human users, implicatures result from the constant need to mean more than conventionalized signs allow us to say. But as speakers exploit the interpretive abilities of hearers, new conventionalized signs emerge. Over time, individuals' attempts to communicate thus become enshrined as conventionalized patterns of polysemy. This interplay makes polysemy a key site for studying how language systems can incorporate culture-specific knowledge into language structure as an "unintended result of the communicative use of signs" (Keller 1998, p. 239).

CULTURE SELECTING FOR GRAMMATICAL STRUCTURE

Though its effects can be seen most easily in the lexicon, the structuration of culture into language systems does not stop there. Hale (1986, p. 234), in the article referred to above, went on to discuss a "World-View-2", defined as "the 'analysis of phenomena' embodied in the system of lexico-semantic themes or motifs which function as integral components in a grammar." Unlike his "World-View-1," it must be shared by all speakers of the language and is necessarily learned as part of the language-learning process. The term ethnosyntax, defined by Enfield (2002a, p. 2) as the direct encoding of cultural meaning in the semantics of morphosyntax, essentially refers to the same class of phenomena that Hale considered as "World-View-2."

The Emergence of Kintax

In this section we discuss one such phenomenon in Australian languages—the obligatory encoding of kinship or moiety relations in core grammar, sometimes called kintax—with an emphasis on the structuration problem. Such phenomena were first described by Hale, who pointed out that

> in some Australian languages a principle which is a proper part of the kinship system also functions as an important principle of opposition within a grammatical paradigm. . . . The intrusion of the kinship system into this portion of the grammar results in the circumstance that a syntactic rule is required to make reference to features normally regarded as outside the domain of grammar. (Hale 1966, pp. 319–20)

Hale showed that, in Lardil, there are two sets of free pronouns in the nonsingular: a harmonic set, for referents related in even-numbered generations, such as siblings, spouses, or grandkin; and a disharmonic set, for referents in odd-numbered generations, such as parents and children. For example, the first-person dual exclusive category has a harmonic form *nyarri*, which can combine with an apposed even-generation term like *ngithun thabu* "my elder brother" (example 2), and a disharmonic form *nyaanki*, used with apposed odd-generation expressions like *ngithun kantha* "father" (example 3). The syntactic rule regulating such appositions must therefore make reference to the kin-based feature of "generational harmony."[3]

(2) *nya-rri*   *(*nya-anki)* *ngithun*   *thabu*   *waangkur*   *riwur.*
    1exc-du.HAR   1exc-du.DIS   my   elder.brother go:FUT   east:FUT
    "My older brother and I will go east."

(3) *nya-anki*   *(*nya-rri)*   *ngithun kantha*   *waangkur riwur.*
    1exc-du.DIS   1exc-du.HAR   my   father   go:FUT   east:FUT
    "My father and I will go east."

More than 20 Australian languages, in a number of distinct regions, have kinship-sensitive constructions of some sort. Lardil exemplifies the most common grammatical site for such information, namely pronouns. But in languages like Martuthunira (Dench 1987), alternating-generation kinship relations (between any two clausal participants) are shown by a verbal suffix (example 4); the same form is used for the collective/reciprocal (example 5), although with singular subjects, as in example (4), the kinship reading is forced.

(4) *ngayu*   *kangku-yarri-lha*   *Panaka-ngurni*   *Karimarra-wuyu-u*
    1sgNOM   take-COLL-PAST   Panaka-BEHIND   Karimarra-SIDE-ACC

    marrari-mulyarra,   *Martuthunira-a*   *nhuura-npa-waa*
    language-ALLAT   language.name-ACC   know-INCH-PURP

> "I took the Karimarra section boy along behind the Panaka boy towards the language, to learn Martuthunira." (the two boys are in the same generation set)

---

[3]I have retranscribed Hale's examples into current Lardil orthography and re-cast his formulation into a more modern idiom. For complexities in the definition of harmonic and disharmonic generations in Lardil, see McKnight (1999).

(5)   *ngaliwa thani-yarri-nguru*
      1pl(inc) hit-COLL-PRES
      "We're hitting each other."

In both Lardil and Martuthunira, the grammaticalized kin relations are generational moiety based, though the reader should note that, whereas in Lardil extra morphological marking codes the disharmonic relation, in Martuthunira it codes the harmonic relation. However, harmonicity is not the only contrast attested.

Mparntwe Arrernte (Wilkins 1989) has a three-way distinction: same versus opposite patrimoiety, then, within the same-patrimoiety category, a further division by generational moiety. Several languages of the Karnic group organize their contrasts on the basis of same versus different matrimoiety in addition to generational moiety. Some languages, such as Dyirbal and Murrinhpatha, have special forms for particular kin dyads (husband/wife, siblings), while Adnjamathanha, the richest of all by number of contrasts (Schebeck 1973, Hercus & White 1973), has around ten distinct categories, some defined at the abstract level of relations between sections and others more specific to particular types of kin relation (e.g., mother-child).

It has been widely asserted that the presence of "kintactic" categories in Australian languages reflects a cultural emphasis on kinship, and kin-derived sociocentric categories like moieties and sections, as the foundation for social relations. However, we have surprisingly few accounts of how structuration of kin categories into the grammar could have actually occurred.

One development that is easy to account for is the Martuthunira type, which merely involves an extension of a cross-linguistically common grammatical category—collective/reciprocals—to take on a new sense, namely same-generation relations between some pair of clausal participants. Dench (1987) argues that this extension would have been motivated by habitual cooperation in ceremonial matters on the part of harmonic relations: In stereotyped descriptions of ceremonies, the way labor is divided up on the basis of generational moiety groupings means that descriptions of activities collectively undertaken would, concurrently, be descriptions of activities undertaken by members of the harmonic generations, setting up the new use of this category.

In the Martuthunira case, we simply need to account for the semantic extension of an existing morpheme into the realm of kinship. However, in the other languages, encoding kinship categories is the sole function, so we are faced with the harder task of showing a pathway by which some free word gets phonologically reduced to a bound affix and in parallel undergoes semantic developments to the sorts of categories we have seen. Though we do not yet have any clear-cut, multi-step account of how any one system has evolved, I sketch a scenario that chains together plausible attested steps from a range of languages.

   (*a*) Formation of dyadic expressions: Expressions yield meanings like "mother and child" from roots meaning "mother" by adding a dyad suffix. Dyad suffixes in Australian languages etymologically derive from words or affixes with meanings like "having," "pair," etc.

(*b*) Apposition: Dyadic nouns are apposed after free pronouns to give phrases of the type "we, father, and son." In Wakaya, for example (G. Breen, unpublished manuscript), the phrase *yibela thungkuthekerrayarl*, literally "you.two younger.sibling:DYAD," means "you and your sister."

(*c*) Reduction and generalization: The dyadic term becomes phonologically reduced and attached to the preceding pronoun, reducing to a suffix expressing dyad-type kinship information. A sub-step of this process is analogical generalization: The newly developed affix spreads to all words in the pronoun paradigm. In Adnyamathanha, whose wealth of kin-specific pronouns was mentioned above, a number of them have suffixes that formally resemble nominal dyad expressions. In the first three given in Table 1, the material that turns into the pronominal suffix is the suffix of the dyad expression, whereas in the fourth it is a lexical root meaning "spouse."

(*d*) Semantic broadening. Step (*c*) gives us pronouns with kin-dyad meanings; however, to get meanings like disharmonic or same patrimoiety we need to broaden the semantics to include all possible kin relations in the relevant sociocentric categories, e.g., from "mother and child" to same matrimoiety. This is plausible semantically—it is a typical case of broadening from a prototype and would fit within the general tendency for grammaticalized meanings to become more abstract. Hercus & White (1973, p. 58) mention an example of just such an extension: In Adnyamathanha the "mother and child" series gets used for "my mother's line" in addition to just "I (female) and my children."

The above account of how moiety-sensitive pronouns have arisen thus involves four chained processes: the formation of dyadic kin terms, their apposition with pronouns in an inclusory construction, their reduction to affixal status and attachment to the pronoun, and their semantic generalization from markers of kin dyads to generalized relationships between types of moiety. This specific series of

TABLE 1   Sample kin-sensitive pronouns in Adnyamathanha and formally related dyadic kin terms (forms from Schebeck 1973 and Hercus & White 1973)

Pronoun	Meaning	Dyadic noun	Meaning
valananji	"they two" (husband and child of speaker)	*vapirinji*	"father and child"
ŋatlaka	"we two" (woman and child)	*ŋamināka*	"mother (or mother's brother) and child"
[*nhu*)*wad**nalpu***	"you plural" [mother (or mother's brother)] and children	*ŋamiŋamiŋalpu*	"mother (or mother's brother) and children"
nhuwaḍupa	"you two, husband and wife"	*aḍupanha*	"married couple"

semantic developments is not known from elsewhere in the world, but the broad outlines are typical of grammaticalization pathways found with other categories, such as tense or mood, and illustrate how grammar can emerge from talk, via processes of lexicalization, phonological reduction, analogical generalization across paradigms, and semantic extension. The result, once again, is the unplanned emergence of a series of culture-specific macro-concepts, powerful new shared representations that come into being through a series of quite unspectacular and general processes.

Toward a Better Methodology: Simpson's Razor

A skeptic could see the above accounts as being post hoc, just-so stories. Could it not simply be a coincidence that kinship-sensitive pronouns develop in Australian languages rather than, say, English or Chinese? After all, no one would seriously claim that the presence in some language of a dative case, or a past tense, is in any way linked to the culture of its speakers. Simpson (2002, pp. 290–91) outlines a useful prophylactic against overenthusiastic postulators of culture ↔ grammar causal connections, proposing the following series of steps that should be followed before any causal claim for cultural selection of grammatical meaning is accepted:

1. Identify the construction
2. Identify an associated meaning (or pragmatic inference or function)
3. Propose a relationship between this meaning and some shared topic of conversation, assumption, or expectation of its speakers
4. Provide evidence that this shared topic of conversation, assumption, or expectation is, or has been, highly salient for the speakers (i.e., something they often mention or do, or which often seems to inform their actions)
5. Provide an explanation based in conversational practice as to how the construction came to exist and bear the proposed meaning (or pragmatic inference or function)
6. Look at similar constructions in other languages and check if the proposed connection between conversational practice and grammatical construction holds. In the strongest case the connection would be causal.

Note that this procedure applies to the emergence of new grammatical categories from free words of similar meaning rather than to the semantic extension of existing categories, such as the Martuthunira collective > harmonic-generations development discussed above. Further principles would need to be added to deal with this, as outlined in The Emergence of Kintax, in particular (*i*) evidence for what the original meaning was, and (*ii*) finding bridging contexts that scaffold the pragmatic extensions that eventually become new meanings for the construction.

Simpson tries out these tests on verbal affixes expressing "associated motion" in Central Australian languages. Such affixes have been claimed to reflect a preoccupation of these cultural groups with discussing travel routes. Particularly difficult, in the study of an individual culturally situated language, is operationalizing steps 4 and 5. Studies addressing the frequency of particular topics in conversation over a properly balanced corpus are vanishingly small, and text collections are skewed, in their representation of frequency, away from multi-party conversation and in favor of genres like mythical narrative. Simpson cites Nash's (1998) observations on the importance to the Warlpiri of "topographical gossip" (about country, trips, navigation) and surveys the collection of texts in Napaljarri Rockman & Cataldi (1994), finding that travel to and from named places is a central part of the action in all stories but one. Clauses headed by motion verbs start the action in about half the stories and end it for most of the stories (Simpson 2002, p. 299). These considerations certainly support the hypothesis that motion is a high-frequency theme in Warlpiri conversation, but the argument cannot be considered proved until we have comparative data on frequency of motion verbs, in a similarly structured corpus, from other languages.

Step 5 includes a requirement to look closely at candidate constructions for grammaticalization. To turn from free word into suffix, it is necessary for the grammaticalizing word to occur regularly in the same order, directly after the host, but Warlpiri is basically a free word-order language, creating a potential explanatory problem. Simpson shows, though, that there is one relevant dependent-verb construction where the order is, unusually, fixed, thus setting the structural stage for reduction to affix status. This underlines the importance of selection by existing structure—the promotion or prevention of certain developments by current typological profile. Returning to kinship-sensitive pronouns, for example, a structural filter on their emergence may be the need for preexisting dyadic nominals and an appositive construction—both of which played a crucial role in our hypothetical grammaticalization path—in addition to the cultural salience of sociocentric kinship categories like moieties.

More complete accounts will also require linguistic practitioners to gather information on "not yet grammaticalized" collocations. The grammar-writing traditions of descriptive linguistics focus on structures that have already emerged; but to explain where they come from, we must look at the messier data of actual speech. This needs larger, more finely transcribed corpora. For example, information on syllable duration helps identify phonetic reduction but is rarely provided within reference grammars.

Finally, Simpson's step 6 underlines the need for a comparative approach, testing for the same correlations across a language sample structured along both cultural and linguistic dimensions. The practical difficulties in constructing such samples mean that few have attempted studies of this type, though see Perkins (1992) for an attempt to correlate types of demonstrative systems with size of speech community.

One more caveat within Simpson's schema concerns temporality. Grammaticalization is a diachronic process that may take centuries to unfold, so the cultural preoccupations that set the stage for grammaticalization may no longer be those identifiable by a modern observer. Again, this adds to the difficulty of fully testing the processes that yield culture-specific structuration.

LANGUAGE IDEOLOGIES AND LECTAL SYSTEMATIZATION

There is growing interest in the question of how linguistic diversity is engendered and maintained and in the social mechanisms that favor its development. Language ideologies were originally defined by Silverstein (1979) as sets of beliefs about language articulated by users as a rationalization or justification of perceived language structure and use. But they may, additionally, act as a selective force favoring particular reconfigurations of structure and of sociolinguistic diversity (Rumsey 1990, p. 357; Woolard & Schieffelin 1994, p. 70; Woolard 1998, p. 12).

Australian groups are remarkable for the ways they organize linguistic variation to systematically index differences in social group membership, often resulting in overarching systems of sociolinguistic differentiation that go beyond the boundaries of any single language. This poses three special problems for the study of language ideologies: firstly, to account for the emergence of systems whose logic transcends any single language community; secondly, to give an evolutionary account of how language ideologies select for distinctive patternings of sociolinguistic diversity; and, thirdly, to show how this evolutionary trajectory can account for the independent emergence of parallel sociolinguistic systems in discontiguous parts of the continent. We focus on two types of lectal variation (where *lect* refers to any distinctive language variety): in Country, Group, Lect, on varieties that reflect place- and moiety-mediated relationships of individuals to social groups; and, in Social Deixis and Kinship-Sensitive Registers, on varieties that index kinship relations between speech-act participants (and sometimes others) through lectal choice.

Country, Group, Lect

The reigning social model over much of Australia posits a direct relationship between land and language (e.g., Merlan 1981), with secondary relationships between language and particular social groupings, such as clans. Individuals then derive the right to be recognized as speakers of particular languages indirectly through their membership in clans or other groups, including higher-order groupings like moieties, which in many areas are aggregated from clans with fixed moiety affiliations (Figure 5).

This direct mapping of language onto country creates an interesting range of sociolinguistic practices (Brandl & Walsh 1982, Trigger 1987). Speakers regularly switch language when entering a new territory, or to address particular locales (e.g., wells or dangerous places) in the local language. Characters in myths switch

Figure 5   The indirect relationship between individuals and "their" languages.

languages as they move about the country, and sometimes this metonymic device may be the only indication that a character has moved from one place to another. Song and myth cycles often incorporate a number of "legs," each in a different language and typically told by different speakers in relay—as if the Odyssey, say, passed through half-a-dozen languages and storytellers as the action shifted.

Typically there is no etiquette that all participants in a conversation should speak the same language, and it is quite normal to witness multilingual conversations where each participant speaks their own language. In Western Cape York (Sutton 1978, p. 228), linguistically exogamous marriage ensures that households are linguistically diverse and multilingual; linguistic exogamy helps give ritualistic recognition to "the three main lines of descent (fathers, mother's father's, mother's mother's) through which economic and political rights and powers were traced." In such circumstances, lectal choice carries a high functional load, indexing the country and social identities of speakers and represented characters. In many areas, such as Western Cape York and Arnhem Land, there is an ideology that each patri-clan has its own way of speaking. The creation of new social groupings, such as splits in clans, results in the rapid development of new patrilects: "[B]ecause of an ideology of clan dialect distinctiveness . . . and the creative role of powerful individuals, there was also constant pressure for diversification" (Sutton 1978, p. 229).

The interaction of diversification and multilingualism may produce Sprachbund phenomena where languages or related dialects converge closely in grammar and phonology, while lexical choice signals lectal difference—see Sutton (1978) and Johnson (1991) on convergent dialects in Western Cape York, and see Rigsby (1997) for grammatical convergence between distinct languages in Eastern Cape York. An interesting variant is reported by Nash (1991) for central Australia, where patrilects of Warumungu and Warlmanpa speakers are distinguished by stereotyped voice qualities rather than lexical differences.

Such systems appear to result from the interaction of convergence (mediated by processing economy in multilingual individuals) and ideological pressure for diversification with senior speakers systematizing lexical variation by "ruling" on the patrilectal status of variants ("Word Y—that's what you say in X language"). Lectal maintenance involves consensual beliefs from the broader community of linked varieties, with adults making sure that children acquire the appropriate patrilect (Smith & Johnson 1986), e.g., by requiring widows to speak their deceased husbands' patrilects as models for their children.

More complex sociolinguistic systems arise when it is not only a matter of symbolizing interclan differences but also of organizing these differences into an overarching system where socially shared features of clans linked in a single moiety are symbolized by shared linguistic features. The clearest example is in North-Eastern Arnhem Land (Morphy 1977, Wilkinson 1991), where each language variety is associated with one of two patrimoieties. Example (6) illustrates how this moiety lect contrast is realized between two adjoining dialects, Gupapuyngu (spoken by some Yirritja moiety clans) and Djambarrpuyngu (spoken by some

TABLE 2   Geographic and social patterning of a pronoun form in some Yolngu dialects (after Wilkinson 1991, p. 187)

	Social (patrimoiety) [Final vowel drop]	
Geographical [initial ŋa-drop]	Yirritja moiety ("Dhuwala varieties")	Dhuwa moiety ("Dhuwal varieties")
Western	Gupapuyngu: (ŋa)napurru	Djamparrpuyngu:(ŋa)napurr
Eastern	Gumatj: ŋanapurru	Djapu: ŋanapurr

Dhuwa moiety clans). A phonological rule truncates most final vowels in Dhuwa clan lects, giving them a staccato effect (Morphy 1977), whereas words in Yirritja moiety lects are predominantly vowel-final.

(6)   Gup: ga balanya   dhäwu-nydja   limurruŋgu   ŋarra-kuŋu

Djamb: ga balanya   dhäwu-ny   limurruŋ   ŋarra-kuŋ

and such   story+PROMINENCE   our   me-from

"And such is our story from me."

Now features like final apocope, which distinguish moiety lects, crosscut features distinguishing dialect groupings set up on geographical grounds, such as the loss of initial syllables of some pronouns. Thus, social groupings contrast on one dimension (Dhuwa versus Yirritja moiety), whereas geographical groupings contrast on the other (western versus eastern dialects)—see Table 2.

We can identify three relevant ideological factors in patterning linguistic diversity in this highly distinctive way:

(a) Each clan should have a different speech variety.

(b) Each clan belongs to just one of two moieties, Yirritja and Dhuwa (this is part of a broader ideology assigning virtually everything—e.g., natural species or territories—to one moiety or another).

(c) General principles are used to categorize moiety membership of entities (plants, animals, designs). In particular, there is a general principle that Dhuwa entities are shorter and yirritja entities are longer. Presumably, at some point in the past, this principle led to the conscious categorization of certain phonetic variants (e.g., truncated, i.e., "short" forms) as belonging to a particular moiety (e.g., Dhuwa), leading to the association of particular lectal variants with particular moieties.[4]

---

[4]However, the operation of these principles does not appear to be uniform over the whole Yolngu area. Waters (1989, p. 254ff) discusses the most northwesterly variety, Djinang, and shows that though there is a native theory of "choppy" versus "undulating" dialects; this doesn't correlate well with moieties among Djinang-speaking clans.

There is a contemporary expansion of Yolngu social categories westward into other parts of Arnhem Land, and it is interesting to observe the emergence of incipient, parallel effects on languages there that are only distantly related to the Yolngu languages. The author has heard senior speakers of Dalabon, well-versed in Yolngu cosmology, claim that there are two types of Dalabon—*Dalabondjurrkdjurrk* (fast Dalabon), associated with Dhuwa clans, and *Dalabon-muduk* (strong or slow Dalabon), associated with Yirritja clans. Distinct lexical items or phonological variants were not given in support of this claim, nor have they been recorded by investigators of the language. However, the speakers mentioned above gave a contrast between reduplicated and unreduplicated verb forms, though such differences have not been noted in natural speech. At present, then, there does not appear to be an observable moiety-based difference within Dalabon varieties, but beliefs such as those held by these senior arbiters of linguistic tradition could easily go on to select for diversification along these lines. As Silverstein (1985, p. 252) puts it, ideological rationalization can impact "language at and through an intersection of structural form and indexical usage, producing tension in the highly charged 'metaphorization' of indexical meanings and forms. The resolution of this tension seems to move the very structural system into new configurations, generally unforeseen by the users of the language."

Social Deixis and Kinship-Sensitive Registers

In many parts of Australia one finds special registers sensitive to kinship relations between speaker and hearer, overhearer or referent; these have been variously designated as "mother-in-law" or "brother-in-law" languages or "respect" or "avoidance" registers (McGregor 1989) (see examples 7a and 7b). In extreme cases, nearly all vocabulary items of the everyday variety must be replaced by separate items in the respect register. For example, in Uw-Oykangand (Cape York), a man talking to a potential mother-in-law must use a special register known as Olkel-Ilmbanhthi. To speak this, one leaves affixes and function words like "I" intact but replaces the remaining vocabulary items (Alpher 1993, p. 98).

(7a) *Alka-nhdh*   *idu-rr*   *ay*
    spear-INSTRUMENTAL   spear-PAST   I
    "I speared it with a spear." (ordinary register)

(7b) *Udnga-nhdh*   *yanganyunyja-rr*   *ay*
    spear-INSTRUMENTAL   spear-PAST   I
    "I speared it with a spear." (respect register)

At the other extreme, only a few special replacements need to be made (e.g., McConvell 1982), or the restrictions affect manner of speaking rather than specific vocabulary items, such as in the Tjalpawangkanytja (oblique) speech style used between co-parent-in-laws in Yankunytjatjara (Goddard 1992).

Respect registers form part of a larger complex of prescribed behaviors for showing respect to certain kin. These include general indirection, giving food, avoiding close physical presence or eye contact, clasping the wrist when passing objects, and general avoidance of conflictual or sexual behavior. However, as Rumsey (1982, p. 178) puts it in his discussion of the *gun-gunma* [GG] avoidance register, "[w]hile the use of 'politeness' strategies thus makes the *majaliway* [avoidance] relationship understandable as a special case within a more general class, the use of distinctive GG formal features singles out the *majaliway* dyad from all others." The development of discrete respect registers is therefore a case of sociolinguistic structuration, in which the outcome of certain sociolinguistic strategies is formalized into a particular pattern of lexical (and sometimes phonological) choices.

Although there are dozens of distinct societies using respect registers in Australian languages, most appear to be independent developments. They occur in genetic subgroups that are only distantly related, in discontiguous blocks, and in general make use of noncognate vocabulary (except in the Gunwinyguan family, where certain respect-language formatives are of significant time-depth, and in the Dyirbal-Yidiny situation described below where there has been mutual borrowing between respect registers in adjacent languages). As with the case of clan lects discussed in Country, Group, Lect, these independent developments appear to result from the impact of language ideologies on practice—this time using the ideology that one should speak differently to certain classes of affine. In some speech communities, this practice leads to the gradual sociolinguistic codification of a range of ad hoc methods of showing respect, whereas in other speech communities the impact of the ideology remains limited to choices of pragmatic strategy or to nonverbal behavior.

Dixon (1990) carried out an etymological study of two adjoining, but not closely related, languages, Dyirbal and Yidiny, each with a respect register known as Jalnguy and called "mother-in-law language" by bilingual consultants. He found three major determinable sources of vocabulary in these registers: borrowings from the everyday register of neighboring dialects or languages, the creation of new Jalnguy forms by phonological deformation of lexemes from the language's own everyday style, and the borrowing of terms that were already in the Jalnguy style of a neighboring language or dialect. Unfortunately, Dixon's article is confined to the results of processes operating some time in the past, and we lack a thorough study of actual practice that would illuminate the operation of structuration processes under our nose. However, at least in the case of loans, several investigators have reported cases of speakers who, unable to recall the "correct" respect register lexeme, have improvisedly borrowed lexemes from neighboring lects.

Another way that many Australian languages index kinship relations between speaker and hearer is through systems of triangular, trirelational, or shared kin terms, which offer a number of alternatives for referring to kin based on simultaneously figuring out the relationship of the referent to speaker and hearer—see Merlan (1989) for an example. Consider the following terms from the *Gun-dembui* register of Gun-djeihmi; all are ways of referring to the mother of speaker and/or hearer in a range of circumstances:

(8) *al-garrng* "the one who is *your mother* and *my daughter*, given that I am your
mother's mother"
al-doingu "the one who is *your daughter* and *my mother*, given that I am your
daughter's daughter"
al-gakkak "the one who is *your maternal grandmother* and *my mother*, given
that I am your mother"
arduk gakkak "the one who is *my maternal grandmother* and *your mother*,
given that I am your daughter"
al-bolo "the one who is *mother of one of us* and *mother-in-law of the other*,
given that we are husband and wife"

These systems are cognitively demanding because they require the speaker to
take two perspectives at once—their own and that of their interlocutor—and are
typically not acquired before speakers reach their twenties. Triangular kinship
systems often coexist with respect registers in the same language. The latter hold
relations between speaker and hearer constant and vary denotation over the whole
universe of discourse, while the former permute speaker-hearer relations but restrict
denotation to the domain of kin.

Over 20 Australian languages have such systems, which are found in many
distinct geographical foci and again appear to be independent developments. As
with respect registers, the independent innovation of numerous triangular systems
again calls for a unified evolutionary explanation in terms of the codifying impact
of language ideology on linguistic practice. In this case, the most likely ingredients
are (*i*) the belief that kin-constituted dyads define behavioral norms between dyad
members, and (*ii*) pragmatic practices governing who should be chosen as propositus or anchor for the kinship expression, in a way that is sensitive to speaker-hearer
kin relationships.

In a given speech community, there may be a number of principles for choosing
between egocentric and altercentric modes of reference and for seeking oblique
modes of reference in certain types of speaker-hearer dyads (Merlan 1982)—
compare the pragmatically determined interpretation of who the anchor is in the
English utterances "Is Mum home?" (adult asking child, anchor is hearer) and
"No, Mum's not home" (child to adult, anchor is speaker). The structuration of
these principles so that they become conventionally attached to particular lexemes,
rather than working as general rules governing choice of anchor, is likely to be
a major means by which some triangular terms arise. Of those given in example
(8) above, for example, the formative *arduk*, which means "my" in other contexts, is a lexicalization of egocentric reference, whereas the use of the feminine
prefix *al-* is a lexicalization of nonegocentric reference. Some of the kin roots
in Gun-dembui are taken over without modification from the regular kin term
set (e.g., *gakkak* "MM"), whereas others (e.g., *garrng* in *al-garrng*) are irregular phonetic modifications of regular kin terms (here *garrang* "mother"). Others
again, such as *nangadjkewarre* for "the one who is your *nakurrng* (WMB) and

my *ngadjadj* (MB), given that we call each other *makkah*" resist synchronic analysis altogether. It seems likely, then, that the system originated as a formalization of a number of principles of centricity, governing who it was polite to take as propositus but blurring into circumspection and obscure usage where certain of these principles came into conflict or where rules of etiquette prescribed indirect reference.

CONCLUSION: STRUCTURATION, CULTURE, AND NATIVISM

We have seen many ways in which culture can select for the emergence of linguistic structure: in the semantics of the lexicon, in grammatical categories, and in the organization of sociolinguistic diversity. A complex of invisible hand processes, including phonological reduction and grammaticalization of frequent sequences, the input of shared cultural knowledge into pragmatic interpretation leading to semanticization, and the input of linguistic ideologies into the systematization of lectal variants, lead to the emergence of structured systems that reflect culturally salient categories, connections, and oppositions.

The result of these processes is a series of linguistic structures that, although common in the Australian culture area, are unknown anywhere else in the world. The author is unaware of any analogues of pronouns reflecting moiety-type categories, of subsections, of moiety lects, or of systems of triangular kin terms.

Such linguistic features are historical products reflecting the impact of various processes of cultural selection on emerging structure. The processes invoked here are broadly familiar within the suite of adaptive, invisible hand processes that functionalist linguists have studied over the last two decades, and, though the semantic content of the outcomes is unfamiliar, the general types of processes are not. Though the existence of culturally shaped linguistic structures is unsurprising to the anthropologically informed descriptivist traditions, it runs directly against the nativist assumptions that have dominated mainstream theoretical linguistics in recent decades. Chomsky (1980), Pinker (1994), Bickerton (1995), and others assume that a knowledge of Universal Grammar is already present in the prelinguistic child, so that individual linguistic structures are simply instantiations of biologically given design principles, with the role of specific input being merely to set a few parameter values. The development of grammatical categories, on this view, is simply a matter of children seeking out, from the flow of speech around them, the exponents of prewired universal concepts that are already part of their "mentalese."

Taking this nativist view makes the goal of characterizing possible language structures a question about human biology: What universal grammar is hard-wired into the mind of the child, so that a biologically driven capacity for language in general can enable the rapid acquisition of particular languages in difficult circumstances?[5] Though this model may seem plausible when confined to grammatical categories that recur in language after language all over the world, like tense on verbs or person in pronouns, it is forced to a *reductio ad absurdum* when faced with the sorts of culture-specific grammatical categories examined here by adopting a hyper-Platonic fallacy that overstates the degree to which we need to have preexisting knowledge of an idea in order to learn it. Did human evolution really equip the child to test for the presence of disharmonic pronouns as part of the parameter-setting process during language acquisition?

An alternative position is to refrain from overdetermining the set of possible linguistic structures through biological constraints. By admitting that languages are at the same time socio-historical products, we can hand over more of the explanation, for both regularity and variation in language structure, to processes of diachronic structuration, which include cultural selection within the constraints imposed by existing structure. And cultural selection, as an invisible hand process, can create complex categories that no member of the culture, and no prewired set of "mentalese" concepts, had foreseen or overtly articulated. The emergence of subsections from a bilingual flux, discussed in The Boundaries of the System, is an emblematic example.

Certainly this point of view does not simplify our goal of explaining how children acquire language. A Fodorian child faces what Levinson (2001) calls a first-degree mapping problem: They must match language-specific phonological units with language-independent semantic units, in the form of preexisting conceptual bundles. But children on the more Boasian view of language espoused here face a third-degree mapping problem: of matching language-specific word-forms to language-specific word-meanings using nonuniversal working concepts. Research into the acquisition of language-specific semantics has just begun (Bowerman & Levinson 2001), and we are far from understanding how it works; however, the phenomena considered in this article suggest that the child faces these third-degree mapping problems precisely because processes of linguistic evolution can lead to the incorporation of culture-specific elements into language structure.

Langacker (1994) suggests one way out of this apparent impasse: by proposing a multi-step cyclic acquisition model in which culture-independent categories play a greater role in initial phases, with successively more elaborate culture-specific elements cutting in later. A further attraction of this cyclic model is the attention it draws to language acquisition later in childhood (or conceivably even later). Because the elaboration of cultural notions is a prerequisite to learning the

---

[5]Cf. Pinker & Bloom (1990, p. 707): "the ability to use a natural language belongs more to the study of human biology than human culture: it is a topic like echolocation in bats or stereopsis in monkeys, not like writing or the wheel." Note that it is not possible to avoid considering data such as that presented in this article by saying that Pinker & Bloom are concerned with "the ability to use a human language" rather than the form a particular language (e.g., Lardil) takes, since that general ability must include the ability to use ANY natural language, including Lardil.

grammatical categories that encode them, some culture-specific categories may in fact be acquired quite late, and Slobin has recently suggested "[o]n closer inspection, crosslinguistic diversity in patterns of grammaticalization points to adult communicative practices as the most plausible source of form-function mappings in human languages, rather than prototypical events in infant cognition" (Slobin 2001, p. 412). This is certainly the case, anecdotally, with kinship-specific pronouns (Wilkins 1989), respect registers, and triangular kin terms, none of which are reportedly mastered in childhood. Unfortunately, though, we lack any studies of how these categories are acquired.

This article has called for a neo-Boasian approach emphasizing that languages, though undoubtedly constrained in many ways by the biological givens of our language faculty, are nonetheless cultural artefacts—though, now, "objects of a third kind" emerging without intentional design. This view is compatible with, but neglected by, more functionalist approaches. And it is interesting that the most recent statement of Chomsky's own views on language evolution opens a space for the culturally selected structuration process described here to operate. In Hauser et al. (2002), a model of human language is set out in which the complexity of individual languages results from three interacting factors: (*a*) a faculty of language in the broad sense, which includes general communicative abilities shared with nonhuman species, "especially those underlying the sensory-motor (speech or sign) and conceptual-intentional interfaces," (*b*) a human-specific faculty of language in the narrow sense (FLN), of which syntactic recursion is the central element, and (*c*) "sociocultural and communicative contingencies," from which "much of the complexity manifested in language derives." This article outlined some of the mechanisms by which these sociocultural and communicative contingencies can shape the evolution and elaboration of particular language structures.

A full and proper working out of how culture affects structuration in language will require some new directions of research focus by linguists. On the one hand, they need to redeploy the tools of the functionalists to study culture-specific processes of structuration from talk. On the other hand they must study, in small and often fragile communities, how culture-specific linguistic categories are acquired, taking care not to neglect older learners so as to pick up on language features that may in fact take longer to acquire. Pinker maintains "when children solve problems for which they have mental modules, they should look like geniuses knowing things they have not been taught; when they solve problems that their minds are not equipped for, it should be a long hard slog" (Pinker 1994, p. 419–20). An important consequence of the model outlined here is that acts of communication can, through invisible hand processes and through the complex, mutually enriching ratcheting-up of culture, language and thought, make categories and structures available to maturing speakers, which, indeed, their minds were not initially equipped for.

ACKNOWLEDGMENTS

I thank Peter Austin, Nick Enfield, Jane Hill, Luise Hercus, Steve Levinson, Pat McConvell, Bill McGregor, Hans-Jürgen Sasse, and Mauro Tosco for comments on this paper and its precursors, and the University of Melbourne and the Humboldt Foundation for supporting its preparation through sabbatical leave and a Humboldt fellowship, respectively.

The *Annual Review of Anthropology* is online at http://anthro.annualreviews.org

LITERATURE CITED

Alpher B. 1993. Out-of-the-ordinary ways of using language. *In Language and Culture in Aboriginal Australia*, ed. M Walsh, C Yallop, pp. 97–106. Canberra, Aust.: Aboriginal Stud. Press

Bickerton D. 1995. *Language and Human Behaviour.* Seattle: Univ. Wash. Press

Boas F, ed. 1966 [1911/1922]. *Handbook of American Indian Languages, Pts. 1 and 2.* Washington, DC: Bur. Am. Ethnol. Bull.

Bowerman M, Levinson SC, eds. 2001. *Language Acquisition and Conceptual Development.* Cambridge, UK: Cambridge Univ. Press

Brandl M, Walsh M. 1982. Speakers of many tongues: toward understanding multilingualism among Aboriginal Australians. *Int. J. Soc. Lang.* 36:71–81

Bybee J. 2000. Lexicalization of sound change and alternating environments. In *Papers in Laboratory Phonology V. Acquisition and the Lexicon*, ed. MD Broe, JB Pierrehumbert, pp. 250–68. Cambridge, UK: Cambridge Univ. Press

Chomsky N. 1980. *Rules and Representations.* New York: Columbia Univ. Press

Dench A. 1987. Kinship and collective activity in the Ngayarda languages of Australia. *Lang. Soc.* 16:321–39

Dixon RMW. 1990. The origin of "Mother-in-Law Vocabulary" in two Australian languages. *Anthropol. Linguist.* 32(1/2):1–56

Dixon RMW. 1991. *Words of Our Country.* St. Lucia, Aust.: Queensland Univ. Press

Du Bois J. 1987. The discourse basis of ergativity. *Language* 63:805–55

Durham WH. 1991. *Coevolution. Genes, Culture and Human Diversity.* Stanford, CA: Stanford Univ. Press

Enfield NJ. 2002a. Introduction. See Enfield 2002b, pp. 1–30

Enfield NJ, ed. 2002b. *Ethnosyntax.* Oxford, UK: Oxford Univ. Press

Enfield NJ. 2003. *Linguistic Epidemiology. Semantics and Grammar of Language Contact in Mainland Southeast Asia.* London: Routledge Curzon

Evans N. 1992. Multiple semiotic systems, hyperpolysemy, and the reconstruction of semantic change in Australian languages. In *Diachrony Within Synchrony*, ed. G Kellerman, M Morrissey, pp. 475–508. Bern, Switz.: Lang Verlag

Evans N. 1997. Sign metonymies and the problem of flora-fauna polysemy in Australian linguistics. See Tryon & Walsh 1997, pp. 133–53

Evans N, Wilkins D. 2000. In the mind's ear: the semantic extensions of perception verbs in Australian languages. *Language* 76(3):546–92

Fodor J. 1975. *The Language of Thought.* Cambridge, MA: Harvard Univ. Press

Giddens A. 1984. *The Constitution of Society.* Berkeley, Los Angeles: Univ. Calif. Press

Goddard C. 1992. Traditional Yankunytjatjara ways of speaking—a Yankunytjatjara perspective. *Aust. J. Linguist.* 12(1):93–122

Hale KL. 1966. Kinship reflections in syntax: some Australian languages. *Word* 22:318–24

Hale KL. 1986. Notes on world view and semantic categories: some Warlpiri examples. In *Features and Projections*, ed. P Muysken, HJ van Riemsdijk, pp. 233–54. Dordrecht: Foris

Haspelmath M. 1999. Optimality and diachronic adaptation. *Z. Sprachwiss.* 19(2):180–205

Hauser MD, Chomsky N, Fitch WT. 2002. The faculty of language: What is it, who has it, and how did it evolve? *Science* 298:1569–79

Heath J, Merlan F, Rumsey A, eds. 1982. *The Languages of Kinship in Aboriginal Australia.* Sydney: Oceania Linguist. Monogr.

Hercus L, White IM. 1973. Perception of kinship structure reflected in the Adnjamathanha pronouns. *Pap. Aust. Linguist.* 6:49–72

Hill JH, Hill KC. 1998. Culture influencing language: plurals of Hopi kin terms in Uto-Aztecan perspective. *J. Linguist. Anthropol.* 7:166–80

Hopper P, Traugott EC. 1993. *Grammaticalization.* Cambridge, UK: Cambridge Univ. Press

Johnson S. 1991. Linguistic change in an unstratified Aboriginal society. In *Linguistic Change and Reconstruction Methodology*, ed. P Baldi, pp. 419–34. Berlin: Mouton de Gruyter

Keen I. 1994. *Knowledge and Secrecy in an Aboriginal Religion.* Melbourne, Aust.: Oxford Univ. Press

Keesing R. 1979. Linguistic knowledge and cultural knowledge: some doubts and speculations. *Am. Anthropol.* 81(1):14–36

Keller R. 1994. *On Language Change: the Invisible Hand in Language.* London: Routledge

Keller R. 1998. *A Theory of Linguistic Signs.* Oxford, UK: Oxford Univ. Press

Langacker R. 1994. Culture, cognition and grammar. In *Language Contact and Language Conflict*, ed. M. Pütz, pp. 25–54. Amsterdam: Benjamins

Levinson S. 2000. *Language as nature and language as art.* Presented to Pontifical Acad. Sci., Rome

Levinson S. 2001. Covariation between spatial language and cognition, and its implications for language learning. See Bowerman & Levinson 2001, pp. 566–88

Lucy J. 1997. Linguistic relativity. *Annu. Rev. Anthropol.* 26:291–312

McConvell P. 1982. Neutralisation and degrees of respect in Gurindji. See Heath et al. 1982, pp. 86–106

McConvell P. 1985a. The origin of subsections in Northern Australia. *Oceania* 56:1–33

McConvell P. 1985b. Time perspective in Aboriginal culture: two approaches to the origin of subsections. *Aborig. Hist.* 9(1):53–80

McGregor WB. 1989. Gooniyandi mother-in-law "language": dialect, register, and/or code? In *Status and Function of Languages and Language Varieties*, ed. U Ammon, pp. 630–56. Berlin: Walter de Gruyter

McKnight DA. 1999. *People, Countries and the Rainbow Serpent.* New York: Oxford Univ. Press

Merlan F. 1981. Land, language and social identity in Aboriginal Australia. *Mankind* 13(2):133–48

Merlan F. 1982. 'Egocentric' and 'altercentric' usage of kin terms in Mangarayi. See Heath et al. 1982, pp. 125–40

Merlan F. 1989. Jawoyn relationship terms: interactional dimensions of Australian kin classification. *Anthropol. Linguist.* 31:227–64

Morphy F. 1977. Language and moiety: sociolectal variation in a Yu:lngu language of North-East Arnhem Land. *Canberra Anthropol.* 1(1):51–60

Morphy H. 1991. *Ancestral Connections. Art and an Aboriginal System of Knowledge.* Chicago, IL: Chicago Univ. Press

Napaljarri Rockman P, Cataldi L, eds. 1994. *Warlpiri Dreamings and Histories: Yimikirli. The Sacred Literature Series.* San Francisco: Harper Collins

Nash D. 1991. Patrilects of the Warumungu and Warlmanpa and their neighbours. In *Language and History: Essays in Honour of Luise A. Hercus*, ed. P Austin, RMW Dixon, T Dutton, I White, pp. 209–20. Canberra, Aust.: Pac. Linguist.

Nash D. 1998. *Ethnocartography: understanding central Australian geographic literacy.* Presented at Aust. Anthropol. Soc. Annu. Conf., Canberra

O'Grady GN. 1990. Pama-Nyungan: the tip of the lexical iceberg. In *Studies in Comparative Pama-Nyungan*, ed. GN O'Grady, DT Tryon, pp. 209–59. Canberra, Aust.: Pac. Linguist.

Perkins RD. 1992. *Deixis, Grammar and Culture.* Amsterdam: Benjamins

Pinker S. 1994. *The Language Instinct.* New York: Morrow

Pinker S, Bloom P. 1990. Natural language and natural selection. *Behav. Brain Sci.* 13:707–84

Rigsby B. 1997. Structural parallelism and convergence in the Princess Charlotte Bay languages. In *Archaeology and Linguistics: Aboriginal Australia in Global Perspective,* ed. P McConvell, N Evans, pp. 169–78. Melbourne, Aust.: Oxford Univ. Press

Rumsey A. 1982. Gun-gunma: an Australian Aboriginal avoidance language and its social functions. See Heath et al. 1982, pp. 160–81

Rumsey A. 1990. Wording, meaning and linguistic ideology. *Am. Anthropol.* 92:346–61

Schebeck B. 1973. The Adnjamathanha personal pronoun and the "Wailpi kinship system". *Pap. Aust. Linguist.* 6:1–45

Silverstein M. 1979. Language structure and linguistic ideology. In *The Elements: a Parasession on Linguistic Units and Levels,* ed. P Clyne, W Hanks, C Hofbauer, pp. 193–247. Chicago, IL: Chicago Linguist. Soc.

Silverstein M. 1985. Language and the culture of gender: at the intersection of structure, usage and ideology. In *Semiotic Meditation: Sociocultural and Psychological Perspectives,* ed. E Mertz, RJ Parmentier, pp. 219–59. New York: Acad. Press

Simpson J. 2002. From common ground to syntactic construction: associated path in Warlpiri. See Enfield 2002b, pp. 287–307

Slobin DI. 2001. Form-function relations: How do children find out what they are? See Bowerman & Levinson 2001, pp. 406–49

Smith I, Johnson D. 1986. Sociolinguistic patterns in an unstratified society: the patrilects of Kugu Nganhcara. *J. Atl. Prov. Linguist. Assoc.* 8:29–43

Sperber D, Wilson D. 1986. *Relevance, Communication and Cognition.* Cambridge, MA: Harvard Univ. Press

Spitzer L. 1947. *Essays in Historical Semantics.* New York: Russell & Russell

Sutton P. 1978. *Wik: Aboriginal society, territory and language at Cape Keerweer, Cape York Peninsula, Australia.* PhD thesis, Univ. Queensland, St Lucia

Sweetser E. 1990. *From Etymology to Pragmatics: Metaphorical and Cultural Aspects of Semantic Structure.* Cambridge, UK: Cambridge Univ. Press

Tomasello M. 1999. The human adaptation for culture. *Annu. Rev. Anthropol.* 28:509–29

Trigger D. 1987. Languages, linguistic groups and status relations at Doomadgee, an Aboriginal settlement in north-west Queensland, Australia. *Oceania* 57:217–38

Tryon D, Walsh M, eds. 1997. *Boundary Rider. Essays in Honour of Geoffrey O'Grady.* Canberra, Aust.: Pac. Linguist.

Von Brandenstein GG. 1970. The meaning of section and subsection names. *Oceania* 41:39–49

Waters B. 1989. *Djinang and Djinba—a Grammatical and Historical Perspective.* Canberra, Aust.: Pac. Linguist.

Wilkins D. 1989. *Mparntwe Arrernte (Aranda): studies in the structure and semantics of grammar.* PhD. thesis. Australian Natl. Univ., Canberra

Wilkins D. 1997. Handsigns and hyperpolysemy: exploring the cultural foundations of a semantic association. See Tryon & Walsh 1997, pp. 413–44

Wilkinson M. 1991. *Djambarrpuyngu. A Yolngu variety of Northern Australia.* Ph.D. thesis. Univ. Sydney, Sydney

Woolard KA. 1998. Introduction: language ideology as a field of inquiry. In *Language Ideologies: Practice and Theory,* ed. BB Schieffelin, K Woolard, P Kroskrity, pp. 3–47. New York: Oxford Univ. Press

Woolard KA, Schieffelin BB. 1994. Language ideology. *Annu. Rev. Anthropol.* 23:55–82

Annu. Rev. Anthropol. 2003. 32:41–62
doi: 10.1146/annurev.anthro.32.061002.093107
First published online as a Review in Advance on April 18, 2003

GENDER AND INEQUALITY IN THE GLOBAL LABOR FORCE

Mary Beth Mills

*Department of Anthropology, Colby College, 4700 Mayflower Hill, Waterville,
Maine 04901; email: memills@colby.edu*

Key Words industrialization, transnational mobility, masculinity and femininity,
informal sector, unions and labor organizing

■ **Abstract** This review examines the convergence of recent anthropological interests in gender, labor, and globalization. Attention to gender and gender inequality offers a productive strategy for the analysis of globalizing processes and their local variations and contestations. Contemporary ethnographic research explores multiple dimensions of labor and gender inequalities in the global economy: gendered patterns of labor recruitment and discipline, the transnational mobility and commodification of reproductive labor, and the gendered effects of international structural adjustment programs, among others. New and continuing research explores the diverse meanings and practices that produce a gendered global labor force, incorporating the perspectives of men and women, masculinities and femininities, and examines how these processes of gender and labor inequality articulate with other structures of subordination (such as ethnicity and nationality) to shape lived experiences of work and livelihood, exploitation and struggle, around the world.

INTRODUCTION

Studies of gender, labor, and globalization do not constitute a clearly bounded or easily definable field of research in anthropology. Nevertheless, the complex intersections of these topics have generated considerable attention and interest in recent years. Numerous edited collections address the overlapping and multifaceted effects of gender and labor inequalities worldwide (see, among others, Elson 1995, Marchand & Runyan 2000, Nash & Fernandez-Kelly 1983, Rothstein & Blim 1992, Ward 1990); whereas, a growing number of focused ethnographies explore the play of these dynamics in specific settings (for example, Finn 1998, Gill 1994, Ong 1987). Much of this work documents the heavily feminized labor forces in free trade zones and similar sites of new industrialization around the world (see Cravey 1998, Freeman 2000, Mills 1999b, Ong 1991, Safa 1995, Wolf 1992). Other work extends the analysis of gender and labor to global processes such as transnational labor migration and domestic service (see Anderson 2000; Constable 1997; Gamburd 2000; Hondagneu-Sotelo 1994, 2001; Parreñas 2001), as well as

0084-6570/03/1021-0041$14.00   **41**

micro-enterprise production and other forms of work in what is often called the informal sector (see Benería & Roldán 1987, Clark 1994, Gill 2000, Rahman 1999, Seligmann 2001). As a whole, the literature encompasses an astonishing range of geographic and occupational settings; yet this eclectic body of research attests to a common phenomenon: a profoundly gendered global economy.

Gender inequalities operate simultaneously, but not identically, as systems of dominant meanings and symbolism; as structured social relations, roles, and practices; and as lived experiences of personal identity. The literature discussed here is notable for engaging all of these divergent dimensions of gender. Of particular interest are the findings of many scholars, which state that gender meanings, relations, and identities do more than merely sustain existing structures of power in global labor relations; these complex dimensions of gender also constitute a dynamic cultural terrain wherein forms of domination may be contested, reworked, and even potentially transformed.

Of course, in any given place or time, gender is only one of "multiple, interlocking systems of domination" (Clark 1994, p. 422). Many ethnographers of globalization explore the ways that gender intersects with other sources of discrimination and exploitation in the lives of working men and women. Gender inequalities represent one dynamic within a global labor force that is also segmented by class, ethnicity and race, nationality and region, among other factors. By tracing these varied systems of domination as they combine in different settings, scholars have begun to illuminate the diverse processes through which gender and labor inequalities shape the global economy. Although this review focuses on gendered forms and experiences of inequality, its aim is not to discount other aspects of identity or ideology that underlie global patterns of labor exploitation and material extraction. Rather the point here is to follow the particular insights that gendered analyses contribute to a broad and dynamic field of study.

Around the globe, gender hierarchies are produced and maintained in relation to transnational circuits of labor mobilization and capital accumulation. In varied and often locally specific ways international capital relies on gendered ideologies and social relations to recruit and discipline workers, to reproduce and cheapen segmented labor forces within and across national borders (see, among others, Enloe 1989, Ong 1991, Safa 1995). These are not new phenomena. Historians of the industrial revolution document the early recruitment of women (particularly young unmarried women) as a highly flexible, inexpensive, and easily disciplined source of labor (Dublin 1979, Tilly & Scott 1978, Tsurumi 1990). Similarly, European colonial regimes relied in part upon the mobilization of colonized women (as well as men) to work, for example, as domestic servants and concubines to colonial officials or as family workers on plantation estates (Stoler 1985, 1991). Yet today, more than in any previous era, the gendered and ethnically segmented labor pool upon which capitalist accumulation depends encompasses every corner of the globe. The first part of this review examines recent contributions to teasing apart the gendered inequalities that produce and sustain these global labor practices in their many variations. The second part of this review explores ongoing efforts by scholars to show how processes of gender and labor inequality articulate with actual women's and men's lived experiences to produce a wide range of struggles and contestations. This division is made for ease of discussion only; both directions of analysis offer critical insights and new questions for further research. Indeed, a central feature of this literature is its consistent attention to the intersections of structure and agency, ideology and practice in tracing out the complex and contested dynamics of gender and labor inequalities around the world.

PRODUCING A GENDERED GLOBAL LABOR FORCE

Feminization and the Disciplining of Global Labor

Around the world, hierarchical gender ideologies serve to cheapen the direct costs of labor to capital by defining key segments of the population (notably women and children) as supplementary or devalued workers (see, for example, Elson 1995, Enloe 1989, Marchand & Runyon 2000). At one level, the pictures appear remarkably consistent; in country after country, industrial employers identify the inherently desirable qualities of their preferred labor force: "nimble-fingered," often youthful, and deferential female workers. Wherever they locate—from Indonesia (Wolf 1992) to Israel (Drori 2000), Mexico (Cravey 1998, Fernandez-Kelly 1983) to Malaysia (Ong 1987)—global factories reproduce similar models of organization wherein women dominate the lowest levels both of pay and authority, whereas men occupy most positions of supervisory and managerial rank (see also Ong 1991 for a comprehensive review of these patterns in Mexican and Asian industrialization through the 1980s). Indeed, it is the hegemonic capacity of patriarchal norms to define women's labor as not only "cheap" but socially and economically worthless (and therefore less worthy of equitable pay and other treatment) that makes a gendered labor force so crucial to the accumulation strategies of global capital (Wright 1999, 2001).

And yet the appearance of sameness is also deceiving. A closer look at the ethnographic record reveals considerable diversity in the discursive forms and material practices that gender hierarchies take within the global labor force. In some cases it is women's status as unmarried and subordinate "daughters" that makes them an attractively cheap and flexible pool of labor (Drori 2000, Kim 1997, Lynch 1999, Wolf 1992). In other contexts, it is women's status as wives and mothers that justifies their lower wages and limited job security (Kondo 1990, Lamphere 1987, Lee 1998, Roberts 1994). Disciplinary strategies may also (and often at the same time) position female workers as sexualized bodies whose subordination is maintained through erotic banter and other forms of sexual harassment (Prieto 1997, Wright 2001, Yelvington 1995). A heightened emphasis on feminine beauty, fashion, and commodified leisure activities associated with wage work can similarly position workers as feminized consumers rather than as productive (and valuable) laborers (Freeman 2000, Lynch 1999, Mills 1999b).

In any given setting the variable interplay of multiple gender roles and meanings can produce a wide range of recruitment and disciplinary regimes. Lee (1998) found that the same company deployed sharply different gendered discourses to deal with its female workforces in Hong Kong (where older women were enlisted in a process of self regulation) and in the nearby free trade zones of South China (where young rural migrants were subject to a much harsher, authoritarian labor process). In the U.S.-Mexico border region, a single, dominant gender discourse constructs Mexican women as the ideal (i.e., docile) labor force for transnational industry; yet on the shop floor the monolithic image of a feminized labor force refracts into divergent forms of labor regulation: from factory regimes that highlight workers' sexualized appearances as idealized objects of managerial consumption and control, to settings in which gendered identities are subordinated to workers' closely monitored performance of piece-rate production quotas (Salzinger 1997). Such studies demonstrate that dominant discourses about gender affect but cannot determine the day-to-day dynamics of labor discipline. Hegemonic ideologies always intersect with local histories and demographies, production processes, and managerial styles to produce site- and even factory-specific regimes of control and contestation.

These patterns are also historically contingent. Longitudinal studies of feminized labor reveal the value of tracing disciplinary regimes over time. Changing demographics and immigration patterns over the twentieth century transformed the preferred labor force of Rhode Island textile and garment factories from unmarried daughters to married mothers (Lamphere 1987). Bao (2001) and Matthews (2003) respectively explore other gendered and ethnicized histories of labor in New York City and California's Silicon Valley. Political transformations can shape these histories as well. The Chinese state's promotion of capitalist production regimes has prompted new gendered labor practices that include the massive recruitment of young rural women for industrial work into urban areas and special economic zones (Lee 1998, L. Zhang 2001); nevertheless, these shifts have not affected all workers in the same ways. Rofel (1999) traces the impact of China's economic reforms in the lives of female silk workers, once members of a revolutionary proletariat whose industrial labor is now no longer an important symbol of national goals. Rosenthal (2002) examines similar processes in a state-owned textile factory in Vietnam.

Labor recruitment into export-oriented agricultural production offers another telling example of the variable ways gender meanings can be used to devalue and control labor. Global agri-business relies on large pools of cheap and seasonally replaceable labor to perform tasks that are typically segregated by gender. Comparing fruit workers in Chile, Brazil, and Mexico, Collins (1995) notes that these gendered norms vary in ways that make clear their arbitrary quality: identical tasks are defined as "men's" work in one place and "women's" in another. Yet in each setting patriarchal norms are manipulated to ensure the low cost structure of the industry. Of particular interest here is the finding that these practices do not mean that women are always positioned at the bottom of the wage scale, if, for example, a more vulnerable population (such as migrants) can be tapped as an even cheaper reserve pool (Collins 1995, pp. 190–92). In other studies of commodified agriculture in Latin America, India, and Africa, scholars explore similar modes of labor segmentation. Varied combinations of gender, class, and ethnic divisions structure agricultural labor inequalities in ways that limit employers' costs and also undermine the possibilities for workers' collective action (Chatterjee 2001, Dolan 2001, Freidberg 2001, Orton et al. 2001, Sachs 1996, Striffler 1999).

Globalizing Reproduction: Gender in the Transnational Service Economy

The feminization of global labor is not limited to third-world sites of export-oriented industry or agriculture; feminized and migrant labor forces are also crucial to reducing the high costs of private consumption and social reproduction at the centers of global privilege and power. Transnational migrants, both women and men, represent a pool of vulnerable, feminized labor in the lowest wage sectors of the world's wealthiest economies (Foner 2000, Kwong 1998, Mahler 1995, Sassen 1998, Yeoh et al. 2000). As sweatshop garment sewers, restaurant workers, domestic servants, and day laborers they provide the undervalued services essential to maintaining both the structures and symbols of global economic power and privilege.

For example, Bonacich & Appelbaum (2000) show how the small subcontracting enterprises that make up the Los Angeles garment trade are essential to maintaining the rapid turnover of clothing styles and fashions in the women's apparel industry. Small shops must produce new products on demand in short periods of time, a process made profitable by their ability to hire predominantly immigrant (often undocumented) and female labor at extremely low wages with minimal protections. Not coincidentally, the gender and ethnic marginalization of this sweated labor force sustains the demands of an industry that is itself crucial to the ideological production of hegemonic femininity as defined through the endless consumption of women's fashion. Similarly, Ingraham (1999) notes the links between sweated labor in the global wedding-gown industry and the consumption and reproduction of hegemonic femininity and patriarchal heterosexuality in U.S. popular culture.

The complex effects of gendered hierarchies on the transnational mobility of global labor is also evident in the international market for domestic servants. Caribbean nannies in New York (Colen 1995); Filipina caregivers in Los Angeles and Rome (Parreñas 2001), in Hong Kong (Constable 1997), and in Malaysia (Chin 1998); Mexican and Latina housecleaners in California and other parts of the United States (Hondagneu-Sotelo 2001, Romero 1992); Sri Lankan maids in Saudi Arabia (Gamburd 2000)—all provide a feminized and racialized support structure for more privileged households. In many cases, this commodification of reproductive labor frees female employers to enter or maintain professional occupations, thereby challenging some gender barriers in their own societies but without a radical reworking of gender responsibilities in the domestic realm. Instead these duties are displaced onto ethnically and legally marginalized women in a complex entanglement of gender, class, racial, and ethnic hierarchies that stretch across the globe.

Ironically, many women and men who provide transnational service labor are themselves pursuing globally inflected desires for class mobility and consumption. The costs of plane fares, agency fees, and other expenses necessary to attain international employment (whether by legal or illegal means) are often very high. Consequently, many of those entering circuits of transnational migration are not the poorest members of their societies; many come from more intermediate strata that face reduced economic opportunities or declining income, perhaps as a result of economic retrenchment and structural adjustment policies in sending countries. Thus, in the Philippines, women with middle-class education credentials—nurses and teachers, for example—find they can earn much more working as domestic servants in Hong Kong, Italy, or Canada (Barber 2000, Constable 1997, Parreñas 2001). Despite the appearance of downward class mobility, these and other transnationally employed domestic workers can secure and even enhance the status of their families left behind. For example, many such migrants use part of their international wages to hire even cheaper domestic help at home. In this way, circuits of transnational labor not only are a product of gendered and ethnic hierarchies within a segmented global labor force, but also they reproduce these same relations of inequality (Parreñas 2001, pp. 72–78).

The Gender and Labor Inequalities of Structural Adjustment

As the preceding discussion suggests, the structuring of gender inequality in one type of employment or one segment of the global economy cannot be viewed in isolation from any other. Further complicating the picture, many scholars argue that the intersections of gender, labor, and globalization extend well beyond the confines of the formal wage economy and conventional arenas of capitalist production. Specifically, ethnographies from Bolivia (Gill 1994, 2000) to Zambia (Hansen 2000), Turkey (White 1994) to Nicaragua (Babb 2001) elucidate the gender and labor inequalities of international structural adjustment policies and related neo-liberal economic programs. These and other scholars highlight the ironies of a global economy in which transnational circuits of labor mobility stretch families and their functions across international boundaries at the same time that international policies of neo-liberal economic restructuring rely upon the resilience of those families to absorb social costs.

Structural adjustment policies require states to cut back or eliminate many social programs and subsidies; this process has had a devastating effect on many communities often with sharply gendered implications. Such programs of economic restructuring—usually implemented at the behest of international financial authorities, such as the International Monetary Fund or World Bank—depend upon the flexible capacities of private households to absorb the loss of state-funded social services (Benería & Feldman 1992, Bergeron 2001, Harrison 1997, Susser 1997). In effect, structural adjustment plans mobilize women's unpaid labor as domestic nurturers and economizers to subsidize costs for international capitalism and to guarantee the debts incurred by poor states. At the same time, the tightened economic conditions that result from economic restructuring programs diminish the security of formal wage employment and increase dependence on informal means of income generation. These sources of livelihood are often largely feminized, including vending and hawking (Babb 1989, Clark 1994, Seligmann 2001), subcontracting and industrial homework (Benería & Roldan 1987, Gringeri 1994, White 1994, L. Zhang 2001), artisanal craft production (Grimes & Milgram 2000, Tice 1995, Wilkinson-Weber 1999), domestic service (Adams & Dickey 2000, Bujra 2000, Gill 1994, Hansen 1992, Ozyegin 2000), and sex work (Maher 1997, Moon 1997, Muecke 1992), among others.

Moreover, women's informal entrepreneurial and artisanal labor has itself been identified as a promising field for international economic development. The growth potential of women's informal sector work is one of the underlying tenets of micro-enterprise investment, also known as the micro-credit movement (Dignard & Havet 1995). Most often modeled on Bangladesh's Grameen Bank, micro-credit financing is viewed by many states and non-state groups alike as an ideal strategy for poverty alleviation and economic development. Most micro-credit programs are targeted primarily if not exclusively at women for investment in small, household-based livelihood projects. Loans typically are secured collectively by small groups of borrowers for whom new loans are dependent on successful repayment by the entire group. Micro-credit is hailed by international sponsors as a means to implement gender-sensitive development, "empowering" women by mobilizing the untapped creativity of their productive and reproductive labor (Mayoux 1999). Nevertheless, micro-enterprise programs rarely challenge the overall sexual division of labor within households and may even reinforce these gendered norms (Milgram 2001, Rozario 1997). Some ethnographic studies suggest that (in practice if not in their original intent) micro-credit programs are more effective at extracting profits from the economic activities of poor women and men than in transforming systems of gender hierarchy or empowering their clients socially and economically (Gill 2000, pp. 142–51; Rahman 1999).

CHALLENGE AND CONTESTATION: GENDERED STRUGGLES IN THE GLOBAL LABOR FORCE

Considering the wide range of settings and the diverse labor practices to which they contribute, it is clear that patriarchal ideologies and related gender inequalities are significant, even constitutive, features of the global economy. In complex and multifaceted ways, gendered hierarchies help to produce a segmented and flexible global labor force. However, the ways in which hegemonic gender meanings structure the lived experiences of actual women and men vary widely. In fact, the forms of gendered inequality that people encounter in their own lives are often sources of conflict and contradiction as gendered ideologies and structures of authority clash with individuals' own lived desires and identities. Slippages between ideological norms and everyday experiences can rupture the disciplinary effects of gender hierarchy whether on the shop floor or in other settings. The resulting disjunctures and inconsistencies can open the way to generate new meanings and practices. Gender inequalities are thus not only sources of exploitation within a global labor force but also, and importantly, critical points of contestation and struggle.

The forms these struggles take, however, are as varied and complex as the hegemonic structures they confront. Some involve explicit oppositional protest, such as strikes and labor organizing, although, as discussed below, the obstacles to such actions are often formidable. In many cases, however, new experiences of global labor give rise to contests that are less obviously confrontational. Nevertheless, these localized processes of what Ong has called "cultural struggle" (Ong 1991, p. 281) are critical to understanding the effects of globalizing labor practices. As individuals and communities confront new modes of exploitation, they also rework experiences of gender and labor inequality in diverse and often unpredictable ways.

Cultural Struggles and Contested Identities

New experiences of wage work and income earning often engage women and men alike in unprecedented forms of social interaction and personal autonomy. Ideological constructions of women as docile and dexterous workers has facilitated their massive recruitment as idealized workers for global industry; at the same time, the experiences and resources of wage labor provide workers, and especially women, with new means to contest their subordination in other arenas of daily life. Around the world, new forms of wage work offer women novel opportunities to challenge or renegotiate the authority of others, particularly parents or husbands, over both their earnings and their activities.

Extensive research challenges assumptions that women's labor is necessarily subordinated to household economic strategies; instead, studies reveal the complex and contested processes through which women's wage work can enhance their relative bargaining power vis-à-vis family and community. For many women, participation in global labor brings new claims to spatial mobility, consumption expenditures, and a wider range of behaviors in which they can engage as respected members of their communities, as "good" daughters, wives, or mothers (Benería & Roldan 1987, Feldman 2001, Freeman 2000, Hondagneu-Sotelo 1994, Kabeer 2000, Lamphere 1987, Silvey 2000a, Tiano 1994, Yelvington 1995).

A theme widely reported in the literature is the pursuit by young women workers of greater autonomy and control over courtship and marriage decisions. Wage workers in rural Malaysia and Indonesia (Ong 1987, Wolf 1992), rural-urban migrants in Thailand (Mills 1999b), factory operatives in Sri Lanka (Lynch 1999), and economic migrants in Shenzen, China (Clark 2001) all use the enhanced autonomy that wage earning gives them to negotiate with parents over desired partners, to postpone or evade arranged marriages, or to experiment with new styles of unsupervised romance and independent matchmaking. A few studies also suggest that new spaces opened up by globalized mobility and labor practices enable expressions of transgressive gender identities and alternative sexualities (Blackwood 1998; Theobald 2002, p. 146).

Transnational migration fosters similar assertions of new identities and shifts in gendered claims to autonomy. For example, both historical and contemporary research on immigration to the United States documents how new income-earning roles allow immigrant women to negotiate a wider scope of autonomy and authority within parental and marital households (Foner 2000, p. 108–41; Gabaccia 1994; Lamphere 1987). Given the potential (and not infrequently, actual) failures of husbands or consensual partners to make reliable contributions to household budgets, many women view their wage work as a source of increased personal independence and security despite the often exploitative conditions of that employment (Grasmuck & Pessar 1991, Hirsch 1999, Hondagneu-Sotelo 1994). For example, studies of Mexican and Caribbean women in the United States often find that they are much more reluctant than their male compatriots to return to the home country, believing that it would likely entail a parallel return to more patriarchal household relations (Goldring 2001; Hondagneu-Sotelo 1994, p. 100; Levitt 2001, pp. 104–6).

An important dimension of women's expanding autonomy in many parts of the world is their ability as independent wage earners to participate in new patterns of consumption linked to desired and often globally oriented standards of "modernity." This points to a complex source of tension surrounding women's new visibility within global labor practices: State-based discourses promote goals of national development and progress in which women's recruitment into export-oriented industrialization or other forms of global labor are often critical components. Thus entrants into new industrial jobs or migrants who remit wages from overseas may be hailed as key contributors to nationalist goals of economic growth and modernization (Lynch 1999; Parreñas 2001, p. 53). However, many new recruits to the global labor force seek to achieve standards of modernity in their own right, particularly as active and sophisticated commodity consumers (Freeman 2000, Gill 1994, Mills 1999b, Rofel 1999).

Wage work and new modes of commodity consumption open up newly imaginable possibilities of personal autonomy and self-expression that are often targeted most forcefully at women. Nevertheless, these images of modernity often carry a contested moral status; women in particular are vulnerable to accusations of immorality owing to "excessive" modernity and inappropriate commodity consumption. Access to new sources of income and consumption possibilities can provoke public fears that autonomous women will spend their wages on "selfish" purchases for personal pleasure or adornment. Furthermore, state-based discourses of development can promote such anxieties by displacing social and political tensions associated with rapid economic changes onto concerns about the inappropriate, immodest, or untraditional behavior of women working outside the home (Brenner

1998, Heng & Devan 1995, Ong 1990, Silvey 2000b). Such charges are only heightened in contexts where economic development relies in part upon the commodification of women's sexual labor, for example, at sites of militarization or for tourism (Law 2000, Moon 1997, Sturdevant & Stolzfus 1992, Truong 1990).

Consequently, for many individual subjects, new experiences of labor and gender autonomy are often marked by ambivalence and conflict, producing actions that simultaneously comply with and resist dominant gender ideals. Thus, young Bangladeshi and Egyptian women adopt the gendered restrictions and respectability of "Islamic dress" to enable easier access to public mobility and wage employment (Feldman 2001, MacLeod 1991). In a different context, women in Barbados off-shore informatics (data entry) industries tolerate patriarchal norms and deteriorating labor conditions within the work place while carving out broader spheres of autonomy elsewhere, particularly as informal entrepreneurs in the "suitcase" trade (i.e., goods acquired through international travel for resale at home; see Freeman 2000, 2001). Similar themes of accommodation and resistance are played out in myriad variations around the globe.

Women's transnational labor offers yet another perspective on the complex ways in which global workers both reproduce and contest the gendered conditions of their subordination. Migrants working as international domestic servants assert pride in their achievements and sacrifices as workers, as contributors to their families and sometimes to their nations as well. Although migrants may assert that they are "better" mothers than their employers, claims that are backed up by substantial financial remittances, many women who leave families behind also negotiate a sharp sense of failure for not being "good" (i.e., physically present) mothers to their own children (Gamburd 2000, pp. 207–8; Hondagneu-Sotelo 2001, pp. 22–27; Parreñas 2001, pp. 119–31). At the same time, for some women transnational migration can be a means to escape violent or abusive partners without abandoning their economic obligations to children or other kin (Arguelles & Rivero 1993; Gamburd 2000, pp. 146–47; Parreñas 2001, pp. 66–69).

Gendered Struggles In/About the Workplace

As the forms of accommodation and resistance discussed above reveal, workers around the world may tolerate tremendous exploitation and hardship in order to achieve other economic or social goals. Gendered encounters with capitalist labor relations do not necessarily direct workers' struggles for greater autonomy toward the workplace. In the case of industrial labor, open resistance to harsh working conditions may be especially unlikely when alternative employment options (such as domestic service or sex work) are even less attractive (Harrison 1997). Nevertheless, new experiences of work and newfound autonomy in other aspects of daily life can also open up avenues for contestation on the job. These may be subtle as in footdragging, withdrawal, or other forms of nonconfrontational resistance to employer demands (Drori 2000, pp. 127–32; Freeman 2000, pp. 208–12; Yelvington 1995, pp. 200–2). Distress and anger may find expression in locally situated idioms of protest such as episodes of mass spirit possession in Malay electronics factories (Ong 1987). Faced with different constraints than industrial workers, transnational domestic servants find indirect ways to resist their isolation and the paternalistic control of employers (Chin 1998). In Rome and Hong Kong, for example, Filipina housekeepers gather visibly in open urban sites on their days off, appropriating public spaces as their own (Constable 1997, pp. 166–70; Parreñas 2001, pp. 202–4).

Strikes, unions, and other organized conflict offer the most obvious evidence of contestation in global labor relations; however, ethnographic research concerning such activities remains rather limited. In part, this gap in the larger literature reflects the formidable obstacles to labor organizing in the global economy. The ease with which capital investment can shift production from one site to another limits the effective bargaining power of workers in any one place; at the same time, many contemporary state regimes seek to attract international investors by sharply restricting (or banning outright) unions and other forms of independent collective organizing for workers. The widespread practice of subcontracting in many industries around the world is also a barrier to worker solidarity: because components of the same end product may be manufactured in several different countries by workers employed by multiple subcontractors. This fragmentation of the global labor force, the distancing of production decisions and marketing from the people and places actually assembling global commodities, may well have curtailed opportunities for labor organizing. It has not, however, prevented labor militancy. Moreover, when strikes and other labor conflicts occur women are often key and sometimes primary figures as, for example, in South Korea (Kim 1997, Koo 2001, Ogle 1990), in Mexico (Cravey 1998, Peña 1995, Tirado 1994), and in Southeast Asia (Hutchison & Brown 2001, Margold 1999, Roha 1994, West 1997).

Strikes, walkouts, and other militant labor actions reveal the outrage and potential for confrontation that are obscured by images of "nimble-fingered" docility in a feminized global labor force. Assumptions about deferential and compliant women workers are challenged by patterns of organizing and activism around the globe (Chhachhi & Pittin 1996, Hutchison & Brown 2001, Louie 2001, Rowbotham & Mitter 1994). Although, to date, few extensive ethnographic studies focus on gendered processes of labor organizing and politicization, this is beginning to change. Kim's (1997) study of women workers in Korea offers a particularly detailed ethnography of militant female labor. Related work includes recent studies of women's labor activism in Asia (Brown 2001, Margold 1999, Mills 1999a, West 1997) and Latin America (Gill 1994, Stephen 1997).

The commodification of women's productive and reproductive labor throughout the global economy has prompted new modes of confrontation and collective struggle. For example, ethnically marginalized domestic servants struggle to unionize in Bolivia (Gill 1994). Transnational Caribbean and Filipina migrants organize for better legal protections and citizenship in Canada (Stasiulis & Bakan 1997). Unions and activist groups represent sex workers in many countries (see Kempadoo & Doezema 1998). Similarly some industrial and artisanal homeworkers join union-like bodies (Prugl 1999, Rose 1992, Rowbotham 1998). Other examples include marketing and production cooperatives through which women can seek greater control over their participation in local and global markets often as handi-craft producers (Babb 2001, Milgram 2001, Tice 1995). Some of these organiza-tions begin as local self-help groups, others as projects sponsored by development or charitable programs; many receive support from and maintain crucial ties to re-gional and transnational networks of women's activist and nongovernmental orga-nizations (cf. Rowbotham & Linkogle 2001, Rowbotham & Mitter 1994, Stephen 1997). As a whole, however, the global record of women's economic organizing reveals the enormous obstacles that their efforts face.

In no small part, these difficulties reflect the fact that, around the world, the pa-triarchal assumptions of employers are often shared by labor organizers. Globally, labor union leadership remains predominantly male; when women do organize their efforts are often perceived as supplementary, subordinate, or constrained by prior domestic roles and responsibilities (Kim 1997, Stephen 1997, West 1997). In an Indian example, male-dominated unions in the Calcutta jute industry actively collaborated with employers to protect men's privileges as full-time skilled work-ers rather than seeking to extend protections to women employed as temporary and unskilled laborers in the same production process (Fernandes 1997). The failure of labor institutions to overcome their own histories of gender inequality remains a critical source of weakness for labor solidarity and activism worldwide.

Masculinities and Global Labor

Women may be especially visible as subordinated labor in the global economy, and the contested quality of their experiences can place them in particularly vulnerable positions. However, gendered struggles in the global economy are not only con-tests about norms and practices of femininity; they are also about meanings and experiences of masculinity. Ethnographers are only beginning to ask how shifting material conditions of labor shape gender roles and relations from the perspective of men. Although overall the gendered dynamics of men's participation in global labor has received far less attention than that of women, ethnographies of transna-tional labor mobility have addressed these questions more consistently than others. For example, high rates of overseas contract labor in South and Southeast Asian men have led some ethnographers to note the effects of this pattern of labor re-cruitment on local gender systems and identities (de Guzman 1993, Gardner 1995, Pinches 2001, Yamanaka 2000).

Filipino men working in the Middle East endured harsh working conditions as well as persistent marginalization as members of an alien ethnic and religious minority. Migrants experienced their legal inferiority and vulnerability as a denial not only of their masculinity but also of their own humanity; the effects of these inversions continued to trouble many migrants even after returning home (Margold 1995). A similar sense of vulnerability affects rural Thai men involved in over-seas contract labor, expressed in part through fears of deadly attacks by female spirits (Mills 1995). Nevertheless, many overseas workers seek a confirmation of masculine pride as intrepid and able workers in high-status sites of globalization. Consequently, rural men in Kerala, India view overseas employment, despite its risks, as increasingly necessary if they are to acquire the material and symbolic capital necessary to claim a fully adult masculine status at home (that is, to establish themselves as responsible and marriageable householders—see Osella & Osella 2000). Similarly, some working class Chinese Malay men have made overseas work experience critical to their assertions of successful masculine identities and authority over other men and women at home (Nonini 1997).

Crises of masculinity also figure into migration studies where transnational mobility involves both sexes or when men are the ones left behind. For many migrant and immigrant communities, the obstacles to achieving economic security in the new setting are often experienced as particularly painful failures for men. No longer able to fulfill traditional provider roles, men are often compelled to renegotiate their status and authority within the household (George 2000, Goldring 2001, Levitt 2001, Rouse 1995). This is the same process that results in the expansion of women's claims to authority in immigrant communities and in men's and women's differing perspectives on the long-term settlement plans of many migrant households (see discussion above). An additional consequence, however, is the elaboration of misogynist discourses among some groups of working class men. These discourses can allow men to deflect their own experiences of subordination or distress in the workplace onto images of women, and sometimes violently onto the bodies of female companions (Ferguson 1999, p. 188; Hondagneu-Sotelo & Messner 1994).

Similar conflicts can arise when women move and men stay behind, as noted above. In Sri Lanka, women migrate to work as maids in Saudi Arabia, reversing the expected order of support between husband and wife; however, men do not assume the feminized status of caregivers in return. Struggling to retain a satisfactory identity as masculine heads of household some men claim their wives' remitted earnings for personal use instead of managing these funds for the household. The persistent power of gender hierarchies in the home community makes it difficult for women to challenge husbands when this happens, in part because husbands' transgressions are viewed as a response to the women's own failures to be good (i.e., present) wives (Gamburd 2000).

Global transformations can also prompt crises of masculinity for long-term residents of the world's wealthier societies as, for example, when nonmigrant men face the loss of relatively high-paying working class jobs to de-industrialization or lose managerial positions under corporate down-sizing (McDowell 2000, Newman 1988). In New York City, young Puerto Rican men reject service-sector jobs as both poorly paid and requiring acts of deference that are demeaning to their masculine self-respect. However, without the educational or social capital to achieve well-paying work in the formal economy some young men find both high earnings and a hyper-masculine (and violent) sense of dominance in the illicit drug trade (Bourgois 1995). The gendered effects of economic restructuring on impoverished urban dwellers in Bolivia are reflected in heightened patterns of masculine violence both toward each other and women, owing in part to the brutalizing effects of military service, one of the few employment options still available to poor men (Gill 2000, pp. 117–28). Similarly the decline of Zambia's Copperbelt compels former mineworkers to reexamine their claims to a "modern" masculine self-identity predicated on secure wage earning and a domestic division of labor that are both increasingly untenable (Ferguson 1999).

Recognizing the persistent privileging of masculine authority within gender hierarchies, a few scholars have begun to examine the production of hegemonic masculinities at the centers of global economic power and prestige. Representations and experiences of gender hierarchy in the global economy are not just concerned with cheapening feminized labor forces; they also reveal the shifting ideological grounds upon which entrepreneurial models of masculinity stand. For example, new demands for "caring" in corporate cultures exist in uneasy relationships with longstanding metaphors of "cowboy" competition and related models of aggression in global business practice (Hooper 2000). The different experiences of capitalists in Italian family firms (Yanagisako 2002), diasporic Chinese entrepreneurial elites (Ong 1999), U.S.-Mexico border factories (Salzinger 1997, Wright 2001), and informal sector entrepreneurs in Beijing (L. Zhang 2001) all promote business practices that assert and refigure hegemonic norms of masculinity but in highly specific and culturally contingent ways.

For example, E.Y. Zhang (2001) examines male-peer culture among new entrepreneurs and state officials in Beijing. This is characterized by ritualized outings to nightclubs where men negotiate globally inflected norms of masculinity through the consumption of imported alcohol and the commodified bodies of women. Such ties between expanding business circuits and the heightened demand for women's labor as sex workers also suggest interesting parallels with the ways women's sexual labor supports similar relations of masculinized power linked to global tourism or military expansion (Enloe 1989, Hyde 2001, Law 2000, Moon 1997, Sinclair 1997, Skrobanek et al. 1997, Truong 1990). In a different context, recent analyses of post-Soviet Russia and Eastern Europe note that the shift to neo-liberal capitalism has meant a reevaluation of economic practices in gendered terms. The entrepreneurial and higher-paying segments of the emerging private sector are often linked with a new sense of globalized masculinity, whereas lower-waged jobs and much of the public sector increasingly represent a domain of feminized and devalued labor (see Gal & Kligman 2000, p. 60; Humphrey 2002, p. 178; True 2000).

Whether hegemonic or subordinate, neither masculinities nor femininities in global economic relations are uniform; nor are they experienced in uniform ways. The gendered practices of women and men, both capitalists and laborers, are always and already culturally and historically situated. As such they constitute appropriate, indeed critical, subjects for ethnographic investigation (cf. Yanagisako 2002, p. 188). The challenge is to explicate globally inflected processes in their locally specific forms while at the same time seeking connections across economic and social contexts.

CONCLUSION

Engaging gender as both a subject and a tool of analysis, the ethnographic and scholarly research discussed above has generated new ways of understanding the intersections between international hegemonies and particular localities in a global labor force. A rich array of case studies and comparative analyses—many more in fact than can be cited in a short review—explore the multiple ways that gendered meanings, practices, and identities mediate these points of contact. The result is an innovative and wide-ranging body of scholarship that illuminates the heterogeneous character of globalizing labor practices and their gendered dynamics.

In a diverse global economy, gender ideologies can support flexible modes of labor control and discipline because of their ability to naturalize arbitrary and constructed claims about whose labor is worth more (or less) and what kinds of bodies are best suited to particular tasks. At the same time, global transformations in production, mobility, and livelihood have specific effects in the lives of gendered subjects, creating tensions and conflicts as well as newly imaginable possibilities. The resulting struggles involve men and women, workers and employers, communities and states in contests that can at times reproduce existing relations of power; however, they can also lead to new, potentially transformative forms of action and identity. Continuing research into the intersections of gender, labor, and globalization must engage all of these varied dimensions of discipline and contestation. Critical as well are studies that can link diverse patterns of gender and labor inequalities with other intertwining sources of power and domination: ethnic-racial divisions, rural-urban conflicts, state ideologies, mass media influences, and more. Whereas women's entry into new forms of employment has focused considerable attention on transformations in experiences and images of femininity in the global economy, far less research has traced how discourses and experiences of masculinity are also implicated in the shifting dynamics of a globalized labor force. Although scholars have begun to ask these and related questions, new research must incorporate closer attention to the constructions of both masculinities and femininities, and the contested experiences of men as well as (and in relation to) women within a gendered labor force.

Comparative work across national boundaries is especially important to illuminate these complexities and contradictions in labor and gender inequalities. Finn (1998) offers an instructive model in her study of a transnational mining corporation and its effects on the men and women of two communities, one in the United States and the other in Chile. Though mining employment in both sites was a masculine preserve, women's domestic work and image were essential to the systems of labor control and struggle in both communities, albeit in different ways. Tracing the interactions of management and workers, men and women, Finn's cross-border and historical analysis unravels the tangled hierarchies of gender, class, ethnicity, and nationality. She highlights the struggles these forces engendered to show how and why they produced differential and shifting experiences of inequality in time and space.

This kind of attention to gender and gender inequalities, in both their material and ideological dimensions, will continue to offer productive strategies for scholarly research. Historically informed and ethnographically rich comparative work is essential to build a more complex understanding of gender and labor in globalizing processes. How do men and women sustain new understandings of themselves and their relations with others while seeking to survive amid often limited options? How and when can people channel new meanings and experiences into actions that may challenge underlying structures of inequality and domination? Under what conditions are such confrontations with inequality more likely to maintain or reproduce structures of power, including gender hierarchies? Ethnographic and anthropological research is and will continue to be particularly well positioned to trace these complexities across settings and times, amid intersecting ideological and symbolic systems, within and between particular industries, states, communities, workplaces, and lives. In so doing, ethnographers of gender, labor, and globalization can and will continue to make gender visible in new ways, to uncover the arbitrary and artificial ways through which gendered inequalities devalue labor and undermine the security and livelihoods of men and women around the world.

ACKNOWLEDGMENTS

I would like to thank Eugenie Montague and Connie Beal, student research assistants who contributed many hours to the preparation of the bibliography for this review. My thanks also to Colby College for the financial support of these positions. I am especially grateful to my colleagues in the Department of Anthropology at Colby College for their generosity and support throughout and to Lesley Sharp for invaluable procedural advice.

The *Annual Review of Anthropology* is online at http://anthro.annualreviews.org

LITERATURE CITED

Adams KM, Dickey S, eds. 2000. *Home and Hegemony: Domestic Service and Identity Politics in South and Southeast Asia.* Ann Arbor: Univ. Mich. Press

Anderson B. 2000. *Doing the Dirty Work?: the Global Politics of Domestic Labour.* London: Zed Books

Arguelles L, Rivero AM. 1993. Gender/sexual orientation violence and transnational migration: conversations with some Latinas we think we know. *Urban Anthropol.* 22:259–75

Babb FE. 1989. *Between Field and Cooking Pot: the Political Economy of Market-Women in Peru.* Austin: Univ. Texas Press

Babb FE. 2001. *After Revolution: Mapping Gender and Cultural Politics in Neoliberal Nicaragua.* Austin: Univ. Texas Press

Bao X. 2001. *Holding Up More Than Half the Sky: Chinese Women Garment Workers in New York City, 1948–92.* Urbana: Univ. Ill. Press

Barber PG. 2000. Agency in Philippine women's labour migration and provisional diaspora. *Women's Stud. Int. Forum* 23:399–411

Benería L, Feldman S, eds. 1992. *Unequal Burden: Economic Crises, Persistent Poverty and Women's Work.* Boulder, CO: Westview Press

Benería L, Roldán M. 1987. *The Crossroads of Class and Gender: Industrial Homework, Subcontracting, and Household Dynamics in Mexico City.* Chicago, IL: Univ. Chicago Press

Bergeron S. 2001. Political economy discourses of globalization and feminist politics. *Signs* 26:983–1006

Blackwood E. 1998. Tombois in West Sumatra: constructing masculinity and erotic desire. *Cult. Anthropol.* 13(4):491–521

Bonacich E, Appelbaum RP. 2000. *Behind the Label: Inequality in the Los Angeles Apparel Industry.* Berkeley: Univ. Calif. Press

Bourgois P. 1995. *In Search of Respect: Selling Crack in El Barrio.* New York: Cambridge Univ. Press

Brenner SA. 1998. *The Domestication of Desire: Women, Wealth, and Modernity in Java.* Princeton, NJ: Princeton Univ. Press

Brown A. 2001. After the Kader fire: labour organising for health and safety standards in Thailand. See Hutchison & Brown 2001, pp. 127–46

Bujra J. 2000. *Serving Class: Masculinity and the Feminisation of Domestic Service in Tanzania.* Edinburgh: Edinburgh Univ. Press Internat. Afr. Inst.

Chatterjee P. 2001. *A Time for Tea: Women, Labor, and Post/Colonial Politics on an Indian Plantation.* Durham, NC: Duke Univ. Press

Chen NN, Clark CD, Gottschang SZ, Jeffrey L, eds. 2001. *China Urban: Ethnographies of Contemporary Culture.* Durham, NC: Duke Univ. Press

Chhachhi A, Pittin R, eds. 1996. *Confronting State, Capital and Patriarchy: Women Organizing in the Process of Industrialization.* New York: St. Martin's Press

Chin CBN. 1998. *In Service and Servitude: Foreign Female Domestic Workers and the Malaysian 'Modernity' Project.* New York: Columbia Univ. Press

Clark CD. 2001. Foreign marriage, "tradition," and the politics of border crossings. See Chen et al. 2001, pp. 104–22

Clark G. 1994. *Onions Are My Husband: Survival and Accumulation by West African Market Women.* Chicago, IL: Univ. Chicago Press

Colen S. 1995. "Like a mother to them": stratified reproduction and West Indian childcare workers and employers in New York. In *Conceiving the New World Order: the Global Politics of Reproduction*, ed. FD Ginsburg, R Rapp, pp. 78–102. Durham, NC: Duke Univ. Press

Collins JI. 1995. Transnational labor process and gender relations: women in fruit and vegetable production in Chile, Brazil and Mexico. *J. Lat. Am. Anthropol.* 1:178–99

Constable N. 1997. *Maid to Order in Hong Kong: an Ethnography of Filipina Workers.* Ithaca, NY: Cornell Univ. Press

Cravey AJ. 1998. *Women and Work in Mexico's Maquiladoras.* Lanham, MD: Rowman & Littlefield

de Guzman AF. 1993. 'Katas ng Saudi': the work and life situation of the Filipino contract workers in Saudi Arabia. *Philipp. Soc. Sci. Rev.* 52:1–56

Dignard L, Havet J, eds. 1995. *Women in Micro- and Small-Scale Enterprise Development.* Boulder, CO: Westview Press

Dolan CS. 2001. The 'Good Wife': struggles over resources in the Kenyan horticultural sector. *J. Dev. Stud.* 37:39–70

Drori I. 2000. *The Seam Line: Arab Workers and Jewish Managers in the Israeli Textile Industry.* Stanford, CA: Stanford Univ. Press

Dublin T. 1979. *Women at Work: the Transformation of Work and Community in Lowell, Massachusetts, 1826–1860.* New York: Columbia Univ. Press

Elson D, ed. 1995. *Male Bias in the Development Process.* Manchester, UK: Manchester Univ. Press. 2nd ed.

Enloe C. 1989. *Bananas, Beaches and Bases: Making Feminist Sense of International Politics.* Berkeley: Univ. Calif. Press

Feldman S. 2001. Exploring theories of

patriarchy: a perspective from contemporary Bangladesh. *Signs* 26:1097–127

Ferguson J. 1999. *Expectations of Modernity: Myths and Meanings of Urban Life on the Zambian Copperbelt.* Berkeley: Univ. Calif. Press

Fernandes L. 1997. *Producing Workers: the Politics of Gender, Class and Culture in the Calcutta Jute Mills.* Philadelphia: Univ. Penn. Press

Fernandez-Kelly MP. 1983. *For We Are Sold, I and My People: Women and Industry in Mexico's Frontier.* Albany, NY: SUNY Press

Finn JL. 1998. *Tracing the Veins: Of Copper, Culture, and Community from Butte to Chuquicamata.* Berkeley: Univ. Calif. Press

Foner N. 2000. *From Ellis Island to JFK: New York's Two Great Waves of Immigration.* New Haven, CT: Yale Univ. Press

Freeman C. 2000. *High Tech and High Heels in the Global Economy: Women, Work and Pink-Collar Identities in the Caribbean.* Durham, NC: Duke Univ. Press

Freeman C. 2001. Is local:global as feminine:masculine? Rethinking the gender of globalization. *Signs* 26:1007–37

Freidberg S. 2001. To garden, to market: gendered meanings of work on an African urban periphery. *Gender Place Cult.* 8:5–25

Gabaccia D. 1994. *From the Other Side: Women, Gender, and Immigrant Life in the U.S., 1820–1990.* Bloomington: Indiana Univ. Press

Gal S, Kligman G. 2000. *The Politics of Gender After Socialism: a Comparative-Historical Essay.* Princeton, NJ: Princeton Univ. Press

Gamburd MR. 2000. *The Kitchen Spoon's Handle: Transnationalism and Sri Lanka's Migrant Housemaids.* Ithaca, NY: Cornell Univ. Press

Gardner K. 1995. *Global Migrants, Local Lives: Travel and Transformation in Rural Bangladesh.* Oxford, UK: Clarendon Press

George S. 2000. "Dirty nurses" and "men who play": gender and class in transnational migration. In *Global Ethnography: Forces, Connections and Imaginations in a Post Modern World,* ed. M Burawoy. pp. 144–74. Berkeley: Univ. Calif. Press

Gill L. 1994. *Precarious Dependencies: Gender, Class and Domestic Service in Bolivia.* New York: Columbia Univ. Press

Gill L. 2000. *Teetering on the Rim: Global Restructuring, Daily Life and the Armed Retreat of the Bolivian State.* New York: Columbia Univ. Press

Goldring L. 2001. The gender and geography of citizenship in Mexico-U.S. transnational spaces. *Identities* 7:501–37

Grasmuck S, Pessar PR. 1991. *Between Two Islands: Dominican International Migration.* Berkeley: Univ. Calif. Press

Grimes KM, Milgram BL, eds. 2000. *Artisans and Cooperatives: Developing Alternative Trade for the Global Economy.* Tucson: Univ. Ariz. Press

Gringeri CE. 1994. *Getting By: Women Homeworkers and Rural Economic Development.* Lawrence: Univ. Press Kansas

Hansen KT, ed. 1992. *African Encounters with Domesticity.* New Brunswick, NJ: Rutgers Univ. Press

Hansen KT. 2000. *Salaula: the World of Secondhand Clothing and Zambia.* Chicago: Univ. Chicago Press

Harrison FV. 1997. The gendered politics and violence of structural adjustment: a view from Jamaica. In *Situated Lives: Gender and Culture in Everyday Life,* ed. L Lamphere, H Ragoné, P Zavella, pp. 451–68. London/New York: Routledge

Heng G, Devan J. 1995. State fatherhood: the politics of nationalism, sexuality and race in Singapore. See Ong & Peletz 1995, pp. 195–215

Hirsch JS. 1999. En el norte la mujer manda: gender, generation and geography in a Mexican transnational community. *Am. Behav. Sci.* 42:1332–49

Hondagneu-Sotelo P. 1994. *Gendered Transitions: Mexican Experiences of Immigration.* Berkeley: Univ. Calif. Press

Hondagneu-Sotelo P. 2001. *Domestica: Immigrant Workers Cleaning and Caring in the*

Shadows of Affluence. Berkeley: Univ. Calif. Press

Hondagneu-Sotelo P, Messner MA. 1994. Gender displays and men's power: the "New Man" and the Mexican immigrant man. In *Theorizing Masculinities,* ed. H Brod, M Kaufman, pp. 200–18. London: Sage

Hooper C. 2000. Masculinities in transition: the case of globalization. See Marchand & Runyan 2000, pp. 59–73

Humphrey C. 2002. *The Unmaking of Soviet Life: Everyday Economies After Socialism.* Ithaca, NY: Cornell Univ. Press

Hutchison J, Brown A, eds. 2001. *Organising Labour in Globalising Asia.* London/New York: Routledge

Hyde ST. 2001. Sex tourism practices on the periphery: eroticizing ethnicity and pathologizing sex on the Lancang. See Chen et al. 2001, pp. 143–62

Ingraham C. 1999. *White Weddings: Romancing Heterosexuality in Popular Culture.* London/New York: Routledge

Kabeer N. 2000. *The Power to Choose: Bangladeshi Women and Labour Market Decisions in London and Dhaka.* London/New York: Verso

Kempadoo K, Doezema J, eds. 1998. *Global Sex Workers: Rights, Resistance, and Redefinition.* London/New York: Routledge

Kim S-K. 1997. *Class Struggle or Family Struggle?: the Lives of Women Factory Workers in South Korea.* Cambridge, UK: Cambridge Univ. Press

Kondo DK. 1990. *Crafting Selves: Power, Gender, and Discourses of Identity in a Japanese Workplace.* Chicago: Univ. Chicago Press

Koo H. 2001. *Korean Workers: the Culture and Politics of Class Formation.* Ithaca, NY: Cornell Univ. Press

Kwong P. 1998. *Forbidden Workers: Illegal Chinese Immigrants and American Labor.* New York: New Press

Lamphere L. 1987. *From Working Daughters to Working Mothers: Immigrant Women in a New England Industrial Community.* Ithaca: Cornell Univ. Press

Law L. 2000. *Sex Work in Southeast Asia: the Place of Desire in a Time of AIDS.* London/New York: Routledge

Lee CK. 1998. *Gender and the South China Miracle: Two Worlds of Factory Women.* Berkeley: Univ. Calif. Press

Levitt P. 2001. *The Transnational Villagers.* Berkeley: Univ. Calif. Press

Louie MCY. 2001. *Sweatshop Warriors: Immigrant Women Workers Take on the Global Factory.* Cambridge, MA: South End Press

Lynch C. 1999. The "good girls" of Sri Lankan modernity: moral orders of nationalism and capitalism. *Identities* 6:55–89

MacLeod AE. 1991. *Accommodating Protest: Working Women, the New Veiling and Change in Cairo.* New York: Columbia Univ. Press

Maher L. 1997. *Sexed Work: Gender, Race and Resistance in a Brooklyn Drug Market.* Oxford, UK: Clarendon Press

Mahler SJ. 1995. *American Dreaming: Immigrant Life on the Margins.* Princeton, NJ: Princeton Univ. Press

Marchand MH, Runyan AS, eds. 2000. *Gender and Global Restructuring: Sighting, Sites and Resistances.* London/New York: Routledge

Margold J. 1995. Narratives of masculinity and transnational migration: Filipino workers in the Middle East. See Ong & Peletz 1995, pp. 274–98

Margold J. 1999. Reformulating the compliant image: Filipina activists in the global factory. *Urban Anthropol.* 28:1–35

Matthews G. 2003. *Silicon Valley, Women, and the California Dream: Gender, Class, and Opportunity in the Twentieth Century.* Stanford, CA: Stanford Univ. Press

Mayoux L. 1999. Questioning virtuous spirals: micro-Finance and Women's Empowerment in Africa. *J. Internat. Dev.* 11:957–84

McDowell L. 2000. Learning to serve?: employment aspirations and attitudes of young working-class men in an era of labour market restructuring. *Gender Place Cult.* 7:389–417

Milgram BL. 2001. Operationalizing micro-finance: women and craftwork in Ifugao, upland Philippines. *Hum. Organ.* 60:212–24

Mills MB. 1995. Attack of the widow ghosts: gender, death, and modernity in Northeast Thailand. See Ong & Peletz 1995, pp. 244–73

Mills MB. 1999a. Enacting solidarity: unions and migrant youth in Thailand. *Crit. Anthropol.* 19:175–91

Mills MB. 1999b. *Thai Women in the Global Labor Force: Consuming Desires, Contested Selves.* New Brunswick, NJ: Rutgers Univ. Press

Moon KHS. 1997. *Sex Among Allies: Military Prostitution in U.S.-Korea Relations.* New York: Columbia Univ. Press

Muecke M. 1992. Mother sold food, daughter sells her body: the cultural continuity of prostitution. *Soc. Sci. Med.* 35(7):891–901

Nash J, Fernandez-Kelly MP, eds. 1983. *Women, Men, and the International Division of Labor.* Albany, NY: SUNY Press

Newman KS. 1988. *Falling From Grace: Downward Mobility in the Age of Affluence.* Berkeley: Univ. Calif. Press

Nonini DM. 1997. Shifting identities, positioned imaginaries: transnational traversals and reversals by Malaysian Chinese. In *Ungrounded Empires: the Cultural Politics of Modern Chinese Transnationalism*, ed. A Ong, DM Nonini, pp. 203–27. London/New York: Routledge

Ogle GE. 1990. *South Korea: Dissent Within the Economic Miracle.* London: Zed Books

Ong A. 1987. *Spirits of Resistance and Capitalist Discipline: Factory Women in Malaysia.* Albany, NY: SUNY Press

Ong A. 1990. State versus Islam: Malay families, women's bodies, and the body politic in Malaysia. *Am. Ethnol.* 17:258–76

Ong A. 1991. The gender and labor politics of postmodernity. *Annu. Rev. Anthropol.* 20:279–309

Ong A. 1999. *Flexible Citizenship: the Cultural Logics of Transnationality.* Durham, NC: Duke Univ. Press

Ong A, Peletz MG, eds. 1995. *Bewitching Women, Pious Men: Gender and Body Politics in Southeast Asia.* Berkeley: Univ. Calif. Press

Orton L, Barrientos S, McClenaghan S. 2001. Paternalism and gender in South African fruit employment: change and continuity. *Women's Stud. Int. Forum* 24:469–78

Osella F, Osella C. 2000. Migration, money and masculinity in Kerala. *J. Roy. Anthropol. Inst. (NS)* 6:117–33

Ozyegin G. 2000. *Untidy Gender: Domestic Service in Turkey.* Philadelphia, PA: Temple Univ. Press

Parreñas RS. 2001. *Servants of Globalization: Women, Migration and Domestic Work.* Stanford, CA: Stanford Univ. Press

Peña DG. 1995. *The Terror of the Machine: Technology, Work, Gender and Ecology on the U.S.-Mexico Border.* Austin: Univ. Texas Press

Pinches M. 2001. Class and national identity: the case of Filipino migrant workers. See Hutchison & Brown 2001, pp. 187–213

Prieto NI. 1997. *Beautiful Flowers of the Maquiladora: Life Histories of Women Workers in Tijuana.* Austin: Univ. Texas Press

Prugl E. 1999. *The Global Construction of Gender: Home-Based Work in the Political Economy of the 20th Century.* New York: Columbia Univ. Press

Rahman A. 1999. *Women and Microcredit in Rural Bangladesh: an Anthropological Study of the Rhetoric and Realities of the Grameen Bank Lending.* Boulder, CO: Westview Press

Roberts GS. 1994. *Staying on the Line: Blue-Collar Women in Contemporary Japan.* Honolulu: Univ. Hawaii Press

Rofel L. 1999. *Other Modernities: Gendered Yearnings in China After Socialism.* Berkeley: Univ. Calif. Press

Roha K. 1994. The conditions and organising activities of women in free trade zones: Malaysia, Philippines and Sri Lanka, 1970–1990. See Rowbotham & Mitter 1994, pp. 73–99

Romero M. 1992. *Maid in the U.S.A.* London/New York: Routledge

Rose K. 1992. *Where Women Are Leaders:*

the SEWA Movement in India. London: Zed Books

Rosenthal M. 2002. Facing a new revolution in Vietnam: state textile workers in the post-reform economy. In *Women and Work in Globalising Asia*, ed. DS Gills, N Piper, pp. 112–30. London/New York: Routledge

Rothstein FA, Blim M, eds. 1992. *Anthropology and the Global Factory: Studies of the New Industrialization in the Late Twentieth Century.* New York: Bergin & Garvey

Rouse R. 1995. Questions of identity: personhood and collectivity in transnational migration to the United States. *Crit. Anthropol.* 15:351–80

Rowbotham S. 1998. Weapons of the weak: homeworkers' networking in Europe. *Eur. J. Women's Stud.* 5:453–63

Rowbotham S, Linkogle S, eds. 2001. *Women Resist Globalization: Mobilizing for Livelihood and Rights.* London: Zed Books

Rowbotham S, Mitter S, eds. 1994. *Dignity and Daily Bread: New Forms of Economic Organizing Among Poor Women in the Third World and the First.* London/New York: Routledge

Rozario S. 1997. Development and rural women in South Asia: the limits of empowerment and conscientization. *Bull. Concern. Asian Schol.* 29:45–53

Sachs CE. 1996. *Gendered Fields: Rural Women, Agriculture and Environment.* Boulder, CO: Westview

Safa HI. 1995. *The Myth of the Male Breadwinner: Women and Industrialization in the Caribbean.* Boulder, CO: Westview Press

Salzinger L. 1997. From high heels to swathed bodies: gendered meanings under production in Mexico's export-processing industry. *Fem. Stud.* 23:549–73

Sassen S. 1998. *Globalization and its Discontents: Essays on the New Mobility of People and Money.* New York: New Press

Seligmann LJ. ed. 2001. *Women Traders in Cross-Cultural Perspective: Mediating Identities, Marketing Wares.* Stanford, CA: Stanford Univ. Press

Silvey RM. 2000a. Diasporic subjects: gender and mobility in South Sulawesi. *Women's Stud. Int. Forum* 23:501–15

Silvey RM. 2000b. Stigmatized spaces: gender and mobility under crisis in South Sulawesi, Indonesia. *Gender Place Cult.* 7:143–61

Sinclair MT, ed. 1997. *Gender, Work and Tourism.* London/New York: Routledge

Skrobanek S, Boonpakdee N, Jantateero C. 1997. *The Traffic in Women: Human Realities of the International Sex Trade.* London: Zed Books

Stasiulis D, Bakan AB. 1997. Negotiating citizenship: the case of foreign domestic workers in Canada. *Fem. Rev.* 57:112–39

Stephen L. 1997. *Women and Social Movements in Latin America: Power from Below.* Austin: Univ. Texas Press

Stoler AL. 1985. *Capitalism and Confrontation in Sumatra's Plantation Belt 1870–1979.* New Haven: Yale Univ. Press

Stoler AL. 1991. Carnal knowledge and imperial power: gender, morality, and race in colonial Asia. In *Gender at the Crossroads of Knowledge: Feminist Anthropology in the Postmodern Era*, ed. M di Leonardo, pp. 55–101. Berkelely: Univ. Calif. Press

Striffler S. 1999. Wedded to work: class struggle and gendered identities in the restructuring of the Ecuadorian banana industry. *Identities* 6:91–120

Sturdevant SP, Stoltzfus B. 1992. *Let the Good Times Roll: Prostitution and the U.S. Military in Asia.* New York: New Press

Susser I. 1997. The flexible woman: regendering labor in the informational society. *Crit. Anthropol.* 17:389–402

Theobald S. 2002. Working for global factories: Thai women in electronics export companies in the Northern Regional Industrial Estate. In *Women and Work in Globalising Asia*, ed. DS Gills, N Piper, pp. 131–53. London/New York: Routledge

Tiano S. 1994. *Patriarchy on the Line: Labor, Gender, and Ideology in the Mexican Maquila Industry.* Philadelphia, PA: Temple Univ. Press

Tice KE. 1995. *Kuna Crafts, Gender, and*

the Global Economy. Austin: Univ. Texas Press

Tilly LA, Scott JW. 1978. *Women, Work, and Family.* New York: Holt, Rhinehart & Winston

Tirado S. 1994. Weaving dreams, constructing realities: the Nineteenth of September National Union of garment workers in Mexico. See Rowbotham & Mitter 1994, pp. 100–13

True J. 2000. Gendering post-socialist transitions. See Marchand & Runyan 2000, pp. 74–93

Truong T. 1990. *Sex, Money and Morality: Prostitution and Tourism in Southeast Asia.* London: Zed Books

Tsurumi EP. 1990. *Factory Girls: Women in the Thread Mills of Meiji Japan.* Princeton, NJ: Princeton Univ. Press

Ward K, ed. 1990. *Women Workers and Global Restructuring.* Ithaca, NY: IRL Press, Cornell Univ.

West LA. 1997. *Militant Labor in the Philippines.* Philadelphia, PA: Temple Univ. Press

White JB. 1994. *Money Makes Us Relatives: Women's Labor in Urban Turkey.* Austin: Univ. Texas Press

Wilkinson-Weber CM. 1999. *Embroidering Lives: Women's Work and Skill in the Lucknow Embroidery Industry.* Albany, NY: SUNY Press

Wolf DL. 1992. *Factory Daughters: Gender, Household Dynamics, and Rural Industri-alization in Java.* Berkeley: Univ. Calif. Press

Wright MW. 1999. The dialectics of still life: murder, women and the maquiladoras. *Pub. Cult.* 29:453–73

Wright MW. 2001. Desire and the prosthetics of supervision: a case of maquiladora flexibility. *Cult. Anthropol.* 16:354–73

Yamanaka K. 2000. Nepalese labour migration to Japan: from global warriors to global workers. *Ethnic Racial Stud.* 23:62–93

Yanagisako SJ. 2002. *Producing Culture and Capital: Family Firms in Italy.* Princeton, NJ: Princeton Univ. Press

Yelvington KA. 1995. *Producing Power: Ethnicity, Gender and Class in a Caribbean Workplace.* Philadelphia, PA: Temple Univ. Press

Yeoh BSA, Huang S, Willis K. 2000. Global cities, transnational flows and gender dimensions: the view from Singapore. *Tijdschr. Econ. Soc. Geog.* 91:147–58

Zhang EY. 2001. Goudui and the state: constructing entrepreneurial masculinity in two cosmopolitan areas of post-socialist China. In *Gendered Modernities: Ethnographic Perspectives*, ed. DL Hodgson, pp. 235–65. New York: Palgrave

Zhang L. 2001. *Strangers in the City: Reconfigurations of Space, Power, and Social Networks Within China's Floating Population.* Stanford, CA: Stanford Univ. Press

Annu. Rev. Anthropol. 2003. 32:63–84
doi: 10.1146/annurev.anthro.32.061002.093244
First published online as a Review in Advance on June 4, 2003

MISSISSIPPIAN CHIEFDOMS: How Complex?

Charles R. Cobb

*Department of Anthropology, Binghamton University, State University of New York,
Binghamton, New York 13902-6000; email: ccobb@binghamton.edu*

Key Words   archaeology, North America, complexity, power, political economy

■ **Abstract**   During the Mississippian period (A.D. 1000–1500) the southeastern
United States witnessed a broadscale fluorescence of polities characterized by impressive earthwork construction, rich mortuary offerings, and intensified agriculture.
Research on the nature of complexity in these so-called chiefdoms has been an enduring issue in North American archaeology, even as this research has undergone several
paradigmatic shifts. This study focuses on the primary dimensions of the archaeological record used to describe and explain variation in Mississippian complexity—
polity scale, settlement and landscape, the organization of labor, mortuary ritual and
ideology, and tribute and feasting. Changing perspectives toward the organization
of complexity and power have become increasingly pronounced in each of these
categories.

INTRODUCTION

Chiefdoms of varying size and complexity emerged with somewhat startling ra-
pidity around A.D. 1000 across a substantial region of the southeastern and midwestern United States (Figure 1). Over 500 years later, the Spaniards who waded
ashore encountered societies that showed a strong continuity with the archaeological complexes now subsumed under the rubric of "Mississippian." Given this
continuity, Mississippian archaeologists have drawn freely from both historical
documents and the archaeological record to address the emergence and variation
of complexity in the late prehistoric era. This development seems to have been
generated primarily by processes internal to the region, building on diverse Late
Woodland (A.D. 400–1000) societies typified by modest communities dependent
to varying degrees on small-scale horticulture (Emerson et al. 2000, Nassaney &
Cobb 1991). Although Mississippian archaeological complexes were originally
defined by such physical criteria as shell-tempered pottery, mound building, large
towns, and maize agriculture, researchers later used the ethnohistoric evidence
from the Southeast to characterize these sites as the remains of polities with powerful leaders who held considerable sway over economic, political, and ritual domains (Griffin 1985, Smith 1986, Steponaitis 1986). The reasons underlying the
widespread fluorescence in social complexity are still subject to considerable debate. This issue is largely sidestepped here, in favor of developing a comparative

0084-6570/03/1021-0063$14.00

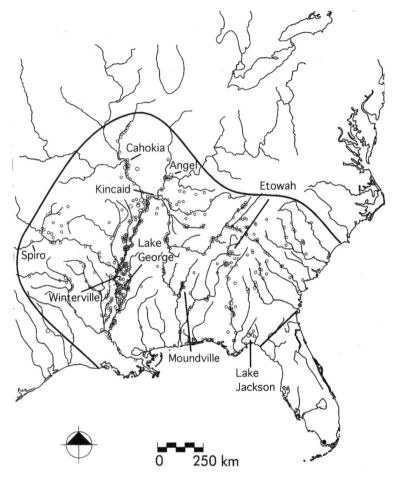

Figure 1 Distribution of significant Mississippian sites in the United States, with sites indicated that are discussed in text (adapted from Payne & Scarry 1998).

perspective on complexity between Mississippian polities in the belief that this approach will at the same time facilitate ongoing discussions on the origins of complexity.

The gross parallels in scale between Mississippian societies and ethnographically described chiefdoms in Polynesia and elsewhere have, to a large measure, made "chiefdom" the centerpiece of debates about Mississippian complexity. As Yoffee (1993) has observed, archaeologists from the University of Michigan in the 1970s and 1980s played a major role in revising the concept of chiefdom that had been forwarded by Service (1962). This group emphasized the political dimensions of chiefly rule, a perspective that strongly influenced Mississippian research from the 1970s onward in part because it was a theoretically compelling view and in part because several of those archaeologists—as well as a subsequent generation of influential archaeologists from Michigan—work in the Mississippian Southeast. Today when archaeologists refer to Mississippian complexity, they usually refer to the political aspects of these chiefdoms.

Yet this is a tacit understanding, and, with few exceptions (e.g., Emerson & Pauketat 2002, Saitta 1994, Schroeder 2003), there has been little explicit discussion in Mississippian circles about the precise meaning of complexity. Variation in complexity is commonly described by subcategories of chiefdoms based on the relative degree of inferred political and economic power. To that end, the most commonly applied terms are "simple," "complex," and "paramount" chiefdoms. It would overstate the case, nevertheless, to argue that considerations of Mississippian complexity are merely exercises in pigeonholing. Lurking behind these categories there is a deeper, implicit interest in the exercise of power and authority. "Complexity" serves as a gloss for these types of relations. Hence, discussions about complexity now tend to be phrased in terms of the political economy, and political economy is commonly tied to the issue of power.

Using political economy as a point of departure, one can discern two trends in research on Mississippian complexity. First, the notion of political economy has expanded from a materialist basis to one that incorporates considerations of ideology, or what some refer to as political culture (Pauketat 1997, Rees 2002). Second, vertical conceptions of power focused on elites have broadened to consider both horizontal characteristics of the political economy (or heterarchy, following Crumley 1987) and the actions of commoners in terms of agency and resistance. These trends can be attributed to the realization that power is not solely a structural feature of chiefdoms that can be expressed as incremental forms of domination. Power also has an experiential quality; it is something that is acted out, reproduced, contested, and transformed in the daily interactions of actors.

It is not easy to parse advocates cleanly into one approach to power or another because there is considerable borrowing across the board. As a consequence, in the remainder of this chapter I use the archaeological record as a guide to examine variation in how practitioners themselves attempt to explain variation in complexity. I begin with a discussion of the scale of Mississippian chiefdoms, an area where there is perhaps the most agreement. Then I turn to settlement systems and landscape, followed by the organization of labor, mortuary ritual and ideology, and tribute and feasting. Finally, I consider diachronic aspects of complexity in Mississippian chiefdoms. Within each category, I present the evidence and reasoning traditionally used to describe and explain complexity and then move on to examine how criteria in that category have broadened in recent years to incorporate concerns with meaning, agency, worldview, and heterarchy. Research within these categories, in conjunction with advances in regional chronologies, has contributed to a growing appreciation of both the complexity of Mississippian chiefdoms at any one point in time and their dynamism through time.

THE SCALE OF MISSISSIPPIAN POLITIES

Mississippian polities varied widely in scale, but discussions about their possible complexity naturally gravitate toward those on the upper end of the spectrum as defined by the physical size, geographic reach, and population of mound centers. The remains of the largest towns are still impressive today, consisting of grand plazas surrounded by mounds of varying sizes and shapes. The earthworks served a number of functions. The largest platform mounds typically were occupied by chiefly leaders, a phenomenon widely observed by European explorers. Conical mounds often contain cemeteries, whereas smaller platform mounds might have served as the bases for charnel houses, domestic structures, or other functions. Residential neighborhoods typically clustered around the periphery of the mound and plaza complexes. Frequently, towns were surrounded by wooden palisades, and even moats, for defense.

The size of these towns has often been used as an initial proxy for complexity. In other words, physical scale is commonly understood as a larger encompassing measure for a loosely conceived amalgamation of power: power to both govern and draw on the labor of a resident population, power to organize public work projects, and even power over life and death. Many researchers have adopted Steponaitis's (1978) distinction between simple (one level of superordinate political offices) and complex (two to three levels) chiefdoms to relate power and scale. Simple chiefdoms have a weakly developed hierarchy, whereas the complex ones have at least an incipient form of class structure. I note that site scale is an initial proxy for complexity because, as can be seen, observers traditionally have used settlement and mortuary data as reinforcing lines of evidence to assess chiefdom organization in a given locale.

Muller's (1997) comparative study of mound volumes from various sites (for which such data could be calculated) shows Cahokia containing 1,007,190 m^3 of mound volume, with the next four on his list—Moundville, Etowah, Winterville, Kincaid—ranging from about 153,000 m^3 down to 93,000 m^3 of fill. Based on the amount of effort vested in mound construction, no other sites are comparable to the enormous size of Cahokia. Likewise, the largest mound at Cahokia, Monk's mound (a huge earthen platform 30 m high and 6 ha at its base), is many magnitudes larger than any of the largest mounds from other sites. Nevertheless, sites like Moundville, Winterville, and Etowah (and many others) are impressive in their own right, consisting of numerous mounds and hundreds of domestic structures spread over scores of hectares. The largest Mississippian towns are presumed to be the seat of polities of considerable size and power commensurate with a complex chiefdom.

The geographic extent of Mississippian polities is commonly gauged by geophysical criteria (especially the borders of floodplain regions), combined with the spacing of mound sites and distribution of diagnostic artifact types. A central difficulty in equating complexity with the spatial dimension is discerning actual power from influence. In historical times, chiefs faced considerable difficulty in retaining the allegiance of independent-minded leaders on the fringes of polities, whereas those closer to home were much easier to monitor. Hence, many of the polity boundaries based on archaeological signatures may more accurately portray threat zones rather than the limits of direct chiefly authority (Blitz 1993a). Many archaeologists now subscribe to Hally's (1993) careful reading of the historical and archaeological evidence for one region of the Southeast, which suggests that, on the average, Mississippian polities were about 40 km in length (typically following drainages). This figure coincides with archaeological data from other regions, such as the Lower Ohio Valley (Kincaid and Angel polities) (Muller 1997). At the higher end, Cahokia may have overseen a territory on the order of 100 km in extent (Scarry 1999). Spanish accounts of the Coosa chiefdom centered in eastern Tennessee and adjoining states describe a very large polity that may have extended 450 km along its longest axis (Hudson et al. 1985). Using Coosa as a model, the term paramount chiefdom (Hudson et al. 1985) has been added to the chiefdom lexicon to describe the largest of Mississippian-style polities, such as Cahokia. Paramount chiefdoms are best viewed as loose and unstable confederations owing to the uncertain power held by their leaders.

The population size of Mississippian towns and polities has elicited some of the strongest discord. Those who lean toward the more complex models of Mississippian organization not surprisingly favor the highest numbers, but all would concede that deriving population estimates from archaeological signatures is exceedingly difficult. There does seem to be a general scaling back in the estimates in recent years. Cahokia in particular has presented a moving target, ranging from an unlikely 40,000 inhabitants (Fowler 1975) to a very high 25,000 (Gregg 1975) to a conservative 1300 (Muller 1997). Holley's (1999) calculation of 3000 to 12,000 seems to be palatable to most archaeologists today. The population of Moundville, one of the largest mound centers aside from Cahokia, has been put as high as 3000 (Peebles 1987), but Steponaitis's (1998) reevaluation of ceramics, burials, and midden deposits suggests a considerably lower number of 1000. With such wildly varying estimates for the sizes of individual towns, estimating the population encompassed by an entire polity seems almost foolhardy. One of our more reliable estimates comes from the Apalachee region of west Florida, the location of what may be construed as a complex chiefdom at the time of European contact. There, considerable survey and excavation data, combined with figures tabulated by Spanish authorities, provide a number of about 30,000 people (Scarry 1999).

Despite disagreements over detail, archaeologists broadly agree that a limited number of impressive complex or paramount chiefdoms were represented during the Mississippian period at any one point in time. The towns at the core of these polities include, but are not limited to, Cahokia, Moundville, Etowah, Spiro, Lake George, Lake Jackson, Winterville, Kincaid, Angel, and one or more sites in the Nashville Basin. Many more simple chiefdoms dotted the landscape, and a large number of hamlets of uncertain affiliation were liberally sprinkled around the Southeast. But complexity involves more than scale, which is, at best, a linear measure. It also involves sets of relations among interest groups and/or individuals.

Mississippian-period research has begun to focus more and more on these relational aspects of complexity in a variety of domains.

SETTLEMENT AND LANDSCAPE

Probably no aspect of the archaeological record better encapsulates shifting theoretical attitudes toward Mississippian complexity than does the spatial dimension—the internal structure of sites and the arrangement of communities across the landscape. The notion of the settlement "system," which so well imparted the idea of a functionally integrated pattern of sites, has now given way to phenomenological views about the way the built environment and the landscape structure everyday life. Although not all Mississippian sites have mounds or other forms of earthworks (in fact, these are in the minority), mounds have become the key attribute for sorting the larger sites that are used to define the most complex regional systems.

The landmark *Mississippian Settlement Patterns* (Smith 1978) presented a series of regional system studies, with a particular eye toward site-size hierarchies. These analyses of both large- and moderate-scale regional systems demonstrated that larger Mississippian chiefdoms typically consisted of a primate, multi-mound center, surrounded by various strata of site types and sizes. The most complex systems appeared to be represented by three or four tiers of sites. A four-tiered system would include a very large multi-mound center, subsidiary centers with a single or only a few mounds, sizable villages without mounds but often with plazas, and a hodgepodge of smaller settlements consisting of as few as one to two structures. More often than not, there is an elegant fit between the relative degree of hierarchy manifest in the settlement system and the levels of status indicated by the associated mortuary assemblages (as described below).

As the number of regional studies surged following the publication of the 1978 volume, two important points became clear. First, only a few regions easily fit the uppermost category of a three- to four-site-size hierarchy, such as the American Bottom (Cahokia) and the Black Warrior Valley (Moundville). These became characterized as complex chiefdoms. Most Mississippian settlement patterns appear to reflect a somewhat ambiguous hierarchy consisting of "a clear top, a clear base, and something fuzzy going on in the middle" (Lewis & Stout 1998b, p. 233), exhibiting a broad range of variation even for the smaller-scale polities. A second concern with Mississippian settlement studies is that there are still very few regions that have been subjected to large-scale, systematic survey. The Black Bottom (Kincaid) in southeastern Illinois was, and remains, one of the most thoroughly surveyed regions—probably as near to 100% coverage as can feasibly be done (Muller 1978). Therefore, the abundance and range of variation of non-mound sites is still poorly known for many areas.

Not surprising, those researchers who have turned their attention to smaller site categories have discovered considerable diversity within categories such as "village" or "hamlet" (Alt 2001, Emerson 1997, Maxham 2000, Mehrer 1995, Thomas 2001). Some of these rural places conducted important communal activities and feasts once thought to be primarily limited to the larger towns. Others appear to have hosted important ritual events. As research has honed in on the character of individual communities, it has become more difficult to accept them as interchangeable units within a site-size category. Further, it is now evident that the development of hinterland occupations did not occur in lock-step with the larger mound centers; residents at these outliers often appear to have simultaneously resisted imposition of a new order at the same time that they sought the advantages of affiliation (Alt 2001, Mehrer 1995).

The shift in settlement perspectives has also moved inward to the mound centers themselves to consider how landscape and the built environment created a spatial crucible for the reproduction of social inequality. Ethnohistoric evidence reveals that the construction of mounds in successive stages evoked purification and renewal and simultaneously reconstituted authority for those individuals or lineages who occupied the top of a mound with each new addition of a mantle (Knight 1989). At a larger scale, mounds may have been arranged to mirror celestial phenomena (e.g., Demel & Hall 1998, Fowler 1996). Even if the evidence for this is problematic, it is likely that towns incorporated ritual dimensions into their planning. The famous woodhenges of Cahokia (circular arrays of large cedar posts) might have been used to mark and control the calendrical cycle (Smith 1992), or they might have been cosmograms that directed the energy of nature and the ascent of spirits (Demel & Hall 1998)—activities that would have strongly reinforced the sacred authority of elites.

The configuration of mound sites created a world where ideological authority was taken for granted among the populace (Cobb & Nassaney 2002, Lewis et al. 1998, Pauketat 1997, Wesson 1998). Grand vistas through plazas and the imposing heights of mounds imbued the built environment with a power of perspective controlled by the elites who supervised construction projects. The denial of perspective could prove powerful, as well. The growth of towns in the Lower Mississippi Valley was characterized by the incremental addition of mounds around plazas, reinforcing the visual and physical segregation of elite space as access to plazas became increasingly limited (Kidder 1998). Similarly, plazas elsewhere seem to have become central for the exercise of power, as elites assumed greater control over areas formerly devoted to public space (Cobb & Nassaney 2002, DeBoer 1993, Lewis et al. 1998). At many sites, large platform mounds simultaneously manifested overt and covert powers of display. On the one hand, they flaunted the symbolic authority of those who resided on their summits, and, on the other hand, mound-top palisades masked the activities of those very same elites.

Passage through a Mississippian mound center thus seems to have involved strategic concealment and revelation as representations of social and political organization. Drawing social distinction in space reflects the importance of ideological alienation in the reproduction of inequality in chiefdoms (Pauketat 1997, Wesson 1998). Power was experienced subjectively as individuals accepted spatial asymmetry as a concrete realization of the natural order. The question remains, however, as to how strongly ideological power carried economic freight. This question is brought most into focus by debates over the organization of labor in Mississippian chiefdoms.

THE ORGANIZATION OF LABOR

Mississippian sites confront us at several scales with impressive residues of human effort, ranging from large earth-moving projects to finely crafted objects. Most obvious are the mounds representing innumerable basket-loads of soil. Lengthy defensive palisades composed of hundreds of sizable posts encircled many Mississippian sites (Cahokia's fortifications were on the order of 3000 m long, Moundville's 2000 m), often with evidence for multiple rebuildings. Many of the portable objects found with burials display a high level of craftsmanship that seem beyond the skill of the average farmer. All of these impressive remains have made the organization of labor a recurring target in debates about Mississippian complexity. These debates typically focus on two issues: What was the degree of elite intervention in production specialization, and in the organization of community projects?

Case studies in Illinois foregrounded the importance of production specialization and underlined the complexity of the methodological and theoretical issues at stake. Yerkes (1983) identified an example of shell-bead production in the American Bottom that he attributed to full-time craft specialization, presumably under the aegis of elites at Cahokia and related centers. This complemented another posited case of "cottage industries" of shell-bead manufacture in the American Bottom and elsewhere, which implied significant specialized production for market exchange at the household level (Prentice 1983). In rejoinder, Muller (1984) used his research on salt production in southern Illinois to make the broader argument that: (*a*) Most cases of presumed Mississippian specialization could be accounted for by models of part-time specialization organized at the household or community level, and (*b*) exchange was relatively unstructured.

Variability in production specialization and its link to elite control continue as one of the more contentious areas of disagreement related to Mississippian complexity. There are a number of notable instances of specialization in the extraction or rendering of regionally restricted resources [Muller's (1984) "regional specialization"], but the relations of production in those areas do not appear to have been strongly hierarchical. The production of hoes at the major chert source areas in Missouri, Illinois, and Tennessee represent part-time specialization embedded in a seasonal cycle of domestic activities (Cobb 2000, Muller 1997, Thomas 2001; cf., Gramly 1992), despite the fact that stone hoes were perhaps the most commonly traded item in the late prehistoric era (Brown et al. 1990, Winters 1981). Other instances for the procurement and/or rendering of geographically restricted, valued raw materials also indicate that Mississippian interest groups rarely monopolized source areas for distinctive economic and political gains [e.g., galena in Missouri (Walthall 1981)], although the procurement of marine shell from the Gulf Coast may represent an exception (Payne & Scarry 1998).

Production carried out under the shadow of mounds and those who occupied them may have been a different matter. There is considerable evidence that clusters of manufacturing debris at Moundville represent workshops for greenstone display goods and shell-bead production (Welch 1991, Wilson 2001), while stylistic commonalities among copper plates at Spiro raise the possibility that they were manufactured in specialized workshops (Phillips & Brown 1978). Likewise, in addition to promoting shell-bead manufacture, elites at Cahokia may have sponsored specialized production of groundstone gaming disks (chunkey stones), megalithic axeheads, fireclay figurines, and copper ornaments (DeBoer 1993; Pauketat 1994, 1997). Mississippian chiefs also had preferred access to nondurable materials rarely recovered by archaeologists, such as high-quality textiles (Phillips & Brown 1978, Drooker 1992, Kuttruff 1993), although inferences about production in such cases must be gleaned from the quality of the final product. Nevertheless, production patterns at certain mound sites indicate elites evinced a keen interest in overseeing the manufacture of valued objects. It is still far from clear whether this represented outright control, patronage, or just preferred access by virtue of propinquity.

As with production specialization, it is not altogether clear whether large-scale endeavors represented by mounds, palisades, and moats required an inordinate degree of effort and coordination. Work estimates for the prominent mound center of Kincaid suggest that, if each household provided only one worker for several days per year, the earthworks for the entire site (93,000 m^3) could have been constructed in a century or less (Muller 1997). As with all production estimates, without knowing the timing and longevity of public-work efforts it is difficult to assess how much labor was mobilized at any one point in time. Because mounds were built in stages, labor efforts may have been punctuated and intensive rather than gradual. If the development of Cahokia was initiated with Pauketat's (1994, 1997) proposed "Big Bang," then many of the rapidly built public projects—ranging from mound construction to the wholesale erection of domestic structures—may have required considerable oversight. Still, Milner's (1998) tabulations for relative energy expenditures at Cahokia are more in line with Muller's estimates for Kincaid, underscoring the divergence of views on the mobilization of labor.

Gender and household studies have provided us with another window on the organization of labor (e.g., Hally & Kelly 1998, Rogers & Smith 1995, Thomas 2001). These still-developing perspectives go beyond issues of elite intervention in major production efforts and examine the organization of labor on a quotidian scale. One of the most important contributions of this research has been to identify considerable variability in production strategies even in fairly small communities, emphasizing the danger of relying on a unit of analysis such as the Mississippian farmstead that is founded on economic stereotypes. Thomas (2001), for instance, makes a well-founded argument that in southern Illinois males produced hoes for exchange, whereas women processed salt for exchange. Hence, one cannot assume that only males were involved in external exchange relations. These studies nicely complement the trend in settlement studies toward examining functional variation in small-scale sites.

Debates over the control of labor highlight one of the key questions pertaining to Mississippian complexity: In the more extreme cases (i.e., the complex or paramount chiefdoms), were relations of production characterized by domination or dominance (Muller 1997)? The former implies an institutionalized form of control over labor, whereas the latter suggests a weak control over labor reliant more on manipulation rather than coercion. The emergence of domination that coincides with expanding control over the means of production is a defining characteristic of class-based societies—and many archaeologists are hesitant to view any Mississippian polities in this light (e.g., Milner 1998, Muller 1997, Saitta 1994). The fact remains, nonetheless, that certain individuals and interest groups were particularly adept at acquiring the physical and symbolic capital that constituted the cornerstone of chiefly authority. Nowhere is this more evident than in the impressive Mississippian mortuary assemblages.

MORTUARY RITUAL AND IDEOLOGY

The elaborate burials associated with many Mississippian sites, in conjunction with earthworks, have served as some of our richest sources of inspiration about the structure of complexity. Several Mississippian case studies published in an influential Society for American Archaeology memoir (Brown 1971a) fashioned a processual link between burial treatment and social complexity. Evidence for superordinate categories of individuals consistent with complex chiefdoms was identified at Etowah (Larson 1971), at Spiro (Brown 1971b), and at Moundville (Peebles 1971; also Peebles & Kus 1977), based on the number and nature of artifacts found with burials. These objects included engraved shell cups and gorgets, repousse copper plates, painted and effigy ceramics, and a host of other exotic artifact types that tend to cluster at Mississippian mound centers. It is important that many of these artifacts (or their raw materials) were imported from considerable distances, attesting to some relationship between elite status and preferred access to long-distance exchange networks.

Numerous case studies followed on the heels of the 1971 publication, all demonstrating more or less the same point: Most Mississippian sites of any size contained cemeteries with individuals who had preferred access (at least at the time of burial) to imported exotic materials and/or finely crafted objects (e.g., Goldstein 1980, Milner 1984, Rothschild 1979). Furthermore, many of the mortuary studies revealed a distinct stratification in the abundance and types of goods, such that two or three (or more) groups could be delineated. Individuals in these groups were usually interred within restricted areas, typically within or around mounds. In certain instances, burials that appeared to represent the apex of the social hierarchy had objects that were unique to those burials, such as copper axes at Moundville (Peebles & Kus 1977), or were placed in special contexts, such as litter interments in the Craig Mound at Spiro (Brown 1971b).

The assumption that abundance and quality of burial goods equate with status still guides much Mississippian mortuary research today. A variation on this theme occurred with the application of the prestige-goods model (Cobb 1989, Brown et al. 1990, Dye 1995, Peregrine 1992). Under this approach, individuals did not merely amass exotic goods throughout their lifetime to have them deposited at death. Instead, valuables first were acquired by elites from distant and ideologically charged places, which endowed the goods with ritual significance. These objects were then distributed among followers to attract their loyalty, labor, and surplus production because nonstratified societies present numerous obstacles through kinship ties and other means that prevent elites from directly accessing the means of production. One could then expect that prestige items would also appear in lower-status burials. Accordingly, although the relative abundance of funerary items could still be viewed as a proxy for status, this could be only a very rough measure given the dynamic circulation of the system.

The classic approach toward prestige-goods economies has been critiqued for Cahokia and the surrounding American Bottom region. There, elites apparently controlled goods that were locally produced (and stamped with symbology more readily comprehended) rather than acquired as finished items from afar (Pauketat 1994). Suffice it to say that the mechanisms and rationale for the movement of prestige goods were varied (including tribute through warfare) and that further attention to these variables is strongly warranted (Dye 1995, King & Freer 1995).

Cahokia continues to elicit some of the strongest divides over the degree of power wielded by elites (Schroeder 2003). At the far extreme are models positing the development of urbanism at Cahokia or far-flung economic control emanating out of the American Bottom (Dincauze & Hasenstab 1989, O'Brien 1989, Peregrine 1992). Then there is the view that Cahokian elites were extremely powerful in some instances, but this power could be attributed more to ideological rather than materialist factors (Emerson 1997; Pauketat 1994, 1997). Finally, there is the possibility that the impressive size differences between Cahokia and other sites could still be accounted for by incremental—rather than true qualitative—differences in power (Milner 1998, Milner & Schroeder 1999, Muller 1997). The Mound 72 mortuary assemblage at Cahokia has become a common referent for these debates (Fowler 1975). Several group burials in this unusually shaped, ridgetop mound contained large amounts of exotic or highly crafted artifacts, including caches of projectile points and groundstone gaming disks, thousands of shell beads, piles of mica, and a large copper tube. Some of the group burials appear to represent sacrifices. An even greater abundance of wealth objects was uncovered from the so-called Great Mortuary at the Craig Mound in Spiro, which held huge deposits of shell beads, engraved shell cups, and copper plates, in addition to an astonishing assortment of other exotics (Brown 1996, Phillips & Brown 1978). No one who is party to the debates over Mississippian complexity denies the spectacular nature of the Mound 72 or Great Mortuary burial complexes. However, a wide variety of power relations can be invoked to account for such assemblages.

One cannot touch on mortuary ritual without mentioning the Southeastern Ceremonial Complex (SECC). The SECC is a recurring set of themes, motifs, and iconography (Figure 2) rendered from a wide range of materials, including copper plates, various forms of worked shell (cups, gorgets), ceramics, and even stone (Brown 1976, Galloway 1989, Howard 1968, Knight 1986). These objects are

Figure 2   Renderings of shell gorgets displaying icongraphy associated with the Southeastern Ceremonial Complex [from Figure 1 in Howard (1968). Reprinted with permission of the Missouri Archaeological Society].

most commonly, though not exclusively, found in mortuary contexts. The skewed distribution of SECC goods among burials is often taken as a marker of social complexity, but archaeologists differ over the meaning that can be attributed to what was originally characterized as a "cult" (Waring & Holder 1945). The variability displayed in objects and motifs associated with the SECC argues against it representing a unified belief system (Muller 1989), although there are recurring themes that may be indicative of a core of ideas that are predominately "otherworldly" in nature (Knight 1986, Knight et al. 2001). Even without universal agreement on what the SECC represents, it is central to discussions about Mississippian complexity because researchers have long relied upon it to consider how elites may have wielded power. The association between leaders and powerful symbols was likely viewed as a manifestation of their control over esoteric knowledge and their pivotal position in maintaining harmony between social and natural worlds.

Power in Mississippian societies was not vested solely in males nor was it only hierarchical in nature.There is strong evidence from both the archaeological and ethnohistoric records that women could hold power in the traditional sense attributed to chiefs (Trocolli 2002). The notion of heterarchy has gained particular favor as a way of emphasizing horizontal relations of overlapping power embedded in gender, age, and lineage, as opposed to the primarily vertical relations of hierarchy (Crumley 1987). As one example, mortuary patterns in the southern Appalachian polities suggest that women's power may have been vested in kin groups (emphasis on burial in domestic structures), whereas men's power may have been linked more to the larger town itself (emphasis on burials in community buildings) (Sullivan & Rodning 2001). The descendents of Mississippian groups were often divided into moities that split powers related to warfare, trade, and civic organization, a pattern that may be seen in the archaelogical record (Dye 1995, Knight 1990). In addition to gender and lineage, other social dimensions of mortuary practices gaining increasing attention include ethnicity and identity (Emerson & Hargrave 2000, Hally & Kelly 1998).

Recent mortuary research—combined with data on settlements, landscape and labor—has begun to paint complexity as a multidimensional phenomenon. Individuals and interest groups often did hold superordinate positions that were hierarchical, and the reproduction of hierarchy involved both material and ideological dimensions. Yet people also assumed multiple identities that extended to gender, clan, and age-group affiliations. These social roles provided alternative frameworks for the negotiation of power relationships acted out daily on stages within the household and other venues. Such arenas did not necessarily involve the direct intervention of chiefs or similar positions that we traditionally link to status and institutionalized power. Whether involving elites or not, power is not an abstract essence; it is made manifest through relations that may be codified by institutions or rationalized through kinship and other means. Research on Mississippian tribute and feasting has highlighted some of the key ways in which individuals and interest groups negotiated relations of power.

TRIBUTE AND FEASTING

The idea that chiefdoms were characterized in large part by redistribution (Service 1962) was laid to rest largely by Earle's (1977) research on Hawaiian chiefdoms, which portrayed leaders as much more interested in mobilizing surplus for self-aggrandizement than for feeding the masses. With a rich ethnohistoric record at their disposal, Mississippian scholars rapidly picked up the theme of elites marshalling surplus and power through various forms of tribute (Peebles & Kus 1977, Steponaitis 1978). Further, it did not go unnoticed that the location of major centers on large drainages provided a particularly strategic location for the accumulation and dispersal of goods (Brain 1978, Kelly 1991). Although there is abundant documentary and archaeological evidence to support the idea that Mississippian chiefs were the recipients of surpluses, it is nonetheless problematic as to what mechanisms were used. Were these willing or coercive? Were they sustained or intermittent? In some cases the argument has been made that chiefs commanded tribute outright. The de Soto accounts relate a number of instances where native chiefs exacted large amounts of goods as gifts and ransom payments for the Spaniards (Clayton et al. 1993). Warfare seems to have played an important role in setting up tributary relationships with vassal chiefs (Dye 1995, Rees 1997). In other cases, family groups typically tithed, surrendering some portion of the season's harvest to lineage heads or chiefs. This does not appear to be the sort of coerced tax associated with highly stratified societies because the surplus seems to have been willingly handed over (Muller 1997).

Archaeological studies of tribute have tended to focus on agricultural surplus and animal products. There are numerous instances in the archaeological record indicating that elites had privileged access to comestibles. Skeletal studies suggest that elites were often (though not always) better fed than the remainder of the population (e.g., Blakely 1995, Hatch et al. 1983). Mounds or mound centers are frequently associated with activities that resulted in accumulations of faunal remains that reflect preferred cuts of meat, such as deer hindquarters (Jackson & Scott 1995a,b; Kelly 1997; Michals 1981; Rudolph 1984). Some small, satellite communities have skewed faunal assemblages compared to those surrounding mounds, suggesting the processing of meat before its movement to the large towns as tribute (Jackson & Scott 1995a). Similar patterns of processing have been described for botanical assemblages, where the remains of maize processing (cobs, cupules) may cluster at outlier sites while the edible portions occur in larger abundance at the mound centers (Pauketat 1994, Welch & Scarry 1995).

The aesthetics of food and animal products also played a strong role in Mississippian political ideology. European chroniclers observed that garments such as bear robes and feather cloaks were often limited to chiefs, and the ostentatious display of large maize granaries under the supervision of elites was a visible reminder of a chief's role in the physical and ritual health of the community (Jackson & Scott 1995b, Rees 1997). The symbolic importance of certain comestibles such as fish may also have conferred them status as prestige goods (Rees 1997, 2002). Tribute thus surrounded chiefs with an aura of economic and ritual privilege tied to consumption.

Mississippian chiefs apparently used their tribute—however gained—to organize feasts for recycling food and gifts to followers in a context of conviviality that further served to bolster personal prestige (Blitz 1993b, Dye 1995, Muller 1997, Rees 1997, Smith & Williams 1994). There is certainly abundant ethnohistorical evidence that attests to the importance of feasts (Muller 1997). The faunal remains surrounding mounds (as described above) have been taken as evidence for feasting behavior, as has the association between mounds and large numbers of serving vessels (Blitz 1993b). A large pit at Cahokia has yielded a variety of ritual-related remains (e.g., tobacco seeds, red cedar) that indicate much more than eating was involved in the feasts (Pauketat et al. 2002). Beneath the revelry, however, there must have been a cynicism reminiscent of the potlatch. Whatever gifts one took home presumably had to be reciprocated at a later date, often multiplied several times over. In this sense, feasting was often elevated to a competitive level of "fighting with property" (Rees 2002), a symbolic form of the warfare that seems to have permeated Mississippian society and relations of power. Notably, studies on feasting bring us back full circle to the issues raised by mortuary studies in connection with elite control over exchange. If certain individuals were in a position to manipulate tribute and exchange, then feasting represents one avenue for redistributing valued objects and food to foster a network of indebtedness and obligations.

POLITICAL AND ECONOMIC CHANGE

It has become increasingly difficult to compare the relative complexity of Mississippian polities owing to the growing recognition that they went through considerable political and economic change, and these changes were not experienced in the same way in all areas (King 2001, Rees 1997, Scarry 1996b, Steponaitis 1991, Sullivan 1995). An earlier tendency to view settlement and mortuary patterns as snapshots of complexity has now been replaced by the appreciation that these patterns are the cumulative effects of transformations in complexity combined with other cultural and natural processes. What appears as a four-site hierarchy to an archaeologist may have been the result of the accumulation of remains of a series of sequential, simple chiefdoms. The discovery that the spectacular mortuary assemblages at Spiro resulted in part from elites curating goods from earlier burials cast further uncertainty on the practice of inferring status primarily from the abundance of burial objects (Brown 1996). Ironically, as archaeologists we had done a poor job of controlling chronology in our models of Mississippian complexity.

Anderson's (1994) research on the trajectory of Mississippian chiefdoms along the Savannah River drainage in Georgia and South Carolina spurred a renewed concern with the development of complexity through time. He demonstrated what he termed "cycling" behavior in chiefdoms, where, instead of following a simple trajectory of increasing complexity, Mississippian chiefdoms continually rose and fell because of their inherent political instability, exacerbated by factors such as warfare and ecological change (see also Blitz 1999, Clay 1997). The relevance of history and the tempo of development to the stochastic nature of chiefdom cycling should not be underestimated. In the rich bottomlands of southeastern Missouri a number of substantial mound centers arose early in the Mississippian period, yet their broadly coeval development may have hampered the emergence of a single, dominant center (although the chronology of the region is still problematic). Etowah's relatively slow development in northwest Georgia suggests a similar pattern of strong competition from other chiefdoms, yet it ultimately became one of the larger Mississippian centers (King 2001). In contrast, the early establishment of powerful elites at Moundville may have hampered the ability of late-bloomers in adjoining polities to compete for access to prestige goods, leading to the development of only simple chiefdoms in those localities (Steponaitis 1991). Yet chiefly primogeniture could not guarantee sustained success; even the most impressive chiefdoms apparently lasted in the range of only 50 to 150 years, whereupon the central towns were either abandoned or lost much of their population (Anderson 1999, Brain 1978, Hally 1996). At a broader scale, there is evidence that wholesale regions may have been largely, if not completely, depopulated at various times in the Mississippian sequence (Anderson 1994, Cobb & Butler 2002, Williams 1990).

The rise and fall of chiefly centers in some localities was attended by changes in site function. As some mound sites (e.g., Moundville, Cahokia) were slowly abandoned by a residential population they became mortuary and ceremonial centers inhabited primarily by caretaker elites (Pauketat 1997, Steponaitis 1998). In an extreme example, Etowah was completely abandoned to be later reoccupied for ceremonial purposes (Hally 1996, King 2001). Other broad shifts in the Mississippian period include the decline of mound-building and the waning of the SECC (particularly from the 1300s onward). Rather than representing a reversal of complexity, however, the argument can be made that these patterns were part of a reorganization related to the increasing importance of secular power focused on individuals, as opposed to corporate or communal forms of authority practiced earlier (Anderson 1999, Trubitt 2000). The broader trends outlined here do present some contradictions, however. Although diminished earthwork construction may indicate that elites no longer needed the security of ostentatious examples of power based on communal labor, the rise of the ritual importance of a number of centers does not seem to square with the simultaneous decline of the ritual complex embodied in the SECC. Such contradictions may dissolve if we decrease the scale and increase the resolution of perspectives on Mississippian complexity, and move to complement comparative studies more rigorously with historical ones. Only then can we hope to achieve an understanding of the reproduction of social inequality in the everyday lives of Mississippian peoples.

CONCLUSION

Approaches to Mississippian complexity underscore the difficulty with materialist, neo-evolutionary models. For the Mississippian case there is not necessarily a continuum from benign redistribution to kin demands on surplus, to some control over the means of production, that neatly correlates with a transition from simple to paramount chiefdoms. Mississippian polities apparently engaged in a variety of hegemonic practices where people willingly reproduced the conditions of their own exploitation. In this sense, even exploitation may be a misnomer if producers were willing to provision elites because those leaders were viewed as essential to the stability of the natural order by virtue of their esoteric knowledge and authority. Perhaps such esteem could not be equated to Louis XIV's "I am the State" because it was a qualitatively different form of power. More likely, a Mississippian chief could proclaim, "I am the Cosmos." Even then, it seems unlikely that such authority was unimpeachable. Nevertheless, it now seems apparent that knowledge-based political economies (McIntosh 1999) that use ritual authority to overcome constraints on political-economic growth are an important facet of chiefdoms in the Mississippian southeast and elsewhere.

If there is a historical trend in studies of Mississippian complexity it is one that first emphasized hierarchy. This was followed by a consideration of the horizontal power links, the heterarchical structure, between segments of society. Finally, some researchers have moved to a practice-based approach that emphasizes agency and relations more than system or structure. Yet the changes in perspective represent more of a Doppler shift than a complete reorientation—scholars may represent different areas on the spectrum, but they do not seem to have lost sight of the importance of the larger spectrum itself. One can see, for example, concerns with Mississippian beliefs, worldview, and social structure in the heyday of adaptation and social systems (Brown 1976, Phillips & Brown 1978) and an interest in inequality and tribute at a time when stasis and redistribution were popular buzzwords (Peebles & Kus 1977, Steponaitis 1978). At the height of the processual era when history was denigrated as too particularistic, Southeastern researchers happily continued combing the ethnohistorical records to animate their perspectives on Mississippian life—a trend that continues today. Many Mississippian archaeologists seem to implicitly adopt Trigger's (1989) view that some broad, empirical generalizations can be drawn from comparative research, which provide lessons for conducting historical studies. In return, historically informed research provides the building blocks of comparative approaches. As we achieve greater success by playing off the particular with the general, we further broaden our capabilities to ask questions about Mississippian political, social, and economic organization, thereby moving from how complex to why complex.

ACKNOWLEDGMENTS

My deepest thanks to Brian Butler, Tim Pauketat, and Sissel Schroeder for taking the time to read an earlier draft of this paper and for providing cogent criticisms. I assume responsibility for the perspective reflected here and errors in fact or logic.

The *Annual Review of Anthropology* is online at http://anthro.annualreviews.org

LITERATURE CITED

Alt S. 2001. Cahokian change and the authority of tradition. See Pauketat 2001, pp. 141–56

Anderson DG. 1994. *The Savannah River Chiefdoms: Political Change in the Late Prehistoric Southeast.* Tuscaloosa: Univ. Ala. Press

Anderson DG. 1999. Examining chiefdoms in the southeast: an application of multiscalar analysis. See Neitzel 1999, pp. 95–107

Blakely RL. 1995. Social organization at Etowah: a reconsideration of paleodemo-graphic and paleonutritional evidence. *S. Archaeol.* 14:46–59

Blitz JH. 1993a. *Ancient Chiefdoms of the Tombigbee.* Tuscaloosa: Univ. Ala. Press

Blitz JH. 1993b. Big pots for big shots: feasting and storage in a Mississippian community. *Am. Antiq.* 58:80–96

Blitz JH. 1999. Mississippian chiefdoms and the fission-fusion process. *Am. Antiq.* 64: 577–92

Brain JP. 1978. Late prehistoric settlement patterning in the Yazoo Basin and Natchez

Bluffs regions of the Lower Mississippi Valley. See Smith 1978, pp. 331–68

Brown JA, ed. 1971a. *Approaches to the Social Dimensions of Mortuary Practices*. Mem. No. 25. Washington, DC: Soc. Am. Archaeol.

Brown JA. 1971b. The dimensions of status in the burials at Spiro. See Brown 1971a, pp. 91–112

Brown JA. 1976. The southern cult reconsidered. *Midcont. J. Archaeol.* 1:115–35

Brown JA. 1996. *The Spiro Ceremonial Center*. Mem. Mus. Anthropol. No. 29. Ann Arbor: Univ. Mich. Press

Brown JA, Kerber RA, Winters HD. 1990. Trade and the evolution of exchange relations at the beginning of the Mississippian period. In *The Mississippian Emergence*, ed. BD Smith, pp. 251–80. Washington, DC: Smith. Inst. Press

Clay RB. 1997. The Mississippian succession on the lower Ohio. *S. Archaeol.* 16:16–32

Clayton LA, Knight VJ Jr, Moore EC, eds. 1993. *The De Soto Chronicles: the Expedition of Hernando de Soto to North America in 1539–1543*. Tuscaloosa: Univ. Ala. Press

Cobb CR. 1989. An appraisal of the role of Mill Creek chert hoes in Mississippian exchange systems. *S. Archaeol.* 8:79–92

Cobb CR. 2000. *From Quarry to Cornfield: the Political Economy of Mississippian Hoe Production*. Tuscaloosa: Univ. Ala. Press

Cobb CR, Butler BM. 2002. The vacant quarter revisited: late Mississippian abandonment of the Lower Ohio Valley. *Am. Antiq.* 67:625–41

Cobb CR, Nassaney MS. 2002. Domesticating self and society in the Woodland southeast. In *The Woodland Southeast*, ed. DG Anderson, RC Mainfort Jr, pp. 525–39. Tuscaloosa: Univ. Ala. Press

Crumley CL. 1987. A dialectical critique of hierarchy. In *Power Relations and State Formation*, ed. TC Patterson, CW Gailey, pp. 155–59. Washington, DC: Am. Anthropol. Assoc.

DeBoer WR. 1993. Like a rolling stone: the chunkey game and political organization in eastern North America. *S. Archaeol.* 12:83–92

Demel SJ, Hall RL. 1998. The Mississippian town plan and cultural landscape of Cahokia, Illinois. See Lewis & Stout 1998a, pp. 200–26

Dincauze DF, Hasenstab R. 1989. Explaining the Iroquois: tribalization on a prehistoric periphery. In *Centre and Periphery: Comparative Studies in Archeology*, ed. TC Champion, pp. 67–87. London: Unwin Hyman

Drooker PB. 1992. *Mississippian Village Textiles at Wickliffe*. Tuscaloosa: Univ. Ala. Press

Dye DH. 1995. Feasting with the enemy: Mississippian warfare and prestige-goods circulation. See Nassaney & Sassaman 1995, pp. 289–316

Earle TK. 1977. A reappraisal of redistribution: complex Hawaiian chiefdoms. In *Exchange Systems in Prehistory*, ed. TK Earle, JE Ericson, pp. 231–59. New York: Academic

Emerson TE. 1997. *Cahokia and the Archaeology of Power*. Tuscaloosa: Univ. Ala. Press

Emerson TE, Hargrave E. 2000. Strangers in paradise? Recognizing ethnic mortuary diversity on the fringes of Cahokia. *S. Archaeol.* 19:1–23

Emerson TE, McElrath DL, Fortier AC, eds. 2000. *Late Woodland Societies: Tradition and Transformation Across the Midcontinent*. Lincoln: Univ. Neb. Press

Emerson TE, Pauketat TR. 2002. Embodying power and resistance at Cahokia. See O'Donovan 2002, pp. 101–25

Fowler ML. 1975. Pre-Columbian urban center on the Mississippi. *Science* 233:92–101

Fowler ML, ed. 1996. The ancient skies and sky watchers of Cahokia: woodhenges, eclipses, and Cahokian cosmology. *Wisc. Archaeol.* 77:1–158

Galloway P, ed. 1989. *The Southeastern Ceremonial Complex: Artifacts and Analysis*. Lincoln: Univ. Neb. Press

Goldstein LG. 1980. *Mississippian Mortuary Practices: a Case Study of Two Cemeteries in the Lower Illinois Valley*. Sci. Pap.

4. Evanston, IL: Northwestern Univ. Arch. Prog.

Gramly RM. 1992. *Prehistoric Lithic Industry at Dover, Tennessee.* Buffalo, NY: Persimmon Press

Gregg ML. 1975. A population estimate for Cahokia. In *Perspectives in Cahokia Archaeology*, ed. JA Brown, pp. 126–36. Bull. No. 10. Urbana: Ill. Archaeol. Surv.

Griffin JB. 1985. Changing concepts of the prehistoric Mississippian cultures of the eastern United States. In *Alabama and the Borderlands: From Prehistory to Statehood*, ed. R Badger, L Clayton, pp. 40–63. Tuscaloosa: Univ. Ala. Press

Hally DJ. 1993. The territorial size of Mississippian chiefdoms. In *Archaeology of Eastern North America: Papers in Honor of Stephen Williams*, ed. J. Stoltman, pp. 143–68. Jackson: Miss. Dep. Arch. Hist.

Hally DJ. 1996. Platform mound construction and the instability of Mississippian chiefdoms. See Scarry 1996a, pp. 92–127

Hally DJ, Kelly H. 1998. The nature of Mississippian towns in Georgia: the King site example. See Lewis & Stout 1998a, pp. 49–63

Hatch JW, Willey PS, Hunt EE Jr. 1983. Indicators of status-related stress in Dallas society: transverse lines and cortical thickness in long bones. *Midcont. J. Archaeol.* 8:49–71

Holley GR. 1999. Late prehistoric towns in the southeast. See Neitzel 1999, pp. 23–38

Howard JH. 1968. *The Southeastern Ceremonial Complex and its Interpretation.* Mem. 6. Columbia: Missouri Archaeol. Soc.

Hudson C, Smith M, Hally D, Polhemus R, DePratter C. 1985. Coosa: a chiefdom in the sixteenth-century southeastern United States. *Am. Antiq.* 50:723–37

Jackson HE, Scott SL. 1995a. Mississippian homestead and village subsistence organization: contrasts in large-mammal remains from two sites in the Tombigbee Valley. See Rogers & Smith 1995, pp. 181–200

Jackson HE, Scott SL. 1995b. The faunal record of the southeastern elite: the implications of economy, social relations and ideology. *S. Archaeol.* 14:103–19

Kelly JE. 1991. Cahokia and its role as a gateway center in interregional exchange. In *Cahokia and the Hinterlands: Middle Mississippian Cultures of the Midwest*, ed. TE Emerson, RB Lewis, pp. 61–80. Urbana: Univ. Ill. Press

Kelly LS. 1997. Patterns of faunal exploitation at Cahokia. See Pauketat & Emerson 1997, pp. 69–88

Kidder TR. 1998. Mississippian period mound groups and communities in the Lower Mississippi Valley. See Lewis & Stout 1998a, pp. 123–50

King A. 2001. Long-term histories of Mississippian centers: the developmental sequence of Etowah and its comparison to Moundville and Cahokia. *S. Archaeol.* 20:1–17

King A, Freer J. 1995. The Mississippian southeast: a world-systems perspective. See Nassaney & Sassaman 1995, pp. 266–88

Knight VJ Jr. 1986. The institutional organization of Mississippian religion. *Am. Antiq.* 51:675–87

Knight VJ Jr. 1989. Symbolism of Mississippian mounds. In *Powhatan's Mantle*, ed. P Wood, G Waselkov, T Hatley, pp. 279–91. Lincoln: Univ. Neb. Press

Knight VJ Jr. 1990. Social organization and the evolution of hierarchy in southeastern chiefdoms. *J. Anthropol. Res.* 46:1–23

Knight VJ Jr, Brown JA, Lankford GE. 2001. On the subject matter of Southeastern ceremonial complex art. *S. Archaeol.* 20:129–41

Kuttruff JT. 1993. Mississippian period status differentiation through textile analysis: a Caddoan example. *Am. Antiq.* 58:125–45

Larson LH Jr. 1971. Archaeological implications of social stratification at the Etowah site, Georgia. See Brown 1971a, pp. 58–67

Lewis RB, Stout C, eds. 1998a. *Mississippian Towns and Sacred Places.* Tuscaloosa: Univ. Ala. Press

Lewis RB, Stout C. 1998b. The town as metaphor. See Lewis & Stout 1998a, pp. 227–41

Lewis RB, Stout C, Wesson CB. 1998. The design of Mississippian towns. See Lewis & Stout 1998a, pp. 1–21

Maxham M. 2000. Rural communities in the Black Warrior Valley, Alabama: the role of commoners in the creation of the Moundville I landscape. *Am. Antiq.* 65:337–54

McIntosh SK. 1999. Pathways to complexity: an African perspective. In *Beyond Chiefdoms: Pathways to Complexity in Africa*, ed. SK McIntosh, pp. 1–30. Cambridge, UK: Cambridge Univ. Press

Mehrer MW. 1995. *Cahokia's Countryside: Household Archaeology, Settlement Patterns, and Social Power*. DeKalb: North. Ill. Univ. Press

Michals L. 1981. The exploitation of fauna during the Moundville 1 phase at Moundville. *S. Archaeol. Conf. Bull.* 24:91–93

Milner GR. 1984. Social and temporal implications of variation among American Bottom Mississippian cemeteries. *Am. Antiq.* 49:468–88

Milner GR. 1998. *The Cahokia Chiefdom: the Archaeology of a Mississippian Society*. Washington, DC: Smith. Instit. Press

Milner GR, Schroeder S. 1999. Mississippian sociopolitical systems. See Neitzel 1999, pp. 189–210

Muller J. 1978. The Kincaid system: Mississippian settlement in the environs of a large site. See Smith 1978, pp. 269–92

Muller J. 1984. Mississippian specialization and salt. *Am. Antiq.* 49:489–507

Muller J. 1989. The southern cult. See Galloway 1989, pp. 11–26

Muller J. 1997. *Mississippian Political Economy*. New York: Plenum

Nassaney MS, Cobb CR, eds. 1991. *The Late Woodland Southeast: Stability, Transformation, and Variation*. New York: Plenum

Nassaney MS, Sassaman KE, eds. 1995. *Native American Interactions: Multiscalar Analyses and Interpretations in the Eastern Woodlands*. Knoxville: Univ. Tenn. Press

Neitzel JE, ed. 1999. *Great Towns and Regional Polities in the Prehistoric American Southwest and Southeast*. Albuquerque: Univ. New Mex. Press

O'Brien PJ. 1989. Cahokia: the political capital of the "Ramey" state? *N. Am. Archaeol.* 10:275–92

O'Donovan MA, ed. 2002. *The Dynamics of Power*. Occ. Pap. No. 30. Carbondale: S. Ill. Univ., Cent. Archaeol. Invest.

Pauketat TR. 1994. *The Ascent of Chiefs: Cahokia and Mississippian Politics in Native North America*. Tuscaloosa: Univ. Ala. Press

Pauketat TR. 1997. Mississippian political economy. See Pauketat & Emerson 1997, pp. 30–51

Pauketat TR. 2001. *The Archaeology of Traditions: Agency and History Before and After Columbus*. Tallahassee: Univ. Fla. Press

Pauketat TR, Emerson TE. 1997. *Cahokia: Domination and Ideology in the Mississippian World*. Lincoln: Univ. Neb. Press

Pauketat TR, Kelly LS, Fritz GJ, Lopinot NH, Elias S, Hargrave E. 2002. The residues of feasting and public ritual at early Cahokia. *Am. Antiq.* 67:257–79

Payne C, Scarry JF. 1998. Town structure at the edge of the Mississippian world. See Lewis & Stout 1998a, pp. 22–48

Peebles CS. 1971. Moundville and surrounding sites: some structural considerations of mortuary practices II. See Brown 1971a, pp. 68–91

Peebles CS. 1987. Moundville from 1000 to 1500 AD as seen from 1849 to 1985 AD. In *Chiefdoms in the Americas*, ed. RD Drennan, CA Uribe, pp. 21–41. Lanham, MD: Univ. Press Am.

Peebles CS, Kus S. 1977. Some archaeological correlates of ranked societies. *Am. Antiq.* 42:421–48

Peregrine PN. 1992. *Mississippian Evolution: a World-System Perspective*. Monog. World Preh. No. 9. Madison: Prehistory Press

Phillips P, Brown JA. 1978. *Pre-Columbian Shell Engravings from the Craig Mound at Spiro, Oklahoma, (Part 1)*. Cambridge, MA: Harvard Univ. Press, Peabody Mus. Archaeol. Ethnol.

Prentice G. 1983. Cottage industries: concepts and implications. *Midcont. J. Archaeol.* 8:17–48

Rees MA. 1997. Coercion, tribute and chiefly

authority: the regional development of Mississippian political culture. *S. Archaeol.* 16:113–33

Rees MA. 2002. Subsistence economy and political culture in the protohistoric Central Mississippi Valley. In *Between Contacts and Colonies: Archaeological Perspectives on the Protohistoric Southeast*, ed. CB Wesson, MA Rees, pp. 170–97. Tuscaloosa: Univ. Ala. Press

Rogers JD, Smith BD, eds. 1995. *Mississippian Communities and Households.* Tuscaloosa: Univ. Ala. Press

Rothschild NA. 1979. Mortuary behavior and social organization at Indian Knoll and Dickson Mounds. *Am. Antiq.* 44:658–75

Rudolph JL. 1984. Earthlodges and platform mounds: changing public architecture in the southeastern United States. *S. Archaeol.* 3:33–45

Saitta DJ. 1994. Agency, class, and archaeological interpretation. *J. Anthropol. Archaeol.* 13:201–27

Scarry JF, ed. 1996a. *Political Structure and Change in the Prehistoric Southeastern United States.* Gainesville: Univ. Fla. Press

Scarry JF. 1996b. Stability and change in the Apalachee chiefdom. See Scarry 1996a, pp. 192–227

Scarry JF. 1999. How great were the southeastern polities? See Neitzel 1999, pp. 59–74

Schroeder S. 2003. Mississippian political organization: economy versus ideology. *The Rev. Archaeol.* 23:6–13

Service ER. 1962. *Primitive Social Organization: an Evolutionary Perspective.* New York: Random House

Smith BD, ed. 1978. *Mississippian Settlement Patterns.* New York: Academic

Smith BD. 1986. The archaeology of the eastern United States: from Dalton to de Soto, 10,500–500 B.P. In *Advances in World Archaeology, Volume 5*, ed. F Wendorf, AE Close, pp. 1–92. Orlando, FL: Academic

Smith BD. 1992. Mississippian elites and solar alignments: a reflection of managerial necessity, or levers of social inequality? In *Lords of the Southeast: Social Inequality and the*

Native Elites of Southeastern North America, ed. AW Barker, TR Pauketat, pp. 11–30. Archeol. Pap. 3. Washington, DC: Am. Anthropol. Assoc.

Smith MT, Williams M. 1994. Mississippian mound refuse disposal patterns and implications for archaeological research. *S. Archaeol.* 13:27–35

Steponaitis VP. 1978. Location theory and complex chiefdoms: a Mississippian example. See Smith 1978, pp. 417–53

Steponaitis VP. 1986. Prehistoric archaeology in the southeastern United States, 1970–1985. *Annu. Rev. Anthropol.* 15:363–404

Steponaitis VP. 1991. Contrasting patterns of Mississippian development. In *Chiefdoms: Power, Economy, and Ideology*, ed. TK Earle, pp. 193–228. Cambridge, UK: Cambridge Univ. Press

Steponaitis VP. 1998. Population trends at Moundville. In *Archaeology of the Moundville Chiefdom*, ed. VJ Knight Jr, VP Steponaitis, pp. 26–43. Washington, DC: Smith. Instit. Press

Sullivan LP. 1995. Mississippian household and community organization in eastern Tennessee. In *Mississippian Households and Communities*, ed. JD Rogers, BD Smith, pp. 99–123. Tuscaloosa: Univ. Ala. Press

Sullivan LP, Rodning CB. 2001. Gender, tradition, and the negotiation of power in southern Appalachian chiefdoms. See Pauketat 2001, pp. 107–20

Thomas L. 2001. The gender division of labor in Mississippian households. In *Archaeological Studies of Gender in the Southeastern United States*, ed. JM Eastman, CB Rodning, pp. 29–56. Gainesville: Univ. Fla. Press

Trigger BG. 1989. *A History of Archaeological Thought.* Cambridge, UK: Cambridge Univ. Press

Trocolli R. 2002. Mississippian chiefs: women and men of power. See O'Donovan 2002, pp. 168–87

Trubitt MBD. 2000. Mound building and prestige goods exchange: changing strategies in the Cahokia chiefdom. *Am. Antiq.* 65:669–90

Walthall JA. 1981. *Galena and Aboriginal*

Trade in Eastern North America. Sci. Pap. 17. Springfield: Ill. State Mus.

Waring AJ, Holder P. 1945. A prehistoric ceremonial complex in the southeastern United States. *Am. Anthropol.* 47:1–34

Welch PD. 1991. *Moundville's Economy.* Tuscaloosa: Univ. Ala. Press

Welch PD, Scarry CM. 1995. Status-related variation in foodways in the Moundville chiefdom. *Am. Antiq.* 60:397–420

Wesson C. 1998. Mississippian sacred landscapes: the view from Alabama. See Lewis & Stout 1998a, pp. 93–122

Williams S. 1990. The vacant quarter and other late events in the Lower Valley. In *Towns and Temples Along the Mississippi*, ed. DH Dye, CA Cox, pp. 170–80. Tuscaloosa: Univ. Ala. Press

Wilson GD. 2001. Crafting control and the control of crafts: rethinking the Moundville greenstone industry. *S. Archaeol.* 30:118–28

Winters HD. 1981. Excavating in museums: notes on Mississippian hoes and Middle Woodland copper gouges and celts. In *The Research Potential of Anthropological Museum Collections*, ed. AE Cantwell, JB Griffin, NA Rothschild, pp. 17–34. Annals 376. New York: New York Acad. Sci.

Yerkes RW. 1983. Microwear, microdrills, and Mississippian craft specialization. *Am. Antiq.* 48:499–518

Yoffee N. 1993. Too many chiefs? (or Safe texts for the '90s). In *Archaeological Theory: Who Sets the Agenda*, ed. N Yoffee, A Sherratt, pp. 60–78. Cambridge, UK: Cambridge Univ. Press

Annu. Rev. Anthropol. 2003. 32:85–109
doi: 10.1146/annurev.anthro.32.061002.093223
Copyright © 2003 by Annual Reviews. All rights reserved
First published online as a Review in Advance on July 30, 2003

DEVELOPMENTAL BIOLOGY AND HUMAN EVOLUTION*

C. Owen Lovejoy,[1] Melanie A. McCollum,[1,2] Philip L. Reno,[1] and Burt A. Rosenman[1]

[1]*Matthew Ferrini Institute of Human Evolutionary Research, Department of Anthropology and Division of Biomedical Sciences, Kent State University, Kent, Ohio 44242;*
[1,2]*Departments of Anatomy and Oral and Maxillofacial Surgery, Case Western Reserve University, Cleveland, Ohio 44106; email: Olovejoy@aol.com, mam17@po.cwru.edu, preno@kent.edu, brosenma@kent.edu*

Key Words   bone, hominid, developmental fields, mechanical loading, limb patterning

■ **Abstract**   Our understanding of developmental biology burgeoned during the last decade. This review summarizes recent advances, provides definitions and explanations of some basic principles, and does so in a way that will aid anthropologists in understanding their profound implications. Crucial concepts, such as developmental fields, selector and realizator genes, cell signaling mechanisms, and gene regulatory elements are briefly described and then integrated with the emergence of skeletal morphology. For the postcranium, a summary of events from limb bud formation, the appearance of anlagen, the expression of *Hox* genes, and the fundamentals of growth plate dynamics are briefly summarized. Of particular importance are revelations that bony morphology is largely determined by pattern formation, that growth foci such as physes and synovial joints appear to be regulated principally by positional information, and that variation in these fields is most likely determined by *cis*-regulatory elements acting on restricted numbers of anabolic genes downstream of selectors (such as *Hox*). The implications of these discoveries for the interpretation of both contemporary and ancient human skeletal morphology are profound. One of the most salient is that strain transduction now appears to play a much reduced role in shaping the human skeleton. Indeed, the entirety of "Wolff's Law" must now be reassessed in light of new knowledge about pattern formation. The review concludes with a brief discussion of some implications of these findings, including their impact on cladistics and homology, as well as on biomechanical and morphometric analyses of both ancient and modern human skeletal material.

---

*Abbreviations and symbols: AER, apical ectodermal ridge; BMP, bone morphogenetic protein; DE, digit enhancer; ECM, extracellular matrix; FGF, fibroblast growth factor; PI, positional information; PA, positional address; Ihh, Indian hedgehog; PTHrP, parathyroid hormone-related peptide; PZ, progress zone; SM, signaling molecule; TF, transcription factor; ZPA, zone of polarizing activity; $\mu\epsilon$, microstrain.

0084-6570/03/1021-0085$14.00

During the past decade, a revolution took place in our understanding of animal structure. Throughout most of the previous century embryology and genetics progressed largely in parallel, with only moderate cross talk (Gilbert et al. 1996). With the advent of modern genetic technology and its novel methods (e.g., gene knock-outs, transgenics, reporter genes, etc.) our understanding of developmental genetics and embryogenesis suddenly burgeoned. Now, in conjunction with simultaneous advancements in biological theory—especially development, positional information (Wolpert 1969), and cell biology (Edelman 1988)—our capacity to accurately analyze mammalian evolution has radically improved. Here we briefly summarize some recent advances in our understanding of skeletal patterning. As can be seen, these advances bear directly on two primary questions fundamental to the study of human evolutionary biology. First, how do adaptations emerge— what is the underlying structure of the genetic variation (i.e., the evolutionarily relevant mutations of Stern 2000) upon which natural selection acts to elicit more favorable morphology? Second, to what degree does the environment contribute to adult skeletal structure, i.e., how great is its phenotypic plasticity? Although neither question can yet be answered definitively, intensive analysis of vertebrate embryogenesis over the past decade has provided substantial new insights.

THE AMPHIBIAN LIMB: AN EXEMPLAR OF THE ROLE OF POSITIONAL INFORMATION IN EMBRYONIC PATTERN FORMATION

When a salamander's forelimb is severed at some point along its length, its tissues undergo a systematic series of cellular events (Bryant & Muneoka 1986, Bryant et al. 1982, French et al. 1976). A wound blastema forms as cells undergo dedifferentiation. Eventually, these cells reactivate the cellular and genetic information originally used during embryogenesis to instruct the cells in the developing limb with respect to which proteins they should synthesize and when; with which cells they should communicate and for how long; and if and when they should change shape, migrate, proliferate, and commit "suicide" (apoptose). In such a way the missing portion of the limb is faithfully regenerated by reconstitution of the missing tissues. Such epimorphosis (Wolpert 1978) is possible because of the PI originally assigned to the cells of the urodele limb during its initial embryonic development. Following amputation, cells of the blastema can somehow recognize their exact position within the severed limb and accurately regenerate all positional values distal to them. How can they do this?

Experimental analysis of this phenomenon has greatly facilitated our understanding of the remarkable proficiency with which cells "talk" to one another (and their daughter cells). Manipulations of urodele blastemata suggest that their PI is deployed like the face of a clock, an informational "map" that allows their cells to reconstruct the missing portions of the limb (see Figure 1). Blastemata cells appear to "know" when their nearest neighbors (e.g., those of the cut end of the humerus) are not appropriate and how to replace any gaps in their "cellular neighborhoods," a process known as intercalation (Keller 2002).

How do cells make this determination? One possible method is by deployment of morphogens—extracellular chemical signals that diffuse to neighboring cells (Gurdon & Bourliere 2000). Cells differentially respond to the chemical's steadily declining concentration (a function of distance). However, simple passive diffusion is only possible for a maximum of about 1 mm (Crick 1970). Alternatively, neighboring cells can actively communicate with one another. For example, transcription of the urodele gene, *Prod 1* (by convention, gene names are italicized but their protein products are not), yields a membrane-bound receptor protein that binds to other copies of itself (homodimerization) (da Silva et al. 2002). Experimental studies of blastemata show that proximal wounds have lower levels of Prod 1 than more distal ones. Therefore, by extension, if a cell lies next to another with a more proximal PA it will have excess undimerized protein. This excess "informs" it that its neighbors are inappropriate and enables it to propagate daughter cells until an appropriate Prod 1 gradient is restored. Each of these new cells will then have a novel PA that will guide its further behavior.

This remarkable example of cell-cell communication tells us a great deal about morphogenesis in general. In the case of urodeles, for example, a faithful copy of the limb (including its skeleton) can be made under two radically different environmental circumstances—one in which the animal is undergoing primary metamorphosis, and the other involving the addition of mature material to the severed limb of an adult. The latter is possible because the original PI is somehow restored in the urodele wound blastema. Although the cell-cell communication mechanisms used are only beginning to be understood, they will undoubtedly prove similar, if not virtually identical, to those used in mammals, just as the genes of the latter have proved to have an almost complete set of homologues in fruit flies (Carroll et al. 2001).

POSITIONAL INFORMATION IN THE MAMMALIAN LIMB BUD

Although adult mammals are not capable of regeneration, their limbs are patterned through the assignment and interpretation of PI just as they are in urodeles (Johnson & Tabin 1997). The processes by which PI is assigned and eventually interpreted have been studied most extensively in avian and, more recently, murine limb buds. Within these particular systems, each cell of the developing limb first acquires positional identities along each of three axes—proximal-distal, anterior-posterior, and dorsal-ventral. This process is followed by a further refinement of PI through the deployment of *Hox* genes in specific limb fields (defined and discussed below).

At its inception the early limb bud consists of a small core of proliferating mesenchymal cells derived from the lateral plate mesoderm covered by an outer layer of ectodermal epithelial cells. At the tip of the growing bud is the AER (Saunders 1948), a collection of specialized, columnar ectodermal cells that maintains

A
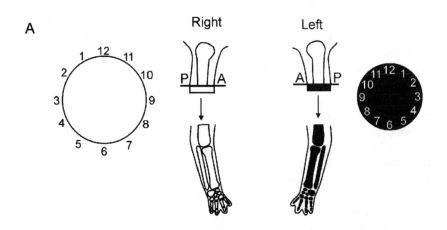

B
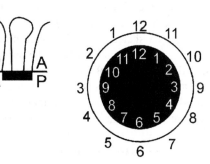

C
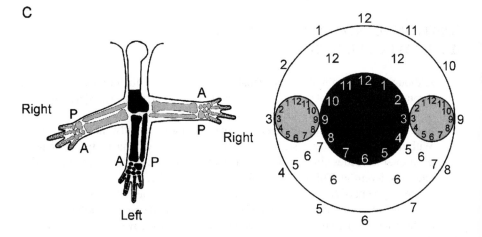

mitosis within a narrow strip of undifferentiated mesenchyme immediately proximal to it, i.e., the PZ, until the cells of the three primary segments of the limb, known embryologically as the stylopod (arm/thigh), zeugopod (forearm/shank), and autopod (hand/foot), have been generated. As limb outgrowth proceeds, mesenchymal cells gradually escape the influence of the AER, drop out of the PZ, and begin their differentiation into limb structures (Wolpert 2002).

As each limb segment is completed, its mesenchyme forms condensations that adumbrate each of its presumptive skeletal elements. These condensations rapidly metamorphose into anlagen, each composed of mitosing chondroblasts. Those fibroblasts at the periphery of an anlagen synthesize the perichondrium, and those entirely external to it guide the disposition of presumptive muscle cells (myoblasts) migrating there from nearby somites (located along the body's main axis). At first, only two muscle masses can be discerned, one dorsal and one ventral, but each progressively divides until all of the named muscles of the limb can be identified (Landmesser & Morris 1975; Whitelaw & Hollyday 1983a,b; Kardon 1998). Very shortly after muscle deployment begins, axons from nerve cells located within the presumptive spinal cord penetrate the limb and initiate synapses with each

←——

Figure 1 Clockface model of PI as evidenced in urodele limb transplantation. Blastema cells can intercalate missing PI values and usually do so by the shortest available route (see text). For example, if a pie wedge (e.g., from two o'clock to five o'clock) is removed from a blastema, the missing cells of the wedge are restored, and regeneration then follows (not shown). In the more elaborate experiment shown here, (*A*) a left forelimb was first truncated just proximal to the elbow and a wound blastema allowed to form. The right forelimb was then truncated at the same location and the left wound blastema transplanted to the stump (the distal right limb is discarded). (*B*) Right (stump) and left (blastemal) surfaces are each represented as clockfaces (clock size differences are for clarity only). Note the left/right asymmetry of the clockface (clockwise—*left*; counterclockwise—*right*). (*C*) Three limbs are often regenerated, which is in exact accord with the clockface PI model as follows: (*1*) regeneration normally occurs only if a complete clockface can be restored by intercalation (which requires at least one half a clockface); (*2*) one complete clockface exists in the form of the transplanted blastema itself—a left limb is regenerated on the stump by the left (transplanted) blastema; (*3*) other areas of intercalation occur between the blastema and the stump (e.g., between values 4 and 8), but only those between 3 and 9 can generate a complete clockface because at these locations there are two equally distant "routes," causing bidirectional intercalation and two complete new clockfaces (one at each 3–9 superimposition site—*grey*). Note that both supernumerary limbs are rights as predicted by the model. Numerous other experiments confirm similar intercalation rules in urodele wound blastemata (and insects), which have been simplified here (for further details see Bryant et al. 1981, Bryant et al. 1982) (modifed from French et al. 1976).

emergent muscle. It is within the PZ that cells acquire their positional identities through processes broadly similar to those observed in urodele regeneration (Wolpert et al. 1998). It is the unique, three-dimensional PA of each cell that will determine its specific role in the embryogenesis of the limb's bones, muscles, nerves, and vascular tissues, just as it does during the regeneration of missing portions of adult urodele limbs.

Axis Specification

Very soon after the limb bud initiates, mesenchymal expression of the TF (a protein that binds directly to DNA) dHand becomes restricted to a small group of cells at its posterior margin (Fernandez-Teran et al. 2000, te Welscher et al. 2002). Shortly thereafter these cells, which define the ZPA, begin to express the signaling molecule Sonic hedgehog (Shh) (Figure 2, see color insert). A classic body of experimental work in chicks attests to the ZPA's role in specifying the anterior-posterior (AP) axis (thumb to little finger) of the vertebrate limb (Summerbell & Honig 1982). For example, if the ZPA from an early wing bud is grafted to the anterior margin of another early wing bud, it develops extra digits with a mirror imaged autopod of the formula 4 3 2 3 4 instead of the normal 2 3 4 (birds lack mammalian digits one and five) (Summerbell et al. 1973, Wolpert & Hornbruch 1990). Based upon these findings it was suggested that the ZPA produces a graded signal that specifies posterior structures (e.g., ulna, digits 4 and 5) at high concentrations and specifies anterior structures in lower concentrations (e.g., radius, digits 1 and 2). That the same autopod mirror imaging caused by transplantation of an extra ZPA can be achieved either by overexpression of *dHand* or by implanting plastic beads soaked in Shh provides compelling evidence that Shh is a key element in this polarizing signal (Riddle et al. 1993, Chiang et al. 1996).

Specification of the proximal-distal axis of the vertebrate limb is less understood. Although distal outgrowth of the limb is clearly regulated by proteins of the FGF family secreted by the AER (Crossley et al. 1996, Fallon et al. 1994, Moon & Capecchi 2000), the most prominent current model holds that limb bud cells acquire their proximal-distal PA by measuring the amount of time spent in the PZ. Those cells that leave the PZ early acquire proximal identities, whereas those that leave it later acquire more distal identities (Wolpert 2002).

The information used to specify the dorsal-ventral limb axis originates within the mesenchyme of the lateral plate mesoderm. Prior to AER formation, this information is transferred to the ectoderm, resulting in the expression of *Wnt7a* in the presumptive dorsal limb bud ectoderm and *engrailed1* (*En1*) in the ventral limb bud ectoderm (Chen & Johnson 2002, Logan et al. 1997, Cygan et al. 1997, Loomis et al. 1996). If the gene *Wnt7a* is knocked out in the developing murine limb, its dorsal tissues become ventralized—and it develops paws with pads on both their palmar and dorsal surfaces. If *engrailed* is knocked out, *Wnt7a* is expressed there and its ventral tissues become dorsalized (i.e., engrailed downregulates *Wnt7a*). Dorsoventral (DV) polarity, established by cell communication similar to that described above for Prod1, is thus thought to establish DV PI in the emerging limb.

Hox Deployment

Hox gene products are transcription factors that contain a 60-amino-acid protein subdomain (the homeodomain encoded by the highly conserved, 180 base-pair homeobox sequence) that binds to DNA in a sequence-specific manner (Figure 3, see color insert). One of several different families of homeobox-containing genes, *Hox* genes are used extensively throughout embryogenesis in tissues as diverse as rhombomeres (i.e., the precursors of the hindbrain), vertebrae, mammary glands, and genitals. Derived from a single set of eight distinct genes organized into two linked gene complexes in *Drosophila* (i.e., Bithorax and Antennapedia), four *Hox* complexes, having as many as 13 genes each (1–13), have arisen in mammals by duplication and translocation (in humans, *Hox*A–D are located on chromosomes 7, 17, 12, and 2, respectively) (Duboule 1994). The duplicated genes within these complexes that derive from the same ancestral gene (i.e., those with the same number) are referred to as paralogues. Of particular importance is the fact that the genes in each complex are arranged as a linear series (in numerical order) on their respective chromosomes, and each gene is typically expressed spatially and temporally according to its sequential position within this series (these phenomena are referred to as spatial and temporal colinearity).

In the limb bud, the most 5' genes (9–13) of *Hox* clusters A and D are used to further refine the PI within the bud's three primary axes (along with some from *Hox* C as well in the hindlimb) (Nelson et al. 1996). For example, if both *Hoxa11* and *Hoxd11* are prevented from being expressed in the mouse limb bud, their forelimbs lack almost any zeugopod (antebrachium) formation (Davis et al. 1995). If denied expression of *Hoxa13* and *Hoxd13*, autopod formation is disorganized and curtailed (Zakany et al. 1997). Such knock-outs have clearly eliminated the PI necessary to specify further development in these two regions of the bud [re-expression of *Shh* and *HoxD* genes in the wound blastemata of urodeles (see above) is one of the mechanisms used to reassign its cells their new fates (Torok et al. 1998, 1999)]. A considerable body of data has accumulated about the manner in which *Hox* genes establish PI in the developing limb.

Hox expression domains are dynamic and occur in multiple phases (Nelson et al. 1996, Shubin et al. 1997). In Phase I, *Hoxd9* and *Hoxd10* are expressed uniformly (e.g., lacking an obvious anterior/posterior gradient) across the entire limb bud. Phase II includes the addition of *Hoxd11* and *Hoxd12* expression and is more complex. In this phase all four D-cluster genes become deployed in nested domains, with higher numbered genes restricted to more distal and posterior regions, generally following the rules of spatial and temporal colinearity (see above). This expression pattern appears to be Shh-dependent and shows the greatest differences between the fore and hindlimb. This may represent a distinct phase (under separate *cis*-regulation—see below), or it may be a temporal continuation of Phase I

(Herault et al. 1999). Finally, Phase III involves expression of *Hoxd10–13* and *Hoxa13* (there is no 12 paralogue in the A cluster) in the most distal portion of the limb bud. In the autopod, the higher numbered *Hox* genes are expressed first (and in more extensive domains), whereas expression of the lower numbered genes is restricted to more posterior territories, i.e., temporal and spatial colinearity are reversed. Although also Shh-dependent, this unusual aspect of Phase III suggests a potentially different regulatory mechanism than in the first two phases (see below) (Herault et al. 1997, Kmita et al. 2002).

Hox Genes as Selector Genes

Hox genes function in this phase of limb development as selector genes; that is, genes that specify cell fate (Pradel & White 1998, Carroll et al. 2001). In the case of the limb bud, developmental fate is being specified by expression of the specific combination of *Hox* genes (a combinatorial [*Hox*] code) in the cells that adumbrate each increasingly specific portion or subdivision of the limb. Furthermore, *Hox* genes play a central role in bone condensation and growth (Goff & Tabin 1997) (Figure 3).

This same phenomenon is particularly well characterized with respect to specification of vertebral identity (Burke et al. 1995, Gaunt 2000, Rosenman et al. 2002). In accordance with spatial and temporal colinearity, *Hox* genes with lower numbers (e.g., *Hox4*) are expressed at more cranial somite levels, whereas those with higher numbers are expressed more caudally (e.g., murine *Hoxd11* normally exhibits a strong anterior limit at the 27th somite, which corresponds to the first sacral vertebra). Although *Hox* genes display a strong cranial border in their expression patterns, their mRNA signal gradually decreases caudally. Therefore, each somite possesses a unique combinatorial *Hox* code, which differs from the codes at other somite levels by the number, expression intensity, and particular combination of its constituent *Hox* genes. Furthermore, the anterior-most expression limits of *Hox* genes correlate well with major morphological transitions along the vertebral column (Burke et al. 1995). For example, *Hox9* paralogues are expressed most strongly at the thoracolumbar junction, whereas *Hox11* paralogues are found at the lumbosacral junction. Experimental manipulations of anterior *Hox* expression limits (see below) always show a concomitant change in the morphological landmark for which the affected gene codes.

A variety of other kinds of selector genes guide other steps in development (as tabulated in Supplemental Table 1 online; follow the Supplemental Material link in the online version of this chapter or at http://www.annualreviews.org/). For example, two genes of the T-box (*Tbx*) family have been implicated as selector genes in specifying fore- and hindlimb identities. Although the specific details are too complex to discuss here, *Tbx4*, in conjunction with the upstream (expressed previously in the regulatory cascade) genes *Ptx1* and *Ptx2*, is expressed strongly in the hindlimb but not the forelimb. Alternatively, *Tbx5* is expressed strongly in the forelimb but not the hindlimb (Ng et al. 2002). These genes, together with

Hox genes, are implicated as selectors of "wingness" and "legness" in chicks (Ahn et al. 2001; Cohn et al. 1997; Gibson-Brown et al. 1996, 1998; Isaac et al. 1998; Lanctot et al. 1999; Logan et al. 1998; Logan & Tabin 1999).

Selector Territories as Developmental Fields

As we have just seen, developing tissues become increasingly more specified with each successive selector gene event. The most important heuristic implication of such canalization is the nature of genetic subprograms initiated by selector genes such as *Hoxes*. Those cells that share the same combinatorial code can be said to comprise a morphogenetic field or module (Opitz 1985, Riddle et al. 1993, Gilbert et al. 1996, Raff 1996). The more intricate details of the cell's successive mitoses, production of receptors and communicating molecules, and eventual structural protein manufacture are all orchestrated by the increasingly specific PI that they acquire with each additional phase of selector expression. In limb development, such fields are originally composed of what appear to be homogenous mesenchyme cells (though their individual PIs or cell fates already must differ substantially), and their progeny will eventually form Sharpey's fibers, muscle epimysia, tendons, cartilage, bone, etc. (Thompson 1988). This means that many daughter cells that later become different cell types (e.g., fibroblast versus chondroblast) can lie adjacent to one another in the early embryo and later in the adult. Thus, even though their final roles differ, their original PI will have often differed (in cases not involving differential migration) by only a single cell diameter along subtle gradients.

Within this context, it is of special importance that fibroblasts determine muscle form and structure—myoblasts are passive and simply made available by their migration from the trunk. This means that the fibroblasts that specify muscle composition and structure emerge from the same fields as the chondroblasts and osteoblasts that later specify bone structure to which these muscles attach (see below)—limb tissues are thus highly integrated and can be presumed to evolve in a holistic fashion (Lovejoy et al. 1999).

Finally, it is important to recognize that selector genes do not directly guide subsequent downstream cellular activities—those are instead determined by the expression of the selector's target genes, which are more immediately involved in local morphogenesis (mitotic rate or apoptosis, cell-cell adhesion, production of the proteins of ECM, etc.) (cf. Supplemental Table 1; see earlier). Such genes are sometimes referred to as realizators. Furthermore, more often than not, realizators are not under direct *Hox* control but are instead guided by other selector gene expression of a more intermediate level. "Therefore, the genetic cascade that controls pattern formation extends to tiers beyond the *Hox* complex genes, before finally reaching the activation of realizator genes thought to provide the basic cellular functions required for differentiation" (Pradel & White 1998). Thus, although loss of *Hoxa13* causes severe autopod deformity, the gene should not be viewed as "the" hand/foot gene (a common error often involved in the description of many other selector genes). It does not determine hand/foot structure per se—rather it activates a cascade of increasingly specific genetic subprograms that guide the details of autopod formation.

The Realization of the Limb Skeleton

The form of any bone is determined predominantly by the history of differential mitosis, cell adhesion, and gene expression within its growth plates and metaphyseal perichondrium as specified by the PI assigned to its ancestral mesenchymal cells prior to cytodifferention and histogenesis (Erlebacher et al. 1995). Although osteoblasts obviously play an important role in bone formation (using PI their lineages acquired as mesenchymal cells), the cells most responsible for bone morphology are its chondroblasts.

The histomorphological events of endochondral ossification have been known for some time (Ogden 1979), but recent work has greatly enhanced our understanding of the genetics of skeletal development (see Karsenty & Wagner 2002 for a more thorough review). During this process, cells go through multiple stages of differentiation that can be characterized by other master transcription factors (i.e., intermediate level selector genes). Skeletal development starts with formation of condensations by mesenchymal cells expressing the transcription factor *Sox9* (de Crombrugghe et al. 2001). These cells then differentiate into chondrocytes and express specific molecular markers such as aggrecan and Type II collagen (Col II) (e.g., products of realizators), while a thin layer of surrounding mesenchymal cells remains to form the perichondrium (Karsenty & Wagner 2002). *Col II* is one of a number of cartilage genes that possess a Sox9 binding domain within its regulatory region, demonstrating that this transcription factor is critical in cartilage development.

At the center of the cartilage model chondrocytes begin to undergo the sequential processes of proliferation, hypertrophy, and ultimately apoptosis. The behavior of the hypertrophic chondrocytes changes radically from their progenitors. They cease proliferation, produce copious amounts of ECM, and greatly expand in size. Not surprising, this is associated with major changes in gene expression including the involvement of a regulatory transcription factor Cbfa1. The ECM that is produced includes Type X collagen (Col X) and becomes calcified. This differentiation process extends centrifugally toward each end of the cartilage model. The perichondrium around the hypertrophic chondrocytes metamorphoses into periosteum and begins to form a bone collar around the hypertrophic chondrocytes. It is interesting that osteoblasts are also characterized by the expression of *Cbfa1*. Under the influence of the hypertrophic chondrocytes (via the expression of angiogenic factors VEGF and MMP9), a periosteal bud invades the model providing an arterial supply to the center of the element (Colnot & Helms 2001). This opens a conduit by which osteoclasts and osteoblasts can enter the cartilage model and replace the calcified matrix with bone, thus forming the primary center of ossification (Figure 4A, see color insert).

In a typical long bone, the progression of the maturing chondrocytes is arrested prior to reaching either end. Here a resting zone of chondrocytes is established that forms the growth plate. The resting zone not only provides a population of progenitor cells for continued growth but also organizes the proliferative chondrocytes into longitudinal columns, which are maintained until they undergo apoptosis (Abad et al. 2002). The relatively undifferentiated hyaline cartilage distal to the resting zone is the chondroepiphysis. Later it will undergo secondary ossification (radially from its center) similar to bones that lack true growth plates, i.e., carpals and tarsals.

A complex regulatory feedback loop acts to maintain and control the timing of chondrocyte maturation (Vortkamp et al. 1996, Vortkamp 2000). As cells leave the proliferative zone and begin to undergo hypertrophy they express *Indian hedgehog* (*Ihh*) (from the same gene family as *Shh*). Its soluble protein product appears to engage a specific signal receptor, Patched (Ptc), in cells of the perichondrium. Upregulation of *Ihh* has also been shown to increase Parathyroid Hormone-related Peptide (PTHrP) expression in periarticular epiphyseal chondrocytes, likely via *TGFβ* expression from the perichondrium (Alvarez et al. 2001). PTHrP receptors are found in proliferating chondrocytes, and PTHrP from the periarticular region acts to maintain these cells in their proliferative state, thus limiting the number that mature to the hypertrophic phase [via the promotion of Sox9 functions (Huang et al. 2001)]. In addition, PTHrP upregulates the expression of *Bcl2*, an apoptosis inhibitor (Amling et al. 1997), which also may have a role in regulating matrix production (Feng et al. 1999). Therefore, Ihh and PTHrP constitute a negative feedback loop that limits the rate of cell maturation and maintains a proliferative pool of chondrocytes in the growth plate throughout ontogeny (see Figure 4*B*) (Lanske et al. 1996).

This feedback model has greatly advanced our understanding of growth plate physiology and has remained largely unchanged since its initial proposal. However, in postnatal and juvenile mammals, intercellular signaling would be required to occur over remarkably large distances. It has therefore been proposed that resting and/or proliferating chondrocytes within the growth plate produce PTHrP themselves, albeit at a lower level than do periarticular chondrocytes, in order to regulate chondrocyte maturation (Reynolds et al. 1998). This hypothesis has been largely supported in multiple postnatal experimental animal models (Vortkamp et al. 1998, van der Eerden et al. 2000, Farquharson et al. 2001, Medill et al. 2001, Yoshida et al. 2001).

One further aspect of skeletal growth is cartilage modeling (Hamrick 1999). The subarticular cartilage of most bones houses another growth zone that is also established by PI and is possibly maintained by its own PTHrP-Ihh loop (Vortkamp et al. 1998). The cells of the two (or more) participating portions of a synovial joint must also transduce mechanical forces (Lovejoy et al. 1999). Because Ihh has been shown to be partially regulated by mechanotransduction (Wu et al. 2001), this may provide a mechanism whereby the two adjacent growth zones of the joint "cooperate" to yield adult surfaces that always exhibit tangential contact force velocities (Frankel et al. 1971, Burstein & Wright 1994). Ihh may also play a role in mediating the tendency for growth plates to continually reorient normal to predominant transarticular forces during development, such as appears to occur in the formation of the bicondylar angle in hominids. These are examples of the kinds of environmental accommodation that sometimes occurs during morphogenesis.

In the final analysis, bones of the limb skeleton are almost entirely determined by the PI of their original cartilage anlagen, primarily as expressed in the differential growth in their physes (for a potential genetic mechanism see Figure 4*B*) and metaphyseal perichondrium, and to a lesser extent modeling of articular cartilage. The diaphysis is thus largely what is left behind in the wake of physis growth, and the length of any long bone is simply the most appropriate (naturally selected) distance separating its joint surfaces (along with appropriate positioning of the joint's musculature) (Reno et al. 2000). Virtually all of these parameters are specified by the PI assigned to each presumptive physis during limb bud formation. So long as the diaphysis is sufficiently stout so as not to fail (primarily in bending for mammals), there is otherwise normally only minimal selection acting on it.

Cis-Regulation and the Evolution of the Limb Skeleton

By now it should be clear that within any given limb field, bone form, muscle attachment and structure, and tendon deployment are all orchestrated by the same genetic subprogram. Changing an adult structure must therefore involve altering the PI of one of its presumptive developmental fields or modules. It is thus the morphogenetic field that constitutes the unit of selection–not the individual bone or any one of its anatomically defined subunits or investing musculature (i.e., soft tissue versus hard tissue traits). One of the most pivotal modern discoveries with respect to morphogenesis is the means by which developmental fields and their subsequent adult structures vary and can be favored or eliminated by selection. The reader is directed to what are now three principal discussions of these phenomena (Carroll et al. 2001, Davidson 2001, Wilkins 2001; see also Weiss 2002 and Chiu & Hamrick 2002), but a brief discussion follows.

The mammalian genome has surprisingly few genes (about 35,000). Of the even smaller number that can be considered developmental genes, i.e., signaling molecules and selector genes, many are used repeatedly during embryogenesis— often for radically different purposes (as tabulated in Supplemental Table 1; see earlier). As detailed above, the bones of the postcranium are essentially all products of the same genes that encode a variety of transcription factors, communicating molecules, cell-adhesion molecules, and growth factors. Of particular importance are growth factors such as BMPs, as well as their receptors (BMPRs), antagonists (e.g., Noggin), and regulators (e.g., retinoic acid), all of which play prominent roles in determining the size and shape of condensations, anlagen, and eventually the growing bone.

The differences between one skeletal site and another are thus, for the most part, not genic (i.e., arising from differences in the exons of genes for structural proteins) but regulatory. A substantial portion of gene expression is regulated by non-coding DNA regions called *cis*-regulatory elements (*cis* means that the regulatory site lies on the same chromosome as the target gene, as opposed to *trans*-regulatory elements, which are the transcription factors that bind them— currently, the best known *cis*-elements are often referred to by the more specific term enhancer). Activity within these regions determines not only which genes are expressed within a particular field but also their timing and degree of expression. For example, in order for a cell to differentiate into an osteoblast, it must express *Cbfa1*, which encodes a transcription factor that binds to the *cis*-regulatory site osteoblast-specific enhancer-2 (OSE2). This expression pathway is regulated, at least in part, by BMPs and other growth factors (Ducy & Karsenty 1995).

Cis-regulatory elements can be found almost anywhere in the vicinity of the genes on which they act—even within the gene's own introns—and their use can be highly specific (i.e., restricted to a single morphogenetic field) and can not only encourage expression in that field (enhancers) but prevent it as well (silencers and insulators). Furthermore, they can be unidirectional, operating only in the 5' or 3' direction, but not the reverse (unidirectionality is an important feature in programming the autopod—see below). Essentially it is the combination of the action of all these elements that determine when and how target genes within selector gene territories (as well as selector genes themselves) operate locally within any specific tissue.

An important variable with respect to this issue is what has been learned about promoter structure in the past several years. As shown in Figure 5 (see color insert), the relationships between enhancers and the gene's primary or basal promoter region (i.e., the binding region for RNA polymerase II and its associated general transcription factors) can be extremely complex, often requiring an adjacent (upstream) second promoter region that binds a variety of small molecules (activators, coactivators, repressors, corepressors). All of these together determine transcription and its rate. Very slight differences in DNA sequence within these non-coding regions can have substantial effects. Furthermore, the particular combination of *cis*-regulatory elements associated with a gene can determine transcription in both discrete and/or continuous fashions (i.e., the combination of *cis*-elements can act as switches and/or rheostats). Several examples may help to illustrate these points.

A primary example is *Hoxc8* expression in the presumptive spinal cord, vertebrae, and limb-producing mesoderm. It is controlled by the binding of at least five transcription factors within a *cis*-element known as the early *Hoxc8* enhancer (Belting et al. 1998a,b; Shashikant & Ruddle 1996). Specific combinations of these binding proteins result in tissue-, spatial-, and temporal-specific *Hoxc8* expression. Moreover, changes of only a few base pairs between mice and chicks result in spatial and temporal expression patterns characteristic for each species (Belting et al. 1998a). Deletion of only four base pairs in one binding site entirely abolishes *Hoxc8* expression in the paraxial mesoderm in baleen whales (Shashikant et al. 1998). Additionally, *cis*-regulation of growth factors such as BMPs and FGFs almost certainly plays an important role in controlling skeletal growth rates (Minina et al. 2001, 2002) (see Figure 4*B*).

Some of the *cis*-regulatory regions acting on the *Hoxd11* locus have also been well characterized (Gerard et al. 1993, 1996, 1997; Zakany et al. 1996). Two highly conserved regions, eight and nine (RVIII and RIX), bind activators and silencers, respectively, to ensure proper *Hoxd11* expression along the main embryonic axis, and thereby to specify the correct placement of the lumbosacral border (see above). Remarkably, a zebrafish homologue to RVIII is able to drive expression of *Hoxd11* in the murine trunk, albeit prematurely and more anteriorly by two somites as compared to the murine RVIII (Gerard et al. 1997). This more anterior expression limit results in a cranial shift of the lumbosacral border. An important corollary of such studies is the phenomenon of transcriptional heterochrony as a mechanism for evolutionary change (i.e., small differences in the timing and spatial expression patterns of loci, as controlled by variants in their *cis*-regulatory architecture, can account for differences in morphology). As noted by Duboule and colleagues, "... changes as subtle as a few hours difference in the activation of a single *Hox* gene can have significant effects on the morphology of the animal" (Gerard et al. 1997, p. 39).

Selection acts primarily upon variation in the sequence, and/or combination of *cis*-regulatory elements (which are themselves modular in construction), rather than in selector or realizator genes (though some particular members of a gene family may be expressed only at some skeletal sites and not others)—that is, the gene tends to be more conserved than the *cis*-elements that specify its local regulation because changes in the latter can be specific to a morphogenetic field whereas those in the former are more likely to have global effects (i.e., all cells expressing that gene). Both types of change are important in evolution, but changes in *cis*-regulation are more likely to be involved in local morphogenetic changes. Intensive investigation of the mammalian autopod has proved particularly illuminating.

Cis-Regulation and Anatomical Structure of the Autopod

As noted earlier, five *Hox* genes act as selectors that regionalize the developing autopod (*Hoxd10–13* and *Hoxa13*). Hoxd13—Hoxd10 transcriptional activity is regulated by the DE, a *cis*-regulatory element that lies some 400,000 base pairs 5′ to the HoxD cluster (Kmita et al. 2002). The *Hoxd* gene, occupying the most 5′ position in this cluster (just 3′ to the conserved region RXII), is always the first and most strongly expressed. Normally, this is *Hoxd13*. However, if *Hoxd13* is removed, *Hoxd12* is then expressed in the *Hoxd13* fashion. Many *Hox* genes have some degree of shared function and can thereby entirely or partially "rescue" missing, closely related genes. This appears to occur with respect to *Hoxd12* and *Hoxd13* because when only the latter is removed there are only minimal morphological effects. This is not true, however, of *Hoxd11*. If both *Hoxd13* and *Hoxd12* are removed, *Hoxd11* is then expressed in the normal *Hoxd13* fashion, and the autopod is grossly deformed (Kmita et al. 2002).

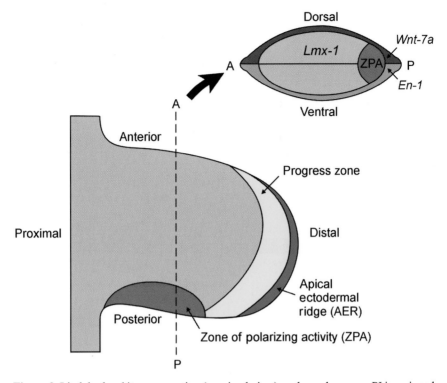

Figure 2 Limb bud and its cross section (proximal view) as shown by arrow. PI is assigned to the mesoderm along three axes by interactions among four organizers: the apical ectodermal ridge (AER, *blue*), the progress zone (PZ, *yellow*), the zone of polarizing activity (ZPA, *red*), and the nonridge dorsal and ventral ectoderm (*purple* and *green*, respectively). The AER maintains distal outgrowth by promoting mitosis of undifferentiated cells in the underlying PZ. Cells are believed to acquire proximal-distal identity along the axis by the time spent in the PZ. Position along the anterior-posterior axis is organized by the ZPA via diffusion of Shh, which establishes a posterior to anterior gradient; therefore, high concentrations of Shh specify the little finger and low concentrations of the thumb. Dorsal and ventral position is established by the nonridge ectoderm as shown in cross section. *Wnt-7a* expression in the dorsal ectoderm assigns dorsal identity to the underlying mesoderm by inducing mesenchymal expression of *Lmx1* (Riddle et al. 1995). In contrast, *En-1* expression in ventral ectoderm blocks the expression of *Wnt-7a*, thus preventing dorsalization via *Lmx1* (adapted from Wolpert et al. 2002).

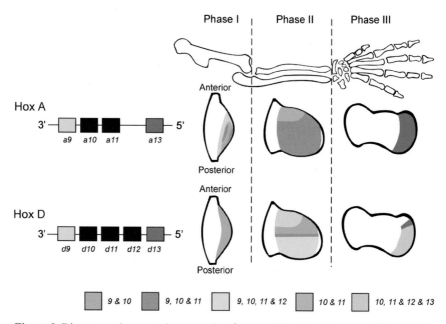

Figure 3 Diagrammatic expression maps for 5′ genes of the Hox A (*top*) and Hox D (*bottom*) clusters during outgrowth of the forelimb. Isolated gene expression domains are coded on the *left* (genes with no singular expression are left uncolored). Combinatorial gene-expression domains are coded along the *bottom*. Each of three proposed phases of expression are shown. Because each gene's expression is dynamic (gene domains and the limb bud itself are both changing continuously), such expression maps can only be very approximate. A digit enhancer is known to exist and to regulate *Hox* patterning of the autopod (Phase III) (for discussion see text). Whether Phases I and II are truly distinct or are actually temporal manifestations of the same expression event cannot be resolved until more data on *cis*-regulation of the clusters become available for the stylopod and zeugopod (Herault et al. 1999). These are in situ mRNA hybridization data for the chick forelimb—the mouse forelimb is shown but known to be similar in general *Hox* expression (data from Nelson et al. 1996, Shubin et al. 1997, Wolpert et al. 1998).

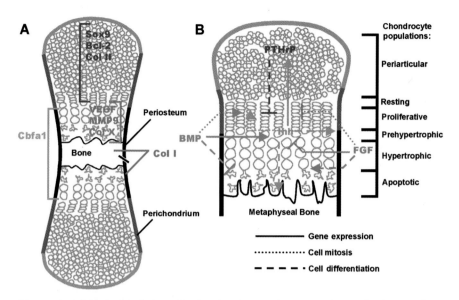

Figure 4 (*A*) Endochondral ossification involves replacement of a cartilaginous anlage with bone. Initially the cartilage cells express the transcription factor *Sox9* and produce an ECM rich in Type II collagen. Subsequently, the chondrocytes become hypertrophic and the surrounding perichondrium differentiates into periosteum. Both processes require the expression of *Cbfa1*. Additionally, hypertrophic chondrocytes secrete Type X collagen and promote calcification of the ECM. They simultaneously synthesize transcription factors (VEGF and MMP9) that promote the invasion of blood vessels, osteoblasts, and osteoclasts from the periosteum. The hypertrophic chondrocytes apoptose, and the remaining ECM is used as a scaffold for the deposition of bone. (*B*) The Ihh/PTHrP feedback loop regulates growth plate chondrocyte proliferation and differentiation (*arrow heads* indicate upregulation, and *bars* indicate downregulation). As cells begin to hypertrophy they synthesize Ihh, which indirectly upregulates the expression of *PTHrP* in periarticular chondrocytes. PTHrP diffuses to PTHrP receptors expressed in proliferating chondrocytes and restrains their further differentiation into the hypertrophic phase. Therefore, Ihh and PTHrP constitute a negative feedback loop that limits the rate of cell maturation and maintains a proliferative pool of chondrocytes in the growth plate throughout ontogeny (Lanske et al. 1996, Vortkamp et al. 1996). In addition, Ihh directly increases the mitotic rate of proliferating chondrocytes, stimulates the differentiation of the perichondrium into periosteum, and promotes bone deposition along the calcified cartilage scaffold by the invading metaphyseal osteoblasts (Karp et al. 2000, St-Jacques et al. 1999).

Growth rate in the physis appears to be regulated by members of the BMP and FGF families. BMPs increase the mitotic rate of proliferative chondrocytes via pathways independent of Ihh. Also, by upregulating the expression of *Ihh* and delaying chondrocyte apoptosis, BMPs enlarge both the proliferative and hypertrophic regions, respectively (Minina et al. 2001). FGFs regulate the same stages of chondrocyte development but have opposite effects. Most important, these signaling factors have been shown to act in a dose-dependent, antagonistic manner (Minina et al. 2002), which suggests that the *cis*-regulation of these genes may be a key heritable mechanism for differential growth within and between physes.

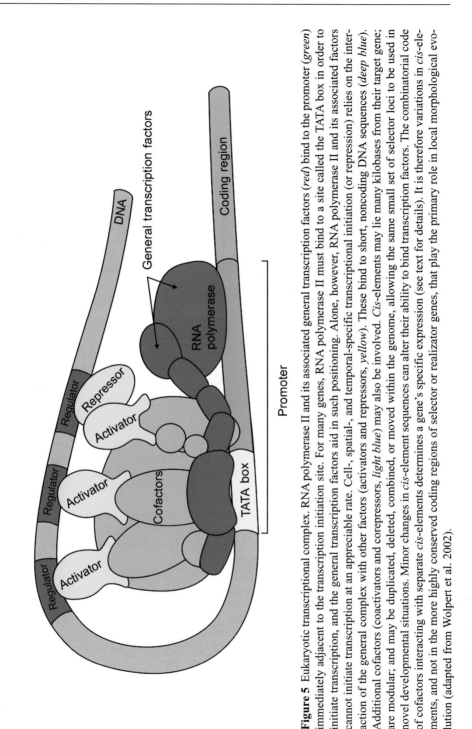

Figure 5 Eukaryotic transcriptional complex. RNA polymerase II and its associated general transcription factors (*red*) bind to the promoter (*green*) immediately adjacent to the transcription initiation site. For many genes, RNA polymerase II must bind to a site called the TATA box in order to initiate transcription, and the general transcription factors aid in such positioning. Alone, however, RNA polymerase II and its associated factors cannot initiate transcription at an appreciable rate. Cell-, spatial-, and temporal-specific transcriptional initiation (or repression) relies on the interaction of the general complex with other factors (activators and repressors, *yellow*). These bind to short, noncoding DNA sequences (*deep blue*). Additional cofactors (coactivators and corepressors, *light blue*) may also be involved. *Cis*-elements may lie many kilobases from their target gene; are modular; and may be duplicated, deleted, combined, or moved within the genome, allowing the same small set of selector loci to be used in novel developmental situations. Minor changes in *cis*-element sequences can alter their ability to bind transcription factors. The combinatorial code of cofactors interacting with separate *cis*-elements determines a gene's specific expression (see text for details). It is therefore variations in *cis*-elements, and not in the more highly conserved coding regions of selector or realizator genes, that play the primary role in local morphological evolution (adapted from Wolpert et al. 2002).

These three genes, which have different (albeit overlapping) territories within the autopod, thus have varying amplitudes of expression determined by their position with respect to *cis*-regulatory elements such as conserved Region XII (RXII) and the DE. This is almost certainly a basis for local anatomical variation. This is indicated by additional experiments related to the one just cited, which demonstrated that the strength of expression of each gene was reduced by the presence of other promoters between it and the target site of the DE. The posterior *HoxD* cluster is thus somewhat similar in this respect to genes of the β-globin cluster, in which simple distance from the locus control region (LCR) impacts preferential activation and expression (Wijgerde et al. 1995). However, the same *Hox* genes and DE are also used in patterning the genital tubercle (Perriton et al. 2002); therefore, substantial modification of intercistronic distances within the *Hox* cluster is an unlikely source of differential expression on which selection can act (though small distances remain as possible sources of such variation).

To summarize, *cis*-regulatory elements can act both as switches and their various combinations as rheostats in gene regulation. They thus play the primary role in altering anatomical structure via slight changes in the deployment or organization of the morphogenetic field(s) they regulate, e.g., the fields that produce the distal femur and proximal tibia differ quantitatively rather than qualitatively. Understanding modification of anatomical structure at this level has profound implications on the way we interpret hominid morphological evolution. Before turning to some of these issues, however, one more important revelation provided by modern developmental biology remains to be discussed.

WOLFF'S LAW: REINTERPRETING THE ROLE OF STRAIN SENSITIVITY IN BONE MORPHOGENESIS

Bone has long been regarded as a very special tissue (and thereby singled out for isolated examination and study) because it is preserved, and thus usually constitutes our singular evidence of extinct vertebrates. Throughout the twentieth century an almost universal presumption was that bone structure broadly derives according to "Wolff's Law." Because bone is sensitive to mechanical loading (or its absence), it has been theorized for decades (especially from an adaptationist perspective) that the skeleton, by activation of unknown mechanisms, is largely mechanoanabolic—bone has an ability to transduce its loading regimens into "definite changes in . . . internal architecture, and equally definite secondary alterations in . . . external conformation in accordance with mathematical laws" (Roesler 1981). Such views have led to a popular hypothetical converse: that bone shape can be used to reconstruct those activities that "produced" it—so long as these "mathematical laws" are known and that adaptations and activities can be directly deduced from geometric analyses of bone structure.

A thoughtful review of these admittedly complex issues can be found in Currey (2002), even though he, himself, largely ignores the anabolic issues of gene expression by relegating it to be "too ill-understood" for discussion. We obviously take an opposite view—that more is now known (or at least rationally suspected) about skeletal genetics than about the "mathematical laws" by which bones hypothetically model themselves. Indeed, a more sagacious review of the vast data that have been accumulated on bone behavior leaves the hypothesis of bone's ability to shape itself by some (unknown) set of mathematical-like transduction functions less than tenuous despite a long tradition of almost heroic attempts to define such laws (Frost 1990a,b). To be sure, bone tissue is responsive to external loads; the potential effects of these, however, can be myriad without invoking mechanoanabolism. The mere addition of bone subperiosteally, for example, is hardly to be heralded as a complex constructive mechanism, nor does it serve as evidence of a capacity to shape itself.

In fact, the cornucopia of twentieth-century observations and experiments on bone behavior can just as readily be interpreted as leading to the opposite conclusion (Bertram & Swartz 1991). For example, the mandible regularly suffers $<1000 \ \mu\epsilon$ (Hylander & Crompton 1986), whereas the canon bones of race horses can experience 5000 $\mu\epsilon$ (Nunamaker et al. 1990). Maximum strain in the latter shows a remarkable lack of uniformity, varying from only 100 $\mu\epsilon$ in some locales to over 2000 $\mu\epsilon$ in others (McLeod et al. 1998). These are hardly data from which to argue that bone form is an integrated syncytial response guided by a systematic repertoire of cues emanating from the simple transduction of the magnitudes of external loading. As Skerry notes, "in rats, sheep, birds, and humans . . . the strains in the skull do not exceed one-tenth . . . those in the long bones even under extreme circumstances" (Skerry 2000, p. 36). Nor does load duration appear to play a significant role—inasmuch as only one min/day of applied load is necessary to prevent loss due to disuse (Rubin & Lanyon 1987), and a mere 5 $\mu\epsilon$ is all that is required to generate an increase in the density of trabeculae in the proximal femora of sheep (Rubin et al. 2001). Even the legendary tennis player data (Jones et al. 1977) are inconsistent with true Wolffian principles because unilateral bone gain (more properly retention since the phenomenon has only been documented in those with a long subadult history of competitive play) occurs both periosteally and endosteally, the latter adding mass in higher proportion than its beneficial effect on section modulus. As emphasized by Fritton and colleagues, "until the mechanism of bone's mechanosensory system is fully understood, all portions of bone's strain history should be considered to possibly play a role in bone adaptation" (2000, p. 317).

Bone's injury response is particularly important for survival, but its disorganized, albeit effective, diffuse reaction to fracture is hardly an example of any inherent organizing constructive capacity. As every anthropologist will recognize, unless completely eliminated by total replacement as a consequence of subsequent growth, bone fractures remain permanently obvious because of their patent irregularity—a truly natural experiment that seems to have entirely eluded those who are enthusiastic about bone's supposed mechanoanabolic powers.

Other mammalian structures and tissues are every bit as organized as bones are (consider the heart, which in some animals does have a calcified "skeleton"), and many are composed of cells that are sensitive to deformation (Banes et al. 1995,

Skerry 2000). However, strain transduction does not play a singular role in their morphogenesis; in fact, such strain sensitivity could readily lead to anabolic chaos. Sarcomeres hypertrophy in response to exercise, indeed much more quickly and dramatically than does bone; yet remarkable mechanoanabolic powers are never attributed to them as well (as well they should not, since they can have virtually none—see earlier).

A far more cogent approach to bone behavior (rather than through elucidation of its material properties) is to acknowledge the degree to which it parallels other tissues. There is no reason to presume that it should not exhibit the same rules of pattern formation and gene expression. In this respect, a common fate of many cells during development is apoptosis—cells require signaling molecules not only to divide but to survive. Cell death may in fact be the default pathway of most cellular differentiation (including osteoblasts), unless there has been alternative specification through PI, cell deformation, and/or communication with other cells (Wolpert et al. 1998). Mammalian innervation of skeletal muscles is achieved by just such methods (save deformation)—why should bone not show these same primary characteristics?

Considerable sense can be made of the distribution and structure of both trabecular and cortical bone if its primary form is assumed to reflect the expression of PI in its anabolic growth zones (as in the other tissues around it), although its material properties and maintenance are also affected by local strain threshold(s) (which may be small and/or at least broadly tissue-specific). If other response regimens are also considered, such as the possibility that Ihh synthesis in physes and articular cartilage may occur in response to strain (Wu et al. 2001), then much of bone structure can be illuminated without assigning osteoblasts the singular and largely unique capacity of guiding morphogenesis via conjectural laws whose execution requires inordinately complex transduction mechanisms at the cellular level.

The most relevant issue for anthropologists is the degree to which adult bone structure is indicative of genetic background versus its history of load transduction. It is of special note that in virtually all cases of bone hypertrophy in noninvasive loading experiments, including the tennis players of Jones et al. (1977) or the exercised pigs of Woo et al. (1981), the subjects were subadult. Comparative cortical thickness data on extinct hominids are thus of very limited value, unless we regard some vague index of the level of subadult play as being important!

Similarly, the demonstration that trabecular design differs in australopithecine ilia from that of modern humans is hardly surprising because iliac form also differs substantially in the two species [largely as a consequence of adaptations to birthing in the latter (Lovejoy 2003)], and therefore so must the anabolic history of their growth plates (which is, in fact, what trabeculae essentially represent). A much more startling finding is the remarkable degree of similarity in the trabecular patterning of the proximal femur in humans compared to those of the great apes (Lovejoy et al. 2002)—among which loading regimens differ dramatically (Kalmey & Lovejoy 2002). Again, such differences are more readily accounted for by presuming that bone retention differs as a consequence of external loading within a broadly similar program of pattern formation (i.e., PI expression) in these various taxa.

DEVELOPMENTAL BIOLOGY AND THE STUDY OF HUMAN EVOLUTION

The history of both phylogenetic assessment and functional analysis has been one of decomposition of anatomical structure into largely arbitrary morphological units. Such procedures tend to systematically ignore Le Gros Clark's maxim on "total morphological pattern" (Le Gros Clark 1978), as well as Dobzhansky's statement of almost 50 years ago: "genes do not determine each a separate trait; they determine, jointly and severally, the developmental processes which result in the appearance of all . . . traits." (Dobzhansky 1956, p. 343). Perhaps most sobering to any cladist resilient to the fundamental truth of these observations is the following principle:

> Other things being equal, many small mutations are consistent with higher rates of progressive evolution than a few large mutations. These most frequent and most important mutations produce small fluctuating effects in developmental fields. They are particulate and for the most part independent, in themselves, but do not ordinarily show any 1:1 correspondence with single structures or unit characters in a morphologically descriptive sense. (Simpson 1944, p. 94)

Such observations, though necessarily vague as a consequence of their age, have become increasingly and systematically ignored in recent hominid paleontology. However, they have been confirmed by modern developmental biology. The implications are clear; the proper units of analysis for both phylogeny and function are not arbitrarily defined traits but the morphogenetic fields that underlie them.

An immediate objection to such a statement is obvious; traits are concrete, discrete units of analysis that can be readily analyzed for mechanical significance and manipulated for phylogenetic investigation. Morphogenetic fields, on the other hand, are neither easily defined nor readily manipulated—they must be determined by examination of large mammalian and vertebrate databases and through experiment (Lovejoy et al. 1999). Nevertheless, we now know that they are the real basis of morphological variation, and as such they are now the proper currency of selection, adaptation, and evolutionary analysis. To continue reliance on entirely artificial categories as a focus of human paleontology is to ignore modern biology's proscription of their relevance (Asfaw et al. 1999a,b). Just as the hominid face is not a compendium of isolated features (McCollum & Sharpe 2001, McCollum 1999), the hominid pelvis does not result from separate selection on both its overall form (e.g., short broad ilium) and anatomical "landmarks" [e.g., the anterior inferior iliac spine (AIIS) of hominids] (Lovejoy et al. 1999, Lovejoy 2003). The latter is almost certainly a mundane (i.e., selectively neutral) byproduct of those changes in *cis*-regulation of hominid pelvic form for bipedality. As a consequence, both reflect the same underlying morphogenetic shift.

The ramifications of these conclusions are obvious. Neither biomechanical nor cladistic analyses can now be properly conducted absent fundamental contextual structuring by modern developmental biology. Unfortunately this will require a major refashioning of both types of analyses—and in some cases total abandonment in favor of more sophisticated embryogenetic approaches. Nor are other similar traditional approaches to morphological analysis any more immune to such requisite restructuring. The demonstration of simple somatic growth patterns and postnatal ontogeny tells us little about the underlying significance of morphology, since their PI is entirely determined during earliest embryogenesis. Postnatal growth is merely the "readout" of such predetermined structural fates.

On the other hand, the glass is half full, so to speak. Application of modern developmental biological methods holds enormous promise to vastly improve our understanding of mammalian and human evolution. In the next few years these methods will play a pivotal role in sorting through the hosts of current historically defined traits and will almost certainly lead to the fashioning of a more accurate comprehension of our evolutionary history. Issues such as the problem of redundancy in cladistic analyses, the putative role of homology in phylogenetic reconstruction, or the often wholesale adaptationism so prominent in twentieth-century hominid biomechanical analyses can now take their place in history and permit their voids to be filled by a more thorough and complete comprehension of the emergence of the human species.

ACKNOWLEDGMENTS

The authors thank Walt Horton, Richard Meindl, Maria Serrat, and Marty Cohn for their critical reading and extensive comments on this manuscript. C.O.L. was supported by NSF SBR 9729060.

The *Annual Review of Anthropology* is online at http://anthro.annualreviews.org

LITERATURE CITED

Abad V, Meyers JL, Weise M, Gafni RI, Barnes KM, et al. 2002. The role of the resting zone in growth plate chondrogenesis. *Endocrinology* 143:1851–57

Ahn K, Mishina Y, Hanks MC, Behringer RR, Crenshaw EB III. 2001. BMPR-IA signaling is required for the formation of the apical ectodermal ridge and dorsal-ventral patterning of the limb. *Development* 128:4449–61

Alvarez J, Horton J, Sohn P, Serra R. 2001. The perichondrium plays an important role in me-

diating the effects of TGF-β1 on endochondral bone formation. *Dev. Dyn.* 221:311–21

Amling M, Neff L, Tenaka S, Inoue D, Kuida K, et al. 1997. Bcl-2 lies downstream of Parathyroid Hormone-related peptide in a signalling pathway that regulates chondrocyte maturation during skeletal development. *J. Cell Biol.* 136:205–13

Asfaw B, White T, Lovejoy O, Latimer B, Simpson S, Suwa G. 1999a. *Australopithecus garhi*: a new species of early hominid from Ethiopia. *Science* 284:629–35

Asfaw B, White TD, Lovejoy CO, Latimer B, Simpson SW, Suwa G. 1999b. Cladistics and early hominid phylogeny: response to Strait and Grine. *Science* 285:1209–10

Banes AJ, Tuan RS, Yamamoto K, Fisher DRJ, Brinckmann J, et al. 1995. Mechanoreception at the cellular level: the detection, interpretation, and diversity of responses to mechanical signals. *Biochem. Soc. Trans.* 73:349–65

Belting HG, Shashikant CS, Ruddle FH. 1998a. Modification of expression and cis-regulation of *Hoxc8* in the evolution of diverged axial morphology. *Proc. Natl. Acad. Sci. USA* 95:2355–60

Belting HG, Shashikant CS, Ruddle FH. 1998b. Multiple phases of expression and regulation of mouse *Hoxc8* during early embryogenesis. *J. Exp. Zool.* 282:196–222

Bertram JE, Swartz SM. 1991. The "Law of Bone Transformation": a case of crying Wolff? *Biol. Rev.* 66:245–73

Bryant SV, French V, Bryant PJ. 1981. Distal regeneration and symmetry. *Science* 212:993–1002

Bryant SV, Holder N, Tank PW. 1982. Cell-cell interactions and distal outgrowth in amphibian limbs. *Am. Zool.* 22:143–51

Bryant SV, Muneoka K. 1986. Views of limb development and regeneration. *Trends Genet.* 2:153–59

Burke AC, Nelson C, Morgan BA, Tabin C. 1995. Hox genes and the evolution of vertebrate axial morphology. *Development* 121:333–46

Burstein AH, Wright TM. 1994. *Fundamentals of Orthopaedic Biomechanics*. Baltimore, MD: Williams & Wilkins

Carroll S, Grenier JK, Weatherbee SD. 2001. *From DNA to Diversity: Molecular Genetics and the Evolution of Animal Design*. Malden, MA: Blackwell Science

Chen H, Johnson RL. 2002. Interactions between dorsal-ventral patterning genes *lmx1b*, *engrailed-1* and *wnt-7a* in the vertebrate limb. *Int. J. Dev. Biol.* 46:937–41

Chiang C, Litingtung Y, Lee E, Young KE, Corden JL, et al. 1996. Cyclopia and defective axial patterning in mice lacking Sonic hedgehog gene function. *Nature* 383:407–13

Chiu C-H, Hamrick MW. 2002. Evolution and development of the primate limb skeleton. *Evol. Anthropol.* 11:94–107

Cohn MJ, Patel K, Krumlauf R, Wilkinson DG, Clarke JDW, Tickle C. 1997. *Hox9* genes and vertebrate limb specification. *Nature* 387:97–101

Colnot CI, Helms JA. 2001. A molecular analysis of matrix remodeling and angiogenesis during long bone development. *Mech. Dev.* 100:245–50

Crick F. 1970. Diffusion in embryogenesis. *Nature* 225:420–22

Crossley PH, Minowada G, MacArthur CA, Martin GR. 1996. Roles for FGF8 in the induction, initiation, and maintenance of chick limb development. *Cell* 84:127–36

Currey JD. 2002. *Bones: Structure and Mechanics*. Princeton, NJ: Princeton Univ. Press

Cygan JA, Johnson RL, McMahon AP. 1997. Novel regulatory interactions revealed by studies of murine limb pattern in *Wnt-7a* and *En-1* mutants. *Development* 124:5021–32

da Silva SM, Gates PB, Brockes JP. 2002. The newt ortholog of *CD59* is implicated in proximodistal identity during amphibian limb regeneration. *Dev. Cell* 3:547–55

Davidson EH. 2001. *Genomic Regulatory Systems: Development and Evolution*. San Diego, CA: Academic

Davis AP, Witte DP, Hsieh LH, Potter SS, Capecchi MR. 1995. Absence of radius and ulna in mice lacking *hoxa-11* and *hoxd-11*. *Nature* 375:791–95

de Crombrugghe B, Lefebvre V, Nakashima K. 2001. Regulatory mechanisms in the pathways of cartilage and bone formation. *Curr. Opin. Cell Biol.* 13:721–27

Dobzhansky T. 1956. What is an adaptive trait? *Am. Naturalist* 40:337–47

Duboule D. 1994. *Guidebook to the Homeobox Genes*. Oxford, UK: Oxford Univ. Press

Ducy P, Karsenty G. 1995. Two distinct osteoblast-specific cis-acting elements control expression of a mouse osteocalcin gene. *Mol. Cell Biol.* 15:1858–69

Edelman GM. 1988. *Topobiology: an Introduction to Molecular Embryology.* New York: Basic Books

Erlebacher A, Filvaroff E, Gitelman S, Derynck R. 1995. Toward a molecular understanding of skeletal development. *Cell* 80:371–78

Fallon JF, Lopez A, Ros MA, Savage MP, Olwin BB. 1994. FGF-2: apical ectodermal ridge growth signal for chick limb development. *Science* 264:104–7

Farquharson C, Jefferies D, Seawright E, Houston B. 2001. Regulation of chondrocyte terminal differentiation in the postembryonic growth plate: the role of the PTHrP-Indian hedgehog axis. *Endocrinology* 142:4131–40

Feng L, Balakir R, Precht P, Horton WE Jr. 1999. Bcl-2 regulates chondrocyte morphology and aggrecan gene expression independent of caspase activation and full apoptosis. *J. Cell. Biochem.* 74:576–86

Fernandez-Teran M, Piedra ME, Kathiriya IS, Srivastava D, Rodriguez-Rey JC, Ros MA. 2000. Role of dHAND in the anterior-posterior polarization of the limb bud: implications for the Sonic hedgehog pathway. *Development* 127:2133–42

Frankel VH, Burstein AH, Brooks DB. 1971. Biomechanics of internal derangement of the knee: pathomechanics as determined by analysis of the instant centers of motion. *J. Bone Jt. Surg.* 53A:945–62

French V, Bryant PJ, Bryant SV. 1976. Pattern regulation in epimorphic fields. *Science* 193:969–81

Fritton SP, McLeod KJ, Rubin CT. 2000. Quantifying the strain history of bone: spatial uniformity and self-similarity of low-magnitude strains. *J. Biomech.* 33:317–25

Frost HM. 1990a. Skeletal structural adaptations to mechanical usage (SATMU): 1. Redefining Wolff's Law: The bone remodeling problem. *Anat. Rec.* 226:403–13

Frost HM. 1990b. Skeletal structural adaptations to mechanical usage (SATMU): 2. Redefining Wolff's Law: the remodeling problem. *Anat. Rec.* 226:414–22

Gaunt SJ. 2000. Evolutionary shifts of vertebrate structures and *Hox* expression up and down the axial series of segments: a consideration of possible mechanisms. *Int. J. Dev. Biol.* 44:109–17

Gerard M, Chen JY, Gronemeyer H, Chambon P, Duboule D, Zakany J. 1996. In vivo targeted mutagenesis of a regulatory element required for positioning the *Hoxd-11* and *Hoxd-10* expression boundaries. *Genes Dev.* 10:2326–34

Gerard M, Duboule D, Zakany J. 1993. Structure and activity of regulatory elements involved in the activation of the *Hoxd-11* gene during late gastrulation. *EMBO J.* 12:3539–50

Gerard M, Zakany J, Duboule D. 1997. Interspecies exchange of a *Hoxd* enhancer in vivo induces premature transcription and anterior shift of the sacrum. *Dev. Biol.* 190:32–40

Gibson-Brown JJ, Agulnik SI, Chapman DL, Alexiou M, Garvey N, et al. 1996. Evidence of a role for T-box genes in the evolution of limb morphogenesis and the specification of forelimb/hindlimb identity. *Mech. Dev.* 56:93–101

Gibson-Brown JJ, Agulnik SI, Silver LM, Niswander L, Papaioannou VE. 1998. Involvement of T-box genes *Tbx2-Tbx5* in vertebrate limb specification and development. *Development* 125:2499–509

Gilbert SF, Opitz JM, Raff RA. 1996. Resynthesizing evolutionary and developmental biology. *Dev. Biol.* 173:357–72

Goff D, Tabin J. 1997. Analysis of *Hoxd-13* and *Hoxd-11* misexpression in chick limb buds reveals that *Hox* genes affect both condensation and growth. *Development* 124:627–36

Gurdon JB, Bourliere F. 2000. Morphogen gradient interpretation. *Nature* 413:797–803

Hamrick MW. 1999. A chondral modeling theory revisited. *J. Theoret. Biol.* 201:201–98

Herault Y, Beckers J, Gerard M, Duboule D. 1999. *Hox* gene expression in limbs: colinearity by opposite regulatory controls. *Dev. Biol.* 208:157–65

Herault Y, Kondo T, Zakany J, Duboule D.

1997. Hox genes and the control of limb development. *Arch. Pediatr.* 4:107s–11

Huang W, Chung U-I, Kronenberg HM, de Crombrugghe B. 2001. The chondrogenic transcription factor Sox9 is a target of signaling by the Parathyroid Hormone-related peptide in the growth plate of endochondral bones. *Proc. Natl. Acad. Sci. USA* 98:160–65

Hylander WL, Crompton AW 1986. Jaw movements and patterns of mandibular bone strain during mastication in the monkey *Macaca fascicularis. Arch. Oral Biol.* 31:841–48

Isaac A, Rodriguez-Esteban C, Ryan A, Altabef M, Tsukui T, et al. 1998. *Tbx* genes and limb identity in chick embryo development. *Development* 125:1867–75

Johnson RL, Tabin CJ. 1997. Molecular models for vertebrate limb development. *Cell* 90:979–90

Jones HH, Priest JD, Hayes WC, Chinn C, Nagel DA. 1977. Humeral hypertrophy in response of exercise. *J. Bone Jt. Surg.* 59A:204–8

Kalmey JK, Lovejoy CO. 2002. Collagen fiber orientation in the femoral necks of apes and humans: Do their histological structures reflect differences in locomotor loading? *Bone* 31:327–32

Kardon G. 1998. Muscle and tendon morphogenesis in the avian hind limb. *Development* 125:4019–32

Karp SJ, Schipani E, St-Jacques B, Hunzelman J, Kronenberg H, McMahon AP. 2000. Indian hedgehog coordinates endochondral bone growth and morphogenesis via Parathyroid Hormone related-dependent and -independent pathways. *Development* 127:543–48

Karsenty G, Wagner EF. 2002. Reaching a genetic and molecular understanding of skeletal development. *Dev. Cell* 2:389–406

Keller R. 2002. Shaping the vertebrate body plan by polarized embryonic cell movements. *Science* 298:1950–54

Kmita M, Fraudeau N, Herault Y, Duboule D. 2002. Serial deletions and duplications suggest a mechanism for the collinearity of *Hoxd* genes in limbs. *Nature* 420:145–50

Lanctot C, Moreau A, Chamberland M, Tremblay ML, Drouin J. 1999. Hindlimb patterning and mandible development require the *Ptx1* gene. *Development* 126:1805–10

Landmesser L, Morris DG. 1975. The development of functional innervation in the hind limb of the chick embryo. *J. Physiol.* 249:301–26

Lanske B, Karaplis A, Lee K, Luz A, Vortkamp A, et al. 1996. PTH/PTHrP receptor in early development and Indian Hedgehog–regulated bone growth. *Science* 273:663–66

Le Gros Clark WE. 1978. *The Fossil Evidence for Human Evolution.* Chicago, IL: Univ. Chicago Press

Logan C, Hornbruch A, Campbell I, Lumsden A. 1997. The role of Engrailed in establishing the dorsoventral axis of the chick limb. *Development* 124:2317–24

Logan M, Simon HG, Tabin C. 1998. Differential regulation of T-box and homeobox transcription factors suggests roles in controlling chick limb-type identity. *Development* 125:2825–35

Logan M, Tabin CJ. 1999. Role of *Pitx1* upstream of *Tbx4* in specification of hindlimb identity. *Science* 283:1736–39

Loomis CA, Harris E, Michaud J, Wurst W, Hanks M, Joiner A. 1996. The mouse *Engrailed-1* gene and ventral limb patterning. *Nature* 382:360–63

Lovejoy CO. 2003. The natural history of human gait and posture: part I. *Gait Posture.* In press

Lovejoy CO, Cohn MJ, White TD. 1999. Morphological analysis of the mammalian postcranium: a developmental perspective. *Proc. Natl. Acad. Sci. USA* 96:13,247–52

Lovejoy CO, Meindl RS, Ohman JC, Heiple KG, White TD. 2002. The Maka femur and its bearing on the antiquity of human walking: applying contemporary concepts of morphogenesis to the human fossil record. *Am. J. Phys. Anthropol.* 119:97–133

McCollum MA. 1999. The robust australopithecine face: a morphogenetic perspective. *Science* 284:301–5

McCollum MA, Sharpe PT. 2001. Developmental genetics and early hominid craniodental evolution. *BioEssays* 23:481–93

McLeod KJ, Rubin CT, Otter MW, Qinghua X. 1998. Skeletal cell stresses and bone adaptation. *Am. J. Med. Sci.* 316:176–83

Medill NJ, Praul CA, Ford BC, Leach RM. 2001. Parathyroid Hormone-related peptide expression in the epiphyseal growth plate of the juvenile chicken: evidence for the origin of the Parathyroid Hormone-related peptide found in the epiphyseal growth plate. *J. Cell. Biochem.* 80:504–11

Minina E, Kreschel C, Naski MC, Ornitz DM, Vortkamp A. 2002. Interaction of FGF, Ihh/Pthlh, and BMP signaling integrates chondrocyte proliferation and hypertrophic differentiation. *Dev. Cell* 3:439–49

Minina E, Wenzel HM, Kreschel C, Karp S, Gaffield W, et al. 2001. BMP and Ihh/PTHrP signaling interact to coordinate chondrocyte proliferation and differentiation. *Development* 128:4523–34

Moon AM, Capecchi MR. 2000. Fgf8 is required for outgrowth and patterning of the limbs. *Nat. Genet.* 26:455–59

Nelson CE, Morgan BA, Burke AC, Laufer E, DiMambro E, et al. 1996. Analysis of Hox gene expression in the chick limb bud. *Development* 122:1449–66

Ng JK, Kawakami Y, Buscher D, Raya A, Itoh T, et al. 2002. The limb identity gene *Tbx5* promotes limb initiation by interacting with *Wnt2b* and *Fgf10*. *Development* 129:5161–70

Nunamaker DM, Butterweck DM, Provost MT. 1990. Fatigue fractures in thoroughbred racehorses: relationships with age, peak bone strain, and training. *J. Orthop. Res.* 8:604–11

Ogden JA. 1979. The development and growth of the musculoskeletal system. In *The Scientific Basis of Orthopaedics*, ed. JA Albright, RA Brand, pp. 41–103. New York: Appleton Century Crofts

Opitz JM. 1985. The developmental field concept. *Am. J. Med. Gen.* 21:1–11

Perriton CL, Powles N, Chiang C, Maconochie MK, Cohn MJ. 2002. Sonic hedgehog signaling from the urethral epithelium controls external genital development. *Dev. Biol.* 247:26–46

Pradel J, White RAH. 1998. From selectors to realizators. *Int. J. Dev. Biol.* 42:417–21

Raff RA. 1996. *The Shape of Life*. Chicago, IL: Univ. Chicago Press

Reno PL, McCollum MA, Lovejoy CO, Meindl RS. 2000. Evolution of the primate postcranium: the radial neck is not a focus of natural selection. *J. Morphol.* 246:59–67

Reynolds SD, Zuscik MJ, Gunter TE, O'Keefe RJ, Puzas JE, et al. 1998. Parathyroid Hormone and Parathyroid Hormone-related peptide effects on growth plate chondrocytes: an overview. *Cells Mater.* 7:289–300

Riddle RD, Ensini M, Nelson C, Tsuchida T, Jessell TM, Tabin C. 1995. Induction of LIM homeobox gene *Lmx-1* by *Wnt7a* establishes dorsoventral pattern in the vertebrate limb. *Cell* 83:631–40

Riddle RD, Johnson RL, Laufer E, Tabin CJ. 1993. Sonic hedgehog mediates the polarizing activity of the ZPA. *Cell* 75:1401–16

Roesler H. 1981. Some historical remarks on the theory of cancellous bone structure (Wolff's law). In *Mechanical Properties of Bone*, ed. G Cowlichaw, pp. 27–42. New York: Am. Soc. Mech. Eng.

Rosenman BA, Lovejoy CO, McCollum MA. 2002. Development of the vertebral column. In *Skeletal and Developmental Anatomy*, ed. RA Walker, CO Lovejoy, ME Bedford, W Yee, pp. 53–79. Philadelphia, PA: FA Davis

Rubin C, Turner AS, Bain S, Mallinckrodt C, McLeod K. 2001. Anabolism. Low mechanical signals strengthen long bones. *Nature* 412:603–4

Rubin CT, Lanyon LE. 1987. Osteoregulatory nature of mechanical stimuli: function as a determinant for adaptive modeling in bone. *J. Orthop. Res.* 5:300–10

Saunders JW. 1948. The proximo-distal sequence of origin of parts of the chick wing and the role of the ectoderm. *J. Exp. Zool.* 108:363–403

Shashikant CS, Kim CB, Borbely MA,

Wang WC, Ruddle FH. 1998. Comparative studies on mammalian *Hoxc8* early enhancer sequence reveal a baleen whale-specific deletion of a cis-acting element. *Proc. Natl. Acad. Sci. USA* 95:15,446–51

Shashikant CS, Ruddle FH. 1996. Combinations of closely situated cis-acting elements determine tissue-specific patterns and anterior extent of early Hoxc8 expression. *Proc. Natl. Acad. Sci. USA* 93:12,364–69

Shubin N, Tabin C, Carroll S. 1997. Fossils, genes and the evolution of animal limbs. *Nature* 388:639–48

Simpson GG. 1944. *Tempo and Mode in Evolution.* New York: Columbia Univ. Press

Skerry T. 2000. Biomechanical influences on skeletal growth and development. In *Development, Growth, and Evolution,* ed. O'Higgens P, Cohn MJ, pp. 29–40. London: Academic Press

Stern DL. 2000. Evolutionary developmental biology and the problem of variation. *Evolution* 54:1079–91

St-Jacques B, Hammerschmidt M, McMahon AP. 1999. Indian hedgehog signaling regulates proliferation and differentiation of chondrocytes and is essential for bone formation. *Genes Dev.* 13:2072–86

Summerbell D, Honig LS. 1982. The control of pattern across the antero-posterior axis of the chick limb bud by a unique signalling region. *Am. Zool.* 22:105–16

Summerbell D, Lewis JH, Wolpert L. 1973. Positional information in chick limb morphogensis. *Nature* 244:492–96

te Welscher P, Fernandez-Teran M, Ros MA, Zeller R. 2002. Mutual genetic antagonism involving GLI3 and dHAND prepatterns the vertebrate limb bud mesenchyme prior to SHH signaling. *Genes Dev.* 16:421–26

Thompson KS. 1988. *Morphogenesis and Evolution.* Oxford, UK: Oxford Univ. Press

Torok MA, Gardiner DM, Izpisua-Belmonte JC, Bryant SV. 1999. *Sonic hedgehog (Shh)* expression in developing and regenerating axolotl limbs. *J. Exp. Zool.* 284:197–206

Torok MA, Gardiner DM, Shubin NH, Bryant SV. 1998. Expression of HoxD genes in developing and regenerating axolotl limbs. *Dev. Biol.* 200:225–33

van der Eerden BCJ, Karperien M, Gevers EF, Lowik CWGM, Wit JM. 2000. Expression of Indian hedgehog, Parathyroid Hormone-related protein, and their receptors in the postnatal growth plate of the rat: evidence for a locally acting growth restraining feedback loop after birth. *J. Bone Miner. Res.* 15:1045–55

Vortkamp A. 2000. The Indian Hedgehog-PTHrP system in bone development. In *Of Fish, Fly, Worm, and Man: Lessons from Developmental Biology for Human Gene Function and Disease,* ed. C Nusslein-Volhard, J Kratzschmar, pp. 191–209. Berlin: Springer

Vortkamp A, Lee K, Lanske B, Segre GV, Kronenberg HM, Tabin CJ. 1996. Regulation of rate of cartilage differentiation by Indian hedgehog and PTH-related protein. *Science* 273:613–22

Vortkamp A, Pathi S, Peretti GM, Caruso EM, Zaleske DJ, Tabin CJ. 1998. Recapitulation of signals regulating embryonic bone formation during postnatal growth and in fracture repair. *Mech. Dev.* 71:65–76

Weiss KM. 2002. Is the medium the message? Biological traits and their regulation. *Evol. Anthropol.* 11:88–93

Whitelaw V, Hollyday M. 1983a. Position-dependent motor innervation of the chick hindlimb following serial and parallel duplications of limb segments. *J. Neurosci.* 3:1216–25

Whitelaw V, Hollyday M. 1983b. Thigh and calf discrimination in the motor innervation of the chick hindlimb following deletions of limb segments. *J. Neurosci.* 3:1199–215

Wijgerde M, Grotewold L, Fraser P. 1995. Transcription complex stability and chromatin dynamics in vivo. *Nature* 377:209–13

Wilkins AS. 2001. *The Evolution of Developmental Pathways.* Sunderland, MA: Sinauer

Wolpert L. 1969. Positional information and the spatial pattern of cellular differentiation. *J. Theoret. Biol.* 25:1–47

Wolpert L. 1978. Pattern formation in biological development. *Sci. Am.* 239:154–64

Wolpert L. 2002. Limb patterning: reports of model's death exaggerated. *Curr. Biol.* 12:R628–30

Wolpert L, Beddington R, Brockes J, Jessell T, Lawrence P, Meyerowitz E. 1998. *Principles of Development*. Oxford, UK: Oxford Univ. Press

Wolpert L, Beddington R, Brockes J, Jessell T, Lawrence P, Meyerowitz E. 2002. *Principles of Development*. Oxford, UK: Oxford Univ. Press

Wolpert L, Hornbruch A. 1990. Double anterior chick limb buds and models for cartilage rudiment specification. *Development* 109:961–66

Woo SL-Y, Kuei SC, Amiel D, Gomez MA, Hayes WC, et al. 1981. The effect of prolonged physical training on the properties of long bone: a study of Wolff's Law. *J. Bone Jt. Surg.* 63A:780–87

Wu Q, Zhang Y, Chen Q. 2001. Indian hedgehog is an essential component of mechanotransduction complex to stimulate chondrocyte proliferation. *J. Biol. Chem.* 276:35,290–96

Yoshida E, Noshiro M, Kawamoto T, Tsutsumi S, Kuwana Y, Kato Y. 2001. Direct inhibition of Indian hedgehog expression by Parathyroid Hormone (PTH)/PTH-related peptide and up-regulation by retinoic acid in growth plate chondrocyte cultures. *Exp. Cell Res.* 265:64–72

Zakany J, Fronmental-Remain C, Warot X, Duboule D. 1997. Regulation of number and size of digits by posterior Hox genes: a dose-dependent mechanism with potential evolutionary implications. *Proc. Natl. Acad. Sci. USA* 94:13,695–700

Zakany J, Gerard M, Favier B, Potter SS, Duboule D. 1996. Functional equivalence and rescue among group 11 Hox gene products in vertebral patterning. *Dev. Biol.* 176:325–28

Annu. Rev. Anthropol. 2003. 32:111–34
doi: 10.1146/annurev.anthro.32.061002.093218
First published online as a Review in Advance on June 4, 2003

ENVIRONMENTAL POLLUTION IN URBAN ENVIRONMENTS AND HUMAN BIOLOGY

Lawrence M. Schell and Melinda Denham

*Department of Anthropology, University at Albany, State University of New York,
1400 Washington Ave., Albany, New York, 12222; email: l.schell@albany.edu,
denham@capital.net*

Key Words   growth, lead, noise, stress, urbanism

■ **Abstract**   The biocultural approach of anthropologists is well suited to understand the interrelationship of urbanism and human biology. Urbanism is a social construction that has continuously changed and presented novel adaptive challenges to its residents. Urban living today involves several biological challenges, of which one is pollution. Using three different types of pollutants as examples, air pollution, lead, and noise, the impact of pollution on human biology (mortality, morbidity, reproduction, and development) can be seen. Chronic exposure to low levels of these pollutants has a small impact on the individual, but so many people are exposed to pollution that the effect species-wide is substantial. Also, disproportionate pollutant exposure by socioeconomically disadvantaged groups exacerbates risk of poor health and well being.

URBANISM AND HUMAN BIOLOGY

Urban growth began slowly several thousand years ago and has accelerated tremendously over the past 300 years. By 2006, half of the world's population will be living in urban places (United Nations 1998). If current trends continue, the characteristic environment of the human species will be urban.

The change from nonurban to urban living has occurred over too few generations to provide much opportunity for evolutionary adaptation to urban challenges. *Homo sapiens* evolved in response to the physical and social demands of a hunting and gathering way of life and death during the Paleolithic and before. Many of these demands are absent from the urban environment today, and new challenges are present in abundance including altered energy budgets from urban activity patterns and diets, psychosocial stress, steep social gradients, increased contact between social groups resulting in increased transmission and evolution of infectious disease, and increased pollution largely from transportation and industry (Schell & Ulijaszek 1999). Given the novelty of so many urban challenges and the antiquity of our response systems, a reasonable question is, "Are we suited for urban living?"

As urban forms are social products, understanding urbanism and human biology involves the study of a complex biocultural interaction. An anthropological approach that integrates sociocultural variables and biological measures of adaptation and health is well suited to the problem. However, understanding effects of industrial pollution on humans requires study designs that differ from those employed to study small-scale societies.

Studies of the effects of urbanism on human health have used two basic designs: studying urban populations and studying people exposed to features of urban environments wherever they may occur. The former approach is exemplified in the urban rural comparison. Urban rural comparisons suffer from the usual flaws inherent in reducing multidimensional differences into a simple dichotomy, each of which exists as a continuum. Today we know that urban rural differences in health vary depending on the particulars of each of the urban and rural places compared. Replication of results, a hallmark of science, is impossible when the identities being compared change. Indeed, urban rural differences may not be apparent even though substantial differences in the factors that influence health exist because these factors, some positive and some negative, may sum to zero. The most obvious urban rural differences, such as those that existed during the height of unregulated industrialization, are now reduced to varying degrees in different countries. Nevertheless, some urban features continue to be highly detrimental to health and well-being.

The second approach, studying urban features, is preferred because it involves the analysis and measurement of individual factors representing dimensions of urbanism (e.g., population size or density, stress levels, activity patterns, specific pollutants). It also involves measuring covariates that if unmeasured, as in urban rural contrasts, may confound the attribution of true causes. This measurement-based approach is more likely to lead to replication and generalization. It is the stronger approach also because in many societies exposure to pollution covaries with socioeconomic disadvantage (Schell & Czerwinski 1998), a known influence on human health. Measuring both the putative causes and the covarying factors is a necessary step in determining the true influence of urbanism on human biology.

The epistemology of urban research is similar to that in epidemiology. Experimental research in which the investigator can randomize exposures is rare or nonexistent, and observational research designs without the investigator's intervention are common. Observational designs produce evidence that is evaluated in terms of Hill's postulates in which proper temporal order of cause and effect, the presence of dose-response relationships, replication, and biological plausibility figure largely (Lilienfeld & Stolley 1994). A special type of observational research design is the natural experiment in which experimental conditions are altered by chance. This approximates randomization but does not involve the investigator's intervention in human circumstances. Sample bias is far less likely to influence results compared to studies without randomization. This review emphasizes results from studies employing measurement-based approaches that meet the epistemological standards of population-based research.

AIR POLLUTION

The air we breathe is polluted with the byproducts of combustion from industry, power generation, and transportation, as well as the manufacture and use of chemicals. Air pollutants are a heterogeneous group of gases and particles that can remain airborne for long periods of time. Common air pollutants are oxides of nitrogen (NO_x), oxides of sulfur (SO_x), ozone (O_3), carbon monoxide (CO), and particulate matter (PM). In sufficient concentrations, these gases and particles can harm human health in the short (burning of eyes and throat, difficulty breathing) and the long term (cancer and long-term damage to the immune, neurological, reproductive, and respiratory systems) (Waldbott 1978). Air pollution is especially problematic in urban areas. In 1999, of the six common pollutants used by the EPA to monitor national air quality, levels of CO, NO_2, SO_2, and PM_{10} were higher in urban areas (U.S. Environ. Prot. Agency 2001).

Mortality (All Cause)

Air pollution is a significant risk factor for all-age, all-cause mortality in urban areas (Brunekreef & Holgate 2002, Schwela 2000). Ozone, CO, SO_x, and PM have each been associated with increased mortality rates (Abbey et al. 1999, Borja-Aburto et al. 1998, Fairley 1999, Lee et al. 1999, Neas et al. 1999, Pope et al. 2002, Xu et al. 2000, Zmirou et al. 1998). Exposure to specific air pollutants has been associated with increased cause-specific mortality rates, especially cardiovascular and respiratory disease deaths (Fairley 1999, Xu et al. 2000, Zmirou et al. 1998). Brunekreef (1997) has estimated that chronic, low-level exposure to air pollution shortens life expectancy by one to two years, a substantial effect compared to other environmental risk factors.

For biological anthropologists, pre-reproductive mortality is especially important because it focuses on the evolutionary impact of air pollution. Fewer studies have considered air pollution and mortality solely in children. Most of these studies have found positive relationships between pollutants and sub-adult mortality (Bobak & Leon 1999, Loomis et al. 1999, Pereira et al. 1998, Woodruff et al. 1997) in varied populations (Mexico, Brazil, Czech Republic, United States) and at different developmental stages (prenatal, neonatal, infant).

Several studies have reported significant associations with mortality even when air pollution levels did not exceed national or World Health Organization standards (Fairley 1999, Lee et al. 1999, Schwartz 1991). For example, Schwartz (1991) demonstrated a dose-response relationship between total suspended particulates (TSP) and daily mortality in Detroit when levels were less than half of the U.S. standard. Recent research suggests that through the mediating effect of socioeconomic factors, air pollution may have a greater impact on mortality in disadvantaged groups (Abbey et al. 1999, Brunekreef 1999, Pope et al. 2002).

Morbidity

Although air pollution can have health effects throughout the body, the target organ for many major urban air pollutants is the respiratory system. In a recent review, Schwela (2000, p. 18) noted these effects: "acute and chronic changes in pulmonary function, increased incidence and prevalence of respiratory symptoms, sensitization of airways to allergens, and exacerbation of respiratory infections, such as rhinitis, sinusitis, pneumonia, alveolitis, and legionnaires' disease." However, the current evidence is mixed as to whether air pollution exposure reduces pulmonary function (Schwartz 1989). For example, PEACE (Pollution Effects on Asthmatic Children in Europe) studied 28 regions of Europe and found no effect of PM or NO_2 on lung function or acute symptoms (Roemer et al. 2000). However, a large cross-sectional analysis including 44 U.S. cities found O_3, NO_2, and TSP to be significantly associated with decrements in several measures of pulmonary function (Schwartz 1989). The 2%–5% reduction in these measures may seem relatively small, but such decrements can impair performance of normal daily activities. Significantly, these relationships were found in areas where pollutants did not exceed national standards. Further evidence for a causal relationship comes from a study that compared pulmonary function before and after an air pollution episode in Western Europe in 1985 (Dassen et al. 1986). Significant deficits in pulmonary function were found to persist for three to four weeks following the episode.

Effects on pulmonary function can be influenced by preexisting morbidity, such as asthma. When asthmatic and nonasthmatic subjects are considered separately, nonasthmatic subjects exhibited little to no effect of air pollution, whereas asthmatic subjects showed declines in measures of pulmonary function (Koenig et al. 1993, Yang & Yang 1994).

Air pollution also causes acute asthma exacerbation (Schwartz et al. 1993, Wjst et al. 1993). Powerful support for this relationship was obtained by a natural experiment in 1996 (Friedman et al. 2001). Investigators compared the number of daily acute asthma events among children 1 to 16 years of age during the Olympics in Atlanta, Georgia, when citywide transportation changes reduced air pollution and improved air quality, to periods before and after the changes. During this period of lower air pollutant levels, the number of Georgia Medicaid claims filed for acute asthma events was reduced by 42% (see Figure 1). Furthermore, Georgia Medicaid claims filed for acute non-asthma events were only reduced by 3%, which indicates that the reduction in acute asthma events was not merely part of an overall change in reporting, hospital use, or improvement in health generally.

Growth

Studies of growth and air pollution are less common than those addressing mortality and morbidity. The scope of public health interests has only recently expanded to include child health generally and growth specifically (Goldman & Koduru 2000, Landrigan et al. 1998). Child growth and development is a measure of health that is sensitive to subtle changes in the environment (Fogel 1986), and alterations

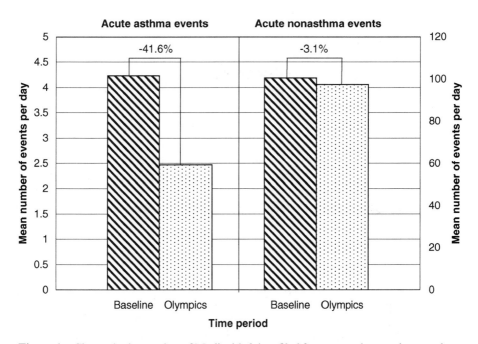

Figure 1 Change in the number of Medicaid claims filed for acute asthma and non-asthma events (emergency care and hospitalizations) among children and youth before and during the 1996 summer Olympics in Atlanta, GA (adapted from Friedman et al. 2001).

in community child growth patterns can signal the presence of a stressor before morbidity or mortality occurs (Schell 1986).

Most studies have adopted an ecological approach comparing child growth in two or more locations that differ in the severity of air pollution. These studies have typically reported reduced weight, height, and skeletal maturation among children in areas with higher pollution levels (Mikusek 1976, Schlipkoter et al. 1986, Thielebeule et al. 1980). A recent study of nine-year-olds in Krakow, Poland compared 434 children living in high pollution areas with 524 children who lived in less polluted areas of the city (Jedrychowski et al. 1999, 2002). Study subjects living in highly polluted areas showed a 1.5-cm-lower growth rate, and the proportion of children classified as having slow growth (less than 10 cm over two years) was 2–3 times higher.

Air pollution may also affect the fetus. Most studies of the relationship between prenatal growth and air pollution have found a negative association (Bobak 2000, Bobak & Leon 1999, Dejmek et al. 1999, Perera et al. 2003, Ritz & Yu 1999, Xu et al. 1995), whereas a few studies have reported no relationship (Alderman et al. 1987, Dolk et al. 2000). The reduction in weight at birth is consistent with studies of cigarette smoking and high altitude where oxygen transfer to the fetus is reduced (Schell & Knutson 2002).

These results suggest an impact of air pollution on prenatal and postnatal growth. However, caution is warranted owing to the small number of studies that has been conducted and a tendency to use an ecological study design. Further research should employ more accurate methods to assess exposure to air pollution. Questions of which components of air pollution reduce growth and which growth stages are most susceptible to air pollution need to be addressed.

Conclusion

The pervasiveness of air pollution means that large numbers of people are adversely affected even if the effect on any single individual is slight. On a community basis, air pollution contributes significantly to increased mortality, morbidity, and growth deficits. These effects are present at levels common in many urban and peri-urban communities.

LEAD

Lead is a legacy pollutant. Lead has entered the air as dust shed from dilapidated, lead-painted housing and from automobile exhaust. During the 1970s lead was eliminated from most paint and gasoline, the primary sources in the United States, but it remains in dust, air, and soil. In the late 1970s lead levels were noticeably higher in urban residents than rural ones (Mahaffey et al. 1982), but the difference across the United States has lessened (Brody et al. 1994).

Most lead enters the body by ingestion rather than respiration. Lead dust in or on food, or on non-food items that are mouthed by toddlers, are the single largest source of exposure (Cent. Dis. Control Prev. 1991). Most of a person's lifelong lead burden is acquired between 12 and 36 months of age unless there is an occupational exposure (Brody et al. 1994). Occupational health studies provide the basis for the CDC (Centers for Disease Control and Prevention) guidelines for effects of high lead exposure, but the more common situation in cities is chronic exposure to a low dose of lead early in life. For this reason and because early human development is so critical for later adult functioning, most of the concern about the health effects of lead focuses on effects during the prenatal period and preschool years.

Lead is deadly at high doses, and at lower ones it causes encephalopathy, anemia, cognitive impairment, and deficits in neurobehavioral development (Cent. Dis. Control Prev. 1988). Until 1970 a blood lead level of 30 μg/dL was considered by the CDC as "elevated," but the current action level established in 1991 is only 10 μg/dL. The change reflects the growth of knowledge regarding subclinical effects of lead and the special vulnerability of children. Despite the new lower action level, it is possible that no level of lead is completely safe.

Pollutant Exposure as Part of Socioeconomic Disadvantage in Cities

The most common sources of lead are abundant in poorer sections of large cities where older housing with peeling paint exists on streets that have been

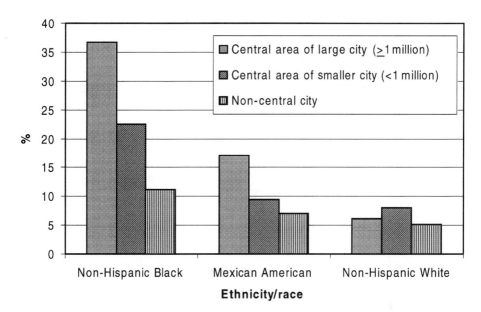

Figure 2   Percentage of 1- to 5-year-old children with elevated lead levels ($\geq$10 μg/dL) by ethnicity/race and urban status: United States, 1988–1991 (adapted from Brody et al. 1994).

heavily trafficked for decades (Agency Toxic Subst. Dis. Registr. 1988). These urban lead belts are disproportionately home to members of minority groups, and the rate of elevated lead levels in urban minority populations is higher than in the rest of the United States (see Figure 2). In the late 1970s the National Center for Health Statistics reported that 1 in 6 African American children from 6 months to 5 years of age who lived in the inner city area of large cities had a blood lead level above the CDC action level (Mahaffey et al. 1982), a level now known to cause deficits in cognitive and neurobehavioral development.

After twenty years of public health policy to prevent lead poisoning in children, the mean level of lead and the frequency of elevated lead burden has decreased in both white and minority U.S. children (Pirkle et al. 1994). Despite the overall decrease in average lead levels, some groups still are disproportionately affected. For example, the frequency of elevated lead among young African American children living in housing built before 1946 is nearly 10 times that of white children living in post-1973 housing. This contrast emphasizes the point that health risk factors covary in urban areas. Minority group status is associated with residence in parts of the city with more older, dilapidated housing and more traffic, as well as a diet that may enhance the toxic effects of lead and other pollutants (Schell et al. 2000). Steep social gradients in urban populations are associated with differences in health, in part from exposure to pollution. Insofar as the abilities needed for socioeconomic mobility may be impaired by lead poisoning during childhood,

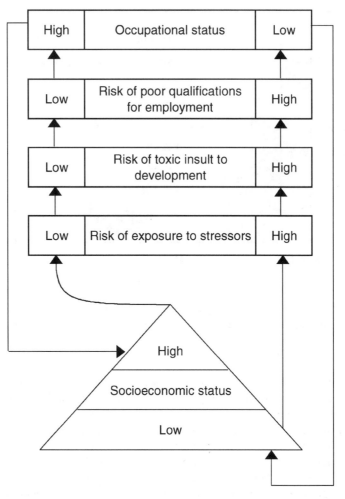

Figure 3   Model of risk focusing on the relationship between socioeconomic position, toxic exposure, and socioeconomic mobility (adapted from Schell 1992).

lead exposure contributes to maintaining or exacerbating socioeconomic gradients (Schell 1992) (see Figure 3).

Effects on Psychological Function and Development

Encephalopathy is a well-known effect of high lead exposure, and nerve conduction velocity is slowed at moderate to low doses (Cent. Dis. Control Prev. 1991). These easily measured effects indicate that the nervous system is susceptible to damage from lead and suggest that more subtle effects on cognition may be caused by lead levels at low exposures.

Recent longitudinal studies of pregnant women and children have shown permanent effects on child development at low lead levels (Bellinger & Needleman 1992). The measure of effect varies with the age of the children studied because some common tests of cognition cannot be administered at early ages. Several longitudinal studies of infants and toddlers have found that neurobehavioral development, as measured by the Bayley Mental Development Index (MDI) scale, is slowed in relation to lead burden: Decrements of 2–8 points per 10 μg/dL increment in blood lead have been found (Grant & Davis 1989) (see Figure 4). Although a reduction of 4 points is not clinically significant to the individual, its meaning for the population is more substantial. An average decrease of 4 points means the entire distribution of scores in the population is shifted down such that there would be 50% more children scoring below 80 on this measure.

In older children, IQ can be measured reliably, and many studies have found it is reduced by 4 to 6 points (Smith 1989). Behavioral measures, specifically attention ability (distractability, organization, impulsivity, frustration tolerance), also may be impaired in relation to lead burden. Taken together, children with moderate or low lead burdens are at increased risk for psychological impairments. In a study of youth whose tooth lead was measured in childhood, the frequency of reading failure (two or more grade years delayed in reading ability) and school failure (not finishing secondary school) (Needleman et al. 1990) were significantly elevated in relation to childhood lead burden. Reports of behavioral problems in lead exposed children are frequent (Sciarillo et al. 1992, Silva et al. 1988). These studies suggest that lead exposure early in life contributes to educational failure with consequences for socioeconomic potential.

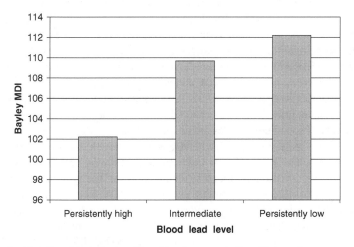

Figure 4 Relationship between blood lead concentration history (as measured at 6, 15, and 24 months) and Bayley Mental Development Index (MDI) at 24 months of age (adapted from Baghurst et al. 1987).

Growth

Effects of lead on cognitive and behavioral development may be part of a general insult to development. Effects on physical growth have been examined in three areas: prenatal growth, child growth, and sexual maturation. Studies of prenatal growth have produced heterogeneous results. Risk of preterm birth is associated with higher lead levels in some studies (Baghurst et al. 1987, Dietrich et al. 1986, McMichael et al. 1986). Reduced size at birth in relation to lead burden of the mother has been found in many studies (Bornschein et al. 1989, Rothenberg et al. 1988, Schell & Stark 1999, Wolf et al. 1987), but not all (Factor-Litvak et al. 1991, McMichael et al. 1986). Reduction in weight at birth varies from 0 to 120 g for each log unit of lead in maternal blood (that is about half the birth weight reduction that may be attributed to moderate maternal cigarette smoking during pregnancy). Differences in results may be caused by differences in control for covarying factors. Lead is related to lower socioeconomic status in the United States and to exposure to other pollutants. Variation across studies in the measurement of lead contributes also. This problem is typical of a science attempting to find the critical variable: When exposure is chronic but development is rapid, as it is during gestation, when is the exposure more influential and its influence best measured?

Several studies stand out in terms of these problems. Two longitudinal studies of births to socioeconomically disadvantaged women in Cincinnati, Ohio (Bornschein et al. 1989) and Albany, New York (Schell & Stark 1999) carefully measured socioeconomic variables, as well as other influences on prenatal development. The Cincinnati study also employed multiple measures of maternal blood lead during pregnancy. The studies detected a significant reduction in birth weight ranging from 114–202 g per log of maternal lead level. A study of middle class Boston mothers found a reduction of 80–100 g in babies with cord blood lead levels above 15 μg/dL compared to those with less lead (Bellinger et al. 1991). Finally, a study of mothers in Mexico City, where lead exposure does not have the same relationship to social variables as it does in the United States, found that women in the highest quartile of maternal tibia lead (a measure of stored lead and long-term exposure) delivered babies weighing 155 g less than those in the lowest quartile (Gonzalez-Cossio et al. 1997). These studies suggest that effects of lead on prenatal growth may be observed if there is a sufficient measure of lead and the effects of social covariables are accounted for.

Large-scale studies of lead and postnatal growth are consistent. Data from the second NHANES survey of U.S. children in the late 1970s showed a reduction of 1.5% in height at 59 months (the mean age of the sample) after controlling for important influences on growth, including dietary variables (Schwartz et al. 1986). U.S. Hispanic children surveyed by NHANES from 1982 to 1984 also showed that children with lead levels below the median were 1.2 cm taller than those with lead levels above the median. Recent data from NHANES III (1988–1994) showed, among non-Hispanic children 1–7 years of age, a reduction of nearly 1.6 cm per 10 μg/dL of lead (Ballew et al. 1999). These studies are very consistent in the magnitude and direction of lead's effect but, being cross-sectional, are not conclusive proof. Animal models have shown that lead can reduce growth, and physiological studies of lead-poisoned children (Huseman et al. 1992) have shown that growth is increased following treatment, which supports a causal relationship between lead and growth in the survey studies. Longitudinal studies of children over time have employed smaller samples and have produced evidence of an effect of lead on head circumference, height, and/or weight (Shukla et al. 1989), but not all studies do so (see Schell 1999 for a detailed review).

The influence of lead on sexual development is little studied as yet. Danker-Hopfe & Hulanicka (1995) examined sexual maturation in relation to lead levels in the environment among a sample of girls from Upper Silesia, Poland ($n = 8090$). Girls from highly polluted areas reached menarche at 13.01 years compared to 13.14 years among girls from less-polluted areas, a significant difference. Earlier age at menarche may seem contrary to findings of less physical growth, but it is consistent with studies showing an endocrine basis underlying growth inhibition in lead-burdened children (Huseman et al. 1987, 1992).

Other Physiological Outcomes

The study of lead's effects on health often focuses on children, but lead exposure can be problematic for adults also. Most adults with elevated lead levels are employed in occupations with the potential for lead exposure (Cent. Dis. Control Prev. 1983). Lower-level lead toxicity and acute lead poisoning can cause changes in heme biosynthesis, anemia, central nervous system dysfunction, and psychomotor and short-term memory impairment. With long-term exposure CNS symptoms grow increasingly severe; peripheral nervous system and renal disorders develop. In addition to these well-established effects, it has been suggested that chronic lead exposure has a detrimental impact on the male reproductive system. Men with blood lead levels elevated for more than five years were significantly more likely to father a low-birth-weight or premature baby than were controls, even after adjustment for confounding social and biological variables (Lin et al. 1998).

Conclusion

The impact of lead on human health is so great that its reduction has been a major health priority in the United States for two decades. Effects on the development of the reproductive system and on adult reproductive function are especially relevant to anthropological interests in the evolution of contemporary societies. Further, the contribution of lead to growth deficits is a clear signal that lead has physiological effects at low doses, doses too low to effect mortality. As with air pollution, the widespread distribution of lead in urban environments means that very large numbers of people experience its effects. Finally, lead is an example of a class of pollutants that are distributed among large numbers of people and may contribute to decreased health and function. Such decrements affect individual and household status because they can contribute to a downward spiral of health, function, and material well-being. This directly impacts the individual and household and contributes to the stratification of society.

ENERGY—NOISE

Energy such as light, radiation, and noise can be pollutants if they occur at unwanted times, places, or levels. Noise is defined as unwanted sound and is a physiological stressor, as seen by classical laboratory experiments on stress (Kryter 1985, Welch & Welch 1970). As such, it serves as a model for effects of stress on human biology. The combination of energy pollutant and psychosocial stressor accounts for the diversity of its effects. It is a well-established cause of hearing impairment and loss, as well as a cause of sleep disturbance, annoyance, chronic cardiovascular effects, increased psychiatric disorder, reduced psychosocial well-being, reduced cognitive performance, and impaired growth (Morrell et al. 1997, Passchier-Vermeer & Passchier 2000, Stansfeld et al. 2000). The public health impact of noise has been recognized since the 1960s and has prompted noise abatement programs. However, because noise is usually louder and more continuous in urban environments (Staples 1997, Westman & Walters 1981), exposure to noise continues to rise as urbanization increases globally.

Auditory Effects

Hearing impairment is defined as a raised hearing threshold, particularly to the point where there is difficulty understanding normal speech with low levels of background noise (Int. Organ. Stand. 1990). Chronic occupational, environmental, and leisure-time exposure to sounds louder than 70 dB(A), especially at higher frequencies, can impair hearing either temporarily or permanently depending on the duration, intensity, and frequency of the noise (Int. Organ. Stand. 1990, World Health Organ. 1980). Hearing impairment can be a serious social handicap insomuch that it can reduce one's ability to understand speech and can ultimately inhibit communication (Passchier-Vermeer & Passchier 2000).

Nonauditory Effects

Stress is the primary mechanism by which noise produces nonauditory effects on physical and mental health. Exposure to a noise stressor provokes short-term physiological responses mediated by the autonomic nervous system and the endocrine system. The nervous system portion of the stress response involves numerous changes including altered blood pressure, heart rate, and respiration (Cohen 1977). Stress also involves the endocrine system, especially the adrenal gland. Endocrine-related effects are systemic and affect such basic functions as basal metabolic rate, the response to injury (tissue repair and inflammation), reproduction, growth and development, and mentation. Studies of noise should be interpreted as studies of stress, and the nonauditory effects of noise represent the potential impact of stress on human biology and health.

CARDIOVASCULAR DISEASE   The strongest evidence for the cardiovascular effect of noise has been the study of blood pressure and occupational noise exposure (Stansfeld et al. 2000). Positive relationships between noise exposure and hypertension or blood pressure have been reported repeatedly in the literature (Belli et al. 1984, Green et al. 1991, Knipschild 1977, Lang et al. 1992, Parvizpoor 1976, Singh et al. 1982, Talbott et al. 1999, Verbeek et al. 1987, Zhao et al. 1991). Failure to control for potential confounders such as obesity, age, sex, cigarette smoking, and use of antihypertensive medication has weakened the results of some of these studies. In general, environmental noise studies of blood pressure have reported greater rates of hypertension and use of hypertension medications in noise-exposed people (Herbold et al. 1989, Knipschild 1977, Knipschild & Oudshoorn 1977) but have shown little or no effect of noise on mean blood pressure (Passchier-Vermeer & Passchier 2000). A recent longitudinal study of two cohorts of approximately 2500 middle-aged men in the United Kingdom addressed the effect of low-level, residential noise on ischemic heart disease (Babisch et al. 1999). The relative risk of heart disease approached significance only in the highest exposure category [66–70 dB(A)]. This finding is consistent with the 70 dB(A) observation threshold for environmental noise exposure suggested by the Health Council of the Netherlands in 1994, based on a meta-analysis of noise and health research to date (Health Counc. Netherlands: Comm. Noise Health 1994).

Several studies of the cardiovascular effects of noise have been conducted with children. Children exposed to high road traffic noise (Cohen et al. 1980, Karsdorf & Klappach 1968) and noisier school environments (Regecova & Kellerova 1995) were found to have increased systolic and diastolic blood pressure. One study compared children living near the new airport in Munich, Germany to controls in a quieter neighborhood (Evans et al. 1998). The airport children had similar levels of epinephrine and norepinephrine before the airport was opened; however, afterwards, the airport children's levels rose significantly and were higher than control area children (see Figure 5).

GROWTH   Studies of noise and postnatal growth are rare but have consistently shown small reductions in children's heights, weights, or both (Schell & Ando 1991, Schell & Norelli 1983, Takahashi & Kyo 1968). More common are studies of prenatal growth, and most of these have compared births in relation to noise from airports. These studies have consistently found reductions in birth weight in the more noise-exposed areas, and the variety of locations (United States, France, the Netherlands, and Japan) supports the validity of the results. Especially convincing evidence comes from two studies in Japan. In one, more than 12,000 births were grouped in five different levels of noise exposure, and a clear dose-response relationship was observed (Ando & Hattori 1973). In a second study (Ando 1988), the frequency of lower birth weight increased in tandem with increases in the amount

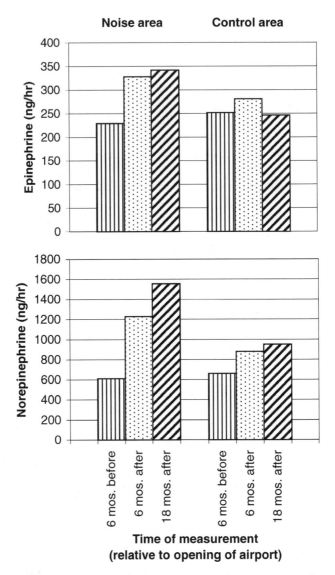

Figure 5 Indicators of stress in third- and fourth-grade children in relation to noise exposure: mean epinephrine and norepinephrine levels (adapted from Evans et al. 1998).

of jet plane activity at the airport, which indicates a temporal association typical of cause and effect (see Figure 6). Evidence from occupational studies where noise is estimated by job description is supportive (Hartikainen et al. 1994, Nurminen & Kurppa 1989); however, in the one study of workers where noise was measured, birth weight was unaffected (Wu et al. 1996). An important consideration is the

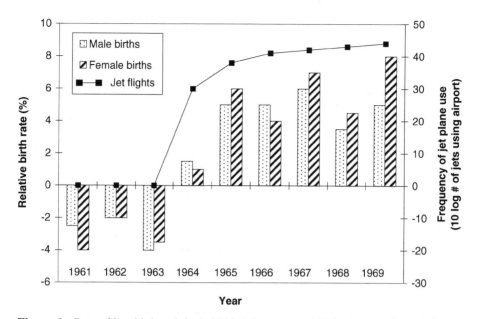

Figure 6   Rate of low birth weight (<3000 g) in an area of high airport noise, relative to a national standard (adapted from Ando 1988).

level of noise experienced. Noise may produce stressful effects that can alter the maternal environment for growth if sufficiently loud and annoying, whereas lower levels of expected noise, as may be found in the workplace, may not be as stimulating and detrimental.

MENTAL HEALTH   Although the causes of mental illness are always difficult to determine, emotional stress is widely recognized to play a role. Noise can be such a stress. Studies of psychiatric hospitalization, drug use, and noninstitutional psychiatric morbidity have yielded mixed results to date (Morrell et al. 1997, Stansfeld et al. 2000). Of two studies of medication use in noise-exposed compared to quiet communities, one found a positive association (Knipschild & Oudshoorn 1977) and the other found no association between noise and medication use (Watkins et al. 1981). The latter study was methodologically weaker because medication use was self-reported, whereas the former study was strengthened by the use of pharmacy dispensation records to determine longitudinal community medication use before and after the opening of a new airport. Although higher rates of some psychiatric symptoms have been reported in populations living in high-noise areas, other studies have failed to find such an association (Stansfeld et al. 2000). Reports of medication use and psychiatric symptomology are both subject to recall bias.

Rates of admission to psychiatric hospitals may be a more objective measure of the impact of noise on mental illness. Early studies with this approach produced inconsistent results owing perhaps to differences in noise exposure and control for confounding variables (Abey-Wickrama et al. 1969, Frerichs et al. 1980, Gattoni & Tarnopolsky 1973, Jenkins et al. 1981, Meecham & Smith 1977). In a survey study of psychiatric hospital admission rates among nearly 1,000,000 people across a wide range of noise exposures, Jenkins et al. (1981) reported no or little effect of noise exposure; however, the analytic method and control for socioeconomic factors may have been inadequate. Kryter (1990) reanalyzed these data adjusting more extensively for socioeconomic variables and found the rate of psychiatric hospital admissions was 40% higher in communities with the greatest exposure to aircraft flyover noise when compared to neighborhoods with the lowest aircraft noise.

The inconsistency of these results likely stems from the complexity of factors influencing both psychiatric morbidity and individual reactions to noise. Noise may not be a large single contributor to mental illness, and the effects seen in studies of noise and mental illness may vary with the presence or absence of other significant variables. Variation in study results is reasonable given the different ways that noise may be measured and the variability in the level of noise studied. In addition, research in noise annoyance suggests that an individual's reaction to noise is not simply a reflection of noise exposure. Noise annoyance, defined as negative feelings provoked by noise that interferes with thoughts or activities, is associated both with noise exposure and psychosocial factors that affect individual noise sensitivity (Borsky 1979, Job 1988, Stansfeld et al. 1985). Thus, noise affects different people in different ways and may contribute to psychiatric symptoms only in certain vulnerable subpopulations (Tarnopolsky et al. 1980, 1978).

COGNITIVE PROCESSING   Laboratory evidence suggests that noise exposure impairs cognitive performance, especially verbal and recall tasks (Loeb 1986, Smith 1989). Noise need not be deafening to impair cognition; even moderate intensity noise can affect memory tasks (Smith & Broadbent 1982, Smith 1989). The quality of noise (controllability and meaning) mediates its effects. Intermittent noise that is out of an individual's control seems to have the greatest impact on performance (Glass & Singer 1972). The anticipation of a loud noise may impair performance even in the absence of noise exposure (Cohen & Spacapan 1984). The meaning attributed to noise also affects the degree to which noise impairs performance. Speech noise (meaningful) has been found to have a greater effect on performance than non-speech noise (Salame & Baddeley 1982, Smith 1985), and irrelevant speech impairs performance perhaps through its effect on memory (Smith & Broadbent 1982, Smith 1989).

Among children, research has consistently demonstrated the role of noise in the impairment of cognitive tasks, such as reading, language comprehension, problem solving, memory, and attention (Cohen et al. 1986, Evans et al. 1995, Haines et al. 2001). This can result in significant developmental delays. Elementary school children in classrooms near a railway line had reading scores three to four months behind children on the opposite side of the school (Bronzaft & McCarthy 1975).

Conclusion

Because of the close relationship between transportation and manufacturing, noise levels in urban areas are higher than in rural ones. Urban populations experience decrements in hearing and a variety of systemic effects related to the ability of noise to activate the stress response. Noise, as a stressor, can affect growth and development, as well as adult functioning, as seen by effects on the cardiovascular system and mental health. Effects of noise on human reproduction have not been studied but are a logical subject for anthropologists interested in evolution.

Noise is only one stressor of urban environments and is used here as an example of stress effects. Urban populations may experience stress from numerous other sources including job stress, crowding and contact with strangers, migration, and social adjustment (Dressler 1993, James et al. 1987, Pollard 1999).

THE ECOLOGICAL FOOTPRINT OF CITIES: PERSISTENT ORGANIC POLLUTANTS

Cities influence populations outside their boundaries because they are not self-sufficient. Circum-urban areas have always provided large cities with food, water, and the disposal of wastes. Modern cities also must provide electrical power from distant sources for residential, commercial, and industrial uses. Manufacturing often is located outside of the cities as well. The extensive influence of cities is its "ecological footprint" (Waskernagel & Rees 1996).

The ecological footprint of cities includes the impact of pollution. Atmospheric and water circulation patterns extend the influence of the city by moving pollutants far from their origins. Remote communities in the North American arctic may have high levels of some pollutants created thousands of miles away. The Arctic Inuit have been affected by consumption of local animals contaminated with persistent organic pollutants (POPs), such as polychlorinated biphenyls, dioxin, and dichlorodiphenyl dichloroethylene (a metabolite of DDT) (Dewailly et al. 1996). POPs are byproducts of manufacturing and incineration, are lipophilic, have long half lives, and enter soil and water through improper disposal practices. They bioaccumulate up the food chain and are concentrated in large fish and sea mammals that are preferred foods for many populations (Johansen 2000). Levels of PCBs, one of the more common POPs, are found in the breast milk of many remote populations (Jensen 1990).

The effects of POPs are not fully known, but evidence from laboratory studies and studies of human populations suggests that the effects may occur by altering the development of the endocrine system and its action later in life (Brouwer et al. 1998). Effects on cognition, behavior, reproduction, growth, and development have been documented among laboratory animals and in human populations.

CONCLUSION

Pollution from industrial and transportation sources has been a characteristic feature of urban environments, but it now reaches far from its origins to affect virtually all human populations. Pollution is a heterogeneous entity and produces highly variable effects on human biology and health, including effects on mortality, morbidity, reproduction, and development. Important knowledge of pollution's association with biological variation has come from large-scale surveys, but proof of the causal nature of these associations has been clarified by critical natural experiments. Mundane pollution exposure tends to produce chronic and sublethal effects, although it can severely affect susceptible subpopulations (e.g., the very young and old) and minority groups who experience disproportionate levels of exposure owing to the broad effects of socioeconomic disadvantage. At this writing, half the world's population lives in cities, which makes small individual effects quite significant to the species as a whole.

The *Annual Review of Anthropology* is online at http://anthro.annualreviews.org

LITERATURE CITED

Abbey DE, Nishino N, McDonnell WF, Burchette RJ, Knutsen SF, et al. 1999. Long-term inhalable particles and other air pollutants related to mortality in nonsmokers. *Am. J. Respir. Crit. Care Med.* 159:373–82

Abey-Wickrama I, A'Brook MF, Gattoni FE, Herridge CF. 1969. Mental-hospital admissions and aircraft noise. *Lancet* 2:1275–77

Agency Toxic Subst. Dis. Registr. 1988. *The Nature and Extent of Lead Poisoning in Children in the United States: a Report to Congress.* Atlanta, GA: US Dep. Health Hum. Serv.

Alderman BW, Baron AE, Savitz DA. 1987. Maternal exposure to neighborhood carbon monoxide and risk of low infant birth weight. *Public Health Rep.* 102:410–14

Ando Y. 1988. Effects of daily noise on fetuses and cerebral hemisphere specialization in children. *J. Sound Vib.* 127:411–17

Ando Y, Hattori H. 1973. Statistical studies on the effects of intense noise during human fetal life. *J. Sound Vib.* 27:101–10

Babisch W, Ising H, Gallacher JE, Sweetnam PM, Elwood PC. 1999. Traffic noise and cardiovascular risk: the Caerphilly and Speed-well studies, third phase–10-year follow up. *Arch. Environ. Health* 54:210–16

Baghurst PA, Robertson EF, McMichael AJ, Vimpani GV, Wigg NR, Roberts RJ. 1987. The Port Pirie Cohort Study: lead effects on pregnancy outcome and early childhood development. *Neurotoxicology* 8:395–402

Ballew C, Khan LK, Kaufmann R, Mokdad A, Miller DT, Gunter EW. 1999. Blood lead concentration and children's anthropometric dimensions in the Third National Health and Nutrition Examination Survey (NHANES III) 1988–1994. *J. Pediatr.* 134:623–30

Belli S, Sani L, Scarficcia G, Sorrentino R. 1984. Arterial hypertension and noise: a cross-sectional study. *Am. J. Indust. Med.* 6:59–65

Bellinger DC, Leviton A, Rabinowitz M, Allred E, Needleman HL, Schoenbaum S. 1991. Weight gain and maturity in fetuses exposed to low levels of lead. *Environ. Res.* 54:151–58

Bellinger DC, Needleman HL. 1992. Neurodevelopmental effects of low-level lead exposure in children. In *Human Lead Exposure,* ed. HL Needleman, pp. 191–208. Boca Raton, FL: CRC Press

Bobak M. 2000. Outdoor air pollution, low birth weight, and prematurity. *Environ. Health Perspect.* 108:173–76

Bobak M, Leon DA. 1999. Pregnancy outcomes and outdoor air pollution: an ecological study in districts of the Czech Republic 1986–8. *Occup. Environ. Med.* 56:539–43

Borja-Aburto VH, Castillejos M, Gold DR, Bierzwinski S, Loomis D. 1998. Mortality and ambient fine particles in Southwest Mexico City, 1993–1995. *Environ. Health Perspect.* 106:849–55

Bornschein RL, Grote J, Mitchell T, Succop PA, Dietrich KN, et al. 1989. Effects of prenatal lead exposure on infant size at birth. In *Lead Exposure and Child Development: an International Assessment*, ed. MA Smith, L Grant, AI Sors, pp. 307–19. Boston: Kluwer

Borsky PN. 1979. Sociopsychological factors affecting the human response to noise exposure. *Otolaryngol. Clin. North Am.* 12:521–35

Brody DJ, Pirkle JL, Kramer RA, Flegal KA, Matte TD, et al. 1994. Blood lead levels in the US population. Phase 1 of the Third National Health and Nutrition Examination Survey (NHANES III, 1988–1991). *JAMA* 272:277–83

Bronzaft AL, McCarthy DP. 1975. The effect of elevated noise on reading ability. *Environ. Behav.* 7:517–27

Brouwer A, Ahlborg UG, van Leeuwen R, Feeley MM. 1998. Report of the WHO working group on the assessment of health risks for human infants from exposure to PCDDS, PCDFS and PCBS. *Chemosphere* 37:1627–43

Brunekreef B. 1997. Air pollution and life expectancy: Is there a relation? *Occup. Environ. Med.* 54:781–84

Brunekreef B. 1999. All but quiet on the particulate front. *Am. J. Respir. Crit. Care Med.* 159:354–56

Brunekreef B, Holgate ST. 2002. Air pollution and health. *Lancet* 360:1233–42

Cent. Dis. Control Prev. 1983. Results of blood lead determinations among workers potentially exposed to lead–United States. *MMWR* 32:216–19

Cent. Dis. Control Prev. 1991. *Preventing Lead Poisoning in Young Children.* Atlanta: US Dep. Health Hum. Serv., Public Health Serv.

Cent. Dis. Control Prev. 1988. Childhood lead poisoning–United States: report to the Congress by the Agency for Toxic Substances and Disease Registry. *MMWR* 37:481–504

Cohen A. 1977. Extraauditory effects of acoustic stimulation. In *Handbook of Physiology. A Critical, Comprehensive Presentation of Physiological Knowledge and Concepts*, ed. DHK Lee, HL Falk, SD Murphy, SR Geiger, pp. 31–44. Bethesda, MD: Am. Physiol. Soc.

Cohen S, Evans GW, Krantz DS, Stokols D. 1980. Physiological, motivational, and cognitive effects of aircraft noise on children: moving from the laboratory to the field. *Am. Psychol.* 35:231–43

Cohen S, Evans GW, Stokols D, Krantz DS. 1986. *Behavior, Health and Environmental Stress.* New York: Plenum. 294 pp.

Cohen S, Spacapan S. 1984. Social psychology of noise. In *Noise and Society*, ed. DM Jones, AJ Chapman, pp. 221–46. London: Wiley

Danker-Hopfe H, Hulanicka B. 1995. Maturation of girls in lead polluted areas. In *Essays on Auxology*, ed. R Hauspie, G Lindgren, F Falkner, pp. 334–42. Welwyn Garden City, UK: Castlemead

Dassen W, Brunekreef B, Hoek G, Hofschreuder P, Staatsen B, et al. 1986. Decline in children's pulmonary function during an air pollution episode. *J. Air Pollut. Control Assoc.* 36:1223–27

Dejmek J, Selevan SG, Benes I, Solansky I, Sram RJ. 1999. Fetal growth and maternal exposure to particulate matter during pregnancy. *Environ. Health Perspect.* 107:475–80

Dewailly E, Ayotte P, Laliberte C, Weber J-P, Gingras S, Nantel AJ. 1996. Polychlorinated biphenyl (PCB) and dichlorodiphenyl dichloroethylene (DDE) concentrations in the breast milk of women in Quebec. *Am. J. Public Health* 86:1241–46

Dietrich KN, Krafft KM, Bier M, Succop PA, Berger OG, Bornschein RL. 1986. Early effects of fetal lead exposure: neurobehavioral findings at 6 months. *Int. J. Biosocial Res.* 8:151–68

Dolk H, Pattenden S, Vrijheid M, Thakrar B, Armstrong BG. 2000. Perinatal and infant mortality and low birth weight among residents near cokeworks in Great Britain. *Arch. Environ. Health* 55:26–30

Dressler WW, Dos Santos JE, Viteri FE. 1993. Social and cultural influences in the risk of cardiovascular disease in urban Brazil. In *Urban Ecology and Health in the Third World. SSHB Symposium 32*, ed. LM Schell, MT Smith, A Bilsborough, pp. 10–25. Cambridge, UK: Cambridge Univ. Press

Evans GW, Bullinger M, Hygge S. 1998. Chronic noise exposure and physiological response: a prospective study of children living under environmental stress. *Psychol. Sci.* 9:75–77

Evans GW, Hygge S, Bullinger M. 1995. Chronic noise and psychological stress. *Psychol. Sci.* 6:333–38

Factor-Litvak P, Graziano JH, Kline JK, Popovac D, Mehmeti A, et al. 1991. A prospective study of birthweight and length of gestation in a population surrounding a lead smelter in Kosovo, Yugoslavia. *Int. J. Epidemiol.* 20:722–28

Fairley D. 1999. Daily mortality and air pollution in Santa Clara County, California: 1989–1996. *Environ. Health Perspect.* 107:637–41

Fogel RW. 1986. Physical growth as a measure of the economic well-being of populations: the eighteenth and nineteenth centuries. In *Human Growth: a Comprehensive Treatise*, ed. F Falkner, JM Tanner, pp. 263–81. New York: Plenum

Frerichs RR, Beeman BL, Coulson AH. 1980. Los Angeles airport noise and mortality–faulty analysis and public policy. *Am. J. Public Health* 70:357–62

Friedman MS, Powell KE, Hutwagner L, Graham LM, Teague WG. 2001. Impact of changes in transportation and commuting behaviors during the 1996 summer Olympic games in Atlanta on air quality and childhood asthma. *JAMA* 285:897–905

Gattoni F, Tarnopolsky A. 1973. Aircraft noise and psychiatric morbidity. *Psychol. Med.* 3:516–20

Glass DC, Singer JE. 1972. *Urban Stress: Experiments on Noise and Social Stressors*. New York: Academic. 182 pp.

Goldman LR, Koduru S. 2000. Chemicals in the environment and developmental toxicity to children: a public health and policy perspective. *Environ. Health Perspect.* 108:443–48

Gonzalez-Cossio T, Peterson KE, Sanin L-H, Fishbein E, Palazuelos E, et al. 1997. Decrease in birth weight in relation to maternal bone-lead burden. *Pediatrics* 100:856–62

Grant LD, Davis JM. 1989. Effects of low-level lead exposure on paediatric neurobehavioral development: current indings and future directions. In *Lead Exposure and Child Development: An International Assessment*, ed. MA Smith, LD Grant, AI Sors, pp. 49–115. Boston: Kluwer

Green MS, Schwartz K, Harari G, Najenson T. 1991. Industrial noise exposure and ambulatory blood pressure and heart rate. *J. Occup. Med.* 33:879–83

Haines MM, Stansfeld SA, Job RF, Berglund B, Head J. 2001. Chronic aircraft noise exposure, stress responses, mental health and cognitive performance in school children. *Psychol. Med.* 31:265–77

Hartikainen A-L, Sorri M, Anttonen H, Tuimala R, Laara E. 1994. Effect of occupational noise on the course and outcome of pregnancy. *Scand. J. Environ. Health* 20:444–50

Health Counc. Netherlands: Comm. Noise Health. 1994. *Noise and Health. nr 1994/15E*. The Hague: Health Counc. Neth.

Herbold M, Hense HW, Keil U. 1989. Effects of road traffic noise on prevalence of hypertension in men: results of the Luebeck Blood Pressure Study. *Soz. Praeventimed.* 34:19–23

Huseman CA, Moriarty CM, Angle CR. 1987. Childhood lead toxicity and impaired release of thyrotropin-stimulating hormone. *Environ. Res.* 42:524–33

Huseman CA, Varma MM, Angle CR. 1992. Neuroendocrine effects of toxic and low blood lead levels in children. *Pediatrics* 90: 186–89

Int. Organ. Stand. 1990. *Acoustics–Determination of Occupational Noise Exposure and Estimation of Noise-Induced Hearing Impairment. International Standard ISO 1999.* Geneva, Switz.: Int. Organ. Stand.

James GD, Baker PT, Jenner DA, Harrison GA. 1987. Variation in lifestyle characteristics and catecholamine excretion rates among young Western Samoan men. *Soc. Sci. Med.* 25:981–86

Jedrychowski W, Flak E, Mroz E. 1999. The adverse effect of low levels of ambient air pollutants on lung function growth in preadolescent children. *Environ. Health Perspect.* 107:669–74

Jedrychowski W, Maugeri U, Jedrychowska-Bianchi I. 2002. Body growth rate in preadolescent children and outdoor air quality. *Environ. Res.* 90:12–20

Jenkins L, Tarnopolsky A, Hand D. 1981. Psychiatric admissions and aircraft noise from London Airport: four-year, three-hospitals' study. *Psychol. Med.* 11:765–82

Jensen AA. 1990. Levels and trends of environmental chemicals in human milk. In *Chemical Contaminants in Human Milk*, ed. AA Jensen, SA Slorach, pp. 45–198. Boca Raton, FL: CRC Press

Job RF. 1988. Community response to noise: a review of factors influencing the relationship between noise exposure and reaction. *J. Acoust. Soc. Am.* 83:991–1001

Johansen BE. 2000. Pristine no more. *Progressive* 64:27–29

Karsdorf G, Klappach H. 1968. Effects of traffic noise on health and achievement of high school students of a large city. *Z. Gesamte Hyg.* 14:52–54

Knipschild P. 1977. V. Medical effects of aircraft noise: community cardiovascular survey. *Int. Arch. Occup. Environ. Health* 40:185–90

Knipschild P, Oudshoorn N. 1977. VII. Medical effects of aircraft noise: drug survey. *Int. Arch. Occup. Environ. Health* 40:197–209

Koenig JQ, Larson TV, Hanley QA, Rebbolledo V, Dumler K, et al. 1993. Pulmonary function changes in children associated with fine particulate matter. *Environ. Res.* 63:26–38

Kryter KD. 1985. *The Effects of Noise on Man.* New York: Academic

Kryter KD. 1990. Aircraft noise and social factors in psychiatric hospital admission rates: a re-examination of some data. *Psychol. Med.* 20:395–411

Landrigan PJ, Carlson JE, Bearer CF, Cranmer JS, Bullard RD, et al. 1998. Children's health and the environment: a new agenda for prevention research. *Environ. Health Perspect.* 106:787–94

Lang T, Fouriaud C, Jacquinet-Salord M-C. 1992. Length of occupational noise exposure and blood pressure. *Int. Arch. Occup. Environ. Health* 63:369–72

Lee J-T, Shin D, Chung Y. 1999. Air pollution and daily mortality in Seoul and Ulsan, Korea. *Environ. Health Perspect.* 107:149–54

Lilienfeld DE, Stolley PD. 1994. *Foundations of Epidemiology.* Oxford, UK: Oxford Univ. Press. 371 pp.

Lin S, Hwang S-A, Marshall EG, Marion D. 1998. Does paternal occupational lead exposure increase the risks of low birth weight or prematurity? *Am. J. Epidemiol.* 148:173–81

Loeb M. 1986. *Noise and Human Efficiency.* Chichester, UK: Wiley. 284 pp.

Loomis D, Castillejos M, Gold DR, McDonnell WF, Borja-Aburto VH. 1999. Air pollution and infant mortality in Mexico City. *Epidemiology* 10:118–23

Mahaffey KR, Annest JL, Roberts J, Murphy RS. 1982. National estimates of blood lead levels: United States, 1976–1980. Association with selected demographic and socioeconomic factors. *N. Engl. J. Med.* 307:573–79

McMichael AJ, Vimpani GV, Robertson EF, Baghurst PA, Clark PD. 1986. The Port Pirie

Cohort Study: maternal blood lead and pregnancy outcome. *J. Epidemiol. Community Health* 40:18–25

Meecham WC, Smith HG. 1977. Effects of jet aircraft noise on mental hospital admissions. *Br. J. Audiol.* 11:81–85

Mikusek J. 1976. Developmental age and growth of girls from regions with high atmospheric air pollution in Silesia. *Rocz. Panstw. Zakl. Hig.* 27:473–81

Morrell S, Taylor R, Lyle D. 1997. A review of health effects of aircraft noise. *Aust. N.Z. J. Public Health* 21:221–36

Neas LM, Schwartz J, Dockery DW. 1999. A case-crossover analysis of air pollution and mortality in Philadelphia. *Environ. Health Perspect.* 107:629–31

Needleman HL, Schell A, Bellinger DC, Leviton A, Allred EN. 1990. The long-term effects of exposure to low doses of lead in childhood. An 11-year follow-up report. *N. Engl. J. Med.* 322:83–88

Nurminen T, Kurppa K. 1989. Occupational noise exposure and course of pregnancy. *Scand. J. Work Environ. Health* 15:117–24

Parvizpoor D. 1976. Noise exposure and prevalence of high blood pressure among weavers in Iran. *J. Occup. Med.* 18:730–31

Passchier-Vermeer W, Passchier WF. 2000. Noise exposure and public health. *Environ. Health Perspect.* 108:123–31

Pereira LAA, Loomis D, Conceicao GMS, Braga ALF, Arcas RM, et al. 1998. Association between air pollution and intrauterine mortality in Sao Paulo, Brazil. *Environ. Health Perspect.* 106:325–29

Perera FP, Rauh V, Tsai W-Y, Kinney P, Camann D, et al. 2003. Effects of transplacental exposure to environmental pollutants on birth outcomes in a multiethnic population. *Environ. Health Perspect.* 111:201–5

Pirkle JL, Brody DJ, Gunter EW, Kramer RA, Paschal DC, et al. 1994. The decline in blood lead levels in the United States: the National Health and Nutrition Examination Surveys (NHANES). *JAMA* 272:284–91

Pollard TM. 1999. Urbanism and psychosocial stress. In *Urbanism, Health and Human Biology in Industrialised Countries*, ed. LM Schell, SJ Ulijaszek, pp. 231–49. Cambridge, UK: Cambridge Univ. Press

Pope CA III, Burnett RT, Thun MJ, Calle EE, Krewski D, et al. 2002. Lung cancer, cardiopulmonary mortality, and long-term exposure to fine particulate air pollution. *JAMA* 287:1132–41

Regecova V, Kellerova E. 1995. Effects of urban noise pollution on blood pressure and heart rate in preschool children. *J. Hypertens.* 13:405–12

Ritz B, Yu F. 1999. The effect of ambient carbon monoxide on low birth weight among children born in Southern California between 1989 and 1993. *Environ. Health Perspect.* 107:17–25

Roemer W, Hoek G, Brunekreef B. 2000. Pollution effects on asthmatic children in Europe, the PEACE study. *Clin. Exp. Allergy* 30:1067–75

Rothenberg SJ, Schnaas L, Mendez CJN, Hidalgo H. 1988. Effects of lead on neurobehavioural developement in the first thirty days of life. In *Lead Exposure and Child Development: an International Assessment*, ed. MA Smith, L Grant, AI Sors, pp. 387–95. Dordrecht: Kluwer

Salame P, Baddeley AD. 1982. Disruption of short-term memory by unattended speech: implications for the structure of working memory. *J. Verbal Learn. Verbal Behav.* 21:150–64

Schell LM. 1986. Community health assessment through physical anthropology: auxological epidemiology. *Hum. Organ.* 45:321–27

Schell LM. 1992. Risk focusing: an example of biocultural interaction. In *Health and Lifestyle Change*, ed. R Huss-Ashmore, J Schall, ML Hediger, pp. 137–44. Philadelphia: Univ. Penn.

Schell LM. 1999. Human physical growth and exposure to toxicants: lead and polychlorinated biphenyls. In *Human Growth in Context*, ed. FE Johnston, PB Eveleth, BS Zemel, pp. 221–38. London: Smith-Gordon

Schell LM, Ando Y. 1991. Postnatal growth of

children in relation to noise from Osaka international airport. *J. Sound Vib.* 151:371–82

Schell LM, Czerwinski S. 1998. Environmental health, social inequality and biological differences. In *Human Biology and Social Inequality*, ed. S Strickland, P Shetty, pp. 114–31. Cambridge, UK: Cambridge Univ. Press

Schell LM, Czerwinski S, Stark AD, Parsons PJ, Gomez M, Samelson R. 2000. Variation in blood lead and hematocrit levels during pregnancy in a socioeconomically disadvantaged population. *Arch. Environ. Health* 55:134–40

Schell LM, Knutson KL. 2002. Environmental effects on growth. In *Human Growth and Development*, ed. N Cameron, pp. 165–95. New York: Academic

Schell LM, Norelli RJ. 1983. Airport noise exposure and the postnatal growth of children. *Am. J. Phys. Anthropol.* 61:473–82

Schell LM, Stark AD. 1999. Pollution and child health. In *Urbanism, Health and Human Biology in Industrialised Countries*, ed. LM Schell, SJ Ulijaszek, pp. 136–57. Cambridge, UK: Cambridge Univ. Press

Schell LM, Ulijaszek SJ. 1999. Urbanism, urbanisation, health and human biology: an introduction. In *Urbanism, Health and Human Biology in Industrialised Countries*, ed. LM Schell, SJ Ulijaszek, pp. 3–20. Cambridge, UK: Cambridge Univ. Press

Schlipkoter HW, Rosicky B, Dolgner R, Peluch L. 1986. Growth and bone maturation in children from two regions of the F.R.G. differing in the degree of air pollution: results of the 1974 and 1984 surveys. *J. Hyg. Epidemiol. Microbiol. Immunol.* 30:353–58

Schwartz J. 1989. Lung function and chronic exposure to air pollution: a cross-sectional analysis of NHANES II. *Environ. Res.* 50:309–21

Schwartz J. 1991. Particulate air pollution and daily mortality in Detroit. *Environ. Res.* 56:204–13

Schwartz J, Angle CR, Pitcher H. 1986. Relationship between childhood blood lead levels and stature. *Pediatrics* 77:281–88

Schwartz J, Slater D, Larson TV, Pierson WE, Koenig JQ. 1993. Particulate air pollution and hospital emergency room visits for asthma in Seattle. *Am. Rev. Respir. Dis.* 147:826–31

Schwela D. 2000. Air pollution and health in urban areas. *Rev. Environ. Health* 15:13–42

Sciarillo W, Alexander GR, Farrell KP. 1992. Lead exposure and child behavior. *Am. J. Public Health* 82:1356–60

Shukla R, Bornschein RL, Dietrich KN, Buncher CR, Berger OG, et al. 1989. Fetal and infant lead exposure: effects on growth in stature. *Pediatrics* 84:604–12

Silva PA, Hughes P, Williams S, Faed JM. 1988. Blood lead, intelligence, reading attainment, and behaviour in eleven year old children in Dunedin, New Zealand. *J. Child Psychol. Psychiatry* 29:43–52

Singh AP, Rai RM, Bhatia MR, Nayar HS. 1982. Effect of chronic and acute exposure to noise on physiological functions in man. *Int. Arch. Occup. Environ. Health* 50:169–74

Smith A. 1989. A review of the effects of noise on human performance. *Scand. J. Psychol.* 30:185–206

Smith AP. 1985. The effects of different types of noise on semantic processing and syntactic reasoning. *Acta Psychol.* 58:263–73

Smith AP, Broadbent DE. 1982. The effects of noise on recall and recognition of instances of categories. *Acta Psychol.* 51:257–71

Smith MA. 1989. The effects of low-level lead exposure on children. In *Lead Exposure and Child Development: An International Assessment*, ed. MA Smith, LD Grant, AI Sors, pp. 3–47. Boston: Kluwer

Stansfeld S, Haines M, Brown B. 2000. Noise and health in the urban environment. *Rev. Environ. Health* 15:43–82

Stansfeld SA, Clark CR, Jenkins LM, Tarnopolsky A. 1985. Sensitivity to noise in a community sample: I. Measurement of psychiatric disorder and personality. *Psychol. Med.* 15:243–54

Staples SL. 1997. Public policy and environmental noise: modeling exposure or understanding effects. *Am. J. Public Health* 87:2063–67

Takahashi I, Kyo S. 1968. Studies on the differences in adaptabilities to the noise environment in sexes and growing processes. *J. Anthropol. Soc. Nip.* 76:34–51

Talbott EO, Gibson LB, Burks A, Engberg R, McHugh KP. 1999. Evidence for a dose-response relationship between occupational noise and blood pressure. *Arch. Environ. Health* 54:71–78

Tarnopolsky A, Barker SM, Wiggins RD, McLean EK. 1978. The effect of aircraft noise on the mental health of a community sample: a pilot study. *Psychol. Med.* 8:219–33

Tarnopolsky A, Watkins G, Hand DJ. 1980. Aircraft noise and mental health. I. Prevalence of individual symptoms. *Psychol. Med.* 10:683–98

Thielebeule U, Pelech L, Grosser P-J, Horn K. 1980. Body height and bone age of school children in areas of different air pollution concentration. *Z. Gesamte Hyg.* 26:771–74

United Nations. 1998. *World Urbanization Prospects: the 1996 Revision. Sales No. E98.XIII.6*, United Nations. New York: Dep. Econ. Soc. Affairs, Popul. Div.

US Environ. Prot. Agency. 2001. *National Air Quality and Emissions Trends Report, 1999. EPA 454/R-01-004.* Research Triangle Park, NC: Off. Air Quality

Verbeek JH, van Dijk FJ, de Vries FF. 1987. Non-auditory effects of noise in industry. IV. A field study on industrial noise and blood pressure. *Int. Arch. Occup. Environ. Health* 59:51–54

Waldbott GL. 1978. *Health Effects of Environmental Pollutants.* St. Louis, MO: Mosby. 350 pp.

Waskernagel M, Rees W. 1996. *Our Ecological Footprint: Reducing Human Impact on Earth.* Gabriola Island, BC: New Society. 160 pp.

Watkins G, Tarnopolsky A, Jenkins LM. 1981. Aircraft noise and mental health: II. Use of medicines and health care services. *Psychol. Med.* 11:155–68

Welch BL, Welch AM. 1970. *Physiological Effects of Noise.* New York: Plenum Press. 366 pp.

Westman JC, Walters JR. 1981. Noise and stress: a comprehensive approach. *Environ. Health Perspect.* 41:291–309

Wjst M, Reitmeir P, Dold S, Wulff A, Nicolai T, et al. 1993. Road traffic and adverse effects on respiratory health in children. *Br. Med. J.* 307:596–600

Wolf AW, Lozoff B, Jimenez E. 1987. Lead and infant development in a developing country. In *Heavy Metals in the Environment*, ed. S Lindberg, T Hutchinson, pp. 165–67. Edinburgh: CEP Consultants

Woodruff TJ, Grillo J, Schoendorf KC. 1997. The relationship between selected causes of postneonatal infant mortality and particulate air pollution in the United States. *Environ. Health Perspect.* 105:608–12

World Health Organ. 1980. *Noise. Environmental Health Criteria Document No. 12.* Geneva: World Health Organ.

Wu T-N, Chen L-J, Lai J-S, Ko G-N, Shen C-Y, Chang P-Y. 1996. Prospective study of noise exposure during pregnancy on birth weight. *Am. J. Epidemiol.* 143:792–96

Xu X, Ding H, Wang X. 1995. Acute effects of total suspended particles and sulfur dioxides on preterm delivery: a community-based cohort study. *Arch. Environ. Health* 50:407–15

Xu Z, Jing L, Yu D, Xu X. 2000. Air pollution and daily mortality in Shenyang, China. *Arch. Environ. Health* 55:115–20

Yang SC, Yang SP. 1994. Respiratory function changes from inhalation of polluted air. *Arch. Environ. Health* 49:182–87

Zhao Y, Zhang S, Selvin S, Spear RC. 1991. A dose response relation for noise induced hypertension. *Br. J. Ind. Med.* 48:179–84

Zmirou D, Schwartz J, Saez M, Zanobetti A, Wojtyniak B, et al. 1998. Time-series analysis of air pollution and cause-specific mortality. *Epidemiology* 9:495–503

Annu. Rev. Anthropol. 2003. 32:135–62
doi: 10.1146/annurev.anthro.32.061002.093207

THE NEOLITHIC INVASION OF EUROPE

Martin Richards

*Department of Chemical and Biological Sciences, University of Huddersfield,
Queensgate, Huddersfield HD1 3DH, United Kingdom; email: m.b.richards@hud.ac.uk*

Key Words   Neolithic farmers, Mesolithic foragers, mitochondrial DNA,
  Y chromosome, phylogeography

■ **Abstract**   Who are Europeans? Both prehistoric archaeology and, subsequently,
classical population genetics have attempted to trace the ancestry of modern Europeans
back to the first appearance of agriculture in the continent; however, the question has
remained controversial. Classical population geneticists attributed the major pattern
in the European gene pool to the demographic impact of Neolithic farmers dispers-
ing from the Near East, but archaeological research has failed to uncover substantial
evidence for the population growth that is supposed to have driven this process. Recently, molecular approaches, using non-recombining genetic marker systems, have
introduced a chronological dimension by both allowing the tracing of lineages back
through time and dating using the molecular clock. Both mitochondrial DNA and Y-
chromosome analyses have indicated a contribution of Neolithic Near Eastern lineages
to the gene pool of modern Europeans of around a quarter or less. This suggests that
dispersals bringing the Neolithic to Europe may have been demographically minor and
that contact and assimilation had an important role.

INTRODUCTION: FARMERS OUR ANCESTORS?

Prehistoric archaeology grew up under the shadow of nationalism, providing the
means by which the newly established European nation-states could create a unitary past for their peoples (Trigger 1989, Kohl & Fawcett 1995). There was traditionally a tendency, therefore, for the narratives of European prehistorians to
divide their actors into "us" and "them." At the deepest level, as Zvelebil (1995a)
argues, this amounted to a founding myth for European culture and civilization
that placed extraordinary emphasis on the Neolithic—a myth that idolizes farmers
at the expense of hunting and foraging ways of life.

There are, Zvelebil believes, three particular reasons why this may have happened. The first arose from the prejudice against hunter gatherers that emerged to
justify the colonial persecution of hunter-gatherer communities in the New World
(Gamble 1992). The second is the rise of urbanism and the resulting idealization
of the rural way of life. The third is the need of many of the new nation-states,
especially in central and northeast Europe, to forge a national identity among their
predominantly peasant populace. The effects were felt not only in archaeology but

0084-6570/03/1021-0135$14.00   **135**

also in literature from Wordsworth and Hardy to Tolstoy, and much more widely throughout the popular culture.

In archaeology, of course, the triumph of these views came with V.G. Childe's proposal that the appearance of the first farming communities in Europe—the future Marxist Childe's "Neolithic revolution"—was the result of immigration of populations from the Near East (Childe 1925). He proposed that following the onset of the Neolithic in the Near East at the end of the last glaciation, about 10,000 years ago, farmers dispersed north and west into Europe, replacing the indigenous, Mesolithic hunting and foraging "savages" by virtue of their superior technology and culture. Zvelebil argues, along with a number of Palaeolithic and Mesolithic archaeologists, that the contribution of Europe's earlier, indigenous inhabitants to European society has been underestimated ever since.

This presumption in favor of what Zvelebil calls "farmers our ancestors" was perpetuated by both Neolithic archaeologists and population geneticists, as the latter became involved in prehistoric reconstruction from the 1970s onward. As recently as the 1980s, Bradley (1984) was able to make his famous observation that "in the literature as a whole, successful farmers have social relations with one another, while hunter-gatherers have ecological relations with hazelnuts." Yet the period since his remark has begun to witness a sea change in our view of the Neolithic and, finally, a rehabilitation of Europe's hunter-gatherer past. This has happened for two reasons: first, a sustained critique of the mass-migration perspective from the archaeological community, stressing in particular the importance of the social context of the Neolithic transition, and, second, by the arrival of molecular genetics on the scene.

The image of an invasion force marching across Europe at the beginning of the Neolithic has always been a caricature, but the question of the relative contribution of newcomers and natives to the European Neolithic has been vigorously fought over during the last 15 years. This question in turn has implications for explaining the social changes that took place with the shift to the Neolithic (e.g., Thomas 1996, 1998; Zvelebil 2000), and perhaps also for the arrival of new languages (Renfrew 1987, Zvelebil 1995b). On the genetic side, however, it appears that some consensus may finally be emerging. This article aims to review that part of the story, in order to assess the state of the argument over "farmers our ancestors" today.

THE WAVE OF ADVANCE

The subject of the genetic history of Europe was more or less created by Luca Cavalli-Sforza and his colleagues in the 1970s. Their work has cast a long shadow, to the extent that today's genetic researchers into the ancestry of Europeans, and even many archaeologists, continue to discuss their subject matter in the terms that they laid down. Cavalli-Sforza's work was pioneering in two ways. It was the first sustained attempt to apply genetic data to a question of major archaeological interest. In addition, however, it helped to bridge the gap between genetics and archaeology by being carried out in collaboration with an archaeologist, Albert

Ammerman. The partnership began in 1970 and culminated in 1984 with *The Neolithic Transition and the Genetics of Populations in Europe*, which remains a seminal work in archaeogenetics.

Ammerman & Cavalli-Sforza (1984) drew upon the new processual archaeology of Lewis Binford (1968) for a scientific model explaining the origins and spread of farming in western Eurasia. Binford's density equilibrium model suggested that farming had arisen in the Near East in areas of optimal wild resources, leading to sedentism, local population growth, and expansion into more marginal environments. Ammerman and Cavalli-Sforza accepted the central role of sedentism, population growth, and the resulting resource pressure in the early farming communities.

Cavalli-Sforza had studied under the founder of orthodox statistics, R.A. Fisher, and was keen to apply quantitative methods to the study of prehistoric Europe. His work with Ammerman began by measuring the rate of the spread of farming into Europe, drawing on the newly available radiocarbon maps compiled by Clark (1965), showing an east-west trend in first Neolithic dates. They observed that there was a complex of elements at Neolithic sites in Europe—the so-called Neolithic package. This included cereal crops—especially emmer wheat, einkorn wheat, and barley, whose wild progenitors occurred only in the Fertile Crescent of the Near East—domestic animals, pottery, ground and polished stone tools, and houses. To maximize their data set, Ammerman and Cavalli-Sforza sometimes chose to rely upon single items, focusing on cereals where possible, as markers for the spread of the Neolithic. They developed the use of isochron maps, plotting similarly dated sites on a map of Europe as a series of isochrons or contour lines. The result was a remarkably uniform rate of about one kilometer per year, or 25 kilometers per generation, with minor variations in different parts of the continent. The entire process, from Greece to the British Isles, had taken place in about 2500 years. This is in fact rather rapid: less time, for example, than it took farming to spread throughout the Near East, where it had originated (Price 2000a).

This discovery that the rate of spread across Europe appeared to be roughly constant suggested a single overarching mechanism, a diffusionary process rather than an old-fashioned model of directed colonization. Ammerman and Cavalli-Sforza introduced the expression demic diffusion to contrast the immigration of farmers themselves with the spread of farming as an idea through the indigenous hunter-gatherer populations—cultural diffusion. Demic diffusion could imply a rather traditional model of migration and colonization, but Ammerman and Cavalli-Sforza argued that the observed rate of spread suggested something different: a "wave of advance."

They took the wave of advance model from Cavalli-Sforza's mentor, Fisher, who had used it to describe the spread of an advantageous gene though a population. The wave of advance combines two features: logistic population growth and random local migratory diffusion or range expansion. The population growth was explained as the result of agriculturalist surpluses and storage in Neolithic societies, which allowed the carrying capacity of the land to rise. The outcome of growth combined with range expansion is a radial expanding population wave, in which the culture spreads with the expansion of people. Ammerman & Cavalli-Sforza (1984) described the wave of advance as "colonization without colonists."

CLASSICAL MARKERS AND THE NEOLITHIC TRANSITION

The wave of advance model appeared to be compatible with the rate of spread of the Neolithic measured from radiocarbon dates. More important, however, was the introduction of genetic data into the equation. At the time, these necessarily comprised only the "classical," non-DNA markers: allele frequencies for blood groups, the tissue antigen HLA system, and some enzymes. Assuming that the Near East and Europe had been relatively isolated during the Upper Palaeolithic and Mesolithic, and had therefore had the opportunity to differentiate genetically, certain predictions were possible that might allow different hypotheses about the spread of agriculture to be distinguished.

A demic diffusion of farmers from the Near East into Europe, involving complete replacement, was thought to predict complete homogeneity of the gene-frequency composition of European and Near Eastern populations (until subsequent differentiation). On the other hand, an entirely cultural spread would leave the two regions with different genetic compositions (assuming that was how they started out). However, a mixed model of demic diffusion involving intermarriage with the Mesolithic population would lead to a gene-frequency cline, or gradient, along the main axis of expansion, with one pole in the Near East and the other in northwest Europe.

It had already been shown by Mourant (1954) that the Rhesus-negative (Rh⁻) blood-group gene was virtually restricted to Europe, North Africa, and the Near East, with its highest frequency amongst the non-Indo-European-speaking Basques of southwest Europe. Mourant became one of the first biologists to use gene-frequency data to write prehistory when he suggested that this might be because the Basques were a relict of an ancient proto-European population who had mixed with newcomers later on. To Ammerman and Cavalli-Sforza, this idea suggested that the newcomers might have been expanding Near Eastern farmers, spreading agriculture into the continent. They were delighted to discover that the Rh⁻ gene was also found at high frequencies in northern and northwest Europe—precisely at the supposed peripheries of the Neolithic expansion.

However, other genes often showed different patterns. Furthermore, the Near East and Europe were not in fact highly differentiated from each other, weakening the picture still further. It was therefore necessary to take a multivariate approach, drawing on the results of many genetic systems, and to find an analytical method that could dissect different patterns. Cavalli-Sforza, with colleagues Menozzi and Piazza, chose principal-component (PC) analysis (Menozzi et al. 1978). They used this to summarize the gene frequencies at a particular location and to represent as much as possible of the information in just a few dimensions. Because the published data sets they used were taken from a variety of sources, there were many gaps, which had to be filled in by interpolation. The results could be graphed as a two-dimensional plot (portraying, say, the first and second or first and third components), or they could be presented as contour maps, component by component, showing the changes in frequency with geography.

The map of the first PC, accounting for about 27% of the total variation in classical marker frequencies across Europe and the Near East (initially using 39 genetic loci; later 95), has become something of an icon in the archaeogenetics of Europe (Figure 1). It showed a gradient from the southeast to the northwest, with the Near East at one pole and Europe at the other. The resemblance to the radiocarbon map for the spread of the Neolithic was immediately obvious. This was, Cavalli-Sforza and his colleagues believed, strong evidence for the mixed demic diffusion hypothesis. The second and third components (accounting for about 22% and 11% of the variation, respectively) showed clines that were oriented roughly southwest-northeast (Figure 2) and east-west. Because their impact on the genetic variation was lower, the processes that generated these were assumed to have taken place more recently than the Neolithic.

The relative proportions of incoming farmers and indigenous hunter-gatherers were difficult to assess, although the process of diffusion and interaction could be simulated using the wave of advance model (Ammerman & Cavalli-Sforza 1984). The simulations showed that the extent of acculturation—modeled as the marrying of hunter-gatherers into the farming community—was critical. With high levels of intermarriage, the survival of Near Eastern genes in the European population could in fact be very low, even with the wave of advance in operation, and a rapid fall-off of Near Eastern genes toward the northwest would be expected. Thus, whereas genetic data could perhaps be used to assess the extent of demic diffusion, testing the wave of advance model was going to be more difficult.

The conclusions of Ammerman and Cavalli-Sforza and their colleagues were supported by work using a different analytical approach: spatial autocorrelation analysis (Sokal et al. 1989, 1991). Again, about a third of the genetic markers analyzed appeared to be arranged in a southeast-northwest cline. Despite Ammerman and Cavalli-Sforza's early caveats about the acculturation coefficient, and despite the fact that only about a quarter to a third of the variation could be explained by these gradients, the assumed model of surplus-driven population growth and expansion led both groups to tend to play up the role of the Neolithic newcomers at the expense of the indigenous Mesolithic peoples. After all, it was the newcomers who had won in the end. No matter how careful and qualified the argument put forward in 1984 was, by the time of the publication of Cavalli-Sforza's magnum opus, *The History and Geography of Human Genes* (Cavalli-Sforza et al. 1994), the view that the genetic data supported an overwhelmingly Neolithic ancestry for modern Europeans had firmly taken root. It was further reflected in the view that much of the remaining variation was the result of subsequent migrations into

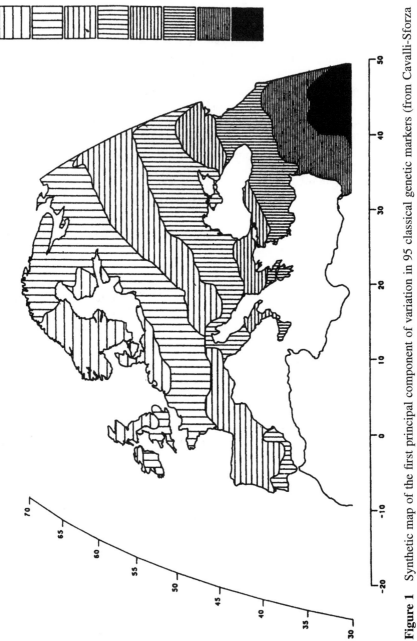

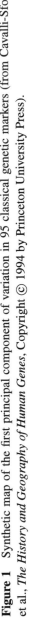

Figure 1 Synthetic map of the first principal component of variation in 95 classical genetic markers (from Cavalli-Sforza et al., *The History and Geography of Human Genes*, Copyright © 1994 by Princeton University Press).

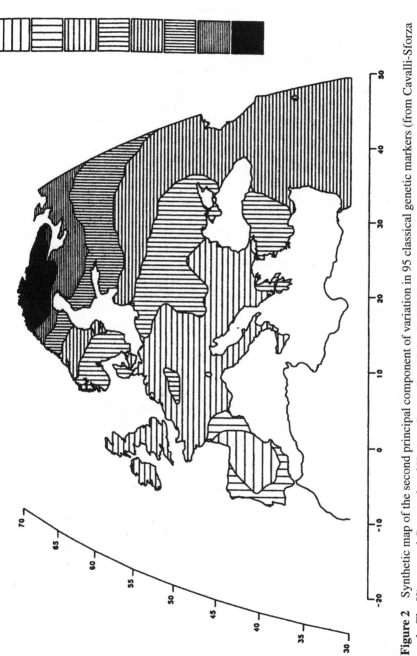

Figure 2   Synthetic map of the second principal component of variation in 95 classical genetic markers (from Cavalli-Sforza et al., *The History and Geography of Human Genes*, Copyright © 1994 by Princeton University Press).

Europe and that the principal components could provide relative dating, like an archaeological stratigraphy (Cavalli-Sforza 1996).

Further consequences ensued. Although he was suitably cautious about the genetic evidence for demic diffusion, Renfrew (1987) enthusiastically embraced the wave of advance model. To Renfrew, it was a good processual model that could be rigorously formulated, anti-migrationist (in the traditional sense) and yet allowing for the expansion of a group of people over, potentially, an enormously wide area. It seemed perfectly suited to Renfrew's radical hypothesis that the spread of Indo-European languages through Europe had been mediated by agriculturalist expansion. He suggested that the Basques were indeed a Palaeolithic relict and that the Indo-European languages had been dispersed through Europe by Neolithic populations originating in Anatolia. The choice of Anatolia was necessitated by the fact that this region was home to a number of extinct Bronze-Age Indo-European languages, which were extremely archaic and believed by some linguists to form a sister branch to the surviving members of the family. Many linguists believed them to be intrusive to Anatolia; Renfrew's suggestion was not popular among Indo-Europeanists, who mostly preferred something akin to the hypothesis of Marija Gimbutas that the Proto-Indo-Europeans had spread west with the Bronze-Age "Kurgan culture" of the eastern European steppe (Mallory 1989, Hines 1991). It was, however, received with considerable interest among archaeologists (Zvelebil & Zvelebil 1988, Sherratt & Sherratt 1988).

CRITIQUES OF THE WAVE OF ADVANCE

Despite some rather vigorous methodological disagreements between the two main proponents of large-scale Neolithic demic diffusion, the Cavalli-Sforza and Sokal groups, the southeast-northwest gradient itself was robust to a number of tests. It appeared there was a genuine pattern that needed explaining, rather than some artefact of the analysis. Nevertheless, interpreting the gradients was not as unproblematic as first thought. This was originally argued not by geneticists, however, but by an archaeologist sympathetic to Renfrew's perspective, Marek Zvelebil.

Firstly, Zvelebil (1989, 1998a) pointed out that there was no strong reason for identifying the first PC solely with a Neolithic expansion. Europe is a small peninsula of the Eurasian landmass and, as such, is likely to have been the sink for many such dispersals throughout prehistory. Movements into Europe may well have taken place many times via Anatolia because this represents one of the main possible points of entry into the continent. The term palimpsest came into play (Renfrew 1998, Zvelebil 1998a): The gradients identified by PC analysis might be the result of many dispersals, each one overwriting the last. The Neolithic may have been one of these, or it may not; if it was, it may or may not have been the most significant. Whereas Zvelebil's argument for "incremental palimpsest" (Zvelebil 2000) focused on post-Neolithic migrations, Richards et al. (1997) compiled a radiocarbon map for the first spread of the Early Upper Palaeolithic into Europe (analogous to the early maps for the Neolithic produced by J.G.D. Clark). They pointed out that the spread of the first modern humans into Europe, from about 45,000 years ago, followed very similar routes to the later spread of the Neolithic—a rapid dispersal around the Mediterranean and a more gradual expansion along the southeast-northwest axis, following the river systems of central Europe. Whereas any patterns set up by the arrival of early modern humans may well have been erased by subsequent demographic events, this reinforced the point that the same routes into Europe may have been used time and time again.

Thus, the idea of "one PC—one migration," suggested quite specifically by Cavalli-Sforza, seemed implausible, as did his analogy between principal components and an archaeological stratigraphy. He and his colleagues arranged principal components in temporal succession, according to their magnitude. The first PC, the supposed Neolithic southeast-northwest gradient, came first, accounting for about 27% of the total variation. The third, running east-west, was attributed to Gimbutas's Proto-Indo-European Kurgan warriors and other invaders from the steppes, and the fourth was ascribed to Greek colonization of the eastern Mediterranean. The second, showing a southwest-northeast gradient and accounting for about 22% of the variation, was thought to be problematic because no plausible demographic explanation in the appropriate time frame (between the early Neolithic and the Bronze Age) could be divined for it. It now seems surprising that the suggestion that the second component might have been in part the result of the Lateglacial re-expansions across Europe from the southwest was not mooted until 1998 (Torroni et al. 1998). Cavalli-Sforza and his colleagues were not ignorant of Palaeolithic processes in Europe, but the fallacious idea that the magnitude of the PCs reflected their age was a blinker to the full range of explanatory possibilities.

Further critiques of the wave of advance have been mounted on archaeological grounds. In the first place, the radiocarbon map of Neolithic spread used by Ammerman & Cavalli-Sforza (1984) was flawed in a number of ways, and the Neolithic package they had used to map the expansion was gradually picked apart. Whereas Ammerman and Cavalli-Sforza took the package as comprising domesticated cereals and animals, ceramics, and so on, various authors showed that these items rarely moved together, except in southeast and central Europe, and that they might often be exchanged into Mesolithic communities (Thomas 1996, Price 2000a). This work suggested that Ammerman and Cavalli-Sforza's strategy of using the presence of pottery, for example, to identify a settlement as "Neolithic" (adopted to maximize the number of sites included) may have led them to overestimate the Neolithic impact and the uniformity of its spread (Zvelebil 1986). Although Ammerman & Cavalli-Sforza (1984) did emphasize that their rate was merely an average, the whole thrust of the wave of advance model was to impose uniformity on the process. Archaeologists now widely agree that the process was very heterogeneous and that there is no evidence in the archaeological record for large-scale continent-wide immigration (e.g., Pluciennik 1998, Zvelebil 2000). Indeed, detailed studies of northern Europe suggest, in fact, that the Neolithic developed in many areas over a very long period of time and did not arrive in the Baltic region, for example, until well into the Bronze Age or even the Iron Age (Zvelebil 1993, 1998b).

Ammerman and Cavalli-Sforza's coupling of Neolithic populations with high population density and Mesolithic ones with low density has been another casualty of further research. Despite the enormous growth potential of agricultural populations—the rationale for the wave of advance—the archaeological and palynological records suggest that this was never remotely approached during the Neolithic itself. Early Neolithic communities in Europe are likely to have been quite small-scale and mobile (Willis & Bennett 1994; van Andel & Runnels 1995; Roberts 1998, pp. 154–58). By contrast, lacustrine, riverine, and coastal Mesolithic communities are likely to have been home to affluent, complex foraging communities, with much greater population densities and a much higher degree of sedentism than used to be assumed. Ethnographic comparisons with Australian aborigines, or the southern African Khoisan-speaking hunter-gatherers, for example, seem to have been inappropriate for these parts of Mesolithic Europe; comparisons with Northwest Coast Native Americans, for example, now seem more suitable (Zvelebil 1986). In this light, the Mesolithic should not be regarded as a mere prelude to the Neolithic revolution but as a western alternative to it. The situation in the forested interior of central Europe, where the Neolithic is known to have spread extremely rapidly, is much less clear: Mesolithic remains are still scanty in these areas. However, it is curious that in this particular case—in which colonization is almost universally accepted to be the best explanation of the archaeological record (the Bandkeramik or LBK horizon)—the spread was in fact far more rapid than the average rate estimated by Ammerman & Cavalli-Sforza (1984) (Gronenborn 1999, Bogucki 2000, Price 2000b). The same is true for the appearance of Cardial ware in the western Mediterranean, which is also thought likely to represent a case of colonization, in this case by sea (Barnett 2000; Zilhão 2000, 2001).

MOLECULAR-GENETIC APPROACHES

Since Cavalli-Sforza and his colleagues formulated their views, it has not only been archaeologists who have moved on. There has also, of course, been a revolution in the study of the human genome. In the 1980s, it became possible to analyze not merely the products of certain genes, as had been done in the "classical" analyses, but also the DNA sequences of the genes themselves. In particular, attention has focused on the two non-recombining genetic loci in humans: the mitochondrial DNA (mtDNA), which is present in both sexes but inherited only down the maternal line, and the Y chromosome, which is present only in males and inherited from father to son.

The new molecular data offer two major advantages over the "classical" approach. The first advantage is the estimation of phylogenies or genealogical trees. Both mtDNA and the Y chromosome, because they are non-recombining—so that variation is not reshuffled between lineages—can be seen as genetic systems in which mutations fall onto an independently formed genealogy: the maternal and paternal lines of descent, respectively. Whereas the genealogies of "family history" involve a substantial dose of fiction to draw attention to particular connections (because the number of ancestors of an individual burgeons alarmingly as one traces them back in time), maternal and paternal ancestry is, by contrast, clearly defined. Any sample of individual subjects will have a defined set of genealogical relations on both the maternal and paternal side so that, in principle, a tree of ancestry could be reconstructed for each. The mtDNA and the Y chromosome both allow us to estimate those trees because both systems have recorded a trace of the pattern of descent, as mutations have inscribed variants into their DNA sequences during the course of history. Because this marks a turn from the collectivist approach of classical population genetics (which necessarily defined "populations" to which allele frequencies were ascribed), it heralds a dramatic increase in resolution for processes involving individuals, such as prehistoric dispersals (Richards & Macaulay 2000). The west Eurasian part of the mtDNA tree is shown in schematic form in Figure 3 (see color insert).

The second major advantage of molecular genetics is dating. Under the neutral theory of molecular evolution, mutations fall onto the genealogy at random and therefore accumulate roughly linearly with time. Just as radiocarbon dating revolutionized archaeology, so the molecular clock has transformed population genetics by providing a timescale. Whether we have reached a stage equivalent to the calibration revolution of radiocarbon in genetics is a subject of some debate. The general consensus is that we haven't; but even so, the introduction of genetic dating does seem to be leading to the collapse of some traditional frameworks for European prehistory in a manner analogous to the famous radiocarbon tree-ring revolution (Renfrew 1973). While always advocating due caution in the interpretation of genetic dates, it is possible to argue that some systems (such as mtDNA) are reasonably well calibrated (Macaulay et al. 1997). The debate does not end here, however. There is also considerable discussion as to how molecular dates can be applied to what is still often seen as the demographic history of populations.

Although many workers have continued to apply (and develop) classical population-genetics methods of analysis to the new molecular data, the new data are different in kind and cry out for new approaches. Of course, one can continue to simply compile frequencies of different forms (or alleles) of a particular gene that are now defined by molecular data. However, the information that this can provide on demographic history is inevitably very impoverished—which is the reason Cavalli-Sforza and his colleagues had to resort to multivariate statistics when analyzing classical markers. By contrast, the non-recombining systems provide us with extremely detailed and fine-grained information about the relations between the alleles, which can be used to reconstruct the genealogical history of the locus. This has led to the development of what has been termed the phylogeographic approach (Richards et al. 1997, Bandelt et al. 2002).

Phylogeography is a heuristic tool for the interpretation of genetic data that attempts to make maximum use of reconstructed trees of descent. It employs the geographic distribution and diversity of genealogical lineages to make inferences about demographic history, in particular, range expansions, migrations, and dispersals. In other words, as Avise (2000, p. 3) has put it, phylogeography is the mapping of gene genealogies in time and space. To some extent, it can trace its ancestry not only from evolutionary genetics but also from the work of Cavalli-Sforza and his colleagues. They also mapped contemporary human genetic variation in space and attempted to interpret it in terms of prehistoric demography—indeed their approach has often been referred to as "gene geography." A subdiscipline of biogeography, phylogeography is inherently interdisciplinary, with input from, for example, molecular genetics, population genetics, phylogenetics, demography, climatology, ecology, and historical geography—plus archaeology, anthropology, and linguistics, in the case of humans, and ethology and palaeontology in the case of other species. This interdisciplinarity is obligate: Phylogeographic inferences are (at least at present) generally rather weak and acquire their force when combined in a context built from a number of disciplines. This need not entail circularity (although it is a risk to be wary of). Phylogeographic hypotheses should, in principle, be capable of testing within a preexisting model-based framework (Richards et al. 2002b). This always entails making assumptions, but the assumptions themselves can be susceptible to empirical investigation and may not always be quite as unrealistic as those of more traditional population-genetics approaches (Richards et al. 2000).

EUROPEAN MITOCHONDRIAL DNA VARIATION

Mitochondrial DNA variation in Europe was studied for the first time by a number of groups in the early 1990s, mostly focusing on sequences from the fast-evolving first hyper-variable segment of the mtDNA control region (HVS-I). Initially, it seemed that the European mtDNA landscape might be so flat as to be almost entirely uninformative with respect to European prehistory (Pult et al. 1994). For example, an attempt by Simoni et al. (2000), using spatial autocorrelation, indicated no southeast-northwest gradient but only a weak gradient along the northern Mediterranean (but see Torroni et al. 2000 for a discussion of flaws hampering this analysis). This finding led to the suggestion that mtDNA may not be a useful demographic marker system, perhaps because of selection or high rates of female gene flow in recent times.

The problem was overcome by supplementing HVS-I data with additional informative variants from the coding region (Torroni et al. 1994, 1996; Macaulay et al. 1999). In this way, mtDNA variation can be dissected into genealogical clades (or haplogroups), which are now strongly supported by analyses of the complete mtDNA genome (Finnilä et al. 2001, Richards & Macaulay 2001) (Figure 3). As shown by Richards et al. (2002a), mtDNA dissected simply into major haplogroups on this basis shows a genetic cline with the Near East at one pole and the Basque country at the other, accounting for 51% of the total variation (Figure 4). The second PC (after subtracting recently migrated African haplogroups) represents the European mtDNAs as a subset of Near Eastern variation. The first PC of mtDNA looks rather similar to the first PC displayed by classical markers: Central and Mediterranean populations group closer to those of the Near

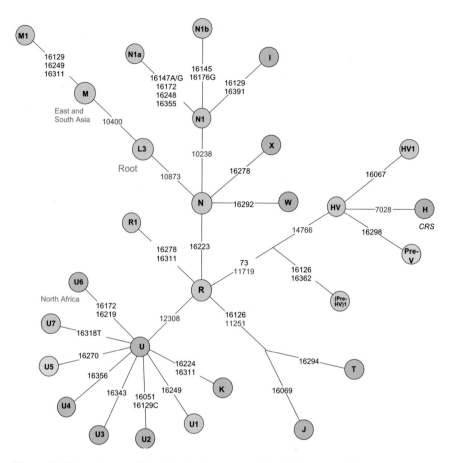

Figure 3 The major west Eurasian haplogroups and their distribution within Europe and the Near East, on the basis of the data in Richards et al. (2000, 2002a). Blue = largely Near Eastern; yellow = largely European; green = found at similar levels in both the Near East and Europe; grey = non-European or undefined. The circles indicate haplogroups, and the branch labels indicate some of the defining mutations of each haplogroup. Numbers in black indicate variants from the CRS at control-region sites, and numbers in blue are coding-region sites. Variants are transitions unless otherwise specified. CRS, Cambridge reference sequence (Anderson et al. 1981).

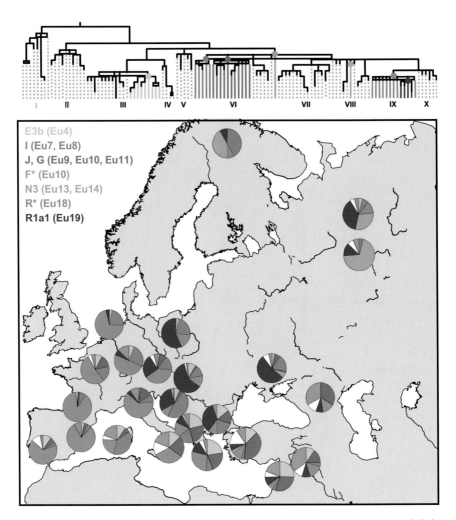

Figure 6 Maximum parsimony tree for the major Y-chromosome haplogroups and their distribution in Europe. The West Eurasian parts of the tree are highlighted and color-coded. The haplogroup nomenclature of Underhill et al. (2000) is indicated beneath the tree; that of the Y Chromosome Consortium (2002) is within the frame; and that of Semino et al. (2000) is in parentheses. See Semino et al. (2000) for further details.

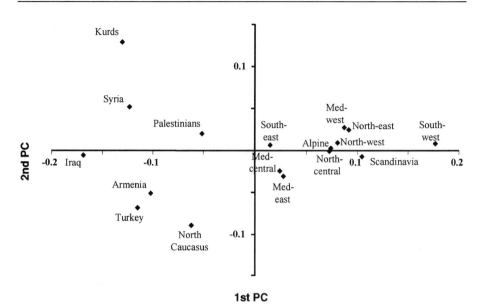

Figure 4   Plot of the first and second principal components of West Eurasian mtDNA haplogroups (after Richards et al. 2002a).

East, with the remaining European regions between these and the outlier Scandinavians and Basques. How is the pattern to be explained? To address this, much more detailed study of the geographical distribution and time depth of the lineages concerned is necessary. The analysis should not, as in the classical analyses, culminate in a PC plot, from which one reads off the prehistoric processes. With the molecular data, the PC plot is simply an impetus to further study (cf. Clark 1998).

Several novel methodological approaches came together in the analysis of European mtDNA. First, employing a new phylogenetic-network approach to tree reconstruction helped to overcome some of the problems associated with traditional phylogenetic methods, which had plagued earlier work based on human mtDNA (Bandelt et al. 1995). Furthermore, new approaches were being developed to study the colonization of a new area using molecular-genetic data. Finally, the approach pioneered by Cavalli-Sforza himself, of taking the archaeological context seriously, was an essential component.

Founder analysis, an approach for dating the colonization of a region using the molecular clock, had been developed by a number of workers, including Stoneking & Wilson (1989), Torroni et al. (1993), and Forster et al. (1996). The approach works by comparing variation in the region that has been settled (the sink population) with the variation in likely source populations, in order to identify founder types and use them to date individual migration events. This involves simply subtracting from the mutational variation in the sink population the fraction of the variation that arose in the source population and has been carried into the sink region by the founders during the colonization process. Effectively, when a founder event occurs, owing to an individual migration event from the source to the sink region, the molecular clock is reset: The descendants of that individual will be effectively members of a new lineage tracing to the time of arrival. This is the date that we are interested in because this is the date of the colonization itself. The molecular age of the founder type in the source population will necessarily be older, and perhaps very much older (Richards & Macaulay 2000).

The first results from European mtDNA (Richards et al. 1996, 1998) suggested that only a small minority of lineages dated to the Neolithic, with the remainder dating back to between 15,000 and about 50,000 years ago. The majority appeared to descend from founders of Middle or Late Upper Palaeolithic origin. These clades were strikingly star-like, indicating dramatic population expansions, which suggested that they were mainly the result of re-expansions in the Lateglacial or Postglacial period. The results were, however, rather tentative because they were reliant on comparisons with a very small and inadequate sample from the Near East.

Further work confirmed these outlines, however. Torroni and his colleagues (1998, 2001), focusing on a particular mtDNA clade known as haplogroup V, have shown that there were indeed dramatic Lateglacial expansions from southwest Europe that repopulated much of the continent from about 15,000 years ago. This is supported by recent work on archaeological dates (Housley et al. 1997, Richards et al. 2003). Moreover, as Torroni et al. (1998) pointed out, Lateglacial re-expansions from the southwest provided a plausible explanation for the mysterious second principal component of classical markers, which was oriented southwest-northeast (Figure 2).

In the meantime, Richards et al. (2000) have used a greatly improved Near Eastern mtDNA database, as well as a more sophisticated founder analysis, to quantify the proportions of lineages surviving from the various major dispersal phases in European prehistory. Although it is difficult to extrapolate to the scale of the immigration at the time, it is possible to estimate the proportion of lineages in the modern population that descend from one or another immigration event. Therefore, at least, the question of "farmers our ancestors" could be addressed.

In this analysis, the long-term complexity of interactions between Europe and the Near East, including what appeared to be substantial back-migration from Europe into the Near East, was a major complicating factor (in comparison with analyses of Native Americans, for example). Furthermore, there was the problem of the high rate of mutation in HVS-I, mimicking founder types by recurrent mutation. It was therefore necessary to perform the analysis in a number of different ways that allowed for these complicating factors. In fact, though, the outcomes were reassuringly similar across the different criteria used.

Under the most plausible set of assumptions, three quarters of the modern mtDNA lineages could be traced to just eleven ancestors (the remaining quarter comprising a much larger set of minor founders) (Figure 5). Under various criteria, the putative Neolithic component in modern Europe—that is to say, those lineages that appeared from the Near East about 9000 years ago—occurs at between

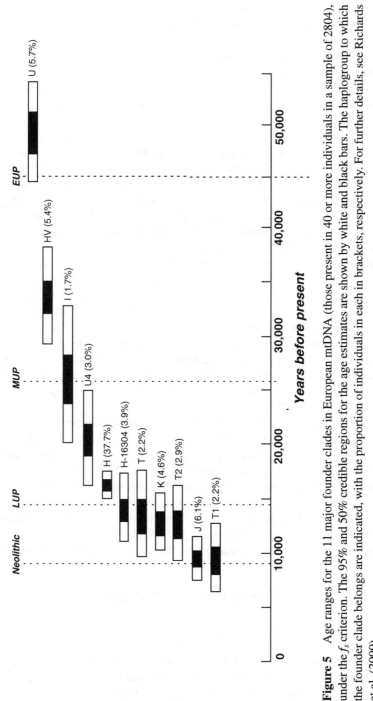

Figure 5   Age ranges for the 11 major founder clades in European mtDNA (those present in 40 or more individuals in a sample of 2804), under the f_s criterion. The 95% and 50% credible regions for the age estimates are shown by white and black bars. The haplogroup to which the founder clade belongs are indicated, with the proportion of individuals in each in brackets, respectively. For further details, see Richards et al. (2000).

12% and 23%; the best estimate would be around 13%. The Early Upper Palae-olithic component was between 2% and 17%, with a most likely value of about 7% or slightly more. Lateglacial expansions were conflated with preceding Middle Upper Palaeolithic immigration; but, between them, they accounted for about two thirds of modern lineages. It appeared that, on the maternal line of descent, only a minority of European ancestors were Near Eastern farmers; in the main, they were indigenous European hunter-gatherers and foragers, who adopted farming later on.

The detailed analysis of these lineages allows us to interpret the mtDNA PC plot in an informed way. The main contributing clades to the first PC are haplogroups H, pre-V, and U5, concentrated at the European pole, and (pre-HV)1 and U1, con-centrated at the Near Eastern pole. The founder analysis suggests that haplogroup U5 appeared in Europe very early, about 45,000 years ago, whereas haplogroups H and pre-V arrived in Europe during the Middle Upper Palaeolithic and re-expanded after the Last Glacial Maximum. Their geographical distributions support this sce-nario. Haplogroups U5 and V are predominantly European, whereas haplogroups (pre-HV)1 and U1 are predominantly Near Eastern, with some probably recent gene flow along the Mediterranean. Haplogroup H is the most frequent cluster in both Europe and the Near East, but it occurs at frequencies of only around 25%–30% in the Near East; whereas its frequency is about 45%–50% in most European populations, reaching about 60% in the Basque country. It is most frequent in western Europe and least frequent in the Near East: quite the opposite of what one would expect had it been distributed by demic diffusion during the Neolithic. Indeed, the founder analysis suggests that the main Neolithic founders are likely to have been members of haplogroups J and T1; neither of these is a determining factor in the first PC.

Furthermore, the pattern of the first PC of mtDNA indicates similarity between Europeans and Near Easterners primarily along the Mediterranean, whereas ar-chaeological evidence would suggest that the main expansion is likely to have been into the Balkans and thence into central Europe. The founder analysis of mtDNA suggests that the similarities along the Mediterranean may be due, at least in part, to substantial recent gene flow rather than solely to the Neolithic expansion. The (pre-HV)1 clade, however, may well have spread along the Mediterranean during the Neolithic. This idea suggests that the first PC of mtDNA is indeed a palimpsest, witness to some processes more recent than the Neolithic and some more ancient.

CRITICISMS OF THE MITOCHONDRIAL DNA WORK

The mtDNA work has been criticized from a traditional population-genetics per-spective by a number of authors (Cavalli-Sforza & Minch 1997; Barbujani et al. 1998; Chikhi et al. 1998, 2002; Barbujani & Bertorelle 2001). The common thread in these critiques is that "the age of a population is not the age of the common molecular ancestor of its set of DNA sequences" (Barbujani & Chikhi 2000), with the implication being that this point has been somehow missed in the analysis. As we have seen, however, this is hardly the case: Founder analysis was explicitly designed to get around this problem (Richards et al. 2000, Richards & Macaulay 2000).

Chikhi et al. (1998) developed a dating approach based on population splits. They used spatial autocorrelation to show that geographical gradients were present not only in classical markers but also in seven autosomal molecular marker systems. Although they did not identify the direction of these clines, they interpreted them as indicating a directional expansion. Of course, simply identifying clines does not tell us anything about when they were generated. More specifically, however, on the evidence of population divergence times estimated from four microsatellite loci, they argued that the clines were the result of Neolithic demic diffusion from the Near East into Europe. This argument was made on the grounds that most of the population splits were estimated to be very recent. In fact, the great majority appeared to be less than 1000 years—not Neolithic at all—and splits involving the supposedly pre-Neolithic Basques did not feature among the very few ancient splits identified, which mostly involved the Saami. However, Saami mtDNA lineages have undergone very severe founder effects, and it is this feature, rather than some innate Palaeolithic qualities that other Europeans lack, that causes them to stand out (Torroni et al. 1998). Such an approach should, at least, allow for regions where the Neolithic is most likely to have been indigenous, such as Iberia and Scandinavia, to act as controls; at the least, these regions should indicate high time depths. But this was not the case in these analyses, which ignore the archaeological evidence in an attempt to read the demographic history directly from the genetic-distance matrices.

In fact, similar results would be obtained from the mtDNA data. Genetic distances can only be used to estimate the time to population fissions under very particular circumstances: The ancestral and daughter populations have to be constant and equal in size, at least for relatively recent events, with no subsequent gene flow. These conditions are hardly likely to be remotely approached for human groups, which have usually undergone founder effects and expansions through time, not to mention multiple fissions and fusions and frequent exchange of genes. As Bandelt et al. (2002) have shown, a similar approach would identify both the Basque and Korean gene pools as having been formed as a result of Neolithic demic diffusion from the Near East.

A subsequent analysis (Barbujani & Bertorelle 2001), this time using haplotype matching to estimate population divergences, similarly placed most of them in the Bronze Age (hence interpreted as supporting Neolithic demic diffusion). It is curious that this analysis relied on a model of exponential expansion over the last 40,000 years (again ignoring archaeological evidence to the contrary), rather than constant size as in the previous analysis, in order to draw the same conclusion (Bandelt et al. 2002).

Perhaps the most important question for the founder analysis concerns the statistical validity of the results, since the analysis relies on the sample size in the source population being adequate to identify all of the most important founder types. Although the founder analysis described here was not sufficiently automated to allow for a resampling test (such as the bootstrap), Richards et al. (2000) did perform a reanalysis in which half of the source data were omitted. This gave very similar results (particularly for the Neolithic contribution) to the analyses using the full source data. This reanalysis uses only the core Fertile Crescent data, omitting Anatolia, Egypt, and the southern Caucasus. It may also help, therefore, to address the Eurocentric bias of the main analyses, drawing as they do sharp dividing lines between "Europe" and the "Near East" at the Bosporus and Caucasus mountains (M. Özdogan, personal communication).

REGIONAL VARIATION IN EUROPE

The founder analysis as described above dates the arrival of mtDNAs in Europe as a whole [or, in the case of the Lateglacial expansions, the timing of a bottleneck within Europe itself (Richards et al. 2000, 2003)]. As mentioned earlier, over the past 25 years archaeology has become much more interested in the regional variation rather than the overall process. Richards et al. (2000) therefore repeated the analysis at the regional level. It has to be stressed that this approach has several limitations. First, the results for any one region are based on fewer data and are therefore naturally associated with greater uncertainty. Second, the data are of variable quality and may poorly represent the deep ancestry of lineages within each region in some cases, such as eastern Europe and Greece. Finally, the results are, at best, estimating the proportion of lineages in the present-day population that can be attributed to each founder event from the Near East (or to bottlenecks within Europe), rather than from the immediate source region. The results are worth discussing, however, as there are both interesting congruences and some conflicts with the archaeological patterns.

   The highest Neolithic impact, according to this analysis, was on southeast Europe, central Europe, and northwest and northeast Europe, which showed values of between 15% and 22% Neolithic lineages each. The Neolithic lineages are mainly from haplogroup J and include a specific subset of J lineages, called J1a, that are restricted to this region and seem to be a marker for the LBK (*Linienbandkeramis-che Kultur*) and post-LBK dispersals (Richards et al. 1996). For southeast and central Europe, a relatively high Neolithic component is very much in agreement with the usual interpretation of the archaeological record. There is some consensus that both the Balkans Neolithic and the central European LBK were the result of direct colonization—although there is debate about the extent to which the process may have involved acculturation as well (cf. Gronenborn 1999, Tringham 2000, Budja 2001). Acculturation may also have taken place in between the two processes, where there was a substantial break in the expansion (Bogucki 2000, Zvelebil 2000). The mtDNA results suggest that colonization from (ultimately) the Near East did indeed take place and that the descendants of Near Eastern colonists are represented in the central European populations of the present day. Nevertheless, more than three quarters of the surviving lineages are the result of acculturation of indigenous foraging peoples. This finding appears to support the integrationist model described by Zvelebil (2000), which involves both pioneer "leapfrog" colonization (directed toward suitable land) and acculturation and genetic exchange across the agricultural frontier during the phase in which aspects of farming become available to the surrounding foraging populations. Strontium isotope analysis has recently suggested immigration, into LBK settlements from very early times (Bentley et al. 2002), of nonlocal people who may have been brought in from the foraging communities (Gronenborn 1999).

The presence of Near Eastern lineages at similar frequencies in the northwest, however, seems to conflict with both Zvelebil's model and the patterns of the classical markers and the Y chromosome (see below). Zvelebil suggests that a long-term frontier was established on the north European plain and that the transition to farming to the north, northwest, northeast, and southwest took place largely by acculturation. The mtDNA picture, however, suggests a value of about 20% for Near Eastern lineages in the northwest (the northeast is more equivocal because the sample may be insufficiently representative). By contrast, both classical markers and the Y chromosome indicate few or no Neolithic markers in the British Isles. In this case, it is perhaps possible that there were female-only exchanges between the post-LBK peoples of the North European plain and the northwest across the agricultural frontier (Wilson et al. 2001). Alternatively, there may have been acculturation at the LBK frontier, after which (by chance) predominantly Near Eastern mtDNAs but predominantly acculturated Y chromosomes moved on to the northwest (Renfrew 2001). Finally, it is possible that the mtDNA lineages were dispersed into the northwest by later processes.

There are fewer Neolithic-derived lineages along the Mediterranean and the Atlantic west, at around 10%, again mainly from haplogroup J. The sample from the eastern Mediterranean is rather small and poorly provenanced but would be compatible with maritime colonization of Greece by Near Eastern pioneer groups (Perlès 2001). Again, there appear to be some mtDNAs that are regionally specific, such as J1b1 along the Atlantic facade. This brings to mind the archaeological view of some colonization alongside acculturation of quite dense, sedentary Mesolithic communities (Barnett 2000; Zilhão 2000, 2001). The Basque region, which was an outlier in the PC analyses of both mtDNA and classical markers, has the lowest Neolithic component, at around 7%. The Basque outlier status may therefore be partly the result of reduced Neolithic penetration, as well as considerable genetic drift due to isolation and small population size. They are little more of a Mesolithic relict than any other European population.

A striking, if perhaps unsurprising, result of the analysis was that there have been very high levels of more recent gene flow in the eastern Mediterranean. In fact, in Greece approximately 20% of lineages have a recent Near Eastern origin. Similarly, in many parts of the Near East, back-migration of lineages from Europe is estimated to be approximately 20%.

Y-CHROMOSOME VARIATION AND THE NEOLITHIC

Around the same time as the early mtDNA work was being published, a number of studies were also attempting to dissect Paleolithic and Neolithic Y-chromosome lineages within Europe. Semino et al. (1996) identified candidates both for an indigenous European clade of lineages, now known as paragroup R* (in the nomenclature of the Y Chromosome Consortium 2002; see also Hammer & Zegura 2002), and a likely Near Eastern Neolithic component, now called haplogroup J (by analogy with the most common putative Neolithic marker in the mtDNA). The Y-chromosome haplogroup J showed a cline similar to Cavalli-Sforza's first PC for the classical markers, whereas R* was most common in western Europe and declined moving east. The highest diversity of haplogroup J appears to be in the Fertile Crescent, possibly Iran (Quintana-Murci et al. 2001).

The work has been developed in more genealogical detail by Semino et al. (2000) (Figure 6, see color insert) using a large series of new markers discovered by Underhill et al. (2000), with fewer markers but many more samples by Rosser et al. (2000), and with greater focus by Scozzari et al. (2001). These studies confirm that the most common diagnostic Near Eastern haplogroups are haplogroup J, referred to above, and haplogroup E3b. Both J and E3b display declining gradients moving from the Near East to Europe, and both may have potentially been spread with the Neolithic. This would imply a Near Eastern Neolithic contribution to Europe, as a whole, of about 20%–25%, similar to the estimates from mtDNA (Semino et al. 2000).

This work has been recently criticized by Chikhi et al. (2002), who have reanalyzed the Y-chromosome data set of Semino et al. (2000) using an admixture approach. They suggested that the Neolithic contribution is much higher—in fact, greater than 50% in most parts of Europe, rather than <25% overall. However, to claim this they have had to assume that the various parts of Europe were formed by a unitary Palaeolithic component (represented by modern Basques or Sardinians), admixing with a unitary Near Eastern component (represented by the modern Near East). No allowance was made for back-migration into the Near East, which the mtDNA data shows has been considerable (Richards et al. 2000). Even when allowing for the implausibility of these assumptions, their approach does not avoid the pitfall of the original classical analyses: the lack of a time scale. Therefore, it seems very unlikely that their analysis improves on the more straightforward approach taken by Semino and her colleagues.

Strangely, however, both of the putative Neolithic Y-chromosome haplogroups are more common along the Mediterranean than in central Europe. This picture differs somewhat both from the mtDNA picture described above and the usual understanding of the archaeological evidence, in which the most likely parts of Europe to have been colonized by substantial numbers of Neolithic immigrants are often thought to be southeast and central Europe. Moreover, without a founder analysis, it is possible that earlier and later processes may be conflated. For example, the mtDNA results suggest substantial very recent gene flow from Turkey to

Greece; this would appear as Neolithic in the calculations of Semino et al. (2000). This is the palimpsest problem all over again.

The issue has been addressed in part by King & Underhill (2002), not by means of a founder analysis (which would require more Y-chromosome data than presently exists) but by using an innovative combination of archaeology and genetics. They have compiled a database of painted pottery and anthropomorphic clay figurines from the Near East. These are thought to have originated in the Pre-Pottery Neolithic B (PPNB) phase of the Levantine and Anatolian Neolithic and to have been carried westward with the Neolithic into parts of Europe, including Greece and the Balkans, as far as the Danube basin and the central Mediterranean coastline. King & Underhill tested the geographical distribution of these artefacts for correlation with the distribution of Y-chromosome lineages. Haplogroup E3b (referred to by them as Eu4) and one subclade within haplogroup J (their Eu9) correlated strongly with the distribution of the archaeological markers. Another subclade within haplogroup J correlated with figurines only, which are more widely dispersed than the painted pottery. However, the western Mediterranean displayed the Near Eastern Y-chromosome lineages but no archaeological correlate. King & Underhill therefore suggested that these latter areas might indeed represent more recent gene flow from the eastern Mediterranean, such as Greek or Phoenician colonization. In cases where the correlation held, they proposed that the Near Eastern lineages could indeed be taken as a signal of Neolithic dispersals or of some other kind of demographic interactions with the PPNB Near East. Furthermore, at least some of the Near Eastern Y-chromosome types in the areas of Neolithic artefacts are also likely to have arrived more recently, and perhaps also even earlier, than the Neolithic (cf. also Malaspina et al. 2001). However, it is also possible that Neolithic colonization of the Mediterranean from the Near East involved maritime pioneers who were predominantly male and that may also help to explain the much higher male contribution of Neolithic lineages in the east and central Mediterranean (Perlès 2001). Overall, it seems fair to say that the mtDNA and the Y chromosome do indeed appear to be moving toward a consensus, consistent with the archaeological evidence, on the scale of Neolithic ancestry in modern Europe (Lell & Wallace 2000).

MODES OF DISPERSAL

It appears, therefore, that the overall Neolithic contribution to modern Europeans is somewhere between 12% and 23% on the female side, with the most likely value being about 13%. It is probably somewhat less than 22% on the male side, depending on how much overwriting there has been in recent times with Near Eastern lineages in southern Europe. From both perspectives, it is clear that the ancestry of the majority of lineages predates the Neolithic in Europe, stretching back to the Last Glacial Maximum and beyond. What is true of the non-recombining marker systems is likely to be true for the autosomal genes as well, and indeed it seems that this may not be inconsistent with the PC maps of classical markers (Cavalli-Sforza & Minch 1997).

What about the demographic mechanisms involved with the arrival of the Neolithic? Renfrew (2001) has pointed out that even the rapid decline in Near Eastern lineages witnessed on the Y chromosome as one crosses into Europe is not inconsistent with the wave of advance model—although the mtDNA pattern is difficult to reconcile with it. But the range of possible models to consider is now much greater than in 1984. Zvelebil (2000) has listed seven possible mechanisms. These are:

1. folk migration, the traditional migrationist explanation: the directional movement of a whole population from one region to another, leading to genetic replacement;

2. demic diffusion by means of a wave of advance;

3. elite dominance, in which a social elite penetrates an area and imposes a new culture on the local population;

4. infiltration of a community by small numbers of specialists fulfilling a particular need, such as livestock farmers;

5. leapfrog colonization by small groups targeting optimal areas to form an enclave surrounded by indigenous inhabitants;

6. frontier mobility, or exchange between farmers and foragers at agricultural frontier zones; and

7. regional contact, involving trade and exchange of ideas.

Clearly, item 1 would involve genetic replacement—the classic migrationist position. Item 7 would involve no movement of genes whatsoever—referred to by some as indigenism (Ammerman 1989). Indigenism includes both cultural diffusion, championed in the 1980s by Dennell (1983), Barker (1985), and Whittle (1996), and a position more akin to separate development, in which the social and ideological, rather than economic, aspects of the Neolithic are regarded as central (e.g., Hodder 1990; Thomas 1996, 1998).

However, items 2–6 would all involve the arrival of new genetic lineages in an area and the eventual acculturation of the indigenous communities: Zvelebil's integrationism. Elite dominance would likely show little evidence of the newcomers and might be unlikely in any case to be relevant in the early Neolithic (Renfrew 1987). The wave of advance model would predict continent-wide genetic clines, as Ammerman & Cavalli-Sforza (1984) showed. There are clines in some classical markers, but those on the Y chromosome believed to associate specifically with the Neolithic fall off steeply, and clines are not evident in the putative Neolithic mtDNAs. Infiltration and leapfrog colonization would be likely to leave traces in the regions where they had occurred but not in the form of clear clines. Frontier mobility would allow for genetic exchange between colonized, newly Neolithic areas such as central Europe and forager strongholds to the north and west. This pattern indeed fits the mtDNA evidence but not exactly in the way that Zvelebil predicted. The northwest of Europe has virtually equilibrated with central Europe with respect to its maternal Neolithic lineages, whereas Iberia and Scandinavia do indeed have a reduced proportion of Neolithic mtDNAs.

Overall, the genetic evidence seems most consistent with pioneer leapfrog colonization of southeast and central Europe, with subsequent infilling acculturation of much larger numbers of indigenous foragers. If there was a wave of advance during the rapid expansion in the LBK area, it is more likely to have involved largely mtDNA and Y-chromosome lineages from assimilated Balkan foraging populations, rather than from the Near East. There seems to have been further colonization from the LBK zone into the northwest, including mainland Britain, but the pattern in Scandinavia might be explained by frontier exchange. Much of the Atlantic west (including western Britain) may also have received mtDNAs by frontier exchange, but the west seems also to have experienced distinct leapfrog colonization events from the direction of the Mediterranean coastline (presumably by boat). The movements into the northwest seem either to not have involved men or (perhaps more plausibly) to have involved male lineages that had undergone acculturation and were therefore indigenous to central Europe. In all or most regions of Europe, there seems to have been local adoption of agriculture. This implies that if, as Renfrew (1987) suggested, the Indo-European languages were also dispersed at this time, then contact-induced language change must have been an important mechanism (Zvelebil 1995b).

It is, of course, rather speculative to try and read a detailed demographic picture from the distribution of present-day genetic lineages. It should perhaps be stressed that nothing intrinsically associates any particular mtDNA, or Y chromosome, with the spread of the Neolithic. These reconstructions are made on the basis of the estimated time of arrival of particular lineages and their geographical distribution; and alternative accounts are certainly possible (Bandelt et al. 2002). For example, it is possible that the initial wave of Neolithic expansion in Europe was entirely the result of cultural diffusion and that it was followed by the lineages we now regard as Neolithic as new social networks were established and men and women moved along them (cf. Budja 2001). Any reconstructions suggested today are likely to become as outmoded as the wave of advance as more detailed accounts become possible by combining regional archaeological and genetic information at an ever-increasing level of resolution. At the more general level, though, it is possible to claim there has been a major shift in opinion on the ancestry of Europeans, driven largely by the combined forces of archaeology and genetics. Near Eastern farmers played their part, but the majority of European genetic lineages have their roots in the European Palaeolithic.

ACKNOWLEDGMENTS

I am very grateful to Hans-Jürgen Bandelt, Detlef Gronenborn, Vincent Macaulay, and Alison Richards for reading and making valuable comments on the text. I thank Princeton University Press for permission to reproduce Figures 1 and 2 and Ornella Semino for permission to use and adapt Figure 6.

The *Annual Review of Anthropology* is online at http://anthro.annualreviews.org

LITERATURE CITED

Ammerman AJ. 1989. On the Neolithic transition in Europe: a comment on Zvelebil and Zvelebil (1988). *Antiquity* 63:162–65

Ammerman AJ, Cavalli-Sforza LL. 1984. *The Neolithic Transition and the Genetics of Populations in Europe.* Princeton, NJ: Princeton Univ. Press

Anderson S, Bankier AT, Barrell BG, de Bruijn MHL, Coulson AR, et al. 1981. Sequence and organization of the human mitochondrial genome. *Nature* 290:457–65

Avise JC. 2000. *Phylogeography.* Cambridge, MA: Harvard Univ. Press

Bandelt H-J, Forster P, Sykes BC, Richards MB. 1995. Mitochondrial portraits of human populations using median networks. *Genetics* 141:743–53

Bandelt H-J, Macaulay VA, Richards MB. 2002. What molecules can't tell us about the spread of languages and the Neolithic. In *Origins and Dispersals of Agricultural Societies and Language Families,* ed. C Renfrew, P Bellwood, pp. 99–107. Cambridge, UK: McDonald Inst. Archaeol. Res.

Barbujani G, Bertorelle G. 2001. Genetics and the population history of Europe. *Proc. Natl. Acad. Sci. USA* 98:22–25

Barbujani G, Bertorelle G, Chikhi L. 1998. Evidence for Paleolithic and Neolithic gene flow in Europe. *Am. J. Hum. Genet.* 62:488–91

Barbujani G, Chikhi L. 2000. Genetic population structure of Europeans inferred from nuclear and mitochondrial DNA polymorphisms. See Renfrew & Boyle 2000, pp. 119–29

Barker G. 1985. *Prehistoric Farming in Europe.* Cambridge, UK: Cambridge Univ. Press

Barnett WK. 2000. Cardial pottery and the agricultural transition in Mediterranean Europe. See Price 2000c, pp. 93–116

Bentley RA, Price TD, Luning J, Gronenborn D, Wahl J, Fullagar PD. 2002. Prehistoric migration in Europe: strontium isotope analysis

of early Neolithic skeletons. *Curr. Anthropol.* 43:799–804

Binford LR. 1968. Post-Pleistocene adaptations. In *New Perspectives in Archaeology,* ed. SR Binford, LR Binford, pp. 313–41. Chicago: Aldine

Bogucki P. 2000. How agriculture came to north-central Europe. See Price 2000c, pp. 197–218

Bradley R. 1984. *The Social Foundations of Prehistoric Britain.* New York: Longman

Budja M. 2001. The transition to farming in Southeast Europe: perspectives from pottery. In *Documenta Praehistorica XXVIII: 8th Neolithic Studies,* ed. M Budja, pp. 27–47. Ljubljana, Slovenia: Zalozila

Cavalli-Sforza LL. 1996. The spread of agriculture and nomadic pastoralism. See Harris 1996, pp. 51–69

Cavalli-Sforza LL, Menozzi P, Piazza A. 1994. *The History and Geography of Human Genes.* Princeton, NJ: Princeton Univ. Press

Cavalli-Sforza LL, Minch E. 1997. Paleolithic and neolithic lineages in the European mitochondrial gene pool. *Am. J. Hum. Genet.* 61:247–51

Chikhi L, Destro-Bisol G, Bertorelle G, Pascali V, Barbujani G. 1998. Clines of nuclear DNA markers suggest a largely Neolithic ancestry of the European gene pool. *Proc. Natl. Acad. Sci. USA* 95:9053–58

Chikhi L, Nichols RA, Barbujani G, Beaumont MA. 2002. Y genetic data support the Neolithic demic diffusion model. *Proc. Natl. Acad. Sci. USA* 99:11,008–13

Childe VG. 1925. *The Dawn of European Civilization.* London: Kegan Paul

Clark GA. 1998. Multivariate pattern searches, the logic of inference, and European prehistory: a comment on Cavalli-Sforza. *J. Anthropol. Res.* 54:406–11

Clark JGD. 1965. Radiocarbon dating and the expansion of farming culture from the Near

East over Europe. *Proc. Prehist. Soc.* 31:57–73

Dennell R. 1983. *European Economic Prehistory: a New Approach.* London: Acad. Press

Edmonds M, Richards C, eds. 1998. *Understanding the Neolithic of North-Western Europe.* Glasgow, UK: Cruithne Press

Finnilä S, Lehtonen MS, Majamaa K. 2001. Phylogenetic network for European mtDNA. *Am. J. Hum. Genet.* 68:1475–84

Forster P, Harding R, Torroni A, Bandelt H-J. 1996. Origin and evolution of Native American mtDNA variation: a reappraisal. *Am. J. Hum. Genet.* 59:935–45

Gamble C. 1992. Uttermost ends of the earth. *Antiquity* 66:252–310

Gronenborn D. 1999. A variation on a basic theme: the transition to farming in southern Central Europe. *J. World Prehist.* 2:23–210

Hammer MF, Zegura SL. 2002. The human Y chromosome haplogroup tree: nomenclature and phylogeography of its major divisions. *Annu. Rev. Anthropol.* 31:303–21

Harris DR, ed. 1996. *The Origins and Spread of Agriculture and Pastoralism in Eurasia.* London: UCL Press

Hines J. 1991. Reviews. *Nor. Archaeol. Rev.* 24:49–54

Hodder I. 1990. *The Domestication of Europe.* Oxford, UK: Blackwell

Housley RA, Gamble CS, Street M, Pettitt P. 1997. Radiocarbon evidence for the Lateglacial human recolonisaton of northern Europe. *Proc. Prehist. Soc.* 63:25–54

King R, Underhill P. 2002. Congruent distribution of Neolithic painted pottery and ceramic figurines with Y-chromosome lineages. *Antiquity* 76:707–14

Kohl PL, Fawcett C. 1995. *Nationalism, Politics and the Practice of Archaeology.* Cambridge, UK: Cambridge Univ. Press

Lell JT, Wallace DC. 2000. The peopling of Europe from the maternal and paternal perspectives. *Am. J. Hum. Genet.* 67:1376–81

Macaulay V, Richards M, Hickey E, Vega E, Cruciani F, et al. 1999. The emerging tree of West Eurasian mtDNAs: a synthesis of control-region sequences and RFLPs. *Am. J. Hum. Genet.* 64:232–49

Macaulay VA, Richards MB, Forster P, Bendall KA, Watson E, et al. 1997. mtDNA mutation rates—no need to panic. *Am. J. Hum. Genet.* 61:983–86

Malaspina P, Tsopanomichalou M, Duman T, Stefan M, Silvestri A, et al. 2001. A multistep process for the dispersal of a Y chromosomal lineage in the Mediterranean area. *Ann. Hum. Genet.* 65:339–49

Mallory JP. 1989. *In Search of the Indo-Europeans.* London: Thames and Hudson

Menozzi P, Piazza A, Cavalli-Sforza LL. 1978. Synthetic maps of human gene frequencies in Europeans. *Science* 201:786–92

Mourant AE. 1954. *The Distribution of the Human Blood Groups.* Oxford, UK: Blackwell

Perlès C. 2001. *The Early Neolithic in Greece.* Cambridge, UK: Cambridge Univ. Press

Pluciennik M. 1998. Deconstructing the Mesolithic–Neolithic transition. See Edmonds & Richards 1998, pp. 61–83

Price TD. 2000a. Europe's first farmers: an introduction. See Price 2000c, pp. 1–18

Price TD. 2000b. Lessons in the transition to agriculture. See Price 2000c, pp. 301–18

Price TD, ed. 2000c. *Europe's First Farmers.* Cambridge, UK: Cambridge Univ. Press

Pult I, Sajantila A, Simanainan J, Georgiev O, Schaffner W, Pääbo S. 1994. Mitochondrial DNA sequences from Switzerland reveal striking homogeneity of European populations. *Biol. Chem. Hoppe-Seyler* 375:837–40

Quintana-Murci L, Krausz C, Zerjal T, Sayer SH, Hammer MF, et al. 2001. Y-chromosome lineages trace diffusion of people and languages in southwestern Asia. *Am. J. Hum. Genet.* 68:537–42

Renfrew C. 1973. *Before Civilization.* London: Penguin

Renfrew C. 1987. *Archaeology and Language.* Harmondsworth, UK: Penguin

Renfrew C. 1998. Comments on Cavalli–Sforza and Otte. *J. Anthropol. Res.* 54:417–19

Renfrew C. 2001. From molecular genetics to

archaeogenetics. *Proc. Natl. Acad. Sci. USA* 98:4830–32

Renfrew C, Boyle K, eds. 2000. *Archaeogenetics: DNA and the Population Prehistory of Europe.* Cambridge, UK: McDonald Inst.

Richards M, Côrte-Real H, Forster P, Macaulay V, Wilkinson-Herbots H, et al. 1996. Paleolithic and neolithic lineages in the European mitochondrial gene pool. *Am. J. Hum. Genet.* 59:185–203

Richards M, Gamble C, Davies W, Pettitt P. 2003. Upper Palaeolithic refugia: genetic and archaeological perspectives. In *The Genetic Revolution and Archaeology*, ed. C Gosden, M Richards, R Ward. Oxford, UK: Oxford Univ. Press. In press

Richards M, Macaulay V. 2000. Genetic data and the colonization of Europe: genealogies and founders. See Renfrew & Boyle 2000, pp. 139–51

Richards M, Macaulay V. 2001. The mitochondrial gene tree comes of age. *Am. J. Hum. Genet.* 68:1315–20

Richards M, Macaulay V, Hickey E, Vega E, Sykes B, et al. 2000. Tracing European founder lineages in the Near Eastern mitochondrial gene pool. *Am. J. Hum. Genet.* 67:1251–76

Richards M, Macaulay V, Sykes B, Pettitt P, Hedges R, et al. 1997. Reply to Cavalli-Sforza and Minch. *Am. J. Hum. Genet.* 61:251–54

Richards M, Macaulay V, Torroni A, Bandelt H-J. 2002a. In search of geographical patterns in European mtDNA. *Am. J. Hum. Genet.* 71:1168–74

Richards MB, Macaulay VA, Bandelt H-J. 2002b. Analyzing genetic data in a model-based framework: inferences about European prehistory. In *Origins and Dispersals of Agricultural Societies and Language Families*, ed. C Renfrew, P Bellwood. Cambridge, UK: McDonald Inst. Archaeol. Res. pp. 459–66

Richards MB, Macaulay VA, Bandelt H-J, Sykes BC. 1998. Phylogeography of mitochondrial DNA in western Europe. *Ann. Hum. Genet.* 62:241–60

Roberts N. 1998. *The Holocene.* Oxford, UK: Blackwell

Rosser ZH, Zerjal T, Hurles ME, Adojaan M, Alavantic D, et al. 2000. Y-chromosomal diversity in Europe is clinal and influenced primarily by geography, rather than language. *Am. J. Hum. Genet.* 67:1526–43

Scozzari R, Cruciani F, Pangrazio A, Santolamazza P, Vona G, et al. 2001. Human Y-chromosome variation in the western Mediterranean area: implications for the peopling of the region. *Hum. Immunol.* 62:871–84

Semino O, Passarino G, Brega A, Fellous M, Santachiara-Benerecetti S. 1996. A view of the neolithic demic diffusion in Europe through two Y chromosome-specific markers. *Am. J. Hum. Genet.* 59:964–68

Semino O, Passarino G, Oefner PJ, Lin AA, Arbuzova S, et al. 2000. The genetic legacy of Paleolithic *Homo sapiens sapiens* in extant Europeans: a Y chromosome perspective. *Science* 290:1155–59

Sherratt A, Sherratt S. 1988. The archaeology of Indo-European: an alternative view. *Antiquity* 62:584–95

Simoni L, Calafell F, Pettener D, Bertranpetit J, Barbujani B. 2000. Geographic patterns of mtDNA diversity in Europe. *Am. J. Hum. Genet.* 66:262–78

Sokal RR, Harding RM, Oden NL. 1989. Spatial patterns of human gene frequencies in Europe. *Am. J. Phys. Anthropol.* 80:267–94

Sokal RR, Oden NL, Wilson C. 1991. Genetic evidence for the spread of agriculture in Europe by demic diffusion. *Nature* 351:143–45

Stoneking M, Wilson AC. 1989. Mitochondrial DNA. In *The Colonization of the Pacific: a Genetic Trail*, ed. AVS Hill, S Serjeantson, pp. 215–45. Oxford, UK: Oxford Univ. Press

Thomas J. 1996. The cultural context of the first use of domesticates in continental Central and Northwest Europe. See Harris 1996, pp. 310–22

Thomas J. 1998. Towards a regional geography of the Neolithic. See Edmonds & Richards 1998, pp. 37–60

Torroni A, Bandelt H-J, D'Urbano L, Lahermo

P, Moral P, et al. 1998. mtDNA analysis reveals a major late Paleolithic population expansion from southwestern to northeastern Europe. *Am. J. Hum. Genet.* 62:1137–52

Torroni A, Bandelt H-J, Macaulay V, Richards M, Cruciani F, et al. 2001. A signal, from human mtDNA, of postglacial recolonization in Europe. *Am. J. Hum. Genet.* 69:844–52

Torroni A, Huoponen K, Francalacci P, Petrozzi M, Morelli L, et al. 1996. Classification of European mtDNAs from an analysis of three European populations. *Genetics* 144:1835–50

Torroni A, Lott MT, Cabell MF, Chen YS, Lavergne L, Wallace DC. 1994. mtDNA and the origin of Caucasians: identification of ancient Caucasian-specific haplogroups, one of which is prone to a recurrent somatic duplication in the D-loop region. *Am. J. Hum. Genet.* 55:760–76

Torroni A, Richards M, Macaulay V, Forster P, Villems R, et al. 2000. mtDNA haplogroups and frequency patterns in Europe. *Am. J. Hum. Genet.* 66:1173–77

Torroni A, Schurr TG, Cabell MF, Brown MD, Neel JV, et al. 1993. Asian affinities and continental radiation of the four founding Native American mtDNAs. *Am. J. Hum. Genet.* 53:563–90

Trigger BG. 1989. *A History of Archaeological Thought.* Cambridge, UK: Cambridge Univ. Press

Tringham R. 2000. Southeastern Europe in the transition to agriculture to Europe: bridge, buffer, or mosaic. See Price 2000c, pp. 19–56

Underhill PA, Shen P, Lin AA, Jin L, Passarino G, et al. 2000. Y chromosome sequence variation and the history of human populations. *Nat. Genet.* 26:358–61

van Andel TH, Runnels CN. 1995. The earliest farmers in Europe. *Antiquity* 68:481–500

Whittle A. 1996. *Europe in the Neolithic.* Cambridge, UK: Cambridge Univ. Press

Willis KJ, Bennett KD. 1994. The Neolithic transition—fact or fiction? Palaeoecological evidence from the Balkans. *The Holocene* 4:326–30

Wilson JF, Weiss DA, Richards M, Thomas MG, Bradman N, Goldstein DB. 2001. Genetic evidence for different male and female roles during cultural transitions in the British Isles. *Proc. Natl. Acad. Sci. USA* 98:5078–83

The Y Chromosome Consort. 2002. A nomenclature system for the tree of human Y-chromosomal binary haplogroups. *Genome Res.* 12:339–48

Zilhão J. 2000. From the Mesolithic to the Neolithic in the Iberian peninsula. See Price 2000c, pp. 144–82

Zilhão J. 2001. Radiocarbon evidence for maritime pioneer colonisation at the origins of farming in west Mediterranean Europe. *Proc. Natl. Acad. Sci. USA* 98:14,180–85

Zvelebil M. 1986. Mesolithic prelude and neolithic revolution. In *Hunters in Transition: Mesolithic Societies of Temperate Eurasia and their Transition to Farming,* ed. M Zvelebil, pp. 5–15. Cambridge, UK: Cambridge Univ. Press

Zvelebil M. 1989. On the transition to farming in Europe, or what was spreading with the Neolithic: a reply to Ammerman (1989). *Antiquity* 63:379–83

Zvelebil M. 1993. Hunters or farmers? The Neolithic and Bronze Age societies of North-East Europe. In *Cultural Transformation and Interactions in Eastern Europe,* ed. J Chapman, P Dolukhanov, pp. 146–62. Aldershot, UK: Avebury

Zvelebil M. 1995a. Farmers our ancestors and the identity of Europe. In *Cultural Identity and Archaeology,* ed. P Graves-Brown, S Jones, C Gamble, pp. 145–66. London: Routledge

Zvelebil M. 1995b. Indo-European origins and the agricultural transition in Europe. In *Whither Archaeology?,* ed. M Kuna, N Venclova, pp. 173–203. Praha, Czech Republic: Inst. Archaeol.

Zvelebil M. 1998a. Genetic and cultural diversity of Europe: a comment on Cavalli-Sforza. *J. Anthropol. Res.* 54:411–17

Zvelebil M. 1998b. What's in a name: the Mesolithic, the Neolithic, and social change at the Mesolithic-Neolithic transition. See Edmonds & Richards 1998, pp. 1–36

Zvelebil M. 2000. The social context of the agricultural transition in Europe. See Renfrew & Boyle 2000, pp. 57–79

Zvelebil M, Zvelebil KV. 1988. Agricultural transitions and Indo-European dispersals. *Antiquity* 62:574–83

Annu. Rev. Anthropol. 2003. 32:163–81
doi: 10.1146/annurev.anthro.32.061002.093158
Copyright © 2003 by Annual Reviews. All rights reserved
First published online as a Review in Advance on June 4, 2003

THE SOCIAL BRAIN: Mind, Language, and Society in Evolutionary Perspective

R.I.M. Dunbar

*School of Biological Sciences, University of Liverpool, Biosciences Building, Crown St.,
Liverpool L69 7ZB, United Kingdom; email: rimd@liv.ac.uk*

Key Words   brain size, social cognition, theory of mind, social group size, culture

■ **Abstract**   The social brain (or Machiavellian Intelligence) hypothesis was proposed to explain primates' unusually large brains: It argues that the cognitive demands of living in complexly bonded social groups selected for increases in executive brain (principally neocortex). The evidence for this and alternative hypotheses is reviewed. Although there remain difficulties of interpretation, the bulk of the evidence comes down in favor of the social brain hypothesis. The extent to which the cognitive demands of bonding large intensely social groups involve aspects of social cognition, such as theory of mind, is explored. These findings are then related to the evolution of social group size, language, and culture within the hominid lineage.

INTRODUCTION

In the century and a half following the discovery of the first Neanderthals, the focus of palaeoanthroplogy has been on the who's who of hominid evolution. How species are defined has come to occupy the central place in that story, with anatomy perhaps inevitably being the central plank of that endeavor. As appropriate as this has been, it does overlook the fact that what makes us human is not our bodies but our minds. The story of hominid—and hence ultimately human—evolution is thus one that must be told in terms of the evolution of mind. As Lewis-Williams (2002) points out, there have been only two serious attempts to grapple with this problem (Donald 1991, Mithen 1996), and both of these have inevitably been somewhat speculative in nature. I here offer a preliminary attempt to grapple with this problem. My focus is the intersection of brain, mind, and language in hominid evolution.

Ever since Jerison's (1973) seminal study, it has been recognized that primates have unusually large brains for body size. Moreover, within the primates, some species have disproportionately large brains for body size, one of these of course being humans. In general, however, differences in brain size do not reflect proportional increases in all brain components. Rather, the size of the neocortex accounts for most of the deviation from overall trend lines (Finlay & Darlington 1995). Primates have larger brains than other species mainly because they have larger neocortices. In effect, then, when asking "Why do primates have unusually large brains?," we are really asking, "Why do primates have unusually large neocortices?"

Traditionally, the assumption has been that changes in brain evolution have been driven by the need to solve ecological problems. Jerison (1973), for example, showed that the brain sizes of ungulates (prey) and carnivores (their predators) covaried across time through the Paleogene and the Neogene, with increases in ungulate brain volume being followed later by a corresponding increase in carnivore brain size. This view has been reflected in the assumption that human intellectual abilities are principally associated with the production and use (in hunting) of tools. However, Byrne & Whiten's (1988) suggestion that primates differed from nonprimates principally in the complexity of their social skills rather than their foraging or survival skills initiated a new interest in alternative hypotheses for brain evolution in primates.

It is important to appreciate in this context that the contrast between the social and more traditional ecological/technological hypotheses is not a question of whether or not ecology influences behavior, but rather is one of whether ecological/survival problems are solved explicitly by individuals acting on their own or by individuals effecting social (e.g., cooperative) solutions to these problems. In both cases, the driving force of selection derives from ecology, but the solution (the animals' response to the problem) arises from contrasting sources with very different cognitive demands (individual skills in one case, social-cognitive skills in the other).

I first briefly summarize attempts to test between alternative hypotheses as to why some primates might have larger neocortices than others, and then I consider some of the implications of these findings for cognitive and social evolution within the hominids. In the latter respect, I consider principally the implications for social group size, language evolution, and core aspects of social cognition.

THE SOCIAL BRAIN HYPOTHESIS

Attempts to test the social brain hypothesis have focused on identifying suitable indices of social complexity and appropriate indices of brain volume against which these indices can be correlated, as well as the implications of alternative statistical procedures. I do not comment here on the latter issues: Useful reviews of methodological issues can be found in Barton & Dunbar (1997), Dunbar (1998a), Barton (1999), and Purvis & Webster (1999).

So far, five separate indices of social complexity or skill have been correlated against neocortex volume in primates. These include social group size (Sawaguchi & Kudo 1990; Dunbar 1992a, 1998a; Barton 1996; Barton & Dunbar 1997), grooming clique size (Kudo & Dunbar 2001), the extent to which social skills are used in male mating strategies (Pawlowski et al. 1997), the frequency of tactical deception (Byrne 1995, 1996), and the frequency of social play (Lewis 2001). Each of these

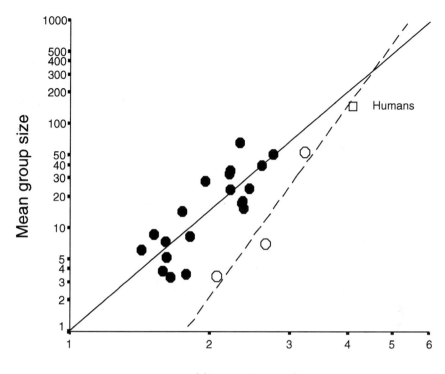

Figure 1   Mean social group size for individual primate taxa (principally, one species per genus) plotted against relative neocortex volume (indexed as neocortex volume divided by the volume of the rest of the brain). Simian (*solid symbols*) and hominoid (*open symbols*) taxa are shown separately. The datapoint for humans is that obtained by Dunbar (1992a). With a logged axis, neocortex ratio is mathematically identical to the more commonly used residuals of logged variables (except that the baseline is taken to be the value of the individual taxon's brain component rather than the scaled average value for the Order or other higher taxonomic grouping). Reproduced with permission from Barrett et al. (2002).

has yielded significant correlations with relative neocortex volume in primates and absolute neocortex volume in the case of group size. Figure 1 plots the relationship for social group size in anthropoid primates. Additional support for the hypothesis comes from two sources: (*i*) The regression equation for primates predicts group size for species not included in the original dataset from which the relationship was derived (Dunbar 1995); and (*ii*) similar relationships for social group size have been reported for carnivores and advanced (but not basal) insectivores (Dunbar & Bever 1998) and cetaceans (Morino 1996). In addition, comparable results have been reported from unpublished analyses of bats and ungulates, which suggests that this relationship may in fact be a general mammalian one.

These tests of the social brain hypothesis have, however, been based on correlational analyses and hence do not allow firm conclusions on causality to be drawn. Nonetheless, testing between competing hypotheses adds significantly to the power of any such analyses if it can be shown that only social indices yield significant relationships with brain component volumes. Dunbar (1992a, 1995) compared social group size (as a nominal index of social complexity) against four ecological indices as predictors of relative neocortex volume in primates. These included the proportion of fruit in the diet, home range size, day journey length, and the species' foraging style [in terms of Gibson's (1986) categories of extractive foraging]. Each of these focuses on a different possible ecological skill that might plausibly be implicated in primates' survival skills (e.g., the greater cognitive demands of frugivory and extractive forms of foraging or the need to manage large mental maps). These analyses yielded nonsignificant relationships between all four ecological indices and relative neocortex size (at least when ecological variables are adjusted for relative body size).

These results were subsequently confirmed in a reanalysis of the data by Deaner et al. (2000) using alternative methods for relativizing neocortex volume and alternative statistical procedures. In their analysis, the ecological variable (range size) was favored over group size only when neocortex volume was scaled against body size (an inappropriate procedure, given that body size is phenotypically more variable than brain component volumes and is hence no longer recommended as a basis for scaling in comparative analyses of the brain) and when range size was not scaled for body size (a questionable procedure because body size must have a significant grain effect on how an animal relates to its spatial environment). All other analyses confirmed that social group size is a better predictor of neocortex volume than is range size.

Reader & Laland (2002) analyzed frequencies of behavioral innovation, social learning, and tool use culled from the literature: All three indices yielded significant positive correlations with both the absolute and relative volume of executive brain (neocortex plus striate cortex) in primates, when appropriate controls are made for phylogeny and research effort (indexed as the frequencies with which individual species have been studied). They found that innovation and social learning covary across species and argued that this undermines the claim that there is an evolutionary trade-off between reliance on social experience and on individual experience. In addition, Reader & Lefebvre (2001) showed that there is no correlation between the social learning index and social group size once brain volume has been taken into account. Reader & Laland (2002) conclude that ecological factors may have been as (or more) important than social factors in primate brain evolution.

Because virtually all the instances of behavior in the Reader/Laland database relate to foraging situations, it is not safe to conclude more than that the cognitive processes underpinning "intelligent behavior" are used (or can be used) in the ecological domain (irrespective of whether the origins of brain evolution in primates have been driven by social or purely ecological forces). What these analyses do not test is whether social situations require different or greater cognitive powers (i.e., executive brain volume) than ecological problem solving. It is important to appreciate that there are two different levels at stake here: One is whether individuals use social transmission of information to solve problems of day-to-day survival and reproduction, and the other is whether individuals are able to exploit and manipulate the mind-states of other individuals in managing the social relationships on which their day-to-day survival and reproduction depend. Social learning competencies are not necessarily an appropriate index of social intelligence in the sense intended by the social brain hypothesis (which principally focuses on the ability to use knowledge about other individuals' behavior—and perhaps mind-states—to predict and manipulate those individuals' behavior). Reader & Laland's findings do, however, allow us to reject unequivocally the first of the two alternatives. In contrast, they do not allow us to dismiss the claim that ecological innovation (including tool use and social learning) is simply a by-product of having large brains (executive or otherwise) for social purposes. Following the lead in developmental psychology, there is a growing view that social intelligence may not be a special module (in the sense that language might be considered a specialized module) but rather is a reflection of the ability to use basic executive functions in a more sophisticated way (for example, by using analogical reasoning, causal analysis, and deeper time depths for predicting future events) as a result of being able to bring greater (or, in terms of the ability to interface different domains, more sophisticated) computing power to bear on the problem at hand (see Mitchell 1997; L. Barrett and R.I.M. Dunbar, submitted).

The lack of correlation between social group size and the social learning index used by Reader & Laland suggests that either (a) there may be specialist cognitive demands for purely social tasks that are not required in foraging tasks, or (b) social (but not foraging) tasks involve components not included in the executive brain. Both options receive some support from the literature. Emery & Perrett (2000) have shown that there are correlations between social group size in primates and the volume of the basolateral complex of the amygdala (which has a direct neural input into the frontal lobe of the brain, the principal seat of executive function). The amygdala (part of the ancient subcortical limbic system) is perhaps an obvious candidate for any social function because one of its more important neurological tasks is the recognition and integration of emotional cues. These are likely to be important in any social context and of rather limited relevance for any strictly foraging problem unless these have a direct emotional component (e.g., sighting a predator or conflict with a conspecific over a resource item). It is important to note that it is only the basolateral complex of the amygdala that exhibits a relationship with social group size and not either the amygdala as a whole or other complexes within that structure (Emery & Perrett 2000, Joffe & Dunbar 1997). Similarly, Joffe & Dunbar (1997) were able to show that removing the primary visual cortex (area V1) from the neocortex volume resulted in a significantly tighter correlation between social group size and the remaining non-striate cortex. Although V1 correlates with social group size, it does so only with much greater variance, and the correlation disappears altogether when non-V1 neocortex volume is partialled out. Indeed, Dunbar (2003) has since shown, using MRI-derived data on brain volume provided by Semendeferi et al. (1997), that frontal lobe volume (widely regarded as the principal site for executive cognitive function) provides an even better fit to social group size (at least for a very small sample of species, principally hominoids).

Reader & Laland's (2002) claim that ecological problem solving might have been the initial impetus that set primate brain evolution in motion does, however, merit serious consideration. They argue that ecological problem solving through behavioral flexibility may have provided the key stimulus to facilitate brain growth within the primates, thus in due course providing the opportunity to exploit the enlarged brains so derived for social purposes. This argument is not implausible. Indeed, a similar argument has been deployed by Barton (1998), who suggested that the dramatic grade shift in relative brain volume found between prosimian and anthropoid primates may owe its origin to the processing demands of color vision associated with a shift in diet from insects to fruits (and the consequent need to be able to detect ripe and unripe fruits against a vegetational background). However, the Reader & Laland (but not the Barton) argument raises questions about why primates should have been singled out in this way. Without knowing exactly where the contrasts between group size and the social learning index lie in relation to the primate phylogenetic tree, it is not possible to decide whether the lack of correlation between these two variables is due to ecological or phylogenetic grade shifts [in their analyses, Reader & Lefebvre (2001) fail to distinguish between prosimians, monkeys, and apes, all of which are now known to exhibit marked grade shifts in brain/behavior relationships; see Dunbar 1993, 1998a; Kudo & Dunbar 2001] or to a genuine discontinuity between ecological and social cognition.

ALTERNATIVE HYPOTHESES

Alternative hypotheses for the evolution of large brains in primates, which view behavioral and cognitive competences as mere by-products of having a large brain, have been proposed. For example, Sacher & Staffeldt (1974) and Martin (1981, 1984) proposed that larger-bodied species incur savings of scale that allow surplus energy to be invested into fetal brain growth in a way that is not possible for smaller-bodied species. The availability of additional brain volume for use in social contexts can thus be seen as a by-product of this brain-to-body-size relationship. However, McNab & Eisenberg (1989) showed that, within mammals, brain size adjusted for body size correlates most strongly with a species' habits and not with its metabolic rate. Similarly, Finlay & Darlington (1995, Finlay et al. 2001) have argued that ontogenetic scaling relationships between brain components are largely responsible for the apparently greater intelligence of larger-brained species.

Although the claim that brain evolution is subject to nothing other than strict scaling laws has been disputed (see Barton & Harvey 2000 and commentaries in Finlay et al. 2000), it remains reasonable to argue that ontogenetic scaling relationships of this kind play an important role in brain evolution when social or ecological selection factors demand it. Thus, when the ability to maintain large group sizes is at a selective premium, it may be necessary to enlarge the whole brain in order to be able to produce the enlarged neocortex required to support large social groups. Either way, however, neither of these developmental arguments addresses the crucial evolutionary fact that large group sizes incur significant costs, both in ecological (van Schaik 1983, Dunbar 1988, Dunbar 1992b) and reproductive terms (Dunbar 1980), not to mention the energetic costs of large brains (Aiello & Wheeler 1995). Large groups simply cannot be an unintended by-product of having a large brain because the costs of living in large groups would inevitably result in their rapid dispersal if there were no intrinsic advantages to living in large groups to offset these costs. Thus, parsimony drives us toward the view that these explanations are in fact perfectly plausible arguments about developmental constraints, but not about evolutionary processes as such. In other words, they are an essential part of the story, but the explanation for why some primates have evolved larger brains than others (or, indeed, why primates in general have larger brains than other mammals) requires something in addition.

In summary, parsimony and biological common sense would suggest that it is group size that drives brain size evolution rather than brain size driving group size and that group size itself is a response to an ecological problem [most probably predation risk (van Schaik 1983, Dunbar 1988, Hill & Dunbar 1998)]. Although the hypothesis has been tested by determining how neocortex volume constrains group size and other social indices, the evolutionary logic is that the need to main-tain coherent groups of a particular size has driven neocortex volume evolution through its demands on cognitive competences. The most succinct and parsimo-nious causal sequence with fewest unsupported assumptions is that the window of opportunity provided for more intensely bonded social groups and the social skills that underpin this was the crucial selection pressure for the evolution of large brains, even though simple ecological pressures (e.g., the shift to a more frugivo-rous diet) may have been instrumental in kicking off the process. In these terms, any associated ecological skills may be seen as the outcome of the opportunity provided by an increase in general purpose intelligence generated off the back of the social requirements. To argue the reverse sequence (that large social groups are a by-product of having evolved large brains to solve simple ecological problems) is, as with the various ontogenetic hypotheses, to leave unanswered the problem of the costs of social living.

SOCIAL VERSUS NONSOCIAL COGNITION

The relationship between indices of social competence and neocortex volume raises questions as to the cognitive mechanisms involved. Social cognition is broadly taken to be synonymous with the phenomenon known as theory of mind (or ToM), the ability to appreciate that another individual has a mind that controls its behavior that cannot be accessed directly but which can be modelled mentally (Tomasello & Call 1998). ToM emerges at an age of about 4–5 years in human children (Leslie 1987). It represents level 2 in a hierarchically reflexive sequence of reflection on belief states known generically as intentional states ["I *believe* that you *suppose* (that something is the case)" identifies two distinct belief or intentional states]. Normal adult humans have been shown to be capable of working at level 4 (Kinderman et al. 1998), but it is widely believed that monkeys can aspire only to level 1 intentionality (Tomasello & Call 1998, Povinelli 1999). However, evidence for chimpanzees (the only great ape tested so far) is ambivalent, with some studies producing negative results (Call & Tomasello 1999) and others more positive findings (Hare et al. 2000; S. O'Connell and R.I.M. Dunbar, submitted).

It is important to appreciate just what is implied by the social brain hypothesis in this particular context. The most plausible interpretation is that some aspect of neocortex size imposes a limit on the number of relationships that an individual animal can maintain as a coherent set within its mental social world. This probably does not refer to the total social group. Rather, the analyses carried out by Kudo & Dunbar (2001) suggest that it is the inner group social group that an individual primate is most concerned about. This seems to correspond to the number of key social partners an individual animal has (as defined by the number of regular grooming partners). This core social group seems to correspond to the limit on the number of individuals who are willing to act as allies during conflicts. Being able to service an effective set of alliances seems to be crucial in allowing the individual animal to maintain the larger social grouping into which it is embedded (the conventional social group).

The effectiveness of an animal's relationships with its key coalition partners appears to be a function in part of its ability to integrate these individuals into its mental social world (a cognitive problem) and the time it can afford to invest in grooming with these individuals (an ecological problem). The latter, at least, is reflected in the fact that time devoted to social grooming increases more or less linearly with social group size (at least in catarrhine primates) (Dunbar 1991); however, this investment in grooming is not evenly distributed around the group but rather becomes increasingly (and disproportionately) focused on the core partners as group size increases (Dunbar 1984, Kudo & Dunbar 2001). It seems that, as group size increases, monkeys and apes endeavor to invest increasingly heavily in their core social partners. This can be interpreted as reflecting the fact that primates need to ensure that these alliances work effectively in order to buffer themselves against the costs of group living. These costs, which increase proportionately (but not necessarily linearly) as group size increases, reflect both the ecological and reproductive costs of living in close proximity to more individuals. Direct ecological costs reflect the energetic and time costs of the increased day journey lengths needed to accommodate extra individuals' feeding requirements, whereas the indirect costs reflect the disruptions to foraging consequent of contests over access to food. For females, these latter costs may be reflected directly in reduced fertility and lower birth rates (Bowman et al. 1978, Harcourt 1987).

Note that this coalitionary effect may find expression in two alternative forms. One is that allies actually come to the aid of the individual when it is under attack. But the same functional effect would be produced simply by the presence of grooming partners acting passively to distance individuals whose physical proximity would stress the individual. Although there is unequivocal evidence for active coalitionary support from some species [e.g., gelada (Dunbar 1980, 1989)], there is equally compelling evidence to suggest that interventions of this kind may not necessarily be all that common in other species [e.g., baboons (Henzi & Barrett 1999, Barrett & Henzi 2002, Combes & Altmann 2001, Silk et al. 2003)]. Nonetheless, the functional consequences of managing group cohesion may be effected equally well by either the active or the passive route (or both).

To survive in a large primate group (and so gain the ecological advantages of group size), an animal has to engage in a sophisticated balancing act in which other group members are kept at just sufficient distance to prevent them imposing serious ecological and reproductive costs while at the same time not driving them away altogether. It is coalitions based on grooming partnerships that appear to allow monkeys and apes to do this. And these coalitions are, in turn, possible because of the social cognitive skills that allow primates to weld these miniature networks into effective social units.

Note that these analyses have all involved mean social group size for a species or genus, whereas the social brain hypothesis is couched in terms of the limits to group size. That limit is set by the point where, for any given species, social groups start to become unstable and fission rather easily. We do not at present know exactly where that value is for more than a handful of species. However, it seems intuitively likely that this value will be correlated with other demographic characteristics of that species, and hence with mean group size, thus explaining why we get the observed significant relationship with mean group size.

Dunbar (2003) has shown that achieved level of intentionality (assuming level 1 for cercopithecine monkeys, level 2 for chimpanzees, and level 4 for adult humans) correlates linearly (and very tightly) with absolute frontal lobe volume for these species, suggesting an important role for the frontal lobe in social cognition. This finding is supported by the results of brain scan studies of human subjects, which indicate that, when solving social cognition tasks, areas within the frontal lobe (specifically the left medial frontal cortex and the orbitofrontal cortex) are active (Happé et al. 1996, Baron-Cohen et al. 1994).

Two distinct views have been expressed, however, as to what ToM or other forms of social cognition actually involve. One is that social cognition consists of one or more specialized modules, most probably situated in the frontal cortex, that are explicitly dedicated to handling mind-reading. The other is that theory of mind (or ToM) itself is an emergent property of other more fundamental cognitive processes associated with executive function (Mitchell 1997). There are cogent arguments for believing that social cognition of the kind that is so fundamental to human social interaction (for review, see Barrett et al. 2002) may in fact be an emergent property of more fundamental and taxonomically widespread cognitive abilities, and that the difference lies not in specialized elements but in the way the power of an enlarged neural network allows these to be integrated and brought to bear on specific problems (see L. Barrett and R.I.M. Dunbar, submitted).

THE SOCIAL BRAIN IN HOMINID EVOLUTIONARY HISTORY

We can use the findings discussed above to throw some light on at least three key aspects of hominid evolutionary history. These are the evolution of social group size, the origins of language, and the origins of culture. I deal briefly with each in turn.

Social Group Size

Primate social groups are complex phenomena (often with several levels of organization) whose size is determined by a number of ecological, demographic, and cognitive variables (Dunbar 1996). Consequently, even though there is a typical value for any given taxon, there is considerable variation in group size across the range of habitats occupied by that taxon. The above analyses do suggest, however, that, for any given taxon, social group size is constrained by relative neocortex size, and we can use this to obtain an estimate of likely changes in group size through time within the hominid lineage. When the regression equation for primates was used to predict social group size in modern humans, it yielded a value of about 150 that turned out to be a remarkably common value at one particular level in the hierarchy of social organization in a wide range of societies (Dunbar 1992b, Hill & Dunbar 2003). This level of grouping appears to be intermediate (in terms of organizational structure) between the overnight camps typical of foraging peoples (typically 30–50) and the size of their tribal units (typically 1500–2000), and roughly equivalent to the set of individuals with whom one has a personal as opposed to formal (or impersonal) relationship (Hill & Dunbar 2003). It is equivalent, for example, to the number of people of whom one feels one can ask a favor and expect to have it granted.

Although neocortex volumes are not available for fossil organisms, Aiello & Dunbar (1993) were able to show that these could be estimated from total cranial volume (which is available for a significant number of fossils) using the scaling relationships between brain components of the kind identified by Finlay & Darlington (1995). With neocortex ratios estimated in this way, Aiello & Dunbar (1993) were able to derive a pattern for group size across hominid specimens. These group sizes are bracketed (and thus delimited) by the observed group sizes for living chimpanzees and humans. Figure 2 shows the pattern, based on a new set of analyses, in which populations rather than individuals are used as the unit of analysis and group sizes are predicted from neocortex ratio using the equation specific to hominoids from Dunbar's (1992a) original analyses. Although there are inevitably problems associated with estimating specific values in all such analyses, the important issue here is not so much individual values as the broad pattern across time, which is much less affected by these kinds of problems. This shows

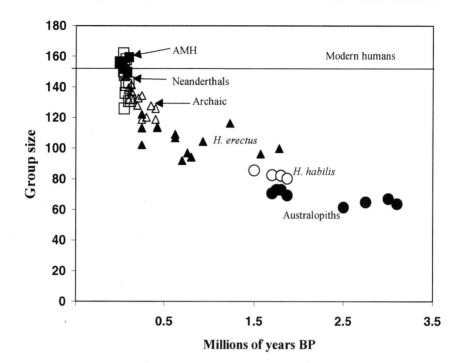

Figure 2   Social group size predicted for individual hominid populations using the regression equation for group size on neocortex ratio for hominoids (including modern humans) shown in Figure 1. The horizontal line represents the value of ~150 predicted for (and found in) modern human populations (see Dunbar 1993). Individual populations are defined as all the crania found within 50,000-year time bands at an individual site; a mean cranial volume for that population is then determined from the values for individual crania within that population. Cranial volume is used to estimate neocortex ratio using the regression equations given by Aiello & Dunbar (1993). Data from Aiello & Dunbar (1993).

that group size probably remained within the broad range for living great apes until well into the *Homo erectus* period and only began to rise significantly above this level from about 1 MY. From that point on, however, group size appears to increase at an exponential rate.

Origins of Language

These results suggest that the pressures exerted by social group size are unlikely to have started to bite until quite late in hominid evolution. Whatever mechanisms are used to bind ape social groups would have sufficed for their hominid counterparts until well into the *erectus* period. These mechanisms were, of course, principally social grooming. The upper limit on time spent grooming by any freeranging primate population is 20%. If modern humans (with their groups of about 150) bonded their social groups using grooming in the conventional primate manner, then the regression equation relating grooming time to group size in Old World monkeys and apes would predict that about 43% of day time would have to be devoted to social grooming. The mean amount of time actually spent in social interaction (principally conversation) by a set of seven modern human populations (with samples from both traditional and postindustrial cultures) is exactly 20% (Dunbar 1998b). Dunbar (1993) argued that language evolved to bridge this gap in bonding time requirement because it allows time to be used more efficiently.

This increased efficiency arises from at least three key features of language. One is that several individuals can be "groomed" at once, in contrast to conventional grooming where only one individual can be groomed at any one time (a problem we still encounter when we resort to the human equivalent of grooming, namely cuddling and petting). The second is that it is possible to timeshare with speech in a way that is not possible with grooming: We can talk and walk or feed, whereas grooming is an exclusive activity (even in modern humans). Third, language allows us to exchange information about events within our social network that happened during our absence: For nonhuman primates, what they do not themselves see they never know about. As a result, humans are able to maintain a better knowledge database on a larger social network than any nonhuman primate.

We can use the regression equation relating social grooming time to group size to estimate grooming time requirements for fossil hominids and, in this way, gain some insight into when language might have evolved. Figure 3 plots the percentage of day time that would have to be devoted to social grooming obtained by interpolating the predicted group sizes for each hominid population shown in Figure 2 into the grooming time equation for Old World monkeys and apes. Because these are simply transformations of brain volume, the pattern across time necessarily reflects the changing size of hominid cranial capacity and is subject to all the usual caveats about compounding error variances. Our concern, however, is less with the exact values than with how this pattern relates to the benchmarks for pongid and modern human grooming time requirements, on the one hand, and the likely limits on how much time could be dedicated to social interaction of this kind.

Recognizing that living catarrhine primates (at least) have an observed upper limit on grooming time at 20% of their time budget, we can make some allowance beyond this for time budgets to be squeezed under strong selection pressure for larger groups. This might allow an additional 5% of time to be allocated to social grooming. If vocal exchanges allow primates to extend the interaction process into foraging and travel by a form of vocal grooming at a distance (as certainly happens in gelada baboons and, perhaps, bonobos and callitrichids), then we can probably add the equivalent of another 5% grooming time. That is to say, the use of vocal exchanges to reinforce grooming relationships may allow group size to increase by an amount equivalent to about 5% of grooming time (but probably not more) without adding significantly to the time budget. This would give us a rubicon at around 30% of grooming time requirement beyond which group size could not increase unless language came into play. Mapping this value onto Figure 3

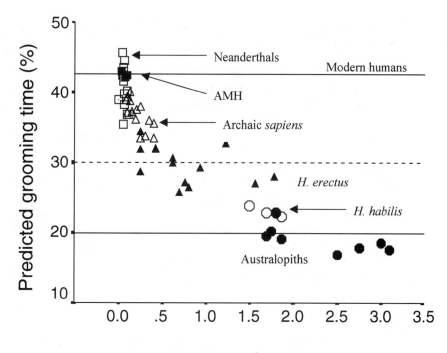

Figure 3 Hominid grooming time requirements plotted against time. Grooming time is determined by interpolating the values for group size shown in Figure 2 into the regression equation for grooming time versus group size obtained from Old World monkeys and apes. The solid horizontal lines represent the maximum grooming time observed in any wild primate group (~20%) and the time investment that would be required to service relationships in modern human groups of ~150 if this was done by social grooming alone (~43%); the dashed line represents the putative threshold at ~30% of time, beyond which group size could not have increased without a method of social bonding that used time more efficiently (i.e., language). Reproduced with permission from Barrett et al. (2002).

suggests that language, at least in some form, would have had to have evolved by around 0.5 MY. The distribution of datapoints on the graph suggests that *Homo erectus* populations, taken as a whole, simply sit astride this rubicon, but *H. sapiens* populations all exceed it. I take this as evidence to support the claim that language (in some form) must have evolved with the appearance of *H. sapiens* and that *H. erectus* almost certainly lacked a language capacity.

This conclusion fits well with two other sources of evidence that point more or less at the same time slot for the evolution of language, namely the size of the hypoglossal canal at the base of the skull and the size of the thoracic vertebral canal. The hypoglossal nerve enervates the tongue, and, because the canal is significantly larger in modern humans than in other primates (when controlling for differences in body size), Kay et al. (1998) proposed that a comparison of its size in fossil hominid crania should tell us when speech evolved. Similarly, MacLarnon & Hewitt (1999) pointed out that the modern human vertebral canal has a distinctive enlargement in its thoracic region that is not present in other living primates, which seems likely to reflect increased enervation for the control of breathing. Because speech requires very fine control over breathing (speech requires a prolonged steady outflow of breath), the relative size of the thoracic canal may give us another benchmark for the appearance of speech. Both indices are of modern proportions in archaic *H. sapiens* but of pongid proportions in all earlier specimens (although there is a considerable time gap separating the latest specimen with the pongid pattern from the first that shows a modern human pattern in both cases).

Although there has been some dispute as to the real significance of these last two anatomical findings, the consistency of these three very different sets of data is surely significant. All three agree that there is evidence for the presence of speech for archaic *H. sapiens* but not for *H. erectus*. This is also in broad general agreement with recent genetic evidence suggesting that two key point mutations, which seem to be associated with grammatical competence (*FoxP2* genes on chromosome 7), are likely to have appeared within the last 200 KY (Enard et al. 2002; see also Lai et al. 2001).

In reviewing the pattern of grooming time in Figure 3, Aiello & Dunbar (1993) argued that we should probably not expect language to have arisen as a single phenotypic or genotypic event but rather as a series of stages. They characterized these as involving (*i*) a conventional primate grooming-based process for the australopiths as a group; (*ii*) increasing use of vocal chorusing to bond groups in the way that gelada and other living primates already do (characteristic of *H. erectus*); (*iii*) the appearance of socially focused language designed to expand the range and quality of interactions needed to support larger groupings (associated with the appearance of archaic *H. sapiens*); and finally (*iv*) language as we now have it (involving extensive use of metaphor and technical knowledge). Aiello & Dunbar (1993) equated the latter with the Upper Palaeolithic Revolution (reflecting the use of language to reflect on, discuss, and teach about other worlds) and argued that this largely involved a software rather than a hardware (i.e., neurological) change.

A plausible interpretation of the suggestion that language evolved out of a phase of increasingly extended vocal exchanges is that such vocal exchanges are likely to have involved chorusing (in the sense of communal singing). This interpretation would imply (*a*) that language evolved out of wordless singing [a view in keeping with the suggestion that language has vocal and not gestural origins (for an overview, see Barrett et al. 2002, pp. 328–34)] and (*b*) that music had an early (and perhaps separate) development as part of the bonding mechanism that welds human groups together.

Two alternative pathways can be envisaged here that have yet to be explored in any detail. One is that music has a very ancient history, dating back to at least the early *H. erectus* period when the demand for grooming time first significantly exceeded the limiting values seen in nonhuman primates (~20%). In this scenario, formal (i.e., grammatical) language evolved with the appearance of archaic humans approximately 0.5 MY, and Neanderthals presumably were capable of speech (though perhaps only in the social sense). The alternative hypothesis is that the sea change in grooming time requirements at ~0.5 MY suggested by Figure 3 marks the point at which musical chorusing evolved into a particularly intense form, with the kinds of vocal exchanges seen before that during the *H. erectus* period being more similar to the counter-calling seen among contemporary primates. Grammatical speech may then be a later development [perhaps associated with anatomically modern humans (AMH) around 200 KY]. This scenario would explain why the anatomical evidence suggests that breathing control and articulation (both as essential for singing as for speech) apparently evolved around 0.5 MY but the genes for grammar did not appear until much later. On this reading, Neanderthals may have been very socially intense, but their groups would have been much smaller than those of AMH because they lacked grammatical language (without which it would be impossible to maintain large dispersed social groups).

Implications for Culture

Culture, and particularly those aspects of high culture that seem to be so crucial to the human condition, depends on advanced social cognition. This is especially clear in the context of religion and its use both in terms of facilitating a more benign world (pleading with or placating supernatural forces to ensure that the natural world behaves in a beneficial way) and in terms of using the supernatural to enforce the social norms of society. It quickly becomes apparent that the cognitive demands of such phenomena are very considerable and rapidly far exceed those required for the much simpler tasks of everyday social interaction. For a supernatural-based religion to have any force in making us toe the social line, I have to *believe* that you *suppose* that there are supernatural beings who can be made to *understand* that you and I *desire* that things should happen in a particular way. This involves four levels of intentionality (marked by the italicized words). Making religion a social as opposed to individual phenomenon thus adds significantly to the cognitive load needed to underpin it. Without working at this level, we will be unable to ensure that our actions are coordinated (as in the performance of rituals) or that we can agree that infringements of the social mores are to be discouraged (i.e., to accept adherence to social norms without the need for punishment). In contrast, conventional interpersonal attempts to insist that you adhere to a social norm require only three levels of intentionality (I *intend* that you *believe* that you must behave in the way that the rest of us *want*). It is the reference to an external supernatural world that cannot be immediately apprehended that adds the key extra layer of intentionality that pushes the cognitive demand to the limits of normal human capacity at level 4. For the individual that conceives all this as a good idea, there is an additional level that he/she needs to aspire to: I *believe* that I can *persuade* you to *believe* that there are some supernatural beings who will *understand* what it is that we all *want*. Kinderman et al. (1998) found that, although level 4 intentionality was the typical level achieved by normal adult humans, a small proportion of individuals can achieve higher levels as a matter of course. It is these individuals that presumably act as the cultural leaders of the societies they live in.

Because Dunbar (2003) found a more or less linear relationship between achievable level of intentionality and frontal lobe volume in the catarrhines, we can interpolate hominid frontal lobe volumes into this equation to see how level of intentionality might have increased through hominid history. We can obtain reasonable estimates of frontal lobe volume by interpolating cranial volumes (corrected to give brain volume) into the regression equation relating frontal lobe volume to total brain size for anthropoid primates following the same logic as that used by Aiello & Dunbar (1993) and exploiting the relationships between brain components noted by Finlay & Darlington (1995). Once again, there will inevitably be some level of error variance in these estimates, but as a first pass it provides us with at least a hypothesis to work from.

The results (Figure 4) suggest that the level-4 intentionality threshold was unlikely to have been breached prior to the appearance of anatomically modern

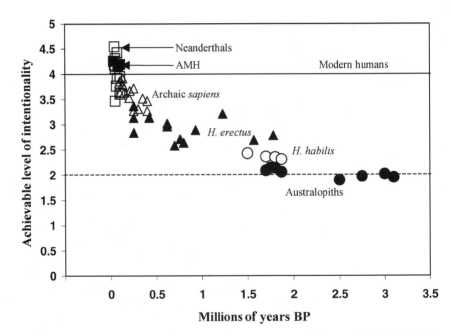

Figure 4   Achievable level of intentionality (or advanced theory of mind) for individual hominid populations, plotted against time. The horizontal lines demarcate level 2 (minimal theory of mind, representing the absolute upper limit for nonhuman primates) and level 4 (the level characteristic of normal human adults and the minimum level required for religion). Frontal lobe volume for fossil hominids is estimated from cranial volume using the regression equation for modern anthropoid primates; these are then interpolated into the regression equation relating achievable level of intentionality versus frontal lobe size in living catarrhines given by Dunbar (2003).

humans (AMH). All archaic *H. sapiens* populations lie just below the critical threshold. Note, however, that Neanderthal populations straddle the line, although there is in fact evidence of increasing cranial volume over time among Neanderthal specimens. In contrast, *H. erectus* populations seem to be more or less evenly distributed around level 3, which would imply a level of cognitive skill much below that required to support advanced human culture. This suggests that religion (at least) and presumably higher culture in general was lacking in *H. erectus* and probably came into being only with the appearance of the earliest populations of archaic *H. sapiens*. This conclusion is broadly in accord with the archaeological record for the Upper Palaeolithic Revolution.

ACKNOWLEDGMENTS

The research on which this article is based forms part of the programme of the United Kingdom's ESRC Research Centre in Economic Learning and Social Evolution (ELSE). The support of the ESRC is gratefully acknowledged.

The *Annual Review of Anthropology* is online at http://anthro.annualreviews.org

LITERATURE CITED

Aiello L, Dunbar R. 1993. Neocortex size, group size and the evolution of language. *Curr. Anthropol.* 34:184–93

Aiello L, Wheeler P. 1995. The expensive tissue hypothesis: the brain and the digestive system in human and primate evolution. *Curr. Anthropol.* 36:199–221

Baron-Cohen S, Ring HA, Moriarty J, Schmitz P, Costa DP. 1994. Recognition of mental state terms: clinical findings in children with autism and a functional neuroimaging study of normal adults. *Brit. J. Psychiatry* 165:640–49

Barrett L, Dunbar RIM, Lycett JE. 2002. *Human Evolutionary Psychology.* Basingstoke: Palgrave/Macmillan; Princeton, NJ: Princeton Univ. Press

Barrett L, Henzi SP. 2002. Constraints on relationship formation among female primates. *Behaviour* 139:263–89

Barton RA. 1996. Neocortex size and behavioural ecology in primates. *Proc. R. Soc. Lond. B* 263:173–77

Barton RA. 1998. Visual specialization and brain evolution in primates. *Proc. R. Soc. Lond. B* 265:1933–37

Barton RA. 1999. The evolutionary ecology of the primate brain. In *Comparative Primate Socioecology*, ed. PC Lee, pp. 167–203. Cambridge: Cambridge Univ. Press

Barton RA, Dunbar RIM. 1997. Evolution of the social brain. In *Machiavellian Intelligence II*, ed. A Whiten, RW Byrne, pp. 240–63. Cambridge, UK: Cambridge Univ. Press

Barton RA, Harvey PH. 2000. Mosaic evolution of brain structure in mammals. *Nature* 405:105–8

Bowman LA, Dilley SR, Keverne EB. 1978. Suppression of oestrogen-induced LH surges by social subordination in talapoin monkeys. *Nature* 275:56–58

Byrne RW. 1995. *The Thinking Ape.* Oxford, UK: Oxford Univ. Press

Byrne RW. 1996. Relating brain size to intelligence in primates. In *Modelling the Early Hominid Mind*, ed. P Mellars, K Gibson, pp. 1–8. Cambridge, UK: Macdonald Inst. Archaeol. Res.

Byrne RW, Whiten A, eds. 1988. *Machiavellian Intelligence.* Oxford, UK: Oxford Univ. Press

Call J, Tomasello M. 1999. A nonverbal theory

of mind test: the performance of children and apes. *Child Develop.* 70:381–95

Combes SL, Altmann J. 2001. Status change during adulthood: life-history by-product or kin selection based on reproductive value? *Proc. R. Soc. Lond. B* 268:1367–73

Deaner RO, Nunn CL, van Schaik CP. 2000. Comparative tests of primate cognition: different scaling methods produce different results. *Brain Behav. Evol.* 55:44–52

Donald M. 1991. *Origins of the Modern Mind.* Cambridge, MA: Harvard Univ. Press

Dunbar RIM. 1980. Determinants and evolutionary consequences of dominance among female gelada baboons. *Behav. Ecol. Sociobiol.* 7:253–65

Dunbar RIM. 1984. *Reproductive Decisions: an Economic Analysis of Gelada Baboon Social Strategies.* Princeton, NJ: Princeton Univ. Press

Dunbar RIM. 1988. *Primate Social Systems.* London: Chapman & Hall

Dunbar RIM. 1989. Reproductive strategies of female gelada baboons. In *Sociobiology of Sexual and Reproductive Strategies,* ed. A Rasa, C Vogel, E Voland, pp. 74–92. London: Chapman & Hall

Dunbar RIM. 1991. Functional significance of social grooming in primates. *Folia Primatol.* 57:121–31

Dunbar RIM. 1992a. Neocortex size as a constraint on group size in primates. *J. Human Evol.* 22:469–93

Dunbar RIM. 1992b. Time: a hidden constraint on the behavioural ecology of baboons. *Behav. Ecol. Sociobiol.* 31:35–49

Dunbar RIM. 1993. Coevolution of neocortex size, group size and language in humans. *Behav. Brain Sci.* 16:681–735

Dunbar RIM. 1995. Neocortex size and group size in primates: a test of the hypothesis. *J. Human Evol.* 28:287–96

Dunbar RIM. 1996. Determinants of group size in primates: a general model. In *Evolution of Culture and Language in Primates and Humans,* ed. J Maynard Smith, G Runciman, R Dunbar, pp. 33–57. Oxford, UK: Oxford Univ. Press

Dunbar RIM. 1998a. The social brain hypothesis. *Evol. Anthropol.* 6:178–90

Dunbar RIM. 1998b. Theory of mind and the evolution of language. In *Approaches to the Evolution of Language,* ed. J Hurford, M Studdart-Kennedy, C Knight, pp. 92–110. Cambridge, UK: Cambridge Univ. Press

Dunbar RIM. 2003. Why are apes so smart? In *Primate Life Histories,* ed. P Kappeler, M Peirera. Cambridge, MA: MIT Press. In press

Dunbar RIM, Bever J. 1998. Neocortex size predicts group size in carnivores and some insectivores. *Ethology* 104:695–708

Emery NJ, Perrett DI. 2000. How can studies of monkey brain help us understand 'theory of mind' and autism in humans? In *Understanding Other Minds: Perspectives from Developmental Cognitive Neuroscience,* ed. S Baron-Cohen, H Tager-Flusberg, DJ Cohen, pp. 274–305. Oxford, UK: Oxford Univ. Press

Enard W, Przeworski M, Fisher SE, Lai CSL, Wlebe V, et al. 2002. Molecular evolution of *FOXP2,* a gene involved in speech and language. *Nature* 418:869–72

Finlay BL, Darlington RB. 1995. Linked regularities in the development and evolution of mammalian brains. *Science* 268:1578–84

Finlay BL, Darlington RB, Nicastro N. 2001. Developmental structure in brain evolution. *Behav. Brain Sci.* 24:263–308

Gibson KR. 1986. Cognition, brain size and the extraction of embedded food resources. In *Primate Ontogeny, Cognition and Social Behaviour,* ed. J Else, PC Lee, pp. 93–105. Cambridge, UK: Cambridge Univ. Press

Happé F, Ehlers S, Fletcher PC, Frith U, Johansson M, et al. 1996. 'Theory of mind' in the brain: evidence from a PET scan study of Asperger syndrome. *Neuroreport* 8:197–201

Harcourt AH. 1987. Dominance and fertility among female primates. *J. Zool. Lond.* 213:471–87

Hare B, Call J, Agnetta B, Tomasello M. 2000. Chimpanzees know what conspecifics do and do not see. *Anim. Behav.* 59:771–85

Henzi SP, Barrett L. 1999. The value of grooming to female primates. *Primates* 40:47–59

Hill RA, Dunbar RIM. 1998. An evaluation of the roles of predation rate and predation risk as selective pressures on primate grouping behaviour. *Behaviour* 135:411–30

Hill RA, Dunbar RIM. 2003. Social network size in humans. *Hum. Nature.* In press

Jerison HJ. 1973. *Evolution of the Brain and Intelligence.* New York: Academic Press

Joffe T, Dunbar R. 1997. Visual and socio-cognitive information processing in primate brain evolution. *Proc. Roy. Soc. Lond. B* 264:1303–7

Kay RF, Cartmill M, Balow M. 1998. The hypoglossal canal and the origin of human vocal behaviour. *Proc. Natl. Acad. Sci. USA* 95:5417–19

Kinderman P, Dunbar RIM, Bentall RP. 1998. Theory-of-mind deficits and causal attributions. *Brit. J. Psychol.* 89:191–204

Kudo H, Dunbar RIM. 2001. Neocortex size and social network size in primates. *Anim. Behav.* 62:711–22

Lai CSL, Fisher S, Hurst JA, Vargha-Khadem F, Monaco AP. 2001. A forkhead-domain gene is mutated in a severe speech and language disorder. *Nature* 413:519–23

Leslie AM. 1987. Pretense and representation in infancy: the origins of theory of mind. *Psych. Rev.* 94:84–106

Lewis K. 2001. A comparative study of primate play behaviour: implications for the study of cognition. *Folia Primat.* 71:417–21

Lewis-Williams D. 2002. *The Mind in the Cave.* London: Thames & Hudson

MacLarnon A, Hewitt G. 1999. The evolution of human speech: the role of enhanced breathing control. *Amer. J. Phys. Anthropol.* 109:341–63

Martin RD. 1981. Relative brain size and metabolic rate in terrestrial vertebrates. *Nature* 293:57–60

Martin RD. 1984. Body size, brain size and feeding strategies. In *Food Acquisition and Processing in Primates*, ed. DJ Chivers, B Wood, A Bilsborough, pp. 73–103. New York: Plenum Press

McNab BK, Eisenberg JF. 1989. Brain size and its relation to the rate of metabolism in mammals. *Am. Nat.* 133:157–67

Mitchell P. 1997. *Introduction to Theory of Mind: Children, Autism and Apes.* London: Arnold

Mithen S. 1996. *The Prehistory of the Mind.* London: Thames & Hudson

Morino L. 1996. What dolphins can tell us about primate evolution. *Evol. Anthropol.* 5:81–86

Pawlowski BP, Lowen CB, Dunbar RIM. 1998. Neocortex size, social skills and mating success in primates. *Behaviour* 135:357–68

Povinelli D. 1999. *Folk Physics for Apes.* Oxford: Oxford Univ. Press

Purvis A, Webster AJ. 1999. Phylogenetically independent comparisons and primate phylogeny. In *Comparative Primate Socioecology*, ed. PC Lee, pp. 44–70. Cambridge, UK: Cambridge Univ. Press

Reader SM, Laland KN. 2002. Social intelligence, innovation and enhanced brain size in primates. *Proc. Natl. Acad. Sci. USA* 99:4436–41

Reader SM, Lefebvre L. 2001. Social learning and sociality. *Behav. Brain Sci.* 24:353–55

Sacher GA, Staffeldt EF. 1974. Relation of gestation time to brain weight for placental mammals: implications for the theory of vertebrate growth. *Am. Nat.* 108:593–615

Sawaguchi T, Kudo H. 1990. Neocortical development and social structure in primates. *Primates* 31:283–90

Semendeferi K, Damasio H, Frank R, van Hoesen GW. 1997. The evolution of the frontal lobes: a volumetric analysis based on three-dimensional reconstructions of magnetic resonance scans of human and ape brains. *J. Hum. Evol.* 32:375–88

Silk JB, Alberts SC, Altmann J. 2003. Patterns of coalition formation by adult female baboons in Amboseli, Kenya. *Anim. Behav.* In press

Tomasello M, Call J. 1998. *Primate Cognition.* New York: Academic Press

van Schaik CP. 1983. Why are diurnal primates living in groups? *Behaviour* 87:120–44

Annu. Rev. Anthropol. 2003. 32:183–204
doi: 10.1146/annurev.anthro.32.061002.093440
First published online as a Review in Advance on June 4, 2003

COMPLEX ADAPTIVE SYSTEMS

J. Stephen Lansing

*Department of Anthropology, 221 Haury Bldg., University of Arizona, Tucson,
Arizona 85721-0030; external faculty, Santa Fe Institute, 1399 Hyde Park Road,
Santa Fe, New Mexico 87501; email: jlansing@u.arizona.edu*

Key Words complexity, self-organized criticality, adaptive agents, evolutionary game theory

■ **Abstract** The study of complex adaptive systems, a subset of nonlinear dynamical systems, has recently become a major focus of interdisciplinary research in the social and natural sciences. Nonlinear systems are ubiquitous; as mathematician Stanislaw Ulam observed, to speak of "nonlinear science" is like calling zoology the study of "nonelephant animals" (quoted in Campbell et al. 1985, p. 374). The initial phase of research on nonlinear systems focused on deterministic chaos, but more recent studies have investigated the properties of self-organizing systems or anti-chaos. For mathematicians and physicists, the biggest surprise is that complexity lurks within extremely simple systems. For biologists, it is the idea that natural selection is not the sole source of order in the biological world. In the social sciences, it is suggested that emergence—the idea that complex global patterns with new properties can emerge from local interactions—could have a comparable impact.

To illustrate the concept of a complex adaptive system, Holland (1995) offers the example of a woman purchasing a jar of pickled herring on an ordinary day in New York City. She fully expects the herring to be there. But grocery stores do not keep large stocks of all kinds of foods to buffer fluctuations; if the daily arrivals were cut off, supplies would last no more than a week or two. How, asks Holland, do cities with millions of inhabitants avoid devastating swings between shortage and glut, year after year, without any form of centralized planning? Invoking Adam Smith's "invisible hand" of the market does not fully satisfy Holland as a solution because it fails to explain the mechanisms that dampen fluctuations. Instead he likens the provisioning of cities to the functioning of immune systems or the interactions of species in ecosystems. Thus for food webs in rainforests to sustain biodiversity, innumerable specific flows of nutrients—equivalent to the jars of pickled herring—must persist in the absence of any form of centralized control. Similarly, an immune system also lacks centralized control and cannot settle into a permanent, fixed structure; instead it must be able to adapt to unknown invaders. Yet despite its protean nature, a person's immune system is coherent enough to distinguish oneself from anyone else; it will attack cells from any other human. Holland suggests that immune systems, cities, and ecosystems share certain

0084-6570/03/1021-0183$14.00

properties that make it useful to consider them as instances of a class of phenomena that he terms complex adaptive systems (CAS) (Holland 1995, pp. 4–6).

The concept of CAS is obviously at a very high level of abstraction. Moreover, it crosscuts the usual categories of anthropological thought, such as culture, nature, and society, and applies only to a rather narrow range of phenomena within them. The insights it offers are essentially mathematical and frequently involve the use of new computational tools. New theoretical ideas about CAS tend to be published initially in physics and mathematics journals; some gradually work their way into biology, the social sciences, and, on occasion, business schools and the popular press. The goal of this review is to provide an introduction to the research that I think may be of most interest to anthropologists. It has two parts: The first offers a historical overview of the broader intellectual currents shaping research on CAS; and the second surveys recent attempts to apply these ideas to anthropological questions.

INTRODUCTION: THE DIVINE TAPE PLAYER

If we could rewind an imaginary videotape of the history of life on Earth, asked biologist Stephen Jay Gould, how much of what we see around us would still be here? Gould's answer was, very little: "[T]he divine tape player holds a million scenarios, each perfectly sensible . . . the slightest early nudge contacts a different groove, and history veers into another plausible channel, diverging continually from its original pathway" (Gould 1989, pp. 320–21). As a paleontologist, Gould saw the living world in terms of phylogenetic trees, each node or species the unique result of a long chain of random evolutionary events. But, as critics of Gould have pointed out, the history of life on this planet shows many examples of convergent evolution, such as the independent evolution of eyes in many taxa, that would be very surprising if Gould were strictly correct (Depew & Weber 1995, pp. 424–27). The divine tape player does not produce exact duplicates of species, but it does generate spectacular examples of convergent evolution like anteaters and pangolins or the marsupial lions and wolves of Australia and Tasmania. At the level of molecular evolution, the phylogenetic history of these species fits Gould's model: African lions and marsupial lions shared a common mammalian ancestor millions of years ago and have been diverging ever since. But the fact that these independent pathways of evolution produced animals that are so similar in morphology and behavior suggests that Gould has captured only part of the story. It seems that random bumps and nudges may be more likely to veer into some grooves than others, producing convergence as well as divergence.

A similar paradox involving the relationship of the parts to the whole intrigued Emile Durkheim in his classic study of suicide. On the one hand, Durkheim observed, the causes of particular suicides are "almost infinite in number . . . one man kills himself in the midst of affluence, another in the lap of poverty; one was unhappy in his home, and another had just ended by divorce a marriage which was making him unhappy" (Durkheim 1979[1897], p. 303). He concluded that no matter how much a researcher knows about a collection of individuals, it is impossible to predict which of them are likely to kill themselves. Yet the number of Parisians who commit suicide each year is even more stable than the general mortality rate. A process that seems to be governed by chance when viewed at the level of the individual turns out to be strikingly predictable at the level of society as a whole.

Among students of complex systems, this phenomenon is known as "emergence." Consider a system or aggregate composed of many interacting parts. If the system is sufficiently complex, it may not be practical or perhaps even possible to know the details of each local interaction. Moreover, local interactions can produce nonlinear effects that make even simple systems impossible to solve (as Newton discovered in attempting to solve the three-body problem). But if we shift our attention from the causal forces at work on individual elements to the behavior of the system as a whole, global patterns of behavior may become apparent. However, the understanding of global patterns is purchased at a cost: The observer must usually give up the hope of understanding the workings of causation at the level of individual elements. "The statistical method," wrote physicist James Clerk Maxwell in 1890, "involves an abandonment of strict dynamical principles" (Vol. 2, p. 253). It is an interesting footnote to the history of the sciences that this discovery occurred in the social sciences and was later borrowed by physicists. "Doubtless it would be too brave," writes Porter in *The Rise of Statistical Thought*, "to argue that statistical gas theory only became possible after social statistics accustomed scientific thinkers to the possibility of stable laws of mass phenomena with no dependence on predictability of individual events. Still, the actual history of the kinetic gas theory is fully consistent with such a claim" (Porter 1986, p. 114).[1]

Late in his career, the philosopher Karl Popper argued that this shift from an atomistic and mechanistic ontology to one based on probabilities was among the most significant intellectual pirouettes in the history of science. "The world is no longer a causal machine," wrote Popper in his last book (1990). "It now can be seen as a world of propensities, as an unfolding process of realizing possibilities and of unfolding new possibilities" (Popper 1990, pp. 18–19). In physics, the application

---

[1]In retrospect, Durkheim's comments on the implications of this point seem remarkably prescient. The key issue is the understanding of chance. If suicides occur for many contradictory reasons, then the overall suicide rate should be governed by chance and fluctuate chaotically. As Durkheim noted, this is what would be predicted by the dominant statistical theory of his day, that of Adolphe Quételet, who held that the behavior of individuals was governed by the sum total of prior influences acting on them. Quételet's theory should accurately predict that the average man would not commit suicide, but it should also predict that the suicide rate should fluctuate randomly. To this, Durkheim responded that "Quételet's theory rests on an inaccurate observation. He thought that stability occurs only in the most general manifestations of human activity; but it is equally found in the sporadic manifestations which occur only at rare and isolated points of the social field" (Durkheim 1979[1897], p. 302). Durkheim concludes that suicides are not mere statistical outliers but the outcome of deterministic processes.

of probability theory to the gas laws and thermodynamics in the nineteenth century was followed by quantum theory in the 1920s, in which the statistical properties of ensembles were pushed down into the very structure of the physical universe. At about the same time, biologists Sewall Wright and R.A. Fisher developed models that depicted natural selection in probabilistic terms. Wright sought to understand what he called "switch-and-trigger mechanisms," which could drive evolutionary processes into new trajectories, and in the 1930s developed a model of adaptive landscapes to facilitate visualizing such patterns. In this model, genetic variation is depicted as clouds of points in a multi-dimensional landscape, often drawn in three dimensions with peaks and valleys representing high and low levels of adaptive fitness. Wright's adaptive landscapes (or fitness landscapes) were used initially to consider the effects of evolutionary forces such as inbreeding (Wright 1932) and genetic drift (Dobzhansky 1937, Mayr & Provine 1980). But recently, complexity theorists have used fitness landscapes to pose more general questions. As biologist Stuart Kauffman has written, "the fitness landscape is a powerful, basic and proper starting point to think about selection" (Kauffman 1989, p. 69).

ADAPTIVE LANDSCAPES

In the 1960s Kauffman posed a simple question: Is Darwinian natural selection, alone, responsible for the patterns of order we see in the living world? Nonliving phenomena like snowflakes exhibit spontaneous order through a process of self-organization. Might self-organizing processes also play a role in biology? To explore this question, Kauffman used computer simulations as a surrogate for Gould's "divine tape player". Although Kauffman's research was originally aimed at understanding evolution at the level of genes, his results suggest that "the range of spontaneous order is enormously greater than we had supposed" (Kauffman 1995). A brief summary of Kauffman's work on adaptive landscapes provides an introduction to some of the methods and perspectives now being used in the study of complex systems.

The original Wright-Fisher model of fitness landscapes assumes a one-to-one correspondence between individual genes and traits that affect fitness. As time goes on, a species can "climb the peak of Mount Fitness" as progressively fitter mutants appear and become dominant. But Kauffman observed that this is an oversimplification. In reality, the adaptive fitness of any particular trait is likely to be determined by several genes; these are known as epistatic connections among genes. Moreover, the fitness of an organism or species depends upon the others with which it interacts: If frogs develop sticky tongues, flies will do better with slippery feet. Thus evolution depends on many interacting (and sometimes conflicting) constraints. But rather than try to analyze the actual epistatic connections in particular instances, Kauffman posed a more general question: What is the relationship between the average connectedness of genes to the ability of organisms to evolve? (Later, Kauffman observed that one can ask analogous questions about the connectedness of firms in an economy or species in an ecosystem).

To see how Kauffman pursued this question, imagine a collection of N Christmas tree lights. Each bulb has one of two possible states, on or off, and is wired up to K other bulbs. A simple rule tells each bulb what to do. For example, let $K = 3$, meaning that each bulb is wired to 3 other bulbs.[2] From one moment to the next, each bulb decides whether to turn itself on or off in accordance with the state of these neighbors. A typical rule is majority wins, meaning that if 2 or 3 of its neighbors are on, the bulb will itself turn on; otherwise it will turn off. How will such a system behave when the electricity goes on? At first, Kauffman found that there are two possible patterns of behavior, ordered and disordered. Later, Langton (1990) pointed out that the behavior of the network at the transition point between order and chaos is different enough to be categorized as a third regime. Thus there are three regimes:

1) chaotic: If K is large, the bulbs keep twinkling chaotically as they switch each other on and off;

2) frozen or periodic: If K is small ($K = 1$), some flip on and off a few times, but most of the array of lights will soon stop twinkling;

3) Complex: If K is around 2, complex patterns appear, in which twinkling islands of stability develop, changing shape at their borders.

Kauffman discovered that the overall behavior of such NK networks (where N is the number of elements and K the number of connections per element) is almost entirely dependent on K, rather than the specific rules implemented along the epistatic pathways (like "majority wins"). Kauffman began these experiments in the days when computers were programmed with punch cards. Changing the order in which the cards were stacked would disrupt ordinary programs. But because he was interested in discovering the average behavior of NK networks, his procedure involved shuffling the cards and running the program again, to the consternation of onlookers (Flake 1998, p. 329). His principal result was that a network that is either frozen solid or chaotic cannot transmit information and thus cannot adapt. But as Langton discovered, a complex network—one that is near the "edge of chaos"—can do both (Langton 1990).

The characteristic patterns of behavior of NK networks can be visualized on a Derrida plot (Figure 1). Here we track the behavior of a network of 1600 elements (light bulbs). To set up the experiment, two versions of the network are created that are identical except for the numbers of bulbs that happen to be on or off at the start. The number of elements that differ (e.g., off or on) is called the Hamming distance between the two instances of the network. Along the X axis, the Hamming distance varies from zero (the two versions of the network are identical) to 1 (the networks are completely dissimilar: If a bulb is off in one, it is on in the other). Imagine that power is switched on and bulbs turn each other on and off in both

---

[2] Rules are defined by Boolean connections like "and" and "or." The "majority wins" rule used here to illustrate the concept of NK Boolean networks will not lead to chaos.

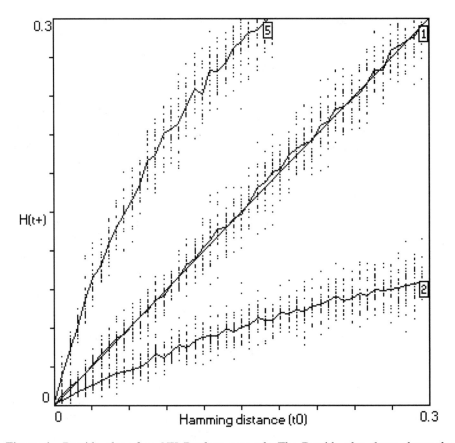

Figure 1   Derrida plot of an NK Boolean network. The Derrida plot above shows the behavior of three *NK* networks (N = 1600). The plot for each network is created as follows: Consider that the network is initialized to two initial states. The two states are identical except for *x* nodes that are changed from on to off or vice versa. The horizontal axis of the graph reflects *x*; its unit is termed the Hamming distance and indicates the number of corresponding nodes with opposite values, scaled by dividing by *N*. At the *left* of the graph the initial states are identical and are progressively more dissimilar to the *right*. Each instance of the network is then allowed to proceed forward for two time steps. The vertical axis shows the Hamming distance between the two final states that result. Several different combinations of initial states are plotted for each initial Hamming distance; each point represents one such trial, and the lines connect the averages of the results. *K* is indicated for each line. For K = 1, the Hamming distance does not change; two initial states that differ on *x* nodes lead to two final states that differ on roughly *x* nodes as well. However, if K = 2, two initial states that differ by a few nodes will tend to converge into a nearby basin of attraction so that after two time steps their initial dissimilarity is significantly decreased. Conversely, if K = 5, the system behaves chaotically so that even two fairly similar initial states will rapidly become dissimilar. This figure was created by John Murphy using A. Wuensch's Discrete Dynamics Lab; see Wuensch & Lesser 1992.

networks, resulting in a new Hamming distance that is plotted on the Y axis. In the extreme case where $K = 0$, the Hamming distance will not change; no bulb will twinkle. At the other extreme, if K is large, even a small initial difference will trigger cascades of twinkles in both networks that will cause them to diverge, and the Hamming distance will increase.

BASINS OF ATTRACTION

If the reader will bear with me, this simple example can be used to explain many of the key concepts involved in the study of complex adaptive systems. As bulbs turn each other on and off, eventually the entire array of bulbs must reach a state that it has encountered before. Once this has occurred, it will cycle back to that configuration forever. This repetitive cycle is called a state cycle or limit cycle. Sometimes more than one configuration of a network will flow into the same state cycle. Start a network with any of these initial patterns and, after passing through a sequence of states, it will settle into the same state cycle or pattern of twinkling. In the language of dynamical systems, the state cycle is called an attractor and the array of initial states that flow into it a basin of attraction. The more initial states that flow into a given attractor, the larger its basin of attraction. So one can ask questions like, how many attractors exist for a given system and how long are the state cycles? For NK networks, the number of states that are possible is 2^N, a hyperastronomical number for all but the smallest networks. But the number of attractors and the size of their basins varies dramatically depending on K. When K = N, the average length of state cycles is 2^N, and the number of attractors is also huge, about N/e. Such networks provide a dramatic illustration of the concept of deterministic chaos. Flip one bulb in a K = N network, and the network moves out of one basin of attraction and into another. It will be a very long time indeed before it encounters a state that it has been in before (and thus completes one tour of its attractor). The network is extremely sensitive to perturbations, which instantly change its entire pattern of behavior; thus such networks cannot store information. At the other extreme, when K is small, networks exhibit stable or periodic behavior. They arrive at their tiny attractors at an exponentially fast rate and then become trapped in simple state cycles. Different sections of the network function as isolated subsections or islands. They can store information, but there is no communication between the islands. So networks with lots of connections exhibit chaotic behavior, whereas networks with very sparse connections decompose into an archipelago of isolated subsystems that either stop twinkling or follow simple repetitive patterns.

However, when K = 2, very different dynamics occur; these networks are in between the chaotic and stable/periodic regimes. Both the number of attractors and their average length are equal to the square root of N, a small number even when N is large. Thus when K = 2, a network of 1600 light bulbs will settle down and cycle through the square root of 1600 states, a mere 40. Initialize a new K = 2 network, and it will soon find itself headed for one of a few relatively stable configurations. The network as a whole does not decompose, nor does it become chaotic. But the most interesting property of K = 2 networks is their response to perturbation. Flip one bulb in a K = 2 network, and in most cases only a few neighbors will twinkle. But occasionally a perturbation will induce large changes, perhaps moving the network into a new basin of attraction. This explains the Derrida plot for K = 2: Most networks are located in just a few large basins of attraction, so networks tend to converge toward one of a relatively few attractors, and the Hamming distance decreases.

These results have dramatic implications for the ability of networks to evolve. To see this, imagine that the N elements are genes and that each one contributes something to the fitness of the whole network. To ensure that the model is very general, let fitnesses be assigned randomly to all the "genes" or elements in the array. When K = 0 (meaning that the fitness of each gene or element does not depend on any others), the fitness landscape shows a single Mount Fuji peak. Start anywhere in this landscape, and you can always find a neighbor one step away with a higher fitness. But as K grows larger there are more and more conflicting constraints. As the complexity of the network increases, selection is progressively less able to alter its properties. When K = N, each gene's fitness contribution depends on all the other genes in the array. This means that the differences in fitness between genes is very small, and the adaptive landscape looks like a lot of tiny hills. As Kauffman observes, "in sufficiently complex systems, selection cannot avoid the order exhibited by most members of the ensemble. Therefore, such order is present not because of selection but despite it" (Kauffman 1993, p. 16).

Complex Systems and the Edge of Chaos

Kauffman emphasized the role of selection in bringing living systems to the edge of chaos, a controversial point to which we shall return. But physicist Per Bak and his colleagues have shown that nonliving systems can also exhibit self-organizing properties that may take them to the edge of chaos (Bak & Chen 1991, Bak 1997). Bak's examples include phenomena like earthquakes, which are unlike biological systems because no process of adaptation is involved; these are known as complex systems rather than complex adaptive systems. Bak's best-known example is a sandpile. If you patiently trickle grains of sand onto a flat surface, at first the sand will simply pile up; but eventually the pile will reach a critical state. At that point, Bak found that the size of the avalanches triggered by dropping another grain of sand follows a power law distribution: The size of avalanches is inversely proportional to their frequency (in other words, there will be many little avalanches, a few medium-sized ones, and on rare occasions a large one). Such a sandpile is at the "edge of chaos," analogous to a K = 2 Boolean network (to picture this, it may help to imagine that a K = 0 pile would be flat, whereas a K = N pile could be a tall and precarious column with a diameter of one grain). Other researchers have found additional pathways that lead to the edge of chaos. The first research on this topic was carried out by Langton, who wrote a dissertation (1991) entitled "Computation at the Edge of Chaos." Langton studied the behavior of cellular automata (CA), a mathematical concept invented by John von Neumann. More recently, mathematician Stephen Wolfram carried out exhaustive computer simulations in an attempt to clarify the dynamics of complex behavior in cellular automata (Wolfram 2002). A simple two-dimensional cellular automata begins with a line of different-colored cells on a grid or lattice. Each cell checks its own color and that of its immediate neighbors and decides on the basis of a rule whether to turn color in the next line of the grid. It is equivalent to a two-dimensional NK model where the K inputs are restricted to the cell's closest neighbors on the lattice. Wolfram noticed the existence of four classes of behavior in CA: (I) fixed, (II) periodic, (III) chaotic, and (IV) complex. Langton became interested in the relationship between these classes and developed a measure, the lambda parameter, that relates the nature of the rules to the overall behavior of the cellular automata (Figure 2). Tuning the lambda parameter leads through Wolfram's classes in the order I-II-IV-III; thus the complex regime (class IV) lies between the periodic and chaotic regimes. This led Langton to propose that class IV behaviors could be associated with a phase transition between order and chaos: the edge of chaos (Langton 1990).

The methods used to study complexity in cellular automata differ from those used to investigate NK models. The study of CA usually involves following a single rule on its journey to its attractor, whereas investigating NK networks requires taking statistics on their average patterns of behavior. It is interesting that each of these independent lines of research—Bak's sandpiles, Kauffman's NK Boolean nets, and Wolfram's Class IV cellular automata—provide intuitive examples of complex behavior near the phase transition between ordered and chaotic regimes (Langton's edge of chaos), but so far there is no satisfactory mathematical definition of complexity.

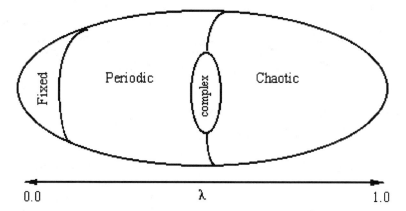

Figure 2   Langton's classification of cellular automata. The behavior of cellular automata depends on the rules that govern their evolution in time. Some rules will map a cell into a quiescent state. Lambda is the fraction of rules that map to non-quiescent states. Langton found that tuning lambda shows that complex behavior (Wolfram's Class IV CA) emerges between classes II and III, at the edge of chaos. See Langton 1990.

A more controversial issue is Kauffman's suggestion that a selective metadynamics may drive complex adaptive systems toward the edge of chaos. Kauffman has demonstrated how this process could occur with computer simulations, but the idea is not easily reconciled with standard models of multilevel selection in evolutionary biology (for a clear statement of this problem, see Levin 2003). Still, from a mathematical standpoint it is clear that systems that find themselves in this region of their state space are advantageously situated for adaptation. As Langton showed, the ability of networks to both store and transmit information is optimized at the edge of chaos. Moreover, as Kauffman observed, this is where the adaptive landscape is most favorable for gains in fitness. At present, physicists (rather than biologists) remain at the forefront of research on the edge of chaos. Two recent examples are noteworthy: One group of physicists found that the rate of entropy increases at the edge of chaos (Latora et al. 2000), whereas de Oliveira confirmed that "the eternal search for new forms, better than the current one, is imperative for evolutionary dynamic systems" and is optimized at the edge of chaos (de Oliveria 2001, p. 1). On the other hand, Mitchell & Crutchfield (1993) report experiments with cellular automata that call into question Langton's suggestion that the ability of cellular automata to perform computational tasks is optimized when lambda values are closest to the edge of chaos.

Although questions remain, the theoretical analysis of complex systems has already produced some intriguing results. Kauffman calls the study of complex adaptive systems "antichaos," because it is concerned with the spontaneous appearance of order in dynamical systems. For mathematicians and physicists, the biggest surprise is that complexity lurks within extremely simple systems. For biologists, it is the idea that natural selection is not the sole source of order in the biological world. As for the social sciences, I suggest that emergence—the idea that complex global patterns with new properties may emerge from local interactions—may someday have a comparable impact. Because space is limited, here I conclude this introduction to the theory of complex systems and turn to some applications of these ideas in the social and behavioral sciences.

THE CRITIQUE OF EQUILIBRIUM THEORY IN ECOLOGY AND ECONOMICS

In a recent article (1999) in the *Annual Review of Anthropology* on "New Ecology and the Social Sciences," Scoones describes the emergence of a "new ecology" beginning in the 1970s. The turning point was May's 1976 paper in *Nature* on "Simple Mathematical Models with Very Complicated Dynamics," which showed that "simple nonlinear systems do not necessarily possess simple dynamical properties" (p. 459). Subsequently, the mathematical foundations of ecology began to shift away from the study of equilibrium (the balance of nature), using simple differential equations, to the study of nonequilibrium theory, with the techniques of nonlinear analysis (Ferriere & Fox 1995, Levin 1999). Scoones suggests that these ideas have so far had little impact on the social sciences and urges "a fuller engagement with the issues raised by the new ecological thinking" (Scoones 1999, p. 496).

May's paper is now seen as a milestone in the first phase of nonlinear analysis, the discovery of chaos. Most of the ecological research discussed by Scoones is also concerned with chaotic dynamics and nonequilibrium systems (it should be noted, however, that a good deal of contemporary research in ecology makes little use of nonlinear methods). More recently, the study of spontaneous order and self-organizing properties in ecosystems has become a major new theme of research. As Levin (2003, p. 3) observes in a recent review article on the mathematics of complex adaptive systems, studying antichaos "involves understanding how cooperation, coalitions and networks of interaction emerge from individual behaviors and feed back to influence those behaviors." Although nonlinear approaches have spread to many areas of ecological research, the aspects that may be of greatest interest to anthropologists have to do with the emergent properties of social and behavioral systems. Here one often encounters broad theoretical pronouncements, such as Schank's contention that "most animal social systems are self-organizing" (Schank 1998, p. 1). But specific applications of nonlinear models to animal behavior have also begun to appear. For example, Bonabeau has investigated the foraging behavior of various species of ants and concludes that they are "a clear example of adaptation to the edge of chaos" (Bonabeau 1997, p. 29). The ants use multiple systems for communication and for recruiting foragers to newly discovered food sources. Species at the edge of chaos, like *Tetramorium caespitum*, can adaptively switch to newly discovered food sources if they are of higher quality, whereas other species do not take advantage of the higher-quality food until the first source is exhausted. Bonabeau's mathematical model shows how the global decision-making processes of the ants emerge from the local interactions between individual foragers (Bonabeau 1997).

Complexity theory is also beginning to have a similar impact on economics: a shift from equilibrium models constructed with differential equations to nonlinear dynamics, as researchers recognize that economies, like ecosystems, may never settle down into an equilibrium. A clear and readable account of this change in perspective is provided by Arthur in his article (1999) on "Complexity and the Economy." Arthur argues that "complexity economics is not a temporary adjunct to static economic theory, but theory at a more general, out-of-equilibrium level. The approach is making itself felt in every area of economics: game theory, the theory of money and finance, learning in the economy, economic history, the evolution of trading networks, the stability of the economy, and political economy" (Arthur 1999, p. 109; see also Arthur et al. 1997). Kauffman draws explicit parallels between biological and economic systems: "[T]he modern corporation is a collectively self-sustaining structure of roles and obligations that 'lives' in an economic world, exchanges signals and stuffs, and survives or dies in ways at least loosely analogous to those of *E. coli* .... Both *E. coli* and IBM coevolve in their respective worlds" (Kauffman 1995, p. 300). Economists have followed up on this idea by investigating the "web structure" of economies, as, for example, in

Kauffman and Scheinkman's analysis of the relationship between the diversity of sectors and rate of economic growth in cities (Kauffman 1995, p. 295).

Today the study of nonequilibrium economics is well under way, for example, in the simulation of stock markets both real and imaginary. The study of the global properties of these economies has been accompanied by research on the behavior of economic actors. Economist Sam Bowles and his colleagues have begun to work with anthropologists to investigate, as an empirical question, how social actors make decisions in game-theoretical or economic contexts (Bowles & Gintis 2002). Based on these results, they propose to supplement *Homo economicus* with a larger and more diverse "family of man." Research in economics on complexity thus proceeds at two levels: the characteristics of individual social actors and the global dynamics of economies or societies. This research draws heavily on mathematical models of nonlinear systems; investigators keep an eye out for power-law distributions of events (such as the growth of firms or the frequency of stock market events) that may signal a system near the edge of chaos (Scheinkman & Woodford 1994).

COOPERATION AND THE "TRAGEDY OF THE COMMONS"

"Common to all studies on complexity," writes Arthur, "are systems with multiple elements adapting or reacting to the patterns these elements create" (Arthur 1999, p. 107). However, what if the elements are not cells or light bulbs but agents capable of reacting with new strategies or foresight to the patterns they have helped to create? As Arthur observes, this adds a layer of complication not experienced in the natural sciences, and much of the current research by social scientists on complex adaptive systems is concerned with precisely this question. One consequence has been to breathe new life into the field of game theory. Like many anthropologists, as a graduate student I had little interest in game theory because it seemed to embody implausible assumptions about human nature, what Marshall Sahlins calls the common average social science wisdom. But the complexity approach has led to a major shift in perspective, from static models of rational choice to the evolution of strategies over time, and from local interactions to their global effects. Perhaps the most active area of research in this field is concerned with the broad subject of social cooperation, which spans topics ranging from the evolution of cooperation in social animals to the human management of natural resources. Here I briefly trace the outlines of this shift from static to dynamic models of the emergence of cooperation.

The obvious place to begin is with Axelrod's famous study of the emergence of cooperation between groups of front-line soldiers who faced each other across the trenches of France in World War One (Axelrod 1984). Axelrod wondered how cooperation could develop between groups of men who could not converse and were in fact trying to kill each other. His approach was to try to identify the strategic choices each group faced in dealing with their opponents across No Man's Land.

Thus a vigorous assault at an unexpected time might lead to a victory, with many enemy dead. But the same option was also available to the enemy. Alternatively, if each group only pretended to attack and made their artillery fire completely predictable, their opponents would have time to take cover. If both sides adopted this strategy, neither side would suffer casualties. In terms of the available options, although a successful attack was deemed the best outcome, to be a victim of such an attack was clearly the worst, while "live and let live" falls somewhere in between. But for a "live and let live" strategy to work, each side must trust the other. Yet such informal truces broke out repeatedly along the trenches and became a major headache for the high command on both sides.

Axelrod suggested that the underlying dynamics of the "live and let live" system could be represented as a game. The advantage to such formalization is that it becomes possible to compare the wartime case with other unlikely instances of spontaneous cooperation to see if similar processes are involved. The particular game is called the Prisoner's Dilemma. As the story goes, two prisoners are each given the choice of giving evidence against the other and so reducing their own sentence. The dilemma arises because if neither defects on the other, the police can convict them both only on a lesser charge. But if one defects (by giving evidence to the police), he goes free, whereas the other goes to jail for a long time. If both defect, both will receive the maximum penalty. These choices and their respective payoffs may be represented in a table (Table 1). Here the rewards are scaled from zero (the worst) to 5 (the best). Mathematician Karl Sigmund suggests that the game becomes more interesting if we think of these payoffs as gold bars, not "measly little numbers" (Sigmund 1993). In Table 1, the numbers in the boxes refer to the payoffs: The first number is the payoff for Player 1 and the second for Player 2. So if Player 1 cooperates and so does Player 2, the payoff for each is 3, as shown in the top left box. But if Player 1 cooperates and Player 2 defects (top right box), Player 1 receives the "sucker's payoff" of zero, whereas the unscrupulous Player 2 reaps the maximum reward: 5 gold bars (or a ticket out of jail in the original anecdote).

The problem is that the optimal strategies for each player create the worst possible joint outcome. Thus, if the other player defects, you are better off defecting (you get one bar instead of none). If the other player cooperates, you are still better off defecting (you get five bars, he gets none). So, cold logic dictates that the best strategy is always to defect. But since the same logic holds for the other player, the outcome is mutual defection, and everyone loses. The chief advantage to defining the problem in this way (as a simple game) is that it can help to reveal the essence of the problem. Indeed one can see that Garrett Hardin's "tragedy of the commons"

TABLE 1   The Prisoner's Dilemma

	Player 2: Cooperate	Player 2: Defect
Player 1: Cooperate	3,3	0,5
Player 1: Defect	5,0	1,1

is another instance of exactly the same game (Hardin 1968, 1998). All fishermen would be better off if they exercised voluntary restraint and did not take too many fish. But in such a situation, an unscrupulous fisherman who decides to take more fish will reap greater rewards than the "suckers" who take only their share, unless there is a common property management system in place (see Agrawal 2003, this volume).

Axelrod suggested that the tragedy of mutual defection can be avoided only if players understand themselves to be in a situation where continuing cooperation can pay off, because the circumstances of the game will recur. In other words, it is worthwhile to cooperate with me today provided I am in a position to repay you by cooperating tomorrow. In the trenches of World War I, Axelrod relates an anecdote in which the artillery from the German side opened up at an unexpected time and killed some British soldiers, thus violating the implicit agreement. Some Germans came out under a flag of truce to apologize and promise that the mistake would not happen again. Subsequent studies emphasized the wide applicability of the Prisoner's Dilemma. For example, sociologists compared the behavior of drivers in large cities versus small towns and villages. Shaking one's fist at other drivers, honking the horn, and other acts of rudeness are more frequent in big city traffic, perhaps because drivers in cities can assume that they are anonymous. Similarly, evolutionary biologists have suggested that cooperation (reciprocal altruism) occurs only among social species that are capable of recognizing other individuals and remembering whether they cooperated on previous occasions. Examples include vampire bats, dolphins, elephants, primates and most especially humans (summarized in Sigmund 1993). Humans turn out to be remarkably good at predicting whether others will cooperate. This was shown in an ingenious experiment: Economist R.H. Frank found that if a group of strangers are asked to play the Prisoner's Dilemma game, their ability to predict who will cooperate (and who will not) improves dramatically if they are given just 30 min to socialize with the other players before the game begins (Frank 1988).

In the original game, rational choice leads to ruin. But if the game continues over time, intuitively it seems possible for cooperation to emerge, as these examples suggest. Axelrod and other researchers accordingly reformulated the game to allow simulated agents to play a series of games with one another, treating their strategies and their memory of the behavior of other players as variables (Axelrod 1997). Because the success of particular strategies is frequency-dependent, the entire game can be treated as a dynamical system evolving over time, with global characteristics that emerge from the local interactions of players and strategies. Under these circumstances, Axelrod found that cooperation would emerge under a wide range of conditions.

Subsequently, physicist Kristian Lindgren embedded game-playing agents on a lattice, adding greater flexibility by making memory length an evolutionary variable. Over tens of thousands of generations, he observed the emergence of spatial patterns that resemble evolutionary processes and that help to clarify preconditions for the emergence of cooperation and competition (Lindgren 1994).

More recently, mathematician Karl Sigmund has developed simulations of games in which players remember encounters they have observed; here cooperation develops very quickly (Sigmund 1993, Nowak & Sigmund 1998). Such simulation results have inspired behavioral ecologists to reexamine biological systems. For example Milinski has studied stickleback fish, which enjoy "a well-earned reputation for keeping abreast of the latest trends in animal behavior." According to Milinski, cooperation in "predator inspection" by the sticklebacks follows the dynamics of the iterated Prisoner's Dilemma (cited in Sigmund 1993, p. 201). The results of these simulations have also been used to model problems in political science and economics (Axelrod 1997).

But cooperation is by no means the only emergent property investigated by social simulations. Philosopher Brian Skyrms has studied the evolution of the social contract by modeling it as a problem in the evolution of dynamical systems. His most ambitious models tackle such large questions as the evolution of justice, linguistic meaning, and logical inference. Skyrms finds that "the typical case is one in which there is not a unique preordained result, but rather a profusion of possible equilibrium outcomes. The theory predicts what anthropologists have always known—that many alternative styles of social life are possible" (1996, p. 81). But this may be a bit too modest. With respect to the evolution of meaning, for example, Skyrms shows that evolutionary processes provide a plausible answer to the fundamental question, "How do the arbitrary symbols of language become associated with the elements of reality they denote?" (Skyrms 1996, p. 81).

COMPLEX SYSTEMS IN ANTHROPOLOGY

There have been several notable studies by anthropologists investigating nonlinear dynamics, such as Park's investigation of the relationship between chaos in flood-recession agriculture and the emergence of social classes (Park 1992). But adaptive agent models have been the main point of entry of complex systems theory into anthropology, beginning with Gumerman's pioneering collaboration with physicist Murray Gell-Mann (Gumerman & Gell-Mann 1994). Gumerman became interested in Axtell and Epstein's Sugarscape, a simulation model developed to study how sociocultural phenomena like trade, warfare, and class structures can arise from simple interactions of adaptive agents. Epstein & Axtell wrote a book about their Sugarscape simulations that provides an excellent overview of research on artificial societies (Epstein & Axtell 1996; for my own critique of this field see Lansing 2002). In Sugarscape, the environment is very simple, consisting of the agents themselves plus some idealized resources, like sugar and spice. Gumerman and his collaborators wondered if more realistic environments could be simulated, with heterogeneous agents and landscapes defined by real archaeological data, observing that "while potentially powerful, agent-based models in archaeology remain unverified until they are evaluated against real-world cases. The degree of fit between a model and real-world situation allows the model's validity to be assessed" (Dean et al. 2000, p. 180). They further observe that the explanatory power of mathematical models may be greatest when they fail because such failures may expose where the researcher's underlying conceptual model or explanation is flawed.

Gumerman & Dean (Dean et al. 2000) worked with Epstein and Axtell to apply the techniques developed for Sugarscape to create an agent-based model of the Anasazi society of Long House Valley in northeastern Arizona from 1800 B.C. to A.D. 1300. Here, the simple lattice environment of Sugarscape is replaced by paleoenvironmental data on a 96-km^2 physical landscape. The environment of "Artificial Anasazi" is populated with human households so that spatiotemporal patterns of settlement formation and household production can be simulated and compared with the archaeological record. A similar approach was developed by Kohler (Kohler & Gumerman 2000) to model human settlements in Mesa Verde circa A.D. 900–1300. Such models enable their creators to test their intuitions about the complex nonlinear processes involved in human-environmental interactions. As Kohler observes, "agent-based approaches admit an important role for history and contingency (and) can also, in principle, accommodate models that invoke heterogeneity among agents, or which drive social change through shifting coalitions of agents, argued by many (e.g., Brumfiel 1992) to be a critical social dynamic" (Kohler & Gumerman 2000, p. 14).

One of the strengths of this type of simulation modeling is that it enables researchers to subject trial explanations for sociocultural phenomena to a rigorous test. Of course this has always been the main justification for mathematical models; what is new about the adaptive agent approach is their ability to capture nonlinear effects that would otherwise be out of reach. But in my view, a more important development is the revelation, foreshadowed by theoretical work on complex adaptive systems, that social institutions can emerge from the bottom up as a result of feedback processes linking social actors to their environments (as Kohler & Gumerman observe in their recent volume). Such institutions might look very different from those that social scientists normally study; they might even be invisible.

Recently my colleagues and I have suggested that the water temple networks with which Balinese farmers manage their centuries-old irrigation systems and rice terraces are a real-world example of a complex adaptive system, whose dynamics resemble those of Lovelock's Daisyworld (Lovelock 1992, Lansing et al. 1998, Lenton & Lovelock 2000). For decades, both social scientists and engineers have marveled at the success of the Balinese in managing complex irrigation systems involving hundreds of villages. But the question of how this was achieved remained mysterious. We developed a simple game-theory formulation of the choices that Balinese farmers face when they make decisions about cooperation in water management, and we verified that this game captured the farmer's views in questionnaires administered to farmers from 15 different irrigation societies. A simulation model of 200 communities was constructed to explore the effects on rice terrace ecology at the watershed scale. We found that even though local communities "do not consciously attempt to create an optimal pattern of staggered cropping schedules for entire watersheds . . . the actual patterns [we] have observed in the field bear a very close resemblance to computer simulations of optimal solutions" (Lansing 2000, p. 313). In subsequent experiments, we pursued the kinds of questions Kauffman posed in *The Origins of Order*, such as the relationship between the structure of connections between farming communities (subaks) and the ability of the entire collection of subaks to self-organize (Lansing et al. 1998).

In the Balinese case, global control of terrace ecology emerges as local actors strike a balance between two opposing constraints: water stress from inadequate irrigation flow and damage from rice pests such as rats and insects. In our computer model, the solution involves finding the right scale of reproductive synchrony, a solution that emerges from innumerable local interactions. This system was deliberately disrupted by agricultural planners during the Green Revolution in the 1970s. For planners unfamiliar with the notion of self-organizing systems, the relationship between watershed-scale synchrony, pest control, and irrigation management was obscure. Our simulation models helped to clarify the functional role of water temples, and, partly as a consequence, the Asian Development Bank dropped its opposition to the bottom-up control methods of the subaks, noting that "the cost of the lack of appreciation of the merits of the traditional regime has been high" (Lansing 1991, pp. 124–25).

An intriguing parallel to the Balinese example has recently been proposed by ecologist Lisa Curran (1999). Forty years ago Borneo was covered with the world's oldest and most diverse tropical forests. Curran observes that during the El Niño Southern Oscillation (ENSO), the dominant canopy timber trees (*Dipterocarpaceae*) of the lowland forests synchronize seed production and seedling recruitment. As in the Balinese case, reproductive success involves countless local-level trade-offs, in this case between competition among seedlings versus predator satiation. The outcome of these trade-offs is global-scale synchronized reproductive cycles. But forest management policies have failed to take into account this vast self-organizing system (Curran et al. 1999). As Curran explains, "With increasing forest conversion and fragmentation, ENSO, the great forest regenerator, has become a destructive regional phenomenon, triggering droughts and wildfires with increasing frequency and intensity, disrupting dipterocarp fruiting, wildlife and rural livelihoods" (p. 2188). As a consequence, the lowland tropical forests of Borneo are threatened with imminent ecological collapse (L.M. Curran, personal communication).

These examples serve to highlight two points emphasized by Holland. The first point is that recognizing complex adaptive systems involves a shift in perception; thus the most fruitful strategy may be "to make cross-disciplinary comparisons in hopes of extracting common characteristics." Holland's second point is to echo the warning sounded by many ecologists: "We, as humans, have become so numerous that we perforce extensively modify ecological interactions, with only vague ideas of longer-range effects" (Holland 1995, pp. 4, 6). Ecologists are beginning to try to quantify these effects; for example, Field recently calculated the fraction of the earth's total biological productivity that is appropriated by *Homo sapiens* at nearly 40% and rising fast (Field 2001). Understanding this phenomenon is an intrinsically interdisciplinary problem, as Holland emphasizes; yet so far it has received far less attention from anthropologists than ecologists (Levin 1999, Solé & Manrubia 1995, Holling 2001, Lenton & Lovelock 2000).

CRITIQUES, REVIEWS, AND RESOURCES

There have been several recent critiques of the field of artificial societies. Thus Smith wrote in the *New York Review of Books* that he has "a general feeling of unease when contemplating complex systems dynamics. Its devotees are prac- tising fact-free science. A fact for them is, at best, the outcome of a computer simulation; it is rarely a fact about the world" (Smith 1995, p. 30). Science writer John Horgan cautions that "as the philosopher Karl Popper pointed out, predic- tion is our best means of distinguishing science from pseudo-science . . . . The history of 20th-century science should also give complexologists pause. Com- plexity is simply the latest in a long line of highly mathematical 'theories of almost everything' that have gripped the imaginations of scientists in this century" (Horgan 1995, p. 104). (Here, Horgan appears to be mostly concerned with the very general theories of emergence developed by Stuart Kauffman and Per Bak, among others.)

A broader critique was recently published by an anthropologist, Stefan Helmreich, who offers an ethnographic account of the researchers working at the Santa Fe Institute in the mid-1990s. In *Silicon Second Nature* (1998), Helmreich argues that artificial-societies models reflect the unconscious cultural assumptions and social prejudices of their creators: "Because Artificial Life scientists tend to see themselves as masculine gods of their cyberspace creations, as digital Darwins exploring frontiers filled with primitive creatures, their programs reflect preva- lent representations of gender, kinship, and race and repeat origin stories most familiar from mythical and religious narratives" (p. 95). For example, Helmreich describes Holland's genetic algorithms as reflecting a "heterosexual" bias: "There are a number of ways we might understand the exchange of bits between strings, but the metaphor of productive heterosex is gleefully emphasized by most authors" (p. 146). Thus for Helmreich, simulation models are like Rorschach tests, revealing the researcher's cultural background and psychological idiosyncrasies. All state- ments, especially theoretical pronouncements, are taken not as statements about the world but as evidence about the author's beliefs and mode of thought. "That many Artificial Life practitioners are white men who grew up reading cowboy sci- ence fiction," observes Helmreich, "is not trivial" (p. 95). Simulation models may also be dangerous (as Helmreich suggests with reference to my own work), urging that "the use and abuse of computer simulations bears watching—especially in situations where there is a notable power differential between those putting to- gether the simulation and those whose lives are the subjects and objects of these simulations" (Helmreich 1999; for my response, see Lansing 2000 and Lansing et al. 2001).

Readers interested in an overview of the field cannot do better than Kohler & Gumerman's (2000) volume, which contains review essays by archaeologists Kohler and Henry Wright, as well as "Modeling Sociality: the View from Europe" by sociologist Nigel Gilbert (2000). There are a large number of popular accounts of research on chaos and complexity; my favorites are Gleick's (1987) *Chaos* and Waldrop's (1992) *Complexity* (though both are rather out of date). More substantial overviews include Langton 1994, Flake 1998, Hofbauer & Sigmund 1988, Depew & Weber 1995, Lansing 2002, and Kauffman 1993. A useful weekly digest of publications pertaining to complexity is available at http://www.comdig.org, and the working papers of the Santa Fe Institute are available for the asking at http://www.santafe.edu. Simulation of cellular automata, random Boolean networks, and Derrida plots can be accomplished using free software created by Andrew Wuensch and is available at http://www.santafe.edu/~wuensch/ddlab.html. Anthropologists may also be interested in mathematical models of "small-world" networks (Watts 1999, Watts & Strogatz 1998), which investigate the topological properties of social and ecological networks.

CONCLUSION

This chapter is already too long, so I will conclude with a single observation. So far, only a handful of anthropologists have taken an interest in complex systems. Yet much contemporary research on complex adaptive systems is concerned with questions that have traditionally formed the subject matter of anthropology. As the distinguished mathematical biologist Simon Levin observed in a review of current research, "there is fundamental interest in the evolution of social norms, or of language, and how such group properties emerge from and feed back to influence individual behavior . . . . [T]he potential payoffs are enormous and the mathematical challenges irresistably seductive" (2003, p. 10). There seems little doubt that such questions will be pursued, if not by anthropologists then by our colleagues.

ACKNOWLEDGMENTS

I am grateful to Christopher Langton, Lisa Curran, George Gumerman, James Kremer, Joseph Watkins, Thérèse de Vet, and John Murphy for helpful comments. Research on complex systems in Bali was supported by grants from the Anthropology and Biocomplexity programs of the National Science Foundation. The Santa Fe Institute, the Center for Advanced Study in the Behavioral Sciences at Stanford, and the University of Arizona provided opportunities for reflection and discussions with colleagues. The views expressed here, however, are entirely my own.

The *Annual Review of Anthropology* is online at http://anthro.annualreviews.org

LITERATURE CITED

Agrawal A. 2003. Sustainable governance of common-pool resources: context, methods, and politics. *Annu. Rev. Anthropol.* 32:In press

Arthur WB. 1999. Complexity and the economy. *Science* 284:107–9

Arthur WB, Durlauf SN, Lane DA. 1997. *The Economy as an Evolving Complex System II.* Reading, MA: Addison-Wesley and the Santa Fe Institute

Axelrod R. 1984. Th*e Evolution of Cooperation.* New York: Basic Books

Axelrod R. 1997. *The Complexity of Cooperation: Agent-Based Models of Cooperation and Collaboration.* Princeton, NJ: Princeton Univ. Press

Bak P. 1997. *How Nature Works: the Science of Self-Organized Criticality.* Oxford: Oxford Univ. Press

Bak P, Chen K. 1991. Self-organized criticality. *Sci. Am.* 264(1):46–53

Bonabeau E. 1997. Flexibility at the edge of chaos: a clear example from foraging in ants. *Acta Biotheor.* 45:29–50

Bowles S, Gintis H. 2002. Homo reciprocans. *Nature* 415:125–28

Brumfiel EM. 1992. Distinguished lecture in anthropology: breaking and entering the ecosystem–gender, class and faction steal the show. *Am. Anthropol.* 94:551–67

Curran LM, Caniago I, Paoli GD, Astiani D, Kusneti M, et al. 1999. Impact of El Niño and logging on canopy tree recruitment in Borneo. *Science* 286:2184–88

Campbell D, Crutchfield J, Farmer J, Jen E. 1985. Experimental mathematics: the role of computation in nonlinear science. *Commun. Assoc. Comput. Mach.* 28:374–84

Dean J, Gumerman G, Epstein J, Axtell R, Swedlund A, et al. 2000. Understanding Anasazi culture through agent-based modeling. In *Dynamics in Human and Primate Societies,* ed. T Kohler, G Gumerman, pp. 179–205. Oxford: Oxford Univ. Press

de Oliveira P. 2001. Why do evolutionary systems stick to the edge of chaos? *Theory Biosci.* 120:1–19

Depew D, Weber B. 1995. *Darwinism Evolving: Systems Dynamics and the Genealogy of Natural Selection.* Cambridge, MA: MIT Press

Dobzhansky T. 1937. *Genetics and the Origin of the Species.* New York: Columbia Univ. Press

Durkheim E. 1979 [1897]. *Suicide: a Study in Sociology.* Transl. JA Spaulding, G Simpson. New York: Free Press. From French

Epstein J, Axtell R. 1996. *Growing Artificial Societies: Social Science from the Bottom Up.* Washington, DC: Brookings Inst. Press, MIT Press

Ferriere R, Fox GA. 1995. Chaos and evolution. *Tree* 10:480–85

Field CB. 2001. Sharing the garden. *Science* 294:2490–91

Flake G. 1998. *The Computational Beauty of Nature: Computer Explorations of Fractals, Chaos, Complex Systems, and Adaptation.* Cambridge, MA, London: MIT Press

Frank RH. 1988. *Passions Within Reason.* New York: Norton

Gilbert N. 2000. Modeling sociality: the view from Europe. See Kohler & Gumerman, pp. 355–72

Gleick J. 1987. *Chaos: Making a New Science.* New York: Penguin Books

Gould SJ. 1989. *Wonderful Life.* Cambridge, MA: Harvard Univ. Press

Gumerman G, Gell-Mann M, eds. 1994. *Understanding Complexity in the Prehistoric Southwest.* Reading, MA: Addison-Wesley and the Santa Fe Institute

Hardin G. 1968. The tragedy of the commons. *Science* 162:1243–48

Hardin G. 1998. Extensions of 'the tragedy of the commons.' *Science* 280:47–48

Helmreich S. 1998. *Silicon Second Nature:*

Culturing Artificial Life in a Digital World. Berkeley: Univ. Calif. Press

Helmreich S. 1999. Digitizing 'development': Balinese water temples, complexity, and the politics of simulation. *Crit. Anthropol.* 19(3):249–65

Hofbauer J, Sigmund K. 1988. *The Theory of Evolution and Dynamical Systems.* Cambridge, MA: Cambridge Univ. Press

Holland JH. 1995. *Hidden Order: How Adaptation Builds Complexity.* New York: Helix Books (Addison Wesley)

Holling C. 2001. Understanding the complexity of economic, ecological and social systems. *Ecosystems* 4:390–405

Horgan J. 1995. From complexity to perplexity. *Sci. Am.* 272(6):104–10

Kauffman S. 1989. Principles of adaptation in complex systems. In *Lectures in the Sciences of Complexity*, ed. E Stein, pp. 619–712. Reading, MA: Addison-Wesley

Kauffman S. 1993. *The Origins of Order: Self-Organization and Selection in Evolution.* New York: Oxford Univ. Press

Kauffman S. 1995. *At Home in the Universe: the Search for Laws of Self-Organization and Complexity.* New York: Oxford Univ. Press

Kohler T, Gumerman G, eds. 2000. *Dynamics in Human and Primate Societies: Agent-Based Modeling of Social and Spatial Processes.* New York: Oxford Univ. Press

Kremer J, Lansing J. 1995. Modelling water temples and rice irrigation in Bali: a lesson in socio-ecological communication. In *Maximum Power: the Ideas and Applications of H.T. Odum*, ed. CAS Hall, pp. 100–8. Niwot, CO: Univ. Press Colorado

Langton CG. 1990. Computation at the edge of chaos: phase transitions and emergent computation. *Physica D* 42:12–37

Langton CG. 1991. *Computation at the edge of chaos: phase transitions and emergent computation.* PhD diss. Univ. Mich.

Langton C. 1994. Artificial life III. *Proc. Santa Fe Inst. Sci. Complex.*, 17th. Reading, MA: Addison-Wesley

Lansing J. 1991. *Priests and Programmers: Technologies of Power in the Engineered Landscape of Bali.* Princeton, NJ: Princeton Univ. Press

Lansing J. 1999. Anti-chaos, common property and the emergence of cooperation. In *Dynamics in Human and Primate Societies: Agent-Based Modeling of Social and Spatial Processes*, ed. T Kohler, G Gumerman, pp. 207–24. Oxford: Oxford Univ. Press

Lansing J. 2000. Foucault and the water temples: a reply to Helmreich. *Crit. Anthropol.* 20:337–46

Lansing J. 2002. 'Artificial societies' and the social sciences. *Artif. Life* 8:279–92

Lansing J, Gerhart V, Kremer J, Kremer P, Arthawiguna A, et al. 2001. Volcanic fertilization of Balinese rice paddies. *Ecol. Econ.* 38:383–90

Lansing J, Kremer J, Smuts B. 1998. System-dependent selection, ecological feedback and the emergence of functional structure in ecosystems. *J. Theor. Biol.* 192:377–91

Latora V, Baranger M, Rapisarda A, Tsallis C. 2000. The rate of entropy increases at the edge of chaos. *Phys. Lett. A* 273:97–103

Lenton T, Lovelock J. 2000. Daisyworld is Darwinian: constraints on adaptiation are important for planetary self-regulation. *J. Theor. Biol.* 206:109–14

Levin S. 1999. *Fragile Dominion: Complexity and the Commons.* Reading, MA: Perseus Books

Levin S. 2003. Complex adaptive systems: exploring the known, the unknown and the unknowable. *Bull. Am. Math. Soc.* 40(1):3–19

Lindgren K. 1994. Evolutionary dynamics of simple games. *Physica D* 75:292–309

Lovelock J. 1992. A numerical model for biodiversity. *Phil. Trans. R. Soc. Lond. B* 338:365–73

Maxwell JC. 1890. *Scientific Papers*, ed. WD Niven. Cambridge, UK: Cambridge Univ. Press. 2 vols.

May R. 1976. Simple mathematical models with very complicated dynamics. *Nature* 261:459–67

Mayr E, Provine WB. 1980. *The Evolutionary*

Synthesis: Perspectives on the Unification of Biology. Cambridge, MA: Harvard Univ. Press

Mitchell M, Crutchfield J. 1993. Revisiting the edge of chaos: evolving cellular automata to perform computations. *Complex Syst.* 7:89–130

Nowak M, Sigmund K. 1998. Evolution of indirect reciprocity by image scoring. *Nature* 393:573–77

Park TK. 1992. Early trends toward class stratification: chaos, common property, and flood recession agriculture. *Am. Anthropol.* 94(1):90–117

Popper K. 1990. *A World of Propensities.* Bristol, UK: Thoemmes

Porter TM. 1986. *The Rise of Statistical Thinking.* Princeton, NJ: Princeton Univ. Press

Schank J. 1998. A new paradigm for animal social systems. *Proc. Int. Conf. Complex Syst. Interjournal.* 240: http://www.interjournal. org/cgi-bin/manuscript_abstract.cgi?49122

Scheinkman JM, Woodford M. 1994. Self-organized criticality and economic fluctuations. *Am. Econ. Rev.* 84(2):417–21

Scoones I. 1999. New ecology and the social sciences: what prospects for a fruitful engagement? *Annu. Rev. Anthropol.* 28:479–507

Sigmund K. 1993. *Games of Life: Explorations in Ecology, Evolution and Behaviour.* London: Penguin Books

Skyrms B. 1996. *Evolution of the Social Contract.* Cambridge, UK: Cambridge Univ. Press

Smith JM. 1995. Review of 'The Origins of Order.' *New York Rev. Books* (March 2):30–33

Solé R, Manrubia S. 1995. Are rainforests self-organized in a critical state? *J. Theor. Biol.* 173:31–40

Waldrop M. 1992. *Complexity: the Emerging Science at the Edge of Order and Chaos.* New York: Touchstone

Watts D. 1999. *Small Worlds: the Dynamics of Networks Between Order and Randomness.* Princeton, NJ: Princeton Univ. Press

Watts DJ, Strogatz SH. 1998. Collective dynamics of 'small-world' networks. *Nature* 393:440–42

Wolfram S. 2002. *A New Kind of Science.* Champaign, IL: Wolfram Media

Wright S. 1932. The roles of mutation, inbreeding, crossbreeding and selection in evolution. *Proc. Sixth Int. Congr. Genet.*, 6th, 1:356–66

Wuensch A, Lesser MJ. 1992. *The Global Dynamics of Cellular Automata: an Atlas of Basin of Attraction Fields of One-Dimensional Cellular Automata.* Reading, MA: Addison-Wesley, Santa Fe Inst. Stud. Sci. Complex.

Annu. Rev. Anthropol. 2003. 32:205–23
doi: 10.1146/annurev.anthro.32.061002.093335
First published online as a Review in Advance on June 4, 2003

IT'S A MATERIAL WORLD:
History, Artifacts, and Anthropology

Elizabeth M. Brumfiel

*Department of Anthropology and Sociology, Albion College, Albion, Michigan 49224;
email: ebrumfiel@albion.edu*

Key Words   colonialism, ethnic and national identities, historical archaeology,
historical anthropology, material culture

■ **Abstract**   History is of critical importance for anthropology because, in human
affairs, the present is intimately linked to the past. Archaeology is important to the
study of history because the material remains of the past supplement and interrogate
historical documents. Collaboration between cultural anthropologists and archaeologists will produce a broader knowledge of past worlds and how those worlds have been
constructed in historical texts, both past and present. Cultural anthropologists and
archaeologists should also compare the ways in which they engage in discussions about
the past with both the American public and local communities—discussions that are
quite different in the two subfields.

INTRODUCTION

Why include archaeology and cultural anthropology within a single scholarly
discipline? A common answer to this question supposes a clear division of labor
between the two subfields: Archaeology studies humans in the past, and cultural
anthropology studies humans in the present. Archaeology's concern with long-term
history complements cultural anthropology's interest in the intimate interactions
of daily life. Archaeology's cross-cultural and comparative perspective balances
cultural anthropology's recognition of each culture's individuality.

Archaeology's comparative and long-term perspective does provide some
unique insights into human nature and the human condition. For example, were
preindustrial humans natural ecologists, or have humans always been the thought-
less exploiters of nature that we see today? Examining contemporary non-Western
cultures, cultural anthropologists might answer that humans can be either natural ecologists or ruthless exploiters, or they can occupy positions between these
extremes, depending on social and natural contexts. But the five million years of
human history accessible to archaeologists supply a different and somewhat more
precise generalization: Humans are terrible pioneers. Over and over again, humans have first degraded their environments and then developed more sustainable
practices.

0084-6570/03/1021-0205$14.00   **205**

For example, human entry into Australia (Miller et al. 1999), North America (Martin & Klein 1984), Cyprus (Simmons 1999), Madagascar (Culotta 1995), New Zealand (Cracraft 1980), and the other Polynesian Islands (Steadman 1995) was followed by the extinction of many large game animals shortly thereafter. This circumstantial evidence seems compelling: The extinctions were due to over-hunting. These extinctions tail off in time and are replaced by less-destructive modes of human habitation, both because the highly vulnerable species were quickly driven to extinction and because humans began to realize their dependence on local resources and to devise more sustainable practices, a process that poet Gary Snyder (1977) refers to as inhabitation. This pattern is not just true of hunters; it also characterized the spread of agriculture. Archaeologists have recorded dramatic incidents of soil erosion in Greece (Runnels 1995), Ireland (Moore 1982), and the Basin of Mexico (Nichols 1982) coinciding with the adoption of agriculture. Episodes of erosion were followed by soil-conserving technologies, such as terracing, but only after most of the soil had washed downslope.

This offers both hope and despair regarding our current ecological crisis. Humans are now engaged in a third great experiment with resource utilization: industrial production. The perspective of prehistory suggests that we are currently in our rape and pillage mode, and that we will probably manage to save ourselves from total destruction, but not before we wreak tremendous harm on the environment with a tragic loss in biodiversity. Of course, we have a better ability to monitor the environment, a greater capacity to control it, and the knowledge of our own history, so this time may be different.

Here is another, less depressing, insight that archaeology provides into the human condition. In several cases, important new technologies were developed for non-utilitarian purposes, and only later were utilitarian applications found for these technologies. For example, Aurignacian bone-working techniques were used first for making beads and only later to shape harpoons and spearheads (White 1989). Clay-firing was used first in the Upper Paleolithic to make clay figurines, not ceramic vessels (Vandiver et al. 1989). In Mesoamerica, metalworkers first produced copper bells and subsequently copper axes (Hosler 1995). Thus, it seems that necessity is not necessarily the mother of invention, and that the most potent stimulus to human creativity is play—or prestige-competition. Prestige-competition is evident in our recent race to the moon, which resulted in the development of freeze-dried and microwave technologies. At any rate, these examples seem to provide a rationale for NSF support of both pure and applied research and deferred timelines of accountability.

However, there are many other fields that complement cultural anthropology in useful and interesting ways, fields such as literary criticism, neuroscience, and religious studies. Is there some special link between archaeology and cultural anthropology that constitutes the basis for a privileged relationship? I believe there is. Archaeology and cultural anthropology share a concern with issues of history, and these issues require mutual cooperation.

In human affairs, the present is intimately linked to the past through material conditions and cultural understandings. The past determines the quality of currently available resources (Redman 1999). The past also determines the store of capital (Netting 1993, Earle 1998) and the distribution of wealth and power in a society (Wolf 1990). These material conditions, inherited from the past, seriously constrain human action in the present. In addition, people continually look to the past to understand their current circumstances, to choose their future course of action, and to justify their choices. As Chanock (1985, p. 15) observes, humans walk into the future facing backward. To understand why people behave the way they do, we must know their past and their understanding of that past. Finally, history provides a potent social weapon. People use history to position themselves with respect to others: to entitle some individuals and to deny others rights to resources, citizenship, and social status (Williams 1989). Social identities are frequently grounded in socially constructed understandings of the past, and this is true both of those identities ascribed to others by outsiders and those identities embraced by individuals for themselves (Hobsbawm & Ranger 1983). Friedman (1992) observes that history is a question of empowerment: People without history are unable to identify themselves for others. Conversely, people use history to identify their common interests and to enter into effective political coalitions. Cultural anthropologists, then, must be interested both in the ways in which humans have actually lived in the past and in the ways history is constructed and deployed in contemporary social contexts (Borofsky 1987, Tonkin 1992, Bond & Gilliam 1994, Haley & Wilcoxon 1997, Kohl 1998, Erikson 1999, Field 1999).

Archaeology is important to the interpretation of history because archaeology controls the material remains of the past. Material remains supplement the historical record in several crucial ways. First, they supply historical information for times and places not recorded in oral and written histories. Material remains are particularly useful in addressing the earliest years of European contact and the effects of contact in rural areas where European visitors were few. Second, material remains reflect the actions and interactions of daily life. These actions—eating, working, moving through space, carrying out rituals—are "the processes that make and transform particular worlds" (Comaroff & Comaroff 1992, p. 31; see Stahl 2001, p. 17). Such taken-for-granted activities often go unrecorded in historical accounts. Third, material remains can correct unconscious bias or deliberate misinformation in historical texts, often in regard to gender, class, and ethnicity. The archaeological record can potentially challenge the "master narratives" preserved in written documents (Johnson 1999, p. 34). Fourth, material remains enable us to gauge the material constraints on action, particularly constraints arising from uneven distributions of resources and labor (Wolf 1990). Thoughts may be free, but action in the physical world is not, and limited resources may impose serious limits on human choice and engender cultural change (Carrier & Heyman 1997; DeMarrais et al. 1996, p. 17).

Finally, material remains are not just a source of information; they are a source of power. Because material remains can be verified through the senses, they carry a special credibility. The control of material remains confers the ability to interpret the past, to speak about it authoritatively.

Cultural anthropologists who study history will want to refer to archaeology to gain a broader knowledge of past worlds and how those worlds have been constructed in historical texts, both past and present. Archaeologists must be concerned with the ways in which the constructs of Western culture shaped archaeological interpretations of the past (Gero et al. 1983, McGuire 1992, Shanks & Tilley 1987, Stahl 2001, Thomas 2000, Trigger 1980).

In addition, cultural anthropologists and archaeologists might compare the way that they engage populations outside of anthropology in discussions about the past, discussions that are quite different in the two subfields.

ARCHAEOLOGY AND HISTORICAL ANTHROPOLOGY

Critiques of anthropology and history extending over the past two decades have shown how anthropology has participated in the ordering of non-Western peoples through the construction and strategic deployment of history—or though the erasure of history (Trigger 1980, 1981; Wolf 1982; Fabian 1983; Thomas 1989; McGuire 1992; Schmidt & Patterson 1995a; Thomas 2000; Stahl 2001). Anthropology's abuses of history are now well known, and archaeology has contributed abuses of its own. For example, archaeologists' uncritical use of ethnographic analogy to interpret archaeological remains succeeded in collapsing the past into the present and reinforced the belief that non-Western cultures had little capacity for change (Trigger 1981, Chance 1996). Archaeologists' focus on prehistoric sites to the exclusion of historic sites created a rupture between descendant populations and their prehistoric heritages, facilitating the dispossession of descendant populations and impeding their collective organization (Lightfoot 1995, Schmidt & Patterson 1995a, Rubertone 2000).

Anthropology has tried to make amends for its misuse of history, principally through historical anthropology (e.g., Comaroff & Comaroff 1991, 1992, 1997; Sahlins 1985; Kirch & Sahlins 1992). Following the lead of Eric Wolf (1982), historical anthropologists have demonstrated that the "natives" taken as the subjects of earlier ethnographies were not living in a pristine state of isolation but rather were subjects of colonial rule and constructs of colonial ideology. In addition, historical anthropologists have shown how local populations mediated the impact of global capitalism. But the success of historical anthropology in constructing more adequate historical accounts has been hampered by methodological and conceptual problems.

Historical anthropology has tended to rely exclusively on historical documents, but, as noted above, documents supply only spotty coverage of indigenous cultures. They are riddled with omissions of place and time period, and the information they supply is refracted through biases of class, gender, and ethnicity. Stahl (2001) notes that historical anthropologists have often tried to fill the gaps in the documentary sources by using information from various times and places to create composite baselines of native culture at the time of contact. Information from documents, ethnographies, and oral histories has been detached from moorings in specific times and places and inserted into the composite picture. The construction of composite baselines introduces anachronisms into the historical record and makes it difficult or impossible to chart the real course of cultural change.

In addition, documents do not extend into prehistory (or not very far), so the result, intended or not, is to emphasize the West as the source of cultural change, as a dynamic and forceful presence, in contrast to a passive, oriental, local population. This is a very limited historicity, stopping short of the longer historical range that local people would find useful in gaining a sense of their own historical identity.

All of this would be much improved if historical anthropologists collaborated with archaeologists in developing local histories. Archaeologists can establish true chronological sequences of events, and they can reconstruct long sequences of pre-contact cultural change. For periods where both documents and archaeological data exist, each can be used to supplement and interrogate the other. The methodology for joining these two data sets is now well understood; it involves tacking back and forth between documents and artifacts, using the new or discordant information presented by one data source to formulate research questions for the other data source (Leone & Potter 1988; Wylie 1999). Kepecs & Kolb (1997) offer innovative approaches to joining historical documents and archaeology; Robertshaw (2000) provides a less optimistic assessment of the prospects for uniting texts and artifacts.

What might collaboration between historical anthropologists and archaeologists accomplish? The best known collaborative effort is *Anahulu*, the monumental, two-volume study of historical change in Hawaii by Kirch & Sahlins (1992). But *Anahulu* must be counted only a modest success, despite exemplary scholarship by both Kirch and Sahlins. Few people read both volumes, and *Anahulu* has not engendered other collaborations. What went wrong? Kirch and Sahlins seem to have suffered from irreconcilable differences of theory. The research questions from one volume did not carry over into the other, and *Anahulu* contains precious little tacking back and forth between documentary and archaeological data. The result is two parallel studies rather than true collaboration. Kirch and Sahlins suggest that this disjuncture is inherent in the differences between documentary and archaeological data: They think that documents provide information on culture, and archaeology provides information on culture's material base [see Smith (1992) for a similar position]. However, it seems to me that the disjuncture in *Anahulu* can be attributed to factors specific to Kirch and Sahlins.

Sahlins shows something of a lack of "archaeological imagination," a lack of ability to envision how archaeological data might relate to his research questions, as when he observes that the later Hawaiian kings demanded tribute, a scheme that "goes back into prehistory—exactly how far no one knows" (Sahlins 1992, p. 27). Actually, tribute collection is rather easy to identify in the archaeological record because it produces change both in the household economy of those responsible for paying the tribute and in the chiefly economy, which allocates the newly acquired resources (Brumfiel 1991, Kolb 1997). At the same time, Kirch, a processual archaeologist trained in prehistoric archaeology, was not attuned to Sahlins' questions of cultural consciousness and how these might be studied through material remains.

Like Sahlins, Comaroff & Comaroff (1997) show a lack of archaeological imagination. The Comaroffs, of course, emphasize the importance of daily routines and material culture in creating new consciousness among colonized Tswana people, to the point of providing floor plans of missionary schools so that readers can consider how movement through space organizes consciousness. But how much better to have actually excavated the school and to discover exactly how that space was used!

I take all this not as evidence of an unbridgeable divide between anthropology and archaeology but as an indication of a need for more informed collaboration between archaeologists and cultural anthropologists. Three recent books clearly demonstrate the value of combining archaeology with historical anthropology. Read as part of graduate training for both cultural anthropologists and archaeologists, they would do much to establish the basis for fruitful collaboration.

The first of these books is *Grave Undertakings* by Patricia E. Rubertone (2001). Rubertone compares the evidence from a sixteenth-century Narragansett cemetery (excavated because it was threatened by development) with the information supplied by the single authoritative text on Narragansett language and culture, Roger Williams' *A Key Into the Language of America* (1973 [1643]). Rubertone finds many points of agreement between text and artifact, but she is more interested in the gaps and differences. For example, Williams describes Narragansett funerary practices, but he fails to mention that the dead were buried in cemetery plots, a practice that archaeologists recognize as a late seventeenth-century innovation. This information alone raises significant issues. Did the cemeteries constitute a more assertive claim for indigenous rights over land and resources than the previous scattered graves? Were the cemeteries intended to provide protection against grave robbing, a Puritan practice which, according to Williams, enraged the Narragansett? The creation of cemeteries suggests pressures generated by the colonial encounter that are suppressed in Williams' account and indicates previously unrecognized inventiveness by the Narragansett in responding to the colonial encounter.

The Narragansett cemetery also subverts the American "master narrative" that the indigenous cultures disintegrated and eventually became extinct under the impact of European contact. In the 47 graves examined by Rubertone, the dead were buried in a highly standardized fashion: on their right sides, in flexed positions, with their heads pointing southwest, and with indigenous cloths or mats spread below and over their bodies. Grave goods included items of both Native and European manufacture, and they varied among individuals. But some grave goods were restricted to individuals of a particular age and sex. The uniform burial program suggests deliberate adherence to a culturally ordered set of rules for disposing of the dead, not cultural disintegration or social disorder. Continuity in Narragansett culture is also evident in continuing efforts to honor the dead, some of which are visible archaeologically (offerings placed in intrusive pits dug some time after the original burial, a burial placed in the cemetery a century after its common use had ended) and others of which are evident in written documents (a nineteenth-century suit by the Narragansett against European Americans who were digging up Narragansett graves, a succession of reports in *Narragansett Dawn*, a twentieth-century magazine of Narragansett language and culture, of encounters between living Narragansett and their long-dead ancestors).

Rubertone points out that Williams' text has been used by the dominant culture to enshrine immutable criteria of cultural authenticity for the Narragansett, criteria that continually undermine contemporary Narragansett claims of identity. But archaeological and documentary data combined can establish continuities of practice that link descendant communities to their ancestral pasts and that permit both cultural change and credible claims of legitimate descent.

Whereas Rubertone focuses on issues of cultural continuity during the colonial encounter, Stahl (2001) emphasizes change. To counter the timeless images of precolonial Africa in anthropology and archaeology, Stahl's *Making History in Banda* examines the occupation of a single region (on the forest edge of northern Ghana) at three points in time, noting the many significant changes that occurred in the course of seven centuries. In the years 1300–1700, the population clustered in large villages with solidly built housing. People hunted a wide variety of forest animals, cultivated indigenous staples, and experimented with New World maize. They produced decorated ceramics and iron tools for regional exchange, and they participated in the trans-Saharan trade for status goods such as gold and cloth. By 1775–1825, under Asante dominance, villages were smaller, though still featuring solidly built houses. Sorghum and maize were well-established crops. Ceramics and iron tools were no longer produced locally, but the presence of spindle whorls suggests local cloth production. Cloth production may have initiated the complex exchanges between women and men that characterize cloth production in the region today. Highly individualized pipes suggest the popularity of New World tobacco. The richly decorated pipes contrast with the subdued and standardized decoration on domestic ceramics, suggesting changes in conventions of social display. From 1875–1925, under British colonial rule, house construction was flimsy, as people resettled the region, which had been abandoned because of intensive warfare. Ceramics were plainer, and standardized clay-ball pipes replaced the individualized pipes of earlier times. Turtle/tortoise, hare/rabbit, rodent, and lizard bones suggest that garden trapping and collecting replaced large game hunting, perhaps because British colonial administrators were appropriating men's labor. European goods increased in frequency and variety, including items such as pipes, glass bottles, and seed beads. However, none of these trade goods noticeably affected the daily routines of household reproduction.

These archaeological data permit Stahl to subvert several master narratives. First, Stahl contests the image of precolonial Africa as timeless and isolated, a view enshrined in the writings of touring colonial officials. The archaeological data record several major shifts in settlement size, residential stability, agricultural staples, household craft production, gender relations, trade networks, and practices of social display, with European colonial rule occurring as only one in a series of significant reorganizations brought about by shifting regional dynamics. Second, Stahl challenges archaeology's preoccupation with narratives of cultural evolution. Of the historical changes evident in the archaeological record, few if any would be recognized as significant evolutionary transitions (Stahl 2001, p. 215). Yet these "non-evolutionary" changes are worthy of study, if only because they were significant in the lives of people in Banda. Finally, both the instability evident in the settlement pattern data and the narratives of migration and ethnic mingling preserved among local populations enable Stahl to narrate a rich and varied history of the Banda region, a history that counters efforts by the Banda chief to limit the scope of history to the affairs of his own noble family and ethnic group.

A third highly successful joining of archaeology and historical anthropology is *Race and Affluence* by Paul R. Mullins (1999). Mullins examines the contents of African American homes in Annapolis, Maryland dating to the late nineteenth and early twentieth centuries. Archaeological excavation revealed many items of consumer culture: patent medicine and mineral water bottles, tea sets set aside from daily dishes, knick-knacks, name-brand products, and canned foods. Mullins asks, do these goods, so similar to the goods of White families of the time, indicate an acceptance of White culture, even though this culture endorsed racism and vigorously opposed Black equality? Or, following Miller (1987) and Thomas (1991), do goods coming from African American contexts deserve a different reading than the same goods coming from Euro-American locales, given the likelihood that racism in America placed African Americans in a distinctive subject position? Mullins accepts the latter possibility.

Drawing on extensive documentary research, Mullins argues that Whites used genteel consumer culture to impute difference to Blacks and Whites, to materialize and naturalize White privilege, and to justify discrimination against Blacks. According to Mullins, Blacks responded by adopting the genteel consumer culture of the day: "African Americans took aim at the racial exclusivity of American consumer culture, launching a subtly politicized, yet profound critique of the very basis of American social privilege" (Mullins 1999, p. 39).

Mullins links specific acts of consumption to different strands of racist discourse and practice. For example, a decline in the consumption of fish and turtle caught by household members is interpreted as a response to racist stereotypes of Blacks as lazy and unreliable workers who would rather fish than take honest jobs. Blacks' purchase of name-brand goods is regarded as an effort to escape well-documented efforts by White storeowners to charge Black customers higher prices for inferior goods. Blacks' use of canned goods might easily be understood as an effort to escape the drudgery of home canning, but it should also be understood as an act of resistance. Whites condemned Black use of canned goods as wasteful, extravagant behavior in an effort to monopolize genteel consumption: an effort that Blacks opposed. Black knick-knack collecting is interpreted as another form of defiance against White efforts to monopolize genteel consumption and also as evidence of

Blacks' desire for the same romanticized escapism from the conflicts of nineteenth-century America as was sought by Whites.

Although the documents of late nineteenth- and early twentieth-century America condemn us to view Black culture and practice mostly through the lens of White racism, archaeology provides less biased, though not unambiguous, evidence of Black daily life. Mullins (1999, p. 186) concludes that the juxtaposition of documentary and archaeological data can provide insight into the very nature of African American culture: "African-American culture is a constantly emerging hybrid forged through struggle against racism, and it is a subjectivity that can both affirm and challenge dominant social conditions."

ARCHAEOLOGISTS AS CHRONOCOPS

As indicated by the examples presented above, archaeologists are able to engage in discussions about the past with many different audiences. First, archaeologists can contend with myth-makers, those who claim that ancient monuments were built by visitors from outer space, or from the lost continent of Atlantis, or by hypermigratory Aryans or Egyptians. Toward these offenders, archaeologists embrace a role as chronocops, the police of prehistory, defending ancient peoples and their modern descendants against the theft of cultural capital. It is true that archaeological data are ambiguous in many ways, permitting the construction of many narratives, but they are also decisively limiting in some ways. Which is to say, there are many stories that are simply not compatible with the physical evidence, as Bruce Trigger (1989, pp. 396–400) makes clear.

The policing activities of archaeology extend to gender issues. Combining archaeological and ethnographic data, archaeologists can destabilize efforts to label some activities as male and then attribute all evolutionary change to those privileged, "male" activities (Watson & Kennedy 1991, Zihlman 1997). Archaeologists have also argued against a utopian stage of the human past where the Goddess reigned supreme (Conkey & Tringham 1995). Archaeologists seem prepared to speak out assertively against what they perceive to be the misuse of prehistory, and the material nature of archaeological data seems to give archaeologists a degree of public credibility, credibility that the public often refuses to grant to cultural anthropologists (Shore 1996, di Leonardo 1999).

Archaeology also has the ability to police more serious ideas, such as the American idea of progress. Some cultural changes do precede others in human prehistory. For example, foraging preceded plant and animal domestication. In American culture, agriculture is usually considered an advance because it can support larger populations, greater material wealth, and more complex divisions of labor than most foraging economies. However, archaeologists point out that the adoption of agriculture was accompanied by a range of adverse outcomes: declining nutrition, increased tooth decay, greater infectious disease, more arthritis, shorter stature, and shorter life spans (Goodman & Armelagos 1985, Larsen 2000, Molleson 1994). Providing more even-handed accounts of important historical transitions gives archaeology a unique and powerful argument against the smug ethnocentrism that currently seems to pervade this country.

Chronicling the effects of capitalism, colonialism, and modernity is a major thrust of historical archaeology today. Historical archaeologists have examined the processes of class formation and class conflict (Burke 1999, Delle 1998, Goodwin 1999, Leone & Potter 1999, Ludlow Collective 2001, Mayne & Murray 2001, Mrozowski et al. 1996, Schavelzon 1999, Shackel 1996, Wurst & Fitts 1999). Issues of race and ethnogenesis have also captured attention (Franklin & Fesler 1999, Funari 1999, Jamieson 2000a, Lightfoot et al. 1998, Mullins 1999, Orser 2001, Praetzellis & Praetzellis 2001, Rodríguez-Alegría 2002, Rowlands 1999, Singleton 1999, Wilkie 2000). Changing gender roles have been examined (Deagan 2001; Delle 2000; Jamieson 2000b; Lawrence 1999; Nassaney 2000; Wall 1994, 2000; Wilkie & Shorter 2001). There are now a dozen important archaeological studies of colonialism (Crowell 1997, Deagan 2001, DeCorse 2001, Delle et al. 1999, Farnsworth 2001, Hall 2000, Lyons & Papadopoulos 2002, Nassaney & Johnson 2000, Perry 1999, Rountree & Turner 2002, Staniforth 2002, Torrence & Clarke 2000, Wesler 1998). In these studies, archaeologists attempt to destabilize self-serving explanations of how things came to be the way they are by focusing on the places and times when social categories were still in flux, thus revealing their artificial and arbitrary nature [Leone 1999, p. 9; note that Comaroff & Comaroff (1992, p. 14) set similar goals for historical anthropologists]. Bioarchaeologists, in particular, can bear witness to the violence that has attended historic appropriations of resources and labor (Blakey 2001, Danforth 1999, Doretti & Fondebrider 2001, Larsen 2000, Martin & Frayer 1997).

Paynter (2000a, 2000b) provides a masterful guide to this literature, as do Delle et al. (2000) and Orser (1996, 2000).

ARCHAEOLOGISTS AS COLLABORATORS

Archaeologists also engage in discussions of history with descendant communities. For descendant communities, archaeology supplies access to objects that are important for cultural heritage. Material remains can physically demonstrate the links between the past and the present, demonstrating the authenticity of local people's ethnic identities. At the same time, material remains can evoke the telling of oral histories, unauthorized histories, histories that narrate the experience of local people at the hands of intrusive, dominant cultures (Erikson 1999, Leone et al. 1995, Perry 1998). Archaeologists, as suppliers and interpreters of material remains, have fallen into the role of collaborators with descendant communities. This collaborative relationship has been more intense within the United States, where Native American treaty rights rest upon maintaining clear lines of descent and where the Native American Graves Protection and Repatriation Act (NAGPRA) forces archaeologists to consult with descendant communities whenever human remains are encountered.

A range of collaborative models has emerged (Dongoske et al. 2000, Swidler et al. 1997). In northwest Washington, the discovery of the prehistoric village of Ozette, miraculously preserved beneath a mud slide, brought outside expertise and funding to supplement an already-well-developed sense of history among the Makah people (Erikson 1999). In these circumstances, archaeologists seem to have acted as technicians and consultants to a historical museum designed and constructed by the local community. In the American Southwest, archaeologists seem to have established a collaboration of equal partnership with Hopi and Zuni people (Dongoske et al. 1997). They have concluded that when the goal is to establish cultural affiliation between modern peoples and ancient archaeological remains, archaeologists should work with tribal consultants to determine culturally appropriate criteria of ethnic identity rather than depending on the stylistic artifact types defined by nonnative archaeologists. This argument has caused archaeologists to rethink the meaning of ethnicity and artifact style in very productive ways.

African-American communities have also asserted their ownership of the past (McDavid & Babson 1997). Collaborations with African Americans have required archaeologists to engage in new forms of activity including critical self-reflection (Franklin 1997), popular writing (Gibb 1997), consulting local populations when designing research (La Roche & Blakey 1997), and developing multivocal interpretations of archaeological remains (McDavid 1997).

Outside the United States, where local histories have been effectively erased by colonialism, archaeologists take a greater leadership role (Schmidt & Patterson 1995b). In Xaltocan, Mexico, townspeople asked me to tell them what I had learned through my archaeological research. I designed an exhibit that I hoped would create a sense of continuity of place, highlight the history of internally generated culture change, and demonstrate Xaltocan's successful resistance to Aztec domination. My goals were to strengthen the Xaltocamecan sense of agency and to increase Xaltocan's solidarity with other towns in the region in order to increase their ability to resist Mexico's powerful state. However, it turns out that many Xaltocamecas prefer to think of themselves as Aztecs, to identify with the conquerors rather than the conquered, and to take pride in domination rather than resistance. In fact, some Xaltocamecas have used what they have learned about local prehistory to claim a higher status than people in surrounding towns. An unexpected outcome of this status rivalry is that neighboring towns are now clamoring for archaeologists of their own (Brumfiel 2000). In Tanzania, Schmidt (1995) designed archaeological research that contributed to nation-building and decreased inter-ethnic competition. He did so (*a*) by focusing research in an area of the country with great ethnic fluidity so that remains could not be claimed by any current group, and (*b*) by researching a single cultural phenomenon, iron-working, in several different parts of the country so that this technology could be regarded as part of a national heritage.

This collaborative work by archaeologists does not seem to have an equivalent in cultural anthropology, where anthropologists more often maintain intellectual control of their research projects (although Rosaldo 1980 and Wiessner & Tumu

1998 might be exceptions). Indeed, there are those such as Friedman (1992) who believe that anthropological investigation will always directly confront others' construction of their identities, as locals strive to construct history in ways that promote their political ends and anthropologists expose the invention of tradition and the arts of memory. If this is true, then the prospects for collaborations between cultural anthropologists and local populations are not very good. Archaeologists, however, have learned to negotiate history. Just as many seeming contradictions between historical documents and archaeological data can be resolved through interpretation, thoughtful interpretation can close the gap between local claims based on oral history and seemingly contrary archaeological evidence. Echo-Hawk (1997), Handsman & Richmond (1995), and Staeck (2000) demonstrate that it is possible to tack back and forth between oral history and archaeological evidence to the enrichment of both data sets. Kohl (1998, p. 243) provides thoughtful ethical standards for archaeologists collaborating with descendant groups.

Collaboration between archaeologists and local communities seems to produce a different kind of history from those produced by historical anthropologists. First of all, histories produced in conjunction with local communities seem to emphasize cultural continuities, whereas the work of historical anthropologists seems to emphasize cultural disjunction. For example, Sahlins (1992, p. 170) describes Hawaiian society in the mid-nineteenth century as one of

> ever-increasing social entropy, as people frequently moved back and forth between their properties in the Anahulu Valley and their upland sites. Families and members of families split up and recombined in a continuous flux. And this apparent incoherence was an aspect only of the more general fact that the *ahupua'a* had lost its political cum economic integrity. Once the system of hierarchy collapsed, nothing could really save the old Hawaiian order.

But according to Friedman (1992, p. 843), the Hawaiian movement today emphasizes the continuities with the past in the form of *ohana*, the extended family, based on a principle of sharing and reciprocity, *aloha*, committing oneself to the needs of others, and *aloha aina*, stewardship of the land. These continuities, persisting at the household level when larger structures have disintegrated or mutated under external pressure, can serve as anchors for Hawaiian ethnic identity.

Additionally, histories produced in conjunction with local communities seem to assume a different voice than those of historical anthropologists. Collaborative histories are inclined toward heroic tales of survival, celebrating local heroes and activists, and providing role models to the young (Schmidt & Patterson 1995a, p. 22).

CONCLUSION

There are individuals who believe that archaeology and cultural anthropology have little common ground. For example, in the centennial issue of *American Anthropologist*, Borofsky (2002) makes a startling announcement: Not only is anthropology not a four-field discipline, it never has been! Borofsky bases his conclusion upon the percentage of *American Anthropologist* articles that have drawn data from two or more subfields. The average for the entire century of *American Anthropologists* is 9.5%, and this low figure characterizes even the early part of the twentieth century, when, according to Borofsky, a legitimate scholarly rationale for four-field anthropology actually existed, which was to account for human variability through evolutionary and historical studies of groups lacking written documents. Now, Borofsky argues, anthropology has moved beyond this problem, and even the ideal of four-field anthropology doesn't make sense for the discipline.

It is interesting that Borofsky's position is at odds with the feelings of the large majority of American anthropologists. In a 1997 membership survey by the American Anthropological Association, 72% of those responding expressed allegiance to the organization because it represented the entire discipline of anthropology, and 90% believed that the governing body should include representatives from all of the major subfields (Moses 1997). What lies behind this loyalty? Should it be attributed to, as Geertz (1985) once proposed, a mix of "sentiment, habit, and broad appeals to the advantages of breadth"? Or is it a result, as Borofsky (2002) suggests, of pragmatic self-interest responding to the academic politics of the moment? I would argue that the majority of anthropologists support multi-field anthropology because they accept two truths about the human condition. The first truth is that humans dwell in a reality that is both material and ideal; that is, humans live in a physical world, but a physical world that they comprehend only through their own constructed models (Rappaport 1994, p. 154). The second is that humans make their own history, but they do so under circumstances transmitted from the past (Marx 1977 [1852], p. 300). These two aspects of the human condition are not likely to change any time soon; hence, there is continuing wisdom in a study of humans that allows for the interplay of the material and the symbolic in human life and that examines the present as a function of the past. Anthropology will never be a field without contradictions, but these tensions should provide an internal dynamic that drives the discipline forward (Brown & Yoffee 1993).

ACKNOWLEDGMENTS

I am grateful to Tim Earle for encouraging me to write this review; left to my own devices, I never would have attempted it. Jill Appel, Jason Antrosio, Don Brenneis, Geoffrey Brumfiel, Vincent Brumfiel, Tim Earle, and Molly Mullin patiently listened to early versions of this piece and offered invaluable comments and suggestions. Their input shaped my ideas in important ways. I also benefited from questions and comments from members of the Anthropology Section of the New York Academy of Sciences and the Department of Anthropology at Northwestern University, where earlier versions of this review were presented.

The *Annual Review of Anthropology* is online at http://anthro.annualreviews.org

LITERATURE CITED

Blakey ML. 2001. Bioarchaeology of the African diaspora in the Americas: its origins and scope. *Annu. Rev. Anthropol.* 30:387–422

Bond GC, Gilliam A, eds. 1994. *Social Construction of the Past*. London: Routledge

Borofsky R. 1987. *Making History: Pukapukan and Anthropological Constructions of Knowledge*. Cambridge, UK: Cambridge Univ. Press

Borofsky R. 2002. The four subfields: anthropologists as mythmakers. *Am. Anthropol.* 104:463–80

Brown PJ, Yoffee N. 1993. Is fission the future of anthropology? *SAA Bull.* 11(1):12, 13, 17

Brumfiel EM. 1991. Weaving and cooking: women's production in Aztec Mexico. See Gero & Conkey 1991, pp. 224–51

Brumfiel EM. 2000. Making history in Xaltocan. See Dongoske et al. 2000, pp. 181–90

Burke H. 1999. *Meaning and Ideology in Historical Archaeology: Style, Social Identity and Capitalism in an Australian Town*. New York: Kluwer Academic/Plenum

Carrier JG, Heyman JMcC. 1997. Consumption and political economy. *J. R. Anthropol. Inst.* 3:355–73

Chance JK. 1996. Mesoamerica's ethnographic past. *Ethnohistory* 43:379–403

Chanock M. 1985. *Law, Custom and Social Order: the Colonial Experience in Malawi and Zambia*. Cambridge, UK: Cambridge Univ. Press

Comaroff JL, Comaroff J. 1991. *Of Revelation and Revolution, Volume 1*. Chicago: Univ. Chicago Press

Comaroff JL, Comaroff J. 1992. *Ethnography and the Historical Imagination*. Boulder: Westview

Comaroff JL, Comaroff J. 1997. *Of Revelation and Revolution, Volume 2*. Chicago: Univ. Chicago Press

Conkey MW, Tringham RE. 1995. Archaeol-

ogy and the goddess: exploring the contours of feminist archaeology. In *Feminisms in the Academy*, ed. DC Stanton, AJ Stewart, pp. 299–347. Ann Arbor: Univ. Mich. Press

Cracraft J. 1980. Moas and the Maori. *Nat. Hist.* 89(10):28–36

Crowell AL. 1997. *Archaeology and the Capitalist World System: a Study from Russian America*. New York: Plenum

Culotta E. 1995. Many suspects to blame in Madagascar extinctions. *Science* 268:1568–69

Danforth ME. 1999. Nutrition and politics in prehistory. *Annu. Rev. Anthropol.* 28:1–25

Deagan K. 2001. Dynamics of imperial adjustment in Spanish America: ideology and social interaction. In *Empires*, ed. SE Alcock, TN D'Altroy, KD Morrison, DM Sinopoli, pp. 179–94. Cambridge, UK: Cambridge Univ. Press

DeCorse CR. 2001. *An Archaeology of Elmina: Africans and Europeans on the Gold Coast, 1400–1900*. Washington, DC: Smithsonian Inst.

Delle JA. 1998. *An Archaeology of Social Space: Analyzing Coffee Plantations in Jamaica's Blue Mountains*. New York: Plenum

Delle JA. 2000. Gender, power, and space: negotiating social relations under slavery on coffee plantations in Jamaica, 1790–1834. See Delle et al. 2000, pp. 168–201

Delle JA, Leone MP, Mullins PR. 1999. Archaeology of the modern state: European colonialism. In *The Companion Encyclopedia of Archaeology*, ed. G Barker, pp. 1107–1159. London: Routledge

Delle JA, Mrozowski SA, Paynter R, eds. 2000. *Lines That Divide: Historical Archaeologies of Race, Class and Gender*. Knoxville: Univ. Tenn. Press

DeMarrais E, Castillo LJ, Earle T. 1996. Ideology, materialization, and power strategies. *Curr. Anthropol.* 37:15–47 di Leonardo M. 1999. The anthropologist's public-image problem. *Chron. Higher Educ.* Mar. 19:B4–5

Dongoske KE, Aldenderfer M, Doehner K, eds. 2000. *Working Together: Native Americans and Archaeologists.* Washington, DC: Soc. Am. Archaeol.

Dongoske KE, Yeatts M, Anyon R, Ferguson TJ. 1997. Archaeological cultures and cultural affiliation: Hopi and Zuni perspectives in the American Southwest. *Am. Antiq.* 62:600–8

Doretti M, Fondebrider L. 2001. Science and human rights: truth, justice, reparation and reconciliation, a long way in Third World countries. In *Archaeologies of the Contemporary Past*, ed. V Buchli, G Lucas, pp. 138–44. London: Routledge

Earle T. 1998. Property rights and the evolution of Hawaiian chiefdoms. In *Property in Economic Context*, ed. RC Hunt, A Gilman, pp. 89–118. Lanham, MD: Univ. Press Am.

Echo-Hawk R. 1997. Forging a new ancient history for Native America. See Swidler et al. 1997, pp. 88–102

Erikson PP. 1999. A-whaling we will go: encounters of knowledge and memory at the Makah Cultural and Research Center. *Cult. Anthropol.* 14:556–83

Fabian J. 1983. *Time and the Other: How Anthropology Makes Its Object.* New York: Columbia Univ. Press

Farnsworth P. 2001. *Island Lives: Historical Archaeologies of the Caribbean.* Tuscaloosa: Univ. Alabama Press

Field LW. 1999. Complicities and collaborations: anthropologists and the "unacknowledged tribes" of California. *Curr. Anthropol.* 40:193–209

Franklin M. 1997. "Power to the people": sociopolitics and the archaeology of Black Americans. See McDavid & Babson 1997, pp. 36–50

Franklin M, Fesler G, eds. 1999. *Historical Archaeology, Identity Formation, and the Interpretation of Ethnicity.* Williamsburg, VA: Colonial Williamsburg Found.

Friedman J. 1992. The past in the future: history and the politics of identity. *Am. Anthropol.* 94:837–59

Funari PPA. 1999. Maroon, race and gender: Palmares material culture and social relations in a runaway settlement. In *Historical Archaeology: Back From the Edge*, ed. PPA Funari, M Hall, S Jones, pp. 308–27. London: Routledge

Geertz C. 1985. Waddling in. *TLS* June 7:623–24

Gero JM, Conkey MW, eds. 1991. *Engendering Archaeology: Women and Prehistory.* London: Basil Blackwell

Gero JM, Lacey D, Blakey M, eds. 1983. *The Sociopolitics of Archaeology. Res. Report, 23.* Dept. Anthropol., Univ. Mass., Amherst

Gibb JG. 1997. Necessary but insufficient: plantation archaeology reports and community action. See McDavid & Babson 1997, pp. 51–64

Goodman AH, Armelagos GJ. 1985. Disease and death at Dr. Dickson's mounds. *Nat. Hist.* 94(9):12–18

Goodwin LBR. 1999. *An Archaeology of Manners: the Polite World of the Merchant Elite of Colonial Massachusetts.* New York: Kluwer Academic/Plenum

Haley BD, Wilcoxon LR. 1997. Anthropology and the making of Chumash tradition. *Curr. Anthropol.* 38:761–94

Hall M. 2000. *Archaeology and the Modern World: Colonial Transcripts in South Africa and the Chesapeake.* London: Routledge

Handsman RG, Richmond TL. 1995. The Mahican and Schaghticoke peoples and us. See Schmidt & Patterson 1995b, pp. 87–117

Hobsbawm E, Ranger T, eds. 1983. *The Invention of Tradition.* Cambridge, UK: Cambridge Univ. Press

Hosler D. 1995. *The Sounds and Colors of Power: the Sacred Metallurgical Technology of Ancient West Mexico.* Cambridge, MA: MIT Press

Jamieson RW. 2000a. *Domestic Architecture and Power: the Historical Archaeology of Colonial Ecuador.* New York: Kluwer Academic/Plenum

Jamieson RW. 2000b. Doña Luisa and her two

houses. See Delle et al. 2000, pp. 142–67

Johnson MH. 1999. Rethinking historical archaeology. In *Historical Archaeology: Back from the Edge*, ed. PP Funari, M Hall, S Jones, pp. 23–36. London: Routledge

Kepecs S, Kolb JM, eds. 1997. Special issue: new approaches to combining the archaeological and historical records. *J. Archaeol. Method Theory* 4(3/4):193–378

Kirch PV, Sahlins M. 1992. *Anahulu: the Anthropology of History in the Kingdom of Hawaii.* Chicago: Univ. Chicago Press

Kohl PL. 1998. Nationalism and archaeology: on the constructions of nations and the reconstructions of the remote past. *Annu. Rev. Anthropol.* 27:223–46

Kolb MJ. 1997. Labor mobilization, ethnohistory, and the archaeology of community in Hawai'i. *J. Archaeol. Method Theory* 4:265–85

La Roche CJ, Blakey ML. 1997. Seizing intellectual power: the dialogue at the New York African Burial Ground. See McDavid & Babson 1997, pp. 84–106

Larsen CS. 2000. *Skeletons in Our Closet: Revealing Our Past Through Bioarchaeology.* Princeton, NJ: Princeton Univ. Press

Lawrence S. 1999. Towards a feminist archaeology of households: gender and household structure on the Australian goldfields. In *The Archaeology of Household Activities*, ed. PM Allison, pp. 121–41. London: Routledge

Leone MP. 1999. Setting some terms for historical archaeologies of capitalism. See Leone & Potter 1999, pp. 3–20

Leone MP, Mullins PR, Creveling MC, Hurst L, Jackson-Nash B, et al. 1995. Can an African-American historical archaeology be an alternative voice? In *Interpreting Archaeology*, ed. I Hodder, M Shanks, A Alexandri, V Buchli, J Carman, J Last, G Lucas, pp. 110–24. London: Routledge

Leone MP, Potter PB. 1988. Introduction: issues in historical archaeology. In *The Recovery of Meaning: Historical Archeology in the Eastern United States*, ed. MP Leone, PB Potter, pp. 1–22. Washington, DC: Smithsonian Inst.

Leone MP, Potter PB, eds. 1999. *Historical Archaeologies of Capitalism.* New York: Kluwer

Lightfoot KG. 1995. Culture contact studies: redefining the relationship between prehistoric and historic archaeology. *Am. Antiq.* 63:199–222

Lightfoot KG, Martínez A, Schiff AM. 1998. Daily practice and material culture in pluralistic social settings: an archaeological study of culture change and persistence from Fort Ross, California. *Am. Antiq.* 63:199–222

Ludlow Collective. 2001. Archaeology of the Colorado Coal Field War 1913–1914. In *Archaeologies of the Contemporary Past*, ed. V Buchli, G Lucas, pp. 94–107. London: Routledge

Lyons CL, Papadopoulos JK, eds. 2002. *The Archaeology of Colonialism.* Los Angeles: Getty Res. Inst.

Martin DL, Frayer DW, eds. 1997. *Troubled Times: Violence and Warfare in the Past.* (Part of *War and Society* series, Vol. 3). Amsterdam: Gordon and Breach

Martin PS, Klein RG, eds. 1984. *Quaternary Extinctions: a Prehistoric Revolution.* Tucson: Univ. Ariz. Press

Marx K. 1977 [1852]. The eighteenth brumaire of Louis Bonaparte. In *Karl Marx: Selected Writings*, ed. D McLellan, pp. 300–25. London: Oxford Univ. Press

Mayne A, Murray T, eds. 2001. *The Archaeology of Urban Landscapes: Explorations in Slumland.* Cambridge, UK: Cambridge Univ. Press

McDavid C. 1997. Descendants, decisions, and power: the public interpretation of the archaeology of the Levi Jordan plantation. See McDavid & Babson 1997, pp. 114–31

McDavid C, Babson DW, ed. 1997. *In the Realm of Politics: Prospects for Public Participation in African-American and Plantation Archaeology. Hist. Archaeol.* 31(1):1–152

McGuire RH. 1992. Archeology and the first Americans. *Am. Anthropol.* 94:816–36

Miller D. 1987. *Material Culture and Mass*

Consumption. Cambridge, UK: Basil Blackwell

Miller GH, Magee JW, Johnson BJ, Fogel ML, Spooner NA, et al. 1999. Pleistocene extinction of *Genyornis newtoni*: human impact on Australian megafauna. *Science* 283:205–8

Molleson T. 1994. The eloquent bones of Abu Hureyra. *Sci. Am.* 271(2):70–75

Moore PD. 1982. Beneath the blanket bogs of Britain. *Nat. Hist.* 91(11):48–55

Moses YT. 1997. Are four fields in our future? *Anthropol. Newsl.* Dec.:8–11

Mrozowski SA, Ziesing GH, Beaudry MC. 1996. *Living on the Boott: Historical Archaeology at the Boott Mills Boardinghouses, Lowell, Massachusetts*. Amherst: Univ. Mass. Press

Mullins PR. 1999. *Race and Affluence: an Archaeology of African American and Consumer Culture*. New York: Kluwer Academic/Plenum

Nassaney MS. 2000. Archaeology and oral tradition in tandem: interpreting Native American ritual, ideology, and gender relations in contact-period southeastern New England. See Nassaney & Johnson 2000, pp. 412–31

Nassaney MS, Johnson ES, eds. 2000. *Interpretations of Native North American Life*. Gainesville: Univ. Florida Press

Netting RMcC. 1993. *Smallholders, Householders: Farm Families and the Ecology of Intensive, Sustainable Agriculture*. Stanford, CA: Stanford Univ. Press

Nichols DL. 1982. A middle formative irrigation system near Santa Clara Coatitlan in the Basin of Mexico. *Am. Antiq.* 47:133–44

Orser CE. 1996. *A Historical Archaeology of the Modern World*. New York: Plenum

Orser CE, ed. 2000. Contemporary issues forum: American historical archaeology. *Am. Anthropol.* 103:621–704

Orser CE, ed. 2001. *Race and the Archaeology of Identity*. Salt Lake City: Univ. Utah Press

Paynter R. 2000a. Historical and anthropological archaeology: forging alliances. *J. Archaeol. Res.* 8:1–37

Paynter R. 2000b. Historical archaeology and

the post-Columbian world of North America. *J. Archaeol. Res.* 8:169–217

Perry WR. 1998. Dimensions of power in Swaziland research. *Transform. Anthropol.* 7(1):2–14

Perry WR. 1999. *The Archaeology of Colonial Impact in Southern Africa, 1500–1900*. New York: Plenum

Praetzellis A, Praetzellis M. 2001. Mangling symbols of gentility in the Wild West: case studies in interpretive archaeology. *Am. Anthropol.* 103:645–54

Rappaport R. 1994. Humanity's evolution and anthropology's future. In *Assessing Cultural Anthropology*, ed. R. Borofsky, pp. 153–66. New York: McGraw-Hill

Redman CL. 1999. *Human Impact on Ancient Environments*. Tucson: Univ. Ariz. Press

Robertshaw P. 2000. Sibling rivalry? The intersection of archaeology and history. *Hist. Africa* 27:261–86

Rodríguez-Alegría E. 2002. *Food, eating and objects of power: class stratification and ceramic production and consumption in colonial Mexico*. PhD thesis. Univ. Chicago. 526 pp.

Rosaldo R. 1980. *Ilongot Headhunting, 1883–1974*. Stanford, CA: Stanford Univ. Press

Rountree HC, Turner ER III. 2002. *Before and After Jamestown: the Powhatans and Algonquins of Virginia*. Gainesville: Univ. Florida Press

Rowlands M. 1999. Black identity and sense of past in Brazilian national culture. In *Historical Archaeology: Back From the Edge*, ed. PPA Funari, M Hall, S Jones, pp. 328–44. London: Routledge

Rubertone PE. 2000. The historical archaeology of Native Americans. *Annu. Rev. Anthropol.* 29:425–46

Rubertone PE. 2001. *Grave Undertakings: an Archaeology of Roger Williams and the Narragansett Indians*. Washington, DC: Smithsonian Inst.

Runnels CN. 1995. Environmental degradation in ancient Greece. *Sci. Am.* 272(3):96–99

Sahlins M. 1985. *Islands of History*. Chicago: Univ. Chicago Press

Sahlins M. 1992. *Anahulu: the Anthropology of History in the Kingdom of Hawaii, Volume I, Historical Ethnography.* Chicago: Univ. Chicago Press

Schavelzon D. 1999. *The Historical Archaeology of Buenos Aires.* New York: Kluwer Academic/Plenum

Schmidt PR. 1995. Using archaeology to remake history in Africa. See Schmidt & Patterson 1995b, pp. 119–47

Schmidt PR, Patterson TC. 1995a. Introduction: from constructing to making alternative histories. See Schmidt & Patterson 1995b, pp. 1–24

Schmidt PR, Patterson TC, eds. 1995b. *Making Alternative Histories: the Practice of Archaeology and History in Non-Western Settings.* Santa Fe, NM: Sch. Am. Res. Press

Shackel PA. 1996. *Culture Change and the New Technology: an Archaeology of the Early American Industrial Era.* New York: Plenum

Shanks M, Tilley C. 1987. *Re-Constructing Archaeology.* Cambridge, UK: Cambridge Univ. Press

Shore C. 1996. Anthropology's identity crisis. *Anthropol. Today* 12(2)(April):2–5

Simmons AH. 1999. *Faunal Extinction in an Island Society.* New York: Kluwer Academic/Plenum

Singleton TA, ed. 1999. *"I, Too, Am America": Archaeological Studies of African-American Life.* Charlottesville, VA: Univ. Virginia Press

Smith ME. 1992. Rhythms of change in Postclassic central Mexico: archaeology, ethnohistory, and the Braudelian model. In *Archaeology, Annales, and Ethnohistory*, ed. AB Knapp, pp. 51–74. Cambridge, UK: Cambridge Univ. Press

Snyder G. 1977. *The Old Ways.* San Francisco: City Lights

Staeck JP. 2000. Echoing the past: reconciling ethnohistorical and archaeological views of Ho-Chunk (Winnebago) ethnogenesis. See Nassaney & Johnson 2000, pp. 88–117

Stahl AB. 2001. *Making History in Banda: Anthropological Visions of Africa's Past.* Cambridge, UK: Cambridge Univ. Press

Staniforth M. 2002. *Material Culture and Consumer Society: Dependent Colonies in Colonial Australia.* New York: Kluwer Academic/Plenum

Steadman DW. 1995. Prehistoric extinctions of Pacific island birds. *Science* 267:1123–31

Swidler N, Dongoske KE, Anyon R, Downer AS, eds. 1997. *Native Americans and Archaeologists: Stepping Stones to Common Ground.* Walnut Creek, CA: Altamira

Thomas DH. 2000. *Skull Wars.* New York: Basic Books

Thomas N. 1989. *Out of Time: History and Evolution in Anthropological Discourse.* Cambridge, UK: Cambridge Univ. Press

Thomas N. 1991. *Entangled Objects: Exchange, Material Culture, and Colonialism in the Pacific.* Cambridge, MA: Harvard Univ. Press

Tonkin E. 1992. *Narrating Our Pasts: the Social Construction of Oral History.* Cambridge, UK: Cambridge Univ. Press

Torrence R, Clarke A, eds. 2000. *Archaeology of Difference: Negotiating Cross-Cultural Engagements in Oceania.* London: Routledge

Trigger BG. 1980. Archaeology and the image of the American Indian. *Am. Antiq.* 45:662–76

Trigger BG. 1981. Archaeology and the ethnographic present. *Anthropologica* 23:3–17

Trigger BG. 1989. *A History of Archaeological Thought.* Cambridge, UK: Cambridge Univ. Press

Vandiver PB, Soffer O, Klima B. 1989. The origins of ceramic technology at Dolni Vestonice, Czechoslovakia. *Science* 246:1002–8

Wall DdZ. 1994. *The Archaeology of Gender: Separating the Spheres in Urban America.* New York: Plenum

Wall DdZ. 2000. Family meals and evening parties: constructing domesticity in nineteenth-century middle-class New York. See Delle et al. 2000, pp. 109–41

Watson PJ, Kennedy MC. 1991. The development of horticulture in the Eastern Woodlands of North America: women's role. See Gero & Conkey 1991, pp. 255–75

Wesler KW, ed. 1998. *Historical Archaeology in Nigeria.* Trenton, NJ: Africa World Press

White R. 1989. Production complexity and standardization in Early Aurignacian bead and pendant maufacture: evolutionary implications. In *The Human Revolution,* ed. P Mellars, C Stringer, pp. 366–90. Edinburgh: Edinburgh Univ. Press

Wiessner P, Tumu A. 1998. *Historical Vines: Enga Networks of Exchange, Ritual, and Warfare in Papua New Guinea.* Washington, DC: Smithsonian Inst. Press

Wilkie LA. 2000. *Creating Freedom: Material Culture and African American Identity at Oakley Plantation, Louisiana, 1840–1950.* Baton Rouge: Louisiana State Univ. Press

Wilkie LA, Shorter G Jr. 2001. *Lucretia's Well: an Archaeological Glimpse of an African-American Midwife's Household.* (Monograph #11). Mobile: Univ. S. Alabama, Cent. Archaeol. Studies

Williams BF. 1989. Class act: anthropology and the race to nation across ethnic terrain. *Annu. Rev. Anthropol.* 18:401–44

Williams R. 1973 [1643]. *A Key Into the Language of America,* ed. JJ Tennissen, EJ Hinz. Detroit, MI: Wayne State Univ. Press.

Wolf ER. 1982. *Europe and the People Without History.* Berkeley: Univ. Calif. Press

Wolf ER. 1990. Distinguished lecture: facing power—old insights, new questions. *Am. Anthropol.* 92:586–96

Wurst L, Fitts RK, ed. 1999. Confronting class. *Hist. Archaeol.* 33(1):1–195

Wylie A. 1999. Why should historical archaeologists study capitalism? See Leone & Potter 1999, pp. 23–50

Zihlman A. 1997. The paleolithic glass ceiling. In *Women in Human Evolution,* ed. LD Hager, pp. 91–113. London: Routledge

Annu. Rev. Anthropol. 2003. 32:225–42
doi: 10.1146/annurev.anthro.32.061002.093426

URBAN VIOLENCE AND STREET GANGS

James Diego Vigil

*School of Social Ecology, University of California, Irvine, California 92697-7080;
email: vigil@uci.edu*

Key Words   urban studies, integrated and holistic frameworks, gang formation
theories

■ **Abstract**   What causes urban street gang violence, and how can we better understand the forces that shape this type of adolescent and youth behavior? For close to
a century, social researchers have taken many different paths in attempting to unravel
this complex question, especially in the context of large-scale immigrant adaptation
to the city. In recent decades these researchers have relied primarily on data gathered
from survey quantitative approaches. This review traces some of these developments
and outlines how frameworks of analysis have become more integrated and multidimensional, as ethnographic strategies have come into vogue again. For the last couple
of decades, either a subculture of violence (i.e., the values and norms of the street
gang embrace aggressive, violent behavior) or a routine activities (i.e., hanging around
high crime areas with highly delinquent people) explanation dominated the discussion.
To broaden and deepen the picture, many other factors need to be considered, such
as ecological, socioeconomic, sociocultural, and sociopsychological, particularly in
light of the immigrant experience. A multiple marginality framework lends itself to a
holistic strategy that examines linkages within the various factors and the actions and
interactions among them and notes the cumulative nature of urban street gang violence.
Questions that are addressed in this more integrated framework are: Where did they
settle? What jobs did they fill? How and why did their social practices and cultural
values undergo transformations? When and in what ways did the social environment
affect them? Finally, with whom did they interact? In sum, in highlighting the key
themes and features of what constitutes urban street gang violence, this review suggests that the qualitative style that relies on holistic information adds important details
to traditional quantitative data.

Urban gang violence has been examined from various sociological and psychological perspectives (Covey et al. 1992, Decker 1996). Though the violence includes
an array of crimes (Zimring 1998), it is the gang conflicts that concern us here: the
turf and drug wars and battles over resources and the drivebys and "counting coup"
escapades. Prior to the 1970s, gang violence was still popularly associated with
white ethnic enclaves in the cities of the Midwest and East, and gang incidents
were typically brawls involving fists, sticks, and knives. Today, gangs are made
up largely of darker-hued ethnic groups, especially African Americans and Latino
Americans, and handguns and other military hardware are the typical vehicles for

the acts of aggression and violent rampages so common in large cities, West and East (Cook & Laub 1998, Sanders 1994, McNulty 1995).

Gangs are now made up, as they were in earlier days, primarily of groups of male adolescents and youths who have grown up together as children, usually as cohorts in a low-income neighborhood of a city. Yet, only about 10% of youth in most low-income neighborhoods join gangs (Vigil 1988, Short 1996, Esbensen & Winfree 2001). Those who do so participate together in both conventional and antisocial behavior (Thornberry 2001). It is the antisocial behavior, however, that attracts the attention of authorities as well as the general public (Decker & Van Winkle 1996, Curry et al. 1994, Bursik & Grasmick 1995).

Hagedorn (1998) has made a distinction between the periods before and since the 1970s, respectively labeling them industrial and postindustrial. He maintains that the latter period has brought more violence because of several factors: "the adoption of economic functions by some urban gangs, the use of violence to regulate illicit commerce, the proliferation of firearms, the effect of prison on neighborhood gangs, and the effect of mainstream cultural values of money and success on gang youth with limited opportunities" (Hagedorn 1998, pp. 369–70).

Access to sophisticated weaponry has made violence easier to carry out, as Canada (1995) has illustrated in his *Fist, Stick, Knife, Gun*. Indeed, in 1968 there were about 80 million guns in the United States, and by 1978 the figure had grown to 120 million; it was 200 million by 1990 (Reiss & Roth 1993). There were 50 million handguns, including those inexpensive pistols often referred to as Saturday Night Specials, in 1991 (Hagedorn 1998). The historical importance of guns in U.S. culture and the strong political support from groups such as the National Rifle Association (NRA) for continued manufacturing and relatively unrestricted sales of firearms have worked to facilitate gang acts of aggression and violence (Lott & Mustard 1997). Meanwhile, drug use and abuse have blurred the thinking of, and in a limited way drug sales have increased motives for, the street youth who perpetrate most of the violence (Blumstein 1995, Klein & Maxson 1994). However, there are also other factors that need to be considered in comprehending gang violence (Spergel & Curry 1998).

Sociologists and social psychologists have extensively examined youth violence. Many, like Farrington (1996, 1998), have generally alluded to violence as an aspect of human aggression (Huesmann & Moise 1999). More recently, others, Messerschmidt (1995) for example, have seen it as an expression of masculinity in working-class culture. In concurrence with anthropological evidence, most agree that males are more physically aggressive than females (Rohner 1976, Ember 1995). However, in recent years female gang members or females affiliated with male gangs have begun to get involved in and participate in gang violence (Chesney-Lind 1999). Female gang members are many fewer in number—from 4% to 15% of all gang members (Campbell 1991, 1990; Curry 2001; Miller 2002, 2001), but studies show that a high percentage of all incarcerated females in the United States belong to gangs (Giordano 1978). Indeed, the arrest rates of young women recently have increased at a faster pace than for nongang males

(OJJDP 1996), and the offenses they are being charged with increasingly involve violence. Of course, some of that increase is probably due to the fact that the criminal justice system is less gender-biased in recent years: Females who engage in deviant gang behavior are more apt today to be treated like their male counterparts rather than being shuttled into counseling sessions, as was likely in the past.

Girls and young women in gangs (usually in auxiliaries of male gangs but sometimes in autonomous groups or even, rarely, in mixed gender groups) are especially severely impacted by street socialization. Like males they must struggle with the same forces that generated their street experience but in addition must contend with their own homeboys, who typically have little respect for them. As gender roles continue to change, however, violence is becoming a more salient aspect of the role of females in gangs (Campbell 1990).

Like young males, many female youths are subjected to: culture conflict, poverty, and associated family and school problems. In addition, they are apt to undergo personal devaluation, stricter child-rearing experiences, tension-filled gender role expectations, and problems with self-esteem stemming from all these forces. Sexual abuse and exploitation experiences, initially with male relatives and later male street peers, can lead to pent-up rage. Not surprising, some young females are now channeling that rage into holding their own in the violence of the street gang world. Thus, some females may take on the persona of a crazy person, as for instance the Chicanas who call themselves Loca and do their best to live up to it (Dietrich 1998). Male gang members are generally dismissive of "gang girls"; but around these extremely violence-prone young women, the males show much more respect.

Nevertheless, most aggressive gang behavior is committed by male youths between 14 and 18 years of age (Hirschi & Gottfredson 1983, Gottfredson & Hirschi 1990, Zimring 1996, Oliver 2003). Erikson (1968) has singled out the psychosocial moratorium in that age span as a status crisis in the transition from childhood to adulthood. Ambivalence and unpredictability characterize that period of human development, as teens face their new social and sexual identities and roles with uncertainty. As a result, they increasingly rely on peers and slightly older male role models as guides. Some teenagers, especially those living in highly stressful conditions, find it particularly difficult to work through this stage of human development. Many gang members, who characteristically have been raised in marginalized, highly stressful families, have their social development arrested and remain peer-dependent well into their thirties and even forties. Of importance to note, sociologists have quantitatively charted a noted increase, high point, and decrease in aggressive, violent actions in that same 14 to 18 age span (Hirschi & Gottfredson 1983, Gottfredson & Hirschi 1990). Because gang members often are organized hierarchically by age, older gang members are able to goad younger members (the 14- to 18-year-olds) to carry out acts of violence against rival gangs (Vigil 1988a,b).

Violence can be defined as a conscious physical act aimed at causing injury, which often includes bodily and psychological trauma and usually is identified with certain neighborhoods (Tonry & Moore 1998, Oliver 2003). Most current theories are framed to explain delinquency or aggression and not youth violence (Farrington 1998). Although there is considerable research still in its infancy focused on bio-logical determinants of youth violence, such as low heart rate, the majority of the investigations and evidence support social and psychological factors (Raine et al. 1997). Indeed, when biological factors are invoked they are usually associated with social and psychological explanations.

Let us summarize the anthropological, ethnographic tradition on the subject. Members of the Chicago School conducted some of the first studies on gangs in the 1920s. These researchers were a group of sociologists and anthropologists who ad-vocated and regularly practiced urban community studies that involved fieldwork observation and intensive interviewing. Thrasher (1927) is the initial researcher credited with studying gangs (and also Ashbury 1927 in New York, but his work was more anecdotal) in detail and establishing the baseline information from which all subsequent studies followed, including those of today (Hagedorn 1988, 1998). Later, Whyte (1943), Yablonsky (1966), Keiser (1969), Suttles (1968), Dawley (1992 [1973]), and Miller (1973, 1975) added to this ethnographic tradition. Soon after, a renewed interest in gangs emerged among ethnographically oriented re-searchers such as Moore (1978, 1991) and Horowitz (1983), and by the late 1980s and 1990s qualitative, anthropological investigations were underway across the nation (Alonso 1999). Anthropologists (e.g., Vigil 1988a, 2002a; Sullivan 1988; Bourgois 1995; Fleischer 1995, 1998) have reworked and reconfigured these per-spectives. Frameworks of analyses are now more holistic (Bronfenbrenner 1979), and methods of research have been broadened as ethnographic approaches have become more popular, even among sociologists (Hagedorn 1988; Padilla 1992; Anderson 1994, 1997, 1998).

In the more recent past, major explanations of gang violence can be fit (usually) into one of two frameworks: subculture of violence (e.g., especially Wolfgang & Ferracuti 1967) and routine activities (e.g., Felson 1987) explanations. In view of recent emphases on multidimensional ways of looking at the subject, I underscore that neither becoming a member of a subculture of violence nor being present where routine activities of a violent nature occur is sufficient, by itself, to explain youth participation in gang violence. Let us take each of these two explanations and describe them in more detail.

The subculture of violence construct posits that it is the normative behavioral systems of groups that support, encourage, and condone violence (Wolgang & Ferracuti 1967). These norms help guide gang members in how and when they react to real or imagined slights and threats to themselves or fellow gang members, such as hostile stares (called "mad dogging" by street youths in Los Angeles), a chance encounter with known gang enemies (e.g., when cruising or walking in non-gang territories), or paybacks (i.e., retaliation by consciously seeking gang enemies to attack). Violence is expected or required under these and other conditions and situations; otherwise the gang member risks being disrespected ("dissed") by other gang members. Failure to live up to these norms brings a loss of honor, and, as

Horowitz (1983) has stated, ones self-image is tarnished for either not promoting or defending these norms.

Many other researchers have relied on one form or another of the subculture of violence explanation. Some of the most knowledgeable of gang writers have focused on heart and courage in fighting (Cohen & Short 1958), the lower-class value of confronting trouble and exhibiting toughness (Miller 1958), or the emphasis on violent behavior in a "conflict subculture" (Cloward & Ohlin 1960). Focusing on disputes between individuals, Luckenbill & Doyle (1989) have underscored that challenges to the notion of self result in a series of events (i.e., naming, claiming, and aggressiveness) that leads to the use of force or violence by members of the subculture.

In contrast to a subculture of violence perspective, a routine activities explanation (Felson 1987) relies on space/time dimensions (e.g., at the wrong place at the wrong time) to substantiate a pattern of violence. The potential for violence is a product of opportunity where one spends more time with criminal offenders who are more likely to participate in offending activities. In short, motivated offenders, suitable targets, and an absence of capable guardians converge in certain times and places to increase the possibility of a crime (Kennedy & Baron 1993, Felson & Cohen 1980). Risky lifestyles of young males on the streets increase contact with similarly adventurous males and thus such associations and interactions heighten the potential for crime and victimization (Sampson & Lauritzen 1990).

A number of other writings reflect the routine activities approach, stressing that it is the " 'criminogenic potential' of certain routines that accounts for their 'victimization potential' " (Kennedy & Baron 1993, p. 92). Most assaults take place in contexts such as bars, parties, and other gatherings. Although ecological factors are paramount in a routine activities explanation, some writers suggest that rational choice is involved even when certain areas or neighborhoods are known as high-risk places (Seigal & Senna 1991, Cornish & Clarke 1986). A whole set of spatial and human factors are reflected in violent episodes.

In sum, both the subculture of violence and routine activities approaches can play a role in broadening our understanding of the issue of gang violence. Some of the shortcomings in the subculture of violence approach are quite obvious. Little empirical evidence has been offered on how violent norms are transmitted, and much of the inferences on subcultural values are derived from the behavior. Moreover, the approach tends to suggest a level of organization in gangs that is not present in the street gangs that others and I have studied, which are more loosely affiliated (Vigil 1988a, 2002a; Fleischer 1998; Klein & Crawford 1967; Short & Strodtbeck 1965; Suttles 1968). On the other hand, a routine activities explanation also has its limitations. For example, this perspective typically provides very little ethnographic evidence, relying mostly on official crime statistics, demographic variables, and victim surveys. Though time/space are crucial, an anthropological perspective suggests that this type of data must be combined with other factors. Thus, other situations and conditions need to be considered in the equation.

Two important considerations will provide examples for why a broader picture must be drawn if we are to better understand gang violence. Embedded in both the subculture of violence and routine activities frameworks are the issues of street realities and the state of mind of the individual. In previous research (Vigil 1987), I have outlined the importance of street socialization and a street state of mind known as "locura" (from loco, crazy, and defined as a spectrum of behavior reflected in a type of quasi-controlled insanity) among Mexican-American gangs and "crazy niggah" among black gang members. A short elaboration of street socialization is followed by the meaning and import of locura.

Street realities insure that a street subculture emerges among children that are bereft of social control from families, schools, and law enforcement, which have all failed to maintain or even gain a guiding influence on their lives. Street socialization is important because some individuals with particularly tarnished, traumatic family and personal backgrounds have had to spend most of their lives in the streets. This begins in early childhood and reaches a high point when an age/gender identity crisis erupts during adolescence. It is then that the more group-oriented preteen activities coalesce and merge into that of the street gang, and in most instances it is a continuous process. As a result, youth who are street socialized dictate the behavioral and attitudinal traits of the streets. The streets have become the arena for what is learned and expected by others to gain recognition and approval. Friendship and counsel, protection from street predators, and a wild, adventurous lifestyle become crucial to street survival. This type of survival through safety in numbers and reliance on friends to "watch your back" can lead to reckless behavior and an early adoption of locura as a way to negotiate the streets and especially to gain the support of street peers.

The culmination of all the street experiences is the shaping of a mindset of locura. It is an attitude that is deeply internalized by some gang members, especially the regular ones who have had particularly traumatic lives and are "crazy-like," but is equally instrumental as an attitude that can be adopted as circumstances dictate. Thinking and acting loco is like playing with insanity, moving in and out of crazy, wild events and adventures, showing fearlessness, toughness, daring, and especially unpredictable forms of destructive behavior. This psychosocial mindset has become a requisite for street survival and a behavioral standard for identification and emulation. Gang members collectively value locura because it helps assuage fear and the anxiety associated with the fight-flight (and even the middle ground of fright) dilemma that street realities impose on a person.

Thus, a complex problem such as gang violence necessitates examining many factors, such as neighborhood effects, poverty, culture conflict and sociocultural marginalization, and social control, among other gang dynamics. Such a combinative approach has been defined and described in other works either as multiple marginality (Vigil 1988a, 2002a; Vigil & Yun 2002) or integrated systems (Elliot 1994, Farrington 1996) or multivariate analysis (Cartwright & Howard 1966). But as we note, it also allows for the inclusion of street socialization (Vigil 1996, Bourgois 1995) and locura [the psychological state of quasi-controlled insanity (Vigil 1988b, Yablonsky 1966)]. In short, an eclectic approach (Bronfenbrenner 1979) is warranted to address the array of facets central to gang violence, and they must be integrated in ways that show the actions and reactions among them.

Multiple marginality (Vigil 2002a, 1988a; Vigil & Yun 1998, 2002) is an integrated framework that allows for the inclusion of the subculture of violence, routine activities, street socialization, locura, and other factors; in short, it combines sociogenic and psychogenic elements and actions (see Figure 1). Klein (1995), Elliot (1994), and Farrington (1996) utilize multidimensional frameworks too but interpret the phenomena more from a sociological perspective (Covey et al. 1992). Multiple marginality addresses the questions of what, where, how, why, and with whom, and it aids in explanations that show dynamic exchanges and interrelationships. As brief examples of how multiple marginality might shed light on these questions, let us take each question in turn to examine how they relate to violence. "What" is a query that is easily answered by defining and describing what

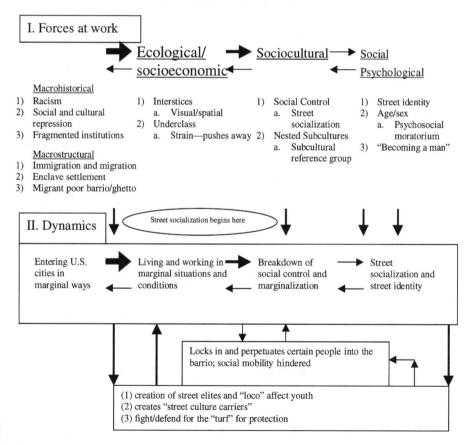

Figure 1   Framework of multiple marginality: "Act and react." From Vigil 2002a.

constitutes a youth gang, including its violent proclivities. "Where" places the gang in a certain locale in sections of urban areas that are usually visually distinct and spatially separate from more upscale neighborhoods and where violence is more likely. "How" requires an explanation of the social mechanisms and psychological predispositions of gang members in carrying out the gang's most salient activities, violent acts among them. "Why" is answered when we describe the situations and motivations that shape the thinking and actions of gang members toward either other gang members or unsuspecting targets for violence. "When" is simply the time and place that is more likely to trigger gang actions that end in violence. Finally, "With Whom" carefully outlines the characteristics of gangs and gang members from different neighborhoods and cohorts who are likely to participate in the violent street rituals that often lead to injury or death. A more detailed analysis follows with examples from various research enterprises and theoretical persuasions.

This review on urban violence and gangs emphasizes a multiple marginality framework as a way to integrate the concepts of subculture of violence, routine activities, street socialization, and locura, while noting other significant factors where appropriate. There are gangs in many ethnic communities to which this more holistic framework applies (Vigil 2002a), and some of the assessments may have limited application to other regions of the world (Klein et al. 2001, Hazlehurst & Hazlehurst 1998, Blanc 1995).

Most important for the purposes of this review is that multiple marginality is more than a laundry list of factors but a model showing sequential, cumulative linkages among factors. For anthropologists particularly, but also for the early gang researchers, the quest for an understanding of urban gangs began when researchers started following peasants and sharecroppers into cities. Thus, immigration and the experiences of immigrants adapting and adjusting to city life form the basis for all else that follows, including and especially the maladaptation that so often occurs among them (Martinez 2000). In this vein, there are multiple areas in which immigrants and especially their children find themselves betwixt and between, beginning with where they settle, what jobs they fill, and how and why their social and cultural values and practices are challenged and typically undermined and revamped. It also takes into account when the social environment shapes personal identities with whom the individuals interact. As noted above, no more than 10% of the youths become gang members in most affected neighborhoods, and the most marginalized families and children in each of these neighborhoods tend to fall into this category.

On a theoretical plane, multiple marginality is, in an essential way, similar to the integrative framework that Farrington (1996, 1998) and Bronfenbrenner (1979) suggest is needed for increased explanatory power. As such, it accounts for the reciprocal actions and reactions among factors, taking stock of sources and modes of human aggression, all the while identifying the interrelationships of social and personal development in the context of rapid urbanization and uneven culture change.

One of the first things to contemplate is that the populations of mostly young ethnic minority populations that contain most of the gang members in the United States do not live in the more comfortable areas of the cities. They did not fall from grace and then settle in the worst, most marginal places of the cities. The overwhelming fact is that they started their city lives in places they could afford, usually rundown, dilapidated, worn-out residences on the East coast where a criminal life style was already in vogue (Venkatesh 1996). In the West, the Los Angeles area primarily, often inferior empty spaces were all that remained for the newcomers, and thus squatter-like settlements arose. Here is where the ecological factor takes center stage (Vigil 2002b).

Place, in this instance, breeds certain human traits and adaptations. This factor gave us the concentric circle explanation of the Chicago School in the early crime and gang research days, a theory that singled out the second circle of the bull's-eye as where immigrants settled, and crime and vice were highly prevalent as compared to the other inner and outer circles of the model (Park et al. 1925, Shaw & McKay 1942). Indeed, as noted previously, it is in place that the routine activities theory builds its case (Felson 1987, Kennedy & Baron 1993). Other writers have also relied on place to explain the propensity for violence or violent incidents (Kornhauser 1978, Covey et al. 1992, Block & Block 1995). Generally, immigrants reside in neighborhoods of cities that are visually distinct (e.g., rundown, inferior) and spatially separate (e.g., across the tracks, freeway, river). In sum, being new to the city and separate from mainstream people and institutions limit the access, exposure, and identification that one has with the dominant culture and customs, which thus blocks avenues for integration. Being thwarted and bottled up in this manner, along with residential overcrowding, which I discuss shortly, engenders frustration and aggression among poor people in general. Space becomes a premium among them; places to congregate, shop, and cultivate romantic liaisons, among other social outlets and activities, become contentious issues, potential battlegrounds for conflict.

Is it an accident that most gang violence, drug sales, and turf wars, among other rivalrous issues, occur between gangs from similar marginal areas? Place alone seems to have an explanatory power beyond most of the other factors because so many other human habits and adjustments emanate from the demands of place. However, let us turn to some of the other elements that frame gang violence.

Socioeconomic status has received as much, perhaps more, attention than ecology in explanations for violence, but certainly both in tandem show the cumulative buildup suggested by multiple marginality. Again, the discussion on status focuses on youth from various ethnic minority populations, and, as with place, it is the marginality of their status that often is the source for aggression and violence. For example, they know that they live on the other side of the tracks; have limited access to entry-level jobs; receive harsh, uneven treatment from authorities, including and especially law enforcement; and are faulted for their own problems (Vigil 1988a, 2002a).

Competition over resources often sparks aggressive behavior and actions that occasionally flare up and get out of control, resulting in very violent, unplanned incidents. In recent years, much has been written about how industries and jobs have vacated the inner city, the places we have mentioned, and set up business in distant suburban environs or foreign nations (Wilson 1987, Hagedorn 1988, Johnson & Oliver 1991). This development has led many residents of the abandoned neighborhoods to participate in illicit, illegal, and informal substitute economic arrangements, of which drug trafficking and competition over markets was a major one (Beckett 1997). Drug trafficking and the conflict for markets, for a time and in some cities but not all (Howell 1996, Maxson 1998), accelerated and heightened gang violence, leading to economic explanations for the increase in gang violence.

Within a multiple marginality framework, however, the drug connection just added to an already dismal status dissonance (Fagan 1999). In fact, quite early in gang research, several social scientists built strong cases for economic theories. The most well known, of course, was Merton's strain theory, which simply refers to the mismatch between the means of low-income peoples to reach the status goals established by dominant society. With such structural barriers in place, differential opportunity paths were sought, such as illicit or illegal ventures that often entailed violence (Merton 1949, Cloward & Ohlin 1960, Kornhauser 1978, Covey et al. 1992, Moore 1978).

Yet, it should be obvious that not everybody in such places or statuses becomes a violent gang member because of where they are and what they do. Indeed, as noted earlier, the great majority of youths in these situations avoid involving themselves in gang activities. Nonetheless, they have to learn how to negotiate and navigate through the aura of aggression and violence that pervades certain places. This variation among low-income peoples in the same neighborhood can involve a number of things. What, then, leads the minority into gangs and violence? Can one live in the poorest house among poor houses? Can he have a much bigger family than other families in the area? Can his family be materially poorer than the others and also have less social capital? And as Anderson (1998) puts it, can poor people be "decent" or "street" irrespective of what demands are made of them? Finally, because of what is present in these marginal places and the strains inherent in a marginal status, can these forces lead youth to spend more time in the street?

The discussion to this point has addressed the questions "where" and "what." Let us turn to "how," "why," and "with whom." It is in these gang research areas that much has been written, but often with such a diffused impact, because what the authors have to say is dependent on place and status as a basis for their explanations. Social and cultural marginality are often intertwined; but for our purposes let us separate them for now. Socialization routines are definitely transformed when immigrants or migrants of low socioeconomic status must adapt to a place in the city. This is particularly the case with social control institutions, such as family, schools, and law enforcement.

Social control theory accounts for how these dynamic changes unfold, and there are many variations of this explanation (Hirschi 1969, Goffredson & Hirschi 1990,

Vigil 2002a, Covey et al. 1992). Families become stressed when their structure and function change as they undergo urbanization, but the stress is greatly increased and intensified under the marginal situations and conditions outlined above (Sampson & Laub 1990, Loeber & Stouthamer-Loeber 1986). For example, in the face of job discrimination, both parents may have to work. In the absence of affordable childcare, without close friends or relatives to care for them, children become latch-keyed and have to fend for themselves during the day. Moreover, cultural strains on rules and duties between first-generation parents and second-generation children, and attenuated father presence and/or single-parent (mostly female) households, often add to a family's stress (Vigil 1988a, 2002a).

Schools generally have a poor record with poor, ethnic minority populations and especially so if there is a sharp cultural contrast between the majority and minority cultures. This becomes painfully obvious when little or no communication or ties between school and home occurs. This void is exacerbated in the classroom when cultural and language differences interfere with learning. More important, the current school practices for students who are experiencing learning difficulties due to poverty and/or cultural differences are narrow and poorly funded. Thus, for the most marginalized segments of the minority populations, the social control mechanisms commonly inculcated by family and school are all but absent. The cumulative effects, as an example, become overwhelming at this point: small dilapidated home; large family under crowded conditions; precarious family structure with attenuated functions, sometimes marked by violence; unaccomodative schools; hostile and aggressive law enforcement; and, in the absence of home and school socialization, street socialization emerges and a multiple-aged peer group becomes a substitute (Vigil 1999).

Already among street youth the sources of aggression and violence become obvious, sometimes starting out with when they are the victims of domestic violence to go along with what the streets have to offer. In short, street socialization leads to a street subculture, and this is where and how the subculture of violence is learned and practiced (Wolfgang & Ferruti 1967). This concept is a variation of Sutherland's much earlier work (1934) and essentially maintains that a violent way of life dominates the streets, and a subcultural group of youth are the carriers that instruct newcomers in the art of street violence. Street socialization combines elements from social control theory (i.e., family, schools, and so on) and the subculture of violence concept; it explains how a person becomes exposed to the streets and then learns the gang subculture to participate in violent acts.

Closely linked to this alteration of the socialization process is the cultural facet of multiple marginality. Enculturation is one process of learning the culture to which one belongs, and acculturation is another process of learning a new culture. What we have with many gang members from different cultural backgrounds is erring acculturation in their adaptation to the city and all that it entails (i.e., place, status, social control and socialization, and so on). It is a core part of marginalization in that fragmented family values and beliefs, uneven schooling and Anglicization, and culture contact and conflict changes lead many youth to identification with the street. What I have referred to as "choloization" for Mexican Americans is simply a form of the cultural marginalization that many other ethnic groups encounter. African Americans, for example, undertook different waves of migration from the mostly rural South to American cities, north, east, and west throughout the twentieth century. The creation of a street gang subculture itself is made up of bits and pieces, fragments, of their past culture as they acculturate to the new, present culture; and in their case, it has been a historical process going back to their abrupt uprooting from Africa.

Miller's theory of "lower-class culture as a generating milieu" (1958) for street violence addresses some aspects of the results of cultural marginality. The new street values and beliefs that stem from these changes can work very well on the streets when surviving violent confrontations is required; oftentimes the threat of violence is used by street youth as a deterrent for having violence used against them. Thus, although street youth aggression and violence stem from various sources and motives, it is the street gang subculture and the complexities of its formation and spread that best explain the level of gang violence today—with drivebys, wanton shootings of innocent bystanders, and other physical harm as the gang takes on a life of its own (Sanders 1994).

As noted earlier, the most aggressive and violent behavior among gang members occurs during that adolescent status crisis, between childhood and adulthood. The social psychology of human development, especially the redefinition of masculinity and capability, is filled with real and symbolic messages. Earlier marginal experiences in these youths' lives lead to a social identity that, not coincidentally, shapes a personal identity during what Erikson referred to as the "psychosocial moratorium" (Erikson 1968). This is a time in human development when ambiguity and conflict reign in the clarification and affirmation of one's age and gender identity. Bloch & Neiderhoffer (1958) underscored in their gang study that "becoming a man" was a strong generator of aggressive and violent behavior. Part of the evidence to this theory was referenced in a cross-cultural study (Burton & Whiting 1961) that assessed male initiation rites that helped youth begin to think of themselves as men, particularly in those societies where young males are raised almost exclusively by women but must abruptly cut the apron strings and become male warriors. It should not escape our attention that most modern-day gangs have an initiation ordeal that helps test and screen novitiates (Vigil 1988a, 1996); and, equally important, many of the gang males come from single-parent families, usually female-headed, and then must adjust to street socialization dominated by experienced gang males.

Humans are so malleable and resilient that, rather than remain lost in this aura of marginality, confused and full of rage, they reconstitute a subculture and identity using bits and pieces of the past mixed with the present but all shaken by the forces of a difficult city reality. Key to this street gang identity is learning to act crazy to survive (i.e., "loco" for Latino gangs and "crazy niggah" for blacks), to be unpredictable, ready for any action, even killing somebody, to show you are "down" for your homeboys and set or "barrio." Many of the gang members, however, have had particularly traumatic lives and, indeed, are crazy; these are usually known as the most loco among Latinos and "ghetto heroes" among African Americans, according to Monster Kody's autobiography (Shakur 1993). Suffering from a type of soul death and sense of worthlessness, leading them to question why anyone else should be worth anything, these crazies can be responsible for most of the gang homicides or, at the least, for instigating more conflicts and confrontations. Strangely, sharing this aura of aggressiveness bordering on a quasi-controlled insanity mindset and behavior makes for a strong street bond. Street gang members look up to one another and show deference and respect for the locos and ghetto heroes. What has happened is that, either because of their own soul death, personal traumas, and wish to prove their masculinity during the adolescent passage, or all of these, a street gang member has joined more than a particular gang but a whole troop of suicidal persons who play a type of street Russian roulette. The mentality is: A bullet is meant for you or me—if you are the one who survives, you, as would be expected, amass more stature and respect. In recent years, unfortunately, the bullets that have moved out of the roulette circle in the streets are marked "To whom it may concern"!

CONCLUSION

In its simplest trajectory, multiple marginality can be modeled as: place/status → street socialization → street subculture → street identity. The literature is rich in certain areas, such as social control, subculture of violence, and socioeconomic factors, but notably lacking is the qualitative information and insight that tell us how and why people become violent if (*a*) their family is dysfunctional, (*b*) they join a violent gang, or (*c*) they need money. The dynamic processes are missing in most of these studies, however useful they may be in other regards. Anthropological theorizing and methods can add significantly to the gang violence literature. As this review has noted, an integrated framework showing actions and reactions among factors is where the research is going, and the multiple marginality framework is merely another step in that direction. Taking a holistic perspective is an essential anthropological enterprise, and talking to and watching people in different settings over a long period of time while they evince different moods and behaviors is also part of that heritage (Bronfenbrenner 1979). In this manner, the actions and reactions are gathered, the reasons and modes for human aggression better understood, and the connections between the street social identity and the personal identity are discerned.

Anthropology and sociology were once one discipline; when they split, sociologists forgot their roots and reached for larger samples to make more general statements about urban issues. Though street gang members are a difficult population to investigate, as many sociologists already clearly understand, it is not that difficult to integrate intensive, in-depth interviewing of gang members as part of large-scale surveys. Large numbers count, but it is in the details that human complexity is better examined and understood.

The contexts of time, place, and people are also an important part of the equation. For example, some gangs have been around for generations and are found in various large and middle-sized cities in the United States (Klein 1995). Studies in larger cities show a tradition of an age-graded gang structure (Moore 1978, Klein 1971). This cohorting network works to maintain the size of the gang as older members "mature out" and the younger gang members, approximately from the ages of 14 to 18, are more likely to be led into and participate in violent behavior. Attention to female gangs and affiliates has also increased (Miller 2001, Campbell 1991) and helped broaden the discussion of gender roles (Messerschmidt 1995, Moore 1991, Moore & Hagedorn 1996). Newer gangs have emerged in different urban enclaves as a result of large-scale immigration, where increasingly more street youth are opting for this lifestyle (Waters 1999). A few of these less-rooted gangs have tried to catch up to the older gangs by becoming just as violent, and they are succeeding.

ACKNOWLEDGMENTS

A hearty "thank you" goes to the many community residents and street gang members who helped me better understand the street life that generates so much violence. Students who helped on this project by digging up references are also appreciated. Although I am responsible for the construction of this review and what is written and emphasized, I would like to express a deep appreciation to my colleague, Cheryl Maxson, who offered critical advice and feedback along the way. Finally, to my long-time friend and co-writer on other projects, John M. Long, goes a heartfelt thanks.

The *Annual Review of Anthropology* is online at http://anthro.annualreviews.org

LITERATURE CITED

Alonso A. 1999. *Territoriality among African-American street gangs in Los Angeles*. MA thesis. Dept. Geogr., Univ. South. Calif.

Anderson E. 1994. The code of the streets. *Atl. Mon.* May:81–94

Anderson E. 1997. Violence and the inner-city street code. In *Violence and Childhood in the Inner City*, ed. J McCord, pp. 1–30. Cambridge, UK: Cambridge Univ. Press

Anderson E. 1998. The social ecology of youth violence. See Tonry & Moore 1998, pp. 65–104

Ashbury H. 1927. *Gangs of New York: an Informal History of the Underworld*. New York: Knopf

Beckett K. 1997. *Crime and Drugs in Contem-

porary American Politics.* New York: Oxford Univ. Press

Blanc CS, with contributors. 1995. *Urban Children in Distress: Global Predicaments and Innovative Strategies*. Florence, Italy: UNICEF

Bloch HA, Neiderhoffer A. 1958. *The Gang: a Study in Adolescent Behavior*. New York: Philos. Libr.

Block CR, Block R. 1995. Street gang crime in Chicago. See Miller et al. 2001, pp. 186–99

Blumstein A. 1995. Youth violence, guns, and the illicit drug industry. *J. Crim. Law Criminol.* 86:10–24

Bourgois P. 1995. *In Search of Respect: Selling*

Crack in El Barrio. New York: Cambridge Univ. Press

Bronfenbrenner U. 1979. The ecology of human development. Cambridge, MA: Harvard Univ. Press

Bursik RJ Jr, Grasmick HG. 1995. Defining gangs and gang behavior. See Miller et al. 2001, pp. 8–13

Burton RV, Whiting WM. 1961. The absent father and cross-sex identity. *Merrill-Palmer Q.* 7:85–95

Campbell A. 1990. Female participation in gangs. See Huff 1996, pp. 163–82

Campbell A. 1991. *The Girls in the Gang.* New York: Blackwell. 2nd ed.

Canada G. 1995. *Fist, Stick, Knife, Gun.* Boston: Beacon Press

Cartwright D, Howard K. 1966. Multivariate analysis of gang delinquency: ecological influences. *Multivar. Behav. Res.* 1:321–37

Chesney-Lind M. 1999. Girls and violence: an overview. See Flannery & Huff 1999, pp. 171–200

Cloward RA, Ohlin LE. 1960. *Delinquency and Opportunity: a Theory of Delinquent Gangs.* New York: Free Press

Cohen AK, Short JF Jr. 1958. Research in delinquent subcultures. *J. Soc. Issues.* 68:452–62

Cook PJ, Laub J. 1998. The unprecedented epidemic in youth violence. See Tonry & Moore 1998, pp. 27–64

Cornish DB, Clarke RV. 1986. *The Reasoning Criminal.* New York: Springer-Verlag

Covey HC, Menard S, Franzese RJ. 1992. *Juvenile Gangs.* Springfield, IL: Thomas

Curry GD. 2001. Female gang involvement. See Miller et al. 2001, pp. 121–33

Curry GD, Richard AB, Fox RJ. 1994. *Gang Crime and Law Enforcement Recordkeeping.* Washington, DC: US Dept. Justice, Natl. Inst. Justice, Res. in Brief

Dawley D. 1992 [1973]. *A Nation of Lords.* Prospect Heights, IL: Waveland Press

Decker SH. 1996. Collective and normative features of gang violence. *Justice Q.* 13:243–64

Decker SH, Van Winkle B. 1996. *Life in the Gang: Family, Friends, and Violence.* New York: Cambridge Univ. Press

Dietrich L. 1998. *Chicana Adolescents: Bitches, 'Ho's, and Schoolgirls.* Westport, CT: Praeger

Elliott D. 1994. Serious violent offenders: onset, developmental, and termination. The Am. Soc. Criminol. 1993 Pres. Address. *Criminology* 32:1–21

Ember CR. 1996. Universal and variable patterns of gender difference. In *Cross-Cultural Research for Social Science,* ed. CR Ember, M Ember, pp. 201–24. Upper Saddle River, NJ: Prentice Hall

Erikson E. 1968. Psychosocial identity. In *International Encyclopedia of the Social Sciences,* ed. D Sills, 7:61–65. New York: McMillan, Free Press

Esbensen F, Winfree LT Jr. 2001. Race and gender differences between gang and non-gang youths. See Miller et al. 2001, pp. 106–20

Fagan J. 1999. Youth gangs, drugs, and socioeconomic isolation. See Flannery & Huff 1999, pp. 145–70

Farrington DP. 1996. The explanation and prevention of youthful offending. In *Delinquency and Crime: Current Theories,* ed. JD Hawkins, pp. 113–31. Cambridge, UK: Cambridge Univ. Press

Farrington DP. 1998. Predictors, causes, and correlates of male youth violence. See Tonry & Moore 1998, pp. 421–76

Felson M. 1987. Routine activities and crime prevention in the developing metropolis. *Criminology* 25:911–31

Felson M, Cohen LE. 1980. Human ecology and crime: a routine activities approach. *Hum. Ecol.* 4:389–406

Flannery DJ, Huff CR. 1999. *Youth Violence: Prevention, Intervention, and Social Policy.* Washington, DC: Am. Psychiatr. Press

Fleisher MS. 1995. *Beggars and Thieves: Lives of Urban Street Criminals.* Madison: Univ. Wisc. Press

Fleisher MS. 1998. *Dead End Kids: Gang Girls and the Boys They Know.* Madison: Univ. Wisc. Press

Giordano PC. 1978. Girls, guys and gangs: the changing social context of female delinquency. *J. Crim. Law Criminol.* 69(1): 126–32

Goffredson M, Hirschi T. 1990. *A General Theory of Crime.* Stanford, CA: Stanford Univ. Press

Hagedorn JM. 1988. *People and Folks: Gangs, Crime and the Underclass in a Rustbelt City.* Chicago: Lake View

Hagedorn JM. 1998. Gang violence in the postindustrial era. See Tonry & Moore 1998, pp. 364–420

Hazlehurst K, Hazlehurst C. 1998. *Gangs and Youth Subcultures: International Explorations.* New Brunswick, NJ: Transaction

Hirschi T. 1969. *Causes of Delinquency.* Berkeley: Univ. Calif. Press

Hirschi T, Gottfredson M. 1983. Age and the explanation of crime. *Am. J. Sociol.* 89(3):552–84

Horowitz RB. 1983. *Honor and the American Dream.* New Brunswick, NJ: Rutgers Univ. Press

Howell JC. 1996. *Youth Gangs, Homicides, Drugs and Guns.* Tallahassee, FL: Natl. Youth Gang Cent.

Huesmann LR, Moise JF. 1999. Stability and continuity of aggression from early childhood to young adulthood. See Flannery & Huff 1996, pp. 73–95

Huff CR. 1996. *Gangs in America.* Thousand Oaks, CA: Sage. 2nd ed.

Huff CR, ed. 2002. *Gangs in America III.* Thousand Oaks, CA: Sage

Johnson J, Oliver M. 1991. Economic restructuring and black male joblessness in U.S. metropolitan areas. *Urban Geogr.* 12(6):542–62

Keiser RL. 1969. *The Vice Lords: Warriors of the Streets.* New York: Holt, Rinehart, & Winston

Kennedy LW, Baron SW. 1993. Routine activities and a subculture of violence: a study of violence on the street. *J. Res. Crime Delinquency* 30(1):88–111

Klein M. 1971. *Street Gangs and Street Workers.* Englewood Cliffs, NJ: Prentice-Hall

Klein M. 1995. *The American Street Gang.* New York: Oxford Univ. Press

Klein M, Crawford LD. 1967. Group, gangs and cohesiveness. *J. Res. Crime Delinquency* 4:63–75

Klein MW, Kerner HJ, Maxson CL, Weitekamp EGM. 2001. *The Eurogang Paradox: Street Gangs and Youth Groups in the U.S. and Europe.* Boston, MA, Dordrecht, The Neth.: Kluwer Acad.

Klein MW, Maxson CL. 1994. Gangs and cocaine trafficking. In *Drugs and the Criminal Justice System: Evaluating Public Policy Initiatives*, ed. D MacKensie, C Uchida, pp. 136–48. Newbury Park, CA: Sage

Kornhauser RR. 1978. *Social Sources of Delinquency.* Chicago: Univ. Chicago Press

Loeber R, Stouthamer-Loeber M. 1986. Family factors as correlates and predictors of juvenile conduct problems and delinquency. In *Crime and Justice*, ed. M Tonry, N Morris, pp. 29–149. Chicago: Univ. Chicago Press

Lott J, Mustard D. 1997. Crime, deterrence and right-to-carry concealed handguns. *J. Legal Stud.* 26:1–13

Luckenbill DF, Doyle DP. 1989. Structural position and violence: developing a cultural explanation. *Criminology* 27(3):419–35

Martinez R Jr. 2000. Immigration and urban violence: the link between immigrant Latinos and types of homicides. *Soc. Sci. Q.* 81(1):365–74

Maxson CL. 1998. Gang homicide. In *Studying and Preventing Homicide*, ed. D Smith, M Zahn, pp. 197–219. Thousand Oaks, CA: Sage

McNulty PJ. 1995. Natural born killers? Preventing the coming explosion of teenage crime. *Policy Rev.* 71:84–95

Merton RK. 1949. *Social Theory and Social Structure.* Glencoe, IL: Free Press

Messerschmidt J. 1995. From patriarchy to gender: feminist theory, criminology, and the challenge of diversity. In *International Feminist Perspective in Criminology: Engendering a Discipline*, ed. NH Rafter, F Heidensohn. pp. 167–88. Philadelphia: Open Univ. Press

Miller J. 2001. *One of the Guys: Girls, Gangs, and Gender.* New York: Oxford Univ. Press

Miller J. 2002. The girls in the gang. In *Gangs in America III*, ed. CR Huff, pp. 175–97. Thousand Oaks, CA: Sage

Miller J, Maxson CL, Klein MW, eds. 2001. *The Modern Gang Reader*. Los Angeles: Roxbury. 2nd ed.

Miller W. 1973. The molls. *Society* 11(1):32–35

Miller WB. 1958. Lower class culture as a generating milieu of gang delinquency. *J. Soc. Issues* 14(3):419–35

Miller WB. 1975. *Violence by Youth Gangs and Youth Groups as a Crime Problem in Major American Cities*. Washington, DC: US Dept. Justice

Moore JW. 1978. *Homeboys*. Philadelphia: Temple Univ. Press

Moore JW. 1991. Going down to the barrio: homeboys and homegirls in change. Philadelphia: Temple Univ. Press

Moore JW, Hagedorn JM. 1996. What happens to girls in the gang? See Huff 1996, pp. 205–18

OJJDP (Off. Juv. Justice Delinquency Prev.). 1996. *Female Offenders in the Juvenile Justice System: Statistic Summary*. Washington, DC: US Dept. Justice

Oliver W. 2003. *The Violent Social World of Black Men*. San Francisco: Jossey Bass. Rev. ed. In press

Padilla F. 1992. *The Gang as an American Enterprise*. New Brunswick, NJ: Rutgers Univ. Press

Park RE, Burgess EW, McKenzie RO, eds. 1925. *The City*. Chicago: Univ. Chicago Press

Raine A, Brennan PA, Farrington DP. 1997. Biosocial bases of violence: conceptual and theoretical issues. In *Biosocial Bases of Violence*, ed. A Raine, PA Brennan, DP Farrington, pp. 99–130. New York: Plenum

Reiss A Jr, Roth JA. 1993. *Understanding and Preventing Violence*. Washington, DC: Natl. Acad. Press

Rohner RP. 1976. Sex differences in aggression: phylogenetic and enculturation perspectives. *Ethos* 4:57–72

Sampson RJ, Laub JH. 1990. Crime and deviance over the life course: the salience of adult social bonds. *Am. Soc. Rev.* 55:609–27

Sampson RJ, Lauritsen JL. 1990. Deviant lifestyles, proximity to crime, and the offender-victim link in personal violence. *J. Res. Crime Delinquency* 27(2):110–39

Sanders WB. 1994. *Gangbangs and Drive-bys: Grounded Culture and Juvenile Gang Violence*. New York: Aldine de Gruyter

Seigal LJ, Senna JJ. 1991. *Juvenile Delinquency*. St. Paul, MN: West Publ. 4th ed.

Shakur S (a.k.a. Monster Kody). 1993. *Monster: the Autobiography of an L.A. Gang Member*. New York: Atl. Mon. Press

Shaw C, McKay R. 1942. *Juvenile Delinquency and Urban Areas*. Chicago: Univ. Chicago Press

Short J. 1996. Personal, gang, and community careers. See Huff 1996, pp. 3–11

Short JF Jr, Strodtbeck FL. 1965. *Group Process and Gang Delinquency*. Chicago: Univ. Chicago Press

Spergel IA, Curry GD. 1998. The national youth gang survey: a research and development process. See Miller et al. 2001, pp. 254–65

Sullivan M. 1988. *Getting Paid*. Ithaca: Cornell Univ. Press

Sutherland EH. 1934. *Principles of Criminology*. Chicago: Lippincott

Suttles G. 1968. *Social Order of the Slum*. Chicago: Univ. Chicago Press

Thornberry TP. 2001. Risk factors for gang membership. In *The Modern Gang Researcher*, ed. J Miller, CL Maxson, MW Klein, pp. 32–43. Los Angeles: Roxbury. 2nd ed.

Thrasher F. 1927/1963. *The Gang*. Chicago: Univ. Chicago Press

Tonry M, Moore MH. 1998. *Youth Violence*. Chicago: Univ. Chicago Press

Venkatesh SA. 1996. The gang in the community. See Huff 1996, pp. 241–56

Vigil JD. 1987. Street socialization, locura behavior, and violence among Chicano gang members. In *Violence and Homicide in*

Hispanic Communities, ed. J Kraus, S Sorenson, PD Juarez, pp. 231–41. Washington, DC: Natl. Inst. Mental Health

Vigil JD. 1988a. *Barrio Gangs: Street Life and Identity in Southern California*. Austin: Univ. Texas Press

Vigil JD. 1988b. Group processes and street identity: adolescent Chicano gang members. *Ethos* 16(4):421–45

Vigil JD. 1996. Street baptism: chicano gang initiation. *Hum. Organ.* 55(2):149–53

Vigil JD. 1999. Streets and schools: how educators can help Chicano maraginalized gang youth. *Harvard Educational Rev.* 69(3):270–88

Vigil JD. 2002a. *A Rainbow of Gangs: Street Cultures in the Mega-City*. Austin: Univ. Texas Press

Vigil JD. 2002b. Community dynamics and the rise of street gangs. In *Latinos! Remaking America*, ed. MM Suarez-Orozco, MM Paez, pp. 97–109. Berkeley, CA: Univ. Calif. Press; Cambridge, MA: David Rockefeller Cent. Lat. Am. Stud., Harvard Univ.

Vigil JD, Yun SC. 1998. Vietnamese youth gangs in the context of multiple marginality and the Los Angeles youth gang phenomenon. In *Gangs and Youth Subcultures: International Explorations*, ed. K Hazlehurst, C Hazlehurst, pp. 117–39. New Brunswick, NJ: Transaction

Vigil JD, Yun SC. 2002. A cross-cultural framework to understand gangs: multiple marginality and Los Angeles. See Huff 2002, pp. 161–74

Waters T. 1999. *Crime and Immigrant Youth*. Thousand Oaks, CA: Sage

Whyte WF. 1943. *Street Corner Society*. Chicago: Univ. Chicago Press

Wilson WJ. 1987. *The Truly Disadvantaged*. Chicago: Univ. Chicago Press

Wolfgang ME, Ferracuti F. 1967. *The Subculture of Violence*. London: Tavistock

Yablonsky L. 1966. *The Violent Gang*. New York: Macmillan

Zimring FE. 1996. Kids, guns, and homicide: policy notes on an age-specific epidemic. *Law Contemp. Probl.* 59:261–74

Zimring FE. 1998. *Youth Violence*. Oxford: Oxford Univ. Press

Annu. Rev. Anthropol. 2003. 32:243–62
doi: 10.1146/annurev.anthro.32.061002.093112

SUSTAINABLE GOVERNANCE OF COMMON-POOL RESOURCES: Context, Methods, and Politics

Arun Agrawal

*Department of Political Science, McGill University, Montréal, Québec H3A 2T7,
Canada; email: arun.agrawal@mcgill.ca*

Key Words   common property, resource management, institutions, sustainability

■ **Abstract**   This paper presents a critical assessment of the field of common property. After discussing briefly the major findings and accomplishments of the scholarship on the commons, the paper pursues two strategies of critique. The first strategy of
friendly critique accepts the basic assumptions of most writings on common property
to show that scholars of commons have discovered far more variables that potentially
affect resource management than is possible to analyze carefully. The paper identifies
some potential means to address the problem of too many variables. The second line of
critique proceeds differently. It asks how analyses of common property might change,
and what they need to consider, if they loosen assumptions about sovereign selves and
apolitical property rights institutions. My examination of these questions concludes
this review with an emphasis on the need to (*a*) attend more carefully to processes of
subject formation, and (*b*) investigate common property arrangements and associated
subject positions with greater historical depth.

INTRODUCTION

The literature on common pool resources and common property has grown swiftly
in the last two decades (see reviews in Ostrom et al. 2002). Globally pervasive
concerns about environmental degradation and resource depletion have stimulated
this growth. Failures attributed to state management and market-oriented policies
have made community attractive to many policy makers as an alternative actor to
govern forests, pastures, water, and fisheries. Insight from students of common
property has found widespread expression as policy innovations, with many governments decentralizing environmental management and promoting community-
based conservation (Li 1996). In many instances, these policy shifts are redefining
communities, resource management, and local arrangements to govern the
commons.

This paper presents a critical assessment of the field of common property. After
discussing briefly the major findings and accomplishments of the scholarship on
the commons, I follow with two distinct strategies of critique. The first strategy
of criticism accepts and uses concepts fundamental to writings on the commons.

0084-6570/03/1021-0243$14.00
243

These concepts include the idea of a sovereign, self-governing self and systems of property that stand above politics. This friendly critique shows that scholars of commons have discovered far more variables that potentially affect resource management than is possible to analyze carefully. I identify some possible ways to address the problem of too many variables. The second line of critique proceeds differently. It asks how analyses of common property might change, and what they need to consider, if they loosen assumptions about sovereign selves and apolitical property rights institutions. My examination of these questions concludes this review with an emphasis on the need to (*a*) attend more carefully to processes of subject formation, and (*b*) investigate common property arrangements and associated subject positions with greater historical depth.

FINDINGS AND ACCOMPLISHMENTS OF THE COMMONS LITERATURE

The major concern of writings on common property is to show that variations in forms of property rights make a difference in resource management outcomes. Such variations affect outcomes by shaping incentives of users and managers. An allied preoccupation of commons scholars has been to demonstrate that markets or private property arrangements and public ownership or state management do not exhaust the range of plausible institutional mechanisms to govern natural resource use. The alternative that commons theorists have identified—community and common ownership and management—is rooted in the practices of millions of households around the world. At the same time, it resonates with theoretical puzzles that concern scholars of social movements and revolutions, voting and other forms of political participation, collusion and cheating, formation of institutions and their maintenance, cooperation, and conflict. In all these situations, participants attempt to solve collective action problems. By focusing on the conditions under which users of renewable resources cooperate to achieve efficient management (or fail to do so), the literature on common property has created the grounds on which its findings can resonate with broader concerns in the social sciences.

In investigating the impact of different institutional structures on resource management, commons theorists have also shown the importance of both formal and informal institutions as an influence on human behavior. They have drawn and built upon the works of other property rights theorists and institutionalists (Bates 1989, Knight 1992, Libecap 1990, North 1990) but have produced additional evidence on the role of informal norms in influencing human actions. Because they conceptualize institutions deliberately in an abstract manner, as sets of enforceable rules that facilitate and constrain human action, their conclusions about property rights, a subset of institutions, possess significant generalizability. For commons theorists, property rights institutions are best seen as sets of rules that define access, use, exclusion, management, monitoring, sanctioning, and arbitration behavior of users with respect to specific resources (Schlager & Ostrom 1992). At the same time as such rules are significant in governing patterns of use, they are also the principal mechanisms through which policies regarding resource management work (Alchian & Demsetz 1973, Furubotn & Pejovich 1974). It is not surprising therefore that findings of common property theorists have found direct application in government policy choices.

Many scholars of the commons have also come to emphasize the political nature of institutions. Institutions come into being as consequences of actions of humans and allow specific individuals and groups to reap advantages from altered social circumstances rather than allowing societies as a whole to capture efficiency gains. In this connection, the work of new institutionalists such as Knight (1992) and Bates (1981, 1989) is especially important. Earlier, property rights theorists had used a functionalist evolutionary logic to suggest that inefficient institutions are eliminated over time and efficient institutions survive (Alchian 1950, Demsetz 1967). But now commons theorists have come to emphasize the fact that institutions change mainly as a result of attempts by specific social actors, and therefore institutional change is likely to occur only when relevant political actors perceive gains from institutional change. The emergence of new institutions thus is a highly political affair (Gibson 1999, Peluso 1992). Further, whether new institutions that emerge will also be efficient for a society depends on the extent to which the interests of groups attempting institutional change intersect or overlap with those of the larger collective.

In their empirical research, scholars of commons have focused primarily on producing case studies of successful community management of coastal fisheries, forests, pastures, irrigation, and ground water (Ascher 1995, Bromley 1992, McCay & Acheson 1987, Peters 1994, Tang 1992). Their work, in conjunction with other writings on participation, indigenous knowledge, and political ecology, has encouraged resource comanagement programs by governments. Comanagement programs assign local communities shares in control over and benefits from renewable resources (Agrawal & Ribot 1999, FAO 1999). Many of them delegate only very limited authority and often communities gain only limited shares. But the altered policy environment constitutes a substantial change over the colonial and immediate postcolonial environment when states saw themselves as best suited to resource control and management. The increase in the stakes of communities has meant a resurgence of interest in community and communal management and contributed to the growth of what might be called the New Commons.

The extensive theoretical and empirical research of commons scholars pays due attention to individuals as decision makers and to the circumstances in which decisions are made. A number of writings have undertaken important theoretical development to focus on the commons dilemmas that confront communities of users (Cheung 1970, Dasgupta & Heal 1979, Oakerson 1992, Ostrom 1990, Runge 1984). These writings have helped clarify the nature of resources that are used jointly, how technological or institutional aspects of use can influence resource characteristics, and how the structure of the situations in which resources are utilized affects use and management decisions and use patterns.

Indeed, it is the institutional nature of the analysis conducted by common property theorists that makes their work so valuable in recent discussions of decentralization of environmental management. Around the world, more than 50 countries have now begun to involve local communities and lower-level decision-making units in protecting and managing the environment (FAO 1999). These new policy trends are based on the recognition that the fiscal capacity of the state to undertake coercive conservation is limited and that communities can often manage their resources better than either private actors negotiating through market-based exchanges or state actors regulating through command and control policies. In many cases, communities are seen also to be characterized by high levels of social capital, which permit them to undertake collective tasks far more efficiently in comparison to state bureaucracies, and to do so far more equitably than market-based solutions. Indeed, recent work on common property has begun to draw upon the vast literature on social capital (Putnam 1993). Several scholars have begun to examine the extent to which common property institutions are based upon stocks of social capital and whether and how they enhance the networks through which social capital is generated (Katz 2000, Muldavin 2000, Robbins 2000).

CRITIQUE FROM WITHIN

A Review of Three Studies

Although scholars of commons have demonstrated that variations in property arrangements matter and that community-based and common property institutions can guide sustainable resource use, there is widespread disagreement among them on what accounts for successful and sustainable resource use. One significant reason for divergent conclusions is that most empirical studies of commons follow the case study method. The multiplicity of research designs, sampling techniques, and data collection methods means that there are few compelling analyses that systematically test findings, compare postulated causal connections across contexts, or carefully specify the contextual and historical factors relevant to success.

These rather bold claims can be illustrated by a comparison of three of the most careful studies of the commons to appear since the mid 1980s. The works by Robert Wade (1994), Elinor Ostrom (1990), and Jean-Marie Baland & Jean-Philippe Platteau (1996) are path-breaking book-length analyses of local, community-based efforts to manage and govern common-pool resources. They are carefully comparative, theoretically informed, and, in contrast to single case-oriented research, they use a relatively large sample of cases to analyze the validity of theoretical insight. Each presents a summary set of conditions critical to sustainability of commons institutions. Together, their conclusions form a viable starting point to analyze the findings of the common property literature.

The three authors differ in their methods and research design. Wade (1994) relies primarily on original data from 31 south Indian villages in a single district. His sample is not representative of irrigation institutions in the region, but at least we can presume that the data collection in each case is consistent. Ostrom (1990) uses detailed case studies that other scholars generated. The independent production of the research she samples means that all her cases may not have consistently collected data. But she examines each case using the same set of independent and dependent variables. Baland & Platteau (1996) motivate their empirical discussion by a wide-ranging review of the economic literature on property rights and the inability of this literature to generate unambiguous conclusions about whether private property is superior to regulated common property. To test the validity of their conclusions, they use information from several different sets of cases. In an important sense, therefore, the model specification is incomplete in each test (King et al. 1994).

Wade's analysis of commonly managed irrigation systems examines when it is that corporate institutions arise in these villages and what accounts for their success in resolving commons dilemmas. He (1994, pp. 215–16) argues for the importance of 14 conditions in facilitating successful management of the commons. According to him, effective rules of restraint on access and use are unlikely to last when there are many users, when the boundaries of the common-pool resource are unclear, when users live in groups scattered over a large area, and when detection of rule-breakers is difficult, and so on (see also Ostrom 1986; Ostrom et al. 1994, p. 319). Wade lists his conclusions in greater detail by classifying different variables under the headings of resources, technology, user group, noticeability, relationship between resources and user group, and relationship between users and the state.

Some of Wade's facilitating conditions parallel findings from other comparative work. Consider Ostrom's (1990) design principles, based on her investigation of 14 cases. A design principle for Ostrom is not part of a blueprint but "an essential element or condition that helps to account for the success of these institutions in sustaining the CPRs and gaining the compliance of generation after generation of appropriators to the rules in use" (1990, p. 90). Like Wade, Ostrom also emphasizes small group size, well-defined boundaries on resources and user groups, and ease of monitoring and enforcement. And in common with Wade, most of the principles are generalizations about local systems and relationships. Nine of her principles are present in a significant manner in all the robust commons institutions she analyzes, and the tenth covers cases that are more complex, such as federated systems.

Baland & Platteau (1996), in their comprehensive and synthesizing review of a large number of studies on the commons, begin with an examination of competing theoretical claims by scholars of property regimes. Carefully comparing features of common property with private property, they suggest that "*regulated common property and private property are equivalent from the standpoint of the efficiency of resource use*" (p. 175, emphasis in original). Note that their result is a formalization of Coase's (1960) insight that property rights are irrelevant in the absence of transactions costs and with full information. Their review of empirical studies of the commons leads them to emphasize small size of a user group, a location close to the resource, homogeneity among group members, effective enforcement mechanisms, and past experiences of cooperation as some of the factors significant to achieve cooperation to manage resources (Baland & Platteau 1996, pp. 343–45).

The brief review above of three landmark works makes evident some of the patterns in their conclusions. They each argue that members of small local groups can design institutional arrangements to help manage resources sustainably. They go further and identify a small set of conditions that are positively related to local self management of resources. Finally, they use theoretical insight to defend and explain the empirical regularities they find.

The regularities in successful management that they discover pertain to one of four sets of variables: (*a*) characteristics of resources, (*b*) nature of groups that depend on resources, (*c*) particulars of institutional regimes through which resources are managed, and (*d*) the nature of the relationship between a group and external forces and authorities such as markets, states, and technology. Characteristics of resources can include, for example, such features as well-defined boundaries of the resource, riskiness and unpredictability of resource flows, and mobility of the resource. Characteristics of groups, among other aspects, relate to size, levels of wealth and income, different types of heterogeneity, power relations among subgroups, and past experience. Particulars of institutional regimes have an enormous range of possibilities, but some of the critical identified aspects of institutional arrangements concern monitoring, sanctions, adjudication, and accountability. Finally, a number of characteristics pertain to the relationships of the locally situated groups, resource systems, and institutional arrangements with the external environment in the form of demographic changes, technology, markets, and different levels of governance. Table 1 summarizes and lists under these four basic categories the different conditions that the three studies under consideration have identified as significant (initials in parentheses following each condition indicate which of the three studies considers that condition important).

Locating Missing Variables

The analysis of the information in Table 1 reveals significant gaps in the collective conclusions of these three authors. They pay relatively little attention to features of resources that affect sustainable governance; they also attend only cursorily to the social, political-institutional, and physical environment in which commons are situated. It is necessary to turn to other studies of commons that investigate these factors more carefully.

The limited attention to resource characteristics is unfortunate. Extensive movements of many forms of wildlife, and unpredictability of these movements, can render them ill suited to local management alone (Naughton-Treves & Sanderson 1995). The extensive spatial impact of greenhouse gases or ozone-depleting chemicals presents similar dilemmas for managers of commons because of mobility, volatility, and unpredictability in the flow of benefits.

In a carefully argued paper on resource characteristics, Blomquist et al. (1994) focus on two physical features of resource systems: stationarity and storage. Stationarity refers to whether a resource is mobile, and storage concerns the extent

TABLE 1 Synthesis of facilitating conditions identified by Wade (1994)—RW, Ostrom (1990)—EO, and Baland & Platteau (1996)—B&P

1) Resource system characteristics
  i) Small size (RW)
  ii) Well-defined boundaries (RW, EO)

2) Group characteristics
  i) Small size (RW, B&P)
  ii) Clearly defined boundaries (RW, EO)
  iii) Shared norms (B&P)
  iv) Past successful experiences—social capital (RW, B&P)
  v) Appropriate leadership—young, familiar with changing external environments, connected to local traditional elite (B&P)
  vi) Interdependence among group members (RW, B&P)
  vii) Heterogeneity of endowments, homogeneity of identities and interests (B&P)

(1 and 2) Relationship between resource system characteristics and group characteristics
  i) Overlap between user-group residential location and resource location (RW, B&P)
  ii) High levels of dependence by group members on resource system (RW)
  iii) Fairness in allocation of benefits from common resources (B&P)

3) Institutional arrangements
  i) Rules are simple and easy to understand (B&P)
  ii) Locally devised access and management rules (RW, EO, B&P)
  iii) Ease in enforcement of rules (RW, EO, B&P)
  iv) Graduated sanctions (RW, EO)
  v) Availability of low-cost adjudication (EO)
  vi) Accountability of monitors and other officials to users (EO, B&P)

(1 and 3) Relationship between resource system and institutional arrangements
  i) Match restrictions on harvests to regeneration of resources (RW, EO)

4) External environment
  i) Technology: low-cost exclusion technology (RW)
  ii) State:
    a) Central governments should not undermine local authority (RW, EO)
    b) Supportive external sanctioning institutions (B&P)
    c) Appropriate levels of external aid to compensate local users for conservation activities (B&P)
    d) Nested levels of appropriation, provision, enforcement, governance (EO)

to which it is possible to "collect and hold resources" (p. 309). After examining the impact of these two physical characteristics of resources on externalities, Blomquist et al. conclude that these factors have an impact on management because of their relationship to information. Greater mobility of resources and difficulties of storage make management more difficult for users because of problems associated with reliability and costs of information. Naughton-Treves & Sanderson (1995) also note that unpredictability adversely affects the ability of users to allocate available resources or undertake activities that augment supply.

Wade's, Ostrom's, and Baland & Platteau's inattention to external social, political-institutional, and physical environment can be illustrated with reference to three important forces that shape the contexts in which common property institutions function: demographic change, market penetration, and state policies. None of the three studies considers demographic issues carefully. Nor do they place much emphasis on market-related demands that may make local pressures on resources seem relatively trivial. But variations and changes in demographic pressures surely influence the ability of those dependent on common-pool resources to create enforceable rules. Indeed, an enormous literature focuses on questions of population and market pressures and asserts their importance.

Writings on the role of population in resource management have a long history and an impressive theoretical pedigree (Ehrlich 1968, Malthus 1960). Many conclude that population growth leads rather straightforwardly to environmental degradation (Low & Heinen 1993, Pimental et al. 1994). A smaller but vocal group of scholars suggests the impact is far more limited (Tiffen et al. 1994, Leach & Mearns 1996). The story is similar where markets are concerned, except that the terms of the debate are less polarized and there is wider agreement that increasing integration with markets usually has an adverse impact on the management of common-pool resources (Colchester 1994, Young 1994). Analogous to market articulation is the question of technological means available to exploit the commons. Sudden emergence of new technological innovations that transform the cost-benefit ratios of harvesting products from commons are likely to affect the sustainability of institutions.

The arrival of markets and new technologies, and the changes they might prompt in existing resource management regimes, is not a bloodless or innocent process (Oates 1999). New demand pressures create varying incentives about the products to be harvested, technologies of harvest, and rates of harvest. In many cases, as new market actors gain access to a particular common-pool resource, they seek alliances with state actors to defend the primacy of their claims (Azhar 1993). State officials can themselves become involved in the privatization of commons (Sivaramakrishnan 1999, Skaria 1999).

As the ultimate guarantor of property rights arrangements, the role of the state and overarching governance structures is central to the functioning of common property institutions. Although the three studies are more attentive to the potential role of central governments than they are to the role of population and market pressures, the nature of local-state relations requires more careful exploration. It is true that a number of scholars have begun to focus on resource management–related laws and national policies (Lynch & Talbott 1995, Repetto & Gillis 1988). But systematic examinations and clear understandings of variations in state-locality relationships are still missing.

One reason scholars of commons have focused relatively little on external factors like markets, technology, states, and population pressures lies simply in the nature of their intellectual enterprise. In trying to demonstrate the importance of local groups, institutions, and resource-system-related factors, they have tended to ignore how the local is created in conjunction with the external and constituted in relation to its context. The almost exclusive focus upon the local has made the work on common property vulnerable to the same criticisms that apply to the work of those anthropologists who saw their field sites as miniature worlds in themselves, changing only in response to political, economic, or cultural influences from outside.

My argument in favor of attention to markets, demography, and the state addresses the nature and importance of contextual factors only to a partial degree. Clearly, the context of any study comprises far more than just markets, demographic changes, and encompassing governance arrangements. Context can be defined as the encompassing variables that remain constant for a given study but not across studies. Precisely because the historical, spatial, social, or political context of a given study likely remains constant for all analytical purposes, it becomes possible to ignore it. But in any real world situation, the state of contextual variables may affect the impact of variables being studied explicitly.

It is worth pointing out that even where the locality itself is concerned, and even where some important features of groups that manage commons are concerned, there are important gaps in our understanding. Take three aspects of groups as an illustration: size, heterogeneity, and poverty.

According to an enormous literature on the commons and collective action, sparked in part by Olson's seminal work (1965), smaller groups are more likely to engage in successful collective action. But later scholars (Hardin 1982) have remarked on the ambiguities in Olson's argument and suggested that the relationship between group size and collective action is not very straightforward. Marwell & Oliver (1993, p. 38) claim, "a significant body of empirical research . . . finds that the size of a group is positively related to its level of collective action." Agrawal & Goyal (2001) use two analytical features of common-pool resources—imperfect exclusion and lumpiness of third-party monitoring—to hypothesize a curvilinear relationship between group size and successful collection action and to test this hypothesis. The current state of knowledge is perhaps best summarized by Ostrom (1997), who says that the impact of group size on collective action is usually mediated by many other variables. These variables include the production technology of the collective good, its degree of excludability, jointness of supply, and the level of heterogeneity in the group (Hardin 1982, pp. 44–49).

Cumulation of knowledge into a consistent and empirically supported theory has proved even more difficult in relation to group heterogeneity. It can be argued fairly that most resources are managed by groups divided along multiple axes, among them ethnicity, gender, religion, wealth, and caste. Especially significant are gender-related differences within groups because of the often critical role women play in the gathering and harvesting of products from common-pool resources. But other forms of heterogeneity within groups can be equally pernicious and, at any rate, can have multiple and contradictory effects on the possibilities of collective action. Empirical evidence on the matter is still highly ambiguous (Baland & Platteau 1999, Quiggin 1993). Thus even in groups that have high levels of heterogeneities of interest, it may be possible to ensure collective action if some subgroups can coercively enforce conservationist institutions (Jodha 1986, Peluso 1993; but see also Libecap 1990). On the other hand, the role of intra-group heterogeneities on distribution may be more amenable to definition. Significant research on the effects of development projects and also on commons suggests that better-off group members are often likely to gain a larger share of benefits from a resource (Agrawal 2001).

Another critical locality-related factor on which much research has been carried out without a consensus is the impact of poverty on common-pool resources. "Does poverty lead to a greater reliance on the commons (Jodha 1986) and their degradation," or "do increasing levels of wealth, at least initially, lead to greater use of commons by users" are questions on whose answer the contours of many commons-related policies would hinge. But to an important degree, government interventions in this arena are based on limited information and even less reliable analysis.

Whether group size, group heterogeneity, and poverty have a positive, negative, or neutral relationship to sustainability of commons institutions seems subject to a range of other contextual and mediating factors, not all of which are clearly understood. Elster (1992, p. 14) suggests about the study of local justice that "it is a very messy business," and that it may be impossible to identify a set of necessary and sufficient conditions that constitute a theory of local justice. His diagnosis for local justice may be equally applicable to the study of commons, as is also his prescription: Instead of making a choice between theory and description, focus on identifying mechanisms or "identifiable causal patterns" (p. 16). Commenting on a similar tendency in political analysis, Ostrom recognizes that "political systems are complexly organized, and that we will rarely be able to state that one variable is always positively or negatively related to a dependent variable" (1998, p. 16).

Table 2 constitutes an effort to supplement the set of variables presented in Table 1. The additional factors presented in the table are the ones that are not followed by the name of a particular author. Although the factors in Table 2 are among those that many scholars of commons would consider most important for achieving institutional sustainability on the commons, they do not form an exhaustive set. Nor is it likely that an undisputed exhaustive set of variables can ever be created.

Some of the factors in Table 2 are also important to the emergence of commons institutions. The overlap between conditions that facilitate emergence and those that facilitate continued successful functioning of institutions points to the close and complex relationship between origins and continued existence, without any suggestion that the two can be stated as an identical set.

Addressing Problems of Method

The list of factors in Table 2 raises some important methodological obstacles. One important problem stems from the fact that most of the conditions cited in the table are expected to pertain to all common-pool resources and institutions, rather

TABLE 2   Critical enabling conditions for sustainability on the commons. Abbreviations: Wade (1994)—RW, Ostrom (1990)—EO, and Baland & Platteau (1996)—B&P

1) Resource system characteristics
 i) Small size (RW)
 ii) Well-defined boundaries (RW, EO)
 iii) Low levels of mobility
 iv) Possibilities of storage of benefits from the resource
 v) Predictability

2) Group characteristics
 i) Small size (RW, B&P)
 ii) Clearly defined boundaries (RW, EO)
 iii) Shared norms (B&P)
 iv) Past successful experiences—social capital (RW, B&P)
 v) Appropriate leadership—young, familiar with changing external environments, connected to local traditional elite (B&P)
 vi) Interdependence among group members (RW, B&P)
 vii) Heterogeneity of endowments, homogeneity of identities and interests (B&P)
 viii) Low levels of poverty

(1 and 2) Relationship between resource system characteristics and group characteristics
 i) Overlap between user-group residential location and resource location (RW, B&P)
 ii) High levels of dependence by group members on resource system (RW)
 iii) Fairness in allocation of benefits from common resources (B&P)
 iv) Low levels of user demand
 v) Gradual change in levels of demand

3) Institutional arrangements
 i) Rules are simple and easy to understand (B&P)
 ii) Locally devised access and management rules (RW, EO, B&P)
 iii) Ease in enforcement of rules (RW, EO, B&P)
 iv) Graduated sanctions (RW, EO)
 v) Availability of low-cost adjudication (EO)
 vi) Accountability of monitors and other officials to users (EO, B&P)

(1 and 3) Relationship between resource system and institutional arrangements
 i) Match restrictions on harvests to regeneration of resources (RW, EO)

4) External environment
 i) Technology
   a) Low-cost exclusion technology (RW)
   b) Time for adaptation to new technologies related to the commons
 ii) Low levels of articulation with external markets
 iii) Gradual change in articulation with external markets
 iv) State
   a) Central governments should not undermine local authority (RW, EO)
   b) Supportive external sanctioning institutions (B&P)
   c) Appropriate levels of external aid to compensate local users for conservation activities (B&P)
   d) Nested levels of appropriation, provision, enforcement, governance (EO)

than being related to or dependent on some aspect of the situation. Consider the first two conditions in Table 2 under the broad class of resource system characteristics: small size and well-defined boundaries. According to Wade, relatively small-sized resource systems are likely to be managed better under common-property arrangements, and, according to both Ostrom and Wade, resources that have well-defined boundaries are likely better managed as common property. But it is possible in principle, and perhaps more defensible, to think of the effects of resource size or boundary definition as dependent on the state of one or more other variables.

For example, well-defined boundaries of resources may promote sustainable use when flows of benefits are predictable and groups relying on them stationary. But when there are large variations in benefit flows, and/or the group relying on the resource is mobile, then fuzzy resource boundaries may better accommodate variations in group needs and resource flows. A large body of research on pastoralists makes this point especially clearly. This example also brings home the importance of context.

As another example, consider the question of fairness in allocation of benefits from the commons. Typically, intuition as well as much of the scholarship on the commons suggests that fairer allocation of benefits is likely to lead to more sustainable institutional arrangements. But in a social context characterized by highly hierarchical social and political organization, institutional arrangements specifying asymmetric distribution of benefits may be more sustainable even if they are entirely unfair. The caste system and racial inequalities constitute two familiar examples of such hierarchical social arrangements.

The most significant problems of method are a consequence of the sheer number of conditions that seem relevant to the successful management of common-pool resources. Wade, Ostrom, and Baland & Platteau jointly identify 36 important conditions. If one eliminates the common conditions across these three studies, 24 different conditions are still to be found (as in Table 1). It is difficult to eliminate *a priori* any of the conditions they consider important. Indeed, the discussion of their substantive conclusions suggests that even the 24 factors they have identified do not exhaust the full set of conditions relevant to common-pool resource management. Once we take into account additional factors identified in the vast literature on the local governance of common-pool resources as being important, it is reasonable to suppose that the total number of factors that affect successful management of commons may be somewhere between 30 and 40 (Table 2 lists a total of 33 factors). At present, we do not have any reliable way to assess the degree of correlation among these factors.

Further, because the effects of some variables may depend on the state of other variables, any careful analysis of sustainability on the commons needs to incorporate interaction effects among variables. As soon as we concede the possibility that somewhere between 30 and 40 variables affect the management of common-pool resources, and that some of these variables may have important interactional effects, we confront tremendous analytical problems.

When a large number of causal variables potentially affects outcomes, the absence of careful research design that controls for factors that are not the subject of investigation makes it almost impossible to be sure that the observed differences in outcomes are indeed a result of hypothesized causes. If commons researchers do not explicitly take into account the relevant variables that affect success, then the number of selected cases must be (much) larger than the number of variables. But no studies of common-pool resources develop their research design by explicitly taking into account the different variables considered critical to successful management as specified in Table 2. In an important sense, then, many of the existing works on the management of common-pool resources, especially those conducted as case studies or those that base their conclusions on a very small number of cases, suffer from the problem that they do not specify carefully or explicitly the causal model they are testing. In the absence of such specification, qualitative studies of the commons are potentially subject to significant problems of method. Two of the most important of these problems are those stemming from "omitted variable bias" and the problem of endogeneity (King et al. 1994, pp. 168–82, 185–95). These biases, resulting from deficiencies of method, have the potential to produce an emphasis on causal factors that may not be relevant, ignoring other factors that may be relevant, and to generate spurious correlations.

The large number of variables potentially affecting the sustainability of institutions that govern common resources, thus, has important theoretical implications for future research. The most important implication is perhaps for research design. Because the requirements of a random or representative selection of cases are typically very hard to satisfy where common-pool resources are concerned (even when the universe of cases is narrowed geographically), purposive sampling easily becomes the theoretically defensible strategy for selecting cases whether the objective is statistical analysis or structured comparative case analysis. In purposive sampling, the selected cases will be chosen for the variation they represent on theoretically significant variables. This strategy can be defended both because it is easier to implement than an effort to select a representative sample, and because it requires explicit consideration of theoretically relevant variables (Bennett & George 2003).

The large number of variables also has implications for data analysis. One of the strategies that scholars on the commons may need to follow is to reduce the number of closely related variables by constructing indices that combine them. Thus for example, several of the factors listed under Institutional Arrangements in Table 2 may be sufficiently correlated to permit the creation of an index of "Enforcement strength." Especially suitable for such an index may be "Graduated sanctions," "Ease in enforcement of rules," and "Availability of low-cost adjudication." Such indices may also be formed out of variables listed under different headings in that table. Thus, an indicator of stress on existing institutions might be revealed by bringing together such factors as "Gradual change in levels of demand," "Low levels of articulation with external markets," and "Gradual change in articulation with external markets."

There is no general theory of purposive sampling apart from formalizations of the commonsensical consideration that selected cases should represent variation on theoretically significant causal factors. Therefore two factors are likely to be critical in research design: awareness of the variables that are theoretically relevant, and deep knowledge of the case(s) to be researched so that theoretically relevant variables can be operationalized. For example, when constructing a research design, where the variables of interest have to do with mechanisms of monitoring and sanctioning, it would be important for the researcher to be aware of the different forms of monitoring that groups can use. The presence or absence of a guard may only be indicative of the presence or absence of third-party monitoring and may reveal nothing about whether the group being studied has monitoring. Other forms of monitoring would include mutual monitoring and rotational monitoring, where households in a group jointly share the tasks related to monitoring and enforcement.

The information presented in Table 2, organized under four major categories, can therefore be useful in the creation of a research design and case selection for comparative studies or data collection for statistical studies. Given a particular context, the information in Table 2 can help in the selection of the variables that need closest attention in the selection of cases. For example, if the cases to be selected lie in the same ecological zone and represent the same resource type, then variables related to resource characteristics may not be very important for case selection. The obvious trade-off for this reduction in the number of variables is that the research is likely to have limited generalizability. Overall, the problems of contingent and multiple causation make it necessary that even those researchers of the commons who use statistical data (*a*) postulate causal relationships among the critical theoretical variables they have identified, (*b*) explain why the variables they do not examine are likely not important for their work, and only then (*c*) test the causal links they have postulated among their variables.

A two-pronged approach to advance the research program, related to institutional solutions to commons dilemmas, then seems advisable. On the one hand, scholars of commons need to deploy theoretically motivated comparative case analyses to identify the most important causal mechanisms and narrow the range of relevant theoretical variables and their interactions. On the other hand commons scholars also need to conduct large N-studies to identify the strength of causal relations (White & Runge 1994, McCarthy et al. 2003). Only then would it be possible to advance our understanding of how institutional sustainability can be achieved on the commons.

CONCLUSION: BEYOND APOLITICAL INSTITUTIONS AND SOVEREIGN SUBJECTS

The arguments advanced in the previous section do not question any of the basic assumptions on which most studies of the commons are founded. Recent developments in social theory, especially the contributions of scholars of resistance, the subaltern collective, and poststructuralist work drawing on insights of Foucault, suggest exciting avenues for exploration by students of commons.

Perhaps the most striking question for theorists of commons lies in arguments about the extent to which they attend to intra-group politics and issues of power and resistance. In their preoccupation with sustainable management and successful institutions, they may have ignored the possibility that all successful enforcement institutions are also coercive, and the burden of coercion tends to fall unequally on those who are less powerful. Indeed, if institutions are the product of conscious decisions of specific individuals and groups, as many commons theorists argue, then it may also be reasonable to suppose that institutional choices by powerful groups deliberately aim to disadvantage marginal and less powerful groups. The other side of the coin of institutional sustainability then turns out to be unequal allocation of benefits from commonly managed resources: not as a by-product but as a necessary consequence!

If existing institutions are the expression of past political alignments, attention to current political relationships within communities can help produce a better understanding of how existing institutions are contested and what future institutions may look like. Institutional arrangements for allocating resources are best viewed as an expression of an idealized status quo. Actual human behavior, even in the context of well-enforced institutional rules, is unlikely to conform precisely to institutional contours. Perfect enforcement is far too costly ever to be achieved. When resources devoted to enforcement of institutions are limited, resource use patterns are far more likely to diverge from what rules specify. Attention to power and micro-politics within communities is therefore critical in understanding how resources are used and managed (Gibson 1999; Moore 1998, 1999). The point is not just to try to understand politics because its effects on resource use and governance are mediated through the prism of institutions. Rather, it is also to try to understand how political relationships imbue resource use even without being mediated by institutional arrangements.

Greater attention to the dynamics of resistance and domination is likely to help explicate better the relationship between property and politics. But the investigation of the nature of power and resistance also possesses significant inherent theoretical and practical merit, as subaltern scholars and writers on everyday protest have argued (Guha & Spivak 1988, Scott 1985). Attention to strategies followed by subaltern actors in relation to resource use is critical to understanding how attempts at control and regulation are always challenged by those who are subjected to control. Issues of agency, the mutually productive relationship between domination and resistance, and the creation of institutional arrangements can be understood only with greater attention to micro-politics. Such a shift in focus can also help address the criticism that scholars of common property have, for the most part, ignored how rural residents can shape attempts by outside agents such as the state or aid agencies to intervene in their lives and modify existing patterns of resource use.

An analogous critique of commons scholarship also aims at their interest in sustainable management of resources. It is suggested by some observers of commons theorists (Goldman 1997) that by not examining the internally differentiated nature of communities commons scholars assume that members of these communities are similarly receptive to ideas of development and efficient resource management, progress, and modernization. But the processes of development and modernization and attempts to make the use and management of commons more efficient can end up increasing state capacities to control and intervene in local affairs. By focusing on how common resources can be more efficiently managed, scholars of commons become enmeshed in the same logic of greater productivity that advocates of privatization talk about (Goldman 1997). This critique of the commons borrows extensively from Foucault's arguments about biopower and biopolitics (1990), effectively deployed by such authors as Mitchell (1991) to critique colonization and modernization in Egypt, by Escobar (1995) to question development, and by Ferguson (1994) to investigate development projects initiated by agencies like the World Bank.

A greater focus on how power works within communities and in the governance of common-pool resources can help strengthen greatly the force of writings on common property. On the one hand, such a shift in focus would facilitate a better understanding of how power and status are related to access and use of resources; on the other hand, it would complement the exclusive focus of common property theorists on institutions and rules. Ultimately, power is not just what planning and management attempt to exclude. Rather, power and politics imbue the process of management thoroughly and unavoidably. Management is not just about providing technical solutions to objective problems of development and environmental conservation. It may be important to consider that these problems and their solutions may themselves be part of a political process. Without attention to the politics that generates underdevelopment and environmental degradation as universal problems, it may be impossible to address poverty, underdevelopment, and environmental degradation effectively.

Finally, one of the most neglected aspects of resource use and management in the commons literature is the changing relationship between the environment and human beings who use environmental resources. If commons scholars consider politics only through the prism of institutions, they fail to attend to human subjectivities in relation to the environment more or less completely. It would be fair to say that changes in human subjectivities, as these occur concomitantly with changes in institutionalized governance of the environment, are the least well understood and investigated of all environment-related changes.

Institutional strategies to govern forests—to allocate, to monitor, to sanction, to enforce, to adjudicate—do not simply constrain the actions of already existing sovereign subjects. Nor is it the case that people's responses to new forms of regulatory strategies are exhausted by the continuum between resistance and conformity. Instead, it is important to recognize how these strategies and their effects on flows of power shape human subjects, their interests, and their agency. By focusing on these strategies as the means through which individuals become different kinds of subjects, it may be possible to specify the micro-mechanisms at work in the reconfiguration of environment-related subjectivities. Explanations of why and when people respond in particular and differentiated ways to new strategies of institutionalized power require attention to their structural locations and the extent to which they are already privileged or marginalized by new strategies of power. To insist on variations in how subject positions change is also to insist on the evident fact that the effects of new institutions are neither totalizing nor permanent (Agrawal 2004). One reason there have been so few studies of the relationship between changes in subjectivities and shifts in institutional regulation is the limited historical scope of most studies of the commons. Diachronic examination of common-property arrangements together with studies of human understandings and subject positions related to the environment have the potential to transform how governance of common property is understood.

Ultimately, the success of institutional changes in prompting better use and governance of environmental resources may depend crucially on changes in human subjectivities. Attempts to change how people act, when such attempts are based solely on coercive threats in hierarchical organizations, are either formidably expensive or evidently impractical (Holmstrom 1982). It is not surprising therefore that concerns about the relationship between changes in subjectivities and emerging social and political forms have historically elicited vast amounts of investigative energies from social theorists, starting from the late nineteenth century onward (Rose 1999). Commons scholars need to focus more clearly and more directly on this underinvestigated relationship between institutions and identities as a fascinating new avenue of inquiry—one that will help build new bridges to scholarship in the social sciences and the humanities.

ACKNOWLEDGMENTS

This paper has gone through multiple iterations and has benefitted from comments at various stages from Ashwini Chhatre, John Galaty, Geoffrey Garrett, Donald Moore, Elinor Ostrom, Paul Stern, and Oran Young, among others. The paper, especially the section titled Critique From Within is based on and draws from earlier versions prepared for the National Academy of Sciences and World Development. Finally, I would like to acknowledge acute questions from audiences of talks based on this paper that I delivered at Indiana University, McGill University, and the International Association for the Study of Common Property.

The *Annual Review of Anthropology* is online at http://anthro.annualreviews.org

LITERATURE CITED

Agrawal A. 2001. State formation in community spaces: the forest councils of Kumaon. *J. Asian Stud.* 60(1):1–32

Agrawal A. 2004. *Environmentality: Technolo-* *gies of Government and the Making of Subjects.* Durham, NC: Duke Univ. Press. In press

Agrawal A, Goyal S. 2001. Group size and

collective action: third party monitoring in common-pool resources. *Comp. Polit. Stud.* 34(1):63–93

Agrawal A, Ribot JC. 1999. Accountability in decentralization: a framework with South Asian and West African cases. *J. Dev. Areas* 33(Summer):473–502

Alchian A. 1950. Uncertainty, evolution and economic theory. *J. Polit. Econ.* 58(3):211–21

Alchian A, Demsetz H. 1973. The property rights paradigm. *J. Econ. Hist.* 33:16–27

Ascher W. 1995. *Communities and Sustainable Forestry in Developing Countries.* San Francisco: ICS Press

Azhar R. 1993. Commons, regulation, and rent-seeking behavior: the dilemma of Pakistan's *Guzara* forests. *Econ. Dev. Cult. Change* 42(1):115–28

Baland JM, Platteau JP. 1996. *Halting Degradation of Natural Resources: Is There a Role for Rural Communities?* Oxford, UK: Clarendon

Baland JM, Platteau JP. 1999. The ambiguous impact of inequality on local resource management. *World Dev.* 27:773–88

Bates RH. 1981. *Markets and States in Tropical Africa: the Political Basis of Agricultural Policies.* Berkeley: Univ. Calif. Press

Bates RH. 1989. *Beyond the Miracle of the Market: the Political Economy of Agrarian Development in Kenya.* Cambridge, UK: Cambridge Univ. Press

Bennett A, George A. 2003. *Case Study and Theory Development.* Cambridge, MA: MIT Press. In press

Blomquist W, Schlager E, Tang SY, Ostrom E. 1994. Regularities from the field and possible explanations. See Ostrom et al. 1994, pp. 301–16

Bromley D, ed. 1992. *Making the Commons Work: Theory, Practice and Policy.* San Francisco: ICS Press

Cheung SNS. 1970. The structure of a contract and the theory of non-exclusive resource. *J. Law Econ.* 13:49–70

Coase R. 1960. The problem of social cost. *J. Law Econ.* 3:1–44

Colchester M. 1994. Sustaining the forests: the community-based approach in South and Southeast Asia. *Dev. Change* 25(1):69–100

Dasgupta P, Heal G. 1979. *Economic Theory and Exhaustible Resources.* Cambridge, UK: Cambridge Univ. Press

Demsetz H. 1967. Towards a theory of property rights. *Am. Econ. Rev.* 57(2):347–59

Ehrlich P. 1968. *The Population Bomb.* New York: Ballantine

Elster J. 1992. *Local Justice: How Institutions Allocate Scarce Goods and Necessary Burdens.* New York: Sage

Escobar A. 1995. *Encountering Development: the Making and Unmaking of the Third World.* Princeton, NJ: Princeton Univ. Press

Ferguson J. 1994. *The Anti-Politics Machine: "Development," Depoliticization, and Bureaucratic Power in Lesotho.* Minneapolis: Univ. Minn. Press

Food Agric. Organ. 1999. *Status and Progress in the Implementation of National Forest Programmes: Outcomes of an FAO Worldwide Survey.* Mimeo, Rome: FAO

Foucault M. 1990. *The History of Sexuality: an Introduction.* New York: Vintage. Vol. 1

Furubotn E, Pejovich S, eds. 1974. *The Economics of Property Rights.* Cambridge, MA: Ballinger

Gibson CC. 1999. *Politicians and Poachers: the Political Economy of Wildlife Policy in Africa.* Cambridge, UK: Cambridge Univ. Press

Goldman M. 1997. "Customs in common": the epistemic world of the commons scholars. *Theory Soc.* 26(1):1–37

Guha R, Spivak GC, eds. 1988. *Selected Subaltern Studies.* Delhi: Oxford Univ. Press

Hardin R. 1982. *Collective Action.* Baltimore, MD: Johns Hopkins Univ. Press

Holmstrom B. 1982. Moral hazard in teams. *Bell J. Econ.* 13(2):324–40

Jodha NS. 1986. Common property resources and rural poor in dry regions of India. *Econ. Pol. Wkly.* 21(27):1169–82

Katz EG. 2000. Social capital and natural capital: a comparative analysis of land tenure and natural resource management in Guatemala. *Land Econ.* 76(1):114–32

King G, Keohane R, Verba S. 1994. *Designing Social Inquiry: Scientific Inference in Qualitative Research.* Princeton, NJ: Princeton Univ. Press

Knight J. 1992. *Institutions and Social Conflict.* Cambridge, UK: Cambridge Univ. Press

Leach M, Mearns R, eds. 1996. *The Lie of the Land: Challenging Received Wisdom on the African Environment.* Oxford, UK, Portsmouth, NH: Currey, Heinemann

Li TM. 1996. Images of community: discourse and strategy in property relations. *Dev. Change* 27(3):501–27

Libecap G. 1990. *Contracting for Property Rights.* New York: Cambridge Univ. Press

Low B, Heinen J. 1993. Population, resources and environment: implications of human behavioral ecology for conservation. *Popul. Env.* 15(1):7–41

Lynch OJ, Talbott K. 1995. *Balancing Acts: Community-Based Forest Management and National Law in Asia and the Pacific.* Washington, DC: WRI

McCarthy N, Dutilly-Diané C, Drabo B. 2003. Cooperation, collective action and natural resources management in Burkina Faso: a methodological note. CAPRi Work. Pap. 27. Washington, DC: CAPRi

McCay BJ, Acheson J, eds. 1989. *The Question of the Commons: the Culture and Ecology of Communal Resources.* Tucson: Univ. Arizona Press

Malthus T. 1960. *On Population* (First Essay on Population, 1798, and Second Essay on Population, 1803). New York: Random House

Marwell G, Oliver P. 1993. *The Critical Mass in Collective Action: a Micro-Social Theory.* Cambridge, UK: Cambridge Univ. Press

Mitchell T. 1991. *Colonising Egypt.* Berkeley: Univ. Calif. Press

Moore DS. 1998. Subaltern struggles and the politics of place: remapping resistance in Zimbabwe's eastern highlands. *Cult. Anthropol.* 13(3):344–81

Moore DS. 1999. The crucible of cultural politics: reworking "development" in Zimbabwe's eastern highlands. *Am. Ethnol.* 26(3):654–89

Muldavin J. 2000. The paradoxes of environmental policy and resource management in reform-era China. *Econ. Geogr.* 76(3):244–71

Naughton-Teves L, Sanderson S. 1995. Property, politics and wildlife conservation. *World Dev.* 23(8):1265–76

North D. 1990. *Institutions, Institutional Change and Economic Performance.* Cambridge, MA: Cambridge Univ. Press

Oakerson R. 1992. Analyzing the commons: a framework. See Bromley 1992, pp. 41–59

Oates JF. 1999. *Myth and Reality in the Rain Forest: How Conservation Strategies are Failing in West Africa.* Berkeley: Univ. Calif. Press

Olson M. 1965. *The Logic of Collective Action.* Cambridge, MA: Harvard Univ. Press

Ostrom E. 1986. An agenda for the study of institutions. *Pub. Choice* 48:3–25

Ostrom E. 1990. *Governing the Commons: the Evolution of Institutions for Collective Action.* Cambridge, MA: Cambridge Univ. Press

Ostrom E. 1997. *Self-governance of common-pool resources.* W97-2, Workshop in Political Theory and Policy Analysis, Indiana Univ., Bloomington

Ostrom E. 1998. A behavioral approach to the rational choice theory of collective action. *Am. Polit. Sci. Rev.* 92(1):1–22

Ostrom E, Gardner R, Walker J. 1994. *Rules, Games and Common-Pool Resources.* Ann Arbor: Univ. Mich. Press

Ostrom E, Dietz T, Dolsak N, Stern PC, Stonich S, Weber E, eds. 2002. *The Drama of the Commons.* Washington, DC: Natl. Acad. Press

Peluso NL. 1992. *Rich Forests, Poor People: Resource Control and Resistance in Java.* Berkeley: Univ. Calif. Press

Peluso NL. 1993. Coercing conservation: the politics of state resource control. *Glob. Env. Change* 3(2):199–217

Peters P. 1994. *Dividing the Commons: Politics, Policy and Culture in Botswana.* Charlottesville: Univ. Virginia Press

Pimental D, Harman R, Pacenza M, Pecarsky

J, Pimental M. 1994. Natural resources and an optimal human population. *Popul. Env.* 15(5):347–69

Putnam R. 1993. *Making Democracy Work: Civic Traditions in Modern Italy.* Princeton, NJ: Princeton Univ. Press

Quiggin J. 1993. Common property, equality, and development. *World Dev.* 21:1123–38

Repetto R, Gillis M, eds. 1988. *Public Policies and the Misuse of Forest Resources.* Cambridge, UK: Cambridge Univ. Press

Robbins P. 2000. The rotten institution: corruption in natural resource management. *Polit. Geogr.* 19(4):423–43

Rose N. 1999. *Powers of Freedom: Reframing Political Thought.* Cambridge, UK: Cambridge Univ. Press

Runge CF. 1984. Institutions and the free rider: the assurance problem in collective action. *J. Polit.* 46:154–81

Schlager E, Ostrom E. 1992. Property rights regimes and natural resources: a conceptual analysis. *Land Econ.* 68(3):249–62

Scott JC. 1985. *Weapons of the Weak: Everyday Forms of Peasant Resistance.* New Haven, CT: Yale Univ. Press

Sivaramakrishnan K. 1999. *Modern Forests: Statemaking and Environmental Change in Colonial Eastern India.* Stanford, CA: Stanford Univ. Press

Skaria A. 1999. *Hybrid Histories: Forests, Frontiers, and Wildness in Western India.* New Delhi: Oxford Univ. Press

Tang SY. 1992. *Institutions and Collective Action: Self-Governance in Irrigation.* San Francisco: ICS Press

Tiffen M, Mortimore M, Gichuki F. 1994. *More People, Less Erosion: Environmental Recovery in Kenya.* Chichester, UK: Wiley

Wade R. 1994. *Village Republics: Economic Conditions for Collective Action in South India.* Oakland: ICS Press

White TA, Runge CF. 1994. Common property and collective action: lessons from cooperative watershed management in Haiti. *Econ. Dev. Cult. Change* 43(1):1–41

Young KR. 1994. Roads and the environmental degradation of tropical montane forests. *Conserv. Biol.* 8(4):972–76

Annu. Rev. Anthropol. 2003. 32:263–85
doi: 10.1146/annurev.anthro.32.061002.093445
First published online as a Review in Advance on June 4, 2003

URBANIZATION AND THE GLOBAL PERSPECTIVE

Alan Smart and Josephine Smart

*Department of Anthropology, University of Calgary, Calgary, Alberta, Canada T2N 1N4;
email: asmart@ucalgary.ca, smart@ucalgary.ca*

Key Words   urban economies, globalization, time-space compression,
transnationalism, entrepreneurial cities

■ **Abstract**   Much of the literature about globalization exaggerates the degree of
novelty. In this review, we concentrate on claims about what has changed about
cities under late capitalism and globalization. Although we suggest that cities have
long been influenced by global forces, we conclude that the roles of cities in the
global system have changed considerably as a result of the time-space compression
made possible by new transportation, communication, and organizational technologies. After discussing what the global perspective means within anthropology, and
how it affects urban anthropological research, our review concentrates on three complex issues. First is whether the global factory and increasing knowledge-intensivity
have decreased or increased the utility of the intermediary or brokerage roles that
cities play. Second, we examine changes in how people live in globalizing cities.
Third, we consider the implications of the construction and maintenance of relationships across borders for processes of citizenship, affiliation, and transnational social
movements.

INTRODUCTION

A global perspective is not new in urban anthropology. A long line of anthropologists from Horace Miner (1953) to Aidan Southall (1998) have urged urban studies
to pay attention to the full range of the urban experience, instead of concentrating
on and generalizing from Western cities (Miner 1953, Southall 1998). Cities have
always been key sites for transcultural connections such as long-distance trade and
the transmission of innovations. Thus although globalization[1] has a much longer
genealogy than credited in recent "global hype" (Wolf 1982, Mintz 1998, Sanjek
1999), this continuity applies particularly to urban settings. The roles that cities
play in the global system, however, have changed considerably, in part owing to

---

[1]Though space does not permit an examination of the related literature on postmodernism,
Leontidou (1993) has argued that Southern European cities possessed many of the cultural and organizational features of postmodernism even before the rise of North Atlantic
Fordism, challenging the teleology and arguing for it as an alternative rather than successor
to modernity.

0084-6570/03/1021-0263$14.00   **263**

time-space compression made possible by new transportation, communication, and organizational technologies.

In this review we consider "urbanization" to include not only the growth of cities, but the transformation of existing urban places. To adequately address the intersection between urbanization and global perspectives, we first provide a brief survey of the contested terrain of the globalization debate. Many authors tend to exaggerate the degree of novelty, and we argue for the need to attend to continuities with the past as well. Cities of the past had many of the features ascribed to "global cities," and early urban anthropologists also made important contributions to the understanding of the global system.

The remainder of our review concentrates on three issues about what has been alleged to have changed about cities under late capitalism (since the 1970s). First, we look at whether the extension of production around the world and increased salience of knowledge have decreased the utility of the intermediary roles that cities play. Second, we examine changes in how people live in globalizing cities, which have been seen as increasingly fragmented and unequal, characterized by social exclusion and an emerging digital divide. At the same time, people continue to resist these pressures and actively construct communities and places. Third, we consider the implications of the construction and maintenance of relationships across borders for the transformation of cities, focusing on translocality (Smith 2001), citizenship in the context of transnational affiliation, and transnational social movements.

THE GLOBAL PERSPECTIVE

Early cities emerged to facilitate trade or as centers of political and/or religious authority. All of these cities brought people of different cultures into close contact and fostered change, either in the form that Redfield & Singer (1954) called orthogenetic transformation (shifts from diverse local traditions toward orthodox Great Traditions) or heterogenetic transformation (fostering new modes of thought associated with the technical order or foreign control). As one example, Keyder (1999, pp. 3–4) insists that Istanbul has, since inception, been a world city: for most of its 1500 years "the largest permanent market place in the area between India and Western Europe" and a capital administering territories in three continents. Complex ethnoscapes and spaces of flows are not novelties in such cities (see also Abu-Lughod 1971).

Dependency and world-system theorists insist that social scientists must go beyond the national level to examine the world as a whole. Accounts of societies that consider only their internal dynamics distort history (Frank 1998). In Wallerstein's framework, cities such as Istanbul or Cairo were centers of world empires but became, at best, part of the semi-periphery in the era of the capitalist world economy. Imperialism is crucial because, as King (1989, p. 1) points out, most contemporary global cities were imperial metropoli, colonial capitals, or ports, so that contemporary urban hierarchies have "largely resulted from colonial rule."

The proportion of the world's population that lives in cities has grown ever since the Industrial Revolution. About 3% of the world lived in urban places in 1800, rising to 13% in 1900, over 40% in 1980 (Brunn & Williams 1983, p. 3), and 47% in 2000, equaling about 2.9 billion people. More Developed Countries (MDCs) were 76% urbanized in 1999, compared to 39% for the Less Developed Countries (LDCs), but the rate of urbanization was much faster in the LDCs from 1950–2000, at 1.62% per year compared to 0.65% for the MDCs (United Nations Pop. Div. 1999). The global distribution of agricultural and medical technologies and world markets for agricultural commodities and inputs has transformed the ways of life even for those who remain in the countryside, challenging anthropological research methods.

Anthropology was among the last of the social sciences to study people in cities, but when those we worked with moved to cities, urban research was inevitable. It seems significant that pioneers of urban anthropology, particularly studies of the Copperbelt cities in Zambia, also broke new ground in the study of world systems. Godfrey Wilson (1941) argued that urban industry, labor migration, and rural villages had to be studied as parts of a single global socioeconomic system. Hunter (1936), Gluckman (1963), Mitchell (1969), Mayer (1961), and Epstein (1958) all addressed issues such as identity and translocal networks, which are still pertinent in addressing global restructuring and the destabilization of identity. Rapid urbanization in the Copperbelt attracted attention because it symbolized novelty and an "epochal leap in evolutionary time" toward industrial modernity (Ferguson 1999, p. 4). Economic decline since the 1970s has resulted in deurbanization (Hansen 1997). Modernity came to be seen as something in the past, an "object of nostalgic reverie, and 'backwardness' the anticipated (or dreaded) future" (Ferguson 1999, p. 13). Social and cultural change during these periods of growth and decline can only be understood through attending to both global dynamics and local responses and interpretations.

The world actually became a less global place for most of the period between World War I and the 1970s, in terms of controls on movement of people, capital, and goods. Developed economies became more self-contained in response to the Depression, as did the South after World War II with decolonization and import substitution. States started to better fit the image of self-enclosed "containers of socio-economic and political-cultural relations" (Brenner 1999, p. 40), in which cities served primarily national or sub-national roles. The crisis of Fordism (i.e., regimes of accumulation based on mass production, unionization, state-sponsored consumerism, and Keynesian fiscal management), owing to declining profits, encouraged offshore production, out-contracting of work, and restructuring of the welfare state (Nash 1989). This combination has come to be referred to as globalization.

Many definitions of globalization assume too much. We use an open-ended definition: the stretching and deepening of social relations across national borders so that everyday activities are more influenced by events at great distances. Most of this activity is not truly global but rather transnational (Hannerz 1992) or translocal

(Smith 2001). Even the largest corporations concentrate their activity in a few of the world's countries: Only firms with key brands or intellectual property rights, such as Coca-Cola or Microsoft, are everywhere. Some issues such as the threat of nuclear war, global warming, or depletion of the ozone layer can be said to be truly global, as can social movements focused on responding to them (Miller 2000).

Transportation and communication technologies have certainly contributed to the "shrinking" of the world, but this is not new. Telegraphs and the world's stock markets produced global real time in the nineteenth century. Maintenance of transnational ties by migrants to New York was as significant in 1900 as in 2000 (Foner 2000).

Supranational organizations such as the World Trade Organization (WTO), North American Free Trade Agreement (NAFTA), the European Union (EU), and the United Nations (UN); technologies such as container terminals, jets, the Internet, electronic funds transfer; and social movements such as human rights and environmentalism do allow people to more easily maintain ties across borders. However, exaggeration of their novelty and inevitability serve political agendas, legitimating changes by claiming that "there is no alternative" in a global world (Hirst & Thompson 1996, Tsing 2000).

We limit ourselves to three dimensions in the debate about globalization, the first of which is whether the world is becoming increasingly homogeneous. Some see global homogenization and the loss of cultural diversity, whether this is equated with Americanization or Westernization or the dominance of consumerism (Sklair 1991, Klein 2000). Others emphasize the proliferation of new hybrid or creolized cultural forms (García Canclini 1997, Hannerz 1992). The second facet of debates concerns whether globalization is driven from above or below. Many see it as the imposition of the hegemony of American/Western institutions such as WTO and the International Monetary Fund (IMF) (McMichael 1998). Others emphasize the agency of migrants, NGOs (Paley 2002), and virtual communities (Wilson & Peterson 2002) in building transnational linkages. The third area of debate concerns whether analysts see globalization as involving the erosion of national sovereignty (deterritorialization) or as preserving or even extending the power of (some) national states (Keating 2001). It has been widely argued that globalization generates the greater salience of both sub-national and supra-national arenas for action at the expense of the nation-state, whereas the explosive growth of global finance constrains the freedom of action of national governments. Once primarily structured by their place within a nested national hierarchy, cities have become more influential in defining or defending roles for themselves within global arenas.

Anthropologists have been important contributors to the deterritorialization (Ong 1991, 1999), globalization from below (Mahler 1998, Schein 1998), and hybridity theses (Howes 1996, Watson 1997, Mathews 2000), perhaps naturally, owing to our grounding in local research and processes. Phenomena such as transnationalism are more apparent from this perspective than from the state-centric data and categories of political science and economics (Smart 1999).

For Appadurai (1996), deterritorialization loosens connections between people, wealth, ideas, and territories (p. 49), resulting in a global "stage characterized by radical disjunctures between different sorts of global flows and the uncertain landscapes created in and through these disjunctures" (p. 43). Increasing lack of connection between different flows produces "fluid, irregular shapes" that he characterizes as ethnoscapes, mediascapes, technoscapes, financescapes, and ideoscapes (p. 33). His extension of the idea of landscape is largely metaphorical, and little sense of changing streetscapes and spatial outcomes can be found in his work (Lin 2003).

Brenner (1999, p. 62) argues that deterritorialization analysts see the relation between global space and territoriality as a zero-sum game and fail to capture the ways in which "territoriality is being reconfigured and re-scaled rather than eroded." Deterritorialization through free trade pacts or global telecommunications presupposes the "fixed socioterritorial infrastructures within, upon, and through which global flows can circulate" (p. 62). Cities acquire new capabilities through engaging with transnational networks. A locality is not a bounded region so much as a "contingent and ever-shifting mesh of interactive processes" (Olds & Yeung 1999, p. 535). We do not live in the borderless world diagnosed by Ohmae (1990); borders are still formidable restrictions for the nonelite (Heyman 1995, Cunningham 1999, De Genova 2002), and governments still have a great deal of influence on what is done and how. Still, as Appadurai (1996) persuasively argues, the imagination combines with new media technology to allow us to affiliate in ways that bring us closer to someone around the globe than to our next-door neighbor. Making sense of opposed tendencies toward deterritorialization and expanded state capacities requires rejecting globalization as a singular process and recognizing the diversity of its projects and outcomes (Yang 2000), described by Rees & Smart (2001) as "plural globalities." Doing so creates major challenges, but also opportunities, for anthropological research strategies.

Urbanization of peoples traditionally studied by anthropology, combined with growing legitimacy for "anthropology at home," resulted in rapid growth of urban anthropology from the 1970s. The Society for Urban Anthropology section of the AAA had 347 members in 1997 when it changed its name and mandate to the Society for Urban, National, and Transnational/Global Anthropology, and membership increased to 712 in 2002 (N. Foner and O. Lynch, personal communication). Urban anthropology has made important contributions to our understanding of migration (Foster & Kemper 2002), housing (Pellow 1999), social and spatial organization (Low & Lawrence-Zuniga 2003), informal economies, and other topics (Smith 2000). However, anthropologists are still poorly represented in the main venues of interdisciplinary urban studies. In a convenience sample of 17 interdisciplinary edited volumes related to this review's topics, the modal number of chapters contributed by anthropologists was zero, accounting for 5.3% of the chapters. We could identify only two articles written by anthropologists out of 173 (1.1%) in the 2002 volumes of three main urban studies journals: *Urban Studies*, *Urban Affairs Review*, and *International Journal of Urban and Regional Research*. Urban anthropology needs to engage itself more with the broader field of urban studies, both to communicate its contributions, but also to find new ways to research transformed urban contexts.

Urban anthropology has tended to assume a rural/urban dichotomy (or sometimes a continuum). Differences between them have become less clear and continue to shrink as a result of new technologies. To a great extent, in developed countries, urban ways of life have become available almost anywhere (Zenner 2002). Global connectivity makes it possible for call centers in Ireland or India to deal with consumer inquiries from Oklahoma (Breathnach 2000) or back-office accounting functions or programming to be done halfway around the globe. Blurring of the urban and rural is particularly pronounced in sprawling urban fields that have emerged in areas like South China (Zhou & Zhang 1995) or Los Angeles. In these areas, the idea of the self-governing urban community has almost completely disappeared. Spatial fragmentation is matched by the growth of "edge cities" in the suburbs and exurbia: clusters of office towers, shopping malls, and other facilities that reproduce some of the main functions that used to be concentrated downtown. Researching fragmented urban fields raises some of the same questions as does the study of globalization: complexity and diversity. In the next section, we examine the issue of the economic role of cities in an era where the shift to a knowledge economy combines with global connectivity to suggest their declining utility.

ECONOMIC NICHES AND URBAN COMPETITION

The rapid growth of cities after 1800 was possible because, with industrialization, cities became centers of production. Economies of scale in manufacturing produced vast agglomerations with all the disorder and human misery described so well by Engels and Dickens. Transportation and other facilities increased the attraction of cities for new industries, and growing populations created demand for services.

Some commentators diagnose trends that reverse this process, potentially resulting in the decline of cities as the main centers of economic activity. These trends include: the shift from material products toward digital or virtual products (Lash & Urry 1994, Thrift & Amin 2002); teleworking, outsourcing, and the separation of back-offices from managerial functions (Graham & Marvin 1996); post-materialist values and environmentalism; fear of and flight from the city (Low 2003). The electronic requiem for the city suggests that telecommunications "displace the need for physical movement between home and work, while urban functions will no longer have a physical presence as services are delivered in electronic form" (Graham & Marvin 1996, p. 243).

If economic activity can be coordinated through phone, fax, or cyberspace, then it becomes less necessary for firms and employees to concentrate in cities, since many costs are higher in large cities (Plotnicov 1991). Whereas economies of scale associated with mass production encouraged large production facilities and agglomeration of suppliers and clients, information technology more readily facilitates the disaggregation of production, networked cooperation, economies of scope, and the "global assembly line." The outcomes of such changes, however, are not determined by technology but through its interaction with the agendas of powerful actors and the structures of the capitalist economy (Blim 2000, Hakken 2003).

Much debate on urban futures focuses on forces countervailing against decentralization: the continued local embeddedness of business, even in finance, the most global of industries (Thrift 1994); the cultural attractions of large cities for knowledge workers and other elites (Florida 2002); the localization of knowledge and expertise (Hsu & Saxenian 2000); and limitations on the outsourcing and decentralization of work and commerce, as increasing velocities of product cycles may make even airfreight seem too slow or quality assurance too difficult (Scott et al. 2001). Urban regions continue to be the most effective platforms on which to construct competitive economies.

Still, it does seem clear that developments in recent decades have increased uncertainties for cities, frequently undermining core industries (Nash 1989). One result is the rise of what has been called urban entrepreneurialism, where cities compete for economic growth, and reconstruct growth machines to enhance their competitive edge and defend old niches from global challenges or craft new opportunities from globalized markets. In some ways little more than an updating of old-fashioned boosterism or place-marketing (Rutheiser 1996), inter-urban competition does seem to have increased, enhancing the importance of turning place-in-itself into place-for-itself, particularly for middle-ranking cities with an opportunity to improve their salience for outside investors. At the same time, urban sprawl and fragmented governance make regional cooperation correspondingly more challenging (Scott et al. 2001).

Outcomes vary considerably so that growth prospects for some cities may be excellent even if the trends are negative for urban places in general. The winners most often nominated are the world cities, global cities, or global command and control centers, which serve to integrate and coordinate the globalized economy (Friedmann 1986, Sassen 1991, King 1991, Abu-Lughod 1999, Yusuf & Wu 2002). While stimulating a great deal of attention, the influence of this approach has also generated academic boosterism ("my city is a global city too") and neglect of more widely distributed processes of transnational urbanism (Smith 2001, p. 71). Although rankings attract interest, there is a danger of misplaced concreteness in such exercises (Beaverstock et al. 2000, Taylor & Walker 2001, Godfrey & Zhou 1999). Tyner (2000) suggests that the approach involves a priori exclusion of Third World cities, even though cities such as Manila and Dhaka are key control sites for the export of global labor. Others have suggested that the evidence for the claims of global city theorists is rather weak (Samers 2002) or ignores differences between Tokyo, the capital of a developmentalist state, and New York/London, centers of leading neoliberal states (Hill & Kim 2000).

Some commentators are not convinced that the increased mobility of manufacturing and routine service work and scope for economic coordination at a distance necessarily advantages global cities such as New York or London. Some smaller cities have managed to wire themselves more effectively and have become as central to Internet data flows as the world cities (Townsend 2001, Zook 2001). Other smaller cities can also be intensely global (e.g., Geneva for international organizations, Zurich for finance, Bermuda for offshore corporations). Thus, we need to attend to globalized cities rather than simply a small set of cities where corporate headquarters are concentrated (Susser & Schneider 2003). Although centralization has so far accompanied other forms of decentralization facilitated by time-space compression, the reduced friction of distance means that centralization need not necessarily follow past patterns.

Even if urban growth increasingly is detached from a city's immediate hinterland and is reliant on competitiveness in transnational arenas, the paths to vitality are not fixed. Smaller cities and rural areas may capitalize on their lower costs and environmental amenities to attract companies and professionals whose work is telemediated and can be carried anywhere. However, the more that entrepreneurial cities compete for the same roles and markets, the less net benefit there may be, at least in zero-sum-type competitions, where rent-seeking may dissipate anticipated gains (Smart 1998). Competition for corporate headquarters or mega-events such as the Olympics are examples (Kipfer & Keil 2002, Olds 2001). Whereas the common emphasis in development plans on tourism (e.g., Kuppinger 1998, Crain 1996) may seem similar, Clark (2000, p. 16) found that the promotion of amenities for citizens has been among the most effective strategies in recent decades. Hannigan (1998) argues that the rich countries are undergoing a shift from service economies to what he calls the experience economy, in which new forms of consumption are increasingly driving economic growth. These developments have been seen as the proliferation of homogeneous American fashions and the promotion of the cultural interests of the professional classes. However, Crewe & Beaverstock (1998) argue that such criticisms overgeneralize specific social and spatial outcomes and neglect other examples where vibrant consumer landscapes have been created.

Friedmann (2001) stresses that mobilizing human, social, natural, and environmental resources of an urban region may not be sustainable if those resources thereby become depleted. Mining assets such as social capital may increase prosperity for a while, but they need to be invested in to continue to underpin growth. Knowledge of how to nurture the social and cultural conditions for cohesion and prosperity in an era of intensifying globalization is still in its infancy.

What of cities in the LDCs? World-system theorists see cities in the periphery and semi-periphery as either mediators of the exploitation of their hinterland or as bases for labor-intensive exports, resulting in overurbanization/underindustrialization and reliance on informal economies (Song & Timberlake 1996). New International Division of Labor theorists focused on the transfer of manufacturing while profits become concentrated in core corporations (Blim 1992). By contrast, Kearney (1995, p. 554) stresses the process of global implosion where the distinction between core and periphery becomes obviated through peripheralization of parts of the core (Halperin 1999) and through the emergence of high-tech sectors in portions of the Third World. At one extreme, former LDC cities have grown rich (Hong Kong, Singapore) and others (Bangalore, Seoul, Taipei, Shanghai) have become centers for computer hardware and software (Hsu & Saxenian 2000) or offshore banking centers (Amit 1997), whereas other LDC cities are at risk of becoming what Castells (1998, p. 162) calls "black holes of informational capitalism": too insignificant in new knowledge economies to even be worth exploiting and potential sources of risk through refugees and instability. Greater diversity, rather than core/periphery dualism, becomes apparent around the world and within cities.

Traditional economic practices in LDC cities, as elsewhere, have come under challenge as they are pried open to competition by structural adjustment policies and WTO rules (McMichael 1998, Applbaum 1998). Bazaar economies are challenged by malls [raising fears of *shoppinizacion* in Buenos Aires (Guano 2002)], McDonald's, and Walmarts (Classen 1996, Dannhaeuser 1996, Watson 1997), garment industries are overwhelmed by the import of used clothes from the West (Hansen 2000), and foreign cultural products displace local ones (Mathews & Lui 2001, Effird 2001). Although informal and illegal economies still pervade most LDC cities (Fernandes & Varley 1998), the informalization that has been identified as a trend in the rich cities (Mingione 1991, Portes et al. 1989, Sassen 1991, Halperin 1999) is matched by pressures toward formalization in the Third World, for example through the medium of political pressure on trade-related intellectual property rights and the removal of restrictions on foreign retailers (Carrier 1998, Babb 1999). Dick & Rimmer (1998) describe convergence between Southeast Asian and American cities, particularly in the blurring of the urban/rural dichotomy, rapid economic growth in the urban peripheries, and increased numbers of gated communities.

Increased inter-urban competition and diverging trajectories for the economic prospects of residents raise crucial issues for urban governance and citizenship. Is redistribution economically counterproductive in an era of urban entrepreneurialism (Gregory 1998, Rosenberger 1999, Jessop 2002)? How are development coalitions constituted and maintained (Logan et al. 1997)? What are the implications of increasing inequality and disenfranchisement for the civility of urban society (Holston 1999)? Are increasingly authoritarian forms of social control required when large populations become undesired by changing local labor markets (Body-Gendrot 2000, Caldeira 1999)? How is welfare restructuring related to competitiveness rhetoric and policy (Jessop 1993, Keating 2001)? Most fundamentally, is the city even the appropriate locus for considering such issues, as cyberspace makes it possible for residents to act simultaneously in more than one place (Thrift & Amin 2002)?

LIVING IN GLOBALIZING CITIES

Globalization and time-space compression have made it more feasible than ever before to break the link between locale, where one lives, and milieu, the environment that is practically relevant to an individual (Durrschmidt 1997). Although transnational involvement by ordinary people is not a new thing, technology makes it much easier to act simultaneously in different places so that anonymous neighbors may be intensely involved in communities that include people from around the globe. What does the possibility of "localities without community and cultures without locality" (Albrow 1997, p. 42) mean for daily life and the social and cultural organization of cities? How do the implications vary by class, occupation, gender, and lifestyle grouping?

Increased connectivity is conjoined with growing divisions. The global city literature suggests that world cities magnify more universal trends toward increased social polarization related to neoliberal global projects, economic restructuring, and welfare reform. Ideas about the increasing salience of knowledge in the economy, or informational capitalism, also raise the prospect of an increasing digital divide between knowledge workers and manual workers or the underclass within cities, or divisions between "fast" and "slow" societies on the global scale. Polarization and divisions have also been alleged to encourage the decline of common civic culture and shared public places and lead to the "fortress city" to protect the haves from the have-nots (Guano 2002, Caldeira 1999, Low 2003). Migration from nontraditional sources may also increase divisions along ethnic lines (Amin 2002), even as it contributes to urban vitality and economic dynamism.

Within these divided and unstable places (Greenhouse 2002), people struggle to create or defend meaningful collective activities and spaces. For example, Darian-Smith (2002) describes the resurrection of old practices of "beating the village bounds" in southern England, despite the fact that most of the participants are middle-class newcomers who commute to jobs in London. Vincent & Warf (2002, p. 30) document the recent growth of *eruvim*, religious Jewish enclaves, in North America and Europe and interpret it as part of a "global surge in ethnic identity that has emerged as a backlash to postmodern capitalism." Srinivas (2001) argues that the Karaga ritual procession in Bangalore enacts earlier landscapes obliterated by urban planning and uncontrolled settlements. The landscape of urban memory is not a personal or cognitive process alone but is achieved by movement through space that renews linkages between different parts of the urban field. In all these cases, actions claim or maintain boundaries around a space and assert commonalities that are continually challenged by broader processes. This process happens at all levels of urban space: block parties, neighborhood watch, and regional planning initiatives. Everywhere, people also organize to protest and resist developments that they believe negatively impact their communities (McDonogh 1999, Parnell 2002, Rotenberg 1999).

There is still no consensus about whether or not inequality is increasing on a global scale. Debates abound concerning the units of analysis and measurement, conflicting results at different geographic scales and timescales, the definition of poverty, whether focus should be on income, income after tax and transfers or wealth, and so on (Fan 1995, Smart 2002). Some argue that unregulated global restructuring is resulting in "labor market dualism, polarized urban social structures, and declining living standards" (Levine 1995, p. 90). Certainly in some contexts inequality has grown considerably: the global cities generally (Logan et al. 1992, p. 131), the United States as a whole (Fainstein 1995, p. 126), and Hong Kong. A major factor has been the decline of industry and a shift to patterns that reduce opportunities for those without high educational qualifications. These trends have been seen as producing an underclass that is socially excluded from the labor market and the resources necessary to promote social mobility. At the same time, discourses of fiscal austerity imposed on local and national governments by globalization have encouraged restructuring of welfare state institutions, particularly in the direction of privatization and workfare (Kingfisher & Goldsmith 2001, Schneider 2001, Clark 2000). The consequences have been documented in ethnographic studies of foodbanks and soup kitchens (Glasser 1988, Curtis 1997, Caldwell 2002), homelessness (Glasser & Bridgman 1999), downward social mobility (Newman 2001), and domestic violence (Susser 1996). In the poorer cities, structural adjustment programs and government deficits have often decimated the ranks of government employees, often the core of the middle class. However, in some cases, restructuring has increased the availability of industrial jobs so that the outcomes are even more diverse than in the MDC cities.

Elsewhere in this volume, Morgen & Maskovsky review studies of urban poverty and welfare reform in the more developed countries, so we concentrate here on complementary studies of middle-class and elite communities. What happens to the middle class and the elite is of course related to what happens to the poor, the clearest expressions of which are the phenomena of gentrification (Smith 1996, 2002; Caulfield 1994, Ley 1996) and the rapid growth of gated communities and other expressions of the "city of fear" (Low 2003). Middle-class flight to "safer" and lower-tax suburbs created funding crises for inner cities with their higher social service and infrastructure costs (Gregory 1998, p. 65), but the return of some of them in the form of gentrification is also causing problems through displacement of the urban poor.

The middle class does not always want to live in areas where similar kinds of people predominate. In the Brixton area of London, Robson & Butler (2001, p. 76) found that 63% of middle-class people surveyed mentioned the area's social mix as a positive feature, compared to 4% who mentioned the positive feature of the presence of "like-minded people." In nearby Telegraph Hill, however, a stronger emphasis on solidifying middle-class networks and associations was related to a sense of the area as a middle-class haven where London's "diversity and delights can be enjoyed from a secure and largely self-contained base" (p. 80). Gregory's (1998) study of a black community in New York emphasizes the political processes by which activists and residents struggled to overcome divisions between the middle class and the poor by emphasizing their common vulnerability to broader structures of racial exclusion.

Many interventions in cities have been seen as efforts to make them more hospitable to the professional middle-class as well as international investors and tourists, usually at the expense of the poor and minorities (Smith 1996, 2002; Cooper 1999; Zukin 1991). Urban revitalization is seen as relying on the reconstitution of a sufficient stock of safety and, if possible, civility. Inter-urban competition demands that major cities be made safe, and attractive, for the transnational elite, as well as their middle-class subordinates. Social polarization increases fear of violence, requiring "pacification." Increasing violence and social tension has generated similar tendencies in many LDC cities as well (Caldeira 1999).

Body-Gendrot (2000) demonstrates that pacification is accomplished in different ways in the United States, where escalation of repressive policing and zero-tolerance policies have been dominant, and in France, where crime prevention through social inclusion is given more emphasis.

Repression is seen as having its limits, not to mention high costs. In reaction, the idea of social capital has had increasing impact on urban policies. Putnam (2000) blames urban problems on the decline of community involvement and argues that recuperating neighborhoods require civically engaged communities. The policy challenge for such analysts is to find ways to rebuild stocks of local social capital (relationships, trust, and membership in voluntary organizations) rather than relying only on disciplinary force to maintain order. Forrest & Kearns (2001, p. 2141) see such approaches as another version of "deficit theory syndrome": identifying something lacking in individuals or communities as a key cause of social problems, rather than looking at broader societal forces. De Soto (2000) takes a different approach in arguing that it is the incompleteness of property rights in poor cities that keeps them poor.

Woolcock (1998) argues that it is possible to have too much social capital, particularly when it is concentrated in communities in such a way as to limit extra-local linkages. What provides the best developmental contexts, he suggests, are community level forms of integration that encourage and foster outside linkages as well as local social cohesion. Ethnic enclaves and established working-class communities may have intense local connectivity, but without the external linkages needed to thrive in a globally competitive "knowledge economy." O'Byrne (1997, p. 76) argues that "awareness of the globe as a perceivable whole" is differentially distributed and that working-class communities may develop a localism that reduces understanding of the challenges and opportunities that globalization poses. As one of his informants stated: "Whatever happens . . . it doesn't affect me. I've got my life and my family to look after. They come first. Nothing that happens out there is going to change that, or help me" (p. 81).

Though hardly a universal characteristic of tightly knit working-class communities, such sentiments do vividly illustrate what has been referred to as the digital divide (Crow & Longford 2000). Graham (2002, p. 34) notes that whereas 2%–5% of the world's population has become superconnected, with access to rich sources of information and contacts at all times, at least 60% of the globe's people have never even made a phone call. While the Internet and telecommunications do have liberatory potential for transcending traditional social and geographical barriers, the trajectories of these industries have not concentrated on this. Instead, promotion of global connectedness has often been combined with increased costs of basic phone service, cutting off an increasing number of the urban poor in the MDC cities (Graham 2002). Global connectivity can be associated with growing disconnection at the local scale. However, Hampton & Wellman (1999) found in their study of the "first interactive new home community" in a Toronto suburb that residents spent much of their online activity interacting with people who lived or worked near each other.

Despite the tendency of technology innovation to extend the power of the powerful and reinforce existing uneven development (Graham 2002, p. 36), at least some remedial efforts are being made. James (2002) describes technological innovations that emphasize reducing costs rather than expanding capabilities. For example, new forms of wireless telephony have reduced cost per connection in remote villages by seven times. Low-cost email can be provided by "store and forward" delivery through satellites. And recycling obsolete computers has the potential to expand in the same way that the global used clothes trade has (Hansen 2000).

Superconnectedness only highlights a more general phenomenon: Living in a globalizing city may involve little interaction with those living nearby. The products of popular culture and the mass media may be much more central to daily routines, dreams, and aspirations. Bodies may inevitably be located in particular places, but imaginations and loyalties need not be, and Appadurai (1996) is right in insisting that the localist prejudices of ethnographic tradition need to be overcome to deal with the contemporary world, particularly as experienced by the middle classes.

In LDC cities, modernity and its trappings have been a consistent vehicle for dreams (Ferzacca 2001, Rofel 1999). The pursuit of modernity generates changes both in the planning and governance of cities (McDonogh 1999, Guano 2002) and in the behavior of their residents. One response is to try to move to the cities of the rich world, partly for pragmatic reasons, but often also in part to partake of true modernity, to be where the action is, whether this is Paris or Silicon Valley. As significant as transnational migration is in globalization, we cannot understand it without seeing it in the continuing centrality of governmental projects (Ong & Nonini 1997), as well as in relation to the possibility of becoming "transnational" while staying at home. Participation in transnational social movements is a particularly crucial dimension of the adoption of a global worldview. The nature of citizenship is affected by eased affiliation with distant individuals, groups, or causes.

TRANSLOCALITY, CITIZENSHIP, AND SOCIAL MOVEMENTS

Globalization involves a vast spider's web of interacting projects. Some of these projects encourage mobility, whereas others try to maintain or impose enclosures, whether of people, goods, capital, or ideas. Some projects inspire resistance to official projects, and everywhere some people manage to get around the rules (Greenhouse 2002, Heyman 1999a). Although the mobility of goods and capital has been greatly enhanced, restrictions on the movement of people have been maintained or reinforced. When promoting migration, rich countries increasingly recruit for skilled and educated migrants. Many who do not qualify have responded by migrating illegally.

Migration, legal or illegal, has a tremendous impact on the demography and landscape of cities because the vast majority of international migrants settle in the largest cities. In Canada, which, after Australia, has the highest percentage of foreign-born population, 71.2% of immigrants settled in Toronto, Vancouver, or Montréal. Nearly half of Toronto's citizens were born outside Canada. The extent of residential segregation and retention of distinct consumption preferences varies considerably between countries and even cities and profoundly influences the texture and vitality of urban spaces (Bauder & Sharpe 2002). The vibrant spaces of diverse cities can serve as powerful magnets for the highly skilled workers and investors attracted to the quality of urban life (Florida 2002), but they can also result in perceptions of urban danger that prompt flight from the central cities. How cities manage diversity seems to be a critical factor in their competitive success.

Glick Schiller et al. (1992, p. 1) defined transnationalism as "the processes by which immigrants build social fields that link together their country of origin and their country of settlement." Smith (2001) argues that these fields are better seen as translocal than transnational (linking Oaxaca and San Diego, for example, more than Mexico and the United States). He sees contemporary cities as being profoundly changed by the "rise of translocalities" (places separated by national borders but united through social and cultural affiliation with groups, categories, networks, and amenities) so that the politics of transforming and defending place have to be seen as resulting from the intersection of bounded jurisdictions with translocal networks and coalitions. Numerous commentators suggest that the first wave of research failed to recognize the high degree of continuity with the past (Portes et al. 1999, Kistivo 2001, Vertovec 1999). Foner (2000, p. 184) notes:

If many academic observers who studied earlier immigrants were guilty of overlooking transnational ties in the quest to document assimilation, there is now a risk of overemphasizing the centrality of transnationalism and minimizing the extent to which contemporary immigrants "become American."

Migrants to New York City in 1900 and 2000 were alike in regular returns, sending remittances, being involved in home community politics and news, and investing in houses and land back home. What has changed is that it has become easier to maintain high levels of contact, there is greater tolerance for cultural diversity, the importance of international business has increased the utility of knowledge of foreign lands and languages, and immigration policies have discriminated in favor of professionals who can afford to maintain closer contacts (Foner 2000). Is transnationalism a one-generation phenomenon? Foner (2000, p. 238) suggests that some of these trends may make it likelier for the second generation to maintain ties than in the past. Louie (2001) is more doubtful about this.

Recent scholarship has illuminated a variety of dimensions of transnationalism: its promotion or suppression as part of state projects (Glick Schiller 1999, Smith 2001); the impact of gender expectations (Salih 2001); limits to involvement in transnational activities and how political coalition building can modify these limits (Anderson 2001); the involvement of religious organizations (Baia 1999, Nagata 1999, Yang & Ebaugh 2001, van der Veer 2002); horizontal linkages across ethnic lines (Baia 1999, Olds & Yeung 1999); and its impact on gender relations

(Willis & Yeoh 2000, Lang & Smart 2002). All of these processes have an impact on the texture and quality of urban landscapes, although these dimensions have often not received as much attention as they deserve (Ma 2003). Shifting the focus from transnationalism, with its implied focus on identity, toward translocality may help turn attention toward the broader implications for rapidly changing urban places.

The involvement of migrants in political and other activities in both the place of residence and place of origin inevitably raises issues of citizenship. Policies of national governments on issues such as dual citizenship, remittances, nonresident voting, pensions, and so on have a major impact on whether and how transnational communities form (Al-Ali et al. 2001, Glick Schiller 1999).

It is not only national governments that influence migrants' access to rights of citizenship. Sometimes, as in China, local governments can limit the access of domestic migrants to crucial resources (Solinger 1999, Smart & Smart 2001). Zhang (2001) has provided a vivid account of how such restrictions affect the daily lives of migrants in Beijing. Migrants have responded by constructing their own unofficial spaces in the domains of housing, education, labor markets, and the maintenance of order. These unofficial translocal spaces have often been subjected to repression owing to fear by local governments that the "political vacuums" developing in these places might "become fertile ground for the growth of social vices and nonstate political forces" (p. 2). Denying migrants rights to the city can create serious problems for authorities intent on disciplining space.

Transnational migrants have also become involved in the construction of new political spaces that cross conventional boundaries between nations and ethnic groups (Anderson 2001). However, research on transnational social movements demonstrates that it is not only migrants who help to constitute transnational social fields: Being an activist in Amnesty International, peace movements (Miller 2000), transnational labor advocacy networks (Trubek et al. 2000), or indigenous rights movements (Mato 2000, Vargas Cetina 2001) often involves acting at a distance without leaving home. The so-called anti-globalization movement is a particularly interesting example of the kinds of transnational linkages and cooperation that can be accomplished while explicitly eschewing any kind of formal organization. Graeber (2002, pp. 64–65) argues that the movement is not actually against global-ization per se but against the kind of globalization that is "limited to the movement of capital and commodities, and actually increases barriers against the free flow of people, information and ideas." These movements all reflect human struggles to transform global milieux into something closer to the human scale of the locales that for most of human existence have been the dominant focus of activity and concern.

CONCLUSION

Most anthropologists maintain a commitment to the twin methodological precepts of holism and ethnographic rigor. Although not necessarily in conflict, the demands of these principles produce a profound sense of inadequacy when approaching research on a large city or global process. Inability to deal with all of the inter-acting forces and their complex outcomes while recognizing the partiality of any artificial delimitation of the subject matter (Devons & Gluckman 1964) creates questions about what anthropology can contribute to such areas. Such limitations apply to this review even more intensely. We have delimited our coverage by con-centrating on claims about what has changed about cities under late capitalism and globalization. Our conclusions have been skeptical: Many claims of novelty suffer from a lack of historical perspective. Globalization was a powerful force centuries before being given that label, and, although time-space compression makes act-ing at a transnational scale easier, many people still maintained close ties across borders a century ago. Still, conditions have changed enough that the distinc-tions between urban and non-urban are much fuzzier than they were a century ago. Is there anything that can justly be described as urbanism when many of its features have become available in what once were radically isolated places, for example for Inuit artists in the Canadian Arctic? Does the urban disappear when it becomes available 24/7 anywhere on the globe? At the same time, concentrating large num-bers of people in relatively close proximity continues to lead to very different landscapes and structures of feeling, opportunity, and risk. Even if the intermedi-ary roles of cities do become less significant for economic processes, they may still retain their magnetism for those who desire experiences that are only available in cities such as live theater or busy streets. However, these attractions will only overcome the costs if a minimum level of livability and safety can be preserved, far from a certain situation if social polarization and urban fortresses become the norm.

We concentrated on three questions: How have the economic roles of cities changed as a result of time-space compression and the greater importance of knowledge in economic activity? How do people live in cities that are becoming more connected to and more dependent on global arenas and forces? How does the maintenance of close social ties across national boundaries influence urban landscapes, citizenship, identity, and affiliation? None of these questions has been answered here, but our survey should clearly indicate that anthropologists do have a great deal to offer in understanding such processes. It is the tension between "experience-near" research and recognition of the interconnections between dif-ferent domains of urban life that gives a different flavor to the contributions of anthropologists to the broader field of urban studies.

ACKNOWLEDGMENTS

The authors appreciate comments on an earlier draft by Byron Miller. This review has also benefited from discussions over the years with too many colleagues to list here, but particularly with Michael Blim, Don Nonini, Sandy Smith-Nonini, Michael Peter Smith, Josiah Heyman, Hilary Cunningham, and Kris Olds. Re-search assistance by Karoline Guelke and Keeley Breibish significantly contributed to this endeavor.

The *Annual Review of Anthropology* is online at http://anthro.annualreviews.org

LITERATURE CITED

Abu-Lughod J. 1971. *Cairo: One Thousand-One Years of the City*. Princeton, NJ: Princeton Univ. Press

Abu-Lughod JL. 1999. *New York, Chicago, Los Angeles: America's Global Cities*. Minneapolis: Univ. Minn. Press

Al-Ali N, Black R, Koser K. 2001. The limits to 'transnationalism': Bosnian and Eritrean refugees in Europe as emerging transnational communities. *Ethn. Racial Stud.* 24:578–600

Albrow M. 1997. Travelling beyond local cultures. See Eade 1997, pp. 37–55. London: Routledge

Amin A. 2002. Ethnicity and the multicultural city: living with diversity. *Environ. Plan. A* 34:959–80

Amit V. 1997. In pursuit of authenticity: globalization and nation building in the Cayman Islands. *Anthropologica* 39:53–63

Anderson B. 2001. Different roots in common ground: transnationalism and migrant domestic workers in London. *J. Ethn. Migr. Stud.* 27:673–83

Appadurai A. 1996. *Modernity at Large: Cultural Dimensions of Globalization*. Minneapolis: Univ. Minn. Press

Applbaum K. 1998. Rationality, morality and free trade: U.S.-Japan trade relations in anthropological perspective. *Dialect. Anthropol.* 23:1–30

Babb F. 1999. "Managua is Nicaragua": the making of a neoliberal city. *City Soc.* 11:27–48

Baia LR. 1999. Rethinking transnationalism: reconstructing national identities among Peruvian Catholics in New Jersey. *J. Interam. Stud. World Aff.* 41:93–109

Bauder H, Sharpe B. 2002. Residential segregation of visible minorities in Canada's gateway cities. *Can. Geogr.* 46:204–23

Beaverstock JV, Smith RG, Taylor PJ. 2000. Geographies of globalization: United States law firms in world cities. *Urban Geogr.* 21:95–120

Blim M. 2000. Capitalisms in late modernity. *Annu. Rev. Anthropol.* 29:25–38

Blim ML. 1992. Introduction: the emerging global factory and anthropology. In *Anthropology and the Global Factory*, ed. FA Rothstein, ML Blim, pp. 1–30. New York: Bergin & Garvey

Body-Gendrot S. 2000. *The Social Control of Cities*. Oxford, UK: Blackwell

Breathnach P. 2000. Globalisation, information technology and the emergence of niche transnational cities: the growth of the call centre sector in Dublin. *Geoforum* 31:477–85

Brenner N. 1999. Globalisation as reterritorialisation: the re-scaling of urban governance in the European Union. *Urban Stud.* 36:431–51

Brunn SD, Williams JF. 1983. *Cities of the World: World Regional and Urban Development*. New York: Harper & Row

Caldeira TPR. 1999. Fortified enclaves: the new urban segregation. See Low 1999, pp. 83–107

Caldwell ML. 2002. The social economy of food poverty in Russia. In *Culture and Economy: Contemporary Perspectives*, ed. U Kockel, pp. 11–34. Aldershot, UK: Ashgate

Carrier JG. 1998. Introduction. See Carrier & Miller 1998, pp. 1–24

Carrier JG, Miller D, eds. 1998. *Virtualism: a New Political Economy*. Oxford, UK: Berg

Castells M. 1998. *End of Millenium: the Information Age, Volume 3*. Oxford, UK: Blackwell

Caulfield J. 1994. *City Form and Everyday Life: Toronto's Gentrification and Critical Social Practice*. Toronto: Univ. Toronto Press

Chen NN, ed. 2001. *China Urban*. Durham, NC: Duke Univ. Press

Clark TN. 2000. Old and new paradigms for urban research: globalization and the fiscal austerity and urban innovation project. *Urban Aff. Rev.* 36:3–45

Classen C. 1996. Sugar cane, Coca-cola and hypermarkets: consumption and surrealism in the Argentine Northwest. See Howes 1996, pp. 39–54. Montreal: McGill-Queen's Univ. Press

Cooper M. 1999. Spatial discourse and social boundaries: re-imagining the Toronto waterfront. See Low 1999, pp. 377–99

Crain MM. 1996. Negotiating identities in Quito's cultural borderlands: native women's performances for the Ecuadorean tourist market. See Howes 1996, pp. 125–37

Crewe L, Beaverstock J. 1998. Fashioning the city: cultures of consumption in contemporary urban spaces. *Geoforum* 29:287–308

Crow B, Longford G. 2000. Digital restructuring: gender, class and citizenship in the information society in Canada. *Citizsh. Stud.* 4:207–30

Cunningham H. 1999. The ethnography of transnational social activism: understanding the global as local practice. *Am. Ethnol.* 26:583–604

Curtis K. 1997. Urban poverty and the social consequences of privatized food assistance. *J. Urban Aff.* 19:207–26

Dannhaeuser N. 1996. Trade concentration in Hassfurt (Germany) and Dagupan City (Philippines): globalization or localization? *J. Dev. Soc.* 12:175–90

Darian-Smith E. 2002. Beating the bounds: law, identity and territory in the New Europe. See Greenhouse et al. 2002, pp. 249–75

De Genova NP. 2002. Migrant "illegality" and deportability in everyday life. *Annu. Rev. Anthropol.* 31:419–47

De Soto H. 2000. *The Mystery of Capital.* New York: Basic Books

Devons E, Gluckman M. 1964. Conclusion: modes and consequences of limiting a field of study. In *Closed Systems and Open Minds*, ed. M Gluckman, pp. 258–61. Edinburgh: Oliver and Boyd

Dick HW, Rimmer PJ. 1998. Beyond the Third World city: the new urban geography of South-East Asia. *Urban Stud.* 12:2303–21

Durrschmidt J. 1997. The delinking of locale and milieu: on the situatedness of extended milieux in a global environment. See Eade 1997, pp. 56–66

Eade J, ed. 1997. *Living the Global City.* London: Routledge

Efird R. 2001. Rock in a hard place: music and the market in nineties Beijing. See Chen 2001, pp. 67–86

Epstein AL. 1958. *Politics in an Urban African Community.* Manchester, UK: Manchester Univ. Press

Fainstein N. 1995. Black ghettoisation and social mobility. In *The Bubbling Cauldron: Race, Ethnicity, and the Urban Crisis*, ed. M Smith, J Feagin, pp. 123–41. Minneapolis: Univ. Minn. Press

Ferguson J. 1999. *Expectations of Modernity: Myths and Meanings of Urban Life on the Zambian Copperbelt.* Berkeley: Univ. Calif. Press

Fernandes E, Varley A, eds. 1998. *Illegal Cities: Law and Urban Change in Developing Countries.* London: Zed Books

Ferzacca S. 2001. *Healing the Modern in a Central Javanese City.* Durham: Carolina Acad. Press

Florida R. 2002. *The Rise of the Creative Class.* New York: Basic Books

Foner N. 2000. *From Ellis Island to JFK: New York's Two Great Waves of Immigration.* New Haven: Yale Univ. Press

Forrest R, Kearns A. 2001. Social cohesion, social capital and the neighbourhood. *Urban Stud.* 38:2125–43

Foster GM, Kemper RV. 2002. Anthropological fieldwork in cities. See Gmelch & Zenner 2002, pp. 89–101

Frank AG. 1998. *ReOrient: Global Economy in the Asian Age.* Berkeley: Univ. Calif. Press

Friedmann J. 1986. The world city hypothesis. *Dev. Change* 17:69–84

Friedmann J. 2001. Intercity networks in a globalizing era. See Scott 2001, pp. 119–36

García Canclini N. 1997. Urban cultures at the end of the century: the anthropological perspective. *Int. Soc. Sci. J.* 153:345–54

Glasser I. 1988. *More Than Bread: Ethnography of a Soup Kitchen.* Tuscaloosa: Univ. Alabama Press

Glasser I, Bridgman R. 1999. *Braving the Street: the Anthropology of Homelessness.* Oxford, UK: Berghahn

Glick Schiller N. 1999. Citizens in transnational nation-states: the Asian experience. In *Globalisation and the Asia-Pacific,* ed. K Olds, P Dicken, PF Kelly, L Kong, HWC Yeung, pp. 202–18. London: Routledge

Glick Schiller N, Basch L, Szanton Blanc C. 1992. Transnationalism: a new analytical framework for understanding migration. In *Towards a Transnational Perspective on Migration,* ed. N Glick Schiller, L Basch, C Szanton Blanc, pp. 1–24. New York: New York Acad. Sci.

Gluckman M. 1963. Gossip and scandal. *Curr. Anthropol.* 4:307–16

Gmelch G, Zenner WP, eds. 2002. *Urban Life: Readings in Urban Anthropology.* Prospect Heights: Waveland Press

Godfrey BJ, Zhou Y. 1999. Ranking world cities: multinational corporations and the global urban hierarchy. *Urban Geogr.* 20: 268–81

Graeber D. 2002. The new anarchists. *New Left Rev.* 13:61–73

Graham S. 2002. Bridging urban digital divides? Urban polarisation and information and communications technologies (ICTs). *Urban Stud.* 39:33–56

Graham S, Marvin S. 1996. *Telecommunications and the City: Electronic Spaces, Urban Places.* London: Routledge

Greenhouse C. 2002. Introduction: altered states, altered lives. See Greenhouse et al. 2002, pp. 1–34

Greenhouse CJ, Mertz E, Warren K, eds. 2002. *Ethnography in Unstable Places: Everyday Lives in Contexts of Dramatic Political Change.* Durham, NC: Duke Univ. Press

Gregory S. 1998. Globalization and the "place" of politics in contemporary theory: a commentary. *City Soc.: Annu. Rev.* 1998:47–64

Guano E. 2002. Spectacles of modernity: transnational imagination and local hegemonies in neoliberal Buenos Aires. *Cult. Anthropol.* 17:181–209

Hakken D. 2003. *The Knowledge Landscapes of Cyberspace.* London: Routledge. In press

Halperin RH. 1999. Third world at home: social banditry as metaphor for urban grassroots leaders in a U.S. Midwestern city. *City Soc.* 11:49–57

Hampton KN, Wellman B. 1999. Netville online and off-line: observing and surveying a wired suburb. *Am. Behav. Sci.* 43:475–92

Hannerz U. 1992. *Cultural Complexity: Studies in the Social Organization of Meaning.* New York: Columbia Univ. Press

Hannigan J. 1998. *Fantasy City: Pleasure and Profit in the Postmodern Metropolis.* London: Routledge

Hansen KT. 1997. *Keeping House in Lusaka.* New York: Columbia Univ. Press

Hansen KT. 2000. *Salaula.* Chicago: Univ. Chicago Press

Heyman JM. 1995. Putting power in the anthropology of bureaucracy: the immigration and naturalization service at the Mexico-United States border. *Curr. Anthropol.* 36:261–87

Heyman JM. 1999a. State escalation of force: a Vietnam/US-Mexico border analogy. See Heyman 1999b, pp. 285–314

Heyman JM, ed. 1999b. *States and Illegal Practices.* Oxford, UK: Berg

Hill RC, Kim JW. 2000. Global cities and developmental states: New York, Tokyo and Seoul. *Urban Stud.* 37:2167–95

Hirst P, Thompson G. 1996. *Globalization in Question.* Cambridge, MA: Polity Press

Holston J. 1999. The modernist city and the death of the street. See Low 1999, pp. 245–76

Howes D, ed. 1996. *Cross-Cultural Consumption: Global Markets, Local Realities.* London: Routledge

Hsu J, Saxenian A. 2000. The limits of guanxi capitalism: transnational collaboration between Taiwan and the US. *Env. Plan. A* 32:1991–2005

Hunter M. 1936. *Reaction to Conquest.* London: Oxford Univ. Press

James J. 2002. Low-cost information technology in developing countries: current opportunities and emerging possibilities. *Habitat Int.* 26:21–31

Jessop B. 1993. Towards a Schumpeterian workfare state? *Stud. Polit. Econ.* 40:7–39

Jessop B. 2002. Liberalism, neoliberalism, and urban governance: a state-theoretical perspective. *Antipode* 34:452–72

Kearney M. 1995. The local and the global: the anthropology of globalization and transnationalism. *Annu. Rev. Anthropol.* 24:547–65

Keating M. 2001. Governing cities and regions: territorial restructuring in a global age. See Scott 2001 pp. 371–90

Keyder C. 1999. The setting. In *Istanbul: Between the Global and the Local*, ed. C Keyder, pp. 3–28. Lanham: Rowman and Littlefield

King AD. 1989. Colonialism, urbanism and the capitalist world economy. *Int. J. Urban Reg. Res.* 13:1–18

King AD. 1991. Introduction: spaces of culture, spaces of knowledge. In *Culture, Globalization, and the World-System*, ed. AD King, pp. 1–18. London: Macmillan

Kingfisher C, Goldsmith M. 2001. Reforming women in the United States and Aotearoa/New Zealand. *Am. Anthropol.* 103: 714–32

Kipfer S, Keil R. 2002. Toronto Inc? Planning the competitive city in the new Toronto. *Antipode* 34:227–65

Kivisto P. 2001. Theorizing transnational immigration: a critical review of current efforts. *Ethn. Racial Stud.* 24:549–77

Klein N. 2000. *No Logo: Taking Aim at the Brand Bullies*. Toronto: Knopf Canada

Kuppinger P. 1998. The Giza pyramids: accommodating tourism, leisure and consumption. *City Soc.: Annu. Rev.* 1998:105–19

Lang G, Smart J. 2002. Industrialization, migration and the "second-wife" in South China. *Int. Migr. Rev.* 36:546–70

Lash S, Urry J. 1994. *Economies of Signs and Space*. London: Sage

Leontidou L. 1993. Postmodernism and the city: Mediterranean versions. *Urban Stud.* 30:949–65

Levine MV. 1995. Globalization and wage polarization in U.S. and Canadian cities: Does public policy make a difference? In *North American Cities and the Global Economy*, ed. PK Kresl, G Gappart, pp. 89–111. Thousand Oaks: Sage

Ley D. 1996. *The New Middle Class and the Remaking of the Central City*. Oxford, UK: Clarendon

Lin G. 2003. Identity, mobility, and the making of the Chinese diasporic landscape in Hong Kong. See Ma & Cartier 2003, pp. 141–61

Logan JR, Taylor-Gooby P, Reuter M. 1992. Poverty and income inequality. In *Divided Cities: New York and London in the Contemporary World*, ed. SS Fainstein, I Gordon, M Harloe, pp. 129–50. Cambridge, UK: Blackwell

Logan JR, Whaley RB, Crowder K. 1997. The character and consequences of growth regimes: an assessment of 20 years of research. *Urban Aff. Rev.* 32:603–30

Louie A. 2001. Crafting places through mobility: Chinese American "roots-searching" in China. *Identities* 8:343–79

Low SM, ed. 1999. *Theorizing the City: the New Urban Anthropology Reader*. London: Rutgers Univ. Press

Low S. 2003. *Behind the Gates: the New American Dream—Searching for Security in America*. New York: Routledge

Low S, Lawrence-Zuniga D, eds. 2003. *Anthropology of Space and Place: Locating Culture*. Oxford, UK: Blackwell

Ma L. 2003. Space, place and transnationalism in the Chinese diaspora. See Ma & Cartier, pp. 1–49

Ma L, Cartier C, eds. 2003. *The Chinese Diaspora: Space, Place, Mobility, and Identity*. Oxford, UK: Rowman & Littlefield

Mahler SJ. 1998. Theoretical and empirical contributions toward a research agenda for transnationalism. See Smith & Guarnizo 1998, pp. 64–100

Mathews G. 2000. *Global Culture/Individual Identity: Searching for Home in the Cultural Supermarket*. London: Routledge

Mathews G, Lui T, eds. 2001. *Consuming Hong Kong*. Hong Kong: Hong Kong Univ. Press

Mato D. 2002. Transnational networking and the social production of representations of identity by indigenous peoples' organizations of Latin America. *Int. Sociol.* 15:343–60

Mayer P. 1961. *Townsmen or Tribesmen.* Cape Town: Oxford Univ. Press

McDonogh G. 1999. Discourses of the city: policy and response in post-transitional Barcelona. See Low 1999, pp. 342–76

McMichael P. 1998. Development and structural adjustment. See Carrier & Miller 1998, pp. 95–116

Miller B. 2000. *Geography and Social Movements: Comparing Antinuclear Activism in the Boston Area.* Minneapolis: Univ. Minn. Press

Miller I. 1994. Creolizing for survival in the city. *Cult. Crit.* 27:153–88

Miner H. 1953. *The Primitive City of Timbuctoo.* Princeton, NJ: Princeton Univ. Press

Mingione E. 1991. *Fragmented Societies: a Sociology of Economic Life Beyond the Market Paradigm.* Oxford, UK: Blackwell

Mintz SW. 1998. The localization of anthropological practice: from area studies to transnationalism. *Crit. Anthropol.* 18:117–33

Mitchell JC, ed. 1969. *Social Networks in Urban Situations.* Manchester: Manchester Univ. Press

Morgen SL, Maskovsky J. 2003. The anthropology of welfare "reform": new perspectives on U.S. urban poverty in the post-welfare era. *Annu. Rev. Anthropol.* 32:In press

Nagata J. 1999. The globalisation of Buddhism and the emergence of religious civil society: the case of the Taiwanese Fo Kuang Shan movement in Asia and the West. *Communal/Plural* 7:231–48

Nash J. 1989. *From Tank Town to High Tech.* Albany: State Univ. New York Press

Newman KS. 2001. Hard times on 125th Street: Harlem's poor confront welfare reform. *Am. Anthropol.* 103:762–78

O'Byrne D. 1997. Working-class culture: local community and global conditions. See Eade 1997, pp. 73–89

Ohmae K. 1990. *The Borderless World: Power and Strategy in the Interlinked Economy.* New York: Harper

Olds K. 2001. *Globalization and Urban Change: Capital, Culture and Pacific Rim Mega-Projects.* Oxford, UK: Oxford Univ. Press

Olds K, Yeung HWC. 1999. Reshaping 'Chinese' business networks in a globalising era. *Env. Plan. D: Soc. Space* 17:535–55

Ong A. 1991. The gender and labor politics of postmodernity. *Annu. Rev. Anthropol.* 20:279–309

Ong A. 1999. *Flexible Citizenship: the Cultural Logics of Transnationality.* Durham: Duke Univ. Press

Ong A, Nonini DM, eds. 1997. *Ungrounded Empires: the Cultural Politics of Modern Chinese Transnationalism.* New York: Routledge

Paley J. 2002. Toward an anthropology of democracy. *Annu. Rev. Anthropol.* 31:469–96

Parnell PC. 2002. The composite state: the poor and the nation in Manila. See Greenhouse et al. 2002, pp. 146–77

Pellow D. 1999. The power of space in the evolution of an Accra *Zongo.* See Low 1999, pp. 277–314

Plotnicov L. 1991. Afterthoughts: old and new directions. *City Soc.* 5:169–71

Portes A, Castells M, Benton LA, eds. 1989. *The Informal Economy: Studies in Advanced and Less Developed Countries.* Baltimore, MD: John Hopkins Univ. Press

Portes A, Guarnizo LE, Landolt P. 1999. The study of transnationalism: pitfalls and promise of an emergent research field. *Ethn. Racial Stud.* 22:217–37

Putnam R. 2000. *Bowling Alone: the Collapse and Revival of American Community.* New York: Simon & Schuster

Redfield R, Singer M. 1954. The cultural role of cities. *Econ. Dev. Cult. Change* 3:53–73

Rees M, Smart J, eds. 2001. *Plural Globalities in Multiple Localities: New World Borders.* Lanham, MD: Univ. Press Am.

Robson G, Butler T. 2001. Coming to terms with London: middle-class communities in a global city. *Int. J. Urban Reg. Res.* 25:70–86

Rofel L. 1999. *Other Modernities: Gendered Yearnings in China After Socialism.* Berkeley: Univ. Calif. Press

Rosenberger NR. 1999. Global capital in small town USA: justice versus efficiency for bus drivers. *Urban Anthropol.* 28:447–81

Rotenberg R. 1999. Landscape and power in Vienna: gardens of discovery. See Low 1999, pp. 138–65

Rutheiser C. 1996. *Imagineering Atlanta: the Politics of Place in the City of Dreams.* London: Verso

Salih R. 2001. Moroccan migrant women: transnationalism, nation-states and gender. *J. Ethn. Migr. Stud.* 27:655–72

Samers M. 2002. Immigration and the global city hypothesis: towards an alternative research agenda. *Int. J. Urban Reg. Res.* 26:389–402

Sanjek R. 1999. Afterword: I'll take rationale and romance, but not globaloney. *City Soc.* 11:117–24

Sassen S. 1991. *The Global City.* Princeton, NJ: Princeton Univ. Press

Schein L. 1998. Forged transnationality and oppositional cosmopolitanism. See Smith & Guarnizo 1998, pp. 291–313

Schneider JA. 2001. And how are we supposed to pay for health care? Views of the poor and the near poor on welfare reform. *Am. Anthropol.* 101:761–82

Scott AJ, ed. 2001. *Global City-Regions: Trends, Theory, Policy.* Oxford, UK: Oxford Univ. Press

Scott AJ, Agnew J, Soja EW, Storper M. 2001. Global city-regions. See Scott 2001, pp. 11–30

Sklair L. 1991. *Sociology of the Global System.* Baltimore, MD: John Hopkins Univ. Press

Smart A. 1998. Economic transformation in China: property regimes and social relations. In *Theorising Transition: the Political Economy of Post-Communist Transformations*, ed. J Pickles, A Smith, pp. 428–49. London: Routledge

Smart A. 1999. Predatory rule and illegal economic activities. See Heyman 1999b, pp. 99–128

Smart A. 2002. The Hong Kong/Pearl River Delta urban region: an emerging transnational mode of regulation or just muddling through? In *The New Chinese City*, ed. J Logan, pp. 92–105. Oxford, UK: Blackwell

Smart A, Smart J. 2001. Local citizenship: welfare reform, urban/rural status, and exclusion in China. *Env. Plan. A* 33:1853–69

Smith ME. 2000. *Trade and Trade-offs.* Prospect Heights: Waveland

Smith MP. 2001. *Transnational Urbanism.* New York: Blackwell

Smith MP, Guarnizo LE, eds. 1998. *Transnationalism from Below.* New Brunswick: Transaction

Smith N. 1996. *The New Urban Frontier: Gentrification and the Revanchist City.* New York: Routledge

Smith N. 2002. New globalism, new urbanism: gentrification as global urban strategy. *Antipode* 34:427–50

Solinger DJ. 1999. *Contesting Citizenship in Urban China: Peasant Migrants, the State, and the Logic of the Market.* Berkeley: Univ. Calif. Press

Song F, Timberlake M. 1996. Chinese urbanization, state policy, and the world economy. *J. Urban Aff.* 18:285–306

Southall A. 1998. *The City in Time and Space.* Cambridge, UK: Cambridge Univ. Press

Srinivas S. 2001. *Landscapes of Urban Memory: the Sacred and the Civic in India's High-Tech City.* Minneapolis: Univ. Minn. Press

Susser I. 1996. The construction of poverty and homelessness in US cities. *Annu. Rev. Anthropol.* 25:411–35

Susser I, Schneider J. 2003. *Wounded Cities: Destruction and Reconstruction in a Globalized World.* Oxford, UK: Berg. In press

Taylor PH, Walker DRF. 2001. World cities: a first multivariate analysis of their service complexes. *Urban Stud.* 38:23–47

Thrift N. 1994. On the social and cultural determinants of international financial centres: the case of the City of London. In *Money, Power and Space*, ed. S Corbridge, N Thrift, R Martin, pp. 327–55. Oxford, UK: Blackwell

Thrift N, Amin A. 2002. *Cities: Reimagining the Urban.* Cambridge, UK: Polity Press

Townsend AM. 2001. Network cities and the global structure of the Internet. *Am. Behav. Sci.* 44:1697–716

Trubek DM, Mosher J, Rothstein J. 2000. Transnationalism in the regulation of labor relations: international regimes and transnational advocacy networks. *Law Soc. Inq.* 25:1187–211

Tsing A. 2000. The global situation. *Cult. Anthropol.* 15:327–60

Tyner JA. 2000. Global cities and circuits of global labor: the case of Manila, Philippines. *Prof. Geogr.* 52:61–74

United Nations Pop. Div. 1999. *World Urbanization Prospects: 1999 Revisions.* http://www.un.orgn/popin/wdtrends.htm

van der Veer P. 2002. Religion in South Asia. *Annu. Rev. Anthropol.* 31:173–87

Vargas-Cetina G. 2001. Postcolonial sites and markets: indigenous organizations in Chiapas, Mexico. *Tamara* 1:68–79

Vertovec S. 1999. Conceiving and researching transnationalism. *Ethn. Racial Stud.* 22:447–62

Vincent P, Warf B. 2002. Eruvism: Talmudic places in a postmodern world. *Trans. Brit. Inst. Geogr.* 27:30–51

Watson JL, ed. 1997. *Golden Arches East: McDonald's in East Asia.* Stanford, CA: Stanford Univ. Press

Willis KD, Yeoh BSA. 2000. Gender and transnational household strategies: Singaporean migration to China. *Reg. Stud.* 34: 253–64

Wilson G. 1941. *An Essay on the Economics of Detribalization in Northern Rhodesia.* Manchester, UK: Univ. Manchester Press

Wilson SW, Peterson LC. 2002. The anthropology of online communities. *Annu. Rev. Anthropol.* 31:449–67

Wolf E. 1982. *Europe and the People Without History.* Berkeley: Univ. Calif. Press

Woolcock M. 1998. Social capital and economic development: toward a theoretical synthesis and policy framework. *Theory Soc.* 27:151–208

Yang F, Ebaugh HR. 2001. Transformations in new immigrant religions and their global implications. *Am. Sociol. Rev.* 66:269–88

Yang MM. 2000. Putting global capitalism in its place. *Curr. Anthropol.* 41:477–509

Yusuf S, Wu W. 2002. Pathways to a world city: Shanghai rising in an era of globalisation. *Urban Stud.* 39:1213–40

Zenner WP. 2002. Beyond urban and rural: communities in the 21st century. See Gmelch & Zenner 2002, pp. 53–60

Zhang L. 2001. *Strangers in the City.* Stanford, CA: Stanford Univ. Press

Zhou D, Zhang YQ. 1997. Rural urbanization in Guangdong' Pearl River Delta. *Chin. Sociol. Anthropol.* 28:47–102

Zook M. 2001. Old hierarchies or new networks of centrality? The global geography of the internet content market. *Am. Behav. Sci.* 44:1679–96

Zukin S. 1991. *Landscapes of Power.* Berkeley: Univ. Calif. Press

Annu. Rev. Anthropol. 2003. 32:287–313
doi: 10.1146/annurev.anthro.32.061002.093116
Copyright © 2003 by Annual Reviews. All rights reserved
First published online as a Review in Advance on June 17, 2003

RESOURCE WARS: The Anthropology of Mining

Chris Ballard

*Division of Pacific and Asian History, Research School of Pacific and Asian Studies,
The Australian National University, Canberra, ACT 0200, Australia;
email: chris.ballard@anu.edu.au*

Glenn Banks

*School of Geography and Oceanography, University College, University of New South
Wales, Canberra, ACT 2600, Australia; email: Glenn.Banks@adfa.edu.au*

Key Words   globalization, corporation, community, state, engagement

■ **Abstract**   The scope for an anthropology of mining has been dramatically transformed since the review by Ricardo Godoy, published in this review journal in 1985. The minerals boom of the 1980s led to an aggressive expansion of mine development in greenfield areas, many of them the domains of indigenous communities. Under considerable pressure, the conventional binary contest between states and corporations over the benefits and impacts of mining has been widened to incorporate the representations of local communities, and broad but unstable mining communities now coalesce around individual projects. Focused primarily on projects in developing nations of the Asia-Pacific region, this review questions the often-monolithic characterizations of state, corporate, and community forms of agency and charts the debate among anthropologists involved in mining, variously as consultants, researchers, and advocates, about appropriate terms for their engagement.

BOOM TIMES? MINING AND ANTHROPOLOGY

During the two decades since this journal published a seminal review of anthropological perspectives on mining (Godoy 1985), the field has been transformed by dramatic developments in the global mining industry and corresponding shifts in the nature and emphasis of related research and theory. An earlier focus on mining labor and the threat posed by transnational mining capital to the sovereignty of newly independent nation-states has given way to a much broader frame for enquiry that addresses the exceptional complexity of the relationships that coalesce around mining projects. Yet, despite the potential of ethnographic studies of mining to address questions of considerable contemporary interest in anthropology, such as globalization, indigenous rights, and new social movements, the anthropology of mining remains largely under-researched and under-theorized (see Knapp & Pigott 1997). It is surprising, given the transnational nature of the industry, that studies of mining have been persistently parochial and regional in their scope.

0084-6570/03/1021-0287$14.00

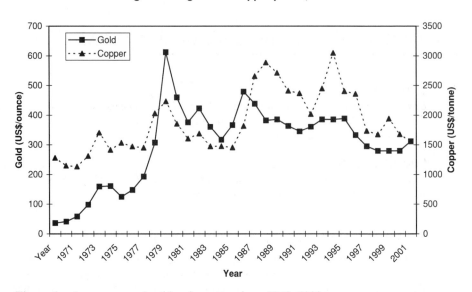

Figure 1   Average annual gold and copper prices, 1970–2002.

This paper reviews the range of developments in the field since Godoy's essay, identifies a number of areas that warrant further consideration, and argues the case for re-conceiving mining projects as sites for critical anthropological research.

The remarkable boom in mineral prices of the late 1970s and early 1980s (Figure 1) promoted an explosion of mineral prospecting activity across the globe, particularly in the largely under-explored Asia-Pacific region. Most of the mining projects realized as a result of the 1980s exploration bonanza have been located in greenfield territories or frontier zones, among relatively remote or marginalized indigenous communities (Howard 1988)—often precisely those communities that have been the classic focus of ethnographic research. These local communities have swiftly assumed a pivotal position in the politics and analyses of the wider global mining community, however unequally they might be positioned with respect to the distribution of the benefits and the negative impacts of the industry.

At least two parallel developments over this same period have further contributed to the strategic significance of mining projects for a broader range of actors. The first has been the growing recognition of the rights of indigenous communities, a process marked by events such as the establishment of the United Nations Working Group on Indigenous Populations in 1982, the subsequent development of a U.N. Draft Declaration on the Rights of Indigenous Peoples, and the increasing prominence of indigenous social movements and non-government organizations (NGOs) dedicated to indigenous rights (Pritchard 1998, Ali & Behrendt 2001). The second has been the institutionalization of impact assessment for large-scale mining operations (often the result of considerable external pressure), allowing for the incorporation of local communities as key players in many of these resource developments (Vanclay & Bronstein 1995, O'Faircheallaigh 1999). The introduction of local communities as stakeholders into the previously binary relationship between states and corporations has led to the widespread adoption by industry analysts of a three-legged or triad stakeholder model (e.g., Howitt et al. 1996a, p. 25).

Although the triad stakeholder model has served usefully as a provisional analytical device allowing for some flexibility in the identification of key agents and their interests, it has not generally served to capture much of the complexity of the relationships that form around mining as a site (Clark & Clark 1999; MMSD 2002, p. 58). As a sense of this broader mining community has developed, so too is there an increasing awareness of the internal complexity of what had previously been considered the monolithic entities of community, state, and corporation. The involvement of national and international NGOs, legal agencies, and individual lawyers, and a globalizing media served by novel means of communication such as the Internet, has produced a multi-sited and multi-vocal arena for interaction of exceptional proportions (Marcus 1995). By introducing this new global cast of agents and a novel range of interconnected locations, mining has the potential to extend conventional lines of anthropological enquiry and, through the engagement of anthropologists as consultants and advocates, to pose a further challenge to ethnographic reflexivity.

That said, mining is no ethnographic playground. Relationships between different actors within the broader mining community have often been characterized by conflict, ranging from ideological opposition and dispute to armed conflict and the extensive loss of lives, livelihoods, and environments. Several of the key low-level conflicts experienced in the Asia-Pacific region during the 1990s have revolved around mining projects, such as the Bougainville rebellion in Papua New Guinea, which started at the Panguna mine (Filer 1990, Denoon 2000), the dispute over the ecological disasters of the Ok Tedi mine (Banks & Ballard 1997, Kirsch 2002), and the human rights abuses associated with the Freeport mine in Indonesian Papua or Irian Jaya (Abrash 2002). The positioning of anthropologists within these "resource wars" (Gedicks 1993) is far from simple, and a parallel war of sorts is being waged within the discipline about the nature and scope of appropriate forms of engagement.

The open-ended nature of the global mining community militates against the possibility of a comprehensive review, either of recent developments or of the relevant literature, and this paper is thus necessarily limited in its focus. Our principal concern is with recent engagements between indigenous communities and large-scale hard-rock mines. Small-scale and artisanal mining, state-owned corporations, and the oil and gas industries are not addressed here, though there are substantial continuities in terms of practices and experiences between these sites and the large-scale mines (for recent studies of small-scale mining, see Godoy 1990; MacMillan 1995; MMSD 2002, Chapter 13). We limit ourselves largely to the literature published since the appearance of Godoy's 1985 review and, through ignorance on our part, to English-language materials. Though we make reference to broader global contexts and cases, our primary regional focus is Asia-Pacific, where a considerable proportion of the post-1980 growth in mining and in related literatures has taken place.

Although we seek to identify some of the limitations of the now-conventional triad stakeholder model, the various institutions that relate to the three central categories—corporation, state, and community—have a persistent presence, demanding that they continue to be treated as fundamental components of any analysis. Accordingly, our review pans across these three principal categories, opening with the corporations, as the primary global players in the field, before turning to states and then local communities. The review closes by considering the politics of engagement for anthropologists and other social scientists embroiled in the arena of large-scale mining—a politics with immediate implications for the nature and direction of academic inquiry.

MINING CORPORATIONS, FROM WITHIN AND WITHOUT

The central, common element in these contemporary resource wars, the stakeholder category which unites the field, is the multinational corporation (MNC). In the context of mining, however, corporations have not generally been subjected to the same level of attention as the other categories of actor in the stakeholder triad. Anthropologists have preferred to maintain their focus on the more familiar "exotic," addressing the position of local communities in the vicinity of mines in preference over the less familiar multinational mining corporations. One consequence of this focus is that the figure of "the mining company" lurks monolithically and often menacingly in the background of many anthropological accounts of communities affected by mining operations. This simple characterization is unfortunate because the dynamics of the corporations involved in mining are often at least as complex, revealing, and challenging as those of governments or local communities. Closer attention to the internal structure and politics of mining corporations has the potential to offer rich insight into the anthropology of multinational capital and its global processes and local entanglements more generally. However, one of the principal reasons for the enduring opacity of mining corporations is their notorious reluctance to expose themselves directly to ethnographic scrutiny, a condition exacerbated by a corresponding willingness to monitor and enforce corporate security.

One outcome of recent studies, by anthropologists and other social scientists, of corporate actors has been a more critical perspective on the nature and diversity of multinational mining corporations. This has led to an examination of the ways in which these corporations function internally, particularly in terms of hierarchy, power, and gender relationships within the corporation and their implications for external relationships with states and local communities. Anthropological perspectives on multinationals have moved beyond the "corporate culture" approach popular in management literature (Rouse & Fleising 1995). Critical elements of this new approach to corporations include analyses of the effects of the new shareholder-driven capitalism on organizational behavior (Emel 2002) and the role of institutions and individual investors in shaping corporate decisions (Evans et al. 2001a), particularly in light of Enron's collapse in 2001 (Bryce & Ivins 2002).

Similarly, attempts by corporations to come to terms with their place in a rapidly changing world and to respond to the negative shift in public perception of the mining industry can be revealing processes. One recent example is the controversial Mining Minerals and Sustainable Development project (MMSD), a major "global" initiative funded by a consortium of the largest mining corporations and administered by the International Institute for Environment and Development (IIED). The MMSD process involved extensive stakeholder consultation and a series of regional and thematic reviews of the current state of the industry and its prospects for contributing toward sustainable development, in anticipation of the Johannesburg Rio+10 Earth Summit (MMSD 2002). Although a number of the larger mainstream NGOs, such as The World Conservation Union (IUCN) and Conservation International, became engaged in the MMSD process, the industry's more trenchant critics have contested the industry's pretensions to sustainability and condemned the project as a further instance of corporate greenwash (Mines and Communities 2001). Under pressure from civil society groups, the World Bank has also initiated a process of review of its participation in oil and mining projects (Extractive Ind. Rev. 2003).

To date there has been little academic commentary on these processes (although see Filer 2002) or their potential to influence the nature of the MNCs themselves and the manner in which they operate. Likewise the effects of the emergence of global NGOs specifically monitoring mining operations have yet to be fully explored. These organizations include the U.S.-based Project Underground and Mineral Policy Centre, MiningWatch Canada, the Mineral Policy Institute (Australia), JATAM (Indonesia), and Partizans (England). Although primarily focused on environmental and human rights campaigns connected with mines, these groups may potentially have an important influence over corporate behavior. Emel (2002, p. 841) offers a useful case study of the impact of NGO-led shareholder protest on the activities of Freeport-McMoRan, concluding that although such strategies "are demonstrably plausible methods to reform the worst corporate social and environmental behaviour," they "put an enormous strain on the scant resources of NGOs." Moves by some of the mining corporations to "constructively engage" with critics have themselves sparked debates within the NGO community about the ethics and effectiveness of such engagement (B. Burton 1998).

Laboring Within the Corporation

Mining has long provided a rich source of material for researchers interested in labor issues and industrial relations, a central feature of Godoy's 1985 review. The "making and undoing of a working class" (Emberson-Bain 1994a, p. 1; Quamina

1987), militancy, and the conflictual nature of labor relations at mine sites are some of the more enduring themes associated with mining in both developed and developing nations (Denoon et al. 1996, Session E). In an important study, the life worlds of generations of African migrant mine workers, their collective organization, their experiences of and responses to violence (intertribal and interracial), and the negotiation of sexuality within mining camps have been documented by Moodie & Ndatshe (1994). A similar analysis of labor relations at the Ombilin coal mines in Sumatra identifies both transformations and continuities in labor conditions over more than a century (Erwiza 1999). Subcontractors can be an important, though often migratory, element in the local community and often are not subject to the same labor standards (or attention from researchers) as mine workers themselves (J.T. Roberts 1995).

Recent studies of indigenous mine workers in Papua New Guinea (Polier 1994, Jorgensen 1998, Imbun 1999) build on the ground-breaking works of Taussig (1980) and Nash (1979) on the intersection of tradition and modernity among South American miner communities. Here the collision between industrialized work practices and remote communities has resulted in the incorporation of mining within indigenous frameworks for the comprehension and apprehension of global processes. In an interesting reversal of the focus on indigenous workers, Cannon (2003) has explored the discourses and practices of expatriates in the mining industries of Papua New Guinea and Indonesia. The strongly patriarchal nature of the industry and its workforce fuels a transnational mining labor culture that places a premium on expressions of masculinity, alcohol, and violence (see Emberson-Bain 1994b and further dicussion below). Prostitution forms a prominent part of this frontier culture and has assumed a new significance in the AIDS era, particularly among migrant labor in South Africa (Campbell 1997, Elias et al. 2001). Mining towns have been a particular focus of studies that explore the dynamics of race and class in Papua New Guinea (Imbun 1995, Polier 1994), Indonesia (Erwiza 1999, Robinson 1986), Chile and the United States (Finn 1998), and Zambia (Ferguson 1999). The mining town frequently functions as a symbol and promise of modernity for local communities and workers alike, though residents all too frequently find themselves betrayed, cast aside, and disconnected from the processes of development and modernity that globalization promises (Ferguson 1999, p. 236).

Mining Discourses

Recently, there have been some provocative explorations into the discursive realms of multinational corporations. Trigger's (1997) exploration of the rhetoric of mining multinationals, and particularly the language and the ethos that underpin relations between corporations and the landscapes and the local communities with which they engage, opens up additional fertile ground for anthropologists (see also McEachern 1995). Tsing's analysis of the Bre-X scandal—an investor bubble built upon a nonexistent gold find in Indonesia—highlights the performative aspects of speculative multinational mining capital, noting that "the self-conscious making of a spectacle" (2000, p. 118) is a critical component of the strategies of mining corporations seeking to raise capital for further exploration. In this context the critique of political economy accounts of global capital advanced by Gibson-Graham (1996) is instructive. Building on work that has its origins in part in the coalfield communities of Australia, Gibson-Graham argues for a querying of globalization and the discourse of a capitalist hegemony. The process of producing discourses of capitalism and anti-capitalism has created a hegemonic "beast" that has "estranged rather than united understanding and action" (1996, p. 1). The implications of this perspective for our understanding of multinational mining corporations are potentially far-reaching and provide an imperative to interrogate conceptions of multinational miners as homogenous, powerful, hierarchical, rational, profit-seeking beasts. Schoenberger (1994) and O'Neill & Gibson-Graham (1999) offer insight into the intensely personal, political, contradictory, and discursive nature of decision making among management within various multinational corporations, suggesting that the logic of capital is routinely undone by other contingent factors:

> Capitalist forms and processes are continually made and unmade; if we offer singular predictions we allow ourselves to be caught by them as ideologies . . . . Attention to contingency and articulation can help us describe both the cultural specificity and the fragility of capitalist—and globalist—success stories. (Tsing 2000, pp. 142–43)

Further fragmentation of the monolithic image of multinational mining capital occurs in the interactions between local, national, and expatriate workers and management, which span cultural, spatial, and temporal divides. Tensions frequently arise within corporations between jobsite staff and headquarters management, particularly in the area of social or community issues (Burton 1996). As Dirlik (2001, p. 26) notes, "corporations as agents of globalization internalise the contradictions that are implicit in the incorporation of different cultural situations with their own productive procedures." The proliferation of functions within mining multinationals over the past two decades contributes to this contradiction, creating departments with conflicting mandates, such as community affairs and company security. In the case of corporate joint ventures, or many of the recent spate of mergers, the intersection of different corporate cultures and agendas can produce further internal tension, such as the unhappy declaration of irreconcilable differences between the cultures of the recently merged BHP and Billiton corporations (FitzGerald 2003). The diversity contained under the rubric of multinational mining capital is a significant, though often overlooked, element of encounters between corporations and other stakeholders. A cursory examination of the *World Mining Directory*, a comprehensive global directory of mining companies, reveals substantial variation in corporate structures, with complex webs of subsidiaries and shared project ownership (Moreno & Tegen 1998). The links between national corporate management and political elites, extensively documented in the cases of Freeport-McMoRan's Indonesian operations (Leith 2002) and Rio Tinto Zinc's failed Cerro Colorado Copper Project in Panama (Gjording 1991), provide valuable insight into global corporate governance that might usefully be pursued by anthropologists elsewhere.

The outwardly opaque, monolithic, and often overwhelming presence of a multinational mining corporation then tends to mask considerable complexity. Mining companies are temporally, spatially, and socially differentiated entities that, as Jackson observed, "are by no means as omniscient or as fiendishly clever as they are usually depicted but are capable of the same lack of foresight and blessed with the same proclivity to create monumental stuff ups as everyone else" (1993, p. 169).

CHALLENGES FOR AND TO THE STATE

Globalized Miners

Globalization marks a useful point of departure for discussion of the role of the state in mining. Hirst & Thompson (1995, p. 409), among others, have argued convincingly that the death of the nation-state has been greatly exaggerated by both critics and proponents of globalization: "While the nation state's capacities for governance have changed and in many respects [. . .] have weakened considerably, it remains a pivotal institution." This holds particularly true in the case of mining because governments tend to play "an exceptionally large role in the resources sector of almost all developing countries" (Ross 1999, p. 305; MMSD 2002, p. 66) for a number of reasons. First, the legal and administrative institutions of nation-states still regulate the entry of multinational miners into a country, despite World Bank and International Monetary Fund prescriptions throughout the 1980s and 1990s that encouraged the relaxation of conditions for foreign investors in the mineral sectors of developing countries (Sassen 2000, p. 228). Although this trend has been reversed in some cases (the Philippines, for example), most states are now inclined to view investment by multinational miners more favorably than in the past (MMSD 2002, p. 172). Nationalization is not currently the threat for mining houses in their dealings with states that it was in the 1970s; indeed, the privatization of existing national companies and mining operations is a more common trend.

A second continuing role for states, and one that is increasingly critical in a competitive global economy, is the setting of financial, labor, and environmental regulations for mining operations and corporations. Here the danger identified by industry critics is of a race to the bottom in terms of environmental and labor regulation, and fiscal regimes, as countries reduce standards in order to secure a share of diminishing global mining exploration funds (Evans et al. 2001b). State responses to the concerns of offshore NGO critics have been couched almost universally in the language of national sovereignty, arguing that independent countries and not western-based NGOs should set these standards. In terms of the relationship between states and the minerals sector, Shafer (1994) advances an argument that the state itself will be shaped fundamentally by the nature of the leading export sector in mineral-dependent economies. Where a small number of large firms with large, fixed capital investments dominate the country's exports, the state tends to focus on tapping revenue from these sectors to the neglect of other sectors of the economy and conflates the interests of the dominant sector with the broader long-term interests of the nation. In this sense, mineral resource exploitation and state policy direction are intimately connected.

Cursed States?

Mining has been central to the evolution of the notion that resources can be a curse that gives rise to a lack of development, internal tensions, human rights abuses, and conflict at the national level. Auty (1993, p. 1) first provided the resource curse label and systematically demonstrated that "not only may resource-rich countries fail to benefit from a favourable endowment, they may actually perform worse than less well endowed countries." In particular, the ore-exporting, resource-rich economies recorded a significantly lower average growth (in the period 1970–1993, it was a 0.2% decline in GDP/capita per annum) than small resource-poor countries (Auty & Mikesell 1998, p. 87). Explanations for this trend have varied but tend to focus on economic and political factors, with an emphasis on the economic distortion that export booms can induce in a mineral-dependent economy. The effects on the non-mining sectors of the economy (including agriculture and manufacturing) can be stifling, with exports becoming less competitive and wages more expensive. In terms of political factors, the mismanagement (or inappropriate economic management) of the economic boom is a key factor. Increased government revenue can lead to myopic policy formulation; greater rent-seeking behavior by individuals, classes, sectors, or interest groups; and the general weakening of state institutions, with less emphasis on accountable and transparent systems of governance (Ross 1999; MMSD 2002, p. 174). Ross (1999, pp. 319–20) contends that a further proximate cause of the resource curse for a country may hinge on the failure of a state to enforce property rights, allowing criminal gangs, private militias, or nascent rebel armies to extract rents themselves from the resource developer.

Collier & Hoeffler (2000) have elaborated on the resource-curse thesis by arguing that economic aspects are only part of the challenge posed to the state by resource wealth. A more sinister characteristic of a dependency on natural resources, and on mineral resources in particular, has been their link with civil conflict (see also MMSD 2002, pp. 192–93). In their analysis of the causes of 73 civil conflicts between 1965 and 1999, Collier & Hoeffler found that the most powerful explanatory factor was whether or not the country derived a substantial share of its GDP from the export of primary commodities. Minerals rate a special mention for Collier (2000, p. 9), as they are especially "vulnerable to looting and taxation because their production relies heavily on assets which are long-lasting and immobile." Switzer (2001) suggests that mining can become a source of conflict over the control of resources and resource territories, the right to participate in decision making and benefit sharing, social and environmental impacts, and the means used to secure access to resources and to personnel; mining operations can then be used to finance conflict but may also both benefit from conflict and themselves become targets for conflict. The presence of mineral wealth has also been a factor in attempts at secession, with Zaire and Bougainville (Papua New Guinea) offering examples of this tendency.

The recent MMSD report (2002, p. 188) notes that human rights abuses associated with mining are most likely to occur where a corporation is "willing to work with repressive regimes or in countries with weak governance or rule of law." In examples of the first case, the presence of an authoritarian, rent-extracting state and a complicit corporation is likely to lead to abuses against opponents of mining operations and particularly local communities (Handelsman 2002; MMSD 2002, pp. 188–89). Dinnen (2001, Chapter 5) provides an example of the second case, suggesting that state violence around mining projects can also manifest in weak states, although in a more chaotic and less deterministic way. In weak states, strategic assets such as mines have been secured by engaging mercenaries, as in the cases of Angola and Ghana in Africa and the failed Sandline affair in Papua New Guinea (Dinnen 1997).

States and Mining Communities

Mineral resources, along with oil, pose particular challenges to states in terms of their relationships with local communities in the vicinity of a project. In part, this stems from the multiple and often conflicting interests being pursued by elements of the state. As one obvious example, departments of finance regularly clash with those involved in regulating the social and environmental impacts of mining projects (MMSD 2002, p. 66). More fundamentally, though, the problems confronting states in the development of natural resources are issues of legitimacy and national identity. Among local communities on the remote resource frontiers of Asia-Pacific, Africa, and South America, the state's claims to mineral ownership are frequently greeted with scepticism or even outright denial. In large part, this derives from the lack of an effective state presence in these resource frontiers: "Where the institutions of the state have little or no presence, material or symbolic, in the village, the ability of the state to insist upon its sovereignty—its voice—is open to challenge" (Ballard 1997, p. 49).

The material evidence of a state's presence has proved to be critical in Papua New Guinea, as elsewhere; a state that delivers services to the village, such as education, health, justice, security, and development, will usually find its claims to authority and legitimacy (and thus its claims to mineral ownership) respected, although not necessarily uncontested. Where state capacity to deliver these services is limited (through political or economic constraints), communities are likely to be more inclined to have less regard for the authority and claims of the state. J. Burton (1998) provides a case study of a "mal-administered mining province" in Papua New Guinea that highlights how "pathologies of provincial administration" can leave regions with no evidence of state or corporate local development initiatives. In such cases, the response of communities is likely to mirror the blunt contention of Lihir Landowners Association Chairman, Mark Soipang, during negotiations over the development of the mine: "The developers are foreigners and the State is only a concept. It is us, the landowners, who represent real life and people" (Filer 1996a, p. 68). Under these conditions, communities are likely to pursue and protect their own interests directly with potential developers, effectively seeking to bypass the state. In Papua New Guinea this has resulted in major concessions by the state in favor of mine-affected communities and increasing pressure on states in the region from host communities to relinquish revenues, control, or even sovereignty over mineral resources. In both the Porgera and Ok Tedi cases, control over government mine-derived development revenues has been returned to the mining companies, with the support of local communities. To developers, this process appears to be, in Filer's (1996b, p. 94) colorful phrase, "the 'Melanesian Way' of menacing the mining industry," a process that is marked by a characteristic diversity and instability of the political relationships between persons, institutions, and communities that constitute their national policy process. There is a multitude of menaces then but very little in the way of moral messages or purposes. The end result is that the development of mineral resources is central to the reshaping of the ideologies and discourses of the state, a political variation on Shafer's economic argument noted above.

CONSTITUTING LOCAL COMMUNITIES

Local Communities and Resource Control

Of the three core categories of stakeholder in the mining community, the so-called local communities are both the most recent addition and the most flexible and extensible group. The boundaries and roles within the mining community of the corporations and the relevant government agencies appear relatively prescribed and, in some respects, mutually complementary. In contrast, local communities are only summoned into being or defined as such by the presence or the potential presence of a mining project. This is not to deny somehow the existence of other forms of community prior to the mine's presence or to suggest that these communities do not play an instrumental role in their own definition. Our intention, instead, is to stress that the composition of the local community in the context of a broader mining community is in no way certain or predictable. Particular, contingent histories of engagement around mining projects yield specific forms of local community, which are themselves subject to continuous processes of transformation over the life of a mining project.

Howard (1994/1995, p. 112) identifies at least four possible constituents of an indigenous local community in the context of mining in Southeast Asia: indigenous communities with pre-industrial life styles; agriculturalists interested in securing benefits from mining; small-scale miners, often in competition with large-scale operations; and mineworkers. Whereas, in some locations such as Kalimantan (Kunanayagam & Young 1998), these different interest groups may map onto distinct communities, in Papua New Guinea all four are likely to be represented within a single ethnic community and to be bound in common alliance against immigrants (or squatters in contemporary parlance) from neighboring communities. The following discussion draws heavily on the extensive literature of the past decade on local communities in Papua New Guinea as one of the better-documented locations for the engagement between mining and indigenous communities.

Membership often poses a substantial problem for local communities (in ways that it does not for governments or corporations) and is the source of much internal and external competition and conflict. The identity of local communities appears in most instances to be constituted largely through discourses of rights claimed (to land, to membership, to compensation, etc.) or rights abused (human rights, land rights, environmental rights, exclusion from membership, etc.), though Gardner (2001, p. 102) issues the important caveat that the "language of rights," read too literally by those seeking to generate legally binding settlements, can obscure "the complex processes which distribute people in space." Li (2000, p. 149) neatly captures the process whereby a local community is generated when she observes that the self-identification of a group as tribal or indigenous is not natural or inevitable, but neither is it simply invented, adopted, or imposed. It is rather a positioning that draws upon historically sedimented practices, landscapes, and repertoires of meaning and emerges through particular patterns of engagement and struggle.

In the process of self-definition in order to represent their interests to government and corporate agencies, or to other local communities, communities in the vicinity of a mining project employ both traditional and novel strategies of inclusion and exclusion. The bases for membership of local communities derive from the tension between competing strategies of inclusion and exclusion, which often turn upon rhetorics of land, kinship, myth, and cosmology. Over time, these strategies have the capacity to introduce inequalities of distribution and marginalization among local communities, along the classic fault lines of gender, age, class, and group identity.

Many local communities in the vicinity of mining projects have been subjected to massive dislocation and negative impacts. Indigenous communities have borne the brunt of much of the exploration and mine development associated with the 1980s boom and are often already marginalized both economically and politically within the nation (Howard 1991). The log of mining-related grievances endured by these communities is remarkable, with countless instances of grave abuses of basic human rights, including dispossession of land and livelihoods, individual murder, and mass killings (Handelsman 2002). A vast reservoir of often well-grounded suspicion harbored by local communities and their supporters thus attaches to the intentions and operations of governments and corporations alike in the context of mining projects.

However, in contrast with analyses that would view grievances over specific issues such as ecological damage as the dominant impetus for local community engagement with mining projects (Hyndman 1994, Kirsch 2001), we contend that most local communities are fundamentally concerned with questions of control over their own destinies, both in relation to the state and in terms of the management of projects, the flow of benefits, and the limitation or redistribution of mining impacts (Wesley-Smith 1990, p. 18; Banks 2002). Community protest over environmental destruction is, at one level and quite obviously, in response to and about environmental destruction; but such protest is not always reducible to a prioritization of environmental concern over other interests, however strongly this image might resonate with western notions of indigenous ecological stewardship (Conklin & Graham 1995).

Distinguishing or singling out ecological from other community interests is a curiously archaic argument, given current anthropological thought on the essential entanglement and integration of the different facets of social life previously conceived of as distinct institutions. Our intention is not to replace an ecological basis for protest with narrowly defined economic interests, as some authors have implied (Hyndman 2001, p. 39; Kirsch 1997, pp. 128–29), but is rather to suggest that a concern with control over fundamental questions of community sovereignty is expressed through a multitude of channels and means and must often appeal to more powerful (and often western) audiences through the most potent and familiar tropes, such as abuses of basic human rights or environmental destruction (Macintyre & Foale 2002).

Strategies of Inclusion and Exclusion

The various strategies of inclusion and exclusion adopted by local communities in the process of defining themselves and their interests cannot be seen as purely instrumental. Seemingly capricious changes in traditional law or in the means of determining community membership reflect both the inherent flexibility of local communities (in defiance of ethnographic attempts to establish fixed forms) and a politics rendered necessary by severe imbalances in the distribution of power (Guddemi 1997, p. 647; Zimmer-Tamakoshi 1997, p. 659): "Complexity, collaboration, and creative engagement in both local and global arenas, rather than simple deceit, imposition, or reactive opportunism, best describe these processes and relationships" (Li 2000, p. 173).

Disputes over access to and ownership of mineral resources have generated protracted confrontations between the legal apparatus of the state and the precepts of local communities, many of which first encounter the full power of the state's sovereign claims to resources only through this process of dispute (Howitt et al. 1996a). Much of the fiercest opposition to mining from local communities has been generated as a consequence of dispossession of land, degradation of a community's resources, and physical relocation of resident communities (Connell & Howitt 1991, Asian Dev. Bank 2000).

For most local communities in Papua New Guinea, land serves as a convenient discursive point of reference to ties to locality and to kin: "A claim to land, rather than some abstract notion of citizenship, is how the majority of Melanesians secure a foothold on the political stage and gain the attention of the state" (Ballard 1997, p. 48). This holds particularly true in the case of mining, where the industry is concerned primarily with securing access and leasehold rights to territory and only secondarily with questions of engagement with local residents. Residence and land ownership thus emerge as the principal bases for corporate and government identification and recognition of local community membership—a priority often swiftly appreciated and strategically incorporated by prospective community members (Jorgensen 2001). The apparent simplicity and neatness of this cadastral form of identity is deceptive, however, precisely because land condenses a host of social relationships for which territory serves as a form of shorthand reference. Filer (1997, pp. 162–68) and Jackson (1992) have both noted how the resources boom of the 1980s led to the development of an ideology of landowners in Papua New Guinea, in which land assumed a new relationship with identity in the national context. As the relative power of local communities in negotiating processes has grown from one mining agreement to the next, that power has increasingly become vested in ever more narrowly defined landowner groups, occasionally to the detriment of neighboring communities.

The self-identification of local communities based on kinship is a critical arena for strategies of inclusion and exclusion. The exceptional diversity among indigenous peoples of modes of social organization, and the flexibility and mobility of social identities, confound easy registration by states and corporations of prospective local community members. For some communities, recognition of their rights (or claims, from the perspectives of the state or corporation) requires some modification in conventional forms of presentation. Ernst (2001, p. 126) describes moves by Papua New Guinea's Onabasulu communities to establish or renegotiate social boundaries in anticipation of the requirements of modernity's outriders, such as mining and oil projects, as a process of "entification": "the making of 'entities,' or things from what have been either implicit or contingent categories." The complex and shifting politics of claims to membership in a local community "becomes an exercise in alignment and self-definition in which the calculus of advantage intersects with questions of identity, all of which is played out against a backdrop of regional political relations" (Jorgensen 2001, p. 93).

Knowledge of myth and cosmology provides a further means through which local communities dispute membership and seek to gain recognition of their sovereignty and rights. Local cosmologies combine and crystallize indigenous understandings of the land and social relations within spatial and temporal frameworks of belief. Respect for indigenous beliefs has slowly, and not without opposition, entered the arena of negotiations and agreements over large-scale mining, particularly in Australia (Gelder & Jacobs 1998, Rumsey & Weiner 2001) and the Pacific (Horowitz 2002).

In the western highlands region of Papua New Guinea, where the Porgera and Ok Tedi mines and the Nena and Mount Kare prospects are located, the presence of regionally extensive rituals and cosmographies has provided a fertile ground for representations to corporations and governments and for competing claims by local communities. Telefol claims to both the Nena prospect and the Ok Tedi mine are founded on the centrality of Telefol ritual experts and sites in regional sacred geography (Jorgensen 2001). More ambitious still is the ownership asserted by more distant Huli-speakers to all of these mining projects, as well as to the oil and gas projects at Lake Kutubu and Hides, on the basis of their pivotal location within a Huli-centric sacred geography that overlaps its Telefol-centric counterpart (Ballard 1994). Ownership of the Mount Kare alluvial gold prospect, which was the site of a spectacular goldrush during 1988 and 1989 (Vail 1995), is similarly disputed in terms of the identity of its ritual custodians and its position within the interlinked sacred geographies of three different ethnic groups (Clark 1993, Biersack 1999, Haley 1996, Wardlow 2001, Stewart & Strathern 2002).

Claims based on ritual knowledge are frequently heard at the District and Supreme courts in Papua New Guinea, yielding decisions as bewildering to the claimants as the substance of the claims must appear to the presiding judges (e.g., Amet 1991 on the decision at the Hides Gasfield). The perceived success of some of these claims has played a part in the widespread revival of interest in the continuing communication and enactment of this knowledge through ritual and initiation (Guddemi 1997, p. 644). Beyond their more limited function of providing further evidence in support of rights to ownership, the mythology and cosmology of a community are also creatively reconfigured to account for disparities in power and for changing circumstances (Kirsch 2001, Wardlow 2001).

Modes of Marginalization

In addition to their position in classic patterns of exploitation of local or migrant labor at large-scale mines (Godoy 1985, p. 206; Robinson 1986, p. 239ff), members of indigenous communities experience marginalization or exclusion on the basis of several other forms of discrimination, including ethnicity or group identity, age, and gender. Encounters with the state and with mining corporations commonly result in a variety of assaults on local understandings of community sovereignty, including dispossession of resources and lands, relocation of communities, and other abuses of fundamental human rights. Exclusion from decision-making processes or from the possible benefits of mining revenues are further forms of marginalization. Kirsch (1997, 2001) has documented the systematic exclusion from decision making about impacts to the environment of Yonggom communities downstream of the Ok Tedi mine. Marginalization on the basis of ethnicity or "race" has also been documented for the area of the Bougainville mine where, in reaction to their own previous experiences of discrimination, indigenous Nagovisi and Nasioi have expressed a common "black" identity in opposition to "redskins" from other parts of Papua New Guinea (Nash & Ogan 1990).

Filer (1990) describes the impact of the systematic marginalization of younger members of the local community at the Panguna mine by older kinsmen identified as the recipients of compensation payments. Filer's argument, which hinges upon the role played by younger men in leading the protests that culminated in the closure of the mine and civil war between Bougainville and the Papua New Guinea state, extends to a prediction that compensation agreements with landowners ossify social relations and act, in the long run, as time bombs that explode after about 20 years, with the passing of decision-making power from one generation to another. Polier (1996, p. 5) records a different dynamic for the Ok Tedi mine, where the fortunes of four different age cohorts are shown to vary considerably, reflecting the opportunities increasingly available to younger Min with better education.

Still more starkly drawn are the forms of marginalization experienced by women in local communities within the ambit of mining projects (see Macdonald & Rowland 2002 for a recent overview). Mining is an exceptionally masculinized industry, in terms of the composition of its workforces, its cultures of production, and its symbolic despoliation of a feminized nature; mining, argues Robinson (1996, p. 137), "is so 'naturally' masculine [that] its gender effects are invisible." There are limited employment opportunities for women in the industry—in either the corporations, the relevant government departments, or the local community workforces (Ranchod 2001). Loss of land and of resources to mining projects impacts most heavily the women of local communities as the key subsistence providers (Emberson-Bain 1994b, Macintyre 1993, Pollock 1996), and women's rights to land, and their role in the transmission of land and other rights, are also commonly diminished (e.g., Guddemi 1997, p. 634), as are their rights to representation within the mining community. Mining often generates additional pressure on women to perform as the maintainers of kinship networks and observers of attendant obligations owing to male absenteeism and the further feminization of subsistence (Polier 1996, p. 10)—a demand that is being met through the emergence of highly effective women's organizations operating both locally and internationally (e.g., Bonnell 1999, Carino 2002). The rapid influx of cash to local communities is also associated with augmented domestic violence and with transformations in patterns of marriage and sexuality (Bonnell 1999; Gerritsen & Macintyre 1991, pp. 47–48; Robinson 1986, 1996), leading to increases in the transmission of HIV/AIDS and sexually transmitted diseases to women of local communities.

Strategies of Engagement

In addition to the issue of control over resources, crucial questions surround "the mechanism and locus of decision-making at the local level" (Weiner 2001, p. 18). The forms of representation generated by local communities to enter into what are often novel engagements with agents of the state and corporations must balance both the requirements of their interlocutors and the internal needs of the community (O'Faircheallaigh 1995). At many mining projects, the initial structures of local community representation tend to be introduced by corporations, state agencies, or consultants acting for either category and are often modeled on similar structures at other projects. Land councils and associations in Australia (Levitus 1991), incorporated land groups in Papua New Guinea (Weiner 2001), and community foundations (*yayasan*) and institutes (*lembaga*) in Indonesia are just some of the structured forms of representation adopted in this way by local communities. Over time, those organizations that persist tend to assume a distinctive, localized character that better suits the needs of the community and that is often more active in the pursuit of community interests.

R. Roberts (1995) describes a continuum of public involvement in decision making that spans the range from persuasion (which can involve considerable violence at mining projects), to consultation, to the selective delegation of authority, and ultimately to self-determination. The history of negotiations for successive large mines in Papua New Guinea illustrates at least part of this progressive sequence (Filer 1999a). During the late 1960s, at the first major mine, Panguna on Bougainville, community "participation" consisted largely of receiving lectures on the impending benefits of the mine for the wider nation (Denoon 2000). As the costs of failing to involve local communities in decision making have become apparent, the community share in financial benefits has gradually been augmented from one mining project in Papua New Guinea to the next, and community representatives increasingly have been introduced into negotiations. Formal project development agreements involving local communities are now almost standard practice in North America, Australia, and Papua New Guinea (Howitt et al. 1996, pp. 17–19; O'Faircheallaigh 2002). In Papua New Guinea, mining agreements have been struck for the Porgera and Lihir mines through a Development Forum process, now incorporated into the national Mining Act and applied retrospectively to other existing projects, which formally identifies project stakeholders and provides a framework for negotiations (Filer 1996b). However, transformations in the extent of community involvement are by no means uniformly progressive. In the case of the Ok Tedi mine, the Papua New Guinea government has repeatedly returned to earlier practices in overriding community concerns about ecological damage and mine rehabilitation (Kirsch 2002). Elsewhere, as in Australia and Canada, considerably more active states have enacted forms of legislation, such as the *Native Title Act 1988* in Australia, which place powerful restrictions on the rights of indigenous communities to negotiate with resource developers (O'Faircheallaigh 2002).

The potential significance of the benefits of mining for local communities can be considerable, particularly for many indigenous communities that "are often badly in need of the additional economic opportunities which mining can generate" (O'Faircheallaigh 1991, p. 230). The principal forms of benefit include direct compensation for lands resumed and damages incurred, royalties on the mineral resource, wage income, equity participation and joint ventures, and access to mine-related infrastructure and services (O'Faircheallaigh 2002). There is enormous variation from project to project in the provision for and scale of such benefits (on compensation in Papua New Guinea, see Banks 1996, Bedford & Mamak 1977, Connell 1991, Filer et al. 2000, Toft 1997). The community share of mining royalty payments in Papua New Guinea rose from an initial 5% at the Ok Tedi mine in the early 1980s (Jackson 1993) to 50% of royalties and an additional 15% equity share at Lihir in the late 1990s, and ultimately to 100% at the Tolukuma mine (Filer 1999a). Another area of increasing prominence for local communities in negotiation over mining agreements is that of ancillary business contracts, though the success of these community businesses is by no means certain (Filer 1997, Banks 1999a).

The extent to which mining "benefits" actually benefit local communities, and the internal mechanisms for their distribution and consumption, are particularly poorly documented (but see Banks 1999b, Connell 1991, Gerritsen & Macintyre 1991, O'Faircheallaigh 2002). Social disruption following the massive influx of cash from gold rushes has been described for the Mount Kare rush in Papua New Guinea (Vail 1995), and Filer (1990) has argued that the payment of compensation is itself a major cause of the process of social disintegration within local communities because of the absence of traditional mechanisms for the distribution of cash and other benefits.

The Fourth Estate

One of the major developments associated with the 1980s mining boom has been the rapid expansion in the significance of additional stakeholders, including a wide variety of NGOs, financial intermediaries, lawyers, business partners, and consultants. Most enter the broader mining community by virtue of connections to or alliances with (rather than membership of) one of the three principal stakeholder categories.

NGOs are a particularly amorphous category, including both those organizations engaged in dialogue with or directly contracted by mining corporations and activist NGOs operating in support of the environment or of local communities, and are often implacably opposed to mining. Several of the major global NGOs, such as Conservation International, have elected to become involved in mining industry initiatives, including the MMSD project (see above). Others operating at a regional level, such as Oxfam Community Aid Abroad in Australia, have assumed a monitoring or ombudsman role, while maintaining their distance from the industry (Atkinson et al. 2001). A loose international alliance of environmental, human rights, and indigenous rights, NGOs have been able to direct attention to particular mining projects through a series of campaigns. Although these campaigns have created substantial negative publicity for certain mining corporations, and may have provoked some of the recent shifts in corporate social and environmental policy, the constraints of limited resources and personnel have tended to reduce the effectiveness of this NGO alliance beyond the horizons of reactions to particular events or the short-lived mobilization of public opinion around a specific topic, such as human rights abuse or ecological damage (Downing et al. 2002, p. 26). Finally, there are also NGOs hired directly by mining corporations to play a mediator or broker role with local communities, as part of a corporate trend to out-source non-core functions conventionally associated with (if in practice often neglected by) state agencies, supplying services such as health or education or assisting communities in negotiation.

In addition to NGOs, mining has begun to attract the involvement of lawyers, particularly in the aftermath of the partial success of the lawsuit brought against

BHP on behalf of the Yonggom people living downstream of the Ok Tedi mine (Kirsch 2002); similar lawsuits have now been lodged against the operators of the Freeport (Indonesia), Panguna (Bougainville), Gold Ridge (Solomon Islands), and Awas Tingni (Nicaragua) projects (Downing et al. 2002, p. 27). As opportunities for business projects develop on the margins of large-scale mines, a host of novel alliances have been formed between local community representatives and entrepreneurs at the national and local levels (e.g., Banks 1999a). Finally, the increase in social impact analysis that has followed in the wake of the 1980s minerals boom has provided a point of entry to a very wide range of consultants, including anthropologists (Goldman 2000). The ethical implications and choices available for consultants are addressed further below.

Human Rights and Mining

In conjunction with the recognition of the scope for legal challenges to mining there has been a convergence on human rights instruments as the most comprehensive and convenient frameworks for monitoring respect for many of the basic rights of local communities and workforces (Handelsman 2002), and a move to hold corporations, and not just states, accountable for abuses (Jochnick 1999). Conceived broadly, human rights comprise five basic categories, including civil, cultural, economic, political, and social rights, which extend to cover issues of property, development, health and safety, and environment (Handelsman 2002); human rights thus potentially address most aspects of mining impact. This is one area in which there has been a relatively constructive dialogue between corporations and NGOs, with groups such as Amnesty International (Sullivan & Frankental 2001) and the Australian Asia Pacific Mining Network (1998) proposing standards for industry practice. The process of defining the relevance and comparative significance of different human rights is still being hotly debated, with the supposedly competing claims of economic and other rights as the principal area of contention.

The most recent advance in this area has been the development by mining companies of individual corporate codes of conduct which subscribe to certain fundamental standards, as laid out in the various universal declarations and conventions (Handelsman 2002, Attachment A). The signing of a set of Voluntary Principles in 2000 by a number of British and American mining and energy companies (Bur. Democracy, Hum. Rights, Labor 2000), and the adoption by individual corporations of operational strategies to ensure and to publicize compliance (e.g., Freeport-McMoRan Copper & Gold 2001, Rio Tinto 2001), may come to mark an important watershed in the scrutiny of conditions at mine sites. However, "it remains to be seen whether [these initiatives] constitute genuine recognition of the importance of corporate integrity, or simply an extension of corporate public relations in the search for comparative advantage within the industry" (Ballard 2001, p. 9). Certainly most corporations, and the states that host their mining projects, have been reluctant to submit to independent, external monitoring; but, while industry critics are unlikely to attribute these developments to corporate philanthropy, a gathering market interest in compliance may render respect for human rights a financial imperative (Spar 1998).

MINING AND ANTHROPOLOGY: TOWARD
AN ETHICS OF ENGAGEMENT

Anthropologists have become engaged as auxiliaries to all parties in the resource wars that revolve around the global mining industry: as consultants to industry, state agencies and local communities, and as advocates in debates both for and against mining. There is no natural position for anthropology in such a contested field, and anthropologists have adopted bitterly opposed stances at several mining projects, such as the Coronation Hill gold prospect in Northern Australia, where debate revolved around claims of neutrality and accusations of partisan advocacy from either side (R. Brunton 1992, Keen 1993). Two broad visions of an appropriate role for anthropologists have been articulated, the first proposing that anthropologists are best suited to an intermediary role as brokers (Downing et al. 2002, p. 22; Filer 1999b; McNamara 1987), and the second that anthropologists must choose between an illusory neutrality, which states and corporations are best positioned to exploit, and a commitment to advocacy on behalf of local communities (B. Brunton 1997, Hyndman 2001, Kirsch 2002).

Although there may be some truth to the observation that anthropologists in resource wars often have an inflated sense of the importance of their contribution, albeit one occasionally shared by local communities (Jorgensen 2001, p. 82), this hardly absolves us of the requirement for sustained reflection on the implications and consequences of our interventions. There is indeed scope for the co-optation of anthropological consultation owing to structural inequalities between different sides in mining disputes (Whiteman & Mamen 2001). State agencies and mining corporations are usually much better positioned to commission and direct ethnographic research or to exploit ethnographic knowledge, though they exercise no monopoly in this respect. However, the distinction between pro- and anti-industry stances appears overdrawn. A number of critics of resistance studies have observed the dangers inherent in oversimplifying or "sanitizing" the politics of local communities in conditions of conflict (Edelman 2001, pp. 310–11; Ramos 1998; Trigger 2000, p. 203)—an often-strategic essentialism characterized by Ortner (1995) as a form of "ethnographic refusal." They instead call for close attention to the contingencies of any given site and for the reclamation of the specific social and historical contexts for particular conflicts (Marcus 1999, p. 12). An adequate ethnography of contemporary resource industries such as large-scale mining will require work at multiple sites and over a sustained period, and the ethics of engagement will vary considerably from one mine site to another, over time at the same site, and from one perspective to the next within a project.

Without seeking yet to prescribe such an ethics, it is possible to predict that the nature of ethnographic research around mining will need to depart in at least one important respect from conventional or existing modes of enquiry. Godoy's (1985, p. 211) concluding plea for an "integrative" approach to the anthropological study of mining, which would combine an understanding of the geological and economic as well as social and cultural dimensions of mining, prefigures at least part of the vision articulated by Marcus (1995) of a multi-sited ethnography: "if anthropology is to be responsible for its own contexts of meaning and the forging of its own arguments from inside the ethnographic process of research itself," argues Marcus (1999, p. 12), then the full spectrum of activities which contribute to and contextualize mining as a site for research must be addressed, if only at the level of the multi-sited "imaginary." Curiously, in his questioning of the orthodoxies of ethnographic practice, Marcus does not appear to place at risk the romantic ideal of the solitary scholar, and yet the pursuit of a multi-sited ethnography of mining appears to lie beyond the competence of any individual researcher. If the complexities of agency, of relationships, and of scales sketched briefly in this review are to be imagined ethnographically and adequately addressed, we shall need to mobilize flexible coalitions or alliances of often-unlikely partners, including industry think-tanks, NGOs, academics, and community activists among others. Jesuit researcher Gjording (1991, pp. xi–xii) describes a transnational coalition formed along these lines to research the potential impact on Guaymí Indians of the proposed Cerro Colorado copper project. The conflicted nature of mining as a site for research and the compelling sense that anthropological skills can contribute to the moderation or resolution of resource wars demand some form of engagement or activism—not necessarily the activism of causes or allegiances but rather a "circumstantial activism" (Marcus 1995, p. 113) that mimics and exploits the labile structure of its own field for enquiry in order to make or re-make the sense of mining, both for the researchers and for their interlocutors.

ACKNOWLEDGMENTS

Colin Filer, Martha Macintyre, Ciaran O'Faircheallaigh, and Kathy Robinson all kindly offered comments on drafts of this paper. Numerous other colleagues, cited or otherwise, have assisted with materials, ideas, and debate.

The *Annual Review of Anthropology* is online at http://anthro.annualreviews.org

LITERATURE CITED

Abrash A. 2002. Development aggression: observations on human rights conditions in the PT freeport contract of work areas with recommendations. Report for the Robert F. Kennedy Meml. Cent. Hum. Rights, Washington DC

Ali S, Behrendt L. 2001. Mining and indige-
nous rights: the emergence of a global social movement. *Cult. Surviv. Q.* 25:6–8

Amet A. 1991. *Decision on Application No. 90/101 (Between the Tuguba Tribe and the Hiwa Tribe).* Port Moresby, Papua New Guinea: Land Titles Comm.

Asian Dev. Bank. 2000. *Resettlement Policy*

and Practice in Southeast Asia and the Pacific. Manila: ADB

Atkinson J, Brown A, Ensor J. 2001. *Mining Ombudsman Annual Report 2000–2001.* Melbourne: Oxfam Community Aid Abroad

Aust. Asia Pac. Mining Netw. 1998. *Principles for the Conduct of Company Operations within the Minerals Industry.* Melbourne: Aust. Asia Pac. Mining Netw.

Auty RM. 1993. *Sustaining Development in Mineral Economies: the Resource-Curse Thesis.* London: Routledge

Auty RM, Mikesell RF. 1998. *Sustainable Development in Mineral Economies.* Oxford: Clarendon

Ballard C. 1994. The centre cannot hold: trade networks and sacred geography in the Papua New Guinea Highlands. *Archaeol. Ocean.* 29:130–48

Ballard C. 1997. It's the land, stupid! The moral economy of resource ownership in Papua New Guinea. In *The Governance of Common Property in the Pacific Region*, ed. P Larmour, pp. 47–65. Canberra: Aust. Natl. Univ.

Ballard C. 2001. Human rights and the mining industry in Indonesia: a baseline study. MMSD Work. Pap. No. 182. http://www.iied.org/mmsd/mmsd_pdfs/indonesia_hr_baseline.pdf

Banks G. 1996. Compensation for mining: benefit or time-bomb—the Porgera case. See Howitt et al. 1996, pp. 223–36

Banks G. 1999a. Business as unusual. See Filer 1999c, pp. 222–59

Banks G. 1999b. The economic impact of the mine. See Filer 1999c, pp. 88–127

Banks G. 2002. Mining and the environment in Melanesia: contemporary debates reviewed. *Contemp. Pac.* 14:39–67

Banks G, Ballard C, eds. 1997. *The Ok Tedi Settlement: Issues, Outcomes and Implications.* Canberra: Aust. Natl. Univ.

Bedford R, Mamak A. 1977. *Compensating for Development: the Bougainville Case.* Christchurch: Univ. Canterbury

Biersack A. 1999. The Mount Kare python and his gold: totemism and ecology in the Papua New Guinea Highlands. *Am. Anthropol.* 101:68–87

Bonnell S. 1999. Social change in the Porgera Valley. See Filer 1999c, pp. 19–87

Brunton R. 1992. Mining credibility: Coronation Hill and the anthropologists. *Anthropol. Today* 8:2–5

Brunton B. 1997. The perspective of a Papua New Guinea NGO. See Banks & Ballard 1997, pp. 167–82

Bryce R, Ivins M. 2002. *Pipe Dreams: Greed, Ego, and the Death of Enron.* New York: Public Aff.

Bur. Democracy, Hum. Rights, Labor. 2000. *Voluntary Principles on Security and Human Rights.* Washington, DC: US Dep. State

Burton B. 1998. Getting engaged? *Mining Monitor* 3(3):2

Burton J. 1996. What is best practice? Social issues and the culture of the corporation in Papua New Guinea. See Denoon et al. 1996, pp. 129–34

Burton J. 1998. Mining and maladministration in Papua New Guinea. In *Governance and Reform in the South Pacific*, ed. P Larmour, pp. 154–82. Canberra: Aust. Natl. Univ.

Campbell C. 1997. Migrancy, masculine identities and AIDS: the psycho-social context of HIV transmission on the South African gold mines. *Soc. Sci. Med.* 45:273–81

Cannon J. 2003. *Men at work: expatriation in the international mining industry.* PhD thesis, Monash Univ., Melbourne

Carino JK. 2002. Women and mining in the Cordillera and the international women and mining network. See Macdonald & Rowland 2002, pp. 16–19

Clark AL, Clark JC. 1999. The new reality of mineral development: social and cultural issues in Asia and Pacific nations. *Resour. Policy* 25:189–96

Clark J. 1993. Gold, sex, and pollution: male illness and myth at Mt. Kare, Papua New Guinea. *Am. Ethnol.* 20:742–57

Collier P. 2000. *Economic Causes of Civil Conflict and Their Implications for Policy.* World Bank Group Policy Res. Pap.

http://www.worldbank.org/research/conflict/papers/civilconflict.pdf

Collier P, Hoeffler A. 2000. Greed and grievance in civil war. Policy Res. Work. Pap. 2355. World Bank, Washington, DC

Conklin BA, Graham LR. 1995. The shifting middle ground: Amazonian Indians and eco-politics. *Am. Anthropol.* 97:695–710

Connell J. 1991. Compensation and conflict: the Bougainville Copper Mine, Papua New Guinea. See Connell & Howitt 1991, pp. 55–76

Connell J, Howitt R, ed. 1991. *Mining and Indigenous Peoples in Australasia.* Sydney: Sydney Univ. Press

Denoon D. 2000. *Getting Under the Skin: the Bougainville Copper Agreement and the Creation of the Panguna Mine.* Carlton South: Melbourne Univ. Press

Denoon D, Ballard C, Banks G, Hancock P, ed. 1996. *Mining and Mineral Resource Policy Issues in Asia-Pacific: Prospects for the 21st century.* Canberra: Aust. Natl. Univ.

Dinnen S. 1997. Trading in security: private military contractors in Papua New Guinea. In *Challenging the State: the Sandline Affair in Papua New Guinea*, ed. S Dinnen, R May, AJ Regan, pp. 112–28. Canberra: Asia-Pacific Press

Dinnen S. 2001. *Law and Order in a Weak State: Crime and Politics in Papua New Guinea.* Adelaide: Crawford House; Honolulu: Univ. Hawaii

Dirlik A. 2001. Place-based imagination: globalism and the politics of place. In *Places and Politics in an Age of Globalization*, ed. R Prazniak, A. Dirlik, pp. 15–51. Lanham, MD: Rowman & Littlefield

Downing TE, Moles J, McIntosh I, Garcia-Downing C. 2002. Indigenous peoples and mining encounters: strategies and tactics. MMSD Work. Pap. No. 57. http://www.iied.org/mmsd/mmsd_pdfs/057_downing.pdf

Edelman M. 2001. Social movements: changing paradigms and forms of politics. *Annu. Rev. Anthropol.* 30:285–317

Elias R, Taylor I, Ramasar V, Buijs G, Holdway A. 2001. HIV/Aids, the mining and minerals sector and sustainable development in Southern Africa. MMSD Work. Pap. No. 163. http://www.iied.org/mmsd/mmsd_pdfs/163_eias.pdf

Emberson-Bain A. 1994a. *Labour and Gold in Fiji.* Cambridge: Cambridge Univ. Press

Emberson-Bain A. 1994b. De-romancing the stones: gender, environment and mining in the Pacific. In *Sustainable Development or Malignant Growth? Perspectives of Pacific Island Women*, ed. A Emberson-Bain, pp. 91–110. Suva: Marama

Emel J. 2002. An inquiry into the green disciplining of capital. *Environ. Plan. A* 34:827–43

Ernst TM. 2001. Land, stories and resources: some impacts of large-scale resource exploitation on Onabasulu lifeworlds. See Rumsey & Weiner 2001, pp. 125–44

Erwiza. 1999. *Miners, managers and the state: a socio-political history of the Ombilin coal-mines, West Sumatra, 1892–1996.* PhD thesis. Univ. Amsterdam, 261 pp.

Evans G, Goodman J, Lansbury N. 2001a. Politicising finance. See Evans et al. 2001b, pp. 37–57

Evans G, Goodman J, Lansbury N, eds. 2001b. *Moving Mountains: Communities Confront Mining and Globalisation.* Sydney: Ortford

Extractive Ind. Rev. 2003. What is the EIR? http://www.eireview.org

Ferguson J. 1999. *Expectations of Modernity: Myths and Meanings of Urban Life on the Zambian Copperbelt.* Berkeley: Univ. Calif. Press

Filer C. 1990. The Bougainville rebellion, the mining industry and the process of social disintegration in Papua New Guinea. *Canberra Anthropol.* 13:1–39

Filer C. 1996a. Participation, governance and social impact: the planning of the Lihir gold mine. See Denoon et al. 1996, pp. 67–75

Filer C. 1996b. The Melanesian way of menacing the mining industry. In *Environment and Development in the Pacific*, ed. B Burt, C Clerk, pp. 91–122. Canberra: Aust. Natl. Univ.; Port Moresby, Papua New Guinea: Univ. Papua New Guinea Press

Filer C. 1997. Compensation, rent and power. See Toft 1997, pp. 156–89

Filer C. 1999a. 'Between a rock and a hard place': mining, 'indigenous people', and the development of states. In *Schatzinseln in der Südsee–Bergbau im Südpazifik: Modernisierungskonflikte in jungen Staaten und Perspektiven nachhaltiger Entwicklung.* Entwicklungs-Politik Special Issue V/99: 7–19

Filer C. 1999b. The dialectics of negation and negotiation in the anthropology of mineral resources development in Papua New Guinea. In *The Anthropology of Power: Empowerment and Disempowerment in Changing Structures*, ed. A Cheater, pp. 88–102. London: Routledge

Filer C, ed. 1999c. *Dilemmas of Development: the Social and Economic Impact of the Porgera Gold Mine, 1989–1994.* Canberra: Aust. Natl. Univ.; Boroko: Natl. Res. Inst.

Filer C. 2002. Should mining companies 'break new ground' in Papua New Guinea? *Dev. Bull.* 58:115–18

Filer C, Henton D, Jackson R. 2000. *Landowner Compensation in Papua New Guinea's Mining and Petroleum Sectors.* Port Moresby: Papua New Guinea Chamber of Mines & Petroleum

Finn JL. 1998. *Tracing the Veins: Of Copper, Culture and Community from Butte to Chuquicamata.* Berkeley: Univ. Calif. Press

FitzGerald B. 2003. Life with Brian bit too scary. *Sydney Morning Herald*, Jan. 11–12: 55–56

Freeport-McMoRan Copper & Gold. 2001. *Human Rights Policy and Implementation.* New Orleans, LA: Freeport-McMoRan Copper & Gold

Gardner D. 2001. Continuity and identity: mineral development, land tenure and 'ownership' among the northern Mountain Ok. See Rumsey & Weiner 2001, pp. 101–24

Gedicks A. 1993. *The New Resource Wars: Native and Environmental Struggles Against Environmental Corporations.* Boston, MA: South End

Gelder K, Jacobs JM. 1998. *Uncanny Australia: Sacredness and Identity in a Postcolonial Nation.* Cartlon South: Melbourne Univ. Press

Gerritsen R, Macintyre M. 1991. Dilemmas of distribution: the Misima gold mine, Papua New Guinea. See Connell & Howitt 1991, pp. 35–53

Gibson-Graham JK. 1996. *The End of Capitalism (As We Knew It): a Feminist Critique of Political Economy.* Cambridge, MA: Blackwell

Gjording CN. 1991. *Conditions Not of Their Choosing: the Guaymí Indians and Mining Multinationals in Panama.* Washington, DC: Smithsonian Inst. Press

Godoy RA. 1985. Mining: anthropological perspectives. *Annu. Rev. Anthropol.* 14:199–217

Godoy RA. 1990. *Mining and Agriculture in Highland Bolivia: Ecology, History, and Commerce Among the Jukumanis.* Tucson: Univ. Arizona Press

Goldman L, ed. 2000. *Social Impact Analysis: an Applied Anthropology Manual.* Oxford: Berg

Guddemi P. 1997. Continuities, contexts, complexities, and transformations: local land concepts of a Sepik people affected by mining exploration. *Anthropol. Forum* 7:629–48

Haley N. 1996. Revisioning the past, remembering the future: Duna accounts of the world's end. *Oceania* 66:278–85

Handelsman SD. 2002. Human rights in the minerals industry. MMSD Work. Paper No. 9. http://www.iied.org/mmsd/mmsd_pdfs/009_handelsman.pdf

Hirst P, Thompson G. 1995. Globalisation and the future of the nation state. *Econ. Soc.* 24:408–42

Horowitz L. 2002. Stranger in one's own home: Kanak people's engagements with a multinational nickel mining project in New Caledonia. RMAP Work. Paper No. 30 http://rspas.anu.edu.au/rmap/Wpapers/rmap_wp30.pdf

Howard MC. 1988. *The Impact of the International Mining Industry on Native Peoples.* Sydney: Univ. Sydney

Howard MC. 1991. *Mining, Politics, and Development in the South Pacific.* Boulder, CO: Westview Press

Howard MC. 1994/1995. Mining, development and indigenous peoples in Southeast Asia. *J. Bus. Adm.* 22/23:93–131

Howitt R, Connell J, Hirsch P. 1996a. Resources, nations and indigenous peoples. See Howitt et al. 1996b, pp. 1–30

Howitt R, Connell J, Hirsch P, ed. 1996b. *Resources, Nations and Indigenous Peoples: Case Studies from Australasia, Melanesia and Southeast Asia.* Melbourne: Oxford Univ. Press

Hyndman D. 1994. *Ancestral Rain Forests and the Mountain of Gold: Indigenous Peoples and Mining in New Guinea.* Boulder, CO: Westview Press

Hyndman D. 2001. Academic responsibilities and representation of the Ok Tedi crisis in postcolonial Papua New Guinea. *Contemp. Pac.* 13:33–54

Imbun BY. 1995. Enga social life and identity in a Papua New Guinea mining town. *Oceania* 66:51–61

Imbun BY. 1999. *Industrial and Employment Relations in the Papua New Guinea Mining Industry.* Waigani: Univ. Papua New Guinea

Jackson R. 1992. Undermining or determining the nature of the state? In *Resources, Development and Politics in the Pacific Islands*, ed. S Henningham, RJ May, L Turner, pp. 79–89. Bathurst: Crawford

Jackson R. 1993. *Cracked Pot or Copper-Bottomed Investment? The Development of the Ok Tedi Project 1982–1991: a Personal View.* Townsville: Melanesian Stud. Cent., James Cook Univ. North Queensland

Jochnick C. 1999. Confronting the impunity of non-state actors: new fields for the promotion of human rights. *Hum. Rights Q.* 21:56–79

Jorgensen D. 1998. Whose nature? Invading bush spirits, travelling ancestors and mining in Telefolmin. *Soc. Analysis* 42:100–16

Jorgensen D. 2001. Who and what is a landowner? Mythology and marking the ground in a Papua New Guinea mining project. See Rumsey & Weiner 2001, pp. 68–100

Keen I. 1993. Aboriginal beliefs vs. mining at Coronation Hill: the containing force of traditionalism. *Hum. Org.* 52:344–55

Kirsch S. 1997. Is Ok Tedi a precedent? Implications of the lawsuit. See Banks & Ballard 1997, pp. 118–40

Kirsch S. 2001. Changing views of place and time along the Ok Tedi. See Rumsey & Weiner 2001, pp. 182–207

Kirsch S. 2002. Anthropology and advocacy: a case study of the campaign against the Ok Tedi mine. *Crit. Anthropol.* 22:175–200

Knapp AB, Pigott V. 1997. The archaeology and anthropology of mining: social approaches to an industrial past. *Curr. Anthropol.* 38:300–4

Kunanayagam R, Young K. 1998. Mining, environmental impact and dependent communities: the view from below in East Kalimantan. In *The Politics of Environment in Southeast Asia: Resources and Resistance*, ed. P Hirsch, C Warren, pp. 139–58. London: Routledge

Leith D. 2002. *The Politics of Power: Freeport in Suharto's Indonesia.* Honolulu: Univ. Hawaii Press

Levitus R. 1991. The boundaries of Gagudju Association membership: anthropology, law, and public policy. See Connell & Howitt 1991, pp. 153–68

Li TM. 2000. Articulating indigenous identity in Indonesia: resource politics and the tribal slot. *Comp. Stud. Soc. Hist.* 42:149–79

Macdonald I, Rowland C, ed. 2002. *Tunnel Vision: Women, Mining and Communities.* Fitzroy: Oxfam Community Aid Abroad

Macintyre M. 1993. Women and mining. In *Papua New Guinea and Australia: Towards 2000*, pp. 43–46. Fitzroy, Aust.: Community Aid Abroad & Freedom from Hunger

Macintyre M, Foale S. 2002. Politicised ecology: local responses to mining in Papua New Guinea. RMAP Work. Paper No. 33. http://rspas.anu.edu.au/rmap/Wpapers/rmap_wp33.pdf

MacMillan G. 1995. *At the End of the Rainbow? Gold, Land, and People in the Brazilian Amazon.* New York: Columbia Univ. Press

Marcus GE. 1995. Ethnography in/of the world

system: the emergence of multi-sited ethnography. *Annu. Rev. Anthropol.* 24:95–117

Marcus GE. 1999. What is at stake—and is not—in the idea and practice of multi-sited ethnography. *Canberra Anthropol.* 22(2):6–14

McEachern D. 1995. Mining meaning from the rhetoric of nature: Australian mining companies and their attitudes at home and abroad. *Policy Org. Soc.* 10:48–69

McNamara JK. 1987. Taking sides in conflict: applied social research in the South African fold-mining industry. In *The Research Relationship: Practice and Politics in Social Policy Research*, ed. GC Wenger, pp. 76–92. London: Allen & Unwin

Mines and Communities. 2001. The London declaration. http://www.minesandcoes.org/Charter/londondec.htm

MMSD (Mining, Minerals and Sustainable Development project). 2002. *Breaking New Ground: Mining, Minerals and Sustainable Development*. London: Earthscan

Moodie TD, Ndatshe V. 1994. *Going for Gold: Men, Mines and Migration*. Berkeley: Univ. Calif. Press

Moreno A-M, Tegen A. 1998. *World Mining Directory*. Surrey: Metal Bull. Books; Stockholm: Raw Mater. Group

Nash J. 1979. *We Eat the Mines and the Mines Eat Us: Dependency and Exploitation in Bolivian Tin Mines*. New York: Columbia Univ. Press

Nash J, Ogan G. 1990. The red and the black: Bougainville perceptions of other Papua New Guineans. *Pac. Stud.* 13(2):1–17

O'Faircheallaigh C. 1991. Resource exploitation and indigenous people: towards a general analytical framework. In *The Challenge of Northern Regions*, ed. P Jull, S Roberts, pp. 228–71. Darwin: North Aust. Res. Unit, Aust. Natl. Univ.

O'Faircheallaigh C. 1995. Negotiations between mining companies and aboriginal communities: process and structure. CAEPR Discussion Paper No. 86. Canberra: Cent. Aborig. Econ. Policy Res., Aust. Natl. Univ.

O'Faircheallaigh C. 1999. Making social im-

pact assessment count: a negotiation-based approach for indigenous peoples. *Soc. Nat. Resour.* 12:63–80

O'Faircheallaigh C. 2002. *A New Approach to Policy Evaluation: Indigenous People and Mining*. Aldershot, UK: Ashgate

O'Neill P, Gibson-Graham JK. 1999. Enterprise discourse and executive talk: stories that destabilise the company. *Trans. Inst. British Geogr.* 24:11–22

Ortner SB. 1995. Resistance and the problem of ethnographic refusal. *Comp. Stud. Soc. Hist.* 37:173–93

Polier N. 1994. A view from the 'cyanide room': politics and culture in a mining town in Papua New Guinea. *Identities* 1:63–84

Polier N. 1996. Of mines and Min: modernity and its malcontents in Papua New Guinea. *Ethnology* 35:1–16

Pollock N. 1996. Impact of mining on Nauruan women. *Nat. Resour. Forum* 20:123–34

Pritchard S, ed. 1998. *Indigenous Peoples, the United Nations and Human Rights*. London: Zed Books

Quamina OT. 1987. *Mineworkers of Guyana: the Making of a Working Class*. London: Zed

Ramos AR. 1998. *Indigenism: Ethnic Politics in Brazil*. Madison: Univ. Wisconsin Press

Ranchod S. 2001. *Gender and Mining: Workplace. Rep. MMSD Southern Africa*, Afr. Inst. Corp. Citizenship, Birnam Park, South Africa

Rio Tinto. 2001. *Human Rights Guidance: Guidance for Managers on Implementing the Human Rights Policy in The Way We Work*. London: Rio Tinto

Roberts JT. 1995. Subcontracting and the omitted social dimensions of large development projects: household survival at the Carajás mines in the Brazilian Amazon. *Econ. Dev. Cult. Change* 43:735–58

Roberts R. 1995. Public involvement: from consultation to participation. See Vanclay & Bronstein 1995, pp. 221–46

Robinson KM. 1986. *Stepchildren of Progress: the Political Economy of Development in an Indonesian Mining Town*. Albany: SUNY Press

Robinson KM. 1996. Women, mining and development. See Howitt et al. 1996, pp. 137–49

Ross M. 1999. The political economy of the resource curse. *World Polit.* 51:297–322

Rouse MJ, Fleising U. 1995. Miners and managers: workplace cultures in a British Columbia coal mine. *Hum. Org.* 54:238–48

Rumsey A, Weiner J, ed. 2001. *Mining and Indigenous Lifeworlds in Australia and Papua New Guinea.* Adelaide: Crawford House

Sassen S. 2000. Spatialities and temporalities of the global: elements for a theorization. *Public Cult.* 12:215–32

Schoenberger E. 1994. Corporate strategy and corporate strategists: power, identity, and knowledge within the firm. *Environ. Plan. A* 26:435–51

Shafer DM. 1994. *Winners and Losers: How Sectors Shape the Developmental Prospects of States.* Ithaca: Cornell Univ. Press

Spar DL. 1998. The spotlight and the bottom line: how multinationals export human rights. *Foreign Aff.* 77(March/April):7–12

Stewart PJ, Strathern A. 2002. *Remaking the World: Myth, Mining, and Ritual Change among the Duna of Papua New Guinea.* Washington, DC: Smithsonian Inst. Press

Sullivan R, Frankental P. 2001. Human rights and the minerals sector. Discuss. Pap. MMSD Workshop Hum. Rights Issues Minerals Sector, Berlin, 6 September 2001

Switzer J. 2001. Armed conflict and natural resources: the cases of the minerals sector. MMSD Work. Report No. 12. http://www.iied.org/mmsd/mmsd_pdfs/jason_switzer.pdf

Taussig MT. 1980. *The Devil and Commodity Fetishism in South America.* Chapel Hill: Univ. North Carolina Press

Toft S, ed. 1997. *Compensation for Resource Development in Papua New Guinea.* Port Moresby: Law Reform Comm.; Canberra: Aust. Natl. Univ.

Trigger DS. 1997. Mining, landscape and the culture of development ideology in Australia. *Ecumene* 4:161–79

Trigger DS. 2000. Aboriginal responses to mining in Australia: economic aspirations, cultural revival, and the politics of indigenous protest. In *Hunters and Gatherers in the Modern World: Conflict, Resistance, and Self-Determination,* ed. PP Schweitzer, M Biesele, RK Hitchcock, pp. 192–205. New York: Berghahn

Tsing A. 2000. Inside the economy of appearances. *Public Cult.* 12:115–44

Vail J. 1995. All that glitters: the Mt. Kare gold rush and its aftermath. In *Papuan Borderlands: Huli, Duna, and Ipili Perspectives on the Papua New Guinea Highlands,* ed. A Biersack, pp. 343–74. Ann Arbor: Univ. Michigan Press

Vanclay F, Bronstein D, ed. 1995. *Environmental and Social Impact Assessment.* Chichester: Wiley

Wardlow H. 2001. The Mount Kare python: Huli myths and gendered fantasies of agency. See Rumsey & Weiner 2001, pp. 31–67

Weiner JF. 2001. The Foi incorporated land group: law and custom in group definition and collective action in the Kutubu Oil Project area, PNG. State, Society & Governance in Melanesia Project Work. Paper 01/2. Aust. Natl. Univ., Canberra. http://rspas.anu.edu.au/melanesia/seminars.htm

Wesley-Smith T. 1990. The politics of access: mining companies, the state, and landowners in Papua New Guinea. *Polit. Sci.* 42:1–19

Whiteman G, Mamen K. 2001. Community consultation in mining. *Cult. Surviv. Q.* 25:30–35

Zimmer-Tamakoshi L. 1997. When land has a price: ancestral gerrymandering and the resolution of land conflicts at Kurukambare. *Anthropol. Forum* 7:649–66

Annu. Rev. Anthropol. 2003. 32:315–38
doi: 10.1146/annurev.anthro.32.061002.093431
Copyright © 2003 by Annual Reviews. All rights reserved
First published online as a Review in Advance on June 4, 2003

THE ANTHROPOLOGY OF WELFARE "REFORM": New Perspectives on U.S. Urban Poverty in the Post-Welfare Era

Sandra Morgen
Center for Study of Women in Society and Department of Anthropology, University of
Oregon, 1201 University of Oregon, Eugene, Oregon 97403;
email: smorgen@oregon.uoregon.edu

Jeff Maskovsky
Department of Urban Studies, Queens College, City University of New York, Flushing,
New York 11367; email: Jeff_Maskovsky@qc.edu

Key Words neoliberalism, difference, inequality, policy, women

■ **Abstract** Anthropological research on welfare restructuring differs from most
poverty research conducted by U.S. policy analysts and many other social scientists
by its situating the study of welfare "reform" within an examination of the production
of poverty and inequality at the center of the global system of advanced capitalism. In
this review we examine urban poverty and welfare-state restructuring in relation to the
ascent of neoliberalism, including the rise of market-oriented assumptions about social
value, productivity, and investment that dominate civic life and public policy. We focus
primarily, though not exclusively, on the United States. After a brief review of four
theoretical frameworks that inform ethnographic research on welfare, we explore five
approaches or themes in anthropological studies of welfare restructuring in the United
States: (*a*) the ethnographic challenge to claims of policy success by documenting
an unfolding crisis in social reproduction for the poor; (*b*) deconstructing the hegemonic discourse on welfare restructuring and juxtaposing it with the lived realities of
impoverished households; (*c*) contesting and moving beyond the behaviorism of mainstream poverty research; (*d*) exploring the multiple perspectives of those differently
situated within the welfare-state apparatus; and (*e*) theorizing the relationship between
welfare restructuring and an eroding social citizenship of the poor. The analysis of
gender, race, and, to a lesser extent, class is central to ethnographic research on welfare-
state restructuring.

INTRODUCTION

The passage of the Personal Responsibility and Work Opportunity Reconciliation
Act (PRWORA) in 1996—commonly referred to as "welfare reform"—is often
viewed as a watershed moment in the restructuring of the U.S. welfare state.

0084-6570/03/1021-0315$14.00

Decades of public confrontation involving business leaders, right-wing ideologues, centrist politicians, and liberal policy experts had placed U.S. welfare policy—and a highly selective slice of the welfare recipient population—under intense scrutiny. Public debate was framed in terms set by neoconservatives in the 1980s around the need to eliminate the socially unproductive "dependency" of welfare mothers. By the mid-1990s, the desire to overhaul welfare policy had achieved support among liberals and conservatives alike. In a moment of bipartisan cooperation that fulfilled then-President Clinton's famous promise to "end welfare as we know it," the 1996 welfare "reform" dramatically altered the goals, objectives, and administrative basis of public assistance.

The legislation ended the federal entitlement for welfare, devolved the program more completely to the states, and imposed a more restrictive set of time-limited policies designed to move welfare recipients rapidly, though not necessarily decisively, beyond "dependency" and into the workforce. Although this was just one moment in a complex history of U.S. poor relief and anti-poverty policy reorganization, it was an important moment that focused a spotlight on welfare-state restructuring and poverty, urban poverty in particular. The anthropological research that has probed the recent overhaul of welfare policy and its implications for the urban poor is the subject of this review. Although welfare policies have been restructured or retrenched throughout Europe and in Australia and New Zealand, restructuring has gone the furthest in the United States, which is widely viewed as a model (or foil) for restructuring elsewhere. Our review focuses on the United States but draws selectively on relevant theoretical and empirical research produced by and about other welfare states as well.

The passage of welfare "reform" inaugurated a period of intense research activity by mainstream poverty scholars in the United States. The apparent vitality of this research climate, however, is belied by the narrowness of their research agenda. With the basic architecture of the new post-welfare policy landscape set, a technocratic optimism has ensued in the policy-oriented research establishment. The task of tweaking the new post-welfare policies to achieve their new stated goals was seen as an opportunity to gain influence and recognition by the policy elite. Far from being freed up by welfare's repeal, however, the main thrust of poverty research remains wedded to new post-welfare policy objectives (O'Connor 2001). Leaving other important aspects of poverty aside, a torrent of research has been produced that focuses singularly on the mechanics of moving people from welfare to work. Not surprising, much of this research has targeted the U.S. urban poor, particularly the African American urban poor, a group that both demographically and symbolically has occupied the center of public policy debates on welfare and other anti-poverty programs and entitlements for decades.

Although the repeal of welfare has also galvanized U.S.-based poverty research in anthropology, the contribution of our discipline to studies of U.S. welfare reform has not been confined to projects that narrowly accord with the welfare-to-work policy agenda. Anthropology has not ignored the policy debates, but anthropologists have refused to analyze welfare "reform" on the narrow terms set by the policy elite. This may account for the discipline's relatively limited influence in the domestic policy arena; however, anthropology is far ahead of the curve in post-welfare poverty studies, having broken through, to a large extent, the welfare "fixation" (Helco 1994; see also O'Connor 2001) that has so limited mainstream poverty studies in recent years.

Anthropologists have taken on the topic of welfare "reform" in several ways:

1) Anthropologists have produced work that calls into question the reputed "success" of welfare's repeal and challenged the paradigms that pathologize both the individual behaviors of poor, inner-city women of color and their household arrangements.

2) Anthropologists have also attempted to broaden the mainstream research and policy agendas by directing attention away from questions about dependency, work, and the myopic fixation on female-headed households and toward questions of poverty reduction, economic security, and, in some cases, the dramatic increase in income polarization and inequality in U.S. cities.

3) Anthropologists have begun to analyze welfare "reform" within the globalization and inequality paradigm. Indeed, some of the most exciting new approaches to the study of urban poverty have theorized welfare-state restructuring in connection with larger questions about the restructuring of race, class, and gender relations in the United States and in relation to global shifts in economy, politics, and governance.

Taken together, this new anthropological work draws on and contributes to theoretical and empirical projects that are at the heart of contemporary anthropological practice. The topic of welfare "reform" invites attention to poverty and inequality at the center of the global system of advanced capitalism and offers a non-parochial view of the U.S. social formation at the turn of the millennium. This view, in turn, offers insight into the production of global inequalities and the contradictions at the core of "millenial capitalism" (Comaroff & Comaroff 2000).

In a review published just after the advent of welfare "reform," Susser (1996) provided a comprehensive assessment of the anthropological contribution to the study of urban poverty and homelessness in the United States. Our objective here is twofold: to describe some new thematic and theoretical interventions in the field since the publication of her review, and to direct attention to welfare "reform" as a power-inflected site in the production of new forms of urban poverty. Central to our endeavor is an analysis of anthropological approaches to the study of U.S. domestic neoliberalism, including the rise of market-oriented assumptions about social value, productivity, and investment that have come to dominate civic life, social welfare policy, and the elaboration of political identities in the post–welfare state era.

THEORIZING URBAN POVERTY IN THE
POST-WELFARE ERA

Different conceptualizations of welfare's repeal, and welfare-state restructuring more generally, relate directly to frameworks for understanding the production of poverty in U.S. cities. Since 1998, welfare receipt has become increasingly concentrated in urban centers, particularly among people of color (Mink 2002, Neubeck & Cazenave 2001), and much public, political, and academic attention has been directed (whether theoretically justified or not) at the inner-city poor.[1] One way in which anthropology's current research program on the topic of post-welfare urban poverty differs from approaches in other disciplines is its near-uniform rejection of William Julius Wilson's "underclass" concept, which has directed disproportionate attention, beyond any demographic imperative, to the "ghetto-specific" behaviors of the poorest of the black inner-city poor—the so-called "underclass" (1997). This perspective focuses on particular behaviors—out-of-wedlock childbearing, female-headed households, and participation in the informal economy, among other characteristics of urban "dislocation"—that Wilson argues are the result of chronic joblessness and the absence, post–affirmative action, of middle-class role models. Conservative analysts, on the other hand, root these behaviors in a culture of dependency associated with welfare (Murray 1984).

Despite an avalanche of scholarship attacking the "underclass" argument from Marxist, feminist, anti-racist, and other perspectives (see, for example, di Leonardo 1998, Reed 1999, Gregory 1998), the "underclass" paradigm prevails in academic and public discussions of urban poverty, many of which ignore Wilson's call for "structural" solutions (demand-side public employment) but embrace his endorsement of ghetto pathology.[2] Recent ethnographic research instead makes links between the historic shifts in the culture and political economy of cities with new modes of survival, resistance, and politicization among the urban poor and integrates Marxist, feminist, post-structuralist, and critical-race approaches to study power relations, governance, and citizenship, and difference and inequality.

Current perspectives move beyond the 1960s and 1970s view of poor urban neighborhoods as encapsulated worlds, bounded and isolated from history and wider political economic developments, to explain the new urban poverty in terms

---

[1]Despite the importance of urban poverty, relative inattention to effects of welfare restructuring in rural communities, including Indian reservations (Biolosi et al. 2002), reinforces stereotypes that make the white poor invisible and ignores problems of labor markets, local economies, and limited social services in rural areas.

[2]That Wilson's ideas continue to dominate poverty research is exemplified by Small & Newman (2001), a review that gives uncritical analytical preeminence to out-of-wedlock and teen births and the ways inner-city "culture" differs from middle-class "culture" as salient aspects of the new urban poverty. Di Leonardo's insightful critique of Wilson explains that the specter of an urban "underclass" reinforces the middle-class white ethnic gender norms that dominate in U.S. popular culture in recent decades (1998).

of changing urban economics, political and spatial transformations, and demographic shifts (for a review of this literature, see Goode & Maskovsky 2001, Hyatt 1995). Susser (1996) explains new patterns of impoverishment as an outgrowth of a new labor regime imposed as part of the new global economy. For Susser, changing constructions of labor, space, time, and identity have created unprecedented economic polarization and new forms of vulnerability, exploitation, violence, and conflict at the center of the global economy and at the "media-visible periphery," as she calls it (1996). This new labor regime is as political as it is economic. Different constituencies—women, children, the aged, and others—have historically been included in or excluded from the reserve army of labor as a consequence of social movement action, shifts in state regulation, and changes in public service provisioning. This point has particular salience for our discussion here because shifts in welfare policy are implicated precisely in the political processes that are given analytical importance by Susser.

Building on this paradigm, Goode & Maskovsky (2001) analyze the rise of U.S. domestic neoliberalism as an important factor in producing new patterns of inequality and new forms of impoverishment. They use the term post-welfare to denote a period of intensely coordinated activity on the part of the business class, suburbanites, and other elite and middle-class constituencies to dismantle the liberal welfare state in accordance with the new ideological and political economic imperatives of neoliberalism. They argue for a conceptualization of the new poverty as a consequence of the historical conjuncture of economic polarization, political demobilization, and market triumphalism, none of which are unprecedented in U.S. society.

But when put together, at their present level of coordination, they produce a new regime of disappearance, "a mode of governance, economy and politics in which the poor are not so much vilified as they are marginalized or erased by the institutional and ideological aspects of work, social welfare and politics that are dominant under neoliberalism" (Goode & Maskovsky 2001, p. 10). Indeed, the post–cold war rise of neoliberalism, marked as it is by privatization, marketization, and the downsizing of the welfare state, all in the name of the nominal enfranchisement of the poor through the market, is key to understanding the political, economic, and ideological arrangements through which urban poverty is produced and maintained (Kingfisher & Goldsmith 2001, Kingfisher 2002, Hyatt 2001, Lyon-Callo 2001).[3] Maskovsky & Kingfisher (2001) define neoliberalism as a "process, not a thing," opening up lines of inquiry into how it is "retooled in the face of its own contradictions" (Maskovsky & Kingfisher 2001, p. 15). New, theoretically sophisticated ethnographic work focuses on race, poverty, and urban "revitalization" (Williams & Prince 2002); transnational migration, flexible

---

[3]Neoliberalism is, of course, not restricted to the U.S. context and has, for example, been addressed more thoroughly in discussions of structural adjustment in Latin America (Edelman 1999, Gill 2000, Gledhill 1995) and as a global form of governmentality (see Ferguson & Gupta 2002).

labor, and state formation (Zavella 2001, Ong 1996, Kwong 2001, Heyman 1998, Schiller & Fouron 2001); racism, predatory lending, and debt (Williams 2001); and power relations, racial and gender ideologies, resistance, and neighborhood politics (Goode 2001, Gregory 1998, Hartigan 1999, Maskovsky 2001b, Mullings 2001, Sanjek 1998).

Despite the obvious descriptive link between welfare-state restructuring and the production of urban poverty, there has been remarkably little discussion in the anthropological literature of contrasting conceptualizations of welfare and their implications for the theorization of the new urban poverty. In the United States, welfare is typically understood as cash assistance, Aid to Families with Dependent Children (AFDC), now Temporary Assistance to Needy Families (TANF), and most anthropological literature on the topic accords with this narrow conceptualization. But it is possible (and more accurate) to interpret the revocation of AFDC and its reincarnation as TANF as part of a broader historical pattern of welfare-state retrenchment affecting both the social wage [what Katz (2001) calls the private welfare state] and universal entitlements such as Social Security and Unemployment Insurance and other means-tested programs such as Medicaid, Food Stamps, and housing assistance programs. The implications of this broader view can be teased out even further in a brief discussion of the comparative approach to welfare-state restructuring.

The literature on comparative welfare states explores the relative power of actors and constituencies, such as labor and conservative, social democratic, and liberal political parties, in shaping the structures, institutions, and policies of welfare-state regimes. A comparative approach to welfare-state restructuring is important (though space restrictions prevent a detailed review of this literature here) because it takes the discussion of U.S. welfare reform outside the confines of U.S. exceptionalism, where reform inside the U.S. is viewed as wholly disconnected from global shifts in economy and their attendant (geo)political realignments. Comparative work has directed attention mostly to the so-called "West"—the U.S., Canada, and the advanced industrialized countries of Western Europe—and has offered a variety of welfare-state typologies as well as theories for welfare-state transformation (see, for example, Finer 1999, Esping-Anderson 1996, O'Connor et al. 1999). Different conceptualizations prioritize different relationships between the state, civil society, and the market, the precise definitions of which are themselves a topic of considerable controversy and debate (see, for example, Comaroff & Comaroff 1999, Gibson-Graham 1996). Here we discuss four interrelated conceptualizations of welfare-state restructuring that are particularly relevant for understanding the U.S. case.

The classic argument derived from Marxist political economy views welfare as a "floor under wages," a Keynesian welfare-state strategy designed to restructure the reserve army of labor to tighten labor markets and generate higher wages for those who are employed (e.g., Piven 2001). In this formulation, welfare "reform" constitutes a form of class warfare, an assault on working-class wages across the board. In the context of declining profitability, the business class has forced the abandonment of welfare-state policies, conceived since the Great Depression as an effective way of achieving long-term economic growth, avoiding capitalist boom-and-bust business cycles, and managing class antagonism. Instead, the welfare state is downsized to loosen labor markets, and the social wage is attacked in an effort to redistribute wealth in an upward direction. The abrogation of the Fordist social compact and the pursuit of cheap labor across the globe join welfare-state downsizing, supply-side corporate welfare, and welfare-to-work as aspects of the post-Fordist strategy of flexible capital accumulation (Harvey 1989). Policy reforms such as devolution can be explained along similar lines as an effort to obscure the class basis of welfare-state restructuring by decentering the federal government as a political target. Urban poverty, according to this view, is an outgrowth of the new kinds of worker vulnerability that are associated with the imposition of a vast global labor pool. This view has been critiqued and embellished to include more substantive discussions of socially and culturally differentiated labor—of how immigration status and racialized and gendered differences push some populations in or out of the labor force at particular moments, how the power of social movements and various class-inflected constituencies shapes the nature and scope of welfare restructuring, and the extent to which welfare-state restructuring can be analytically subsumed under nation-state restructuring as an aspect of globalization (Susser 1996, Clarke 2001).

A second conceptualization places more emphasis on the mandate for productivity in the new global informational economy. The urban poor—the residual labor force of formerly industrialized cities—have been rendered irrelevant, and their labor superfluous, in the new global economy. According to Castells (2002 [1989]), the logic of informationalism, where new technologies and knowledge form the basis of the new economy and society, has new implications for the welfare state. With the need for industrial labor significantly diminished, welfare "reform" functions not so much to suppress wages (though it does that) but to reorient the labor pool toward the more productive dimensions of the new economy. Moreover, it is not that welfare-state expenditures are no longer affordable but that these expenditures do not perform the proper function of the state in accordance with the logic of informationalism (see, for example, Susser 1997). Devolution and other strategies that augment federal bureaucratic control over the welfare state can similarly be interpreted as new organizational forms that are designed to accord with this new "network society." For Castells, the patterns of inclusion and exclusion through which urban poverty is created, and the relation of these patterns to the specifics of welfare-state restructuring, are a matter for empirical investigation.

A third approach draws from post-structuralism to treat welfare as "a set of policies, practices and relations that are central to the management of subject-populations and their conduct" (Clarke 2002, p. 7). Here the emphasis is on the extension of governmentality through the advent of neoliberal forms of subjectification, where political and social domains are "economized" through the elaboration of new, individuated, marketized subjectivities. For example, the market orientation of new policies such as Medicaid managed care requires the reconfiguration of the poor from passive recipients of welfare-state services into self-empowered and self-governing health care consumers (Maskovsky 2000; see also Cruikshank 1999; Goldstein 2001; Hyatt 1997, 2001 for related examples). This perspective focuses less on the coercive modes of regulating the poor through welfare provision (Piven & Cloward 1971) than on the refashioning of the subjectivity of the poor. Along similar lines, the welfare state is reterritorialized or respacialized through devolution, the invocation of community as a site of governance, and other practices that index a rethinking of spatial and scalar hierarchies and containments (Clarke 2002, Ferguson & Gupta 2002). Clarke (2001) cautions against an over-unified view of neoliberalism in which every aspect of social policy is viewed as an expression of this new form of governance. He suggests instead that we treat neoliberalism as a "social-political project that *attempts* to conform the world to its logic" (Clarke 2001, p. 10, emphasis in original). By treating welfare reform as a set of unstable, hybridized governance practices, new areas of ethnographic inquiry are opened.

A fourth perspective places race and gender at the center of analysis of welfare-state restructuring. Feminist perspectives have argued that the welfare state has historically been gendered, treating men as workers, entitled to social insurance, and women as "mothers," entitled to welfare benefits. The two-tiered welfare state devalued women and reinscribed the dominant organization of gender relations (and public/private dichotomies) in the domains of the family, household, and community and in the domain of the workforce (Abramovitz 1996, Orloff 1996, Kingfisher 2002). Similarly, work that has placed race at the center of analysis shows how the persistent pattern of "welfare racism" (Neubeck & Cazenave 2001; see also Buck 1996, Mink 1998) reinforces racial hierarchies and redefines the terms of citizenship to exclude poor families of color from even the meager protections offered by the social safety net (Mullings 1997, Roberts 1997). Taken together this literature directs attention beyond narrowly construed terms of class to look at wider patterns of social reproduction. It details the ways social citizenship—defined here in terms of entitlements to social welfare benefits—has been constituted in racialized and gendered ways. In this formulation, welfare "reform" reinforces—and may even intensify—gender- and race-based inequalities by reforms such as welfare-to-work. Welfare "reform" also indexes a fundamental disregard for non-remunerative forms of work, such as caring for children and families, housework, and community work (Hirschmann & Lierbert 2001, O'Connor et al. 1999). In this view, welfare restructuring is fundamentally about the devaluation of care work (Meyer 2000, O'Connor et al. 1999) and results in an intensification of class- and race-based inequalities among women.

Kingfisher combines elements of each of these conceptualizations in a recent comparative study of five liberal welfare states (2002). Her project directs attention to the relationship between the emergence of neoliberalism and welfare-state restructuring, demonstrating the parallels and points of difference in these states. She argues that different conceptions of possessive individualism are operative in different western welfare states and that these conceptions are gendered in various ways. Her work emphasizes the importance of locating the U.S. case in global perspective, something too rarely done by many other scholars. By drawing comparisons that focus on the scope and scale of different "reforms," and how they are contested, we see how particular constellations of services, programs, and entitlements organized under the rubric of "welfare states" change in articulation with different political projects, such as neoconservatism and the New Right in the U.S. (Goode 2002). Edgar & Russell (1998) place the cultural processes of welfare practice in comparative perspective as well. Moreover, different sets of meanings and different forms of state (and non-state) "welfare" practices also come into view in analyses that go beyond the so-called West, such as those that focus on the neo-Confucian corporatist/family form of welfare in East Asia (Ong 1999, Tang 2000) and those that focus elsewhere (Bibars 2001).

ETHNOGRAPHIES OF WELFARE RESTRUCTURING: BETWEEN A ROCK (POLICY) AND A HARD PLACE (THEORY)

Most anthropological research on welfare conducted in the U.S. in the past decade responds explicitly or implicitly to the assumptions and conclusions that have been framed by narrow public policy debates about urban poverty and welfare (Morgen 2002b, Schram 1995). Ethnographers, claiming access to insight overlooked in the largely quantitative research of policy science, have produced findings to intervene strategically in the policy debate with a variety of objectives: to humanize welfare recipients and to deconstruct, complicate, and contest the ideologically saturated policy discussions of welfare. In this section we examine how these putatively strategic interventions provide new perspectives on welfare-state restructuring as an aspect of the neoliberalization of U.S. urban poverty. We are reading this literature somewhat unconventionally, teasing out insight frequently submerged, rather than overtly articulated, in this scholarship.

The dominant policy narrative argues that welfare "reform" is successful because (*a*) national cash assistance (TANF) caseloads have been halved since 1996; (*b*) roughly two thirds of those who leave welfare are employed when they go off TANF; and (*c*) the national poverty rate has declined modestly (Glazer 2001). Although this narrative acknowledges that many families have experienced material hardship and economic insecurity in the wake of welfare's repeal, this has not undermined the claims of policy success. This narrative performs the important ideological function of harnessing welfare "reform" to the national interest, imagining that the integration of former welfare recipients into the workforce will promote self-sufficiency and material well-being for all. The celebration of reduced TANF rolls reinforces the ideological basis of post-Keynesian supply-side economics that has dominated U.S. domestic economic policy since the late 1970s. Ethnographies of welfare restructuring, despite their multiple theoretical perspectives and varying emphases, contest this mainstream narrative, suggesting it distorts the experiences of the poor and ignores the combination of ideological and political-economic forces that produce poverty. They therefore have the potential to challenge more than just the narrow arena of post-welfare policy but also the major tenets of U.S. domestic neoliberalism.

CONTESTING POLICY SUCCESS BY DOCUMENTING A CRISIS IN SOCIAL REPRODUCTION

Neoliberal welfare restructuring, like structural adjustment programs in developing countries, has exacerbated a crisis in social reproduction for the poor (Abramovitz 2000, Morgen 2002a, Okongwu & Mencher 2000). Neoliberal policies reduce state income maintenance and other means-tested programs that ameliorate the harsh impact of market forces on economically disadvantaged groups, compelling greater reliance on earnings and child support. Not surprising, ethnographers have shown that the effect has been to increase economic insecurity for the poor and to exacerbate the hardship for families left with insufficient resources because private, market-based solutions do not generate adequate resources to meet their basic needs.[4]

In studies of household economics harkening back to the urban ethnographic tradition of the 1960s, researchers have shown that poor families rarely make ends meet by relying either on welfare alone or solely on low wages (Edin & Lein 1997, Scharff 1998). Before and after welfare "reform" poor families packaged income sources, including wages from informal sector work, various forms of public and private assistance, and support from family, friends, and partners, including court-ordered and informal child support (Hartmann & Spalter-Roth 1996, Scott et al. 2003a). The new welfare policies have undermined the strategies many poor families had developed to survive when welfare "work requirements" interfere with informal sector revenue-generating activities and mutual aid of kin (Newman 2001). Changes in eligibility criteria for means-tested programs (especially the exclusion of legal and illegal immigrants), and program rules that allow states to divert, time limit, and sanction welfare recipients, combine to curtail, delay, or discourage public assistance receipt, engendering material hardship and economic insecurity (Acker et al. 2002, Cherlin et al. 2001, Curtis 1999, Dodson 1998).

The most consistent and basic finding of researchers is the failure of low-wage employment as a strategy to escape poverty or attain self-sufficiency. The insufficiency of the wages paid to workers for the jobs that are allegedly leading families to self-sufficiency is a development that is at the center of a mounting

---

[4]The term family is often used without adequate specification. Here, we use the term cautiously, recognizing the extensive ethnographic and historical evidence that poor households are not co-terminus with poor families and that the prevailing assumption of heteronormativity that undergirds most research on welfare ignores the effects of welfare "reform" on sexual minorities (except see Maskovsky 2002).

crisis of social reproduction (Ehrenreich 2001, Lein et al. 2002, Riemer 2001). Anthropologists have produced extensive evidence that most jobs the poor get provide neither living wages nor the health insurance or job stability that are essential for a modicum of economic security (Acker et al. 2002, Davis et al. 2002). Furthermore, anthropologists counter the human capital explanations offered by policy analysts to explain why low-income breadwinners end up in "bad" jobs, documenting job unavailability, especially in inner cities and rural areas, and to explain the continuing impact of racial and gender discrimination on job opportunity (Biolosi et al. 2002, Mullings 2001, Riemer 2001, Weinberg 1998). This work weds empirical findings about jobs, earnings, and unemployment to a theoretically informed appreciation of the impact of global economic restructuring to explain why the rhetoric of employment-based self-sufficiency does not work for those relegated to the low-wage sector of the labor force.

Reading across regional differences compounded by the 50+ variations of welfare programs produced by devolution, ethnographers have depicted the economic consequences behind the well-worn statistical summary of welfare "reform:" that at least one third of families who leave welfare are not employed, and of those who are, over half remain poor and face spells (sometimes extended) of unemployment or underemployment (Glazer 2001). They show the ramified consequences of inadequate incomes are insecurity and hunger, homelessness and inadequate or unstable housing, debt accumulation, and reliance on kin or friends who often can ill afford to help (Acker et al. 2002, Connolly 2000, Hays 2003, Seccombe 1999). Yet the link between the crisis in social reproduction brought on by the imposition of TANF and the wider processes of deindustrialization, gentrification, and private and public disinvestments that have shaped cities over the past two decades has been conspicuously absent in much of the literature on welfare reform (but see, for example, Davis 2001, Mullings & Wali 2001).

DECONSTRUCTING "DEPENDENCY," "SELF-SUFFICIENCY," AND "WORK"

Ethnographers have deconstructed the hegemonic discourse on welfare restructuring, juxtaposing dominant ideologies with the so-called realities of impoverishment. This work explores the centrality of a racialized, demonizing dependency discourse in the assault on welfare (Dill et al. 1999, Fraser & Gordon 1994, Mullings 1997, Naples 1997). Support for public assistance was undermined by political rhetoric defining families on welfare as "undeserving" welfare dependents whose immoral, deviant, dysfunctional lifestyles and family structures lead to intergenerational poverty and an unacceptable tax burden on hard-working middle- and working-class families. Anthropologists have contested the accuracy of this depiction, sometimes depicting poor single mothers as "just like the rest of us" in terms of their values, morals, and dreams (Newman 1999); sometimes humanizing the poor by explaining the economic or social reasons why they are not "just like us" (Hays 2003, Waterston 1999); and, in either case, arguing that the tremendous diversity among poor families belies reductionist causal explanation (Goode 2001, Schneider 2002).

Ethnographers have also challenged the ideological assumptions that define much welfare use as dependency. Edin & Lein (1997) showed that welfare use, rather than being a lifestyle, is for most families a critical resource that supplements low wages or is used between unstable or temporary jobs or when a job cannot be retained because of illness, childcare problems, or other family needs (see also Acker et al. 2002, Dodson et al. 2002, Hays 2003, Scharff 1998, Seccombe 1999). Scholarship such as this reveals the inaccuracy of the invidious distinction between the "working poor" and the "welfare dependent," a distinction that is functionally innocent of the ways that race and gender inflect class relations in contemporary capitalism and that has been retooled, post–welfare reform, around the issue of productivity instead of being based on race, gender, and impoverished status alone (Kingfisher 2002, Maskovsky 2001a, Wacquant 2002). Other ethnographers directly counter and complicate the association of welfare and dependency by showing how poor women use welfare to support themselves while they work toward independence or self-sufficiency through higher education, which they hope will improve their job prospects (Kahn & Polakow 2002), or as a source of income that allows them to leave violent partners (Davis 2001). Welfare policies that make it more difficult for poor women to leave abusive partners (Brush 2001, Scott et al. 2002) or to secure education or training appear to promote dependency on male partners (including abusive men) or on the low-wage jobs to which they are consigned (Susser 1998) instead of promoting (as the rhetoric implies) true self-sufficiency.

Another important critique of dependency discourse emerges from research that theorizes "care work" as socially valuable, but unpaid, labor that constitutes an important activity of single mothers on welfare (Albelda 2002, Meyer 2000). Researchers show that the labor of women caring for infants, other children, and friends and family members with health problems, disabilities, or special needs is a non-commodified form of work (Kingfisher 2001, Little 1999, Oliker 2000). By depicting welfare-reliant mothers as providing essential care for dependents rather than being dependents themselves, this work reveals the limits of privatized, hyper-individualized notions of productivity (Meyer 2000, O'Connor et al. 1999). When welfare rules demand that poor mothers subordinate care work to employment, race and class inequalities are increased as poor women of color, and especially immigrants, are transformed from "undeserving" unpaid givers of care for their families to the primary workers in the low-paid personal services sector of the labor force (Davis 2002, Hondagneu-Sotelo 2001).

BEYOND BEHAVIORISM

At its core, welfare restructuring promotes privatization by shifting the responsibility for many services and functions from the state to the private sector and by emphasizing the ideology of "personal responsibility" (Morgen 2001). This reversal of New Deal policies based on the assumption that the state should play a redistributive role in ameliorating the consequences of capitalism has affected welfare and other social policies (Greenbaum 2002, Horton et al. 2001). Ethnographic research reveals the adverse consequences of privatization and the fallacy of conceiving of the many problems poor families confront as matters of personal, rather than social, responsibility.

For example, ethnographers have shown that in the absence of strong family policies, poor mothers construct fragile, often inadequate, childcare arrangements in order to work. Frequently they must trade quality for affordability and/or flexibility (Hays 2003, Heyman 2000, Scott et al. 2003b, Weigt 2002), and some face insurmountable problems finding care for children who are sick, disabled, or have special needs (Cancian et al. 2000). Similarly, in the absence of national health insurance, because few low-wage employers provide health insurance, and because welfare "reform" has caused a precipitous decline in Medicaid coverage, access to health care has been reduced for millions of poor families (Burton et al. 2003, Schneider 1999a, Seccombe 2002). This serious problem can hardly be resolved through "personal responsibility," and millions of families face a chronic struggle to retain or cope without Medicaid or private insurance. Indeed, researchers have shown that many poor breadwinners are forced to turn down modest pay raises, increases in work hours, or promotions because they would otherwise lose Medicaid but be unable to afford private coverage (Acker et al. 2001). Approaches that examine the intertwined effects of converging or contradictory policies reveal the policy logic of multiple state policies that have fostered a deepening structural inequality in the United States and elsewhere in the past two decades (O'Connor et al. 1999).

Some researchers, adopting an ecological approach, focus on the resources and strategies of organizations that serve poor communities, including state, nonprofit, and private (including faith-based) organizations. Research focused on the investigation of social networks and social capital reveals that welfare policies that ignore or rely solely on social capital-enhancing strategies often do not help families escape poverty and sometimes even fail to address immediate needs because of inadequate organizational resources or narrow missions (Curtis 2001, Schneider 1999b). Ethnographers show further how welfare restructuring undermines the vitality of community organizations that since the 1960s have served as an institutional base for grassroots anti-poverty activism (Curtis 1997, Reisch & Bischoff 2002, Withorn 2002). Jennings documents how welfare policy in Massachusetts impedes the building of social capital and discourages civic participation in black and Latino neighborhoods by altering the goals, activities, and capacity of the community-based organizations in poor communities (2002). Although the process of co-opting poor people's organizations is not new (Morgen & Weigt 2001, Naples 1998), neoliberal welfare policies have particularly insidious effects as organizations are changed in ways that dampen collective action by the poor and that foster individual, entrepreneurial, or apolitical self-help survival strategies (Hyatt 2001, Lyon-Callo 2001). Moreover, local and state political elites often evidence a stunning disregard for the needs of the poor and may, as Stack has shown, interfere with grassroots efforts to attract federal funds for needed programs for organizations in poor communities (1996). Here we see how neoliberal policy shifts have "destroyed" social capital in poor neighborhoods, as Wacquant once put it (Wacquant 2002; see also Lopez & Stack 2002).

THE GOOD, THE BAD, AND THE UGLY: POSITIONALITY AND WELFARE RESTRUCTURING

Ethnographies of the welfare bureaucracy offer insight about policy implementation, including analysis of how organizational cultures mediate the different concerns of welfare managers, workers, and clients (Brodkin 1986, Edgar & Russell 1998). Ethnographers typically explore welfare as a contested site in which different groups accommodate and resist dominant ideologies about poverty, welfare, and politics (Bloom 1999; Horton & Shaw 2002; Kingfisher 1996, 2001; Morgen 2001). This research demonstrates that although hegemonic discourses about welfare and poverty shape the perspectives of all groups, welfare policy makers, managers, workers, and clients construct different meanings and express different perspectives about the practices and policies that constitute welfare "reform" (Churchill 1995, Hays 2003, Little 1999, Morgen 2001, Riemer 2001, Seccombe 1999).

Although it is a mistake to homogenize the views of the poor regarding welfare restructuring, ethnographers have sought to include the "voices of the poor" in policy debates from which they have been largely excluded. This is not to say that the voices of the poor are given epistemological preeminence in this literature; rather, this research emulates the priorities of the welfare rights movement by bringing recipients to the table, so to speak. For example, there is ample documentation that recipients of public assistance are acutely aware of the flaws of welfare, particularly the inadequacy of benefit levels, the stigmatization of welfare, the bureaucratization of need and eligibility, the limits of welfare services, and the failure of programs to help them escape poverty (Hays 2003, Little 1999, Limoncelli 2002, Seccombe 1999, Weigt 2003). These are not the concerns that drove welfare "reform," but their airing is important in policy contexts.

Perspectives that treat welfare bureaucracy as a site of ideological and institutional struggle have shown how worker/client relations are reworked and new hierarchies established in the context of "reform." What is experienced as positive change by welfare workers (e.g., increased discretion in case management) is often experienced by clients as arbitrary or unfair (Morgen 2001). Kingfisher (1996) argues that the conditions of welfare work (including very high caseloads) and neoliberal ideologies about poverty promoted by welfare agencies foster hierarchical, often adversarial, relationships between workers and recipients, undermining potential alliances even though both groups contend with unrealistic agency expectations.

Class analysis is conspicuously absent in much of the literature on welfare. For example, the oft-repeated conclusion that the greatest flaw in the new welfare policies is the focus on caseload rather than poverty reduction (Acker et al. 2002,

Schneider 2002, and many others) is a crucial insight. But if the researcher understands that U.S. urban poverty is produced by the dynamics of class under advanced capitalism, combined with the politics of neoliberalism and the mutual constitution of gender, race, and class relations, the strategic intervention of refocusing on poverty reduction may be simply a retreat to welfare statism without an overall analysis of the political economic developments that have brought about its demise in the first place. This leaves the theoretically engaged researcher caught between a rock (policy) and a hard place (theory).

NEOLIBERAL CITIZENSHIP: COERCION, CONSENT, AND ENTITLEMENT IN WELFARE-STATE RESTRUCTURING

Welfare reform claims to empower the poor by bringing them into the mainstream of society, i.e., the workforce. But many of those affected by welfare "reform" experience quite the opposite: intensified surveillance, punishment, and ultimately the abrogation of their citizenship rights. Ethnographers have explored multiple facets of the relationship between citizenship and welfare restructuring: the erosion of citizenship rights for poor women through the abridgement of choice about key decisions; the construction of legal citizenship as a thicker border around the welfare state; and a changing balance between consent and coercion in welfare practice that affects the rights, responsibilities, and entitlements of citizenship. At its core, this work theorizes citizenship in terms of the material and ideological aspects of race, class, and gender. From this perspective, welfare-state restructuring can be seen as an important moment in the reshaping of social citizenship through the reconfiguration of state, market, and family relations. Welfare "reform" casts out a significant number of poor women from neoliberal citizenship, now defined in terms of independence (from dependency) and self-sufficiency through labor-force attachment and productivity. Kingfisher argues that neoliberalism "degenders" women by defining them primarily as productive citizens (i.e., workers), disarticulating their identities as mothers and caregivers from their identities as citizens (Kingfisher 2002; see also Henrici 2002). The entitlement to social provision that depended on a conceptualization of mothers as "deserving," if only to enable the care of their children, has been eliminated.

Along similar lines, Roberts (1997, 2002) and Mink (1998, 1999) theorize welfare restructuring as an attack on the citizenship rights of poor women, especially women of color. Full citizenship has historically been categorical, not universal, accorded to different social groups at different times, often in accordance with the victories of popular movements for civil rights. Welfare restructuring imperils those gains, repositioning poor single mothers as sub-citizens with reduced rights and heavy state-enforced social restrictions and penalties to which other women are not subject (Mink 1998, 1999). By tracing how policies such as the family cap deny additional dollars in a family's welfare grant for children born while the mother is on welfare, Roberts links welfare restructuring to the diminished reproductive freedom of women of color, an effect produced by other policies intended to curb childbearing (Roberts 1997) and policies that disproportionately remove poor children from their mothers (Roberts 2002). Race, class, and gender come together in the cultural image of the "bad" mother (Connolly 2000, Roberts 2002) whose poverty or noncompliance with welfare policy can be defined by social service personnel as a sign of neglect.

But even "good" mothering does not constitute deservingness in accordance with the work imperatives of the neoliberal welfare regime. Beyond the extensive ethnographic research that shows how welfare restructuring intensifies the difficulties poor, single mothers face balancing the competing demands of employment, children, and other household responsibilities (Dodson et al. 2002, Goode 2002, Hays 2003, Limoncelli 2002, London et al. 2001, Weigt 2002), their lack of choice and subjugation to intense surveillance and punishment reveals the erosion of basic citizenship rights.

Given the disproportionate poverty of women of color and continuing racial discrimination in the labor force (Browne 1999, Burnham 2002, Mullings 1997), women of color are hardest hit by the new, more-punishing, welfare-state policies. Empirical research showing how communities of color have been disproportionately and most negatively affected by the new welfare policies calls for an analysis of "welfare racism" (Neubeck & Cazenave 2001). States with a higher concentration of people of color on their welfare caseloads tend to have the harshest state welfare policies, including the family cap, punitive sanctions for failure to comply with work requirements, and shorter time limits for receipt of cash assistance (Soss 2001). Researchers have shown that women of color are more likely than their white counterparts to be required to perform "workfare"; less likely to receive job training; more likely to encounter negative attitudes, insults, and disrespect from welfare caseworkers; less likely to be referred to services for domestic violence; and more likely to have been sanctioned (Davis 2001, Gooden 1998, Gordon 2001, Weinberg 1998).

One of the important findings in the burgeoning field of border studies has been the connection between welfare restructuring and anti-immigrant racial politics. This literature has demonstrated a parallel rhetoric of "personal responsibility" in two major pieces of legislation passed in 1996: the Personal Responsibility and Work Opportunity Reconciliation Act and the Illegal Immigrant Reform and Immigrant Responsibility Act. Researchers conceive of the combined effects of welfare and immigration policies as creating a new border around the welfare state based on legal citizenship status rather than family need or residence (Fujiwara 1999, Stephen 2001). For their part, ethnographers have documented the adverse effects of denying public assistance to legal and illegal immigrants, who, overwhelmingly, are people of color (Becker & Beyene 2000, Ng 2002). But researchers are also quick to point out that immigrant communities have not passively accepted these new borders, mobilizing at the grassroots level to restore some benefits (Fujiwara 1999) and thus contesting their rejection as legitimate claimants on the state.

Welfare-state restructuring can also be conceived as one of a number of sites where the boundary between coercion and consent is being redrawn in the remaking of the neoliberal state. This is evidenced in work that shows how more punitive state policies have been implemented and time limits, diversion programs, and more-punishing sanctions have been enforced (Goode 2002). Those who can take advantage of the "carrots" (work incentives and supports) surely experience welfare restructuring more positively (Hays 2003) than those who confront the overtly coercive face of reform (Davis et al. 2002, Gordon 2001). For many women who cannot work outside the home—because of health problems and disabilities (Skinner et al. 2002), because decent jobs or childcare are unavailable, because they do not want to leave young children or children with special needs, because of domestic violence or other problems—welfare has become more punitive and dehumanizing. Evidence is accumulating that the most disadvantaged TANF recipients (e.g., by race, level of education or work experience, number of young children) are sanctioned more often and more severely than others (Cherlin et al. 2001). Although resistance to dehumanizing, stigmatizing, and patrolling welfare practices is evident (Dodson 1998, Little 1999), the expanded arsenal of regulatory mechanisms rewards accommodation and punishes resistance.

A more "punishing" welfare state is consistent with other policies that regulate and control the poor as economic polarization has intensified. The criminal justice system, including the prison industry, has grown exponentially, whereas social service programs have been slashed, both of these disproportionately affecting poor communities of color (Parenti 1999). The so-called war on drugs replaced the war on poverty in inner-city neighborhoods, leading to high rates of incarceration and slashed community resources. Another way the poor are criminalized is by the frequent reference to welfare fraud ("cheats") by policy makers, a claim that receives media attention at key moments of economic restructuring such as the early 1980s and that is thus central to political efforts designed to undermine public support for welfare and to legitimize heightened surveillance against the poor (Susser & Kreniske 1987). The very low benefits levels for AFDC/TANF and the complexity of welfare rules often do result in intentional and unintentional rule breaking (Edin & Lein 1997). Here, the criminalization of the poor provides the ideological rationale for the more punishing state. Welfare is thus a major site where coercion meets consent. In the aftermath of September 11, 2001, it has become clear that anthropology needs to pay closer attention to the reconfiguration of material domination on the home front. Welfare-state restructuring should be part of this discussion.

CONCLUSION: REFORMING THE POVERTY RESEARCH AGENDA

The Bush administration is poised to enact more restrictive welfare policies, ignoring an extensive body of research documenting adverse effects of welfare restructuring and advocating a policy shift to target poverty, not just caseload, reduction. Clearly, we need, as O'Connor has advocated, a "new poverty knowledge" (2001) that goes beyond behaviorism to address the ideological and political-economic production of poverty. We show how anthropological research on welfare moves beyond the behaviorism so rampant across poverty studies in other disciplines and also beyond the "workism" (Maskovsky 2001a) that has been uncontested in most welfare research. Indeed, the neoliberalization of the welfare state has ensured that employment will be the central focus of post-welfare policies in the immediate future. This is not to say that we think work is unimportant. The anthropological literature tells us otherwise. But it insists that work cannot be understood outside of a broader perspective on social reproduction and the global political-economic processes that produce poverty, racial and gender inequality, and the massive income polarization that has intensified in the past two decades. It is important that anthropology continues to define its research agenda in ways that go beyond the narrow concerns, neoliberal assumptions, and ideological confines of the public-policy debate. This does not mean anthropologists should abandon the policy arena. But given that politics and vested disciplinary and institutional interests are so deeply entrenched, anthropological research on welfare restructuring should also see itself as part of the larger project of deconstructing neoliberalism and contesting its attendant patterns of racial and gender inequality and class polarization.

There are several promising research trends that we believe should continue. First, and at the very least, anthropologists can maintain their policy-relevant stance that welfare and other policies should be reoriented toward the stated goal of eliminating poverty. Second, anthropology can use ethnographic research to show the dynamics of accommodation and resistance to the new post-welfare work regime (Fine & Weis 1998). Sometimes that resistance means noncompliance with regulations and policies the poor find dehumanizing or that stand in the way of what is in the best interest of their families—continuing to go to school when they are supposed to be seeking work, turning down "bad" jobs, finding a way to stay home with infants and children, and other means (Bloom 1999, Seccombe 1999). Sometimes it means creating or joining anti-poverty or welfare rights organizations (Abramovitz 2000, Baptist & Bricker-Jenkins 2002, Naples 1998). There is too little research on the everyday resistance or political mobilization of the poor in the face of welfare-state retrenchment or the increasingly punitive state. Finally, anthropologists can identify the limits, instabilities, and contradictions brought on by neoliberalism. Indeed, neoliberal hegemony may not be as totalizing or as triumphant as its proponents claim it to be, as Kingfisher (2002) suggests. In these ways, anthropological work on welfare-state restructuring can be part of a process of envisioning alternatives and can play an important role in calling attention to and linking with the fragile but growing grassroots movements across the world that have begun to challenge neoliberalism and the most egregious forms of inequality that have accompanied its onset.

ACKNOWLEDGMENTS

We wish to thank Barbara Sutton and Seth Long for research assistance, numerous colleagues for bibliographical suggestions, and Ida Susser, John Clarke, Molly Doane, and Catherine Kingfisher for helpful comments on earlier drafts of this article.

The *Annual Review of Anthropology* is online at http://anthro.annualreviews.org

LITERATURE CITED

Abramovitz M. 1996. *Regulating the Lives of Women: Social Welfare Policy from Colonial Times to the Present*. Boston, MA: South End Press

Abramovitz M. 2000. *Under Attack, Fighting Back: Women and Welfare in the United States*. New York: Monthly Review Press

Acker J, Morgen S, Gonzalez L. 2002. *Welfare Restructuring, Work, and Poverty: Policy Implications for Oregon*. Eugene: Univ. Oregon Press

Acker J, Morgen S, Heath T. 2001. *Oregon Families Who Left Temporary Assistance to Needy Families (TANF) or Food Stamps: a Study of Economic and Family Well-Being From 1998–2000*. Salem and Eugene, OR: Adult Fam. Serv. Div./Cent. Stud. Women Soc.

Albelda R. 2002. Fallacies of welfare to work policies. See Albelda & Withorn 2002, pp. 79–94

Albelda R, Withorn A. 2002. *Lost Ground: Welfare Reform, Poverty and Beyond*. Cambridge, MA: South End Press

Baptist W, Bricker-Jenkins M. 2002. A view from the bottom: poor people and their allies respond to welfare reform. See Albeda & Withorn 2002, pp. 195–209

Becker G, Beyene KP. 2000. Health, welfare reform, and narratives of uncertainty among Cambodian refugees. *Cult. Med. Psychiatry* 24(2):139–63

Bibars I. 2001. *Victims and Heroines: Women, Welfare and the Egyptian State*. London: Zed Books

Biolosi T, Cordier R, Douville M, Eagle T, Weil M. 2002. Welfare reform on Rosebud reservation: challenges for tribal policy. *Wicazo Sa Rev.* 17(1):131–58

Bloom RL. 1999. "I'm poor, I'm single, I'm a mom and I deserve respect": advocating in schools as and with single mothers in poverty. *Educational Stud.* 32(3):300–16

Brodkin EZ 1986. *The False Promise of Admin-istrative Reform: Quality Control in Welfare*. Philadelphia, PA: Temple Univ. Press

Browne I. 1999. *Latinas and African American Women at Work*. New York: Sage

Brush L. 2001. Poverty, battering, race and welfare reform: black white differences in women's welfare-to-work transitions. *J. Poverty* 5(1):67–89

Buck PD. 1996. Sacrificing human rights on the altar of "morality": white description, far right and punitive social welfare reform. *Urban Anthropol.* 25(2):195–210

Burnham L. 2002. Welfare reform, family hardship, and women of color. See Albeda & Withorn 2002, pp. 43–56

Burton LM, Tubbs C, Odoms AM, Oh HJ, Mello ZR, Cherlin A. 2003. Welfare reform, poverty, and health: ethnographic perspectives on health status and health insurance coverage in low-income families. *Kaiser Comm. Medicaid and the Uninsured*. http://www.kff.org

Cancian F, Kurz D, London AS, Reverie R, Tuominen M. 2002. *Childcare and Inequality: Rethinking Carework for Children and Youth*. New York: Routledge

Cancian FM, Oliker SJ. 2000. *Caring and Gender*. Thousand Oaks, CA: Pine Forge Press

Castells M. 2002 [1989]. The informational mode of development and the restructuring of capitalism. In *Castells Reader on Cities and Social Theory*, ed. I Susser, pp. 255–84. Malden, MA: Blackwell

Cherlin A, Burton L, Grancis J, Henrici J, Lein L, et al. 2001. *Sanctions and Case Closings for Rules Violations: Who is Affected and Why. Policy Brief 01-1. Welfare, Children and Families: a Three City Study*. Baltimore: John Hopkins Univ.

Churchill N. 1995. Ending welfare as we know it: a case study in urban anthropology and public policy. *Urban Anthropol.* 24(1–2):5–35

Clarke J. 2001. Globalization and welfare

states: some unsettling thoughts. In *Globalization and European Welfare States*, ed. R Sykes, B Palier, P Prior, pp. 19–37. New York: Palgrave

Clarke J. 2002. *Reinventing community? Governing in contested spaces.* Presented at Spacing Social Work—On the Territorialization of the Social Conference, Bielefeld, UK

Comaroff JL, Comaroff J. 1999. *Civil Society and the Political Imagination in Africa.* Chicago: Univ. Chicago Press

Comaroff JL, Comaroff J. 2000. Millennial capitalism: first thoughts in a second coming. *Public Cult.* 12(2):291–343

Connolly DR. 2000. *Homeless Mothers: Face to Face with Women and Poverty.* Minneapolis: Univ. Minn. Press

Cruikshank B. 1999. *The Will to Empower: Democratic Citizens and Other Subjects.* Ithaca, NY: Cornell Univ. Press

Curtis K. 2001. Welfare dependency in Delaware: a study of the state's program reform and advocacy for change. *J. Poverty* 5(2):45–66

Curtis KA. 1997. Urban poverty and the social consequences of privatized food assistance. *J. Urban Aff.* 19(2):207–26

Curtis KA. 1999. 'Bottom up' poverty and welfare policy discourse: ethnography to the rescue? *Urban Anthropol.* 28(2):103–14

Davis DA. 2001. Surviving welfare reform: battered black women's strategies for survival. PhD Diss. Dep. Anthropol., The City Univ. New York

Davis DA. 2002. *The burdens of service: economic restructuring, welfare reform and battered black women.* Presented at Soc. Anthropol. N. Am. Conf., Windsor, Ontario

Davis DA, Aparicio A, Jacobs A, Kochiyama A, Queely A, et al. 2002. *The Impact of Welfare Reform on Two Communities in New York City.* New York: New State Sch. Prac. Team, CUNY Graduate Cent.

Di Leonardo M. 1998. *Exotics at Home: Anthropologies, Others, American Modernity.* Chicago: Univ. Chicago Press

Dill BT, Zinn MB, Patton S. 1999. Race, family values, and welfare reform. In *A New Introduction to Poverty: the Role of Race, Power, and Politics*, ed. L Kushick, J Jennings, pp. 263–83. New York: New York Univ. Press

Dodson L. 1998. *Don't Call Us Out of Name: the Untold Lives of Women and Girls in Poor America.* Boston, MA: Beacon Press

Dodson L, Manuel T, Bravo E. 2002. *Keeping Jobs and Raising Families in Low-Income America: It Just Doesn't Work.* Cambridge, MA: Radcliffe Inst. Adv. Study, Harvard Univ.

Edelman M. 1999. *Peasants Against Globalization: Rural Social Movements in Costa Rica.* Stanford, CA: Stanford Univ. Press

Edgar IR, Russell A. 1998. *The Anthropology of Welfare.* London: Routledge

Edin K, Lein L. 1997. *Making Ends Meet: How Single Mothers Survive Welfare and Low-Wage Work.* New York: Sage

Ehrenreich B. 2001. *Nickel and Dimed: On (Not) Getting By in America.* New York: Metropolitan Books

Esping-Anderson G. 1996. *Welfare States in Transition: National Adaptations to Global Economies.* London: Sage/UNRISD

Ferguson J, Gupta A. 2002. Spatializing states: toward an ethnography of neoliberal governmentality. *Am. Anthropol.* 29(4):981–1002

Fine M, Weis L. 1998. *The Unknown City: the Lives of Poor and Working-Class Young Adults.* Boston, MA: Beacon Press

Finer CJ. 1999. Trends and developments in welfare states. In *Comparative Social Policy: Concepts, Theories and Methods*, ed. J Clasen, pp. 15–33. Oxford, UK: Blackwell

Fraser N, Gordon L. 1994. A genealogy of dependency: tracing a keyword of the U.S. welfare state. *Signs* 19(2):309–36

Fujiwara LH. 1999. Asian immigration communities and the racial politics of welfare reform. In *Whose Welfare?*, ed. G Mink, pp. 100–31. Ithaca, NY: Cornell Univ. Press

Gibson-Graham KT. 1996. *The End of Capitalism (As We Know It).* Oxford, UK: Blackwell

Gill L. 2000. *Teetering on the Rim: Global Restructuring, Daily Life, and the Armed*

Retreat of the Bolivian State. New York: Columbia Univ. Press

Glazer S. 2001. Welfare reform. *The CQ Res.* 11(27):603–24

Gledhill J. 1995. *Neoliberalism, Transnationalization and Rural Poverty: a Case Study of Michoacán Mexico.* Boulder, CO: Westview

Goldstein D. 2001. Microenterprise training programs, neoliberal common sense, and the discourses of self-esteem. See Goode & Maskovsky 2001, pp. 236–72

Goode J. 2001. How ethnography counters myths about the poor. In *Urban Life: Readings in the Anthropology of the City*, ed. G Gmelch, WP Zenner, pp. 279–95. Prospect Heights, IL: Waveland Press

Goode J. 2002. From the New Deal to bad deal: racial and political implications of U.S. welfare reform. See Kingfisher 2002, pp. 65–89

Goode J, Maskovsky J. 2001. *The New Poverty Studies: The Ethnography of Power, Politics, and Impoverished People in the United States.* New York: New York Univ. Press

Gooden ST. 1998. All things not being equal: differences in caseworker support toward black and white welfare clients. *Harvard J. Afr. Am. Public Policy* 4:23–33

Gordon R. 2001. *Cruel and Unusual: How Welfare "Reform" Punishes Poor People of Color.* Oakland, CA: Appl. Res. Cent.

Greenbaum S. 2002. Social capital and deconcentration: theoretical and policy paradoxes of the Hope VI program. *N. Am. Dialogue* 5(1):9–13

Gregory S. 1998. *Black Corona: Race and the Politics of Place in an Urban Community.* Princeton, NJ: Princeton Univ. Press

Hartigan J. 1999. *Racial Situations: Class Predicaments of Whiteness in Detroit.* Princeton, NJ: Princeton Univ. Press

Hartmann H, Spalter-Roth R. 1996. Poverty alleviation and single-mother families. *Natl. Forum* 76(3):24–28

Harvey D. 1989. *The Condition of Postmodernity: an Enquiry into the Origins of Cultural Change.* Oxford: Blackwell

Hays S. 2003. *Flat Broke With Children:* *Women in the Age of Welfare Reform.* Oxford, New York: Oxford Univ. Press

Helco H. 1994. Poverty politics. In *Confronting Poverty: Prescriptions for Change*, ed. SH Danzinger, GD Sandefur, DH Weinberg, pp. 396–437. New York: Sage; Cambridge, MA: Harvard Univ. Press

Henrici J. 2002. U.S. women and poverty. See Morgen 2002a, pp. 27–31

Heyman J. 2000. *The Widening Gap.* New York: Basic Books

Heyman JM. 1998. State effects on labor exploitation: the INS and undocumented immigrants at the Mexico-United States border. *Crit. Anthropol.* 18:155–79

Hirschman NJ, Liebert U. 2001. *Women and Welfare: Theory and Practice in the United States and Europe.* New Brunswick, NJ: Rutgers Univ. Press

Hondagneu-Sotelo P. 2001. *Domestica: Immigrant Workers Cleaning and Caring in the Shadows of Affluence.* Berkeley: Univ. Calif. Press

Horton J, Shaw L. 2002. Opportunity and Control: Living Welfare Reform in Los Angeles County. See Piven et al. 2002, pp. 197–212

Horton S, McCloskey J, Todd C, Henriksen M. 2001. Transforming the safety net: responses to Medicaid managed care in rural and urban New Mexico. *Am. Anthropol.* 103(3):733–46

Hyatt SB. 1995. Poverty and difference: ethnographic representations of "race" and the crisis of "the social." In *Gender and Race Through Education and Political Activism: The Legacy of Sylvia Forman*, ed. D Shenk, pp. 185–206. Arlington, VA: Am. Anthropol. Assoc.

Hyatt SB. 1997. Poverty in a 'post-welfare' landscape: tenant management policies, self-governance and the democratization of knowledge in Great Britain. In *Anthropology of Policy: Critical Perspectives on Governance and Power*, ed. C Shore, S Wright, pp. 217–38. London: Routledge

Hyatt SB. 2001. From citizen to volunteer: neoliberal governance and the erasure of poverty. See Goode & Maskovsky 2001, pp. 201–35

Jennings J. 2002. Welfare reform and neighborhoods: race and civic participation. See Albelda & Withorn 2002, pp. 129–44

Kahn P, Polakow V. 2002. Struggling to live and to learn: single mothers, welfare, policy and post-secondary education in Michigan. See Piven et al. 2002, pp. 157–71

Katz MB. 2001. *The Price of Citizenship: Redefining the American Welfare State*. New York: Holt

Kingfisher C. 2001. Producing disunity: the constraints and incitements of welfare work. See Goode & Maskovsky 2001, pp. 273–92

Kingfisher C. 2002. *Western Welfare Decline: Globalization and Women's Poverty*. Philadelphia: Univ. Penn. Press

Kingfisher C, Goldsmith M. 2001. Reforming women in the United States and Aotearoa/New Zealand: a comparative ethnography of welfare in a global context. *Am. Anthropol.* 103(3):714–32

Kingfisher CP. 1996. *Women in the American Welfare Trap*. Philadelphia: Univ. Penn. Press

Kwong P. 2001. Poverty despite family ties. See Goode & Maskovsky 2001, pp. 57–78

Lein L, Benjamin A, McManus M, Roy K. 2002. Economic roulette: when is a job not a job? Presented at Annu. Meet. Am. Soc. Assoc., Chicago

Limoncelli S. 2002. Some of us are excellent at babies: paid work, mothering, and the construction of need in a welfare-to-work program. See Piven et al. 2002, pp. 81–93

Little DL. 1999. Independent workers, dependable mothers: discourse, resistance, and AFDC workfare programs. *Soc. Polit.* Summer:161–202

London A, Scott E, Edin K, Hunter V. 2001. *Juggling Low Wage Work and Family Life: What Mothers Say about Their Children's Well Being in the Context of Welfare Reform*. New York: Manpower Dev. Res. Corp.

Lopez ML, Stack CB. 2002. Social capital and the culture of power: lessons from the field. In *Building Social Capital to Combat Poverty*, ed. M Warren, P Thompson, S Sagert, pp. 31–59. New York: Sage

Lyon-Callo V. 2001. Homelessness, employment and structural violence. Exploring constraints on collective mobilizations against systemic inequality. See Goode & Maskovsky 2001, pp. 293–320

Maskovsky J. 2000. 'Managing' the poor: neoliberalism, Medicaid HMOs and the triumph of consumerism among the poor. *Med. Anthropol.* (19):121–46

Maskovsky J. 2001a. Afterword: beyond the privatist consensus. See Goode & Maskovsky 2001, pp. 470–82

Maskovsky J. 2001b. The other war at home: the geopolitics of U.S. poverty. *Urban Anthropol. Stud. Cult. Syst. World Econ.* 30 (2–3):215–39

Maskovsky J. 2002. Do we all 'reek' of the commodity?: Consumption and the erasure of poverty in lesbian/gay studies. In *Out in Theory*, ed. E Lewin, W Leap, pp. 264–86. Urbana and Chicago: Univ. Ill. Press

Maskovsky J, Kingfisher C. 2001. Introduction to globalization, neoliberalism and poverty in Mexico and the United States. *Urban Anthropol. Stud. Cult. Syst. World Econ.* 30 (2–3):105–23

Meyer MH. 2000. *Care Work: Gender, Labor and the Welfare State*. New York: Routledge

Mink G. 1998. *Welfare's End*. Ithaca, NY: Cornell Univ. Press

Mink G. 1999. *Whose Welfare?* Ithaca, NY: Cornell Univ. Press

Mink G. 2002. Violating women: rights abuses in the welfare police state. See Albelda & Withorn 2002, pp. 95–112

Morgen S. 2001. The agency of welfare workers: negotiating devolution, privatization and self sufficiency. *Am. Anthropol.* 103(3):747–61

Morgen S. 2002a. *The Impoverishment of Women*. Arlington, VA: Am. Anthropol. Assoc.

Morgen S. 2002b. The politics of welfare and of poverty research. *Anthropol. Q.* 75(4):741–53

Morgen S, Weigt J. 2001. Poor women, fair work, and welfare-to-work that works. See Goode & Maskovsky 2001, pp. 152–78

Mullings L. 1997. *On Our Own Terms: Race, Class and Gender in the Lives of African-American Women*. New York: Routledge

Mullings L. 2001. Households headed by women: the politics of class, race and gender. See Goode & Maskovsky 2001, pp. 37–56

Mullings L, Wali A. 2001. *Stress and Resilience: the Social Context of Reproduction in Central Harlem*. New York: Kluwer Acad./Plenum

Murray C. 1984. *Losing Ground: American Social Policy, 1950–1980*. New York: Basic Books

Naples N. 1997. The 'new consensus on the gendered social contract': the 1987–88 U.S. congressional hearings on welfare reform. *Signs: J. Women Cult. Soc.* 22(4):907–45

Naples NA. 1998. *Grassroots Warriors: Activist Mothering, Community Work, and the War on Poverty*. New York: Routledge

Neubeck KJ, Cazenave NA. 2001. *Welfare Racism: Playing the Race Card Against America's Poor*. New York: Routledge

Newman K. 1999. *No Shame in My Game: the Working Poor in the Inner City*. New York: Knopf/Sage

Newman K. 2001. Hard times on 125th street: Harlem's poor confront welfare reform. *Am. Anthropol.* 103(3):762–78

Ng D. 2002. From war on poverty to war on welfare: the impact of welfare reform on the lives of immigrant women. See Piven et al. 2002, pp. 277–88

O'Connor A. 2001. *Poverty Knowledge: Social Science, Social Policy, and the Poor in Twentieth Century U.S. History*. Princeton, NJ: Princeton Univ. Press

O'Connor JS, Orloff AS, Shaver S. 1999. *States, Markets, Families: Gender, Liberalism and Social Policy in Australia, Canada, Great Britain, and the United States*. Cambridge, UK: Cambridge Univ. Press

Okongwu AF, Mencher JP. 2000. The anthropology of public policy: shifting terrains. *Annu. Rev. Anthropol.* 29:101–24

Oliker SJ. 2000. Examining care at welfare's end. See Meyer 2000, pp. 167–85

Ong A. 1996. Citizenship as subject making: new immigrants negotiate racial and ethic boundaries. *Curr. Anthropol.* 37(5):737–62

Ong A. 1999. *Flexible Citizenship: the Cultural Logics of Transnationality*. Durham, NC: Duke Univ. Press

Orloff A. 1996. Gender in the welfare state. *Annu. Rev. Sociol.* 22:51–78

Parenti C. 1999. *Lockdown America: Police and Prisons in the Age of Crisis*. London: Verso

Piven FF. 2001. Welfare reform and the economic and cultural reconstruction of low wage labor markets. See Goode & Maskovsky 2001, pp. 135–51

Piven FF, Acker J, Hallock M, Morgen S. 2002. *Work, Welfare and Politics: Confronting Poverty in the Wake of Welfare Reform*. Eugene: Univ. Oregon Press

Piven FF, Cloward R. 1971. *Regulating the Poor: the Functions of Public Welfare*. New York: Random House

Reed A. 1999. *Stirrings in the Jug: Black Politics in the Post-Segregation Era*. Minneapolis: Univ. Minn. Press

Reisch M, Bischoff U. 2002. Welfare reform strategies and community-based organizations: the impact on family well-being in an urban neighborhood. See Piven et al. 2002, pp. 333–46

Riemer FJ. 2001. *Working at the Margins: Moving Off Welfare in America*. New York: State Univ. N.Y. Press

Roberts D. 1997. *Killing the Black Body: Race Reproduction and the Meaning of Liberty*. New York: Pantheon Books

Roberts D. 2002. *Shattered Bonds: the Color of Child Welfare*. New York: Basic Civitas Books

Sanjek R. 1998. *The Future of Us All: Race and Neighborhood Politics in New York City*. Ithaca, NY: Cornell Univ. Press

Scharff JW. 1998. *King Kong on 4th Street: Families and the Violence of Poverty on the Lower East Side*. Boulder, CO: Westview Press

Schiller NG, Fouron G. 2001. *Woke Up Laughing: Long-Distance Nationalism and the*

Search for Home. Durham, NC: Duke Univ. Press

Schneider JA. 1999a. And how are we supposed to pay for our health care? Views of the poor and the near poor on welfare reform. *Am. Anthropol.* 101(4):761–82

Schneider JA. 1999b. The dialectic between research and practice: learning from welfare reform. *Res. Polit. Soc.* 7:135–59

Schneider JA. 2002. *TANF Reauthorization Policy Suggestions: Committee on Public Policy. Am. Anthropol. Assoc.* http://www.aaanet.org/committees/ppc/tanf

Schram SF. 1995. *Words of Welfare: the Poverty of Social Science and the Social Science of Poverty.* Minneapolis: Univ. Minn. Press

Scott E, Edin K, London AS, Kissane RJ. 2003a. Unstable work, unstable income: implications for family well-being in the era of time-limited welfare. *J. Poverty.* In press

Scott E, Hurst A, London A. 2003b. *Out of Their Hands: Patching Together Care for Children when Parents Move from Welfare to Work.* New York: Manpower Demonstr. Res. Corp.

Scott E, London AS, Myers N. 2002. Dangerous dependencies: the intersection of welfare reform and domestic violence. *Gender Soc.* 16(6):878–97

Seccombe K. 1999. *So You Think I Drive a Cadillac: Welfare Recipients' Perspectives on the System and Its Reform.* Needham Heights, MA: Allyn and Bacon

Seccombe K. 2002. Integrating meaningful health and welfare reforms. See Piven et al. 2002, pp. 289–99

Skinner D, Slattery E, Lachicotte W, Cherlin A, Burton L. 2002. *Disability, Health Coverage and Welfare Reform.* Kaiser Comm. Medicaid and the Uninsured, Washington, DC

Small ML, Newman K. 2001. Urban poverty after the truly disadvantaged: the rediscovery of the family, neighborhood, and culture. *Annu. Rev. Sociol.* 27:23–45

Soss J. 2001. Setting the terms of relief: explaining state policy choices in the devolution revolution. *Am. J. Polit. Sci.* 45(2):378–96

Stack CB. 1996. Holding hands: African

Americans reclaim the rural south. *Dissent* Spring:85–91

Stephen L. 2001. Globalization, the state, and the creation of flexible indigenous workers: Mixtec farmworkers in Oregon. *Urban Anthropol. Stud. Cult. Syst. World Econ.* 30:189–214

Susser I. 1996. The construction of poverty and homelessness in U.S. cities. *Annu. Rev. Anthropol.* 25:411–35

Susser I. 1997. Flexible woman: regendering labor in the informational society. *Crit. Anthropol.* 17(4):389–402

Susser I. 1998. Inequality, violence and gender relations in a global city: New York, 1986–1996. *Identities* 5(2):219–47

Susser I, Kreniske J. 1987. The welfare trap. In *Cities in the United States,* ed. L Mullings, pp. 51–68. New York: Columbia Univ. Press

Tang KL. 2000. *Social Welfare Development in East Asia.* New York: Palgrave

Wacquant L. 2002. Scrutinizing the street: poverty, morality and the pitfalls of urban ethnography. *Am. J. Sociol.* 107(6):1468–503

Waterston A. 1999. *Love, Sorrow and Rage: Destitute Women in a Manhattan Residence.* Philadelphia, PA: Temple Univ. Press

Weigt J. 2003. *The work of mothering: welfare reform and the care work of poor and working class women.* PhD thesis. Univ. Oregon

Weinberg SB. 1998. Mexican-American mothers and the welfare debate: a history of exclusion. *J. Poverty* 2:53–76

Williams B. 2001. What's debt got to do with it? See Goode & Maskovsky 2001, pp. 79–102

Williams B, Prince S. 2002. Urban legends. *Urban Anthropol.* 3(1):1–4

Wilson WJ. 1997. *When Work Disappears: the World of the New Urban Poor.* New York: Vintage Books

Withorn A. 2002. Friends or foes? Non-profits and the puzzle of welfare reform. See Albelda & Withorn 2002, pp. 145–62

Zavella P. 2001. The tables are turned: immigration, poverty, and social conflict in California communities. See Goode & Maskovsky 2001, pp. 103–31

Annu. Rev. Anthropol. 2003. 32:339–61
doi: 10.1146/annurev.anthro.32.061002.093228
Copyright © 2003 by Annual Reviews. All rights reserved
First published online as a Review in Advance on June 4, 2003

HUNTER-GATHERER ARCHAEOLOGY IN SOUTH AMERICA

Vivian Scheinsohn
*Consejo Nacional de Investigaciones Científicas y Técnicas (CONICET)/Instituto
Nacional de Antropología y Pensamiento Latinoamericano (INAPL), 3 de Febrero 1370,
1426 Capital Federal, Buenos Aires, Argentina; email: scheinso@mail.retina.ar*

Key Words Pleistocene, Holocene, Pre-Clovis, adaptive strategies

■ **Abstract** A general overview of hunter-gatherer archaeology in South America is given by recognizing the main problems in a South American context. Environmental framework and Paleoecological changes are summarized. Pleistocene and Holocene archaeology is reviewed in terms of these particularities. With respect to the Pleistocene, I review Pre-Clovis human presence in South America, technological differences between North and South America, variability in South American subsistence strategy, colonization and demographic models, and migratory routes. The Holocene archaeology is divided into Early and Late. For the former, I consider establishment of adaptive strategies (as marine adaptations), new artifact designs, and mortuary behaviors. For the latter, I consider exchange networks, emergence of complex hunter gatherers, mortuary behavior, origins of food production, and the contact with European populations.

INTRODUCTION

South American hunter-gatherer archaeology has been strongly influenced by North American archaeology. Automatic application of North American models in South America and a tendency to overemphasize similitude on both continents were the consequences (see discussions in Anderson & Gilliam 2000; Borrero 1997b, 1999, 2001; Dillehay 2000; Gnecco 1990; Muñoz & Mondini 2002; Pineau et al. 2000; Politis 1999, 2002). In the North American sequence, the first colonizers, "Paleoindian," were big game hunters, and more generalized "Archaic" hunter gatherers followed. I intend to show that the North American Paleoindian and Archaic labels mask the diversity of South American hunter gatherers. Many South American archaeologists have been criticizing this sequence with little impact on their North American counterparts. In addition, most North American archaeologists have discussed South American archaeology as it appears in English-language publications. Because South American archaeologists have investigated much of the record of South American hunter gatherers and most of their papers

0084-6570/03/1021-0339$14.00

are written in Spanish, the North American view is at best partial (Ardila & Politis 1989).

The recognition of these problems has guided me in writing this paper. It would be vain to present a detailed inventory of hunter-gatherer archaeology. Several books deal with this subject (e.g., Dillehay 2000, Fiedel 1992, Sanders & Marino 1970, and Schobinger 1969 among others). Two excellent works also deal with research history, sociopolitical factors, and theoretical frameworks (Politis 2002, Politis & Alberti 1999). I have decided to describe the main trends and subjects that have arisen when discussing hunter-gatherer archaeology in South America. I establish three criteria for review. First, I assess South American particularities (cf. Pineau et al. 2000) in order to evaluate the challenges and opportunities that South America posed to humans. Second, I abandon traditional archaeological periodifications made on the basis of North American archaeology (see Gnecco 2000) and use only a chronological separation between Pleistocene and Holocene. And third, I focus this review on general trends and more recent works.

The New Archaeology has relied heavily on the concept of hunter gatherer. In spite of the current criticisms, some authors still consider the term to be useful (e.g., Dunnell 1994, Kelly 1995). Then, for practical purposes and following Kelly (1995), I consider hunter gatherers to be those groups who procure most of their food from hunting, gathering, and fishing, even while growing some food, trading with agriculturists, or participating in cash economies as complementary activities.

History of Research

Archaeological research in South America began almost contemporaneously with the development of scientific archaeology in the Old World, but only at the middle of the twentieth century was it included as a subject in university studies (Politis 2002). This research has been characterized as empiricist (Politis 2002). The main theoretical frameworks were North American culture history, German *kulturkreise* (Politis 2002), and the French school (López Mazz 1999). Social Archaeology was the only theoretical development originated locally (Arenas & Sanoja 1999, Bate 1977, Lumbreras 1974), which achieved only a limited repercussion. Processualism arrived at the beginning of the 1980s and became especially strong in the Southern Cone. Postprocessualism arrived at the beginning of the 1990s and slowly began to add more proponents. Today, in spite of a still-dominant empiricism, some theoretical variability exists among South American archaeologists, but serious pitfalls also prevented the development of original elaborations. First, publications in South America often take a long time. Some papers are published long after they were written, which renders their content old even before they are read. Second, little information flows between South American researchers. At the present time, some researchers are trying to avert this tendency. Several countries have organized many meetings jointly, and researchers from different countries attend national congresses held in neighboring countries.

THE SOUTH AMERICAN WAY: ENVIRONMENTAL FRAMEWORK

South America (Figure 1) lies mainly in the Southern Hemisphere, stretching from 12° N to 55° S (Morello 1984), and shows high latitudinal variation, going from tropics to subpolar regions. More than half the surface is located between intertropics; its maximum W-E width is located over the Equator (Morello 1984). Its main characteristics are:

1) Three great river basins (Orinoco, Amazonas, and Paraná) covering 10,000,000 km² (Clapperton 1993) presenting then the biggest hyperhumid space in the world, provided by the Orinoco and Amazonas basins (Morello 1984).

2) A large arid and semiarid surface that goes from Caribbean Coast to Caatinga on the NE and the Diagonal Arreica de América del Sur (South American Arid Diagonal) stretching N-S, from the Equator to 54° S (Morello 1984).

3) The Cordillera de Los Andes organizing the South American space. The Andes create, in a short distance, mosaics of different ecosystems at different altitudes (Morello 1984). Also there are other more ancient and lower highlands (Brasilia, Guyana, Tandilia, Ventania, and Southern and Northern Patagonian) with lesser effects on the continent (Clapperton 1993).

4) A great oceanic influence in the Southern Cone: The shape of the continent presents a narrowing. This coincides with the more temperate and colder latitudes, where marine influence is stronger, thus moderating summer and winter extreme temperatures. This results in environments that are less harsh than expected by latitude alone. Thus we can find gradients of increasing oceanity, decreasing interoceanic distances, and a more ecosystemic and morphostructural simplicity in the southern portion (Morello 1984). This explains the lack of subpolar conditions and the current lack of tundra and permafrost in ice-free zones (Morello 1984).

5) Existence of unexpected natural phenomena derived from climatic anomalies (e.g., ENSO; see below) or unpredictable events (e.g., volcanic activity).

Phytogeographically we can define three main zones (Clapperton 1993):

1) East of Andes:

   a) Tropical vegetation: as Caatinga (low arboreal deciduous scrubland, NE of Brazil), Cerrado (savanna grassland and forest, around Amazon rainforest and Brazilian planalto), Transition forests (belt between rainforest and Cerrado), Inundated and Terra rainforest

   b) Subtropical vegetation: palm trees, parkland, and savanna, Pantanal (SW Brazil)

   c) Temperate vegetation: Pampas and Chaco (grasslands and thorn forest)

   d) Patagonian steppe: semidesert with dry resistant grasses and shrubs

Figure 1   Map of South America showing regions mentioned in the text.

2) West of Andes (from North to South):

a) Tropical rainforest in NW coast

b) Tropical desert from South Ecuador to Northern Chile

c) Evergreen broadleaf forest and maquis from Central Chilean Valley to 38°

d) Valdivian rainforest and deciduous forest in Southern Andes

e) Magellanic moorland in Southern Chile

3) Mountain vegetation:

a) Páramo: high-altitude grassland in Northern Andes

b) Puna: high-altitude grassland in Central South Andes

c) Andean and subandean forest belt in Southern Andes

d) Planalto (Brazilian Highlands): Tropical and subtropical forest and grasslands

Paleoecology

During the Pleistocene, South American glaciations were milder and more restricted than in the Northern Hemisphere and occurred only in the Southern Andes (Clapperton 1993).

The Late Glacial Stage began between 19,000 and 14,000 BP and ended between 11,000 and 10,000 BP (Dillehay 2000). Paleoforms suggest that the climate was drier, cooler, and windier than at present. The most important influences attributed to glaciations were:

1) in the Lowlands: There is persuasive evidence of aridity in the Orinoco savannas, western Amazonia, and wide areas of the Chaco-pampas plains. The presence of rainforest in Amazonia during glacial times is still under discussion. Some researchers argued that wet tropical lowlands could be transformed into dry savannas and that the rainforest receded to isolated refugia. Others concluded that, although tropical rainforest underwent change during the glaciations, no data demonstrate aridity. Clapperton (1993) considers both perspectives and proposes a substantial rainforest reduction in transitional zones with preservation of coverage in zones with high precipitation.

2) in the Uplands/Highlands: Glaciations were denoted by geocryogenic, solifluction, and rock-wasting processes. Southern Patagonian Highlands show eolian relic features that suggest dryness, stronger and persistent winds, and less effective evaporation. Permafrost occurred south of 51° S (Clapperton 1993).

3) in the Andean cordillera: Features related to glacial activity and geocryogenic processes exist in periglacial zones. Icefields were created as a result of glaciations.

For the Late Pleistocene, Clapperton (1993) differentiates the following glacial cycles:

1) Early Late-Glacial Interval: Full glacial conditions returned worldwide between 15,000 and 14,000 BP.

2) Termination 1: Temperate conditions existed in southern South America between 14,000 and 12,000 BP.

3) Late-Glacial Interval (12,500–10,000 BP) equivalent to Younger Dryas from NW Europe. Most scientists continue to argue about the existence of this deterioration in South America. There is an extensive debate about the effects on the vegetation. According to Clapperton (1993), if a Late-Glacial cooling occurred in South America, it did not reach more than 2° below current temperatures.

During the Holocene a wide record of fluctuations occurred that should have influenced human populations. A thermally optimum climate is implied at most sites for the Middle Holocene centered around 8500–5500 BP, warmer and drier than at present (Clapperton 1993). Three neoglacier advances have been modeled, following a scheme similar to the one suggested for the Northern Hemisphere, but new research suggests additional events. Re-advances were dated between 4700 and 4200 BP, 2700 and 2000 BP, and the last, known as the Little Ice Age, between 1340 and ca. 1850 AD (see Clapperton 1993, Villalba 1994). In spite of the poor resolution of polinic records (Clapperton 1993), there is a broad agreement from different sources (Rabassa 1987, Villalba 1994) to confirm this model. The effects of the global warming event known as the Medieval Warm Epoch were recognized in South America and dated between 1080 and 1250 AD.

Also, after 5800 BP, with the return to Neoglacial conditions, the phenomenon called El Niño Southern Oscillation (ENSO) was onset first less frequent and weak, then increased in frequency and intensity around 3200–2800 BP (Sandweiss et al. 2001).

LIVING IN THE FRONTLINE: LATE PLEISTOCENE ARCHAEOLOGY

A set of main subjects could be followed in the available literature about this period.

Pre-Clovis Human Presence in South America

Currently, an intense debate exists regarding when and how South America was peopled. Once determined, the evaluation of South America's first settlement would directly impact the evaluation of North America's first settlement, given the current view of America's human peopling that sustains an entry from Beringia, going from North to South. At present, more pre-Clovis sites exist in

South America than in North America, which challenges the view that Clovis was among the first settlers of North America (Clovis First Model). Thus, South American sites that are contemporaneous with or pre-dating Clovis have been subjected to intense scrutiny (Politis 2002). This scrutiny explains the interest and direct participation of some North American researchers in early site research in South America, though from different positions [e.g., Bryan 1973; Bryan & Gruhn 1992; Lynch 1974, 1990a,b; Roosvelt (see Roosvelt et al. 1996), and others]. Because a detailed account of these early sites can be found in Dillehay (2000), I use only two of the best known cases to show different appreciation: Monte Verde and Pedra Furada.

The 12,500 BP component of Monte Verde, situated in Central Chile, represents a forest-adapted economy, based on the collection of plants and hunting. Evidence indicates a low-density colonizing population, adapted to cool temperate wetland and forest environment with a unifacial industry, bipointed projectile points, and bola stones. A wide variety of plants remains and wooden objects were recovered, along with features that were interpreted as tent structures (see Dillehay 1997, among others). After initial rejection followed by a long debate (e.g., Borrero 2001, Politis 2002), archaeologists finally accepted Monte Verde as pre-Clovis. This site also presents a deeper component dated to 33,000 BP, but even Dillehay doubts its anthropogenic nature (Dillehay 2000).

The situation in Pedra Furada, located in NE Brazil, is different and has been severely criticized. The sociopolitical aspects of these critics were detailed in Politis (2002). The fact that artifacts are made from quartzite obtained on a gravel bar situated 100 m above the site is among the more important of the scientific criticism. The chutes from this gravel bar could be seen from either side of the site, which renders it difficult to distinguish geofacts from artifacts (Dillehay 2000, Politis 2002). There is no megafauna or conclusive evidence of human activity at this site before 11,500 BP (Dillehay 2000).

Despite the rejection of other sites (e.g., Alice Boer, Toca da Esperanza), many are now accepted, and a growing record provides firm evidence of pre-Clovis sites. These are very different from what should be expected under the Paleoindian label. Even in Amazonia, where old models assumed that the lack of resources made life difficult for foragers (Politis 2002), early sites are being recovered (Roosvelt et al. 1996). Today, some researchers support the idea that, during the Pleistocene, people created their own patches of resources in order to increase their effectiveness in that environment (Gnecco 2000, Politis 2002).

Technological Differences Between North and South America

UNIFACIALITY AND BIFACIALITY   Traditionally, the absence of bifacial artifacts (Pre-Projectile Point Stage formulated by Krieger, see Gnecco 1990) identified sites as early, but currently strong evidence exists of early bifacial artifacts. Debitage analysis documents the presence of bifacial reduction in southern South

America (Nami 1993) and contemporaneous bifacial and unifacial industries (Dillehay 2000; see Ardila & Politis 1989, Aschero 2000, Borrero 2001), with one predominating over the other according to necessity. The presence of one or the other could be related to site function, transportability (sensu Nelson 1991), and raw material availability (see Kuhn 1994).

PROJECTILE POINTS   Early sites include a variety of projectile points, such as El Jobo, Paiján, triangular, willow, and fishtail points (Gnecco 1990), albeit their sequence is still unclear (Dillehay 2000).

Lanceolate El Jobo points show a limited distribution (northern South America) with the exception of those registered in Monte Verde, Argentinean Northwest, and Northern Chile (Bryan 1999). However, a case of convergence could be argued based on the generality of its design (Borrero 2001).

Fishtail points or *cola de pescado* are stemmed points with an end similar to a fish tail. Between 11,600 and 10,200 BP, they were widespread in South America from Southern Patagonia to the Pampas and Central Chile. They were discovered for the first time in the Cueva Fell site, in the southern tip of the continent, and characterized the first archaeological period termed Bird or Magallanes I (see Aschero 2000, Bryan 1999). Since many of them present fluting, some investigators have linked them with Clovis points (i.e., Morrow & Morrow 1999), regardless of differences in their morphology (Politis 1991) and reduction sequences that suggest separate origins (Nami 1996). Other researchers interpreted the dispersion of fishtail points as the result of functional effectiveness and a shared technology among different highly mobile populations, in which circulation of information played an important role (Aschero 2000, Politis 2000).

Bryan (1999) postulated a model explaining the dispersal of these points. Whereas Clovis projectile points thrived in North America (10,900–11,200 BP) and then spread to the South, fishtail, almost contemporaneously, dispersed to the North from the Magallanes Strait. Both traditions converged in Ecuador and Central America around 9000 BP. In contrast, Dillehay (2000) considers that El Jobo points and unifacial industries were developed between 13,000 and 11,000 BP and that regional cultural variation was in place between 11,000 and 10,500 BP, resulting in the use of fishtail, Restrepo, willowleaf (a kind of projectile point with a willowleaf-like morphology), and triangular projectile points. Politis (1999) has questioned such models considering it risky to propose relationships or connections between different sites based on similar traits of only one class of artifacts. Cultural transmission models could help explain the dispersion of such artifact types, as Cardillo (2002) had proposed to do with lanceolate forms in the Puna.

Variability in Subsistence Strategies

Although guanaco is the main prey species in many contexts, humans were developing several subsistence strategies from the very beginning.

BESIDE THE SEA   Current evidence supports an early exploitation of marine resources on the Pacific Coast (Bryan 1999, Richardson 1998), as shown by Peruvian sites (e.g., Talara, Quebrada Tacahuay, Pampa de los Fósiles, and Quebrada Jaguay). Some sites have evidence of transhumance between the coast and the interior (Richardson 1998). They include a unifacial industry (Amotope), as well as Paiján and fishtail points. Paiján developed as an adaptation to a grassy coastal plain. Lizards, snails, deer, birds, and fish were recorded in these sites, but not marine mammals (Chauchat 1988). In contrast, Southern Peruvian and Northern Chilean sites represent seasonal coastal exploitation. Fish remains suggest net fishing, given the lack of other specialized equipment (Dillehay 2000, Llagostera Martínez 1999).

THE BEAST MUST DIE? MEGAFAUNA ROLE   In spite of the reliable association between artifacts and megafauna at many sites (e.g., Tibitó, Tagua-Tagua, Piedra Museo, Cueva del Medio, Cueva Lago Sofía), the place of these fauna remains in the early hunter-gatherer diet is still unclear. Megafauna presence could merely indicate contemporaneity between humans and large animals (as in Gruta del Indio, Argentina, Aschero 2000), or human bone exploitation (as Borrero 2001 suggested for Monte Verde). In any case, it is not the same kind of exploitation argued for the Clovis case.

In those sites where evidence of consumption is clear, megafauna is an opportunistic resource not highly ranked and may have been obtained by scavenging or hunting (Borrero 2001, Mengoni 1988). For instance early sites in Patagonia with megafauna—Los Toldos Cueva 7 and AEP1 at Piedra Museo are among the best known, the latter presenting the most ancient occupation of Patagonia at almost 13,000 BP (see Miotti et al. 1999)—present those remains in the context of a hunting strategy that preferred camelids (Aschero 2000). Also, some authors explain megafauna extinction through multicausality instead of human pressure alone (Borrero 1984, 1997a; Mengoni 1988; among others). In any case, most agree that hunting was an additional but not definitive factor.

BETWEEN A ROCK AND A HARD PLACE: ALTITUDE ADAPTATION   Highlands occupation appears after 10,500 BP, although Lauricocha, Guitarrero, and Pachamachay have questionable evidence of earlier occupation (Dillehay 2000). In these regions, the physiological adaptation to hypoxia (low oxygen density) was critical and probably took some time (Bonavía & Monge 1999). Aschero (2000) suggests that people in Argentinean and Chilean Puna may have optimized the use of resources from three environments (Puna, quebradas, and valleys), located at different altitudes. Resources from valleys and forests were recorded in various archaeological Puna sites, in spite of the lack of sites in those areas where these resources came from (Aschero 2000). Puna exploration and later colonization are characterized by: (*a*) lack of unifacial or core flake tradition; (*b*) triangular and later willow-shaped projectile points; (*c*) camelid remains dominating the archaeofaunal record but with the important presence of rodents and Cervidae; and (*d*) lack of megafauna consumption (Aschero 2000).

THE SECRET GARDEN: IMPORTANCE OF PLANT RESOURCES   Colombian La Elvira and San Isidro sites (Gnecco 2000) were located in the tropical forest. Gnecco (2000) believes these sites date back to the end of the Pleistocene, and exploitation or perhaps early manipulation of plant resources has been interpreted from evidence of tree clearance and artificial concentration of useful plants in certain areas. Lithic raw material was locally available in all of these early sites. Some Colombian early sites indicate sporadic and specialized use (Tibitó), but others, such as San Isidro, show non-specialized occupations and a wide variety of activities (Gnecco 2000).

Colonization and Demographic Models

Dillehay (2000) developed a model considering different stages of human dispersion, migration, and colonization. At least three different populations may have existed: (*a*) populations equipped with a bifacial stone tool technology adapted to hunting in multiple habitats—their archaeological traces are El Jobo, fishtail, and Paiján projectile points, and they fed on megafauna and camelids; (*b*) populations possessing unifacial and bifacial technologies, adapted to multiple resources in specific habitats—they exploited environmental boundaries such as ecotones; and (*c*) populations with unifacial and curated bifacial technologies, who adapted to one environment and curated technology for specialized tasks with intensively occupied sites.

Borrero (2001) developed expectations for the Patagonian case, though they could be applicable to the entire continent for the same time period. Assuming that all exploring groups need to maintain contact with their groups of origin, he proposed that it takes time to successfully colonize a continent and that some failed attempts must have occurred. Low population density may have resulted from environmental instability in Patagonia in the Late Pleistocene and caused a discontinuous distribution of settlement and artifacts (Borrero 2001).

In sum, population density was probably low in Pleistocene times. Neighbors would have been few or none, but relationships with the original group would need to have been maintained, in order to ensure the group's survival. Therefore, the expected archaeological record should be scattered and hard to locate but should present some common characteristics in distant places.

Migratory Routes: The Southern Highway

Migratory routes may be recognized by knowing site distribution (Dillehay 2000). Bonavia & Monge (1999) proposed an oriental migratory route into Amazonia and another that followed the Cauca and Magdalena river valleys into other Andean valleys and further south. But this model assumes such a pace that the route should have remained as part of an intergenerational memory by oral tradition (Bonavía & Monge 1999, p. 347). Because "first human populations moved along the Pacific and Atlantic coasts" (Dillehay 2000, p. 63), this situation should have determined a genetic isolation that could have caused differences between eastern and western cultures. This isolation ended when the glaciers receded, thus establishing the first horizon trait, namely the fishtail point (see above).

These models are hard to test archaeologically. Factors such as site visibility are not contemplated, and the "routes" are not stated from chronological gradients or technological sequence but by diffusionist mechanisms (Politis 1999). Currently new models, postulated from an ecological perspective (i.e., Anderson & Gilliam 2000, Steele et al. 1998, see below), are testable. Also, instead of considering migratory routes, it would be more fruitful to consider increases in range size predicted by biogeographical models (see Ruggiero et al. 1998), which should result in testable archaeological predictions.

WARMING UP: THE HOLOCENE

Following the Pleistocene patterns, the beginning of the Holocene presents a wide diversity of hunter-gatherer adaptations in South America. After 10,000 BP the archaeological signal becomes so intense that it is difficult to talk about hunter gatherers on a continental scale because of the record richness that is generated. The Pleistocene/Holocene transition should not have made an important impact on human populations because they were in the process of adjusting to new environments (Borrero 2001). In fact, human populations thrived. From the Middle Holocene onward, humans had acquired a certain sedentarism and had developed complex hunter-gatherer societies (see below), had given place to a new way of life based on food production and, finally, had developed chiefdoms and states. This process changed the hunter gatherers' social environment. Their neighbors were not solely hunter gatherers anymore. Given this varied social environment, most of this section focuses on two regions where hunter gatherers remained until historic times, notably the Southern Cone and Brazil.

The richness of the archaeological record has resulted in the use of various periodifications, most of them revolving around the term archaic or preceramic and based on regional idiosyncrasies. Industries, traditions, and phases flourished in the literature. Most of them departed from an essentialist and/or cultural-historical perspective. Following Borrero (2001), I divide the Holocene into Early (10,000–5000 BP) and Late (5000 BP to present).

Getting Better: Early Holocene

By 9000 BP, the marked increase in temperature that started the Holocene was clear. This climatic amelioration prompted many researchers to postulate a demographic increase and resource exploitation intensification. Thus, a steady proliferation of industries and a faster rate of culture change, along with increases both in size and complexity of settlement growth and overall population levels, took place, especially in the coastal zones and arid grasslands (Dillehay 1993). In Patagonia, this intensification was expressed as changes in mobility, with less extensive circuits that would, in turn, take advantage of strategic sites for guanaco hunting, coupled with the emergence of blade technology, saving raw material and standardizing production (Aschero 2000). We should expect decreasing home ranges as well as founder effects and a high rate of innovation (Borrero 2001).

Although population expansion was taking place in some areas, the increasing temperatures showed different effects in other areas. For example, in the Chilean Puna (Atacama), a *silencio arqueológico* (archaeological silence) (see Nuñez et al. 2002) is postulated. This archaeological silence refers to the lack of human occupation between 8000 and 5500 BP, when aridity increased. Some authors (e.g., Aschero 2000, Nuñez et al. 1999) maintain that this *silencio arqueológico* should not be attributed to the abandonment of the region but instead to a retreat to strategic sites with concentrated resources. Seasonal programming, transhumant mobility with complementary resource use between high and low areas, information flow in wide ranges, and symbolic systems followed (Aschero 2000, Nuñez et al. 2002).

At a continental level, the most outstanding characteristics of this period are:

1) Establishment of adaptive strategies. Certain dominant adaptive strategies began to delineate. The most outstanding are the maritime coastal adaptations and some of them would set the foundations for the ulterior appearance of complexity and sedentarism (see below). Three main areas show this adaptation:

   a) Peru, Ecuador, and Northern Chile: Marine hunter gatherers were established by 9700 BP (see above); they started exploiting deep sea resources, at first with simple hooks made of shell and then with composite hooks (shell and Cactacea thorn), nets, and harpoons. The traditional literature suggests that these resources allowed the development of complexity, as in the Complejo Chinchorro (Northern Chile, see below). The Peruvian Coast shows this adaptation represented in Las Vegas (9700–8000 BP) and Nanchoc, among others (Dillehay 2000).

   b) The Brazilian Atlantic Coast: *Sambaquí* is the term that describes the shell mounds that proliferated here from 6500 BP. People living there were specialized gatherers and fishers (see below).

   c) Southern South America: According to Orquera & Piana (1999, 2000), specialized gatherers and fishers existed from 6000 BP at many sites of the southern tip of Patagonia (Túnel I, Grandi I, Englefield, etc.). Their main staples were pinnipeds, albeit included in shell mounds (Orquera & Piana 2000). A characteristic of this kind of adaptation was the abundance of bone tools (Scheinsohn 1997).

Other hunter gatherers, especially those living in the Andean Highlands and Patagonia, focused on camelids, particularly guanaco (*Lama guanicoe*). Since then, coevolutionary relationships developed between humans and camelids, first as wild prey (guanacos, see L'Heureux 2002) and eventually as domesticated camelids (llama) in the Andean region. The guanaco is one of the biggest herbivores in South America and was commonly available in various environments (Borrero 2001, Muñoz & Mondini 2002). Thus, in some South American sites (e.g., Pampas and Patagonia) faunal diversity decreased, reflecting megafauna extinction and a concomitant increase of guanaco exploitation (i.e., Miotti et al. 1988).

2) A great variety of new artifact designs. In Patagonia, fishtail points were apparently replaced by bola stones, which were found in many grassland sites and even recorded in rock art at Cueva de las Manos. Hunting strategies probably changed (i.e., collective versus individual) and explain the lack of projectile points in open environments, though projectile points should be expected in forested environments (Aschero 2000). Also, on the whole continent plant-processing tools increased in frequency and variety. They are associated with both wild plant exploitation and the development of the first cultigens. For instance, in Central Chile, the lithic polyhedron or indented circular cogged stones are conspicuously as long as *piedras de tacita*, interpreted as mortars (Mostny 1971). Also, in northern South America unifacial technology is associated with plant resource exploitation (Correal Urrego 1990, Uribe 1999). As mentioned for Patagonia, in terms of lithic production, behaviors tending to save and standardize lithic artifacts, such as blade production, also emerged (Borrero 2001). Finally, related to marine adaptations, new bone tools and special techniques adapted to this raw material were developed (Scheinsohn 1997, 2002).

3) Emergence of complex mortuary behavior, in contrast with the scarcity of human burials in Late Pleistocenic times (for an explanation on this last subject, see Barrientos 2002). Climax was reached with artificial mummification in Complejo Chinchorro. This practice started around 7000 BP. Individuals were skinned, butchered, eviscerated, dried, and then reconstructed, stuffed with wool and plant fibers, and modelated with clay forming a complex *fardo funerario* or funerary bundle (Mostny 1971, Llagostera Martínez 1999). These techniques allowed the conservation of bodies, which were accompanied by abundant offerings such as textiles, mats, and feather bundles. *Fardos funerarios* are also recorded in the Puna (Incacueva and Huachichocana) and Northern Argentina (Tarragó 1999), albeit without artificial mummification.

Here, There, and Everywhere: Late Holocene

Increased density of sites and intensification of resource exploitation characterize the Late Holocene period. The increased density is evident, for instance, in Patagonia, where some sites are constantly reoccupied [e.g., Cerro de los Indios I (Aschero 2000)]. Humans were irregularly distributed not only along rivers and lakes but also in lowlands, exploiting the highlands (Borrero 2001) and forests (Bellelli et al. 2000). Few places remained without human populations.

The intensification process was accompanied by the development of sedentarism based in pastoralism and agriculture. One debated issue is why humans in certain places developed agriculture or domestication, whereas in other places they remained as hunter gatherers. Food production arose within a narrow time range in many parts of the world and in different environments. Many have sought to explain this phenomenon (see, among the classics, Binford 1968, Braidwood 1960, Childe 1952, Cohen 1977, Rindos 1980), but there is no single answer. Environmental changes or population pressure are not the only factors. It should be taken into account that the hunter-gatherer intensification affects the impact of the changes in the resource through time on the human population (Winterhalder & Goland 1993). Clearly, in South America, as in other parts of the world, post-Pleistocene environmental changes were influential. For instance, the confluence of humans and animals at certain favorable points [ecorefugia (sensu Nuñez et al. 1999)] during the arid interval, which caused *silencio arqueológico* in the rest of the Puna, could lead to a logistic strategy, which in turn stimulated animal domestication, as was registered in Puripica-1 and other Puna sites (Nuñez et al. 1999, Yacobaccio et al. 1994).

However, environmental factors will not lead all human populations into food production. As mentioned earlier, increasing temperature produced different effects in other areas. Also, the human answer was variable. In any case, domestication started at the beginning of the Holocene and gradually increased but did not initially produce important changes (Politis 2002, see below). Because these developments took place in non-hunter-gatherer societies they are reviewed only in terms of their influence on hunter-gatherer societies, since many of them incorporated some agricultural products. In Figure 2, which corresponds to ca. 1000 BP, the areas with hunter gatherers (<20% food production), mixed hunter gatherers and horticulturists (20%–80% food production), and agriculturalists and pastoralists (>80% food production) are presented (specific zones of complex hunter gatherers are omitted).

Main characteristics for this time period are:

1) Wide exchange networks. A study where obsidian artifacts from Chubut (Patagonia) were chemically analyzed (Stern et al. 2000) established that obsidian was transported from different sources located at moderate distances (200 km); however, at least in the case of one artifact, the source was located 800 km away from the site of discovery. In one burial site from Rawson (Patagonian Atlantic Coast), dating back to the Spanish arrival in this area, a bronze ax similar to those produced in northwestern Argentina was found about 2000 km away (Gómez Otero & Dahinten 1997–1998). Exchange took place between hunter-gatherer populations and their non-hunter-gatherer neighbors. The relationships between them should take the form not only of interchanges but also of oscillations between foraging and production, symbiosis and dependence (Layton 2001), and those options should be explored archaeologically. For instance, the process called *araucanización* (the cultural expansion of Chilean Mapuches over Pampas and Patagonian populations initiated around the sixteenth century), documented ethnohistorically, should express some of those relationships and deserves archaeological treatment (for an example see Berón 1999).

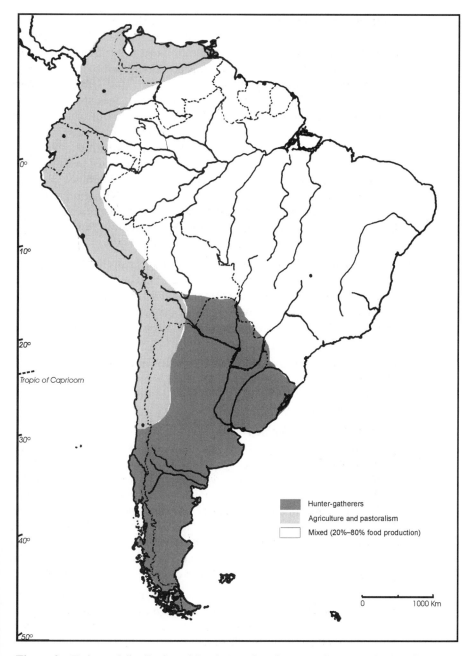

Figure 2   Estimated distribution of South American hunter gatherers, agriculturalists, pastoralists, and horticulturalists in the Late Holocene.

2) Cultural complexity among hunter gatherers became widespread after the Pleistocene (Dillehay 2000). Recent studies suggest the development of complexity with dense settlements and earthworks in Amazonia, Venezuela Llanos, Upper Magdalena River, Sierras de Tairona, and southern *cerritos* [SE Brazil and E Uruguay (Politis 2002)]. Also, after 1000 BP, earthen burial mounds and small hamlets or agricultural villages appeared in the cool temperate rainforests of the Central Chilean region (Dillehay 1993). But this complexity is related to sedentarism (which takes place first in coastal areas) and food production (Politis 2002). In the northern Pacific Coast, Preceramic Ceremonial Centers developed and were related to the climatic change that took place between 8000 and 5000 BP, which resulted in coastal desertification and increasing use of oceanic resources (Richardson 1998). In the Central Andes and toward 3000 BP, the sedentary centers were followed by Chavin, the first Pan-Andean Horizon, Tiawanaku-Wari Horizon (400 AD to 1000 AD), and finally the Inca State (1470 to 1536 AD).

3) In the Brazilian Atlantic Coast, *sambaqui* sites are conspicuous, and in the South they rise up to 30 m. These mounds were built by complex hunter gatherers and date back to between 6000 and 1000 BP. Many were interpreted as burial structures but others were semi- or permanently residential. Larger mounds could indicate the emergence of territorial circumscription (De Blasis et al. 1998).

4) Complex burial practices became widespread. In Patagonia, for instance, *chenques* (i.e., stone mounds marking single or multiple burials) were constructed and cemeteries can even be found (see Berón et al. 2000, Castro & Moreno 2000, Goñi & Barrientos 2000).

5) Food production. In Central Andes, people handled early forms of cultigens at least by 8000 BP. In other areas, early cultigens also appeared in a hunter-gatherer context (e.g., Huachichocana, in Argentinean Puna). By 4500 BP, cultigens were widespread. Camelid domestication took place in Central Andes between 6000 and 5000 BP. Also Puna de Atacama has been proposed as a peripheral center of domestication by 4300 BP (Llagostera Martínez 1999, Nuñez 1982). But even herding control did not imply abandoning hunting. In sites where food was abundant wild camelids were still present during this period. Thus, hunter-gatherer societies did not end; instead forager and production practices complemented each other (Yacobaccio et al. 1994).

6) European contact. European presence affected hunter gatherers in many ways, some of which had an archaeological expression. Before direct domination occurred, European presence was felt as a scarcity of traditional prey [as in the southern tip of South America owing to European whaling and pinniped overexploitation (see Orquera & Piana 1999, 2000)] and the appearance of new prey (European livestock). Originally, Spanish settlers in the Pampas did not thrive and they returned home, abandoning their livestock to become *cimarrón* (wild). By the sixteenth century, wild cattle became so widespread that native populations, and later new Spanish settlers, adopted

them as their main staple, hunting them intensively in what was called *vaquerías*. Between the eighteenth and nineteenth centuries, when this wild cattle population began to dwindle, native populations took their prey from the growing *estancias* (ranches) by means of *malones* [Indian raids (Palermo 2000)]. They kept some and sold the rest in Chile to acquire new products (see below). The archaeological signal of this commercial circuit was found by Goñi (1986–1987) in Malleo River Valley (Northern Patagonia). The evidence consists of a chain of stone constructions, which can be seen one to the next, as geared to territorial surveillance.

Among the European livestock, which was quickly incorporated by native populations (Politis 2000), the horse was critical. What North American anthropologists called the "horse complex" also appeared in South America, owing to the introduction of European habits related to the horse, coupled with the development of new inventions. Goñi (2000) studied the archaeological signal of the horse incorporation. Because horses require special care (constant access to grasslands and water), according to Goñi, human population home ranges increased, but in what Binford (cited in Goñi 2000) has called extensification. This term refers to an intense use of wide home ranges out from more permanent settlements. Thus, while home ranges were widening, a certain degree of sedentarism was developing.

The exchange of foreign goods generated a dependence (among hunter gatherers) on European settlers and promoted changes in local technologies. For instance, in comparing Tierra del Fuego bone tool samples obtained by nineteenth-century travelers and from archaeological excavations, important differences are observed. The nineteenth-century sample presented raw material and design impoverishment. The sample was composed almost exclusively of harpoon heads, which exhibited larger sizes than the archaeological ones. This increase must have negatively affected their effectiveness. Thus, some tools may no longer have served a technological function but instead as a commodity to obtain European goods. The increase in size may have made those harpoons more attractive to European travelers (Scheinsohn 1993).

When Europeans settled, hunter gatherers reacted in different ways. Some in need of the new European goods (weapons, iron, alcohol, etc.) were attracted by these first settlements, and they made long trips to reach them (see Musters 1997). Others, like Fuegian Selk'nam, avoided contact (Borrero 2001). European appropriation saturated the available spaces (sensu Borrero 2001) and, along with the spread of new illnesses, resulted in the disappearance of hunter gatherers. Currently their descendants are trying to recover their ethnic identity. Most are rural wage workers, but some still practice hunting and gathering.

CONCLUSION

South America presents particular characteristics that make difficult the application of concepts and models created for North American archaeology. For instance, South America is a more oceanic continent, presenting more variety of biomes and milder Pleistocene glaciations. It is not that comparisons are useless but rather that cultural sequences may not be the correct basis for them. Archaeological comparison would be more fruitful in areas that were ecologically similar, as for example Great Basin and Patagonia (Morello 1984).

Additionally, new theory is needed. As Politis notes in *South American Archaeology*, "There is a technical and methodological progress unaccompanied by a parallel theoretical development" (Politis 1999, p. 45). South American hunter-gatherer archaeology could and should contribute to hunter-gatherer archaeology in general. In this sense, I wish to mention some interesting results obtained by applying ecological models. Among them, the peopling model put forward by Borrero (Borrero 1989–1990) has been regularly applied in Patagonia (Borrero 1994–1995), and much work has been developed from it. On a continental scale, other interesting proposals based in ecology are those of Steele et al. (1998) and Anderson & Gilliam (2000). In the latter case, the results are of particular interest because the peopling model proposes that the main path into South America leads through the central part of the continent, east of the Andes, a region that has received minimal archaeological attention (Anderson & Gilliam 2000).

However, much ecological and biogeographical work is waiting to be applied. For instance, Ruggiero et al. (1998) have modeled an environmental resistance index (used to infer the effects of physical and biological barriers on the size of the geographical distributions) and an anisotropy index (which quantifies the extent to which the perimeter:area ratios of geographical ranges depart from a circle) for South American mammals. Their results could generate some archaeological expectations for hunter gatherers on a continental scale. For instance, the following could be expected: (*a*) smaller home ranges for human populations in the tropics; (*b*) fewer differences in a N-S direction (especially along the Andes) than E-W; and (*c*) a wider dispersal in environments that have less variation in their environmental resistance index. Thus, dispersal could be modeled in neighboring environments with equal or similar environmental resistance [Steele et al. (1998) had proposed something similar]. These research fields should provide new insight. In spite of the challenges that still remain, a lot of work has been done, elaborated on by many archaeologists for more than a century. New perspectives arising in South American archeology will profit from it, under the insight of more and better theory.

ACKNOWLEDGMENTS

To acknowledge all the people who helped me in this work would be almost impossible, but I would like to express my gratitude to my South American colleagues who informed me about their current research. For brevity's sake, I could not include all the information they shared with me. My apologies for that. I also wish to acknowledge the help of Silvia Chinen in tracking the literature, Mónica Berón for her recommendations, and Luis Borrero for his comments on a previous version of this paper. Thanks also to the anonymous *ARA* reviewer who helped to improve this paper. My appreciation is endless for the hard work of María José

Figuerero and Victoria Horwitz in the translation revision. And thanks to Silvia Gataffoni for the figures. Finally I wish to thank Cristina Bellelli, Rafael Goñi, Daniel Olivera, and the colleagues who integrated the Archaeology and Evolution Group (Alejandro Acosta, Ramiro Barberena, Marcelo Cardillo, Isabel Cruz, Pablo Fernández, Mariana Mondini, Sebastián Muñoz, Hernán Muscio, Virginia Pineau, Atilio Zangrando). Their discussions oriented me on many issues. Part of this work was developed with the help of CONICET and Fundación Antorchas.

The *Annual Review of Anthropology* is online at http://anthro.annualreviews.org

LITERATURE CITED

Anderson DG, Gilliam JC. 2000. Paleoindian colonization of the Americas: implications from an examination of physiography, demography, and artifact distribution. *Am. Antiq.* 65(1):43–66

Ardila G, Politis G. 1989. Nuevos datos para un viejo problema. Investigación y discusión en torno del Poblamiento de América del Sur. *Bol. Museo Oro* 23:2–45

Arenas I, Sanoja M. 1999. Archaeology as a social science: its expression in Latin America. See Politis & Alberti 1999, pp. 59–75

Aschero C. 2000. El poblamiento del territorio. In *Los Pueblos Originarios y la Conquista, Nueva Historia Argentina,* ed. M Tarragó, Tomo I:17–60. Buenos Aires: Sudamericana

Barrientos G. 2002. The archaeological analysis of death-related behaviors from an evolutionary perspective: exploring the bioarchaeological record of early American hunter-gatherers. See Martínez & Lanata 2002, pp. 221–54

Bate LF. 1977. *Arqueología y Materialismo histórico.* México: ed. Cultura Popular

Belardi J, Carballo Marina F, Espinosa S. 2000. *Desde el País de los Gigantes. Perspectivas Arqueológicas en Patagonia.* Río Gallegos: UNPA

Belardi J, Fernández P, Goñi R, Guráieb A, De Nigris M. 1999. *Soplando en el Viento, Actas de las III Jornadas de Arqueología de la Patagonia.* Neuquén: Univ. Nac. Comahue, Inst. Nac. Antropología Pensam. Latinoam.

Bellelli C, Scheinsohn V, Fernández P, Pereyra F, Podestá M, Carballido M. 2000. Arque-

ología de la Comarca Andina del Paralelo 42. Localidad de Cholila. Primeros resultados. See Belardi et al. 2000, pp. 587–602

Berón M. 1999. Contacto, intercambio, relaciones interétnicas e implicancias arqueológicas. See Belardi et al. 1999, pp. 287–302

Berón M, Baffi I, Molinari R, Barrientos G, Aranda C, Luna L. 2000. Estructuras funerarias de momentos tardíos en Pampa-Patagonia. El Chenque de Lihué Calel. See Belardi et al. 2000, pp. 123–40

Binford L. 1968. Post-Pleistocene adaptations. In *New Perspectives in Archaeology,* ed. SR Binford, LR Binford, pp. 313–41. Chicago: Aldine

Bonavia D, Monge C. 1999. El hombre Andino. See Rojas Rabiela & Murra 1999, pp. 343–58

Borrero LA. 1984. Pleistocene extinctions in South America. *Quat. S. Am. Antarct. Penins.* 2:115–215

Borrero LA. 1989–1990. Evolución cultural divergente de la Patagonia Austral. *An. Inst. Patagonia* 19:133–40

Borrero LA. 1994–1995. Arqueología de la Patagonia. *Palimpsesto* 4:9–55

Borrero LA. 1997a. La extinción de la megafauna en la Patagonia. *An. Inst. Patagonia* 25:89–102

Borrero LA. 1997b. *Paleoindians Without Mammoths and Archaeologists Without Projectile Points?: the Archaeology of the First Inhabitants of the Americas.* Presented at Annu. Meet. Soc. Am. Archaeol., 62nd, Nashville, Tenn.

Borrero LA. 1999. The prehistoric exploration and colonization of Fuego-Patagonia. *J. World Prehist.* 13:321–55

Borrero LA. 2001. *El Poblamiento de la Patagonia. Toldos, Milodones y Volcanes.* Buenos Aires: Emecé

Braidwood RJ. 1960. The agricultural revolution. *Sci. Am.* 203:130–41

Bryan A. 1973. Paleoenvironmental and cultural diversity in Late Pleistocene South America. *Quat. Res.* 3(2):237–56

Bryan A. 1999. El Poblamiento originario. See Rojas Rabiela & Murra 1999, pp. 41–68

Bryan A, Gruhn R. 1992. La discusión sobre el Poblamiento Pleistocénico de América del Sur. *Revista Arqueol. Americana* 5:233–41

Cardillo M. 2002. Transmisión cultural y persistencia diferencial de rasgos. Un modelo para el estudio de la variación morfológica de las Puntas de Proyectil Lanceoladas de San Antonio de los Cobres, Provincia de Salta, Argentina. See Martínez & Lanata 2002, pp. 97–120

Castro A, Moreno E. 2000. Noticia sobre enterratorios humanos en la costa norte de Santa Cruz, Patagonia, Argentina. *An. Inst. Patagonia* 28:225–31

Chauchat C. 1988. Early hunter-gatherers on the Peruvian Coast. In *Peruvian Prehistory*, ed. RW Keating, pp. 41–66. Cambridge, UK: Cambridge Univ. Press

Childe VG. 1952. *New Light on the Most Ancient East.* London: Routledge & Kegan Paul

Clapperton CM. 1993. *The Quaternary Geology and Geomorphology of South America.* Amsterdam: Elsevier

Cohen MN. 1977. *The Food Crisis in Prehistory.* New Haven: Yale Univ. Press

Correal Urrego G. 1990. Evidencias culturales durante el Pleistoceno y Holoceno de Colombia. *Revista Arqueol. Americana* 1:69–89

De Blasis P, Fish S, Gaspar M, Fish P. 1998. Some references for the discussion of complexity among the Sambaqui mound-builders from the southern shores of Brazil. *Revista Arqueol. Americana* 15:75–106

Dillehay TD. 1993. Archaeological trends in the southern cone of South America. *J. Archaeol. Res.* 1(3):235–66

Dillehay TD. 1997. *Monte Verde: a Late Pleistocene Settlement in Chile. The Archaeological Context.* Washington, DC: Smithsonian Inst. Press. Vol. II

Dillehay TD. 2000. *The Settlement of the Americas.* New York: Basic Books, Perseus Book Group

Dunnell R. 1994. Why is there a hunter-gatherer archaeology? See Lanata & Borrero 1994, pp. 7–16

Fiedel S. 1992. *Prehistory of the Americas.* Cambridge, UK: Cambridge Univ. Press. 2nd ed.

Gnecco C. 1990. El paradigma Paleoindio en Suramérica. *Revista Antropología Arqueol.* VI(1):37–78

Gnecco C. 2000. *Ocupación Temprana de Bosques Tropicales de Montaña.* Popayán: Editorial Univ. Cauca

Gómez Otero J, Dahinten S. 1997–1998. Costumbres funerarias y esqueletos humanos: variabilidad y poblamiento en la costa nordeste de la Provincia de Chubut (Patagonia Argentina). *Relaciones* XXII–XXIII:101–24

Goñi R. 1986–1987. Arqueología de sitios tardíos en el Valle del río Malleo, Provincia del Neuquén. *Relaciones* XVII(1):37–66

Goñi R. 2000. Arqueología de momentos históricos fuera de los centros de conquista y colonización: un análisis de caso en el sur de la Patagonia. See Beraldi et al. 2000, pp. 283–96

Goñi R, Barrientos G. 2000. Estudio de chenques en el Lago Salitroso, Provincia de Santa Cruz. See Belardi et al. 2000, pp. 141–60

Kelly R. 1995. *The Foraging Spectrum. Diversity in Hunter-Gatherer Lifeways.* Washington, DC: Smithsonian Inst. Press

Kuhn S. 1994. A formal approach to the design and assembly of mobile toolkits. *Am. Antiq.* 59(3):426–42

Lanata JL, Borrero LA. 1994. *Arqueología de Cazadores-Recolectores. Límites, Casos y Aperturas.* Special Issue of *Arqueología Contemporánea* 5. Buenos Aires: PREP

Layton R. 2001. Hunter-gatherers, their neighbours and the nation-state. In *Hunter-Gatherers. An Interdisciplinary Perspective*, ed. C Panter-Brick, R Layton, P Rowley-Conwy, pp. 292–321. Cambridge, UK: Cambridge Univ. Press

L'Heureux G. 2002. *Estudio arqueológico del proceso coevolutivo entre las poblaciones humanas y las poblaciones de guanacos en Magallania (Patagonia Meridional y Norte de Tierra del Fuego)*. Presented at XIV Congreso Nac. Arqueol. Argentina, Rosario

Llagostera Martínez A. 1999. Sociedades del Sur Andino: los desiertos del norte y el centro húmedo. See Rojas Rabiela & Murra 1999, pp. 445–64

López Mazz JM. 1999. Some aspects of the French influence upon Uruguayan and Brazilian archaeology. See Politis & Alberti 1999, pp. 38–58

Lumbreras L. 1974. *La Arqueología Como Ciencia Social*. Lima: Ediciones Histar

Lynch T. 1974. Early man in South America. *Quat. Res.* 4(3):356–77

Lynch T. 1990a. Glacial-age man in South America: a critical review. *Am. Antiq.* 55:12–36

Lynch T. 1990b. El hombre de la edad glacial en Suramérica: una perspectiva Europea. *Revista Arqueol. Americana* 1:141–85

Martínez G, Lanata JL. 2002. *Perspectivas Integradoras Entre Arqueología y Evolución. Teoría, Métodos y Casos de Aplicación*. Serie Teórica, Volumen I. Olavarría: INCUAPA-UNC

Mengoni G. 1988. Extinción, colonización y estrategias adaptativas paleoindias en el extremo austral de Fuego-Patagonia. In *Precirculados de las Ponencias Científicas Presentadas a los Simposios del IX Congreso Nacional de Arqueología Argentina*, pp. 119–29. Buenos Aires: Facultad Filosofía Letras, Inst. Cienc. Antropológicas, Univ. Buenos Aires

Miotti L, Salemme M, Menegaz A. 1988. El manejo de los recursos faunísticos durante el Pleistoceno Final y Holoceno Temprano en Pampa y Patagonia. *Precirculados de las Po-*

nencias *Científicas Presentadas a los Simposios del IX Congreso Nacional de Arqueología Argentina*, pp. 102–18. Buenos Aires: Facultad Filosofía Letras, Inst. Cienc. Antropológicas, Univ. Buenos Aires

Miotti L, Vázquez M, Hermo D. 1999. Piedra Museo, un Yamnagoo pleistocénico de los colonizadores de la meseta de Santa Cruz. El estudio de la arqueofauna. See Belardi et al. 1999, pp. 113–36

Morello J. 1984. *Perfil Ecológico de Sudamérica. Características Estructurales de Sudamérica y su Relación con Espacios Semejantes del Planeta*. Barcelona: ICI–Ed. Cultura Hispánica

Morrow J, Morrow T. 1999. Geographic variation in fluted projectile points: a hemispheric perspective. *Am. Antiq.* 64(2):215–30

Mostny G. 1971. *Prehistoria de Chile*. Santiago: Editorial Universitaria

Muñoz S, Mondini M. 2002. *Long term human/animal interactions and their implications for hunter-gatherer archaeology in South America*. Paper presented at CHAGS 9, Edinburgh

Musters GC. 1997. *Vida Entre los Patagones*. Buenos Aires: El Elefante Blanco

Nami HG. 1993. Observaciones sobre desechos de talla procedentes de las ocupaciones tempranas de Tres Arroyos (Tierra del Fuego, Chile). *An. Inst. Patagonia* 22:175–80

Nami HG. 1996. Investigaciones actualísticas para discutir aspectos técnicos de los cazadores-recolectores del tardiglacial: el problema Clovis-cueva Fell. *An. Inst. Patagonia* 25:151–86

Nelson M. 1991. The study of technological organization. *Archaeol. Method Theory* 3:57–100

Nuñez L. 1982. Asentamientos de cazadores-recolectores tardíos de la Puna de Atacama. *Chungara* 8:137–38

Nuñez L, Grosjean M, Cartajena I. 1999. Un ecorefugio oportunístico en la Puna de Atacama durante eventos áridos del Holoceno Medio. *Estud. Atacameños* 17:125–74

Nuñez L, Grosjean M, Cartajena I. 2002. Human occupations and climate change in the

Puna de Atacama, Chile. *Science* 298:821–24

Orquera LA, Piana EL. 1999. *Arqueología de la Región del Canal Beagle (Tierra del Fuego, República Argentina)*. Buenos Aires: Publ. Soc. Argentina Antropología

Orquera LA, Piana EL. 2000. El extremo austral del continente. In *Nueva Historia de la Nación Argentina*, Tomo I:233–57. Buenos Aires: Academia Nac. Historia-Editorial Planeta

Palermo MA. 2000. A través de la frontera. Economía y sociedad indígenas desde el tiempo colonial hasta el siglo XIX. See Tarragó 2000, pp. 343–82

Pineau V, Zangrando A, Scheinsohn V, Mondini M, Fernández P, et al. 2000. Las particularidades de Sudamérica y sus implicancias para el proceso de dispersión de Homo sapiens. In *Análisis, Interpretación y Gestión en Arqueología*, ed. R Curtoni, ML Endere. Serie teórica, Volumen 2. Olavarría: INCUAPA, UNCPBA

Politis G. 1991. Fishtail projectile points in the southern cone of South America: an overview. In *Clovis. Origins and Adaptations*, ed. R Bonnichsen, KL Turnmire, pp. 287–301. Corvallis: Cent. Stud. First Am., Oregon State Univ.

Politis G. 1999. La estructura del debate sobre el poblamiento de América. *Bol. Arqueol.* 14(2):25–51

Politis G. 2000. Los cazadores de la llanura. See Tarragó 2000, pp. 61–104

Politis G. 2002. South America: in the garden of forking paths. In *Archaeology. The Widening Debate*, ed. B Cunliffe, W Davies, C Renfrew, pp. 193–244. Oxford, UK: Oxford Univ. Press

Politis G, Alberti B. 1999. *Archaeology in Latin America*. London: Routledge

Rabassa J. 1987. The Holocene of Argentina: a review. *Quat. S. Am. Antarct. Penins.* 5:269–90

Richardson J III. 1998. Looking in the right places: pre-5000 BP maritime adaptation in Peru and the changing environment. *Revista Arqueol. Americana* 15:33–56

Rindos D. 1980. Symbiosis, instability and the origins and spread of agriculture: a new model. *Curr. Anthropol.* 21:751–72

Rojas Rabiela T, Murra J. 1999. *Historia General de América Latina*. Paris: Editorial Trotta, Ed. Unesco. Vol. I. 660 pp.

Roosvelt AM, Lima da Costa C, Lopes Machado M, Michab N, Mertier H, et al. 1996. Paleoindian cave dwellers in the Amazon: the peopling of the Americas. *Science* 272:373–84

Ruggiero A, Lawton JH, Blackburn TM. 1998. The geographic ranges of mammalian species in South America: spatial patterns in environmental resistance and anisotropy. *J. Biogeogr.* 25:1093–103

Sanders W, Marino J. 1970. *New World Prehistory: Archaeology of the American Indian*. Englewood Cliffs: Prentice Hall

Sandweiss D, Maasch K, Burger R, Richardson J III, Rollins H, et al. 2001. Variations in Holocene El Niño frequencies: climate records and cultural consequences in ancient Peru. *Geology* 29(7):603–6

Scheinsohn V. 1993. El sistema de producción de los instrumentos óseos y el momento del contacto: un puente sobre aguas turbulentas. *Relaciones* XVIII:121–38

Scheinsohn V. 1997. *Explotación de materias primas óseas en la Isla Grande de Tierra del Fuego*. PhD thesis, Univ. Buenos Aires, Buenos Aires

Scheinsohn V. 2002. Un modelo evolutivo en Argentina. Resultados y perspectivas futuras. See Martínez & Lanata 2002, pp. 187–204

Schobinger J. 1969. *Prehistoria de Suramérica*. Barcelona: Editorial Labor

Steele J, Adams J, Slickin T. 1998. Modelling paleoindian dispersals. *World Archaeol.* 30:286–305

Stern C, Gómez Otero J, Belardi J. 2000. Características químicas, fuentes potenciales y distribución de diferentes tipos de obsidiana en el Norte de la Provincia del Chubut, Patagonia Argentina. *An. Inst. Patagonia* 28:275–90

Tarragó M. 1999. Las sociedades del Sudeste

Andino. See Rojas Rabela & Murra 1999, pp. 465–80

Tarragó M. 2000. *Los Pueblos Originarios y la Conquista, Nueva Historia Argentina*. Tomo I, Buenos Aires: Sudamericana

Uribe MV. 1999. Las sociedades del norte de Los Andes. See Rojas Rabela & Murra 1999, pp. 315–42

Villalba R. 1994. Tree-ring and glacial evidence from the Medieval Warm Epoch and the Lit-

tle Ice Age in Southern South America. *Clim. Change* 26:193–97

Winterhalder B, Goland C. 1993. On population, foraging efficiency and plant domestication. *Curr. Anthropol.* 34:710–15

Yacobaccio H, Elkin D, Olivera D. 1994. El fin de las sociedades Cazadoras? El proceso de domesticación animal en los Andes Centro-Sur. See Lanata & Borrero 1994, pp. 23–32

Annu. Rev. Anthropol. 2003. 32:363–92
doi: 10.1146/annurev.anthro.32.061002.120046
Copyright © 2003 by Annual Reviews. All rights reserved
First published online as a Review in Advance on June 4, 2003

INTERGROUP RELATIONS IN CHIMPANZEES

Michael L. Wilson
The Jane Goodall Institute's Center for Primate Studies, Department of Ecology, Evolution, and Behavior, University of Minnesota, 100 Ecology Building, 1987 Upper Buford Circle, St. Paul, Minnesota 55108; email: wilso198@tc.umn.edu

Richard W. Wrangham
Department of Anthropology, Harvard University, Peabody Museum, 11 Divinity Ave., Cambridge, Massachusetts 02138; email: wrangham@fas.harvard.edu

Key Words   aggression, territoriality, *Pan troglodytes*, warfare, coalitionary killing

■ **Abstract**   In the 1970s, researchers provided the first detailed descriptions of intergroup conflict in chimpanzees. These observations stimulated numerous comparisons between chimpanzee violence and human warfare. Such comparisons have attracted three main objections: (*a*) The data supporting such comparisons are too few, (*b*) intergroup aggression is the result of artificial feeding by observers, and (*c*) chimpanzee data are irrelevant to understanding human warfare. Recent studies provide strong evidence against these criticisms. Data from the five long-term sites with neighboring groups show that intergroup aggression is a pervasive feature of chimpanzee societies, including sites where artificial feeding never took place. Recent studies have clarified questions about the functional goals and proximate mechanisms underlying intergroup aggression. Male chimpanzees compete with males in other groups over territory, food, and females, base their decisions to attack strangers on assessments of numerical strength, and strive for dominance over neighboring groups. Human males likewise compete over territory, food, and females and show a preference for low-risk attacks and intergroup dominance. Chimpanzee studies illustrate the promise of the behavioral biology approach for understanding and addressing the roots of violence in our own species.

INTRODUCTION

A widespread assumption in the 1960s and 1970s was that warfare resulted from features unique to the human lineage, such as weapons or the dense populations created by agriculture (e.g., Lorenz 1966, Montagu 1976). The observation of lethal intergroup attacks in wild chimpanzees challenged this view (Goodall et al. 1979). Numerous comparisons between chimpanzee aggression and human warfare followed these first observations (e.g., Trudeau et al. 1981, Goodall 1986, Ghiglieri 1987, Alexander 1989, van Hooff 1990, Hamburg 1991, Manson & Wrangham 1991, Boehm 1992, van der Dennen 1995, Wrangham & Peterson 1996). Shared traits, such as the cooperation of males to defend group resources and the occurrence of lethal intergroup attacks, suggested that key features of human warfare evolved either in the common ancestor of humans and chimpanzees or independently in the two lineages for similar reasons (Ghiglieri 1989, Manson & Wrangham 1991).

Until recently, however, these comparisons rested on a narrow foundation. Most of the detailed information on intergroup aggression came from two sites in Tanzania, Gombe and Mahale, raising the possibility that patterns of intergroup aggression observed there resulted from some unusual feature of those sites, such as artificial feeding by observers (Power 1991).

In recent years, however, a new generation of studies has advanced our understanding of intergroup relations (reviewed in Wrangham 1999, Boesch & Boesch-Achermann 2000, Mitani et al. 2002). New descriptions of intergroup aggression are emerging from unprovisioned sites, including Taï National Park, Côte d'Ivoire (Boesch & Boesch-Achermann 2000), Kibale National Park, Uganda (Watts & Mitani 2001, Muller 2002), and Budongo Forest Reserve, Uganda (Newton-Fisher 1999). New technologies and methods have enabled researchers to ask new questions and answer previously unanswerable old questions. Entry of data into increasingly powerful computer systems is enabling researchers to examine long-term ranging and grouping data in unprecedented detail (e.g., Williams et al. 2002b). Genetic analysis has enabled researchers to test the proportion of infants born from intergroup mating (Gagneux et al. 1997, Constable et al. 2001, Vigilant et al. 2001). Field experiments have made possible controlled tests of hypotheses that are difficult to test using only observational data (Wilson et al. 2001; I. Herbinger and C. Boesch, submitted manuscript).

In this chapter we review the current information on chimpanzee intergroup relations and discuss how results from recent studies affect prior generalizations. First, we describe the emerging consensus regarding chimpanzee social structure, territory characteristics, and intergroup interactions. Then we examine how recent studies have clarified questions about the functional goals and proximate mechanisms underlying intergroup aggression. Finally, we discuss the relevance of these findings to intergroup aggression in humans.

The comparisons of chimpanzee and human intergroup aggression have attracted three main objections. First, critics claim that the data on intergroup aggression are too few to support claims that chimpanzees are inherently violent (Sussman 1999, Marks 2002). Second, some argue that intergroup aggression results from human influence, especially provisioning chimpanzees with artificial food (Power 1991, Sussman 1999). Third, it has been suggested that chimpanzee violence is irrelevant to understanding human behavior (Sussman 1999, Ferguson 2001, Marks 2002). According to this view, we already know that humans can be violent and that humans can be peaceful as well; what matters for humans are environmental factors such as culture rather than biology.

As we discuss below, recent studies provide strong evidence against these criticisms. First, evidence from classic and more recent studies shows that intergroup aggression, including lethal attacks, is a pervasive feature of chimpanzee societies. Second, the occurrence of intergroup aggression at unprovisioned sites allows us to reject the hypothesis that intergroup aggression and other patterns of social be-havior were the result of provisioning. Instead, chimpanzee intergroup aggression is best explained by principles of behavioral biology that apply to other species such as lions, wolves, and hyenas (e.g., McComb et al. 1994, Mech et al. 1998, Boydston et al. 2001). Third, the argument that, because humans can be both warlike and peaceful, war is not the result of biology or instinct is aimed at an outdated view of biology. Animals, especially large-brained animals such as pri-mates, are no longer viewed as response-stimulus robots but rather as strategic ac-tors who make decisions based on assessments of costs and benefits (Archer 1988, Huntingford & Turner 1987). Recent studies have improved our understanding of the costs and benefits underlying intergroup aggression for chimpanzees. These studies illustrate the promise for obtaining a better understanding of human inter-group aggression using principles generated by behavioral biology.

LONG-TERM STUDY SITES

Chimpanzees have been studied at over forty sites across Africa (Wrangham et al. 1994). Many years are required to fully habituate chimpanzees to the presence of researchers, to learn the identity and group membership of individuals, and to identify patterns of ranging behavior and intergroup interactions. Detailed data on intergroup relations are thus available only from the five long-term study sites with neighboring communities: Gombe, Mahale, Taï, Kibale, and Budongo (Figure 1). [One additional long-term study site, Bossou, Guinea, consists of a single semi-isolated chimpanzee community surrounded by villages (Sugiyama 1989) and therefore is not considered here.] Since 1960, these long-term studies have accumulated over 190 years of demographic and behavioral data from 11 different communities. Researchers at these sites are currently studying nine habituated communities, more than ever before.

In addition to "common" chimpanzees (*Pan troglodytes*), the genus *Pan* includes one other species, bonobos (*Pan paniscus),* which are also (rather misleadingly) called pygmy chimpanzees. Bonobos differ strikingly from chimpanzees in their intergroup relations. Although both species defend group territories (Hohmann et al. 1999, Kano 1992), no indications of attempts to conduct lethal violence have been recorded among bonobos (reviewed in Stanford 1998b, Wrangham 1999). Furthermore, parties from neighboring bonobo communities with friendly relations may intermingle for several hours, during which time members of different com-munities sometimes groom and copulate without aggression (Idani 1991, White 1996). No comparable peaceful associations have been recorded among chim-panzees. Possible reasons for this difference are discussed elsewhere (Wrangham 1986, Wrangham & Peterson 1996). Because comparisons of human and ape in-tergroup aggression have focused on chimpanzees, we focus, in this chapter, on the chimpanzee evidence.

Researchers commonly distinguish three chimpanzee subspecies: eastern (*P. troglodytes schweinfurthii*), central (*P. troglodytes troglodytes*), and western (*P.*

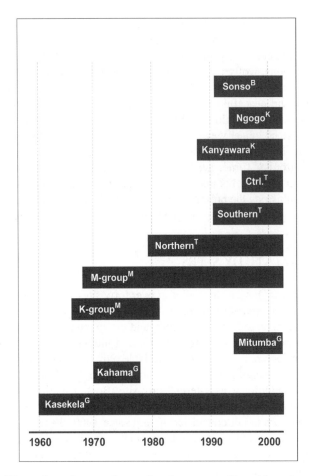

Figure 1 Years of continuous observation for communities at long-term study sites with neighboring communities. Following the community name, a superscript letter indicates whether the community's site is Gombe, Mahale, Taï, Kibale, or Budongo. Start times are approximate and exclude earlier short-term studies; see text for details on duration of habituation and systematic study.

troglodytes verus) (Hill 1969). Apart from Taï chimpanzees, which belong to the western subspecies, the communities with long-term data on intergroup relations are eastern chimpanzees. The subspecies are not very distinct in appearance or behavior (Boesch & Boesch-Achermann 2000, Wrangham 1984). Population differences in behavior appear to depend more on habitat and local traditions than on genetic differences (Boesch & Boesch-Achermann 2000).

The first and longest-running chimpanzee study site is in Gombe National Park, which currently contains three chimpanzee communities: Mitumba, Kasekela, and Kalande. Observers have studied the Kasekela community since 1960 (Goodall

1986). A fourth community (Kahama) separated from Kasekela in the early 1970s and was subsequently exterminated by attacks from Kasekela (Goodall 1986). Efforts to habituate the Mitumba community began in the mid-1980s, with more systematic observations beginning in the mid-1990s [The Jane Goodall Institute's Center for Primate Studies (JGICPS), unpublished data]. Attempts to identify and monitor the Kalande chimpanzees began in 1998 (Greengrass 2000).

A second Tanzanian site, Mahale, has been operating since 1966 (Nishida 1990). Observations initially focused on K-group, which declined in numbers from over 30 individuals in 1974 to effective extinction with the death of the group's last adult male in 1982 (Nishida et al. 1985). Researchers speculated that K-group's decline resulted from attacks by the larger M-group, studied from 1968 to the present (Nishida et al. 1985).

Researchers at both Gombe and Mahale provisioned chimpanzees with cultivated food (mainly bananas and sugarcane) to facilitate habituation and observation. At Gombe, the intensity of provisioning was initially decreased in 1969 (Wrangham 1974) and then halted entirely in 2000 (JGICPS, unpublished data). At Mahale, provisioning was reduced in 1981 and halted in 1987 (Nishida 1990). Due to concerns that provisioning might affect chimpanzee behavior and health, researchers did not provision chimpanzees at sites established in later years (see, for example, Ghiglieri 1984, Boesch & Boesch-Achermann 2000).

Researchers studied chimpanzees without provisioning in Uganda and Côte d'Ivoire. Short-term studies occurred in Uganda as early as 1960. In Budongo, chimpanzees were observed intermittently through the 1960s (Reynolds & Reynolds 1965, Suzuki 1971), with long-term study starting in 1990 (Newton-Fisher 1999). In Kibale, studies have focused on the Ngogo and Kanyawara communities, which are separated from one another by 12 km of forest occupied by unhabituated chimpanzees. Researchers conducted short-term studies at Ngogo from 1976–1978 and in 1981 (Ghiglieri 1984) and at Kanyawara from 1983–1985 (Isabirye-Basuta 1988). Kanyawara has been studied continuously since 1987 (Wrangham et al. 1996). Habituation of Ngogo resumed in 1989, with intensive study continuous since 1995 (Watts & Mitani 2001). The Northern community at Taï has been observed continuously since 1979 (Boesch & Boesch-Achermann 2000). Habituation of Taï's central and southern communities began in 1996 and 1991, respectively (Herbinger et al. 2001; I. Herbinger, personal communication).

SOCIAL ORGANIZATION

Chimpanzees live in groups called communities (van Lawick-Goodall 1968) or unit-groups (Nishida 1968) containing up to at least 150 individuals (Watts et al. 2002). Rather than traveling in a cohesive unit, chimpanzees exhibit fission-fusion grouping patterns. Individuals travel, feed, and sleep in parties containing 1 to 20 or more individuals (Chapman et al. 1994). The entire community rarely or never comes together. Males tend to be more gregarious than females, especially mothers with infants (e.g., Nishida 1968, Wrangham 2000). Mothers spend much of their time alone with their offspring or in nursery parties with other mothers and young (Wrangham & Smuts 1980, Goodall 1986). During the 10 to 15 days preceding ovulation, female chimpanzees experience a conspicuous swelling of the ano-genital skin and an increase in sexual proceptivity (Graham 1981, Tutin & McGinnis 1981). Mothers are more likely to join mixed-sex parties when they have full sexual swellings (e.g., Matsumoto-Oda 1999; Williams et al. 2002a). Females with offspring typically use an individual home range that is smaller than the total range used and defended by males (Wrangham 1979, Chapman & Wrangham 1993, Wilson 2001, Williams et al. 2002b).

Males and females differ strikingly in their residence and dispersal patterns. Female chimpanzees usually emigrate to another community at adolescence, whereas males remain in their natal group (Pusey 1979). Gombe is unusual among chimpanzee sites in that roughly half of all females remain in their natal community (Pusey et al. 1997).

TERRITORY CHARACTERISTICS

The degree to which chimpanzees occupy and defend distinct territories remained unclear for the first decades of chimpanzee field studies. At least one early report from Gombe described chimpanzees as "strongly territorial," but this was entirely guesswork (Thomas 1961). Other early observers assumed that chimpanzees did not defend discrete territories (Reynolds 1966, van Lawick-Goodall 1968) and were "free to come and go as they please without restraint by territorial borders" (Power 1991, p. 62).

Various difficulties inherent in studying chimpanzees contributed to the late understanding of territorial behavior. Even in the richest habitats, chimpanzees live at low densities [1–4 per km^2 (e.g., Table 7.4 in Boesch & Boesch-Achermann 2000, Herbinger et al. 2001)] and occupy large home ranges [of 10–38 km^2 (Herbinger et al. 2001, Wilson et al. 2001)]. Under such circumstances, it is challenging to simply find and follow any chimpanzees. Moreover, individuals frequently join and leave temporary parties, giving early observers the mistaken impression that friendly relations existed among all chimpanzees in the population. In species that live in stable troops, such as baboons, researchers studying a new troop can see and be seen by all the troop's members every time they encounter the troop. In such species, habituation and identification of individuals proceed rapidly, taking perhaps a few months. In contrast, in chimpanzees, observers studying an unhabituated chimpanzee community encounter only a few group members at a time. Without provisioning, fully habituating and learning the identity of all community members—necessary steps to learning group and territory boundaries—can take five years or more (Boesch & Boesch-Achermann 2000). An additional obstacle to understanding territorial behavior is that, during the 1960s, observations at Gombe focused on behavior at the feeding station. Observations of territorial behavior did not occur until researchers began conducting all-day follows of individuals throughout the forest in the 1970s (Goodall 1986).

As habituation improved at Gombe and Mahale, and once researchers began following chimpanzees away from the feeding station at Gombe, researchers found clear evidence for territoriality, including boundary patrolling and hostility to members of neighboring communities (Kawanaka & Nishida 1974, Goodall et al. 1979, Nishida 1979). The striking difference between early and later reports of territorial behavior at Gombe and Mahale suggested to Power (1991) that these reports represented a change in behavior, rather than a changing understanding of existing behavior. Power argued that by provisioning chimpanzees with food, and by limiting access to that food, researchers caused chimpanzee intergroup relations to change from peaceful to hostile. Now that long-term data from several studies of unprovisioned chimpanzees are available, however, it is clear that territorial competition is a pervasive feature of chimpanzee societies, rather than the product of human interference (Wrangham 1999, Boesch & Boesch-Achermann 2000, Watts & Mitani 2001).

Rather than wandering about nomadically, as some early observations suggested, chimpanzees use well-defined home ranges. Barring such disruptions as deforestation or community extinction, a given chimpanzee community can use the same locations for decades. At Gombe, the Kasekela chimpanzees still focus their activities in the valleys they used over 40 years ago, despite variation in the total size of their range (e.g., Williams et al. 2002b).

Recent quantitative analyses of chimpanzee ranging have shown that chimpanzee territories include a heavily used central area surrounded by a less frequently used periphery that may overlap extensively with neighboring territories (Herbinger et al. 2001, Wilson 2001). This pattern of ranging suggests that chimpanzees actively avoid border areas. For example, at Taï, chimpanzees spent 75% of their time in the central 35% of the range (Boesch & Boesch-Achermann 2000, Herbinger et al. 2001). Likewise, at Kanyawara, chimpanzees spent 90% of their time in the central 40% of their total range (Wilson 2001). At Taï, chimpanzees rarely visited border areas even though food was at least as abundant in those regions as in the center of their range (Anderson et al. 2002). Indeed, preliminary evidence suggests that some food items, such as preferred animal prey, may be more abundant in border regions (Stanford 1998a, Wrangham 1999).

Although communities on both sides visit borders infrequently, the risk of encountering neighbors in those regions affects behavior during border visits. Chimpanzees often appear tense or cautious during such visits (Bygott 1979, Boesch & Boesch-Achermann 2000, Watts & Mitani 2001). At Gombe (Bauer 1980) and Kibale (Chapman & Wrangham 1993, Wilson 2001), chimpanzees are more likely to visit borders when in parties with many males. Success during intergroup encounters depends greatly on the number of males on each side (Manson & Wrangham 1991). Chimpanzees thus appear to seek safety in numbers before visiting borders.

INTERGROUP INTERACTIONS

The overall pattern of intergroup interactions is similar across long-term study sites (for detailed accounts, see Boesch & Boesch-Achermann 2000, Chapter 7; Goodall 1986, Chapter 17; Mitani et al. 2002). Hostile intergroup relationships are the norm, in the sense that, in the majority of cases where members of one community detect the presence of neighbors, interactions are immediately aggressive (Boesch & Boesch-Achermann 2000, Wrangham 1999). Within the overall hostile relationship between communities, the nature of a particular interaction depends on the age, sex, and reproductive state of the individuals involved.

Intergroup interactions are most likely to occur during visits to borders. Goodall (1986, p. 489) distinguished two kinds of border visit: patrols and excursions. During patrols, parties consisting mainly of males travel quietly along borders, apparently searching for evidence of neighbors (Bygott 1979, Watts & Mitani 2001). Males on patrol sometimes pause to sniff the ground or listen for distant calls, and they may destroy chimpanzee nests found in border areas (Goodall 1986, p. 490). During excursions, large parties that may include mothers and offspring travel to border areas to feed in particularly rich food patches (Goodall 1986).

Despite the importance of intergroup interactions, both to human observers and to chimpanzees themselves, such interactions occur infrequently. Parties that were followed at least 6 h in a day heard or saw strangers of either sex on 9.5% of follows at Gombe and 11.8% of follows at Taï (Table 7.11 in Boesch & Boesch-Achermann 2000). At Kanyawara, encounters occurred even less frequently [2.8% of days with at least 6 h of observation, January 1998–May 2002 (R.W. Wrangham, unpublished data)]. When chimpanzees do encounter their neighbors, most interactions involve only auditory contact rather than direct visual or physical contact. For example, during a 14-year period at Taï, 70% of intergroup encounters were limited to auditory contact (Table 7.5 in Boesch & Boesch-Achermann 2000).

Auditory encounters typically involve "pant-hoot" calls (Marler 1976), which can be heard for 2 km or more in dense forest (Ghiglieri 1984). Both sexes produce pant-hoots, but males pant-hoot more often than females, with high-ranking males pant-hooting most frequently (Clark 1993, Mitani & Nishida 1993). Most pant-hoots are produced during within-community contexts, such as arrival at fruit trees, during reunions with other community members, and as exchanges between allies that are nearby but out of sight (Mitani & Nishida 1993). The long distance over which pant-hoots are audible enables chimpanzees to advertise their presence and numerical strength to rival communities (Clark 1993, Ghiglieri 1984) and to assess the numerical strength of rivals from a safe distance (Boesch & Boesch-Achermann 2000).

Hearing calls from neighbors usually generates a striking response, including signs of apparent fear and/or excitement, such as open-mouth grinning and bristling of hair, and reassurance gestures, such as embracing and mounting other party members (Goodall et al. 1979, Nishida 1979). They may either listen quietly or respond with a chorus of loud calls. They may retreat, hold their ground, or approach the calls with varying degrees of apparent caution and excitement. Generally, all members of a party show similar responses, but on occasion differences can occur. Males tend to act more boldly than females, but even among males there can be a mixture of reactions (e.g., Goodall 1986, p. 518).

The circumstances vary under which visual and physical encounters occur. Parties may converge by accident, such as at a shared food resource, in which case approaches to as close as <100 m can occur before the chimpanzees realize each other's presence. Such events are rare, however. More often, encounters appear to be intentional, in which members of one party move rapidly and directly toward pant-hoots or other calls made by neighbors. Such approaches can either be silent, resembling a hunt, or vocal (Boesch & Boesch-Achermann 2000, Watts & Mitani 2001).

Males and females differ in their willingness to approach neighbors. Upon hearing strangers, males often approach them with the apparent intention of attacking, as evidenced by stalking and swift silent movements during their approach, followed by directed aggression after they arrive (Goodall 1986, Boesch & Boesch-Achermann 2000). Females are less likely to join patrols, but they do seek out members of other communities during adolescent dispersal (Pusey 1979). Females usually visit a new community only if they have a full sexual swelling, in which case they are more attractive to resident males. Mothers with infants generally avoid encounters with neighboring communities (Goodall 1986). Mothers rarely transfer unless their current community contains few males (Nishida et al. 1985, Williams et al. 2002b). Females are usually intolerant of stranger females and sometimes attack immigrating females (Pusey 1980, Goodall 1986, Nishida 1989). In contrast to other sites, females at Taï often join males during patrols and intergroup encounters, but they rarely take part in direct physical attacks (Boesch & Boesch-Achermann 2000).

The outcome of direct encounters varies according to each side's party composition. Males are least likely to act aggressively if the stranger is an adolescent female with a sexual swelling. Males may groom and mate with such females, although they may attack if the female attempts to run away (Goodall 1986). Males are sometimes tolerant of stranger mothers, especially when they have a sexual swelling. Remarkably, however, males often attack females, and these attacks can involve considerable brutality, especially if the female has young offspring (Goodall 1986; J. Williams and A.E. Pusey, submitted manuscript). At Gombe, males attacked stranger mothers in 76% of encounters (Goodall 1986). In some cases, males focus their attacks on the female's infant, which they may kill and eat (e.g., Bygott 1972, Watts et al. 2002). At other times, however, males appear focused on attacking the mother rather than the infant [e.g., many cases at Taï (Boesch & Boesch-Achermann 2000)]. Attacks on stranger females can result in severe wounds and, in at least one case, death (Goodall 1986).

Males almost always show fear or hostility to stranger males (Goodall 1986, Boesch & Boesch-Achermann 2000, Watts & Mitani 2001). Males sometimes flee from neighboring parties, particularly if they appear outnumbered (Goodall 1986,

Boesch & Boesch-Achermann 2000, Watts & Mitani 2001). Direct intergroup interactions among males include battles and gang attacks (Manson & Wrangham 1991). In battles, both sides contain many males. Both sides may exchange pant-hoots and other loud calls while displaying at and charging their opponents. The outcome is often indecisive, and severe injuries rarely occur, unless males from one side manage to isolate and surround a rival (Goodall 1986, Boesch & Boesch-Achermann 2000). Gang attacks involve many males attacking a lone individual and are the main source of severe injuries, including fatal ones (Manson & Wrangham 1991).

TERRITORIAL GAINS

Intergroup aggression appears to yield territorial benefits. At Mahale, the larger M-group seasonally invaded the range of the smaller K-group to exploit abundant food resources (Nishida 1979). Following the disappearance of the K-group males, K-group's neighbors (B-group to the north and M-group to the south) expanded their ranges, dividing all of K-group's former range between them (Nishida et al. 1985). Likewise, during the years of the attacks on Kahama chimpanzees, the Kasekela community expanded into Kahama's former range (Goodall 1986). Kasekela's gains proved fleeting, however, when the powerful Kalande community to the south expanded northward (Goodall 1986). Kahama had apparently acted as a buffer state between Kasekela and Kalande (Goodall 1986).

LETHAL ATTACKS: ADULTS

Lethal attacks against both infants and weaned individuals have been observed or inferred at both provisioned and unprovisioned sites. Because theoretical considerations suggest different motivations for killing infants and older individuals (e.g., Arcadi & Wrangham 1999, Wrangham 1999), we discuss the age classes separately, starting with older victims. Table 1 lists all cases with either direct observation of intergroup attacks on adults and adolescents that were known or inferred to result in fatalities or compelling evidence of fatal attacks, such as a freshly killed body with wounds consistent of chimpanzee attack (N = 14). Such evidence exists for three sites: Gombe, Mahale, and Kibale. A comparable number of males that disappeared suddenly, without evidence of disease or other factors, are suspected to have died from intergroup aggression. Suspicious disappearances include up to six adult males (and one adolescent) from Mahale (K-group) (Nishida et al. 1985), at least five adult males and four juveniles from Gombe (Kasekela) (Williams et al. 2002b), and five adult males from Kanyawara (R.W. Wrangham, unpublished data).

Until recently, the best-described cases were those that occurred at Gombe in the 1970s. By 1972, the main study community at Gombe had split into two:

TABLE 1   Intercommunity killings of adults and adolescents, 1972–2002

Site	Year	Victim[a]	Aggressors' community	Victim's community	Evidence[b]
Gombe	1972	**Unknown**	Kahama?	Kalande?	Inf.[1]
Gombe	1974	*Godi*	Kasekela	Kahama	Obs.[2]
Gombe	1974	*Dé*	Kasekela	Kahama	Obs.[2]
Gombe	1975	*Goliath*	Kasekela	Kahama	Obs.[2]
Gombe	1975	**Madam Bee**	Kasekela	Kahama	Obs.[2]
Gombe	1977	*Sniff*	Kasekela	Kahama	Obs.[2]
Gombe	1977	*Charlie*	Kasekela	Kahama	Inf.[2]
Gombe	1998	*Unknown*	Kasekela	Kalande	Obs.[5]*
Gombe	2002	*Rusambo*	Kasekela	Mitumba	Inf.[5]
Kibale	1992	*Ruwenzori*	Rurama	Kanyawara	Inf.[3]
Kibale	1998	*Unknown*	Kanyawara	Sebitole	Inf.[3,4]
Kibale	2002	*Unknown*	Ngogo	Unknown	Obs.[6]
Kibale	2002	*Unknown*	Ngogo	Unknown	Obs.[6]
Kibale	2002	*Unknown*	Ngogo	Unknown	Obs.[6]

[a]**Females** in bold, *males* in italics.

[b]Whether the attack was observed directly (Obs.) or inferred from strong evidence such as finding a body with wounds consistent with chimpanzee attack (Inf.).

References: [1]Wrangham (1975); [2]Goodall (1986); [3]Wrangham (1999); [4]Muller (2002); [5]M.L. Wilson, W. Wallauer, and A.E. Pusey, submitted; [6]D.P. Watts and J.C. Mitani, personal communication.

*Attack was observed but whether the victim survived is unknown.

Kasekela in the north and Kahama in the south (Bygott 1979). From 1974 to 1977, Kasekela males brutally attacked at least five and probably six or more Kahama chimpanzees. Observers directly witnessed attacks on five individuals (Godi, Dé, Goliath, Madam Bee, and Sniff). The body of a sixth individual, Charlie, was found after fisherman heard sounds of fighting and saw a large group of habituated males, almost certainly from Kasekela (Goodall 1986). With the death of Sniff in 1977, the Kahama community became extinct, and the surviving females joined neighboring communities. One Kasekela male, Faben, disappeared in 1975 and was suspected have been a victim of intergroup aggression (Goodall 1986, p. 64).

Following Kahama's extinction, intergroup relations remained hostile at Gombe. From 1979 to 1990, four juveniles and four adult males disappeared in the absence of injury or illness (Williams et al. 2002b). In recent years, observers have found direct evidence of additional intergroup killing of weaned individuals. In 1998, observers at Gombe witnessed a brutal and possibly fatal attack on a young male from Kalande (M.L. Wilson, W. Wallauer, and A.E. Pusey, submitted manuscript; for video footage from this attack, follow the Supplemental Material link from the Annual Reviews home page at http://www.annualreviews.org). In 2002, the day after an incursion into Mitumba's range by a large party of Kasekela males, observers found the body of an adolescent Mitumba male, Rusambo, whose numerous wounds included severe bites to the throat and elsewhere, bruises, and a torn-off scrotum and penis (M.L. Wilson, W. Wallauer, and A.E. Pusey, submitted manuscript).

At Mahale, K-group (initially about 30 individuals) lost all six of its adult males and one adolescent male from 1970 to 1982 (Nishida et al. 1985). Although K-group was described as "effectively extinct" by 1982 (Nishida et al. 1985), sporadic sightings indicate that a remnant, including a male who was an adolescent in 1982, persisted at least through the 1990s (Nishida et al. 1990, Uehara et al. 1994). Researchers speculated that the K-group males died from attacks by the large M-group (90–100 individuals) (Nishida et al. 1985). In contrast to Gombe, observers at Mahale neither directly observed intergroup killing nor found bodies of victims. Nonetheless, aggressive intergroup encounters did occur during K-group's decline, including the intergroup killing of infants (Nishida et al. 1979). As the number of K-group males declined, M-group expanded its range to include former K-group territory, and most of K-group's females joined M-group.

What caused the disappearance of K-group's males remains unknown. Alternatives to intergroup aggression include disease and predation. In contrast to known disease epidemics (e.g., Nishida et al. 1990), the K-group males were all healthy at the time of their disappearance. Both lions and leopards sometimes prey on chimpanzees and are capable of killing adult males (Boesch 1991, Inagaki & Tsukahara 1993). During the disappearances of the K-group males, however, observers found no evidence of predation—such as wounded survivors of attacks—and/or fresh carcasses with carnivore wounds (cf., Boesch 1991). Circumstantial evidence thus supports intergroup aggression as the cause of at least some of these deaths.

At Kibale, evidence for intergroup killing of adults exists for both the Kanyawara and Ngogo communities. The freshly killed body of a Kanyawara male, Ruwenzori, was found near the site of recent intergroup encounters, huddled face down at the edge of an area trampled by what was apparently the charges and fighting of chimpanzees (Wrangham 1999). In 1998, observers found a large party of Kanyawara males beating on and displaying around the freshly killed body of a male from the Sebitole community (Muller 2002). The victim's body bore numerous wounds consistent with chimpanzee attack, including broken ribs, removal of testes and fingernails, and a ripped-out trachea (Muller 2002). At Ngogo in 2002, observers witnessed lethal intergroup attacks on two adult males and one juvenile male (D.P. Watts and J.C. Mitani, personal communication).

In most cases, the victims did not die immediately after these attacks. Instead, their death was inferred from their subsequent disappearance or the discovery some days later of the victim's body. Nonetheless, observers had the impression that killing was the goal of these attacks (e.g., Goodall 1986). The attacks on Kahama individuals included an intensity of wounding not seen in other contexts, such as prolonged beating, biting, twisting of limbs, tearing off strips of flesh, and, in one case, drinking blood from the victim's nose (Goodall 1986). Among the more recent attacks, evidence for immediate death of the victim exists in five cases. At Kanyawara, Ruwenzori's body was found on the site of trampled vegetation, indicating he died during or soon after the attack (Wrangham 1999). The Sebitole male inferred to have been killed by Kanyawara males presumably died soon after his trachea was ripped from his throat (Muller 2002). At Gombe, Rusambo had massive damage to the throat and is unlikely to have survived long after receiving those wounds (M.L. Wilson, W. Wallauer, and A.E. Pusey, submitted manuscript). During two of the three fatal intergroup attacks at Ngogo in 2002, the victim died before the attackers left (D.P. Watts and J.C. Mitani, personal communication).

Fatal coalitionary killing attacks are not limited to intergroup contexts (Wrangham 1999). Intragroup killings have occurred at Budongo (Fawcett & Muhumuza 2000), Mahale (Nishida 1996), and Ngogo (D.P. Watts and J.C. Mitani, personal communication). For example, at Budongo, during a time of intense competition for mates, males ganged up on and killed a young male from their own community (Fawcett & Muhumuza 2000). At Mahale, males overthrew and killed Ntologi, who had spent nearly 16 years as alpha male (Kitopeni et al. 1995).

LETHAL ATTACKS: INFANTS

Although discussions of lethal intergroup aggression often focus on conflict between adults (e.g., Gat 1999, Sussman 1999), intergroup attacks have resulted in a comparable number of infant victims. For example, compared to the 14 or more killings of adults (Table 1), 15 infants are known or inferred to be victims of intergroup attack (Table 2). In addition to intergroup infanticide, a similar number of intragroup infanticides have been reported [N = 12 in which the mother was known to be a stranger and 3 in which the mother's community was uncertain (Table 6 in Arcadi & Wrangham 1999)].

Intergroup infanticide is more widespread than killing of adults, having been reported for four of the five long-term sites: Budongo, Gombe, Kibale, and Mahale. Six cases of intergroup infanticide occurred at Gombe and Mahale in the 1970s. In three of these cases the attack was observed directly, and in the other cases three males were found eating the infant's freshly killed carcass (reviewed in Arcadi & Wrangham 1999). Recent cases of infanticide include two from Budongo (Newton-Fisher 1999), two from Gombe (M.L. Wilson, W. Wallauer, and A.E. Pusey, submitted manuscript), four from Kibale (Ngogo) (Watts et al. 2002, Watts & Mitani 2000), and one from Mahale (Kutsukake & Matsusaka 2002).

A single ambiguous case of infanticide has been reported for Taï. Observers found females eating an infant, presumably an infanticide victim, near the boundary

TABLE 2   Observed and inferred intercommunity infanticides, 1967–2002

Site	Date	Infant's sex	Aggressors' community	Victim's community	Evidence[a]
Budongo	1995	Unknown	Sonso	N15	Inf.[5]
Budongo	1995	M	Sonso	N15	Obs.[5]
Gombe	1971	Unknown	Kasekela	Unknown	Obs.[1]
Gombe	1975	M	Kasekela	Unknown	Inf.[2]
Gombe	1975	F	Kasekela	Unknown	Obs.[2]
Gombe	1979	Unknown	Kasekela	Unknown	Obs.[4]
Gombe	1993	F	Kasekela	Mitumba	Obs.[9]
Gombe	1998	Unknown	Kasekela	Kalande	Obs.[9]
Kibale	1999	Unknown	Ngogo	Unknown	Obs.[6]
Kibale	1999	Unknown	Ngogo	Unknown	Obs.[6]
Kibale	2001	Unknown	Ngogo	Unknown	Obs.[7]
Kibale	2001	Unknown	Ngogo	Unknown	Inf.[7]
Mahale	1974	M	K-group	M-group	Inf.[3]
Mahale	1976	M	M-group	K-group	Sus.[3]
Mahale	2000	M	M-group	Unknown	Inf[8]

[a]Whether the fatal attack was observed directly (Obs.), inferred from strong evidence such as finding males eating a freshly killed infant (Inf.), or suspected from the sudden disappearance of a healthy individual (Sus.).

References: [1]Bygott (1972); [2]Goodall (1977); [3]Nishida et al. (1979); [4]Goodall (1986); [5]Newton-Fisher (1999); [6]Watts & Mitani (2000); [7]Watts & Mitani (2002); [8]Kutsukake & Matsuska 2002; [9]M.L. Wilson, W. Wallauer, and A.E. Pusey, submitted.

of the community's range, but it was not clear whether the infant was from the study community (Boesch & Boesch-Achermann 2000). On a number of occasions, Taï males captured a female "prisoner" and attacked her with sufficient severity that blood was observed on the female and on the ground following the attack (Boesch & Boesch-Achermann 2000). During such attacks, mothers with infants cowered protectively over their infants, suggesting that Taï infants do face some risk from male attackers.

Intergroup infanticide typically involves many males attacking a strange mother. Males may beat the mother severely. In contrast to attacks on adults, attacks on infants usually result in the victim's immediate death. In most cases, the attackers killed the infant quickly with a bite to the head or bowels and ate at least part of the carcass (Arcadi & Wrangham 1999). In most cases, the attackers overwhelmingly outnumbered the mother, who was unable to effectively defend herself or her infant. Attackers thus face little risk of injury. In the recent case at Mahale, however, the presumed mother of the infanticide victim attacked and severely injured two human observers, whom she apparently regarded as allies of her attackers (Kutsukake & Matsusaka 2002).

FUNCTIONS OF INTERGROUP AGGRESSION

It is now clear that chimpanzees across Africa defend group territories and respond to members of neighboring groups with aggression, including lethal attacks. Debate continues, however, over the relative importance of different benefits that chimpanzees gain from intergroup aggression. Recent studies have helped clarify long-standing questions about the degree to which males are successful in excluding rival males, the degree to which males can gain females by expanding territory or killing their infants, and the extent to which territorial behavior involves feeding competition.

Excluding Rival Males

For males in many species, females are the limiting resource for reproductive success (Trivers 1972). The primary cause of chimpanzee intergroup aggression is thus widely assumed to be competition for mates: Males cooperate to defend their females from other males (e.g., Ghiglieri 1989, Manson & Wrangham 1991). The routine aggression toward stranger males supports this assumption. Researchers were thus surprised when early genetic paternity tests of Taï chimpanzees indicated that over 50% of infants had fathers from outside the community (Gagneux et al. 1997, 1999). These results suggested that intercommunity mating is widespread and an important feature of chimpanzee social evolution (e.g., Boesch & Boesch-Achermann 2000). Subsequent studies, however, found the earlier reports to be mistaken. Improved lab work and data analysis methods identified within-community fathers for most infants at Taï (Constable et al. 2001, Vigilant et al. 2001). Genetic testing at Gombe found within-community fathers for all infants (Constable et al. 2001). These results indicate that males are largely successful in defending their females from outside males and/or that females choose not to mate with extragroup males.

Gaining Females by Expanding Territory

In addition to defending their females from extragroup males, various authors have proposed that a goal of male intergroup aggression is to obtain females from rival groups (e.g., Boesch & Boesch-Achermann 2000, Ghiglieri 1989, Manson & Wrangham 1991). The degree to which females are obtainable from rivals depends on both the female's age and the extent to which females are loyal to particular communities. Male demonstrations of power during intergroup encounters potentially influence the transfer choices of adolescent females. Direct evidence for factors underlying the decisions of which community females join is limited, however. Females usually have several communities to choose from, with at best one or two of them known to researchers. Nonetheless, some evidence suggests that females choose communities with more males. For example, during K-group's decline, many of K-group's adolescent females transferred to the much larger M-group, and one M-group female that had immigrated to K-group transferred back to M-group (Nishida et al. 1985).

More questionable is the degree to which male intergroup aggression can influence the group membership of adult females with offspring (parous females). Whether male chimpanzees can add parous females to their community by expanding their territory depends on the degree to which females identify with a particular community (Williams et al. 2002b). The degree to which female ranging patterns depended on male territorial boundaries remained unclear for many years. Females spend much of their time alone, and most studies have focused on more conspicuous male behavior such as hunting and fighting.

Wrangham (1979) proposed three alternative models in which female home ranges are either (*a*) entirely overlapping with male ranges, (*b*) smaller than male ranges and dispersed within boundaries defended by males, or (*c*) smaller than male ranges and dispersed independently of boundaries defended by males. The first model can be rejected, with the possible exception of Taï (Boesch & Boesch-Achermann 2000, Wrangham 1979). Distinguishing between the second and third models has proved difficult, but these two models provide contrasting predictions regarding the extent to which males can acquire new females. In the second model, because females identify closely with a single territory defended by males, males cannot directly increase their access to females by expanding territory. Instead, male access to females depends on female immigration patterns. In contrast, in the third model, males can increase their access to females by taking over more land occupied by those females.

Analyzing 18 years of ranging data from Gombe, Williams and colleagues (2002b) found evidence for a variation of Wrangham's second model that might be termed the neighborhood model. Rather than being evenly distributed across the landscape, females settle in different neighborhoods within the male-defended range. Most females live in centrally located neighborhoods, avoid borders, and mate exclusively with males of one community. These females' home ranges expanded when the community's total area grew and contracted when the total area shrank. Some females, however, lived in peripheral neighborhoods and may have maintained friendly relations with more than one community. One possible advantage to having a peripheral home range is that food resources may be more plentiful in the no-man's-land between communities (Boesch & Boesch-Achermann 2000, Wilson 2001). Despite possible access to more abundant food, however, females using the periphery face a higher risk of intergroup aggression and infanticide (Williams et al. 2002b). These observations from Gombe indicate that, over all, males are unlikely to add females to their community simply by expanding their territory. Nonetheless, the diversity of female strategies suggests that, in some cases, peripheral females could change their community loyalties when faced with territorial expansion.

Rival Extermination

The community extinctions reported for Gombe and Mahale suggest that one strategy for males to add females to their community is to kill all the males from a rival community. The extent to which this strategy occurs is difficult to interpret. Of the two reported community extinctions, Gombe and Mahale, lethal attacks were observed only at Gombe, and extensive female transfers were observed only at Mahale.

At Gombe, Kahama contained at least three adult females and two adolescent females (Goodall 1986). One of these adolescent females, Little Bee, joined Kasekela in the early 1970s, though it is unclear whether Little Bee's immigration was the result of intergroup aggression. The other adolescent, Honey Bee, was briefly seen in Kasekela but then disappeared. Both adolescents were daughters of Madam Bee, who was killed by the Kasekela males through a series of at least five attacks that occurred over the course of a year (Goodall 1986). One additional but uncertain case is that of Joanne, who immigrated to Kasekela in 1978 with her five-year-old son. Based on facial resemblance and the age of her son, researchers suspect that Joanne was the daughter of Wanda, a likely Kahama resident (Williams et al. 2002b). It is thus unclear whether the attacks on Kahama chimpanzees yielded any direct gains in female members for the Kasekela males.

The case for large-scale transfer of females is clear from Mahale. K-group contained a maximum of 6 males and 14 females in the early 1970s. Including females who immigrated and natal females who grew to maturity, a total of 28 females resided in K-group during the group's decline (1970–1983) (Nishida et al. 1985). Seventeen of these females transferred to M-group and five disappeared, presumably transferring to an unhabituated group. Only six females had not emigrated from K-group by 1983; three of these had died. Of the 17 females that transferred to M-group, 5 were K-group natal females that presumably would have left their natal group in any case. (A sixth natal female had returned to K-group to breed, then transferred to M-group after her son was weaned.) The remaining females included females with infants, who usually do not transfer, as well as young females born in M-group who probably would not have returned to their natal group if K-group had survived. In general, K-group females with young infants did not transfer to M-group until their infants were weaned, presumably to minimize infanticide risk (Nishida et al. 1985).

M-group males clearly gained females because of K-group's decline. As discussed above, however, the reasons for K-group's decline remain uncertain. Whether K-group's males were killed mainly by M-group males, as Nishida and colleagues (1985) proposed, or by some other factor, K-group's females showed a strong preference to reside in the group with more males, despite all the potential costs of transferring, such as aggression from the new community's males and females and the risk of infanticidal attacks.

The large-scale transfer of K-group females to M-group suggests that exterminating rival males would be an effective way to gain females. Whether such extermination is the goal of intergroup killing remains unclear. Killing all the males of a rival community takes many years and occurs rarely. Existing evidence suggests that rather than being the goal of intergroup aggression, exterminating all of a rival group's males is an extreme outcome of a more general strategy: killing individual rivals whenever possible (see below, Imbalances of Power).

Recruiting Females Through Infanticide

In some species, such as gorillas (Watts 1989) and Thomas' langur monkeys (Sterck 1995, Steenbeek 1999), females whose infants were killed by a stranger male during an intergroup encounter have subsequently joined the attacker's group. The logic underlying such transfers is that by killing a female's infant a male demonstrates the inability of a female's current male(s) to protect her and her offspring from such attacks. In chimpanzees, however, there is little or no evidence that females whose infants were killed during intergroup infanticide subsequently joined the attackers' community (reviewed in Arcadi & Wrangham 1999, Watts et al. 2002). Obtaining such evidence is difficult, however, in that the mothers in such cases are usually unhabituated and not individually recognized. Intergroup infanticide seems more likely to result from either attempts to reduce the coalitionary strength of neighboring communities (Nishida & Kawanaka 1985, Takahata 1985) or from a more general strategy of defending feeding territory from all members of rival groups (Pusey 2001; J. Williams and A.E. Pusey, submitted manuscript).

Defending a Feeding Territory

Williams and Pusey (J. Williams and A.E. Pusey, submitted manuscript) argue that males defend a feeding territory for themselves, females, and their offspring. In this view, male territoriality represents parental effort rather than mating effort. Males indirectly gain fitness benefits by providing more territory and thus more food for females and their offspring. In a given habitat, larger territories presumably contain more food such as fruit trees and animal prey. Recent analyses of long-term data at Gombe reveal that females travel in larger parties and have shorter interbirth interval when territory size is larger, both indications of more abundant food (Pusey 2001; J. Williams and A.E. Pusey, submitted manuscript). Additional evidence in support of the view that intergroup aggression involves male parental effort comes from data on participation in border patrols. At Ngogo, males with more mating success, and hence greater probability of having offspring in the community, participated in patrols more often than other males (Watts & Mitani 2001).

The pattern of aggression toward females supports the view that males defend a feeding territory for themselves, their mates, and offspring. If males were attempting to recruit females, they would be expected to affiliate with them rather than attack them. In general, male hostility to a stranger female depends on both the female's cycling status and the presence of offspring. Swollen females without infants receive the least aggression, and nonswollen females with infants receive the most. This pattern of aggression appears based on the female's reproductive value, a measure of a female's expected future reproduction (Wolf & Schulman 1984). Young females without infants are likely to transfer and thus represent possible recruits, whereas older females with infants represent competitors for food and the source of future male rivals.

IMBALANCES OF POWER

Chimpanzees, like many social mammals, compete over territory, food, and females. Why should chimpanzees, but few other mammals, engage in lethal intergroup attacks? The imbalance-of-power hypothesis developed by Wrangham and colleagues (Manson & Wrangham 1991, Wrangham & Peterson 1996) attempts to answer this question by drawing attention to the costs, rather than the benefits, of aggression. A growing number of studies support the view that animals use aggression strategically, when the benefits are likely to outweigh the costs of aggression (Archer 1988, Huntingford & Turner 1987, Wilson 2003). Proximate mechanisms underlying aggression should therefore be sensitive to both costs and benefits. Costs of aggression include the risk of injury and/or death as well as energetic and opportunity costs (time spent fighting could be spent feeding or mating instead). Benefits of aggression include food and females. Decisions about how to interact with neighbors should therefore depend on a variety of factors, including resource distribution and assessing the motivations and capabilities of potential opponents. The imbalance-of-power hypothesis proposes that in chimpanzees fission-fusion social structure, combined with coalitionary bonds among males, creates opportunities for low-cost killing of rivals.

Chimpanzees travel in parties of varying size and composition, which may result in large disparities in party size during intergroup encounters, even among communities that are similar in overall size. In such cases, members of the larger group can kill rivals at very low risk of injury to themselves. During observed lethal intergroup attacks, three or more attackers ganged up on a single victim, who was immobilized by some of the attackers while others beat and bit the victim. Attackers themselves rarely received injuries. The imbalance-of-power hypothesis thus argues that intergroup attacks are lethal not because of unusually high benefits to be obtained from killing, but because the costs of killing are low during gang attacks.

The primary benefit of intergroup killing is thought to be the reduction of the coalitionary strength of rival communities. By reducing the fighting strength of a given community, males increase their chances of success in future battles with that community. More frequent success in battles should result in territory expansion and thus more food for group members, including females and offspring.

Both observational and experimental evidence support the prediction that chimpanzees modify their response to intergroup threat based on the relative number of opponents. At both Ngogo and Taï, parties containing many males were more likely to approach intruders (Boesch & Boesch-Achermann 2000, Watts & Mitani 2001). The actual number of intruders was unknown in these cases. To obtain a more controlled test, Wilson and colleagues (2001) used playback experiments to simulate intergroup encounters. These experiments involved playing a single pant-hoot from a stranger male to parties of varying size and composition. Parties with only females remained silent, and in some cases females dropped down from the trees and moved away from the speaker. Parties with one or two males also remained silent, but in about half the cases the males moved slowly and cautiously toward the speaker. Parties with three or more males usually responded with loud calls immediately after the playback and quickly approached the speaker. These results indicate that chimpanzees are able to assess the numerical strength of their own side compared to the opposition and are more likely to respond aggressively when the odds are in their favor. More recent experiments conducted at Taï will refine our understanding of how numerical assessment interacts with other factors, such as familiarity with the opponent(s) (I. Herbinger and C. Boesch, submitted manuscript).

Additional observational evidence supports the view that the number of males in a community is crucial to the community's success in intergroup encounters. At Taï, the Northern group's territory was larger when it contained more males (Lehmann & Boesch 2003). At Gombe, territory size did not depend on the number of adult males alone but did depend on the number of adult males divided by an index of intergroup threat (J. Williams and A.E. Pusey, submitted manuscript). The exceptionally large Ngogo community in Kibale has over 150 members, including 23 adult males (Watts et al. 2002). The large number of males at Ngogo enables that community to engage in high rates of cooperative aggression, both within and between species. In a single year, 2002, Ngogo males killed two adults and a juvenile male from neighboring communities and also killed an adult male in their own community (D.P. Watts and J.C. Mitani, personal communication). In addition to killing adults, Ngogo males have killed four infants from neighboring communities in the past four years (Watts et al. 2002). The large number of males at Ngogo also leads to extraordinary success in coalitionary killing of their preferred prey, red colobus monkeys (Mitani & Watts 1999).

Killing Future Rivals

The imbalance-of-power hypothesis predicts that a primary benefit of intergroup infanticide is to reduce the future coalitionary strength of rival communities. To ensure the killing of future rivals rather than potential future mates, attackers should kill male rather than female infants. Observers were able to determine the sex of the victim in 7 of 14 infanticide cases (Table 2). Two victims were female and five were male. The occurrence of female victims suggests either that intergroup infanticide serves some function besides reducing the number of future male rivals or that attackers do not face a high cost from making mistakes in identifying the victim's sex.

RELEVANCE TO HUMANS

The first four decades of research on wild chimpanzees have produced evidence of important similarities between aspects of chimpanzee and human intergroup aggression. Comparisons between the two species are made difficult, admittedly, by many factors. In chimpanzees, the description of intergroup aggression is still in an early phase. In humans, quantitative data from the most relevant groups (hunter gatherers) are so rare that different authors reach widely differing conclusions about the frequency of aggression (e.g., Ferguson 2000, Gat 2000a).

Yet despite these problems, it is clear that intergroup aggression has occurred among many, possibly all, hunter-gatherer populations and follows a rather uniform pattern (Gat 1999). From the most northern to the most southern latitudes, the most common pattern of intergroup aggression was for a party of men from one group to launch a surprise attack in circumstances in which the attackers were unlikely to be harmed. Attacks were sometimes unsuccessful but were, at other times, responsible for the deaths of one or many victims. Women and girls were sometimes captured (Gat 1999).

One factor that complicates efforts to compare patterns of intergroup aggression in humans and chimpanzees is that in chimpanzees the only large social group is the community, whereas no precise equivalent of the chimpanzee community exists for humans. Instead, human group membership always exists on several levels: residential group, clan, tribe, nation, and so on (Boehm 1992, Durkheim 1933). The existence of these multiple types of group complicates the comparison of aggressive patterns between chimpanzees and humans because it means that aggression between groups can occur at many more levels among humans than among chimpanzees. At one extreme, aggression can be found between residential groups that both belong to the same linguistic, cultural, and tribal unit, within which individuals can move and intermarry [internal warfare (Otterbein 1997)]. At the other extreme, it can occur between culturally distinct groups having different languages (or dialects) and little or no tendency for intermarriage or friendly contact (external warfare).

Despite this variation, a useful comparision can be made between chimpanzees and humans by identifying the level at which relations are essentially anarchic, i.e., characterized by the lack of any central or cultural authority. Human societies normally feature such a level (Rodseth & Wrangham 2003). The Ache, for example, lived in bands of 10 to 70 individuals who, in turn, formed groups of up to 550 (Hill & Hurtado 1996). Within these regional groups, the only form of culturally sanctioned violence among men was the club fight. By contrast, "anyone not in the group, including other Ache, could be shot on sight" (Hill & Hurtado 1996, p. 70).

Among foraging societies, such regional groups frequently included around 500 individuals (e.g., Birdsell 1968, Tindale 1974). Both the size and internal structure of such groups varied extensively, however, in relation to ecological and cultural factors, as indicated by the wide variety of terms used to describe them (e.g., dialect group, maximum band, tribe).

Whatever the name used, this level of grouping suggests a similarity to the chimpanzee community because aggressive interactions at this level are not regulated by the predictable intervention of allies (Rodseth & Wrangham 2003). This essential similarity suggests that shared principles may help explain the occasionally intense escalation of interactions between such groups. But of course the similarity gives way to major differences in scale and organization, given that humans can expand their regional groupings all the way to nation-states containing hundreds of millions of individuals living in complex networks.

Chimpanzees and hunter gatherers, we conclude, share a tendency to respond aggressively in encounters with members of other social groups; to avoid intensely aggressive confrontations in battle line (typically, by retreating); and to seek, or take advantage of, opportunities to use imbalances of power for males to kill members of neighboring groups.

These similarities have been explained in parallel ways in the two species, using concepts from evolutionary ecology (Gat 2000b,c; Wrangham 1999). The essential notion is that natural selection has favored specific types of motivational systems (Gat 2000b). In particular, motivations have been favored that have tended, over evolutionary time, to give individuals access to the resources needed for reproduction.

The motivations that drive intergroup killing among chimpanzees and humans, by this logic, were selected in the context of territorial competition because reproduction is limited by resources, and resources are limited by territory size. Therefore, it pays for groups to achieve dominance over neighboring groups so that they can enlarge their territories. To achieve dominance, it is necessary to have greater fighting power than the neighbors. This means that whenever the costs are sufficiently low it pays to kill or damage individuals from neighboring groups. Thus, intergroup killing is viewed as derived from a tendency to strive for status (Gat 2000c, Wrangham 1999). According to this view, these several aspects of human intergroup aggression do not appear exceptional compared to other animals (Gat 2000a).

Many other aspects of human intergroup aggression, however, differ extensively from chimpanzees, such as the ability of residential groups to form alliances, the possibilities for expressing formal peace relations, the capacity for symbolic domination [through cannibalism, for example (Gat 2000c)], the ability to kill large numbers at a time, and the integration of intergroup relations with ideology. Such differences suggest to some critics that human warfare cannot usefully be compared to chimpanzee aggression (Lewontin 1999, Marks 1999, Sussman 1999). No ultimate explanation has yet been offered, however, as an alternative to the hypothesis that territorial competition for resources for reproduction favors a drive for intergroup dominance (cf., Gat 2000a).

Finally, it is important not to confuse levels of explanation. The comparison of chimpanzees and humans is useful in suggesting common principles generating evolved psychological tendencies. But it is not useful in directly accounting for intraspecific variation, which is the central concern of the anthropology of war (e.g., Otterbein 2000). As with chimpanzees and other species, however, models based on evolutionary principles (such as behavioral ecology) provide powerful tools for understanding intraspecific variation (e.g., Daly & Wilson 1988, Mesquida & Wiener 1996).

LETHAL RAIDING IN *PAN* AND *HOMO*: HOMOLOGY OR HOMOPLASY?

It is currently unclear whether the patterns of intergroup aggression seen in humans and chimpanzees result from homology (shared evolutionary history) or homoplasy (convergent evolution). Various lines of evidence suggest that our common ancestor with chimpanzees was very much like a chimpanzee (Wrangham & Pilbeam 2001). In the five to seven million years that followed the divergence of the lines leading to *Pan* and *Homo*, however, the human lineage developed into a bushy tree (Wood & Collard 1999). A variety of woodland apes (Wrangham & Peterson 1996) evolved, including *Ardipithecus*, *Australopithecus*, and *Paranthropus*. These creatures do not closely resemble any living species, and we can make only educated guesses about their feeding ecology and social structure. Considerable behavioral diversity exists among extant apes; woodland apes probably varied as well, with societies that evolved to meet different ecological challenges. We know that social behavior can change quickly over evolutionary time. The two extant species of *Pan*, chimpanzees and bonobos, differ considerably in their intergroup relations despite generally similar feeding ecology, morphology, and recent date of divergence. Fossils can provide only a limited amount of information about social behavior. For example, lions and tigers differ strikingly in their social behavior, despite being closely related enough to interbreed. If we had only fossils of lions and tigers, it is hard to imagine that we would be able to infer cooperative territory defense for the one and solitary seclusion for the other.

The relevance of chimpanzee violence to the evolution of human warfare does not depend on the possibility that both species inherited this trait from a common ancestor. Instead, chimpanzees provide a valuable referential model. Before observers reported accounts of chimpanzee intergroup aggression, anthropologists assumed that human warfare resulted from some factor unique to the human lineage, such as social stratification, horticulture, high population density, or the use of tools as weapons. The observation of warlike behavior in chimpanzees demonstrated that none of these factors was required. A similar lesson could be drawn from the warlike behavior of social carnivores, such as lions, wolves, and spotted hyenas (Wrangham 1999). The relevance of carnivore behavior to human evolution might be discounted, however, given that carnivores possess many specialized traits; intergroup killing in carnivores could be a byproduct of morphological and behavioral evolution for cooperative hunting. The benefit of using chimpanzees as a referential model is that, as our evolutionary cousins, they give us a more realistic picture of traits our ancestors may have possessed.

The benefits and limitations of using chimpanzee data to understand the evolution of human warfare are similar to those presented by data on another trait shared by chimpanzees and humans: hunting. In both species, hunting is conducted mainly by males, who often hunt in groups. As Mitani & Watts point out (2003), chimpanzee hunting differs in various ways from human hunting. For example, chimpanzees pursue prey through the trees and kill with their hands and teeth, whereas humans pursue prey on the ground and kill with weapons. Chimpanzees hunt opportunistically, and the degree of cooperation involved remains the subject of debate, whereas human hunting clearly involves planning and cooperation. We don't know if *"Pan prior"* (Wrangham 2001) hunted, and the extent to which the various early woodland apes hunted or scavenged continues to be debated. Nevertheless, much like the case with intergroup aggression, data from chimpanzees (and other primates, such as baboons) challenged previous views that humans were the only hunting primate, and ongoing studies continue to provide valuable insight for guiding our thinking about human evolution.

CONCLUSION

Recent studies have shown that the patterns of intergroup aggression reported from Gombe and Mahale in the 1970s are, in many ways, typical of chimpanzees. Chimpanzees at all long-term study sites defend group territories, and chimpanzees at four out of five sites have conducted lethal attacks on members of neighboring groups. Studies of unprovisioned communities demonstrate that these patterns of intergroup aggression are not the result of provisioning. Indeed, the Ngogo community, which Power (1991) considered a prime example of peaceful intergroup relations, turns out to have an exceptionally high rate of intergroup violence.

Instead of being a maladaptive aberration, chimpanzee intergroup aggression appears to be typical of aggression in other wild animals in that it tends to provide fitness benefits for the aggressors. Two sets of genetic paternity tests demonstrate that males successfully kept outside males from mating with females in their community, a result supported by consistent behavioral observations. Females reproduced more quickly when territories were larger, indicating that both females and males benefit from defense and acquisition of feeding territory.

The chimpanzee studies suggest that our understanding of human intergroup aggression, particularly small-scale non-state violence, would benefit from more extensive testing of hypotheses generated by behavioral biology. The few studies that have focused on testing evolutionary principles (e.g., Chagnon 1988, 1992) have provoked hostile critiques (e.g., Ferguson 2001, Tierney 2000). The hostility apparent in such critiques reflects a widespread concern that "biological" is equivalent to "fixed" or "unchangeable." Contemporary behavioral biology, however, views primate aggression as a strategic response to appropriate environmental conditions. Rather than viewing human aggression as inevitable, an approach rooted in behavioral biology would provide more focused predictions for when aggression is likely to occur and how aggression can be reduced.

Even among chimpanzees, rates of intergroup aggression vary considerably among sites and over time within sites. Understanding the factors responsible for that variation constitutes the next frontier in studies of chimpanzee intergroup relations. The range of variation may well prove greater than so far observed. For example, under appropriate conditions, captive chimpanzees can be induced to accept new adult males into their group, something not yet observed in the wild (Seres et al. 2001). Newly introduced males are predictably aggressive to one another, but appropriate management can lead to eventual acceptance.

Such observations indicate both that biology provides chimpanzees with clear dispositions (e.g., hostility toward stranger males) but also that even chimpanzees, under the right conditions, can learn to overcome such hostility. A fully developed behavioral biology of human intergroup aggression offers similar hope for understanding—and addressing—the roots of violence in our own species.

ACKNOWLEDGMENTS

Anne Pusey, John Mitani, Bill Wallauer, and Becky Sun provided helpful comments and discussion. Ilka Herbinger, John Mitani, Anne Pusey, David Watts, and Jennifer Williams generously provided access to unpublished data.

The *Annual Review of Anthropology* is online at http://anthro.annualreviews.org

LITERATURE CITED

Alexander RD. 1989. Evolution of the human psyche. In *The Human Revolution*, ed. P Mellars, C Stringer, pp. 455–513. Edinburgh: Edinburgh Univ. Press

Anderson DP, Nordheim EV, Boesch C, Moermond TC. 2002. Factors influencing fission-fusion grouping in chimpanzees in the Tai National Park, Côte d'Ivoire. In *Behavioral Diversity in Chimpanzees and Bonobos*, ed. C Boesch, G Hohmann, LF Marchant, pp. 90–101. Cambridge, UK: Cambridge Univ. Press

Arcadi AC, Wrangham RW. 1999. Infanticide in chimpanzees: review of cases and a new within-group observation from the Kanyawara study group in Kibale National Park. *Primates* 40:337–51

Archer J. 1988. *The Behavioural Biology of Aggression*. Cambridge, UK, New York: Cambridge Univ. Press

Bauer HR. 1980. Chimpanzee society and social dominance in evolutionary perspective. In *Dominance Relations: Ethological Perspectives of Human Conflict*, ed. DR Omark, FF Strayer, D Freedman, pp. 97–119. New York: Garland

Birdsell J. 1968. Some predictions for the Pleis-

tocene based on equilibrium systems among recent hunter-gatherers. In *Man the Hunter*, ed. DR Lee, I DeVore, pp. 229–40. Chicago: Aldine

Boehm C. 1992. Segmentary 'warfare' and the management of conflict: comparison of East African chimpanzees and patrilineal-patrilocal humans. In *Coalitions and Alliances in Humans and Other Animals*, ed. AH Harcourt, FMB de Waal, pp. 137–73. Oxford, UK: Oxford Univ. Press

Boesch C. 1991. The effects of leopard predation on grouping patterns in forest chimpanzees. *Behaviour* 117:220–42

Boesch C, Boesch-Achermann H. 2000. *The Chimpanzees of the Taï Forest: Behavioral Ecology and Evolution*. Oxford, UK: Oxford Univ. Press

Boydston EE, Morelli TL, Holekamp KE. 2001. Sex differences in territorial behavior exhibited by the spotted hyena (Hyaenidae, *Crocuta crocuta*). *Ethology* 107:369–85

Bygott JD. 1972. Cannibalism among wild chimpanzees. *Nature* 238:410–11

Bygott JD. 1979. Agonistic behaviour and dominance among wild chimpanzees. See Hamburg & McCown 1979, pp. 405–27

Chagnon NA. 1988. Life histories, blood revenge, and warfare in a tribal population. *Science* 239:985–92

Chagnon NA. 1992. *Yanomamo.* Fort Worth, TX: Harcourt Brace

Chapman CA, White FJ, Wrangham RW. 1994. Party size in chimpanzees and bonobos: a reevaluation of theory based on two similarly forested sites. In *Chimpanzee Cultures,* ed. RW Wrangham, WC McGrew, FBM de Waal, PG Heltne, pp. 41–58. Cambridge, MA: Harvard Univ. Press

Chapman CA, Wrangham RW. 1993. Range use of the forest chimpanzees of Kibale: implications for the understanding of chimpanzee social organization. *Am. J. Primatol.* 31:263–73

Clark AP. 1993. Rank differences in the production of vocalizations by wild chimpanzees as a function of social context. *Am. J. Primatol.* 31:159–79

Constable JL, Ashley MV, Goodall J. 2001. Noninvasive paternity assignment in Gombe chimpanzees. *Mol. Ecol.* 10:1279–1300

Daly M, Wilson M. 1988. *Homicide.* Hawthorne and New York: Aldine de Gruyter

de Waal FBM, ed. 2001. *Tree of Origin.* Cambridge, MA: Harvard Univ. Press

Durkheim E. 1933. *The Division of Labor in Society.* New York: Free Press

Fawcett K, Muhumuza G. 2000. Death of a wild chimpanzee community member: possible outcome of intense sexual competition. *Am. J. Primatol.* 51:243–47

Ferguson RB. 2000. The causes and origins of "primitive warfare": on evolved motivations for war. *Anthropol. Q.* 73:59–65

Ferguson RB. 2001. Materialist, cultural and biological theories on why Yanomami make war. *Anthropol. Theory* 1:99–116

Gagneux P, Boesch C, Woodruff D. 1999. Female reproductive strategies, paternity and community structure in wild West African chimpanzees. *Animal Behav.* 57:19–32

Gagneux P, Woodruff DS, Boesch C. 1997. Furtive mating in female chimpanzees. *Nature* 387:358–59

Gat A. 1999. The pattern of fighting in simple, small-scale, prestate societies. *J. Anthropol. Res.* 55:563–83

Gat A. 2000a. The causes and origins or "primitive warfare": reply to Ferguson. *Anthropol. Q.* 73:165–68

Gat A. 2000b. The human motivational complex: evolutionary theory and the causes of hunter-gatherer fighting. Part I. Primary somatic and reproductive causes. *Anthropol. Q.* 73:20–34

Gat A. 2000c. The human motivational complex: evolutionary theory and the causes of hunter-gatherer fighting. Part II. Proximate, subordinate, and derivative causes. *Anthropol. Q.* 73:74–89

Ghiglieri M. 1984. *The Chimpanzees of Kibale Forest: a Field Study of Ecology and Social Structure.* New York: Columbia Univ. Press

Ghiglieri MP. 1987. Sociobiology of the great apes and the hominid ancestor. *J. Hum. Evol.* 16:319–58

Ghiglieri MP. 1989. Hominid sociobiology and hominid social evolution. See Heltne & Marquardt 1989, pp. 370–79

Goodall J. 1977. Infant killing and cannibalism in free-living chimpanzees. *Folia Primatol.* 22:259–82

Goodall J. 1986. *The Chimpanzees of Gombe: Patterns of Behavior.* Cambridge, MA: Belknap Press

Goodall J, Bandora A, Bergman E, Busse C, Matama H, et al. 1979. Intercommunity interactions in the chimpanzee population of the Gombe National Park. See Hamburg & McCown 1979, pp. 13–53

Graham CE. 1981. Menstrual cycle physiology of the great apes. In *Reproductive Biology of the Great Apes,* ed. CE Graham, pp. 286–303. New York: Academic Press

Greengrass E. 2000. The sudden decline of a community of chimpanzees at Gombe National Park. *Pan Africa News* 7:http://jinrui.zool.kyoto-u.ac.jp/PAN/7(1)/7(1)-05.html

Hamburg DA. 1991. An evolutionary perspective on human aggression. In *The Development and Integration of Behavior: Essays in Honor of Robert Hinde,* ed. P Bateson, pp.

419–58. Cambridge, UK: Cambridge Univ. Press

Hamburg DA, McCown ER. 1979. *The Great Apes*. Menlo Park, CA: Benjamin/Cummings

Heltne PG, Marquardt LA. 1989. *Understanding Chimpanzees*. Cambridge, MA: Harvard Univ. Press

Herbinger I, Boesch C, Rothe H. 2001. Territory characteristics among three neighboring chimpanzee communities in the Tai National Park, Ivory Coast. *Int. J. Primatol.* 22:143–67

Hill K, Hurtado MA. 1996. *Ache Life History: the Ecology and Demography of a Foraging People*. New York: Aldine de Gruyter

Hill WCO. 1969. The nomenclature, taxonomy, and distribution of chimpanzees. In *The Chimpanzee*, ed. GH Bourne, pp. 22–49. Basel, Switz.: Karger

Hohmann G, Gerloff U, Tautz D, Fruth B. 1999. Social bonds and genetic ties: kinship association and affiliation in a community of bonobos (Pan paniscus). *Behaviour* 1999:1219–35

Huntingford F, Turner A. 1987. *Animal Conflict*. New York: Chapman and Hall

Idani G. 1991. Cases of inter-unit group encounters in pygmy chimpanzees at Wamba, Zaire. In *Primatology Today: Proceedings of the XIIth Congress of the International Primatological Society*, ed. A Ehara, pp. 235–38. Amsterdam: Elsevier

Inagaki H, Tsukahara T. 1993. A method for identifying chimpanzee hairs in lion feces. *Primates* 34:109–12

Isabirye-Basuta G. 1988. Food competition among individuals in a free-ranging chimpanzee community in Kibale Forest, Uganda. *Behaviour* 105:135–47

Kano T. 1992. *The Last Ape: Pygmy Chimpanzee Behavior and Ecology*. Stanford, CA: Stanford Univ. Press

Kawanaka K, Nishida T. 1974. Recent advances in the study of inter-unit-group relationships and social structure of wild chimpanzees of the Mahale Mountains. In *Proceedings of the 5th Congress of the International Primatological Society*, ed. S Kondo, M Kawai, A

Ehara, S Kawamura, pp. 173–85. Tokyo: Jpn. Sci. Press

Kitopeni R, Kasagula M, Turner L. 1995. Ntologi falls??! *Pan Africa News* 2:9–11

Kutsukake N, Matsusaka T. 2002. Incident of intense aggression by chimpanzees against an infant from another group in Mahale Mountains National Park, Tanzania. *Am. J. Primatol.* 58:175–80

Lehmann J, Boesch C. 2003. Social influences on ranging patterns among chimpanzees (*Pan troglodytes verus*) in the Taï National Park, Côte d'Ivoire. *Beh. Ecol.* In press

Lewontin RC. 1999. The problem with an evolutionary answer. *Nature* 400:728–29

Lorenz K. 1966. *On Aggression*. New York: Harcourt Brace

Manson JH, Wrangham RW. 1991. Intergroup aggression in chimpanzees and humans. *Curr. Anthropol.* 32:369–90

Marks J. 1999. Demonic males: apes and the origins of human violence (review). *Hum. Biol.* 71:143–46

Marks J. 2002. *What It Means to Be 98 Percent Chimpanzee: Apes, People, and Their Genes*. Berkeley: Univ. Calif. Press

Marler P. 1976. Social organization, communication and graded signals: the chimpanzee and gorilla. In *Growing Points in Ethology*, ed. PPG Bateson, RA Hinde, pp. 239–77. Cambridge, UK: Cambridge Univ. Press

Matsumoto-Oda A. 1999. Mahale chimpanzees: grouping patterns and cycling females. *Am. J. Primatol.* 47:197–207

McComb K, Packer C, Pusey A. 1994. Roaring and numerical assessment in contests between groups of female lions, *Panthera leo*. *Animal Behav.* 47:379–87

Mech LD, Adams LG, Meier TJ, Burch JW, Dale BW. 1998. *The Wolves of Denali*. Minneapolis: Univ. Minn. Press

Mesquida CG, Wiener NI. 1996. Human collective aggression: a behavioral ecology perspective. *Ethol. Sociobiol.* 17:247–62

Mitani JC, Nishida T. 1993. Contexts and social correlates of long-distance calling by male chimpanzees. *Animal Behav.* 45:735–46

Mitani JC, Watts DP. 1999. Demographic

influences on the hunting behavior of chimpanzees. *Am. J. Phys. Anthropol.* 109:439–54

Mitani JC, Watts DP. 2003. Seasonality in hunting by nonhuman primates. In *Primate Seasonality: Implications for Human Evolution*, ed. DK Brockman, CP van Schaik. Cambridge, UK: Cambridge Univ. Press. In press

Mitani JC, Watts DP, Muller MN. 2002. Recent developments in the study of wild chimpanzee behavior. *Evol. Anthropol.* 11:9–25

Montagu A. 1976. *The Nature of Human Aggression*. New York: Oxford Univ. Press

Muller MN. 2002. Agonistic relations among Kanyawara chimpanzees. In *Behavioural Diversity in Chimpanzees and Bonobos*, ed. C Boesch, G Hohmann, LF Marchant, pp. 112–23. Cambridge, UK: Cambridge Univ. Press

Newton-Fisher NE. 1999. Infant killers of Budongo. *Folia Primatol.* 70:167–69

Nishida T. 1968. The social group of wild chimpanzees in the Mahale Mountains. *Primates* 9:167–224

Nishida T. 1979. The social structure of chimpanzees of the Mahale Mountains. See Hamburg & McCown 1979, pp. 73–121

Nishida T. 1989. Social interactions between resident and immigrant female chimpanzees. See Heltne & Marquardt 1989, pp. 68–89

Nishida T. 1990. A quarter century of research in the Mahale Mountains: an overview. In *The Chimpanzees of the Mahale Mountains: Sexual and Life History Strategies*, ed. T Nishida, pp. 3–35. Tokyo: Univ. Tokyo Press

Nishida T. 1996. The death of Ntologi, the unparalleled leader of M Group. *Pan Africa News* 3:http://jinrui.zool.kyoto-u.ac.jp/PAN/3(1)/nt.death.html

Nishida T, Hiraiwa-Hasegawa M, Hasegawa T, Takahata Y. 1985. Group extinction and female transfer in wild chimpanzees in the Mahale National Park, Tanzania. *Z. Tierpsychol.* 67:284–301

Nishida T, Kawanaka K. 1985. Within-group cannibalism by adult male chimpanzees. *Primates* 26:274–85

Nishida T, Takasaki H, Takahata Y. 1990. Demography and reproductive profiles. In *The Chimpanzees of the Mahale Mountains:* *Sexual and Life History Strategies*, ed. T Nishida, pp. 63–97. Tokyo: Univ. Tokyo Press

Nishida T, Uehara S, Nyundo R. 1979. Predatory behavior among wild chimpanzees of the Mahale Mountains. *Primates* 20:1–20

Otterbein KF. 1997. The origins of war. *Crit. Rev.* 11:251–77

Otterbein KF. 2000. A history of research on warfare in anthropology. *Am. Anthropol.* 101:794–805

Power M. 1991. *The Egalitarians—Human and Chimpanzee: an Anthropological View of Social Organization*. Cambridge, UK: Cambridge Univ. Press

Pusey A, Williams JM, Goodall J. 1997. The influence of dominance rank on the reproductive success of female chimpanzees. *Science* 277:828–31

Pusey AE. 1979. Intercommunity transfer of chimpanzees in Gombe National Park. See Hamburg & McCown 1979, pp. 464–79

Pusey AE. 1980. Inbreeding avoidance in chimpanzees. *Animal Behav.* 28:543–82

Pusey AE. 2001. Of genes and apes: chimpanzee social organization and reproduction. See de Waal 2001, pp. 9–38

Reynolds V. 1966. Open groups in hominid evolution. *Man* 1:441–52

Reynolds V, Reynolds F. 1965. Chimpanzees of the Budongo forest. In *Primate Behavior: Field Studies of Monkeys and Apes*, ed. I DeVore, pp. 368–424. New York: Holt, Rinehart & Winston

Rodseth L, Wrangham RW. 2003. Human kinship: a continuation of politics by other means? In *Kinship and Behavior in Primates*, ed. B Chapais, CM Berman. New York: Oxford Univ. Press. In press

Seres M, Aureli F, de Waal FBM. 2001. Successful formation of a large chimpanzee group out of two preexisting subgroups. *Zoo Biol.* 20:501–15

Stanford CB. 1998a. *Chimpanzee and Red Colobus: the Ecology of Predator and Prey*. Cambridge, MA: Harvard Univ. Press

Stanford CB. 1998b. The social behavior of chimpanzees and bonobos: empirical evidence and shifting assumptions. *Curr. Anthropol.* 39:399–420

Steenbeek R. 1999. Tenure related changes in wild Thomas's langurs. I. Between-group interactions. *Behaviour* 136:595–625

Sterck EHM. 1995. *Females, foods and fights: a socioecological comparison of the sympatric Thomas langur and long-tailed macques.* Unpubl. PhD thesis, Univ. Utrecht, Utrecht

Sugiyama Y. 1989. Population dynamics of chimpanzees at Bossou, Guinea. See Heltne & Marquardt 1989, pp. 134–45

Sussman RW. 1999. The myth of man the hunter, man the killer and the evolution of human morality (evolutionary and religious perspectives on morality). *Zygon* 34:453–72

Suzuki A. 1971. Carnivory and cannibalism observed in forest-living chimpanzees. *J. Anthropol. Soc. Nippon* 74:30–48

Takahata Y. 1985. Adult male chimpanzees kill and eat a newborn infant: newly observed intragroup infanticide and cannibalism in Mahale National Park, Tanzania. *Folia Primatol.* 44:161–70

Thomas DK. 1961. The Gombe Stream Game Reserve. *Tanganyika Notes Rec.* 56:34–39

Tierney P. 2000. *Darkness in El Dorado: How Scientists and Journalists Devastated the Amazon.* New York: Norton

Tindale NB. 1974. *Aboriginal Tribes of Australia.* Los Angeles: Univ. Calif. Press

Trivers RL. 1972. Parental investment and sexual selection. In *Sexual Selection and the Descent of Man 1871–1971*, ed. B Campbell, pp. 136–79. London: Heinemann

Trudeau MB, Bergmann-Riss E, Hamburg DA. 1981. Towards an evolutionary perspective on aggressive behavior: the chimpanzee evidence. In *Biobehavioral Aspects of Aggression*, ed. DA Hamburg, MB Trudeau, pp. 27–40. New York: Alan Liss

Tutin CEG, McGinnis PR. 1981. Chimpanzee reproduction in the wild. In *Reproductive Biology of the Great Apes*, ed. CE Graham, pp. 239–64. New York: Academic Press

Uehara S, Nishida T, Takasaki H, Kitopeni R,

Kasagula MB, et al. 1994. A lone male chimpanzee in the wild: the survivor of a disintegrated unit-group. *Primates* 35:275–81

van der Dennen JMG. 1995. *The Origin of War: the Evolution of a Male-Coalitional Reproductive Strategy.* Groningen, The Neth.: Origin Press

van Hooff JARAM. 1990. Intergroup competition and conflict in animals and man. In *Sociobiology and Conflict: Evolutionary Perspectives on Competition, Cooperation, Violence and Warfare*, ed. JMG van der Dennen, VSE Falger, pp. 23–54. London: Chapman and Hall

van Lawick-Goodall J. 1968. Behaviour of free-living chimpanzees of the Gombe Stream area. *Animal Behav. Monogr.* 1:163–311

Vigilant L, Hofreiter M, Siedel H, Boesch C. 2001. Paternity and relatedness in wild chimpanzee communities. *Proc. Natl. Acad. Sci. USA* 98:12,890–95

Watts DP. 1989. Infanticide in mountain gorillas: new cases and a reconsideration of the evidence. *Ethology* 81:1–18

Watts DP, Mitani JC. 2000. Infanticide and cannibalism by male chimpanzees at Ngogo, Kibale National Park, Uganda. *Primates* 41: 357–65

Watts DP, Mitani JC. 2001. Boundary patrols and intergroup encounters in wild chimpanzees. *Behaviour* 138:299–327

Watts DP, Mitani JC, Sherrow HM. 2002. New cases of inter-community infanticide by male chimpanzees at Ngogo, Kibale National Park, Uganda. *Primates* 43:263–70

White FJ. 1996. Comparative socio-ecology of *Pan paniscus*. In *Great Ape Societies*, ed. WC McGrew, LF Marchant, T Nishida, pp. 29–41. Cambridge, MA: Cambridge Univ. Press

Williams JM, Liu H, Pusey AE. 2002a. Costs and benefits of grouping in female chimpanzees at Gombe. In *Behavioral Diversity in Pan*, ed. C Boesch, G Hohmann, L Marchant, pp. 192–203. Cambridge, UK: Cambridge Univ. Press

Williams JM, Pusey AE, Carlis JV, Farm BP, Goodall J. 2002b. Female competition and male territorial behavior influence female chimpanzees' ranging patterns. *Animal Behav.* 63:347–60

Wilson ML. 2001. *Imbalances of power: how chimpanzees respond to the threat of intergroup aggression.* Unpubl. PhD thesis, Harvard Univ., Cambridge, MA

Wilson ML. 2003. Environmental factors and aggression in non-human primates. In *Neurobiology of Aggression: Understanding and Preventing Violence*, ed. M Mattson. Totowa, NJ: Humana Press. In press

Wilson ML, Hauser MD, Wrangham RW. 2001. Does participation in intergroup conflict depend on numerical assessment, range location, or rank for wild chimpanzees? *Animal Behav.* 61:1203–16

Wolf K, Schulman SR. 1984. Male response to "stranger" females as a function of female reproductive value among chimpanzees. *Am. Nat.* 123:163–74

Wood B, Collard M. 1999. The human genus. *Science* 284:65–71

Wrangham R. 1974. Artificial feeding of chimpanzees and baboons in their natural habitat. *Animal Behav.* 22:83–93

Wrangham RW. 1975. *The behavioural ecology of chimpanzees in Gombe National Park, Tanzania.* Unpubl. PhD Thesis, Cambridge Univ., Cambridge, UK

Wrangham RW. 1979. Sex differences in chimpanzee dispersion. See Hamburg & McCown 1979, pp. 481–89

Wrangham RW. 1984. Chimpanzees. In *The Encyclopedia of Mammals*, ed. DW MacDonald, pp. 422–42. New York: Andromeda Oxford Ltd.

Wrangham RW. 1986. Ecology and social relationships in two species of chimpanzee. In *Ecological Aspects of Social Evolution:*

Birds and Mammals, ed. DI Rubenstein, RW Wrangham, pp. 352–79. Princeton, NJ: Princeton Univ. Press

Wrangham RW. 1999. The evolution of coalitionary killing. *Yearb. Phys. Anthropol.* 42:1–30

Wrangham RW. 2000. Why are male chimpanzees more gregarious than mothers? A scramble competition hypothesis. In *Primate Males: Causes and Consequences of Variation in Group Composition*, ed. PM Kappeler, pp. 248–58. Cambridge, UK: Cambridge Univ. Press

Wrangham RW. 2001. Out of the *Pan*, into the fire: from ape to human. See de Waal 2001, pp. 119–43

Wrangham RW, Chapman CA, Clark-Arcadi AP, Isabirye-Basuta G. 1996. Socio-ecology of Kanyawara chimpanzees: implications for understanding the costs of great ape groups. In *Great Ape Societies*, ed. WC McGrew, LF Marchant, T Nishida, pp. 45–57. Cambridge, UK: Cambridge Univ. Press

Wrangham RW, McGrew WC, de Waal FBM, Heltne PG. 1994. *Chimpanzee Cultures.* Cambridge, MA: Harvard Univ. Press

Wrangham RW, Peterson D. 1996. *Demonic Males: Apes and the Origins of Human Violence.* Boston: Houghton Mifflin

Wrangham RW, Pilbeam D. 2001. African apes as time machines. In *All Apes Great and Small. Volume 1: Chimpanzees, Bonobos, and Gorillas*, ed. BMF Galdikas, N Briggs, LK Sheeran, GL Shapiro, J Goodall, pp. 5–18. New York: Plenum/Kluwer

Wrangham RW, Smuts BB. 1980. Sex differences in the behavioural ecology of chimpanzees in the Gombe National Park, Tanzania. *J. Reprod. Fertil., Suppl.,* 28:13–31

Annu. Rev. Anthropol. 2003. 32:393–410
doi: 10.1146/annurev.anthro.32.061002.093341

MADDENING STATES

Begoña Aretxaga

Department of Anthropology, University of Texas, Austin, Texas, 78712-1104

Key Words fantasy, governmentality, nationalisms, state theory, violence

■ **Abstract** Despite transformations in the character of the state in an age of globalization, news of its demise is certainly exaggerated. Even as operations of state (or
state-like) power exceed the boundaries of the nation-state to be deployed by actors
such as transnational nongovernmental organizations, private corporations, guerrilla
groups, or narcotraffickers, the state form shows remarkable tenacity and adaptability.
Invested with a kind of meta-capital, the state remains a crucial presence, a screen
for political desires and identifications as well as fears. This review addresses recent
academic reflection on the field of knowledge we call the state. It asks how the state
becomes a social subject in everyday life, examining the subjective experience of state
power and tracing its effects on territories, populations, and bodies. Finally, it considers the ways violence, sexuality, and desire work in the intimate spaces of state
power.

*Begoña Aretxaga's essay was left among her papers in an almost complete
form at the time of her untimely death. A collective, consisting of James Brow,
Charles Hale, Yael Navaro-Yahsin, Geeta Patel, Brandt Peterson, and Pauline
Strong, worked to fill in citations, answer questions Begoña posed to herself,
which were unresolved, and to lightly edit the final form of this essay. This
piece has not been changed substantially. In an effort to keep to the form
and spirit of Begoña's interrogations the essay stands as it was, without a
literal conclusion. Perhaps a conclusion can be supplied by readers engaged
in an ongoing analysis of contemporary political situations, to which Begoña's
work speaks profoundly, as a legacy that this essay and her extended oeuvre
bequeathed to us.*

INTRODUCTION

During the past decade the field of knowledge that we call the state has become
the object of renewed academic reflection by anthropologists and scholars in other
fields. During the 1980s and mid-1990s studies of globalization seemed to point to
the radical weakening and transformation, if not disappearance, of the modern state
(Appadurai 1993, 1996; Hannerz 1996; Kearney 1995; Ong 1999; Tsing 2000).
States' borders and economies were being challenged, if not erased, by neoliberal

transnational corporations, by higher-order political processes of unification such as the formation of the European Union, or by those set in motion by the fall of the Berlin Wall and the transitions from authoritarian regimes to democratic ones. War and war economies in Africa, Latin America, and Asia made a joke of the monopoly of state violence by showing the crucial role of other actors (warlords, guerrillas, narcotraffickers) in inflicting violence, displacing populations, and organizing economic and political networks (Steinmetz 1999). Refugees and migrants were crossing state borders and challenging both territorial sovereignty and homogeneous definitions of the nation-state. Diasporic forms of identification coexisted (if not competed) with nationalist identities. So too the traditional functions of the state as regulator of diverse areas of social life such as law, education, health, crime, national security—what Althusser (1971) called the "state apparatus"—were being substituted by private companies and institutions. To give just one example, the penal system, which was once the paradigm of the modern, panoptic disciplinary sovereignty accompanying the emergence of the modern state, has become in the United States a large, private, profitable business that has abandoned any pretension to reform and has embraced a racialized logic of pure containment and abandon, where the simultaneous enticement to and suppression of violence seem to be the only rule (Hallinan 2001). So too have nongovernmental organizations (NGOs), aid organizations, and transnational entities like the World Bank, rather than local communities or state officials, determined development and political projects (Ferguson 1990, Gupta 1998, Hale 2002, Trouillot 2001). And yet, in spite of this inexorable logic of neoliberal capitalist globalization, or as Comaroff & Comaroff call it "millennial capitalism" (Comaroff & Comaroff 2000a), which has eroded those functions of the Weberian state that were once its defining feature, the state form can hardly be said to have withered away (Comaroff & Comaroff 2000a, Trouillot 2001). Since 1945, the number of states has more than quadrupled. From 1989, when the Berlin Wall fell, to 1994 there were 22 new states created (Nagengast 1994), and the number has increased since then. The desire for statehood continues to be intense in many parts of the world, in spite, or perhaps because of, the hollowed-out character of the state. Struggles for statehood help to sustain ethnic conflicts, processes of insurgency and counterinsurgency, war economies, international interventions, refugee camps, and torn societies. The commanding power of the state form can partly be understood because the state holds a sort of meta-capital (Bourdieu 1999), its hallowed form commanding an imagery of power and a screen for political desire as well as fear. There is also real capital circulating through the elusive body of the state in the form of international aid, development projects, and capitalist ventures of various kinds. This aura of capital associated with the state is often transformed into a discourse of corruption when people encounter the doubtful practices of local bureaucrats (Gupta 1995). The corrupt state also acquires visibility through highly publicized events highlighted by the mass media (Navaro-Yashin 2002). In marginal locales the images of corruption mix with those of consumption giving rise to discourses and sentiments of abandonment by the state (Berdahl 1999). Globalization is not only compatible with statehood; it has actually fueled the desire for it, whether to have access to resources and powers experienced, imagined, or glimpsed or to defend an ethnic group against the violence of another state, one of the arguments forwarded by Basque insurgents in the Basque country.

Foucault's analysis of power as a field of multiple forces challenged the notion of the state as a unitary center of power, and more specifically it challenged the notion that the state was necessarily the most important target of political struggles (Foucault 1978, 1979, 1991). His inquiries of governmentality and bio-power inspired a whole field of research of power that were outside the field of state studies. The notions of governmentality as well as bio-power have returned, however, to rethink the notion of the state in a new light as a contradictory ensemble of practices and processes (Brown 1995, Mitchell 1991, Trouillot 2001) and as new managements of life and death (Agamben 1998). Repositioning the question of the state in relation to the meaning of sovereignty also seems to me particularly crucial, especially after September 11, 2001.

The question of desire as well as fear becomes most crucial in rethinking the kind of reality the state might be acquiring at this moment of globalization, not only of capital, services, and culture but also of security operations and states of emergency. The question of subjectivity emerges as critical in a variety of ways. On the one hand, there are the subjective dynamics that link people to states, something that Weber already pointed out; on the other hand is what one could call the subjectivity of the state being (Taussig 1992, 1997). How does it become a social subject in everyday life? This is to ask about bodily excitations and sensualities, powerful identifications, and unconscious desires of state officials (Aretxaga 2000a, 2001a); about performances and public representations of statehood; and about discourses, narratives, and fantasies generated around the idea of the state. The state cannot exist without this subjective component, which links its form to the dynamics of people and movements. A major part of this essay is therefore devoted to this problem.

There are other dimensions of statehood I have left out for reasons of space and preference, not for reasons of importance. These are questions relative to state formation and postcolonial state practices. I use state form to emphasize the notion of a powerful state devoid of content, which then serves as a screen for a variety of identifications and as a performative mask (Abrams 1988) for a variety of power discourses and practices. In using the notion of state form I echo Balibar's notion of national form as a repository of ideas, images, and ideologies, which are not predetermined (Balibar & Wallerstein 1991, Zizek 1993). In this way I attempt to leave the state as both an open notion and an entity, the presence and content of which is not taken for granted but is the very object of inquiry. By thinking about the state in this way, I want to emphasize the power it still conveys; its social and political presence can hardly be ignored.

THE UNTENABLE HYPHEN

It has been difficult to think of the state outside the hyphenated dyad "nation-state." States have appeared as actively promoting national cultures (Handler 1988), creating national narratives (Borneman 1993, 1998) that could organize and give shape to collective subjectivities. They have actively engaged in the production of national fantasies of communitas (Berlant 1993, Grant 2001) in a variety of ways, from monumentalization of heroism aimed at creating collective memory and myth, to monumentalization of fable and folktale projecting the erasure of memory and the infantilization of the nation. In studies of nationalism, states often figure as being actively involved in creating "imagined (national) communities" (Anderson 1991 [1983]), cultural intimacies through narrative, media, ritual, pageantry, and public works that link the public sphere to the domestic and local scenes (Borneman 1998, Herzfeld 1997). Nationalist movements have also aspired and fought for states of their own, linking the desire for statehood to nationalist proclamations and often to opposition to another state (perhaps seen as oppressor or colonizer).

Yet if the nation and state are joined in ambiguous ways (Trouillot 1990), the notion of the nation-state has also obscured the instability and deeply problematic nature of such a seemingly self-evident link. On the one hand, the fantasy of a unified, imagined nationalist community clashes with internal differences and power struggles. Differences in class, gender, ethnicity, and status create de facto differences in citizenship. The impact of state power is felt differently at various levels of the national community. At the margins of the polity and at the local level, encounters with the state are often experienced in an intimate way where power is experienced close to the skin, embodied in well-known local officials, through practices of everyday life (Das 2003). This encounter with the state at the local level often takes the form of a discourse of corruption (Gupta 1995), but it can also take the form of profound ambivalence and a discourse of abandonment, as in the remote areas of Colombia where who acts as the state is disputed among a number of actors: the military, the guerrilla, the drug lords (Ramirez 2001). Local officials are caught in a situation divided by impotence and responsibility to their communities, always uncertain about the impact of state power in its different incarnations. The imagined national state, which is supposed to provide for its citizens, seems remote and careless, not fulfilling its obligations and generating a discourse of state deficit, an insufficient state which has abandoned its citizens. In fact, there is not a deficit of state but an excess of statehood practices: too many actors competing to perform as state. Longings for a good paternalistic state coexist with a nationalist discourse of citizenship. At the margins of polities and global economies, the desire for a good state can take the form of struggles for full citizenship (Aretxaga 1997, Hardt & Negri 2000, Ramirez 2001, Warren 1993). The nationalist discourse of citizenship remains attached in the social imaginary to the state but clashes with the actual experience of marginalization, disempowerment, and violence.

The experience of disjunction in the status of citizenship is sometimes covered up by what Girard (1979) called the "scapegoat," an outsider, or an outsider-insider, a ritual repository of the jarring violence inhabiting the national community. Riots against ethnic others can be an example of such attempts to rid the imagined national space of its inherent violence (Tambiah 1997). While it is certainly the case that all sorts of manipulations and political interests are part of what triggers ethnic violence (Brass 1997, Das 1990, Warren 1993), we should also direct close attention to a recurrent dynamic that exceeds strategic manipulation in which violence within the national community is displaced to an insider-outsider, a familiar stranger forcefully cast out of the polity.

In the centers of global power such displacements have also become the norm. In Europe, immigrants often become targets of practices of violence by state institutions, right-wing organizations, and disaffected citizens (Balibar & Wallerstein 1991, Zizek 1997). Processes of unification, such as those of eastern and western Germany, have created their own targeted lesser citizens too (Berdahl 1999). In societies where old regimes have given rise to new ones there are often deep fissures between state and government, a corollary of a situation in which the bureaucracy and the administration are left in place while the government changes. In places like Russia, organized crime can function as a veritable para-state (Comaroff & Comaroff 2000a).

Discourses of patriotism and practices of war against a magnified enemy such as terrorism disguise differences in power and the internal violence of the nation around a national unity to combat a common enemy (Aretxaga 2001a, Zulaika & Douglass 1996). Yet the violence of security apparatuses can also turn into the homeland policing of the state's own citizens in a paranoiac gaze that curtails civil rights and extends terror through the social field. It is in the studies of violence that the state—what we imagine as the state, what we call the state, that ensemble of discourses and practices of power, that elusive subject that can so much affect the life of citizens—appears most clearly as working against the nation (Trouillot 1990). The very concept at the heart of the nation, "the people," becomes an object of fear and violence by a state that wants to have absolute control of a nation it is at once dividing and destroying. "The people" is invoked and torn apart through the creation of ever-present enemies: criminals, communists, subversives, guerrillas, terrorists (Daniel 1996, Denich 1994, Nelson 1999, Ramirez 2001, Siegel 1998, Taylor 1997).

There is also a gender dimension to the instability of the nation-state link. In societies torn by the terror of the violence of military rule such as Argentina and Guatemala, the state is represented and enacted through military performances of masculinity while the nation is feminized into idealized, desexualized maternity. Actual women, who remain outside this imaginary of idealized motherhood, are a reminder of what cannot be fully controlled in the nation—the object of sexual-political violence in endless performances of violent control of the body of the nation by the state body (Nelson 1999, Taylor 1997). So too in societies torn by ethnic violence or war, women have become the embodiment of a threatening nation or a threatening ethnic other; their bodies become the field through which violent statehood not only enacts but draws its power (Aretxaga 2000a, Das 1996). This is the case not only in Bosnia but also in Algeria, India, Rwanda, and South Africa. The imaginary of the nation-state is organized in a variety of ways: as romance or idealized domestic space and inhabited by an ongoing nightmare of sexualized and racialized violence in which the masculinity of statehood becomes a constant threat rather than a benevolent agent. This is a situation in which a repetition-compulsion of violence might be coupled with a compulsion of desire for a harmonic but illusory nation-state. The state should then be thought of in ways that are not necessarily totally dislodged from the nation but neither attached to it. Rather one should consider a variety of relations that are ambivalent, ambiguous, hostile, violent, porous . . . in which the nature of the hyphen is more a cipher than a self-evident reality.

THE GOVERNMENT OF BODIES

The violence and terror spread by totalitarian regimes or/and military bodies has often been considered an attack of the state on civil society; yet this sharp distinction between state and civil society has been questioned in recent scholarship on the state (Alonso 1994, Aretxaga 2000b, Borneman 1998, Brown 1995, Gupta 1995, Mitchell 1991, Navaro-Yashin 2002, Trouillot 2001). The separation between civil society and the state does not exist in reality. Rather, the state as phenomenological reality is produced through discourses and practices of power, produced in local encounters at the everyday level, and produced through the discourses of public culture, rituals of mourning and celebration, and encounters with bureaucracies, monuments, organization of space, etc. The state has to be considered as the effect of a new kind of governmentality (Mitchell 1991); it appears as an open field with multiple boundaries and no institutional or geographical fixity (Trouillot 2001). It is recognizable through its multiple effects. The state has lost many of the ordering functions that produced the effect of a unitary force such as the organization of health care, education, economic production, imprisonment, and military and policing interventions, which are, in many cases, contracted to private companies; on the other hand, aid organizations, NGOs, private entrepreneurs, security companies, and warlords are acting as state and producing the same powerful effects. "The paradox of what we call the state is at once an incoherent, multifaceted ensemble of power relations and a vehicle of massive domination . . . despite the almost unavoidable tendency to speak of the state as an 'it' the domain we call the state is not a thing, system or subject, but a significantly unbounded terrain of powers and techniques, an ensemble of discourses, rules and practices cohabiting in limiting, tension ridden, often contradictory relation to each other" (Brown 1995, p. 174). One strategy for studying the state will be to "focus on the multiple sites in which state processes and practices are recognized through their effects" (Trouillot 2001, p. 126), looking for encounters that are not immediately transparent. The sites of everyday life become "a central domain for the production and reproduction of the state" (Navaro-Yashin 2002, p. 135).

Critiques of the state as a unitary center of power have drawn on Foucault's critique of state as the structure (Poulantzas 1978) or apparatus (Althusser 1971) that defines the locus of power. Foucault's studies of governmentality suggested the rise of a new kind of sovereign power from the eighteenth-century, one in which the power of the absolute sovereign was replaced by an array of practices and discourses aimed at the ordering and control of bodies and populations. The emergence of statistics, new notions about health and contagion, madness and sanity, sexuality and reproduction, techniques of surveying and mapping and census, new institutions such as the clinic and the prison, and the discourses of the social sciences were aimed at rendering populations and bodies legible, disciplined, and controlled. State officials deployed this legibility to create their own fictions of reality. These fictions of the state then turn into nightmares animated by utopian visions of efficiency and technological and bureaucratic control:

> The economic plan, survey map, record of ownership, forest management plan, classification of ethnicity, passbook, arrest record and map of political boundaries acquire their force from the fact that these synoptic data are the points of departure from reality as state officials apprehend and shape it. In dictatorial settings where there is no effective way to assert another reality, fictitious facts-on-paper can often be made eventually to prevail on the ground, because it is on behalf of such pieces of paper that police and army are deployed. . . . [T]he categories used by state agents are not merely means to make their environment legible, they are an authoritative tune to which most of the population must dance. (Scott 1998, p. 83)

In the era of globalization, practices of legibility and control are carried by a variety of organizations and take a variety of forms that nevertheless produce state-like effects so that the state continues to be a powerful object of encounter even when it cannot be located. In the margins and borders of global spaces and polities, but perhaps also in the marginal spaces of western cities (Aretxaga 1997, Balibar & Wallerstein 1991), the will to legibility present in the violence of the checkpoint or the police questioning of immigrants turns into a repetition of illegibility and uncertainty about the outcome of the encounter; de facto, an arrest of temporality (Das 2003), an intimate secrecy in which the fictions of the state about the people it fears, gets locked in with the fictions people at the margins have about the state (Taussig 1997). What is interesting here is that it is not only the people who imagine the state but also the state itself in its multiple incarnations that has, and enacts, its own fantasies (Siegel 1998). This mirroring dynamic between the imaginary relation of those embodying the state and those who encounter their effects in everyday life emerges indirectly from studies of the state (Taussig 1993, 1997). This idea suggests a subjective dynamic that produces and reproduces the state as objects of fear and attachment, of identification or disavowal, as subjects of power, elusive, unlocatable, ever present, immensely powerful, or impotent. It alerts us to what Judith Butler has called "the psychic life of power" (1997).

THE POWER OF A FICTION

The subjective dynamic that sustains the state as a powerful, inescapable, social reality has been noted by anthropologists and other social theorists. Weber, who defined the state as "a compulsory association which organizes domination" through the means of physical force (Gerth & Mills 1946), also understood that "in reality, obedience [to the legality of the state] is determined by highly robust motives of fear and hope—fear of the vengeance of magical powers within the power-holder, hope for reward in this world or in the beyond—and besides all this, by interests of the most varied sorts" (Gerth & Mills 1946). So too does George Simmel call attention to this subjective dynamic that makes the state a powerful reality (1955). Early political anthropology also wrestled with the notion of the state. In his introduction to the classic *African Political Systems*, Radcliffe-Brown makes explicit that the state as a unitary entity is a fiction:

> In writing on political institutions there is a good deal of discussion about the nature and origin of the State, which is usually represented as being an entity over and above the human individuals that make up a society, having as one of its attributes something called "sovereignty," and sometimes spoken of as having a will (law being often defined as the will of the State) or as issuing commands. The State in this sense does not exist in the phenomenal world; it is a fiction of the philosophers. (Fortes & Evans-Pritchard 1940, p. xxiii; Taussig 1992; Trouillot 2001)

In a seminal paper Phillip Abrams also calls attention to the fictional character of the State (Abrams 1988), strongly questioning (like Radcliffe-Brown) the materiality of this "fictional reality" (Aretxaga 2000a). The difficulty in studying the state resides in the fact that the state—as unified political subject or structure—does not exist; it is a collective illusion, the reification of an idea that masks real power relations under the guise of public interest:

> [T]he state is not the reality which stands behind the mask of political practice. It is itself the mask which prevents our seeing political practice as it is [. . .] It starts its life as an implicit construct; it is then reified—as the *res publica* [. . .] and acquires an overt symbolic identity progressively divorced from practice as an illusory account of practice. The ideological function is extended to a point where conservative and radicals alike believe that their practice is not directed at each other but at the state. The world of illusion prevails. (Abrams 1988, p. 58)

The illusion of the state as the subject of domination hiding behind political practice is sustained in no small measure by a shroud of secrecy surrounding the being of the state (Taussig 1992, 1997). The secrecy and the anxiety that accompanies this ungraspable character of power is elaborated in public culture in a variety of ways, including news reporting (Navaro-Yashin 2002) and television series like the American-produced "X-Files," generating a derealization of reality, or a sense of the state as virtual reality (Aretxaga 1999), as the powerful Wizard of Oz determining people's lives. In locations where the state is felt as arbitrary violence, the force of the state is experienced as a traumatic emergence of the Real that breaks the parameters and assumptions of ordinary reality—as, for example, with the discovery of the extent of information about people accumulated by the Stasi secret police in East Germany or the discovery that close relatives had acted as spies (Rosenberg & Lukens 1993). This sense of an invisible, all-powerful subject has been elaborated beautifully in creative literature as well. One only has to think of Milan Kundera's *The Book of Laughter and Forgetting* (1981), in which the Soviet state appears as the invisible hand that alters history by erasing public figures from official photographs. This is the kind of traumatic power over life and death held by the fictional reality of the state elaborated by Kafka in *The Trial* (1964) and other stories. In places like Argentina, with its spectacular disappearances, Guatemala, Colombia, Sri Lanka, the former Yugoslavia, and a great part of Africa, violence enacted by different armies, not just by the state but by those aspiring to statehood, has created un-nameable "spaces of death" (Taussig 1986) without borders, nightmarish realities in which the habitual references that organize reality have been systematically broken, giving rise to powerful phantasmatic states or state-like organizations (Comaroff & Comaroff 2000b, Daniel 1996, Malkki 1995, Nelson 1999, Suárez-Orozco 1992, Tambiah 1996, Taylor 1999, Warren 1993).

For Abrams as for other scholars, the mystifying illusion of a center of power called the state must be unmasked for the reality of disparate relations of power to emerge. Yet to gaze into the labyrinthine interiority of state being (as in truth commissions or when the archives of the Stasi were opened) does not necessarily dispel its mystifying, magical power. On the contrary, such mystifying power often seems to be augmented by such unveiling of the state's scandalous life, triggering an endless proliferation of discourses about the state at all levels of social life. But to talk of the state as a fiction does not necessarily mean falsity but rather, as Clifford Geertz (1973) said long ago, a certain genre of representation, a particularly powerful one. If the fictional reality of the state is socially powerful, then scholars must focus not only on those discourses and practices that produce this state form as real but also on the actual social and subjective life of this formation we call the state. If the state appears and acts as having a life of its own, then we are in the presence of a fetish and must ask for the powerful ways in which this fetish works (Nelson 1999; Taussig 1993, 1997). To look for state effects is also to follow the ways in which those identified as the state enact their fantasy vis-à-vis those others it considers its enemies (Taussig 1997, Zulaika & Douglass 1996).

FANTASY, FETISH, SENSUALITY

One of the areas where fantasy has entered state discourse and practice has been the expanding field of terrorism. On the one hand, official documents reproduce plots and narrative forms from novels or films about terrorism. On the other hand, journalists covering terrorist subjects often turn to fiction writing about terrorism (Zulaika & Douglass 1996). In much of the literature about terrorism, "the brandishing of stark facts goes hand in hand with great leaps into discursive fantasy" (Aretxaga 2001a; Zulaika & Douglass 1996, p. 4). The boundaries between fiction and reality become indistinguishable, endowing encounters between the state and terrorism with a phantom quality (Aretxaga 2001a; Zulaika & Douglass 1996, p. 14). Such indistinguishability creates not only forceful interventions within particular political fields (military interventions, unjustified arrests, torture) but also political cultures "of uncertainty and fear [that] mark the bodies of its subjects to the point of haunting them" (Navaro-Yashin 2002, p. 181). Such haunting by the persecutory power of the state does not face in only one direction. Those identified as state—government officials, politicians, military personal, policemen, judges, prosecutors etc.—are also haunted by the perceived power of terrorists, subversives, guerrillas, or criminals (Aretxaga 2000a, Siegel 1998, Taussig 1986). This mirroring paranoid dynamic often takes the form of powerful identifications and obsessive fascination as when the state engages in terrorist or criminal practices in order to appropriate the power it attributes to its enemies, criminals, subversives, or terrorists (Taylor 1997). These are not just moments of repression against enemies that are already there; they are fields in which the state and its enemies are created and recreated as powerful fictional realities (Siegel 1998) through what Derrida has called "a phantomatic mode of production" (1994, p. 97), a structure and *modus operandi* that produces both the state and its threatening Other as fetishes of each other, constructing reality as an endless play of mirror images. It is in the act of killing, kidnapping, disappearances, and imprisonment that the state materializes as a powerful spectral reality, which marks the bodies and souls of those subjected to its practice. In some parts of the world, the increase in criminal "phantom states" has been associated with the development of an increasingly spectral neoliberal economy, the violence of which has called into being old specters such as witches, zombies, and ghosts (Comaroff & Comaroff 1999, 2000a).

Criminal states alert us to the fact that the power of the state is harnessed not so much from the rationality of ordering practices as from the passions of transgression, in which the line between the legal and the illegal is constantly blurred. One has to recall Bataille and Foucault and think of what this particular blurred border may mean for the exercise of state power. To go back to fantasy, a good deal of the literature on the state and violence shows the state not as the product of rational technologies of control but as the subject of excess that bypasses any rational functionality. What articulates this excess is fantasy (the fantasy of statehood, the fantasy of total control, the fantasy of appropriation of the other, the fantasy of heterosexual domesticity...), which appears as a major component of political life and a key factor structuring power relations. Fantasy here is not meant as a purely illusory construction but as a form of reality in its own right, a scene whose structure traverses the boundary between the conscious and the unconscious (Laplanche & Pontalis 1989). Fantasy in this sense belongs to the "objectively subjective" (Zizek 1997). It is not opposed to social reality but constitutes its "psychic glue." The state can be considered then as "a privileged setting for the staging of political fantasy in the modern world" (Agamben 1998; Rose 1996, p. 4).

This is not to say that rational technologies of control are unimportant to the materialization of state power; it is to say that they are animated by a substrate of fantasy scenes that betray complicated kinds of intimacy, sensualities, and bodily operations. If the state is constituted as an effect of discourses and practices, this is an embodied and sensual effect. It depends on the continuous recreation of the body of national heroes (Navaro-Yashin 2002, Weiss 2002), on corpses and funerals as acts of possession and rebirth. The corpse mediates between the state and the people (Siegel 1998, Taussig 1997) in a process that seems intrinsic to the materialization of the state. In Indonesia, the emergence of a notion of criminality coincides with the suppression of the people under Suharto's New Order. The obsession with the criminal springs from the fact that the criminal mediates a realm of death "leading towards a force the state felt it lacked and which in mastering the criminal [massacring them], it hopes to have for itself" (Siegel 1998, p. 6). Is this process not also undergirding the obsession with guerrillas, ethnic rebels, and terrorists? There is an uncanny quality to the production of the state through the production of an enemy because often the criminal or terrorist or threatening Other is a familiar face, familiar but strange, strange in its familiarity, such as neighbors. Nothing distinguishes them from the rest except the fact of their death, kidnapping, disappearance, or arrest (Balibar & Wallerstein 1991, Siegel 1998, Taussig 1997, Warren 1993).

It is impossible, with all this, to ignore the discourses and practices of sexuality involved in the production and reproduction of the state. The systematic rapes of women and men that often accompany state formation, and that reached the proportions of genocide in the case of Bosnian Muslims and in Rwanda, have been linked by some scholars to the institutions of territorial sovereignty and heterosexuality. This collective sexual-political violence "is not the cause of anything but the effect of sexual political categories—of the interimplication of heterosexuality and territorial sovereignty" (Borneman 1998, p. 284). The embodied being of what counts as the state is not a neutral body but is instead a thoroughly sexualized one, whose sexual operations are invested with political power (Aretxaga 2001b, Das 1996, Taylor 1997). There is a strange intimacy between the state and the people. The state excises from the polis those subjects and practices that question or threaten homogeneous models of territorial sovereignty and heterosexual forms of political control, which are fundamental to national narratives of harmonious domesticity. This intimacy that filters and subverts modern disciplinary practices and rational technologies of control was already noticed by Foucault in his study of modern forms of punishment:

> The training of behavior by a full time-table, the acquisition of habits, the constraints of the body, imply a very special relation between the individual who

is punished and the individual who punishes him . . . .The agent of punishment must exercise total power which no third party can disturb; the individual to be corrected must be entirely enveloped in the power that is being exercised over him. Secrecy is imperative and so too is autonomy at least in relation to this technique of punishment. (Foucault 1979, p. 129)

The modern will to reform seems to have been abandoned to mere forms of confinement of those who are excluded from the social-political community. The camp as a form of exclusion and total control seems to have replaced the Foucauldian prison as a model of total control over life (Agamben 1998). Yet such total control over life and death only makes more acute the presence of terrifying forms of intimacy. In some ways, "the 'estrarity' of the person held in the sovereign ban is more intimate and primary than the extraneousness of the foreigner" (Agamben 1998, p. 110; Agamben 2000; Berlant 1997; Siegel 1998; Zizek 1993).

There is a relation of simultaneous attraction and repulsion that holds together this sovereign power and those reduced to bare life, life that can be killed without accountability (Agamben 1998, Hardt & Negri 2000). There is a will to legibility here as a state effect that is focused on bodies perceived as both familiar and opaque, an object of fascination and threat. The official gaze constantly scans these bodies for signs (of the criminal, the terrorist, the immigrant, the undocumented), in an attempt to render them transparent, to extricate the secret opacity of its uncanny familiarity. Practices of legibility are not detached but invested with affect. Ideologies of difference take the form of bodily diacritics that fuel the obsession to render threatening bodies and people legible. Yet these intense practices of legibility often produce more opacity, as subjects manipulate stereotypes, so that the state in its military, police, or legal embodiment may see everything and yet see nothing, as in the case noticed by Fanon (1967) of women in the Algerian anticolonial war who don the veil in order to carry arms unnoticed while the army focuses on veiled women as the object of terrorist threat (Aretxaga 1997, 2000a; Bhabha 1990; Das 2003; Fanon 1967). The terrifying force of the management of bodies and people that characterizes the modern state, coupled with the intimacies that invest it, is not unrelated to the power of the law as it has come to represent the sovereign power of the state. The intense affect of this power, its "obscene enjoyment" (Zizek 1993), ingeniously portrayed by Kafka in his famous novel *The Trial*, has a hold not only on one's life but also on one's soul. It has the capacity to drive people mad, madness that comes from being "oversaturated with law" (Berlant 1991), with the force of law without signification (Aretxaga 2000a, Santner 1996).

THE STATE OF EXCEPTION

On the one hand, for some scholars it is precisely when we set aside the problem of sovereignty that the state comes into view as a complex problem of power, an ensemble of techniques and tactics of domination that Foucault defines as more crucial than the state for those interested in power (Foucault 1979, 1991). Yet for others, the continuous desire for political sovereignty in the form of statehood makes unavoidable the question of what sovereignty means in the age of Empire (Hardt & Negri 2000). On the other hand, sovereignty takes the form of homogeneous territorial sovereignty justifying all sorts of violence against those defined as outsiders (Borneman 1998). Yet the claim to sovereignty from states and those aspiring to statehood entails a larger problematic of how power is articulated and imagined today in a global world where democracy has become the form and discourse of political legitimation. It entails also a reflection of the mystifying force of the law (Derrida 1991). What defines sovereignty for some scholars is the power to call a state of exception, a social-political space of force ruled by a law beyond the law, where the distinction between fact and law has become blurred (Agamben 1998, Hardt & Negri 2000, Schmitt 1985 [1922]). The state of exception is not decided by a situation of conflict or chaos, although this is often its discourse of legitimation; rather it is decided to affirm a juridical order in which lawfulness, right, is suspended in the name of law.

In this particular order, lawfulness and unlawfulness, execution and transgression of the law become indistinguishable "such that what violates a rule and what conforms to it coincide" (Agamben 1998, p. 57). Sovereignty then presents itself as the law, which stands outside the law. In this sense, to claim state sovereignty is to embody a juridical order that cannot be held accountable. The state in this sense is and is not the law. The lack of distinction between transgression and execution of the law that characterizes the state of exception, within which anything can happen, leaves the law as a terrifying force devoid of meaning from which one cannot escape. There is no position of exteriority to the power of a law that shows itself as arbitrary, ruthless, and invested with excitement (Zizek 1997), as Kafka so masterfully illustrated. And "what after all is a state that survives history, a state sovereignty that maintains itself beyond the accomplishments of its telos, is it not a law that is in force without signifying?" (Agamben 1998, p. 60). The question is "What is the place of this law that is beyond the law?" (Foucault 1982, p. 198).

In his "Theses on the Philosophy of History," Walter Benjamin noted that "the state of emergency in which we live is not the exception but the rule" (Benjamin 1968, p. 257). What the state of exception brings to the fore is the spectral domain of the law in the form of military and police violence, which takes, in the state of exception, an autonomy that was previously hidden. In this sense "the exception gives rise to a form of right which is really a right of the police" (Hardt & Negri 2000, p. 17). Yet the spectral domain of the law as the form of the state not only pertains to situations of military alert but also is the rule in the life of democratic states. Such spectrality comes from the violence of pure performativity in which the law simply affirms itself in a tautological form: "the law's interest in a monopoly of violence is not explained by the intention to preserve legal ends but, rather, by that of preserving the law itself; that violence when not in the hands of the law, threatens it not by the ends that it may pursue but by its mere existence outside the law" (Benjamin 1978, p. 281). More than in any other act, law (as the state) reaffirms itself in the exercise of power over life and death (Agamben 1998; Benjamin 1978; Hardt & Negri 2000; Siegel 1998; Taussig 1992, 1997). This lack of ultimate legitimation of law reveals something disturbing: "[A]t its foundation the rule of law is sustained . . . by the force/violence of a tautological enunciation—'the law is the law'" (Santner 1996, p. 10). Emptied of content, the violence of law, as sovereign power, becomes ghostly and persecutory, giving rise to forms of paranoiac acting from the state as much as from the subjects who encounter it. The ghostly, persecutory power of law is incarnated in the police, a haunting figure invested with formless power (Benjamin 1978), whose effects are seen as disappearances, corpses, arrests, and internments but whose identity remains mysterious, as objects of constant speculation, rumor, and fear. "The police becomes hallucinatory and spectral because they haunt everything; they are everywhere, even there where they are not, in their *Fort Dasein* to which we can always appeal. Their presence is not present, but the presence of its spectral double knows no boundaries" (Derrida 1991, p. 1011). Like in the king's two bodies, Kantorovitch's famous theory of sovereignty, the spectral double of the police acts like the permanent body of the state, a presence interiorized as the law, at once fearful and paternalistic, familiar and strange, uncanny, a presence that one cannot shake out of oneself. Is this not what is at stake in Althusser's famous example of interpellation, when a hail by the police "Hey you" compels one to turn around even when one knows one has done nothing wrong (Althusser 1971)? It is not the particular policeman as much as the spectral double, the state's other body wrenched with sovereign power, which, as a haunting law, makes one turn around when being hailed by the police. For Althusser this hailing is not about meaning or significance but about performative force. What transpires in this performance of the spectrality of the state is an imaginary and violent relation with the state but also a paternalistic one.

This confluence of annihilating violence and paternalistic intimacy present in the regulations of the law/state is precisely what produces an uncanny feeling in relation to the police (Brown 1995; Freud 1958 [1919], 1967; Gerth & Mills 1946). It is what can drive people mad as it did German Judge Daniel Paul Schreber, Freud's famous case of paranoid schizophrenia (Santner 1996). It is not only the coupling of rationality and violence as Weber suggested (Gerth & Mills 1946, Taussig 1992) that defines the state, for what is at stake in modern forms of sovereignty is not merely the management of bodies and populations, the power over life, but the intensification of bodies and intimacies that result from those technologies of management. What Schreber's diary of his illness illustrates is what happens "when law becomes entangled in the management of life," a state of affairs that for Foucault characterized modern forms of sovereignty: "a sustained traumatization induced by exposure to, as it were, fathers who knew too much about living human beings" (Santner 1996). Schreber's father was obsessed with disciplining the body through a variety of modern regimes and disciplines. But the question one can extract through his case is that one could easily replace *fathers who knew too much* with *states who knew too much* about the bodies and lives of people. The confluence of violence and paternalism, of force and intimacy, sustains the state as an object of ambivalence, an object of resentment for abandoning its subjects to their own fate and one desired as a subject that can provide for its citizens (Brown 1995, Ramirez 2001). The state is split into good and bad state, triggering an imaginary of the state in which desire and fear are entangled in a relation of misrecognition from which one cannot be extricated. Such inextricability from the state as law rests on an imaginary relationship with the state, which presupposes a passionate attachment to the law (Butler 1997). The hold of the law, the impossibility of extricating oneself from it, rests on the force of its performance which, lacking symbolic content, can create an obsessive attempt at interpretation, at translation of mere force into the language of reason. What is ultimately untranslatable about the performance of the law, the dimension of pure performativity that constitutes the law's authority, is the arbitrariness of its power to decide life and death.

The relationship to the law is one of being abandoned to the force of its own performance, of being transformed into bare life, at least for those who are excluded from its domain. This exclusion is always present as a potentiality, a sine qua non of the law and the state as an embodiment of its form. The state needs constant exclusions: Those who are excluded are included through their exclusion. These exclusions are always present as potentiality, a sine qua non of the law and the state as embodiments of its form, best seen in the camp as the emerging nomos of the political and as the space where the state of exception coincides with life, in which anything can happen (Agamben 1998).

The *Annual Review of Anthropology* is online at http://anthro.annualreviews.org

LITERATURE CITED

Abrams P. 1988. Notes on the difficulty of studying the state. *J. Hist. Sociol.* 1:58–89

Agamben G. 1998. *Homo Sacer: Sovereign Power and Bare Life*. Stanford, CA: Stanford Univ. Press

Agamben G. 2000. *Remnants of Auschwitz: The Witness and the Archive*. New York: Zone Books

Alonso AM. 1994. The politics of space, time and substance: state formation, nationalism and ethnicity. *Annu. Rev. Anthropol.* 23:379–405

Althusser L. 1971. Ideology and ideological state apparatuses. Notes towards an investigation. In *Lenin and Philosophy and Other Essays*, pp. 127–86. New York: Mon. Rev. Press

Anderson B. 1991 (1983). *Imagined Commu-* *nities. Reflections on the Origins and Spread of Nationalsm*. London: Verso

Appadurai A. 1993. Patriotism and its futures. *Public Cult.* 5:411–29

Appadurai A. 1996. *Modernity at Large: Cultural Dimensions of Globalization*. Minneapolis: Univ. Minn. Press

Aretxaga B. 1997. *Shattering Silence. Women, Nationalism and Political Subjectivity in Northern Ireland*. Princeton, NJ: Princeton Univ. Press

Aretxaga B. 1999. Lo 'real': violencia como realidad virtual. In *La Cuestión Vasca: Claves de un Conflicto Cultural y Político*, ed. JBaR Fernandez, pp. 106–17. Barcelona: Projecto A Ediciones

Aretxaga B. 2000a. A fictional reality: paramilitary death squads and the construction of state terror in Spain. In *Death Squad: The Anthropology of State Terror*, ed. JA Sluka, pp. 47–69. Philadelphia: Univ. Penn. Press

Aretxaga B. 2000b. Playing terrorist: ghastly plots and the ghostly state. *J. Span. Cult. Stud.* 1:43–58

Aretxaga B. 2001a. Terror as thrill: first thoughts on the 'war on terrorism.' *Anthropol. Q.* 75:139–53

Aretxaga B. 2001b. The sexual games of the body politic: fantasy and state violence in northern Ireland. *Cult. Med. Psychiatry* 25:1–27

Balibar E, Wallerstein IM. 1991. *Race, Nation, Class: Ambiguous Identities*. London; New York: Routledge

Benjamin W. 1968. Theses on the philosophy of history. In *Illuminations: Essays and Reflections*, ed. H Arendt, pp. 253–64. New York: Schocken Books

Benjamin W. 1978. Critique of violence. In *Reflections: Essays, Aphorisms, Autobiographical Writings*, ed. P Demetz, pp. 277–301. New York: Harcourt Brace Jovanovich

Berdahl D. 1999. *Where the World Ended: Re-Unification and Identity in the German Borderland*. Berkeley: Univ. Calif. Press

Berlant L. 1991. *The Anatomy of National Fantasy*. Chicago: The Univ. Chicago Press

Berlant L. 1993. The theory of infantile citizenship. *Public Cult.* 5:395–410

Berlant L. 1997. *The Queen of America Goes to Washington City. Essays on Sex and Citizenship*. Durham, NC: Duke Univ. Press

Bhabha H. 1990. *Nation and Narration*. London: Routledge

Borneman J. 1993. Uniting the German nation: law, narrative and historicity. *Am. Ethnol.* 20:288–311

Borneman J. 1998. *Subversions of International Order. Studies in the Political Anthropology of Culture*. Albany: State Univ. New York

Bourdieu P. 1999. Rethinking the state: genesis and structure of the bureaucratic field. In *State/Culture. State Formation After the Cultural Turn*, ed. G Steinmetz, pp. 53–72. Ithaca: Cornell Univ. Press

Brass PR. 1997. *Theft of an Idol. Text and Context in the Representation of Collective Violence*. Princeton, NC: Princeton Univ. Press

Brown W. 1995. *States of Injury: Power and Freedom in Late Modernity*. Princeton, NJ: Princeton Univ. Press

Butler J. 1997. *The Psychic Life of Power*. Stanford, CA: Stanford Univ. Press

Comaroff J, Comaroff J. 1999. Alien-nation: zombies, immigrants, and millenial capitalism. *South Atl. Q.* 4:779–806

Comaroff J, Comaroff J. 2000a. Millenial capitalism: first thoughts on a second coming. *Public Cult.* 12:291–343

Comaroff J, Comaroff J. 2000b. Naturing the nation: allies, apocalypse, and the postcolonial state. *Hagar. Int. Soc. Sci. Rev.* 1:7–40

Daniel VE. 1996. *Charred Lullabies. Chapters in an Anthropography of Violence*. Princeton, NJ: Princeton Univ. Press

Das V. 1990. *Mirrors of Violence: Communities, Riots, and Survivors in South Asia*. Delhi; New York: Oxford Univ. Press. 407 pp.

Das V. 1996. Sexual violence, discursive formations and the state. *Econ. Polit. Wkly.* 31:2411–25

Das V. 2003. *The State at its Margins: Comparative Ethnographies*. Santa Fe: Advanced Seminar Series, SAR. In press

Denich B. 1994. Dismembering Yugoslavia: nationalist ideologies and the symbolic revival of genocide. *Am. Ethnol.* 21:367–90

Derrida J. 1991. Force of law: the mystical foundations of authority. *Cardozo Law Rev.* 11:921–1045

Derrida J. 1994. *Specters of Marx*. New York: Routledge

Fanon F. 1967. *A Dying Colonialism*. New York: Grove Press

Ferguson J. 1990. *The Anti-Politics Machine: "Development," Depoliticization, and Bureaucratic Power in Lesotho*. Cambridge, UK; New York: Cambridge Univ. Press

Fortes M, Evans-Pritchard EE, eds. 1940. *African Political Systems*. London: Int. Inst. Afr. Lang. Cult./Oxford Univ. Press

Foucault M. 1978. *The History of Sexuality*. New York: Vintage Books

Foucault M. 1979. *Discipline and Punish: The Birth of a Prison.* New York: Random House

Foucault M. 1982. *I Pierre Riviere, Having Slaughtered my Mother, my Sister and my Brother...* Lincoln: Univ. Neb. Press

Foucault M. 1991. Governmentality. In *The Foucault Effect: Studies in Governmentality,* ed. G Burchell, C Gordon, P Miller, pp. 87–104. Chicago: The Univ. Chicago Press

Freud S. 1958 (1919). The uncanny. In *On Creativity and the Unconscious,* ed. B Nelson, pp. 122–61. New York: Harper Torchbooks

Freud S. 1967. *Moses and Monotheism.* New York: Vintage Books

Geertz C. 1973. *The Interpretation of Cultures.* New York: Basic Books

Gerth HH, Mills CW, eds. 1946. *From Max Weber: Essays in Sociology.* New York: Oxford Univ. Press

Girard R. 1979. *Violence and the Sacred.* Baltimore: Johns Hopkins Univ. Press

Grant B. 2001. New Moscow monuments, or, states of innocence. *Am. Ethnol.* 28:332–62

Gupta A. 1995. Blurred boundaries: the discourse of corruption, the culture of politics, and the imagined state. *Am. Ethnol.* 22:375–402

Gupta A. 1998. *Postcolonial Developments: Agriculture in the Making of Modern India.* Durham, NC: Duke Univ. Press. 409 pp.

Hale CR. 2002. Does multiculturalism menace? Governance, cultural rights and the politics of identity in Guatemala. *J. Lat. Am. Stud.* 34:485–524

Hallinan JT. 2001. *Going Up the River. Travels in a Prison Nation.* New York: Random House

Handler R. 1988. *Nationalism and the Politics of Culture in Quebec.* Madison: Univ. Wisc. Press

Hannerz U. 1996. *Transnational Connections.* New York: Routledge

Hardt M, Negri A. 2000. *Empire.* Cambridge, MA: Harvard Univ. Press

Herzfeld M. 1997. *Cultural Intimacy: Social Poetics in the Nation-State.* New York: Routledge

Kafka F. 1964. *The Trial.* New York: Modern Library

Kearney M. 1995. The local and the global: the anthropology of globalization and transnationalism. *Annu. Rev. Anthropol.* 24:547–65

Kundera M. 1981. *The Book of Laughter and Forgetting.* New York: Penguin

Laplanche J, Pontalis JB. 1989. *New Foundations for Psychoanalysis.* Oxford; New York: Basil Blackwell

Malkki LH. 1995. *Purity and Exile: Violence, Memory and National Cosmology Among Hutu Refugees in Tanzania.* Chicago: The Univ. Chicago Press

Mitchell T. 1991. The limits of the state: beyond statist approaches and their critics. *Am. Polit. Sci. Rev.* 85:77–96

Nagengast C. 1994. Violence, terror, and the crisis of the state. *Annu. Rev. Anthropol.* 23: 109–36

Navaro-Yashin Y. 2002. *Faces of the State: Secularism and Public Life in Turkey.* Princeton, NJ: Princeton Univ. Press

Nelson DM. 1999. *A Finger in the Wound. Body Politics in Quincentennial Guatemala.* Berkeley: Univ. Calif. Press

Ong A. 1999. *Flexible Citizenship: The Cultural Logics of Transnationality.* Durham, NC: Duke Univ. Press

Poulantzas N. 1978. *State, Power, Socialism.* London: New Left Books. 269 pp.

Ramirez MC. 2001. *Entre el Estado y la Guerrilla: Identidad y Ciudadania en el Movimiento de los Campesinos Cocaleros del Putamayo.* Bogota: Inst. Colomb. Antropologia Hist.

Rose J. 1996. *States of Fantasy.* Oxford: Clarendon Press

Rosenberg D, Lukens N, eds. 1993. *Daughter's of Eve: Women's Writing from the German Democratic Republic.* Lincoln: Univ. Neb. Press

Santner EL. 1996. *My Own Private Germany: Daniel Paul Schreber's History of Modernity.* Princeton, NJ: Princeton Univ. Press

Schmitt C. 1985 (1922). *Political Theology. Four Chapters on the Concept of Sovereignty.* Cambridge, MA: MIT Press

Scott JC. 1998. *Seeing Like a State: How Certain Schemes to Improve the Human Condition Have Failed.* New Haven, CT: Yale Univ. Press. 445 pp.

Siegel JT. 1998. *A New Criminal Type in Jakarta: Counter-Revolution Today.* Durham, NC: Duke Univ. Press. 145 pp.

Simmel G. 1955. *Conflict.* Glencoe, IL: Free Press

Steinmetz G. 1999. *State/Culture. State Formation After the Cultural Turn.* Ithaca, NY: Cornell Univ. Press

Suárez-Orozco M. 1992. Grammar of terror: psychocultural responses to state terrorism in dirty war and post-dirty war Argentina. In *Paths to Domination, Resistance, and Terror.* Berkeley: Univ. Calif. Press

Tambiah SJ. 1996. The nation state in crisis and the rise of ethno-nationalism. In *The Politics of Difference,* ed. EN Wilmsen, P McAllister, pp. 124–43. Chicago: The Univ. Chicago Press

Tambiah SJ. 1997. *Leveling Crowds: Ethnonationalist Conflicts and Collective Violence in South Asia.* Berkeley: Univ. Calif. Press

Taussig M. 1986. *Shamanism, Colonialism and the Wild Man: A Study in Terror and Healing.* Chicago: The Univ. Chicago Press

Taussig M. 1992. Maleficium: state fetishism. In *The Nervous System,* pp. 111–40. New York: Routledge

Taussig M. 1993. *Mimesis and Alterity: A Particular History of the Senses.* New York: Routledge

Taussig M. 1997. *The Magic of the State.* New York: Routledge

Taylor D. 1997. *Disappearing Acts. Spectacles of Gender and Nationalism in Argentina's "Dirty War."* Durham, NC: Duke Univ. Press

Taylor J. 1999. *Agency, Trauma, and Representation in the Face of State Violence: Argentina.* Brasilia: Univ. Brasilia Dep. Antropologia. 16 pp.

Trouillot M-R. 1990. *Haiti: State Against Nation.* New York: Mon. Rev. Press

Trouillot M-R. 2001. The anthropology of the state in the age of globalization. Close encounters of the deceptive kind. *Curr. Anthropol.* 42:125–38

Tsing A. 2000. The global situation. *Cult. Anthropol.* 15:327–60

Warren KB. 1993. *The Violence Within: Cultural and Political Opposition in Divided Nations.* Boulder, CO: Westview Press. 262 pp.

Weiss M. 2002. *The Chosen Body: The Politics of the Body in Israeli Society.* Stanford, CA: Stanford Univ. Press

Zizek S. 1993. *Tarrying with the Negative: Kant, Hegel, and the Critique of Ideology.* Durham, NC: Duke Univ. Press

Zizek S. 1997. *The Plague of Fantasies.* London: Verso

Zulaika J, Douglass W. 1996. *Terror and Taboo. The Follies, Fables and Faces of Terrorism.* New York: Routledge

Annu. Rev. Anthropol. 2003. 32:411–29
doi: 10.1146/annurev.anthro.32.061002.093449

HIGHLIGHTS AND OVERVIEW OF THE HISTORY OF EDUCATIONAL ETHNOGRAPHY

Daniel A. Yon

*Department of Anthropology, York University, Toronto, Ontario, M6E 3N1, Canada;
email: dyon@edu.yorku.ca*

Key Words   schooling, postmodern, correspondence theory, symbolic production,
countercultures/resistance theory

■ **Abstract**   In broad brush strokes, this essay identifies and reviews key trends and
theoretical orientations that have shaped the field of educational ethnography from the
period of its inception to the closing decade of the twentieth century. It demonstrates
how the growth of educational ethnography as a subfield within anthropology reflects
a growing focus on prescriptive, applied, and reformist research within urban contexts.
It maps the transition from modernist formulations of the field in its formative days,
when ethnographies laid claim to being sealed and scientific texts, to the more recent
formulations shaped by postmodern and poststructural ideas that undermine earlier
meanings of culture and call attention to the explanatory limits of ethnography. This
review draws on examples from North America and Britain and makes no claim to being
exhaustive of the vast and growing field. Although it delineates what distinguishes
successive decades of educational ethnography, the essay argues for understanding the
developments not as distinct phases but as overlapping moments in the evolution of
the field of study. Attention is drawn to how developments in theory and method, in
particular a move toward reflexivity in educational ethnography, mirror developments
in the discipline of anthropology at large.

CONTEXT AND SCOPE OF THE FIELD

Long-established anthropological concerns about the socialization and enculturation of children in different cultural settings formed the historical context for the
evolution, in the latter part of the twentieth century, of a distinct field of research
focused on ethnographic accounts of schools and educational settings, broadly
defined as the anthropology of education. The history and scope of this field of
research has been fairly well documented (Banks 1993; Burnett 1974; Eddy 1985;
Fisher 1998; Heshusius & Ballard 1996; Spindler 1984, 2000; Wax et al. 1971;
Wilcox 1982), and reflections on its future have looked backward and forward to
establish the kinds of questions that continue to preoccupy ethnographers of education and schooling (Bratlinger 1999). Spindler (1984, 2000) notes the "meteoric
rise" in the volume of educational ethnographies in the later decades of the

0084-6570/03/1021-0411$14.00   **411**

twentieth century. This rise, evidently, is concerned with how the genre of inquiry draws practitioners not only from anthropology but also from psychology and sociology, and, more recently, cultural studies. Furthermore, growing ethnographic research in education has to do with the attractiveness and promise of ethnography not only as a process and product that embody novelty and pleasurable reading but also as a method that claims to take the reader into the actual world of its subjects in order to reveal the cultural knowledge that is working in a particular place, as it is actually lived through its subjects (Britzman 1995). Ethnographic research is doubly attractive for the qualitative child-centered and culturally sensitive insights it offers to a field of research traditionally preoccupied with quantitative measurements.

The volume and scope of educational ethnography undertaken in the period surveyed here is vast. This review does not attempt to document the scope, rehearse the histories, or reaffirm the key figures that occupy and shape the field. Instead the reader is reminded that *Anthropology and Education Quarterly* continues to be the flagship for the dissemination of reviews and research in the field. This essay identifies, in broad brush strokes, some of the key trends and theoretical developments shaping the field from the period of its inception to the closing decades of the twentieth century. This focus is confined to North America and Britain. Such a focus, however, should not overlook more recent and extensive research in colonial, postcolonial, and late neoliberal contexts (deserving of a another review) in which ethnographic research draws attention to the operations and enculturating projects of schools as unique institutions in their respective social landscapes and historical contexts (see, for example, Bond 2000; Bryant 2001; Dolby 2001; Foley 1977, 1991; Kaplan 1996).

The aim of this review is to chart some of the theoretical developments in educational ethnography from its earlier formulation as a subdiscipline in anthropology roughly in the period following the First World War to its state in the closing decade of the twentieth century. This focus reveals an overall transition from the formative modernist formulations and promises of educational ethnography as sealed and scientific texts to the later postmodern and post-structuralist orientations that acknowledge multiple meanings of culture, paying attention to the implication of both ethnographers and readers in their ethnographic endeavors and recognizing the explanatory limits of ethnography genres. This reading is neither smooth nor linear and, while I attempt to break this account into periods, there are no clear breaks in educational ethnography. Instead of neat breaks, what emerges is a continuing set of tensions as modernist and postmodernist orientations and notions of structuralism and post-structuralism vie for authority. Or, taking a different glance at the same account, we see how concerns with the impact of structure upon agency in earlier ethnographic accounts of schooling are reworked and reordered to focus on how agency produces structure. In this sense, the review shows how trends in the making of educational ethnographies essentially mirror the same kinds of tensions, continuities, and shifts that are discerned in the working of theory and ethnography since the 1960s (Ortner 1994).

THE FORMATIVE YEARS

Eddy (1985) provides an extensive list of anthropologists whose work has variously engaged formalized systems of education and issues of enculturation during what is described as the formative years of educational ethnography, 1925–1954. *Highlights in the History of the Council of Anthropology in Education* offers an insightful summary of the key concerns, meetings, and specific projects for this period. These formative years, and the decade following them, were distinguished by beliefs about the ethnographer as a detached and objective observer. However, the convening of a conference by Margaret Mead in 1949, for the purpose of exploring the educational problems of special cultural groups, foreshadowed the direction of future educational ethnography and challenged notions of the detached observer. Educational ethnography came increasingly to champion the rights and interests of marginalized groups, initially in the United States. Among the early examples of the overarching concern with the marginalized was a six-year social action program on Native American personality, education, and administration, designed to collect scientific data (by using participant observation) for the U.S. Department of the Interior and Commissioner of Indian Affairs in 1941 (Mead 1951). Such interest in the education of Native American children suggests that the beginnings of educational ethnography in North America grew out of anthropology's conventional preoccupation with native "others," within the dominant paradigm of cultural relativism, albeit the native was "at home." Also significant was British structural functionalism, which offered a holistic model for engaging the socialization of the child in environments perceived to be structured by cultural norms and traditional institutions. Holistic paradigms thus structured early research on education in North American Indian cultures (Pettit 1946).

The seminal role played by the Spindlers in the institutional and disciplinary development of educational ethnography is now well recognized, and George Spindler's convening of the first Educational Anthropology Conference at Stanford in 1954 was a significant moment in this history. He writes:

> Anthropology can help shed light on human behavior in educational situations just as it has on behaviour in factories, hospitals, peasant communities, air force installations, Indian Reservations, New England towns, and various primitive societies . . . . [D]irectly relevant are the concepts and data of specialized and relatively new fields in anthropology, such as personality and culture ("psychological anthropology") and cultural dynamics (culture change and acculturation). (1955, p. 58)

Spindler's interest in culture and personality focused on the evolving, enduring, and situated self, with culture increasingly being seen as heritage and a resource that can be utilized in the processes of making the self. Culture, in the formative years of educational ethnography, was increasingly understood as dynamically changing in the process of transmission. This, coupled with a shift toward an anthropological approach informed by social responsibility of the researchers and the ethical implications of the research, was significant for subsequent directions of educational ethnography in the 1960s and 1970s. These kinds of shifts toward engaged, and what later became "activist," research are evoked by Margaret Mead's (1951) *The School in American Culture*, in which images of the little red schoolhouse as the symbol of stability, democracy, and gradual change in American society, are juxtaposed with the modern city school as lacking in architectural personality for the children of poor, immigrant, and "others." This contrast between rural and urban, modern and traditional worked within the modern/primitive trope, which also evoked assumptions about the pathology of American culture as contrasted with the "harmony and stability" of the "primitive cultures" that had occupied Mead elsewhere. Mead's interest in the contrasting personalities of schools also reflects the significance of personality and cultural change as dominant themes in the formative period of educational ethnography.

Important to these formative years is the work of Franz Boas and in particular his interest in "the problems of modern life" (Boas 1962). Three ideas in particular foreshadowed the kinds of preoccupations that came to distinguish educational ethnography in the subsequent decades: (*a*) the challenge Boas' work posed to prevailing beliefs in the immutability of racial characteristics and his insistence that cultural forms are not reducible to race; (*b*) the attention he drew to how bodily developments are related to the economic state and conditions of families; (*c*) his reminder that while anthropological research may help understand social phenomena, it offers no predictability. These kinds of early theorizations undermined prevalent assumptions about primodialism and, with respect to ethnographic research, insisted upon a methodology that calls attention to how groups are socially produced. By destabilizing assumptions about innate characteristics of "race," for example, the ground was laid for works that fleshed out the accounts of how seemingly innate meanings are made and culturally sustained. Such ideas and methodological assumptions became the "common sense" givens of educational ethnography in the decades that followed.

THE SIXTIES: CONSOLIDATING THE FIELD

Singleton (1984) describes the convergence of anthropological interests at what was at times a "highly charged and confrontational" session at the annual AAA meetings in Seattle in 1968. The outcome of this meeting of separate networks of educational ethnographers was the formation of a new coalition and network, encouraged by Margaret Mead among others, to organize formally in pursuit of the anthropology of education. The establishment of the *Council of Education's Newsletter*, which became the *Education Quarterly Journal* in 1970, confirmed the institutionalization of the field in North America.

The institutionalization of educational ethnography reflects tendencies away from the historic preoccupation in Western anthropology with "exotic others" toward doing fieldwork "at home." This move coincided with a growing theoretical focus in the social sciences on links between geographic, social, and economic integration as well as segregation. Experiences of high mobility, upheaval, and dramatic demographic change associated with the development of the metropolis and the suburb in the postwar era are also the context for this evolving field of study. Thus, a central theme during this era was the problems of social change and the transition from an agrarian to a technological society with the metropolitan city as the dominant form of community life (Bloom et al. 1965; Eddy 1967; Havighurst & Levine 1971; Reiss 1965; Schrag 1967; Spindler 1955, 1959). These kinds of concerns were widely shared in the social sciences and humanities, and the ethnographic method, traditionally associated with anthropology, was increasingly taken up as a most effective research method for addressing them as evidence in, for example, the work of the Chicago School of Sociology.

In the United States, ethnographies focused not only on increasing immigration and the imperatives of assimilation—the notion of the melting pot—but also on movements within the U.S. population, namely that of African Americans to the northern cities as well as substantial migrations of Puerto Rican and Southern Appalachian white populations to cities where they collectively came to constitute the urban poor (Bloom et al. 1965, Eddy 1967, Havighurst & Levine 1971, Landes 1965, Leacock 1969, Schrag 1967, Smith & Geoffrey 1968, Wax et al. 1964, Wax & Wax 1964). In this context, the focus on applied, operational, prescriptive, and reformist research viewed the metropolis as a special unit of analysis for looking at culture in progress with education as the key to rational, planned, and directed change (Brameld 1957, Havighurst & Levine 1971, Landes 1965, Mead 1951, Schrag 1967). Indeed, it was argued that a proper appreciation of society was indispensable to a proper appreciation of what education should mean in reference to it. But the prescriptive and reformist trends in educational ethnography began to push the perceived functions of schooling. Thus Seeley (1964, p. 46) argued that although the school may be instituted by society its purpose is not to represent society as it is but rather to recall it to that which it would wish to be.

The kinds of shifts in focus effected by educational ethnographic research described thus far, from exotic others in far-flung places to the exotic and marginalized "at home" and from detached observation to ethical engagement, also paralleled growing interest in social and cultural differentiations based on race, class, and ethnicity. This must be related to the fact that anthropology as a whole became increasingly interested in the West and in mainstream modern institutions in the late twentieth century. Education was perceived as integral to this shift in focus. The period was also marked by anthropological theory and practice becoming increasingly linked to the availability of government funding for poverty and desegregation/integration-related research aimed at adaptation, adjustment, enculturation, assimilation, and the socialization of minorities and the marginalized into dominant cultures. Jackson's (1968) *Life in Classrooms* emerges as a seminal work in fleshing out societal and school-based linkages and establishing the school as a microcosm of the society it serves. Constituting the classroom as a stable and standardized environment characterized by intense ritualistic and cyclical activities, Jackson demonstrated the importance of participant observation to educational researchers. He identified the disjunctures between the theories and practices of teaching and learning. Jackson noted the teacher's multiple roles as gatekeeper, supply sergeant, and timekeeper, these being the unpublicized features of school life. He also stressed the value of studying the dominant features of instructional interchange and curriculum design. Although much of his view was conceptualized through the lens of a normative understanding of culture, Jackson noted the "infinitely complex" picture of adjustment within the school environment, including withdrawal on the part of school participants. But perhaps most significant for the future directions of school ethnography was his insistence upon an ethnographic method that pays attention to "things that come and go" such as "twinkling-things like a students yawn or a teachers frown," given that, "such transitory events may contain more information about classroom life than might appear at first glance" (Jackson 1968). These are the sentiments that would be echoed in the call for "thick description" and the significance of the "nods" and "winks" in educational research as in anthropology at large (Jackson 1968). Similarly, in Smith & Geoffrey's (1968) *Complexities of an Urban Classroom*, we might discern precursors to the kinds of methodological anxieties and ethical dilemmas about the processes of information-gathering, including reviewing letters from parents, that have preoccupied subsequent ethnographers.

Looking back at the 1960s and the preceding decades, we find educational ethnographies preoccupied with the apparent contradiction between the official goals of and their actual effects on schooling. In the best tradition of humanist thinking, education was perceived as a normative enterprise whose obligation was:

> not only to help personalities come to terms with the dominant goals of their respective cultures, but to help them analyze, express, implement, and often reconstitute these goals as fully as they are able to and as comprehensively as they see fit. (Brameld 1957, p. 196)

These kinds of assumptions, about both the normative enterprise and role of schooling, are structured by normative understandings of culture, and a persisting interest in cultural transmission and enculturation within formalized systems of education. Educational ethnography, however, offered a critique of both official goals and the means to achieving them. Thus attention was increasingly paid to the unintended consequences of the "natural" processes of schooling and the hidden cultural influences that, in everyday practices, superseded conscious attention (Spindler 1959). Out of this tension came a growing focus on what variously came to be understood as the hidden curriculum as well as attention to subcultures as units of analysis within the larger cultural context of education. This trend was evident at the onset of the 1960s as educational ethnography moved far beyond schools and beyond the discipline of anthropology to include critical cultural studies.

The continuing backdrop of social change (brought about by urbanization, migration, and industrialization), concerns with psychological adaptation, the resolution of culture conflicts, generational transmission of culture, and the kinds of symbolic meaning that came to be attached to repetitive behaviors such as rituals continued as dominant themes in the 1970s (see, for example, Leemon 1972). Concerns with personality and culture persisted, and functionalism, which had provided the dominant conceptual and analytical frame, was reproduced as the school continued to be viewed as a society within itself, having its own dominant system of values, pervasive ideologies, and characteristic networks of interrelations within and outside. Thus, Wolcott's (1973) *Man in the Principal's Office: An Ethnography* emphasized the social rather than the physiological and psychological aspects of behavior through theories of cultural deprivation. This work focused on the processes by which Ed Bell, the principal of a "comfortable" suburban elementary school in a lower-middle to middle-class and predominantly white community, was linked to the broader set of social and economic relations in which he lived his life. Bell was found to perform a stability-maintaining role as monitor for community, an agent of its rhetoric, rather than a source for actual change. Wolcott saw the role of ethnographer as the participant-as-observer, emphasizing description over interpretation, in arriving at the themes of principalship. The test of ethnography, he wrote, is "whether it enables one to anticipate and interpret what goes on in a society or social group as appropriately as one of its members" (1973, p. xi). But Wolcott's desire for both ethnographer and reader to "go native" in this "test" was already compromised by the dilemma posed by his friendship with his own "native," the principal. This friendship produced its own anxieties for the author and his capacity to "go native." Significantly too, such work called attention to the general tendency toward conservatism in functionalism. This was one of the faultlines in the field of educational ethnography that would be occupied by Marxism as the 1970s progressed.

THE SEVENTIES: STRUCTURALISM AND MARXISM

Rist's (1973) *The Urban School: A Factory of Failure*, published in the same year as Wolcott's text, documented the classroom as the face-to-face level of a complex system that operates to keep the poor and black oppressed. This longitudinal study of an all-black school inside a black community "persistently and doggedly contained by surrounding whites" (1973, p. xiv) remained within a functionalist analytical frame, constituting the classroom as a microcosm of the larger society in which the attitudes and assumptions necessary for perpetuating inequality were legitimated (1973, p. 245). Rist argued for the need to disabuse oneself of assumptions about the mythical functions of schools so that "we can begin to meet the needs of children in humane ways that do not require them to be more than simply children" (1973, p. 254). Demystifying the functions of school implied a critique of dominant ideologies of social mobility by calling attention to the role of schools in normalizing social inequality (Clement et al. 1979; Ogbu 1974, 1978; Rist 1973).

In the 1970s, we thus see educational ethnography redefining its orientation in relation to taken-for-granted assumptions about structural functionalism and the integration imperatives of earlier eras. Education was no longer viewed as the unproblematic key to rational, planned, and directed change, as in Mead's call for new educational forms as adaptive strategies for dealing with the new metropolitan conditions or the need for urban renewal. The meaning of culture in educational anthropology, following trends in the discipline at large, was reconceptualized in terms of competing and conflicting interests constituted by, and within, unequal relations of power. With the beginning of discourses of multiculturalism and antiracism, and amid continuing concerns with the effects of immigration, notions of desegregation and assimilation assumed more ambiguous meanings. Far from being an accepted goal of education, acculturation and assimilation, in their efforts to "accommodate" differences, became the problem and were viewed as the source of new kinds of subordination, discrimination, and marginalization. Ethnographies began to pay increasing attention to the social significance of difference premised on sex, race, class, and ethnicity. Older concerns with culture and personality, which idealized views of schools as democratic engines, were eclipsed by critiques of schooling as perpetuating academic failure among minorities (Rist 1973; Ogbu 1974, 1978).

Thus, Ogbu (1974), a West African living in America (an "anthropologist as stranger"), addressed the question of the disproportionate school failure of city children from minority groups. The conceptual thrust was premised on the Durkheimian view that when the behavior of a large number of people within a society, or any segment thereof, departs from the norm, then the problem has to be explained in terms of the behavior of the group and not that of its individual members. The high rates of failure were considered to be both a reaction as well as an adaptation to the pervasive racism in American society and to the limited opportunities for the racially marked. Challenging psychological themes of "cultural deprivation," Ogbu stressed the importance of looking at different folk systems and theories of education based in experiential reality rather than "social reality," concluding that "the real source of school-based failure lies in the wider community. The schools—administrators, counselors, teachers, pupils and so on—are merely playing the roles that the community assigns to them" (1974, p. 16). He argued that school failures should not be viewed as abnormal but as influenced by historical, cultural, and structural factors and by the location of those who failed within systems of unequal power relations (taxpayers/non-taxpayers and patron-client relationships). Here we might note the influence and echoes of cultural ecology, specifically its focus on adaptation for explaining the adaptive functions of particular social groups such as African Americans. Adaptation, in this sense, explains the development, maintenance, and transformation of social forms (Ortner 1994, p. 378). Ogbu thus identified the caste-like status—that is, the inferior social and occupational positions—held by minorities, specifically African

Americans, as generating and sustaining patterns of unequal school performance. Ethnographic studies that followed from this conceptualization pointed to how school knowledge itself is racialized as demonstrated, for example, in the extent that African Americans who embrace it are perceived among their racial groups as acting white (Fordham & Ogbu 1986; Ogbu 1978, 1988; Rist 1979; Weis 1985).

On the other side of the Atlantic, anthropology's virtual monopoly of the ethnographic method was being challenged as the 1970s progressed with the rise of cultural studies. Working within this new multidisciplinary perspective, proposed by the Birmingham School, Paul Willis' (1977) *Learning to Labour* addressed the gaps in the Marxist-oriented ethnography of working-class students and schools' roles in reproducing labor power. His analysis illustrated ethnographically how working-class kids reproduce their working-class status not simply as dupes of structure but as active agents. Contextualized within the culture of schooling, *Learning to Labour* became the inspiration for studies of school subcultures and countercultures found under the umbrella of resistance theory (Everhart 1983, Delgado-Gaitan 1988, Goodson & Ball 1984, Sefa Dei 1996, Soloman 1992, Weis 1988). The masculinity and toughness of the culture of the "lads" of *Learning to Labour* was constituted in the image of "shop-floor culture," i.e., as a form of masculine chauvinism. The strategies of working-class kids to take control of their own unofficial timetables were viewed as efforts to control their own routines and life spaces (Willis 1977, pp. 52–53). The "lads" were thus somewhat romantically constituted not as dupes of the capitalist system but as agents actively involved in reproducing it. This ethnography called attention to self-induction as a significant aspect of regenerating working-class culture and to the paradoxical ways by which schooling fulfills its unrecognized objective of directing a proportion of working-class kids "voluntarily" to skilled, semi-skilled, and unskilled manual labor. This "cultural Marxist" account demonstrated how cultural forms could neither be reduced to, nor be regarded simply as, epiphenomenal expressions of structural factors.

Willis argued instead that cultural forms mediate the real structural relationships of society and are a necessary part of the dialectic of reproduction (1977, p. 174). Cultural forms provide the materials and the context for the construction of subjectivities and identities. Resistance theory addresses what is less explicit in correspondence and reproduction theory, namely how society is reproduced culturally. One of the most influential theoretical influences of this resistance theory came from Gramsci's (1971) notion of hegemony and counter-hegemony, which stressed the creation of a cultural sphere wherein people are socialized into different levels of class awareness and consciousness. In positing a more nuanced account of reproduction theory, agents are reconstituted as mutually implicated in the production of the structures through which life is organized as opposed to being simply products of structures. Thus, following what Giddens (1984) calls structuration theory, there is a duality and mutual implication of structure and agency.

As the 1970s gave way to the 1980s, social structure was increasingly recognized as being unstable, contradictory, and no longer the taken-for-granted, all-determining object "out there." Ethnomethodology, which concentrated on the everyday and seemingly trivial but practical activities of everyday life, challenged concentrations on the larger questions of social structures (Benson & Hughes 1983, Turner 1974). It was used as a tool for studying rites of passage in schooling and classroom life and for ascertaining, in the language of ethnomethodology, the "practical reasoning" that underpins social interactions. It highlighted the revitalization mechanism of school culture and how it reconfirmed the organizational scheme of society by producing in students a tacit understanding and acceptance of their social position by constituting it as an objective social fact (Mehan 1979). This particular emphasis on social processes continued to stress school/community/societal linkages (the micro-macro model) and the networks spanning all three. But the need to recognize the more dynamic nature of social processes and interpersonal interaction beyond the traditional structural-functional framework was also emphasized (Apple & Weis 1983, Ogbu 1988, Rist 1979, Sullivan 1979). Reproduction and correspondence theory began to take different forms, moving away from the structural determination by which structures are perceived as merely producing agents, to pay attention to how schools are sites for competing meanings of culture. This more nuanced account of structure and agency also benefited from Bourdieu's notion of habitus and his theory of practice (Bourdieu 1977). A theory of practice focused on decoding the cultural forms through which people live their lives and on how individuals come to embody and assume those forms as the taken-for-granted basis for their everyday social activity. The influence of language and discourse was also significant. Discourse, in this context, is viewed in the Durkheimian sense as a distinctive social reality with the classroom being constituted through speech events or routinized forms of behavior (Collins 1996, Schecter & Bayley 2002). Following the rise of multiculturalism, attention was increasingly called to the failure of schools to respond to cultural, linguistic, and cognitive differences; to different linguistic codes; and to the "ethnosemantic domain" where labeling maintained social boundaries, reinforced in turn by school curricula (Clement et al. 1979; Everhart 1983; Hymes 1972, 1974; Mehan 1979; Rist 1973; Sullivan 1979; Varenne 1982; Wilcox 1982).

Bringing together Marxist theory of labor processes and Habermas' concern with symbolic action to interpret the ties between popular culture and social formations, Everhart's (1983) ethnography of male youth in an American junior high school saw culture as the ground on which ideologies work, the subjects having agency that could be deployed to resist, mediate, and transform the domination and exploitation they experience. In contrast to Willis' "lads" in Britain, Everhart points to the tensions between the reified knowledge of the school and the regenerative knowledge of students. He shows, too, how youth do not totally reject the formal curriculum but rather resist by giving only what is necessary so as to not endanger their possible social mobility. Everhart notes the role of forces of symbolic production, including language, communication patterns, and belief systems, that enter the whole project of schooling as a means of knowledge transmission. Thus, the everyday humor and "goofing" that characterized a significant aspect of adolescent practices reaffirmed group membership in a pervasive manner and provided a sense of control and collective meaning greater than the acts themselves. Resistance theory, especially with respect to class inequalities, thus challenged older models, conceptualized though correspondence theory, which, as in the work of Bowles & Gintis (1976) for example, saw schooling as the site for the transmission of ideology and structural integration. Ethnographic studies paid attention, instead, to notions of autonomy and internal contradictions.

INTO THE EIGHTIES AND THE NINETIES: MULTI-VOCALITY AND THE SHIFTING MEANINGS OF CULTURE

As the 1980s progressed, the theoretical influences and conceptual tools available for writing educational ethnographies multiplied and competed. There was a continued focus on schools as institutions of cultural and economic reproduction, theorized through a functionalist analytical framework, with the classroom as a replicating microcosm of the wider society (Gearing & Epstein 1982, Peshkin 1982). But the over-determination of correspondence theory and structural functionalism encountered the increasing interest in, and concern with, questions of voice, multi-vocality, and agency. Feminism and antiracism competed and converged with neo-Marxism. Debates about culture in education also paralleled the increasingly central question of identity and identifications as culture became the ground on which identities and ideologies were contested and worked out. Challenging earlier unidirectional micro-macro dynamics, education and schooling were conceptualized as lived hegemony and habitus, created and recreated as culture from within, not just from outside; the crucial links between knowledge and power were emphasized not simply as a force that comes from outside but that is also present in notions of cultural capital (Anyon 1981; Apple 1982; Bourdieu & Passeron 1977; Delpit 1988; Everhart 1983; Player 1984; Weis 1985, 1988).

Throughout the 1980s and into the 1990s, feminist ethnographers noted the gendered assumptions of established models of resistance theory (Grant et al. 1994, Hall & Sandler 1982, Holland & Eisenhart 1990, Kelly & Nihlen 1982, Leadbeater et al. 1996). In this view, the focus for school ethnographies should not just be on the contested production of class relations but also on the simultaneous self-formative cultural reproduction of raced, gendered, classed identities and subjectivities. The intersection of these categories of identity came to be viewed not only as a structure but also as experience embodied in live actors and cultures (Bourdieu 1977). However, ethnographic works demonstrated that embodied experiences and identities were rarely smooth. Thus McCarthy (1990) coins the notion nonsynchrony, which emphasized the interruptions, discontinuities, and attenuations of the effects of identity categories in social and institutional settings, while noting that these catagories do not simply reproduce each other. Identity formations through class, gender, and race came to be viewed in educational ethnographies as dynamic and relational rather than static and foreclosed. Furthermore, the identities invoked by these categories are not unidimensional. Class, for example, cannot be easily disarticulated from gender or gender from race.

Thus, bringing feminist theory to bear upon neo-Marxism, Weis (1990) undertook a seminal study of white, working-class male youth in the context of the deindustrialization of the American economy. She stresses social action over reproduction, demonstrating how gendered identities and subjectivities are also simultaneously racialized and sexualized. Weis notes the dialectical relationship between youth identity formation and competing social movements. She maps ways in which student identities, specifically those of white male and female working class, are forged in relation to a constructed racialized "other." Male identities, by comparison, emerge in relation to the construction of female "others" and through affirmation of patriarchal divisions of the private (women's) and public (men's) spheres, as well as in relation to constructed black "others" who, whether male or female, are relegated to the sexual realm. Weis emphasizes the ways in which struggles take place over school knowledge as symbolic capital (Bourdieu & Passeron 1977) and over the realm of information and the production of culture. She points to how schools promote contradictory relationships with official school knowledge and culture, as teachers and students view the formal structure of schooling instrumentally for getting through rather than engaging with its substance. Weis also notes significant political implications of her study: Although white female identities are shaped in relation to white males, they remain individualistic and not yet aligned with the politics of feminism, which is largely middle-class oriented. On the other hand, white male working-class identity is likely to embrace the New Right and its patriarchal agenda in the face of the decline of a labor movement. Weis illustrates ethnographically how, through their organization and the knowledge they promote, schools may actually foster an increase in domestic and racialized violence, furthering the identity of working-class males while constraining potential for public critiques of working-class females.

Cousins (1999) also uses a symbolic and relational framework to examine how class unfolds with race and gender in a predominantly black high school. He demonstrates how students in their play between classes negotiate identities through the behavioral and verbal symbols of social class, which intersect with race and gender. Social class categories are complicated by the ways students live within and against dominant sexual and racial narratives. Cousins describes the "deep play" of these subalterns, in which—both intentionally and unintentionally—they adopt, manipulate, contradict, and signify the symbols of social class as they intersect race and gender (1999, pp. 296–97). These kinds of insights challenged further the determinism of earlier correspondence theories.

As the 1990s progressed, ethnographies built around nonsynchronous workings of identity categories extended those that combined an ethnohistorical approach with a performative one (see Foley 1991, Gordon 2001). Critiques of neo-Marxist theories recognized the plurality of processes within the economic as well as cultural and political spheres as they explored and emphasized contradictions and discontinuities within the institutional setting of schooling spheres (Aggleton & Whitty 1985, Apple & Weis 1983, Fine 1991, Gillborn 1997, McCarthy 1990). Thus, there was an increasing move away from essentialism toward a view of race, gender, and class as social processes linked to competing interests in education and society. Accordingly, minorities were positioned in multiple struggles as knowledge production was viewed as systematically relational and heterogenous (Alpert 1991, Cousins 1999, Fordham 1996, Hemmings 1996, McCarthy 1990, Miron & Lauria 1998, Weis 1990, Winbush 1993). As ethnographers of education at the end of the 1990s staked out their own theoretical and political investments, Stambach (1999) raised questions about the prospect of ethnography for understanding the ways in which gender links to conceptualizations of the educated citizen, the formation of rights, and local discourses of power and authority.

By the close of the twentieth century, the period of writing educational ethnographies over which I make a broad sweep, ideas about culture and society were no longer what they were at the beginning of the period. By now, theories of postmodernism, post-structuralism, and the postcolonial had gained significance and in their various ways eroded the ground upon which earlier ethnographies were built. No longer could culture be viewed as the property of social groups, bounded, determined, and internally coherent, and the kinds of certainty that characterized ethnographic findings in earlier eras could no be longer guaranteed. Post-structuralism reminds ethnographers and their readers of the interestedness that is brought to bear upon ethnographic writing, undermines assumptions about the unitary nature of ethnographic texts, and reminds us of how the ethnography is always a partial representation. Indeed, as Haraway (1985) notes, postmodernism calls for an appreciation of the tension of holding incompatible perspectives together because both or all are necessarily true. Furthermore, it is the tensions of competing perspectives, rather than efforts to resolve them, that make for new reflections and questions about the situations and cultural settings that ethnographies engage. These kinds of methodological and theoretical developments are significant departures from the holistic models of earlier educational ethnographies as they insist upon debate and avoid the rush to concensus.

Haraway's sense of holding together incompatible perspectives parallels the working of Bakhtin's (1981) concepts of dialogism and heteroglossic discourses. Thus, poststructuralist educational ethnographies move beyond realist preoccupations to engage the precarious and textual construction of the ethnographic account. Paying attention to textual constructions implies being mindful of the identities not only of the subjects of ethnography but also of ethnographers themselves and the ways they grapple with the tensions of competing discourses—both the authorative educational discourses that are officially sanctioned as well as those internally persuasive discourses that run counter to them (Britzman 2003, Lather 1991). Similarly, postcolonial theory interrupts the foundational practices of "othering" in ethnographic work as it breaks down the insider/outsider binary upon which anthropology and histories of imperialism have been premised. In this context of competing theories and intertextuality, the ethnographic method in educational ethnography, as elsewhere, becomes more self-reflective, recognizing the subjective factors that shape all parties involved in the production of the text (Foster 1995, Hicks 1996, Levinson et al. 1996, Rockwell 2000).

Notions such as elusive culture and schooling as a discursive space are coined to capture the ambivalent and contradictory ways that students relate to schools and to the older attribute theory of culture that set the discourses not only of culture and identity but also of school ethnography (Yon 1999, 2000). The emphasis on the discursive production of subjects of ethnographies retains elements of older notions of correspondence theory; however, as it captures the crosscutting of discourses at the site of schooling, it acknowledges that subjects work on discourses just as discourses work on subjects. Such ideas push further the nonsynchronous workings of race, gender, and class as they pay attention to the instability of these categories and critique the ways they are represented in ethnographic works. They open educational ethnographies to the surprises, contradictions, conflicting desires, ironies, and ambivalence of the everyday life of students and teachers, inside and outside the classroom, and they do so without trying to domesticate the incongruities for the sake of theoretical coherence.

CONCLUSIONS

As noted at the outset, this review makes no attempt to provide an exhaustive account of educational ethnography over the decades surveyed. Instead, I have merely called attention to some of the themes, theoretical and operational, that have come to shape the field. I show how, in its formative days, educational ethnography was tied to the development of applied anthropology, which has tended to be focused on "others" at home over "exotics" abroad, and to the increasing application of ethnographic methodology to the study of institutions "at home." Significant too was the growth of educational ethnography, as a subfield of anthropology, which also coincided with increasing interest in the "problems" of immigration and urbanization and the attendant growth and development of urban anthropology. Although these developments set educational ethnography apart as a subfield, they also ensured connections with allied fields in the social sciences. Thus ethnography as a method is taken up by sociology and by cultural studies. These kinds of multidisciplinary approaches to the field help account for what Spindler describes as a "meteoric rise" in the production of educational ethnographies. Educational ethnographies, as this overview suggests, were the means for engaging disjuctions between official goals and actual effects, as well as the symbolic meanings and adaptive strategies evident in cultures of schools. Whereas schools, in essentially functionalist frameworks, were viewed as microcosms of the society they served, new perspectives enabled them to be seen as sites for addressing concerns with differentiation and discrimination based on class, race, and gender.

I attempted to place the broad brush strokes that mark this overview in the context of theoretical and conceptual developments taking place in the discipline of anthropology at large. Thus, we see the transitions from objectivist and scientific orientations to educational ethnography in the formative years to the subjectivist, reflexive, and various materialist perspectives that shaped directions in subsequent years. While these various perspectives and theoretical orientations may be read as distinct, I argue that they are best understood as overlapping and convergent.

At the end of the twentieth century, the kinds of concerns—with social justice and emancipatory projects—that shaped the field of educational ethnography in the first place continue to prevail. Concerns about the problems of representation, with conflicted and contradictory meanings as stressed by postmodernism as well as post-structuralism, all variously influence these essentially modernist projects. These kinds of turn-of-the-century theoretical developments have raised concerns (see Brantlinger 1999) about educational ethnography losing its emancipatory potential. These are the sorts of questions that will continue to haunt the field of educational ethnography in the twenty-first century.

ACKNOWLEDGMENTS

I would like to acknowledge and thank Marc Lafleur and Radhika Johari, both graduate students in the York University program in Social Anthropology, who were research assistants for this project. I am also thankful for the suggestions of the AR reviewer.

The *Annual Review of Anthropology* is online at http://anthro.annualreviews.org

LITERATURE CITED

Aggleton P, Whitty G. 1985. Rebels without a cause? Socialization and subcultural style among the children of the new middle class. *Sociol. Education* 58(1):60–72

Alpert B. 1991. Student's resistance in the classroom. *Anthropol. Education Q.* 22(4):350–66

Anyon J. 1981. Social class and school knowledge. *Curriculum Inq.* 11:3–42

Apple M, ed. 1982. *Cultural and Economic Reproduction in Education: Essays on Class, Ideology and the State.* London: Routledge, Kegan and Paul

Apple MW, Weis L, eds. 1983. *Ideology and Practice in Schooling.* Philadelphia: Temple Univ. Press

Bakhtin MM. 1981. *The Dialogical Imagination*, ed. M Holquist. Austin: Univ. Texas Press

Banks J, ed. 1993. Multicultural education: historical development, dimensions and practice. In *Review of Research in Education*, ed. L Darling-Hammond, 19:3–49. Washington, DC: Am. Educational Res. Found.

Benson D, Hughes JA. 1983. *The Perspective of Ethnomethodology.* London: Longmans

Bloom BS, Davison A, Hess R. 1965. *Compensatory Education for Cultural Deprivation.* New York: Holt, Rinehart and Winston

Boas F. 1962. *Anthropology and Modern Life.* New York: Norton

Bond GC. 2000. *Contested Terrains and Constructed Categories: Contemporary African in Focus.* Boulder, CO; Oxford, UK: Westview

Bourdieu P. 1977. *Outline of a Theory of Practice*, transl. R Nice. Cambridge, MA; New York: Cambridge Univ. Press

Bourdieu P, Passeron J-C. 1977. *Reproduction in Education, Society and Culture*, transl. R Nice. London; Beverly Hills, CA: Sage

Bowles S, Gintis H. 1976. *Schooling in Capitalist America*. London: Routledge and Kegan

Brameld TBH. 1957. *Cultural Foundations of Education: An Interdisciplinary Exploration*. New York: Harper

Bratlinger EA. 1999. Inward gaze and activism as moral new steps in inquiry. *Anthropol. Education Q.* 30(4):413–29

Britzman D. 1995. Beyond innocent readings: educational ethnography as a crisis of representation. In *Continuity and Contradiction: The Futures of the Sociology of Education*, ed. W Pink, GW Noblit, p. 133. Cresskill, NJ: Hampton

Britzman D. 2003. *Practice Makes Practice, a Critical Study of Learning to Teach*. Albany: SUNY Press. Rev. ed.

Bryant R. 2001. An aesthetics of self: moral remaking and the Cypriot education. In *Comp. Stud. Soc. Hist.* 43(3):583–614

Burnett JH. 1974. *Anthropology and Education: An Annotated Bibliographic Guide*. New Haven, CT: Hum. Relat. Areas Files Press

Clement DC, Eisenhart M, Harding JR. 1979. The veneer of harmony: social-race relations in a southern desegregated school. In *Desegregated Schools: Appraisals of an American Experiment*, ed. R Rist, 1:15–64. New York: Academic

Collins J. 1996. *Negotiating Identities: Education for Empowerment in a Diverse Society*. Ontario, CA: Calif. Assoc. Biling. Education

Cousins LH. 1999. "Playing between classes": America's troubles with class, race and gender in a black high school and community. *Anthropol. Education Q.* 30(3):294–316

Delgado-Gaitan C. 1988. The value of nonconformity: learning to stay in school. *Anthropol. Education Q.* 19(4):354–81

Delpit L. 1988. The silenced dialogue: power and pedagogy in educating other people's children. *Harv. Educational Rev.* 58(3):280–98

Dolby N. 2001. *Constructing Race: Youth, Identity and Popular Culture in South Africa*. Albany: SUNY Press

Eddy EM. 1967. *Walk the White Line: A Profile of Urban Education*. New York: Anchor Press

Eddy EM. 1985. Theory, research, and application in educational anthropology. *Anthropol. Education Q.* 16(2):83–104

Everhart R. 1983. *Reading, Writing and Resistance: Adolescence and Labour in a Junior High School*. London: Routledge, Kegan and Paul

Fine M. 1991. *Framing Drop Outs: Notes on the Politics of an Urban High School*. Albany: SUNY Press

Fisher AD. 1998. Anthropology and education in Canada, the early years (1850–1970). *Anthropol. Education Q.* 29(1):89–102

Foley D. 1977. Anthropological studies of schooling in developing countries: some recent findings and trends. *Comp. Education Rev.* 21:311–28

Foley D. 1991. Rethinking school ethnographies of colonial settings: a performance perspective of reproduction and resistance. *Comp. Education Rev.* 35(3):532–51

Fordham S. 1996. *Blacked Out: Dilemmas of Race, Identity and Success at Capital High*. Chicago: The Univ. Chicago Press

Fordham S, Ogbu J. 1986. Black students' school success: coping with the burden of 'acting white.' *Urban Rev.* 18(3):176–206

Foster M. 1995. Talking that talk: the language of control, curriculum and critique. *Linguist. Education* 7:129–50

Gearing F, Epstein P. 1982. Learning to wait: an ethnographic probe into the operations of an item of hidden curriculum. In *Doing the Ethnography of Schooling: Educational Anthropology in Action*, ed. G Spindler, 8:240–67. New York: Holt, Rinehart and Wilson

Giddens A. 1984. *The Constitution of Society: Outline of the Theory of Structuration*. Cambridge: Polity Press

Gillborn D. 1997. Ethnicity and educational performance in the United Kingdom: racism, ethnicity and variability in achievement. *Anthropol. Education Q.* 28(3):375–93

Gordon JA. 2001. *Why They Couldn't Wait: A Critique of Black-Jewish Conflict Over*

Control in Ocean-Hill Brownsville, 1967–1971. New York: Routledge/Falmer

Goodson I, Ball SJ. 1984. *Defining the Curriculum: Histories and Ethnographies of School Subjects.* London, New York: Falmer Press

Gramsci A. 1971. *Selections for Prison Notebooks.* London: Lawrence and Wishart

Grant L, Horan PM, Watts-Warren B. 1994. Theoretical diversity in the analysis of gender and education. *Res. Sociol. Education Socialization* 10:71–109

Hall RM, Sandler B. 1982. *The Classroom Climate: A Chilly One for Women?* Washington, DC: Assoc. Am. Coll.

Haraway D. 1985. A manifesto for cyborgs: science, technology, and socialist feminism in the 1980s. *Social. Rev.* 80:65–107

Havighurst RJ, Levine DU. 1971. *Education in Metropolitan Areas.* Boston: Allyn and Bacon

Hemmings A. 1996. Conflicting images? Being black and a model high school student. *Anthropol. Education Q.* 27(1):20–50

Heshusius L, Ballard K, eds. 1996. *From Positivism to Interpretivism and Beyond: Tales of Transformation in Educational and Social Research.* New York: Teachers Coll. Press

Hicks D. 1996. *Discourse, Learning and Schooling.* New York: Cambridge Univ. Press

Holland DC, Eisenhart MA. 1990. *Educated in Romance: Women, Achievement, and College Future.* Chicago: The Univ. Chicago Press

Hymes DH, ed. 1972. *Reinventing Anthropology.* New York: Pantheon Books

Hymes DH, ed. 1974. *Studies in the History of Linguistics: Traditions and Paradigms.* Bloomington: Indiana Univ. Press

Jackson P. 1968. *Life in Classrooms.* New York: Holt, Rinehart, and Winston

Kaplan S. 1996. *Education and the politics of national culture in a Turkish community circa 1990.* PhD Diss., Univ. Chicago

Kelly GP, Nihlen AS. 1982. Schooling and the reproduction of patriarchy: unequal workloads, unequal rewards. In *Culture and Economic Reproduction in Education: Essays on Class, Ideology and the State,* ed. M Apple, Ch. 5. London: Routledge and Kegan Paul

Landes R. 1965. *Culture in American Education: Anthropological Approaches to Minority and Dominant Groups in the Schools.* New York: Wiley

Lather P. 1991. *Getting Smart: Feminist Research and Pedagogy Within the Postmodern.* New York: Routledge

Leacock EB. 1969. *Teaching and Learning in City Schools: A Comparative Study.* New York: Basic Books

Leadbeater R, Bonnie J, Way N, eds. 1996. *Urban Girls: Resisting Stereotypes, Creating Identities.* New York: New York Univ. Press

Leemon T. 1972. *Rites of Passage in a Student Culture.* New York: Teachers Coll. Press

Levinson BA, Foley DE, Holland DC, eds. 1996. *The Cultural Production of the Educated Person: Critical Ethnographies of Schooling and Local Practice.* Albany: SUNY Press

McCarthy C. 1990. *Race and Curriculum: Social Inequity and the Theories and Politics of Difference in Contemporary Research on Schooling.* London; New York; Philadelphia: Falmer Press

Mead M. 1951. *The School in American Culture.* Cambridge, MA: Harv. Univ. Press

Mehan H. 1979. *Learning Lessons. Social Organization in the Classroom.* Cambridge, MA: Harv. Univ. Press

Miron LF, Lauria M. 1998. Student voice as agency: resistance and accommodation in inner city schools. *Anthropol. Education Q.* 29(2):189–213

Ogbu J. 1974. *The Next Generation: An Ethnography of Education in an Urban Neighborhood.* New York: Academic Press

Ogbu J. 1978. *Minority Education and Caste: The American System in Cross-Cultural Perspective.* New York: Academic Press

Ogbu J. 1988. Class stratification, racial stratification, and schooling. In *Class, Race, and Gender in American Education,* ed. L Weis, 7:163–82. Albany: SUNY Press

Ortner SB. 1994. Theory in anthropology since the sixties. In *Culture/Power/History, a*

Contemporary Reader in Social Theory, ed. NB Dirks, G Eley, S Ortner, pp. 372–411. Princeton, NJ: Princeton Univ. Press

Peshkin A. 1982. The researcher and subjectivity: reflections on an ethnography of school and community. In *Doing the Ethnography of Schooling: Educational Anthropology in Action*, ed. G Spindler, 2:48–65. New York: Holt, Rinehart and Wilson

Pettit GA. 1946. Primitive education in North America. *Univ. Calif. Publ. Am. Archeol. Ethnol.* XLIII:11–82

Player J. 1984. The amorphous school. In *Defining the Curriculum: Histories and Ethnographies*, ed. IF Goodson, SJ Ball, pp. 219–38. London; Philadelphia: Falmer Press

Reiss AJ, ed. 1965. *Schools in a Changing Society*. New York: Free Press

Rist R. 1973. *The Urban School: A Factory of Failure*. Cambridge, MA: MIT Press

Rist R. 1979. *Desegregated Schools: An Appraisal of an American Experiment*. New York: Holt, Rinehart and Winston

Rockwell E. 2000. Teaching genres: a Bakhtinian approach. *Anthropol. Education Q.* 31(3):260–82

Schecter S, Bayley R. 2002. *Language as Cultural Practice, Mexicanos en el Norte*. Mahwah, NJ; London: Erlbaum

Schrag P. 1967. *Village School Downtown. Politics and Education—A Boston Report*. Boston: Beacon Press

Seeley JR. 1964. Mankind as fact by faith. In *Education and the Idea of Mankind*, ed. R Ulrich, 2:34–48. New York: Harcourt, Brace and World

Sefa Dei G. 1996. *Anti-Racism Education: Theory and Practice*. Halifax: Fernwood

Singleton J. 1984. Origins of the AEQ: rituals, myths and cultural transmission. *Anthropol. Education Q.* 15:11–16

Smith L, Geoffrey W. 1968. *Complexities of an Urban Classroom*. New York: Holt, Rinehart and Winston

Soloman P. 1992. *Black Resistance in High School: Forging a Separatist Culture*. Albany: SUNY Press

Spindler G. 1959. *The Transmission of American Culture*. Cambridge, MA: Grad. Sch. Education Harv. Univ.

Spindler G, ed. 2000. *Fifty Years of Anthropology and Education 1950-2000. A Spindler Anthology*. Mahwah, NJ: Erlbaum

Spindler GD, ed. 1955. *Education and Anthropology*. Stanford, CA: Stanford Univ. Press

Spindler GD. 1984. Roots revisited: three decades of perspective. *Anthropol. Education Q.* 15:3–10

Stambach A. 1999. Gender-bending anthropological studies of education. *Anthropol. Education Q.* 30(4):441–45

Sullivan 1979. Contacts among cultures: school desegregation in a polyethnic New York City High School. In *Desegregated Schools: Appraisals of an American Experiment*, ed. R Rist, 6:201–40. New York: Academic Press

Turner R, ed. 1974. *Ethnomethodology*. Harmondsworth, UK: Penguin

Varenne H. 1982. Jocks and freaks: the symbolic structure of the expression of social interaction among American senior high school students. In *Doing the Ethnography of Schooling: Educational Anthropology in Action*, ed. G Spindler, 7:210–39. New York: Holt, Rinehart and Winston

Wax M, Diamond LS, Gearing F, eds. 1971. *Anthropological Perspectives on Education*. New York: Basic Books

Wax M, Wax R. 1964. Cultural deprivation as an educational ideology. *J. Am. Ind. Education* 3(2):15–18

Wax M, Wax RH, Dumont RV. 1964. Formal education in an American Indian community. *Soc. Prob.* 11(4, Suppl.):1–25

Weis L. 1985. *Between Two Worlds: Black Students in an Urban Community College*. Boston: Routledge, Kegan and Paul

Weis L. 1988. *Class, Race and Gender in American Education*. Albany, NY: SUNY Press

Weis L. 1990. *Working Class Without Work: High School Students in a De-industrializing Economy*. New York: Routledge

Wilcox K. 1982. Ethnography as a methodology and its application to the study of schooling: a review. In *Doing the Ethnography of*

Schooling: Educational Anthropology in Action, ed. G Spindler, 15:456–88. New York: Holt, Rinehart and Wilson

Willis P. 1977. *Learning to Labour: How Working Class Kids Get Working Class Jobs*. New York: Columbia Univ. Press

Winbush O. 1993. Who has to change? African-American oral traditions in multicultural classrooms. *Pathways: Forum Progressive Educators* 9(2):13–16

Wolcott H. 1973. *The Man in the Principal's Office: An Ethnography*. Prospect Heights, IL: Waveland

Yon DA. 1999. Pedagogy and the 'problem' of difference: on reading community in 'The Darker Side of Black.' *Qual. Stud. Education* 12(6):623–41

Yon DA. 2000. *Elusive Culture: Schooling, Race and Identity in Global Times*. Albany: SUNY Press

Annu. Rev. Anthropol. 2003. 32:431–46
doi: 10.1146/annurev.anthro.32.061002.093345
Copyright © 2003 by Annual Reviews. All rights reserved
First published online as a Review in Advance on June 4, 2003

CHILDREN, CHILDHOODS, AND VIOLENCE

Jill E. Korbin

*Department of Anthropology, Case Western Reserve University, 10900 Euclid Avenue,
Cleveland, Ohio 44106-7125; email: jek7@po.cwru.edu*

Key Words   child abuse, culture, aggression, risk, child rearing

■ **Abstract**   Anthropological literature on children and violence has been constrained by similar considerations that have limited an anthropology of childhood more
generally, and by difficulties in conceptualizing children both as victims of violence and
as violent themselves. A review of the anthropological literature on violence directed
toward children reveals a litany of violence to which children may be subjected that
includes child abuse and neglect, bullying, violent cultural rites, warfare, and structural
violence stemming from poverty and inequality. Aggression in childhood has been the
subject of a robust and long-standing literature that has examined socialization for or
against aggressive behavior in children. An emerging literature considers children's
own violent behavior from the perspective of child agency. Children's own voices and
perspectives have been largely absent from the anthropological literature on childhood
and violence. This review highlights several issues at the intersection of childhood and
violence that demand a synthesis and reformulation in anthropology.

> *"There is a growing consciousness of children* at risk ... *there is also a grow-
> ing sense of children themselves as* the risk ... "

(Stephens 1995, p. 13)

INTRODUCTION

Anthropological literature on children and violence has been constrained by similar
considerations that have limited an anthropology of childhood more generally (e.g.,
Christensen & James 2000, James et al. 1998, Mayall 2000), and by difficulties
in conceptualizing children both as victims of violence and as violent themselves
(Boyden 1990; Ennew 1998; Korbin 1981; Scheper-Hughes 1987a, 1992; Scheper-
Hughes & Sargent 1998; Stephens 1995). Increased interest in children over the
past several decades has led to an awareness of the multiple harms experienced by
children and the "unacceptably poor condition" of childhood itself (Mayall 2000,
p. 132). The International Year of the Child in 1979 posed an international wake-up
call to the deplorable state of children in many parts of the world (James & Prout
1997, Stephens 1995). In contrast to the idealized Western view of childhood
as a life stage filled with play, school, friends, and family, attention turned to
children devastated by famine, warfare, and preventable diseases as documented by

publications from organizations such as UNICEF and Save the Children. Following the cornerstone article on child abuse and neglect in the United States (Kempe et al. 1962), the First International Congress on Child Abuse and Neglect held in Geneva in 1976, and the founding of the International Society for the Prevention of Child Abuse and Neglect, attention also focused on abused and neglected children around the world (Donnelly 2002). The United Nations' Convention on the Rights of the Child in 1989 represented concerted international efforts to apply basic human rights to children, who, as it had become increasingly apparent, had not necessarily been the beneficiaries of such considerations. The Convention on the Rights of the Child has, at this date, been ratified by all but two nations (one of which is the United States). The Convention, with its 54 articles, has 3 guiding principles. The first principle is the *provision* of necessary resources for children's survival and well being. The second principle, *protection*, holds that children should be shielded from harm. The third provision, *participation*, mandates that children and youth should be involved in decisions concerning their lives and welfare insofar as their age and maturity allow. These considerations are relevant to an understanding of children and violence.

The intersection of childhood and violence raises several problematic issues that demand a synthesis and reformulation. Although it is perhaps simplistic to say that both childhood and violence are culturally constructed categories, it is nevertheless the case that violence is not a unitary phenomenon nor is childhood experienced similarly everywhere (e.g., James & Prout 1997). Without making this basic assumption explicit, it is impossible to understand the variability of experience involving children and violence. This review considers both violence directed toward children and violence exhibited by children.

VIOLENCE DIRECTED TOWARD CHILDREN

Anthropological interest in violence directed at children had to overcome two major barriers. First, conventional wisdom holds that children are to be treated with solicitousness and care, to be nurtured and protected. Increasing evidence of children suffering from a range of harms forced the recognition that children indeed were not immune from violence. Second, the role of sociocultural anthropology has traditionally been to explain and make comprehensible behavior and beliefs different from one's own, with a reliance on cultural relativism as a hallmark of anthropology. Confrontations with issues of human rights, however, precipitated a reexamination of the basic tenets of an unquestioned adherence to cultural relativism.

A review of the anthropological literature on children and violence reveals a litany of violence to which children may be subjected. There are multiple ways to organize a discussion of the anthropological literature on children and violence. First, children and violence can be organized by the setting in which violence occurs. Children experience violence in situations of war, in dangerous neighborhoods, on the streets, in factories, and in settings that conventional wisdom, but not empirical evidence, suggests would be havens of safety such as the home, school, and playground. Second, violence can be categorized based on whether the perpetrator is a parent, stranger, another child, the child himself/herself, or a larger political entity. Third, violence can be organized by type and severity. Violence toward and by children can be physical, sexual, verbal, and emotional and can range from being relatively mild to serious and life threatening. Fourth, one can take an approach that links violence to categories of age and/or gender. Fifth, discussions can be organized by definitions of culture and violence that may vary within and across cultural contexts. Thus, violence toward children can be categorized by setting, perpetrator, type and severity, age and gender, and cultural context.

Violence toward children may be individually perpetrated as in child maltreatment; collective as in culturally sanctioned rites or disciplinary practices; or structural as in the harms that befall children as a result of poverty, inequality, lack of opportunity, and local, national, and global hostilities. In addition to categories of violence, there is an important source of variability in that some children are at greater risk of experiencing violence than their peers in similar circumstances.

Regardless of how appealing categorizations of violence as individualized, collective, or structural might be, such distinctions have permeable boundaries. Individual violence directed at children is rooted both in individual pathology and in structural inequalities that compromise parents' abilities to care for their children. Child abuse and neglect, for example, have been linked with poverty, but not all poor families abuse or neglect their children. Structural or collective violence is differentially distributed. Not all families are affected, and not all children in a single family have similar experiences. Thus, we need to reconceptualize the relationships across types of violence directed at children as potentially arising at multiple levels.

The settings in which violence occurs also are not neatly bounded. Children may experience violence at home, in school, on the playground, in the streets and community, or in conditions of war and hostility. The permeability of boundaries argues against a neat framework. Warfare, for example, is obviously not limited to a battlefield. More than this, however, settings that should be bastions of safety from larger hostilities become embroiled in the violence. Approximately two thirds of "the disappeared" in Argentina were abducted from their homes. Some were children, and some witnessed their parents or older relatives and siblings being taken (Robben 2000).

The following section uses the framework of a cross-cultural and international perspective on child maltreatment to illustrate some of the considerations in forging a synthesis of violence toward children. Cross-cultural and international attention to child abuse and neglect has tended to lump together harms that come to children. The following brief discussions of child maltreatment, physically harsh rites of passage, and structural violence of poverty and warfare can be used as illustrations for moving toward a more comprehensive theoretical perspective on violence toward children.

Child Abuse and Neglect in Cross-Cultural and International Perspectives

As child abuse and neglect came to public and professional attention, questions arose as to whether child maltreatment was limited to North American and Western European nations, where it was first identified, or whether it occurred throughout the world. Debates ensued as to what, precisely, should be included under the rubric of child maltreatment. To address this issue, three levels of consideration were suggested to organize thinking about child maltreatment cross-culturally (Korbin 1980, 1981, 1997). First, cultural-level acts, practices, and rites or rituals may be differentially viewed as abusive or neglectful by other societies, but not by the culture in question. This is the level at which cultural conflict is most likely to occur and also the level at which sociocultural anthropology has been the most active in seeking to translate across cultural boundaries. The second level reflects idiosyncratic departure from cultural standards that results in harm to a child or compromises his or her well-being. The third level encompasses societal abuse and neglect of children, or the structural violence of poverty, inadequate health care, and lack of educational and employment opportunities. These conditions have been implicated as powerfully contributing to the incidence of individually perpetrated child maltreatment or as abusive and neglectful in their own right.

At the first level of consideration, anthropology has displayed an ambivalence about culturally sanctioned practices that may cause children pain, suffering, or harm. Charged with the mantle of understanding and explaining cultural diversity, anthropologists have gone to great efforts to explain how such rites, although physically painful and emotionally frightening, fall outside the rubric of "abuse" in that they are collective expressions of cultural values (e.g., Korbin 1981). As such, not only adults who perform and perpetuate the rites, but also children who are subjected to them, view these rites, however painful and terrifying, as having a positive long-term value. The child's view of his or her experience and treatment has long been recognized as an important consideration in differentiating cultural practices from idiosyncratic abuse (Ennew 1998, Korbin 1977). In the words of Camara Laye, from his autobiographical account of his experience of initiation rites, including circumcision, in an African context:

> However great the anxiety, however certain the pain, no one would have dreamed of running away from the ordeal . . . and I, for my own part, never entertained such thoughts. I wanted to be born, to be born again. I knew perfectly well that I was going to be hurt, but I wanted to be a man, and it seemed to me that nothing could be too painful if, by enduring it, I was to come to man's estate. (Laye 1954, p. 113)

Not all children, however, necessarily view such rites in the same way; nor do all children view cultural practices designed "for their own good" as necessarily so. Among the Pueblo Indians, whom Benedict portrayed as extraordinarily peaceful and gentle, or "Apollonian," in her best selling *Patterns of Culture* (1934), another autobiographic account of childhood, this time by Sun Chief, a Hopi, portrayed his view as anything but accepting even though this was, as above in Laye's description, a collective event:

> I stood them (the blows) fairly well, without crying and thought my suffering was past; but then the Ho Katchina struck me four more times and cut me to pieces. I struggled, yelled, and urinated . . . . Blood was running down over my body . . . . (Simmons 1942, p. 83)

Using a framework drawn from Western-based conceptions of child abuse and neglect, anthropology has, in its efforts to show how acts may be differentially defined, in some ways privileged a Western view of "abuse" by cataloguing the harms that children may come to, in a range of cultural contexts, as "abuse." In this light, it is sobering to view many Western child-rearing practices that would be viewed as abusive from the vantage point of other cultures (Korbin 1980, 1981, 1987a). In one of the earliest systematic cross-cultural comparisons of child-rearing practices (Whiting & Child 1953), United States and Western European cultures were more often than not on the far end of the continuum. Isolation for sleep at night, for example, is widely regarded cross-culturally as detrimental to children, yet it is the ideal practice in middle-class families in the United States. Although conceptions of child abuse in North America and Western Europe have had a focus on physical violence, in some societies verbal violence toward children is regarded as much more serious than physical violence (Korbin 1990).

Nevertheless, despite an anthropological mandate for translation and explanation across cultural contexts, it is less clear that the collectivity of a painful act removes that act from the discourse of harm and indefensible treatment of children, whether or not the label "abuse" is applied. Initiation rites, for example, may be culturally sanctioned situations for adult expression of hostility toward children. Children who might have misbehaved in the past may be singled out for harsher application of deprivations and violent acts in the context of such rites (Langness 1981). Anthropology has increasingly come to grips with the possibility that cultural relativity falls short in the effort to reconcile painful acts with understanding other cultures (Edgerton 1992). "But can we ultimately take a stance of cultural relativism to systems that systematically use pain, fear, and deception to dominate boys and subordinate, demean, and oppress women . . .?" (Keesing 1982, p. 37).

Additionally, anthropology as the purveyor of culture has also been careful to point out that culture can be used as an excuse or justification (Korbin 1987a, 1997). Similar to abusive parents using their own upbringing as justification for their own violent behavior, so too can parents rely on culture as a justification. In its most blatant form, parents or other perpetrators may simply misrepresent their own culture, whether consciously or unconsciously. For example, once a Navajo girl undergoes a puberty ceremony, she traditionally is considered eligible for marriage. This cultural practice has been misused by some men to justify the rape of teenage girls who have undergone this ceremony, but who are not, in reality, considered ready for marriage (Hauswald 1987). Similarly, leaving children alone and unsupervised is a frequent source of child maltreatment reports among the Navajo. Parents who are reported for child neglect may justify their behavior as traditional Navajo child-rearing patterns of sibling caretaking and the high level of responsibility entrusted to children that is characteristic of that culture, despite interview data that contradict this view (Hauswald 1987). These examples, then, are not cultural patterns but departures from cultural norms and values exacerbated by problems of poverty, unemployment, and alcoholism among some residents of the reservation.

At the second level of idiosyncratic abuse and neglect of children, discussion can be directed toward two issues. First, can we determine which children are at risk? The cross-cultural record suggests that certain categories of children are more likely to be maltreated. Scrimshaw's (1978) demographic analysis found that girls, later-born children, and second children of the same gender were less likely to survive owing to selective neglect. The cross-cultural record suggests that there are categories of children at risk that may be identified through, for example, female gender in societies with a strong preference for sons (e.g., Poffenberger 1981), although gender as a risk factor may be mediated by economic factors (Miller 1981, 1987) or improved health care (Minturn 1984). Other categories of children at risk may depend on the cultural context, for example, twins in societies with ambivalent or negative beliefs about multiple births from a single pregnancy (Johnson 1981, Levy 1964).

Despite increasing international awareness, child abuse and neglect are often difficult to recognize or make sense of in small populations. Because child maltreatment is a low base-rate behavior, it may be rare in a small population during a single year of fieldwork. Among the Inuit, for example, anthropologist Graburn observed a few cases of what could be described as the classic battered child. These cases were not only rare, but also contradicted past literature on Inuit peoples and Graburn's overall impression of nurturant, indulgent, and non-punitive Inuit parenting. Descriptions of these cases were not published for many years after Graburn's fieldwork (Graburn 1987), thereby leaving intact a literature that would lead one to believe that child abuse was virtually nonexistent among Inuit peoples living in traditional circumstances (Briggs 1970, Graburn 1987). Similarly, in my own fieldwork among rural Hawai'ian Polynesian Americans, child maltreatment seemed so aberrant from the larger pattern of loving and attentive care of children that the few cases that came to my attention also did not find their way into the literature for many years (Korbin 1990).

In addition to categories of children at increased risk (Korbin 1987b), attention can reorient to considering protective factors. The discussion by Counts et al. (1992) of wife beating cross-culturally suggested that women were protected if there were "sanctions" against wife beating that were enforced, or if there was the possibility of "sanctuary," or networks in place to protect the woman. Although sanctions against abuse do not protect all children, there is some evidence that embeddedness in strong and protective social networks, or sanctuary, protects children (Fraser & Kilbride 1980, Korbin 1981, LeVine & LeVine 1981, Olson 1981).

If child-care tasks and children are shared, rather than considered the property of one or two biological parents, a situation in which "no one needs an invitation to intervene in the case of an overly severe spanking" (Olson 1981) is more likely. Among rural Hawai'ian Polynesian Americans, relatives do not hesitate to yell from one house to the next that a spanking has gone on long enough or is too severe a response to the child's misbehavior. Children are aware of this protection. They often scream or cry more quickly and loudly than a spanking warrants as an effective strategy to summon help and disarm an angry parent (Korbin 1987a, 1990).

At the third level, structural violence is at the root of much child suffering (Kleinman et al. 1997). Children absorb more than their fair share of suffering from war and hostilities, as combatants, as civilians, and through forced emigration and displacement, either with their parents or as unaccompanied minors (Janzen & Janzen 2000, Peters & Richards 1998, Povrzanovic 1997, Quesada 1998, Suarez-Orosco & Robben 2000). Parents, guardians, the home armies, and international aid agencies are too often unable to shield children from injury or death, or to provide for their basic needs of food, water, and shelter. Children are subject to injury not only from the direct hostilities but also from dangerous armaments left behind in areas where children play or roam (Povrzanovic 1997). Children as the quintessential noncombatants are targeted in war as a measured strategy: "... [An] obvious reason why children are maimed, molested, and killed in war has to do with the subjugation and humiliation of 'the enemy.' This is part of the symbolic war, fought out using the physical bodies of those least able to protect themselves and least implicated in the war effort" (Nordstrom 1999, p. 73). Among the most terrifying aspects of the "dirty war" in Argentina was the group torture of families in which parents were unable to protect their children and children had to watch helplessly as their parents were assaulted (Suarez-Orozco 1987). Suarez-Orozco & Robben (2000, p. 4) further underline the impact of violence on children, noting the "intergenerational transmission from parents to children to grandchildren" in which "social violence continues to pursue its victims long after the slaughter ends and the peace treaties are signed" (2000, p. 5).

Another aspect of structural violence is that children are subject to violence simply from the nature of the poor, disinvested, and dangerous urban neighborhoods in which their families live, where they are exposed to drug- and street-related violence (Bourgois 1995, 1998; Garbarino et al. 1992).

CHILDREN AS VIOLENT AND AGGRESSIVE

In addition to anthropological attention to children as recipients of violence, anthropologists also have focused on children as perpetrators of violence and aggression. This literature can be organized into two major groupings. First, aggression in childhood has been the subject of a robust and long-standing literature that has examined socialization for or against aggressive behavior in children. This literature has attended primarily to the antecedents of children's aggressive behavior. Childhood aggression is seen as one of many behaviors to be socialized and is generally viewed as within the range of normal child behavior as defined within its cultural context. This literature is largely based on participant observation, systematic observations of children, and interviews with parents (primarily mothers) and other caretakers. Children's own views are rarely sought (Korbin 1978).

With respect to the literature on the socialization of aggression, anthropologists interested in culture took up the challenge of questioning whether aggression was rooted in biology and human nature or in cultural patterns of child rearing. Although a detailed history of the field is beyond the scope of this review, interest can be traced back to the early work on children and adolescents, the configurationist approach, in which Margaret Mead (1928) and Ruth Benedict (1934) promoted the view that children absorb whichever culture they are born into by the simple experience of living it. Simply put, children in aggressive cultures become aggressive. In a later work, Mead (1935) more explicitly linked patterns in early childhood to later adult expressions of violence and aggression. In this genre, the interest was not strictly in young children but in what they would become as adults of their culture.

The Whiting School developed interests not only in whether a culture was aggressive, but also in the processes and mechanisms involved. Interest shifted from the product to the process and from viewing children as a *tabula rasa* (blank slate) to examining the aspects of the setting, such as a mother's workload, children's task assignments, or rural versus urban residence, in which children were socialized. Aggression was gendered: Boys showed more aggression except in those societies in which boys and girls engaged in similar tasks. The term aggression was not consistently used—terms that included dominance and egoism substituted (e.g., Weisner 1979, Whiting & Child 1953, Whiting & Edwards 1988, Whiting & Whiting 1975).

Not necessarily associated with any school, a number of ethnographic accounts sought to explain children's aggressiveness, or lack of it, as emanating from the cultural context of child-rearing and child-care patterns. The ethnographic record is replete with examples of cultures that promote violent behavior in children (e.g., Chagnon 1968, Langness 1981, Turnbull 1972) and cultures that promote nonviolence (e.g., Briggs 1970, 1978; Denton 1978; Draper 1978; Johnson 1981; Turnbull 1961). Keesing, implicating initiation rites as not simply inculcating culture and male solidarity, suggests that these experiences promote aggression. "New Guinea initiation rites enact a philosophy of growth, of human and cultural nature; they define the separation of men and women as a biological and religious as well as social imperative; and they *transform gentle boys into warriors capable of killing rage, stealthy murder* and bravery" (Keesing 1982, p. 3, emphasis added).

Although this first body of literature is focused primarily on children being socialized, the possibility was raised of children's aggressiveness having an impact on the adults around them. For example, in the mothers' interviews from the Six Cultures project, aggression was more severely socialized against in extended than in nuclear households, regardless of culture, because it would spill over into adult conflicts (Minturn & Lambert 1964). More contemporary research also has found children's aggressiveness to have wider effects. In urban neighborhoods, interethnic and racial violence among children reverberates into conflicts among their parents and the wider community of adults (Merry 1981). In Cleveland, Ohio, neighborhood adults expressed hesitancy to intervene with other people's children because they feared that not only the parents but also the child would retaliate with aggression (Korbin & Coulton 1997).

The second body of literature on violent and aggressive children has emerged in the past few decades. This literature stems from the recognition of contemporary social conditions and has been influenced by the extensive discussions that have surrounded the United Nations Convention on the Rights of the Child. The post-Columbine era in the United States and the post–Jamie Bulger era in the United Kingdom are but two examples of how adult society has been forced to acknowledge the violent capacities of children and youth. The dramatic nature of these events captured public attention, perhaps out of proportion. Although such comparisons are always problematic, the daily homicide rate on the streets of major U.S. cities takes a greater toll on young people's lives than did the shooting at Columbine. The number of infants and young children killed by their parents each year is also greater than the death toll of Columbine. Nevertheless, Columbine and the other school shootings that followed struck at the heart of society's sense that children were safe in middle-class schools, and the murder of the toddler Jamie Bulger by two 10-year-old boys challenged beliefs in the innocence of childhood. Hostilities and war around the world also added to the picture of children as violent and aggressive, as stories of youthful soldiers came to popular and professional attention.

In contrast to the first body of literature on the socialization of aggression, this second literature has relied on participatory research and children's own voices and perspectives. This literature has sought to elaborate on the violent acts that children and youth commit that are not situated within the range of "normal" child development. Children's violent behavior is too easily minimized or relegated to a childhood stage that will pass and thus need not be taken seriously. "Using the euphemism 'bullying' . . . may allow adults to ignore behavior in children that they would perceive as criminal if the perpetrators were adults. Because they [certain acts] are perpetrated by children they may be seen as a transient problem or as 'childish' behavior that will be outgrown" (LaFontaine 1991, p. 16). Similarly, it took concerted professional efforts to gain recognition that child-to-child sexual assault needed to be taken more seriously than a boys-will-be-boys stage of sexual curiosity (Vizard et al. 1995) or that violence that is tolerated in the home would be unacceptable in other settings (Straus et al. 1980).

Two examples from this literature are discussed in this review: child-to-child violence and bullying, and children in war. These are, of course, not the only circumstances in which children's own violent behavior has been considered (see, for example, Hecht 1998 or Panter-Brick 2002 on street children; and Andersen 1992 or Vigil 1988, 2003 on gangs). Several anthropologists have noted the violence that occurs among children and youth in urban schools, including those in the United States (Bourgois 1998), Australia (Burbank 1994), and Britain (LaFontaine 1991). In Japan, school bullying is a major factor in "school refusal syndrome" (Field 1995). Children bullied in Britain may be advised by their parents to respond with violence (LaFontaine 1991).

Children are both victims of war and combatants. In Croatia, young children play games of war, mimicking and elaborating on what they have seen and experienced. Adults do not attempt to prohibit these games, even though children are sometimes hurt by other children in the course of such games (Povrzanovic 1997). Children and youth may elect to participate in hostilities, particularly when it is clear that they cannot be protected from them. Child and youth soldiers are not only conscripted but also may choose a more active than passive role in the hostilities swirling around them. Some children and youth fight because they believe in the cause, some are conscripted, and some join because they see this as a way to secure survival necessities such as food, water, and shelter in the absence of other avenues to obtain these resources (Peters & Richards 1998, Reynolds 1996). But, as Quesada (1998, p. 57) cautions, confronted with "... the conditions experienced by children in the context of war, scarcity, destruction, and lack of food and affection, the options to act freely are limited. Children must make Manichean choices between picking up arms or running away, resisting or giving in."

Children and youth may be effective combatants, valued by their commanding officers. Young soldiers have likely been victimized themselves or witnessed violence against family members and peers. If they have been orphaned or left without family, they may form a fierce loyalty to their unit and officers as a substitute for their own lost families. If they have been victimized or lost loved ones, they may be dedicated fighters operating under the motivation of revenge. They are not inhibited by thoughts of their own children or dependents. Combat may be a way to increase self-esteem and adulation, gaining "instant adult respect" (Peters & Richards 1998, p. 82). As soldiers, children are at risk of other threats, such as drugs given to them to help them in battle (Peters & Richards 1998).

Furthermore, children and youth demonstrate their agency not only during the actual hostilities, but also afterward. "... [Y]oung Africans are conscious of their agency in opting to fight, and often wise beyond their years in understanding their subsequent predicament" (Peters & Richards 1998, p. 77). A focus on the trauma and recovery of young soldiers and children impacted by war diverts attention from underlying structural conditions of poverty and lack of educational and employment opportunities. Although these conditions may have been present prior to the hostilities, they may be exacerbated in the aftermath as youth find themselves crippled by the same structural conditions. Peters & Richards (1998) point to the importance of addressing the concerns of children and youth in demobilization programs. Youth themselves argue that talking about their experiences and feelings is of less use to them than job training that will allow them to support themselves. Traditional healing by the n'anga to cleanse both adults and children may be more effective, in context, than outside trauma relief aid and efforts that attempt a more universalized approach to trauma and recovery (Reynolds 1996). A view of children as only traumatized victims leads to a reliance on psychological issues in trauma recovery work and not on the repair of larger structural conditions (Peters & Richards 1998).

FUTURE DIRECTIONS AND CONCLUDING REMARKS

This review considers the anthropological literature on children and violence. This area of work requires that anthropologists accept both that children are recipients of violence in a range of settings and that children are capable of violence toward others. At this juncture, anthropological work on the relationship between children and violence is poised to make substantial steps forward. This concluding section briefly suggests some future directions.

Descriptive work on children experiencing violence, in general, is better developed than theoretical frameworks are to explain the causes or consequences of such violence. A litany of the types of violence experienced and perpetrated by children will only take the field far enough to understand that children suffer, which they clearly do. Anthropology is in a position to understand how violence is situated and to act within the bounds of cultural contexts when ensuring provision, protection, and participation to children.

Despite increasing calls for the child's perspective, less is understood about how meaning and agency act as mediating forces between violence and its impact. Along these lines, consideration needs to broaden from a focus on risk to include resilience and protective factors. Children can sustain broken bones with no long-lasting effects. They cannot so easily recover from broken spirits, when their bones are broken purposively out of malevolence or disregard. There are important differences among children and youth in the extent to which events are experienced as traumatic (Cairns 1987, 1995). Pervasive violence may even take on a sense of normality (Stephens 1995). Children's perceptions of risk do not necessarily match those of adults (Kelley et al. 1997). Furthermore, "children may be perceived by adults as reluctant to talk when often their silence may be a manifestation of their despair at the absence of any solution to their problems [of being bullied]" (LaFontaine 1991, p. 31). It is also important to understand how children act in the face of danger and violence, for example, making choices that may not be obvious to adults about who they will rely on for help (Spilsbury 2002, Spilsbury & Korbin 2003).

That both violence and childhood are culturally constructed cannot be overemphasized. The cultural construction of violence is influenced by its portrayal. What kind of violence comes to adult and societal attention? LaFontaine (1991) argues that bullying may be conceptualized as childish and therefore insignificant, and Nordstrom (1999) suggests that the more dramatic and exotic, such as purported selling of body parts, may dwarf other widespread issues, such as rape.

In addition, childhood is gendered and is variable by age and experiences. An 8-year-old combatant has different issues than one who is 18 years old. It is important not to gloss over all of these individuals as "children." Children may be redefined as adults depending on the offense they commit. Further, gender plays a role in children's experiences of war and hostilities, both in how children are victimized and the attention directed to this victimization. Nordstrom (1999) argues that boys forced to be soldiers receive greater media attention than girls forced to be prostitutes.

Children exposed to violence and children acting violently may be at odds with adults' conventional wisdom and cherished beliefs about human nature and childhood as a protected life stage. Nevertheless, this is a daily reality for too many of the world's children, and anthropology is in a position to take a stand to fulfill the United Nation's commitment to offer provision, protection, and participation.

NOTES

Because of the broad nature of this review, there are certain literatures that cannot be comprehensively reviewed. The chapter does not consider the extensive literature on infanticide (e.g., Hausfater & Hrdy 1984), on emotions such as anger and shame that are implicated in violence (e.g., Gilligan 1996, Lutz 1988), or on language socialization for anger (Schieffelin 1990). It does not review the extensive literature on child abuse and neglect, including the literature on child sexual abuse cross-culturally (Korbin 1987c, LaFontaine 1990), nor does it include detailed analyses of initiation rites (e.g., Herdt 1981) or female genital operations (e.g., Gruenbaum 2001). The inward-directed violence of suicide also is not included (Institute of Medicine 2002).

ACKNOWLEDGMENTS

The author thanks the editors of Annual Reviews and the production editor, Jennifer Mann, for assistance with this project. All errors and omissions are the sole responsibility of the author.

The *Annual Review of Anthropology* is online at http://anthro.annualreviews.org

LITERATURE CITED

Andersen E. 1992. *Streetwise. Race, Class, and Change in an Urban Community*. Chicago: Univ. Chicago Press

Benedict R. 1934. *Patterns of Culture*. Boston: Houghton Mifflin

Bourgois P. 1995. *In Search of Respect. Selling Crack in El Barrio*. Cambridge, UK: Cambridge Univ. Press

Bourgois P. 1998. Families and children in pain in the U.S. inner city. See Scheper-Hughes & Sargent 1998, pp. 331–51

Boyden J. 1990. Childhood and the policy makers: a comparative perspective on the globalization of childhood. In *Constructing and Reconstructing Childhood*, ed. A James, A Prout, pp. 184–216. London: Falmer

Briggs JL. 1970. *Never in Anger. Portrait of an Eskimo Family*. Cambridge, MA: Harvard Univ. Press

Briggs JL. 1978. The origins of non-violence. Inuit management of aggression. *In Learning Non-Aggression. The Experience of*

Non-Literate Societies, ed. A Montagu, pp. 54–93. New York: Oxford Univ. Press

Burbank V. 1994. *Fighting Women: Anger and Aggression in Aboriginal Australia.* Berkeley and Los Angeles: Univ. Calif. Press

Cairns E. 1987. *Caught in the Crossfire: Children in Northern Ireland.* Syracuse, NY: Syracuse Univ. Press

Cairns E. 1995. *Children and Political Violence.* Oxford: Blackwell

Chagnon N. 1968. *Yanomomo: The Fierce People.* New York: Rinehart Winston

Christensen P, James A. 2000. *Research with Children. Perspectives and Practices.* London: Routledge

Counts D, Brown J, Campbell J. 1992. *Sanctions & Sanctuary. Cultural Perspectives on the Beating of Wives.* Boulder, CO: Westview

Denton R. 1978. Notes on childhood in a nonviolent context: the Semai case. *In Learning Non-Aggression. The Experience of Non-Literate Societies*, ed. A Montagu, pp. 94–143. New York: Oxford Univ. Press

Donnelly AC, ed. 2002. *An International Movement to End Child Abuse. The Story of ISPCAN.* Carol Stream, IL: ISPCAN

Draper P. 1978. The learning environment for aggression and anti-social behavior among the !Kung. *In Learning Non-Aggression. The Experience of Non-Literate Societies*, ed. A Montagu, pp. 31–53. New York: Oxford Univ. Press

Edgerton RB. 1992. *Sick Societies: Challenging the Myth of Primitive Harmony.* New York: Free Press

Ennew J. 1998. Shame and physical pain: cultural relativity, children, torture and punishment. In *Childhood Abused. Protecting Children Against Torture, Cruel, Inhuman and Degrading Treatment and Punishment*, ed. G Van Bueren, pp. 7–34. Aldershot, UK: Ashgate

Field N. 1995. The child as laborer and consumer: the disappearance of childhood in contemporary Japan. In *Children and the Politics of Culture*, ed. S Stephens, pp. 51–78. Princeton: Princeton Univ. Press

Fraser G, Kilbride P. 1980. Child abuse and neglect–rare, but perhaps increasing, phenomenon among the Samia of Kenya. *Child Abuse Neglect* 4(4):227–32

Garbarino J, Dubrow N, Kostelny K, Pardo C. 1992. *Children in Danger.* San Francisco, CA: Jossey-Bass

Gilligan J. 1996. *Violence. Our Deadly Epidemic and Its Causes.* New York: Grosset/Putnam

Graburn N. 1987. Severe child abuse among the Canadian Inuit. See Scheper-Hughes 1987b, pp. 211–25

Gruenbaum E. 2001. *The Female Circumcision Controversy. An Anthropological Perspective.* Philadelphia: Univ. Penn. Press

Hausfater G, Hrdy S, eds. 1984. *Infanticide. Comparative and Evolutionary Perspectives.* New York: Aldine

Hauswald L. 1987. External pressure/internal change: child neglect on the Navajo Reservation. See Scheper-Hughes 1987b, pp. 145–64

Hecht T. 1998. *At Home in the Street. Street Children of Northeast Brazil.* Cambridge, UK: Cambridge Univ. Press

Herdt GH. 1981. *Guardians of the Flutes: Idioms of Masculinity.* New York: McGraw-Hill

Herdt GH, ed. 1982. *Rituals of Manhood. Male Initiation in Papua New Guinea.* Berkeley and Los Angeles: Univ. Calif. Press

Inst. Med. 2002. *Reducing Suicide.* Washington, DC: Natl. Acad. Press

James A, Jenks C, Prout A. 1998. *Theorizing Childhood.* Cambridge, UK: Polity

James A, Prout A. 1997. *Constructing and Reconstructing Childhood: Contemporary Issues in the Sociological Study of Childhood.* London: Falmer

Janzen J, Janzen R. 2000. *Do I Still Have a Life? Voices from the Aftermath of War in Rwanda and Burundi.* Publ. Anthropol. 20. Lawrence: Univ. Kansas

Johnson O. 1981. The socioeconomic context of child abuse and neglect in Native South America. See Korbin 1981, pp. 56–70

Keesing RM. 1982. Introduction. See Herdt 1982, pp. 1–43

Kelley P, Mayall B, Hood S. 1997. Children's accounts of risk. *Childhood* 4(3):305–24

Kempe CH, Silverman F, Steele B, Droegmueller W, Silver H. 1962. The battered child syndrome. *JAMA* 181:17–24

Kleinman A, Das V, Locke M. 1997. Introduction. In *Social Suffering*, ed. A Kleinman, V Das, M Locke, pp. ix–xxvii. Los Angeles/Berkeley: Univ. Calif. Press

Korbin J. 1977. Anthropological contributions to the study of child abuse. *Child Abuse Neglect* 1(1):7–24

Korbin J. 1978. *Caretaking patterns in a rural Hawaiian community: congruence of child and observer reports*. PhD thesis. Univ. Calif., Los Angeles

Korbin J. 1980. The cross-cultural context of child abuse and neglect. In *The Battered Child*, ed. CH Kempe, RE Helfer, pp. 21–35. Chicago, IL: Univ. Chicago Press. 3rd ed.

Korbin J, ed. 1981. *Child Abuse and Neglect: Cross-Cultural Perspectives*. Berkeley/Los Angeles: Univ. Calif. Press

Korbin J. 1987a. Child abuse and neglect: the cultural context. In *The Battered Child*, ed. RE Helfer, RS Kempe, pp. 23–41. Chicago, IL: Univ. Chicago Press. 4th ed.

Korbin J. 1987b. Child maltreatment in cross-cultural perspective. Vulnerable children and circumstances. In *Child Abuse and Neglect: Biosocial Dimensions*, ed. R Gelles, J Lancaster, pp. 31–55. Chicago, IL: Aldine

Korbin J. 1987c. Child sexual abuse: implications from the cross-cultural record. See Scheper-Hughes 1987b, pp. 247–65

Korbin J. 1990. Hana 'ino: child maltreatment in an Hawaiian-American community. *Pac. Stud.* 13:7–22

Korbin J. 1997. Culture and child maltreatment. In *The Battered Child*, ed. M Helfer, R Kempe, R Krugman, pp. 29–48. Chicago, IL: Univ. Chicago Press. 5th ed.

Korbin J, Coulton C. 1997. Understanding the neighborhood context for children and families: epidemiological and ethnographic approaches. In *Neighborhood Poverty: Context and Consequences for Children*. ed. J Brooks-Gunn, L Aber, G Duncan, pp. 77–91. New York: Sage

LaFontaine J. 1990. *Child Sexual Abuse*. Cambridge, UK: Polity

LaFontaine J. 1991. *Bullying: The Child's View*. London: Calouste Gulbenkian Found.

Langness LL. 1981. Child abuse and cultural values: the case of New Guinea. See Korbin 1981, pp. 13–34

Laye C. 1954. *The Dark Child. The Autobiography of an African Boy*. New York: Farrar, Straus and Giroux

LeVine S, LeVine R. 1981. Child abuse and neglect in Sub-Saharan Africa. See Korbin 1981, pp. 35–55

Levy J. 1964. The fate of Navajo twins. *Am. Anthropol.* 66:883–87

Lutz C. 1988. *Unnatural Emotions*. Chicago, IL: Univ. Chicago Press

Mayall B. 2000. The sociology of childhood: children's autonomy and participation rights. In *Advocating for Children. International Perspectives on Children's Rights*, ed. A Smith, M Gollop, K Marshall, K Nairn, pp. 126–40. Dunedin, New Zealand: Univ. Otago Press

Mead M. 1928. *Coming of Age in Samoa*. New York: Morrow

Mead M. 1935. *Sex and Temperament in Three Primitive Societies*. New York: Morrow

Merry SE. 1981. *Urban Danger: Life in a Neighborhood of Strangers*. Philadelphia, PA: Temple Univ. Press

Miller B. 1981. *The Endangered Sex. Neglect of Female Children in Rural North India*. Ithaca, NY: Cornell Univ. Press

Miller B. 1987. Female infanticide and child neglect in rural North India. See Scheper-Hughes 1987b, pp. 95–112

Minturn L. 1984. Changes in differential treatment of Rajput girls in Khalapur: 1955–1975. *Med. Anthropol.* 8(2):127–32

Minturn L, Lambert W. 1964. *Mothers of Six Cultures. Antecedents of Childrearing*. New York: Wiley

Nordstrom C. 1999. Girls and war zones. Troubling questions. In *Engendering Forced*

Migration. Theory and Practice, ed. D Indra, pp. 63–82. New York: Berghahn

Olson E. 1981. Socioeconomic and psychocultural contexts of child abuse and neglect in Turkey. See Korbin 1981, pp. 96–119

Panter-Brick C. 2002. Street children, human rights, and public health: a critique and future directions. *Annu. Rev. Anthropol.* 31:147–71

Peters K, Richards P. 1998. Fighting with open eyes: young combatants talking about war in Sierra Leone. In *Rethinking the Trauma of War*, ed. P Bracken, C Petty, pp. 76–111. New York/London: Free Assoc. Books

Poffenberger T. 1981. Child rearing and social structure in rural India: towards a cross-cultural definition of child abuse and neglect. See Korbin 1981, pp. 71–95. Berkeley/Los Angeles: Univ. Calif. Press

Povrzanovic M. 1997. Children, war and nation. Croatia 1991-4. *Childhood* 4(1):81–102

Quesada J. 1998. Suffering child: an embodiment of war and its aftermath in Post-Sandanista Nicaragua. *Med. Anthropol. Q.* 12(1):51–73

Reynolds P. 1996. *Traditional Healers and Childhood in Zimbabwe*. Athens, OH: Ohio Univ. Press

Robben A. 2000. The assault on basic trust: disappearance, protest, and reburial in Argentina. See Robben & Suarez-Orozco 2000, pp. 70–101

Robben A, Suarez-Orozco M, eds. 2000. *Cultures Under Siege: Collective Violence and Trauma*. Cambridge, UK: Cambridge Univ. Press

Scheper-Hughes N. 1987a. The cultural politics of child survival. See Scheper-Hughes 1987b, pp. 1–29

Scheper-Hughes N, ed. 1987b. *Child Survival. Anthropological Perspectives on the Treatment and Maltreatment of Children*. Boston: Reidel

Scheper-Hughes N. 1992. *Death Without Weeping. The Violence of Everyday Life in Brazil*. Berkeley and Los Angeles: Univ. Calif. Press

Scheper-Hughes N, Sargent C, eds. 1998. *Small Wars: The Cultural Politics of Childhood*. Berkeley/Los Angeles: Univ. Calif. Press

Schieffelin B. 1990. *The Give and Take of Everyday Life*. Cambridge, UK: Cambridge Univ. Press

Scrimshaw S. 1978. Infant mortality and behavior in the regulation of family size. *Pop. Dev. Rev.* 4:383–403

Simmons L, ed. 1942. *Sun Chief*. New Haven, CT: Yale Univ. Press

Spilsbury J. 2002. "If I don't know them, I'll get killed probably": how children's concerns about safety shape help-seeking behavior. *Childhood* 9(1):101–17

Spilsbury J, Korbin J. 2003. Negotiating the dance: social capital from the perspective of neighborhood children and adults. In *Rethinking Childhood*, ed. P Pufall, R Unsworth. New Brunswick, NJ: Rutgers Univ. Press. In press

Stephens S. 1995. Introduction: children and the politics of culture in "late capitalism." In *Children and the Politics of Culture*, ed. S Stephens, pp. 3–48. Princeton, NJ: Princeton Univ. Press

Straus M, Gelles R, Steinmetz S. 1980. *Behind Closed Doors. Violence in the American Family*. New York: Anchor

Suarez-Orozco M. 1987. The treatment of children in the "dirty war": ideology, state terrorism, and the abuse of children in Argentina. See Scheper-Hughes 1987b, pp. 95–112

Suarez-Orozco M, Robben A. 2000. Interdisciplinary perspectives on violence and trauma. See Robben & Suarez-Orozco 2000, pp. 1–41

Turnbull C. 1961. *The Forest People*. New York: Simon & Schuster

Turnbull C. 1972. *The Mountain People*. New York: Simon & Schuster

Vigil D. 1988. *Barrio Gangs: Street Life and Identity in Southern California*. Austin, TX: Univ. Texas Press

Vigil D. 2003. Urban violence and street gangs. *Annu. Rev. Anthropol.* 32:225–42

Vizard E, Monch E, Misch P. 1995. Child and

adolescent sex abuse perpetrators: a review of the research literature. *J. Child Psychol. Psychiatry* 36(5):731–56

Weisner T. 1979. Urban-rural differences in sociable and disruptive behavior of Kenya children. *Ethnology* 18(2):153–72

Whiting B, Edwards C. 1988. *Children of Different Worlds. The Social Formation of Social Behavior*. Cambridge, MA: Harvard Univ. Press

Whiting B, Whiting JWM. 1975. *Children of Six Cultures*. Cambridge, MA: Harvard Univ. Press

Whiting JWM, Child I. 1953. *Child Training and Personality*. New Haven, CT: Yale Univ. Press

Annu. Rev. Anthropol. 2003. 32:447–74
doi: 10.1146/annurev.anthro.32.061002.093412
Copyright © 2003 by Annual Reviews. All rights reserved
First published online as a Review in Advance on June 17, 2003

ANTHROPOLOGY, INEQUALITY, AND DISEASE: A Review

Vinh-Kim Nguyen[1] and Karine Peschard[2]

[1]Department of Social Studies of Medicine, McGill University, Montréal, Québec,
Canada H2A 1X1; email: vinh-kim.nguyen@staff.mcgill.ca
[2]Department of Anthropology, McGill University, Montréal, Québec, Canada H3A 2T7;
email: karineeliane.peschard@mail.mcgill.ca

Key Words embodiment, biopolitics, structural violence, commodification, infectious diseases, biomedicine

■ **Abstract** Anthropological approaches broaden and deepen our understanding of the finding that high levels of socioeconomic inequality correlate with worsened health outcomes across an entire society. Social scientists have debated whether such societies are unhealthy because of diminished social cohesion, psychobiological pathways, or the material environment. Anthropologists have questioned these mechanisms, emphasizing that fine-grained ethnographic studies reveal that social cohesion is locally and historically produced; psychobiological pathways involve complex, longitudinal biosocial dynamics suggesting causation cannot be viewed in purely biological terms; and material factors in health care need to be firmly situated within a broad geopolitical analysis. As a result, anthropological scholarship argues that this finding should be understood within a theoretical framework that avoids the pitfalls of methodological individualism, assumed universalism, and unidirectional causation. Rather, affliction must be understood as the embodiment of social hierarchy, a form of violence that for modern bodies is increasingly sublimated into differential disease rates and can be measured in terms of variances in morbidity and mortality between social groups. Ethnographies on the terrain of this neoliberal global health economy suggest that the violence of this inequality will continue to spiral as the exclusion of poorer societies from the global economy worsens their health—an illness poverty trap that, with few exceptions, has been greeted by a culture of indifference that is the hallmark of situations of extreme violence and terror. Studies of biocommodities and biomarkets index the processes by which those who are less well off trade in their long-term health for short-term gain, to the benefit of the long-term health of better-off individuals. Paradoxically, new biomedical technologies have served to heighten the commodification of the body, driving this trade in biological futures as well as organs and body parts.

0084-6570/03/1021-0447$14.00   **447**

INTRODUCTION: INEQUALITY AND DISEASE

This review examines how the relationship between social inequality and health has been opened up to anthropological investigation. Epidemiological evidence claims a robust relationship between socioeconomic inequality and health outcomes, although the mechanisms by which this relationship occurs remain poorly understood. Drawing on cross-cultural work on the body and affliction, this article examines how anthropologists through the prism of embodiment have viewed the impact of inequality on health. This review starts with the standard definitions of inequality and health, understood as the socioeconomic disparities captured in quantitative population surveys and the biological outcomes measured in epidemiological research respectively, to explore how anthropological research can generate insight into the relationship between the two by recasting them within anthropological considerations of how the body is fashioned by cultural, political, and historical processes (Diamond 1997). Understanding the body as deeply historicized and socialized enables a cross-cultural framework for understanding how social relations condition disease patterns and, more broadly, states of individual and collective affliction. For anthropologists, the inequality/disease relationship is a form of violence enacted through cultures and rationalities. A distinction has been made between social relations, where the violence of inequality is most often expressed in ritualized form, leaving visible traces on the body, and those where the violence of inequality is transcribed into the body as biological difference and expressed as "risk" to be managed through techniques of government. This distinction differentiates "modern" political spaces of health, where misfortune is managed through specialized therapeutic institutions and violence is sublimated into hierarchies of disease; "pre-modern" spaces of therapy, where anthropologists have classically operated, producing of witchcraft, spirit possession, and other "traditional" medical systems; and "a-modern" (Latour 1993) spaces, where the lines between therapeutic and political power are once again blurred.

More contemporary anthropological work on health and disease points to an increasingly a-modern therapeutic economy, where competing powers and therapeutic claims vie for legitimacy and the right to manage misfortune. The massive global scaling-back of public health in a neoliberal economic climate has conjugated with globalization to magnify the health impact of transnational inequalities and the way these are manifested and administered (Kelley 2003). From this conjuncture a new political configuration of health has emerged that marshals nongovernmental organizations (NGOs) and humanitarian governmentalities, biomedical discourses and technologies, and diseased bodies on an increasingly conflict-ridden terrain (Elyachar 2002). These extreme health inequalities constitute a form of structural violence that has come under increased ethnographic scrutiny. This research has described a striking culture of indifference to affliction present in areas of extreme inequality and expressed through the rationalities used to manage it. This culture of inequality facilitates a pathogenic biosocial spiral of socioeconomic exclusion and deteriorating health. Growing attention has been paid by anthropologists to how biomedical technologies conjugate with material inequalities to create novel markets that have intensified and accelerated the commodification of the body and its futures, a phenomena of which the organ trade is only the most visible element. These markets are emblematic of the processes by which the poor trade in their long-term health for survival while the rich, although increasingly shielded from most disease threats, are able to purchase better health.

SOCIAL DETERMINANTS OF HEALTH

The relationship between poverty and ill health is well established. The nefarious effects of poverty on health, as historically demonstrated by the McKeown thesis—which showed that improvements in health were due to decreases in poverty in England and had little to do with improved medical care—have been widely confirmed and reviewed (Subramanian et al. 2002, Wagstaff 2002), validating the common view that poverty is the only robust social determinant of health. The mechanisms by which poverty causes disease are, by now, well understood. They include weakened immunity and neurophysiological development because of malnutrition, ease of spread of pathogens because of insalubrious living conditions, and the precariousness of social support networks. More recently, the role of increased exposure to environmental pollutants, to which the poor may be more exposed, has been implicated (Evans & Kantrowitz 2002, Faber & Krieg 2002, Woodward & Boffetta 1997). It is the material deprivation poverty entails that is unhealthy. For epidemiologists, the first hint that the deleterious effects of poverty might not be due to material deprivation alone came from a now landmark study, the Whitehall study (Marmot 1986). It was found that life expectancy among British civil servants increased with their rank, even when standard factors influencing the risk of death—such as smoking, lack of exercise, and so on—were factored in. This finding held even between those with very similar ranks who would have had the same kinds of jobs in adjacent offices and lived in the same neighborhoods and had the same leisure activities; in other words, the finding could not be ascribed to differences in working conditions such as those that might be found between laborers and managers, nor could it be attributed to cultural or class differences in lifestyle. The observation of this hierarchy effect suggested that poverty could not be the sole social factor accounting for adverse health outcomes.

A growing body of epidemiological research now indicates that social inequality contributes to ill health independently of income level, providing evidence that hierarchy effects can act across large populations and not just within discrete groups. This gradient effect means that, at the same absolute level of income, an individual in a more-egalitarian society will be healthier than one in a less-egalitarian society. This gradient effect not only affects those who are lower, or poorer, in the social hierarchy but also impacts health across all income levels (Donohoe 2003, Kawachi et al. 1999). This observation suggests that the concept of social class, although a conceptually robust first approximation of social inequality, is too blunt an instrument to capture the fine-grained differences that occur within groups that share the same material conditions of reproduction (such as British civil servants), nor does it adequately account for spread within and between classes. Finally, class-based analyses may not be completely transposable across societies with different degrees of industrialization and, therefore, different historical trajectories of class formation (Forbes & Wainwright 2001).

Criticisms that the observation is spurious, merely a statistical aberration or an artefact of measurement, appear to be unfounded (Wolfson et al. 1999). The observation that there is a correlation between socioeconomic inequality and health has proven to be robust and is, therefore, a novel finding of major significance. Previously, it had been thought that absolute poverty, rather than relative poverty, was the only robust social determinant of ill health and that this effect was unidirectional, affecting only those lower on the social ladder. That health outcomes in those who live in inegalitarian societies are inferior to those who live in more egalitarian societies has led to the observation that some societies are, indeed, "unhealthy" (Kawachi & Kennedy 2002, Wilkinson 1996). Globalization, increasing evidence of heightened inequalities, increasing poverty and ill health in many parts of the world, and emerging transnational threats to health invite talk of an "unhealthy planet" and have focused considerable attention most recently on how health equity is to be achieved globally today (Whitehead & Evans 2001).

WHAT MAKES INEQUALITY UNHEALTHY: THREE HYPOTHESES

This finding has major implications for social policy and public health; as a result considerable energy has been spent on identifying the mechanisms responsible. A significant body of research that details this finding and explores possible mechanisms to explain it has emerged in the field of public health. However, the underlying mechanism for the inequality/disease relationship remains poorly understood. Anthropologists can contribute to advancing attempts to understand the mechanisms through which hierarchy is translated into disease and to inscribe this relationship into a broader historical and sociocultural framework. Considerable attention has been paid to identifying the mechanisms responsible. The elucidation of the pathways—neurodevelopmental, physiological, and behavioral—by which social inequality produces adverse health outcomes has stimulated considerable interest among researchers in these sciences (Evans et al. 1994, Graham 2002). A principal methodological difficulty in examining the inequality/disease relationship has been isolating the adverse impact of inequality, per se, from poverty (Clarke et al. 2002). For instance, how can we know whether worsening health outcomes in a situation of deepening inequality are not just due to the fact that there are more people who are poor? Epidemiologists rely on quantitative methods to tease out the contribution of inequality, or relative poverty, from absolute poverty.

Yet these methods are limited in their ability to segregate the relative contribution of environmental, biological, and social factors to the mechanisms by which inequality exerts its unhealthy effects. Although no clear mechanism for explaining how inequality translates into ill health has emerged, consensus exists around three broad hypotheses.

The role of social cohesion has been emphasized, building on a body of clinical epidemiologic studies (Kawachi et al. 1997, Lomas 1998, Wilkinson 1996). Although lacking a singular definition, these studies point out that the density of social networks correlates with better disease outcomes and decreased mortality, a finding that is understandable in settings of poverty where social ties can be called upon to weather ill health but is more difficult to explain in more affluent surroundings. This observation has triggered a search for a quantifiable proxy for the density of social ties and the presumed correlate, social cohesion. Considerable attention has focused on social capital, a term first advanced in this sense by Jacobs (1961) and that has received considerable interest from epidemiologists, sociologists, and economists (Anheier & Kendall 2002, Cattell 2001, Campbell & McLean 2002, Pearce & Smith 2003, Putnam 1995) as both a potentially quantifiable measure of social cohesion and a goal of policy initiatives.

A host of psychosocial mechanisms have been implicated to account for how hierarchy exerts deleterious effects on the health of populations and individuals. Research has attempted to link psychosocial factors to biological pathways that explain how greater inequality can lead to negative developmental and physiological effects. The emerging field of the biology of inequality is centrally concerned with this hypothesis (Brunner 1997). Stress has emerged as the common psychosocial entry point or trigger for these biological pathways. For instance, stressed mothers have lower-birth-weight babies who are, in turn, at higher risk for adverse health outcomes in adulthood (Mullings & Wali 2001). In adulthood, chronic stress elevates cortisol levels, which decreases resistance to infectious insults (Evans 1994). The initial and persistent emphasis on stress as a determinant subsequently led to cognitivist notions of self-efficacy as well as to approaches that draw on the sociology of emotion, which seeks to complexify the psychosocial triggering of biological pathways (Elstad 1998). These pathways may allow biological effects to be exerted much later on in life, generating cohort or generational effects that make epidemiological ascertainment of cause difficult, as historical events may lead to later biological effects through complex pathways that entangle biology, culture, and environment, pointing to the need for life-course approaches (Graham 2002).

Neomaterialists have countered that material factors can explain the observed gradient effect on ill health. Their reasoning is such that in inegalitarian societies the poor are more deprived than in comparatively egalitarian societies because fewer investments are made in infrastructure and social services (Navarro & Shi 2001). These material investments, which are not captured by aggregate data on income, help to shield those lower on the social ladder from a broad range of environmental, behavioral, and social risks—from environmental toxins to endemic violence (Wilkinson et al. 1998, Galea et al. 2002)—that would otherwise compromise their health outcomes. Moreover, material deprivation in childhood, which is more prevalent in inegalitarian societies, has been shown to perpetuate "unhealthy" behavior later on in life, leading to worse health outcomes that persist even as individuals climb the social ladder (Lynch 1997).

ANTHROPOLOGICAL PERSPECTIVES ON THE THREE HYPOTHESES

Anthropological research contributes to greater understanding of the complex, multifactorial mechanisms by which inequality leads to ill health. The strength of this research has been its ability to investigate, from the ground up, both the effects of inequality and the way in which it is perceived and acted upon. What has this research contributed to furthering the three hypotheses?

The notion of social capital has been drawn upon extensively to attempt to explain what makes a society "healthy." However, closer examination shows that the concept of social capital has been lacking analytic clarity. Definitions have ranged from trust to density of social ties. Surveying the uses of social capital in the literature on health inequality and disease, it is difficult to avoid a nagging suspicion that this lack of analytic clarity leads to a tautology: Societies are healthy because they are trusting, and there is a lot of trust because societies are healthy. Although part of the confusion stems from different usages of the term by economists and sociologists, conceptual clarity will not necessarily be helpful in the absence of research that can place social capital within local, historical dynamics and understandings of trust (Anheir & Kendall 2001, Kunitz 2001). The plea for local context questions the idea of social capital as a historical and cultural essence, arguing instead for understanding how social ties are produced in historically and culturally conditioned networks of reciprocity and exchange, result from asymmetrical relations of power that are highly hierarchized (Elkana et al. 2002), or may simply be artefacts of bodily practice.

A theoretically important critique of the biology-of-inequality hypothesis has been advanced by medical anthropologists. Several important studies question the universality of the biology that is assumed to express the pathways through which inequality exercises biological effects. Rather than deny the relevance of biology to understanding social phenomena, these studies, which take biology very seriously, point out that biology—from the genetic to the ecological—is more plastic than otherwise acknowledged and is extraordinarily permeable to social events (Lock 1995, Lewontin 2000). An important caveat, these studies tell us, is not to confuse cause and effect: For example, biological differences between populations may not so much be the cause of observed social differences as their effect. These studies indicate that rigid notions of causality—such as that implied by terms like social determinants—may oversimplify what are highly complex biosocial interactions between environment, culture, diet, and history and may endorse longitudinal or life-course approaches that take into account how individuals shape their environments based on the ways in which they understand their positions in the world. These life-course approaches provide a glimpse into how history is embodied; they point to how complex social, historical, and physiological interactions are overly simplified by reducing them to uniquely biological phenomena. Such biologizing, and by extension medicalizing, of social ills can be a form of social control and, perhaps more dangerously, paves the way for attempts at "magic bullet" solutions to these complex problems, with potentially deleterious results (Conrad 1992, Illich 1977, Zola 1972).

Medical anthropologists are largely sympathetic to the neomaterialist hypothesis, adding to it a more overtly political perspective by seeking to link local inequalities to a broad range of large-scale social forces by working "up" from field sites. Building on the social epidemiology that sought to track the hidden injuries of class in the 1970s (Baer 1996, Turshen 1984, Waitzkin 1981), the impact on health of social policy and, furthermore, of the broader political economy has received renewed attention, with a focus on how contemporary changes in macroeconomic policy and the role of the state impact the health of populations in general and the poor in particular (Kim et al. 2000, Navarro 2002). Here, by using social theory to provide the crucial link between large-scale social change and the lives of individuals, medical anthropologists have joined forces with critical scholars of public health to more sharply politicize the materialist hypothesis. Increasing attention has been paid to linking material "determinants" of health to social policy, how social policy is translated into material action, and, more generally, to the ideological and political commitments that shape the environments within which policy is formulated (Coburn 2000).

In summary, anthropological perspectives on the three hypotheses advanced to explain the inequality/disease correlation call for an approach that links local context to broader analysis. This approach requires that materialist factors be placed within a broader geopolitical context (Coburn 2000, Popay et al. 1998), that discussions of biological or social determinants be opened up to include exploration of the full complexity of biosocial interactions, and that analytically robust definitions of social capital be developed from fine-grained empirical studies that examine the historical and cultural coproduction of social cohesion and inclusiveness.

THE EMBODIMENT OF INEQUALITY: A THEORETICAL FRAMEWORK

Anthropologists may work within an epidemiological framework to integrate sociocultural and historical approaches with the research agenda, as is the case with research that examines why inequality leads to the poor health outcomes measured in epidemiological surveys. The epidemiological framework relies on quantitative understandings of inequality and health: respectively, income distribution and biomedically measurable morbidity and mortality events. Outside of the epidemiological framework, anthropologists have more broadly conceived the inequality/health relationship as being one between the body and society and fleshed out by ethnographically driven approaches. Before exploring the implications of ethnographically driven work on inequality and disease, this section first examines how theoretically driven approaches have enlarged epidemiological notions of health and inequality to allow for consideration of the processes that produce and legitimate inequalities both in societies and in bodies.

Medical anthropologists have long argued that biomedical and epidemiological categories are socially constructed rather than naturally given. The social construction of biomedical facts—that is, their production through different combinations of institutional, technical, social, cultural, and political operations—does not mean they are not real; rather, it is through these very operations that the biological world becomes real and available for intervention (Cambrosio & Keating 1992, Latour 1993). As a result, the categories through which the biological world is understood and acted upon may reflect and perpetuate existing inequalities (Adas 1989, Lippman 1991, Sharp 2002, Wright & Treacher 1982). A complementary tradition within anthropology more generally has rejected the biomedical definition of disease (seeing it as too narrow, even ethnocentric) in order to better study the forms affliction takes across cultures—from witchcraft and spirit possession to infestation by various nonhuman agents (Lewis 1991, Samuelson 2001, Geissler 1998). The evidence that biological categories—biomedical nosologies—do not adequately cover the spectrum of afflictions present across the world has prompted anthropologists to seek more inclusive definitions of affliction and, therefore, a fuller picture of how inequality translates into affliction. More recent work informed by social studies of science has problematized the social and technical processes through which disease entities are constructed and embodied.

Within medical anthropology, a phenomenological school sees the biomedical inscription of disease as one cultural elaboration among many of a precultural, existential form of suffering that is considered defining of the human condition (Good 1993). In this view, while biomedicine shares with Christian religions a soteriological structure, it offers treatment without salvation. An engaged anthropological critique of social suffering has joined forces with critics of medicalization to denounce the depoliticization of health and to mount a powerful critique of the social forces that shorten the lives of the poor (Farmer 1997). However, the notion of a precultural existential ground of suffering does not offer firm theoretical purchase on how affliction is to be historicized—according to this view, it is the enculturation of suffering that is historicized, not affliction. Social suffering approaches also foreclose the possibility that what is at stake in anthropological considerations of the body may include issues other than affliction. Medical systems are not only preoccupied with pain and suffering, it is argued, but also are intimately concerned with pleasures and passions (Farquhar 1994a).

Eschewing the search for a transcendental theory of suffering and soteriological approaches to biomedical systems, other medical anthropologists have instead focused on the materiality of the body, drawing on a tradition of scholarship on the anthropology of the body that has shown how social relations invest and express the body, either as inscription (Turner 1980), experience and its embodiment as traces in the body (Pandolfi 1990), or practice, sedimented into what Bourdieu has called habitus (Farquhar 1994b). This social dimension makes for a politics of the body, visible in the political economy of the body (Goodman & Leatherman 1998) or through the scrutiny of the processes through which the body may express resistance to dominant political forms (Comaroff 1985). By focusing on how the body is located within historical and social relations, this literature provides an important theoretical stepping stone to formulating an anthropological problematic that is more sharply focused on the relationship between social inequality and disease.

A phenomenon of such great significance as the disease/inequality relationship calls for examination in cross-cultural and translocal perspectives—whether this is to validate the findings or to challenge and sharpen the hypotheses it raises. The anthropology of the body offers a theoretical framework that allows comparative research into how social processes and local meaning inform and produce affliction (Lock 1993). Quantitative measures such as income spread, gini coefficients, and so on are invaluable for generating hypotheses, providing comparative markers, and indicating new avenues for research. However, the rich tradition of anthropological scholarship reviewed in this volume indicates that understanding what makes a society inegalitarian requires qualitative research for understanding how local actors understand, enact, and respond to inequalities and, as a result, how these translate into embodied effects.

Whether the classical object of anthropological research is taken to be culture or society, recent work has reread both in light of the opening up of field sites to development, globalization, technoscience, and new social movements (Haraway 1996, Richey 1999, Werbner 1999). Ethnographic research in previously out-of-the-way places (Tsing 1994) and in a plethora of new field sites closer to home has moved beyond debates concerning structure, agency, and meaning to reposition culture firmly within the nexus of power, history, and subjectification. Whether one subscribes to a modernist or postmodernist program, common new social forms have become available to ethnographic scrutiny. Although these new objects of study have not been viewed through the lens of inequality, their focus on the processes of social change means that they have either addressed new forms of inequality or their consequences. Studies of new social movements that respond to these inequalities, especially NGOs and the humanitarian industry (Pandolfi 2001), can be cited alongside those of various urban subcultures, violent conflicts (Ellis 1999), displaced populations (Malkki 1995), emerging and resurgent infectious threats to human health (Farmer 1999), and "natural" catastrophes (Steinberg 2000). As can be seen from the ethnographic spread of this work, the challenge is to integrate a scattered body of empirical work within a cohesive theoretical paradigm that allows the disease/inequality relationship to be ethnographically fleshed out.

The insistent presence of the suffering body in medical anthropology (Butt 2002a) means that the question of power—the power to wound, to heal, or to prevent injury—is more acute than in other domains of anthropological inquiry.

Power offers a compelling framework for opening up consideration of inequality to include historical and cultural processes, rather than reifying it in terms of social structure or cultural essence or individualizing it in terms of human agency. As a result, a political anthropology of health offers an appealing theoretical project for reconciling culture, inequality, and disease. Fassin (1996) has developed a genealogical model to bring anthropological scholarship on "traditional" societies into a dialogue with more contemporary work. This model represents the most definitive statement of the form such a political anthropology should take. Rather than being a comparative enterprise framed by a structuralist understanding of society, or a humanist notion of agency, this model draws on the Foucaultian distinction between premodern and modern political societies. This opposition can be used to delineate contrasting political spaces of health, constituted along three axes: the ways in which inequalities are embodied, therapeutic power is legitimated, and collectivities respond to misfortune. This genealogical approach identifies the outlines of a political regime of health that articulates affliction, therapeutic power, and collective management of misfortune in contingent ways. Rather than advocating a teleological or evolutionary view of "progress" toward a modern medicalized society, this approach permits the identification of ruptures as well as the tracing of continuities between premodern political health apparatuses, such as witchcraft and spirit possession, and their equivalents in the modern world (Fassin 1996).

THE VIOLENCE OF INEQUALITY

Social inequality is manifest in the body; however, it is not limited to biomedical manifestations (i.e., disease). Rather than proceeding from a strictly biomedical definition of disease and correlating it with social inequalities, anthropological approaches to the body invite us to compare how inequality is embodied across societies and times. Rites and social procedures that mark the body and place it in a social order are a paradigmatic example of this phenomenon (Maertens 1978, Turner 1980). Similarly, various forms of initiation, spirit possession, and witchcraft can be viewed as manifestations that express and enact social hierarchy, fixing them in a fluctuating social world. However, these examples show us that the body is not merely a passive recipient of social inscriptions; indeed, the body can serve as a site for organizing forms of resistance to dominant social inscriptions, such as those exercised by patriarchy (Boddy 1989), capital (Ong 1987), the state (Arnold 1993), or colonialism (White 2000). Resistance operates through diverse mechanisms, either by furnishing counter-hegemonic meanings (Hebdige 1979), constituting therapeutic communities whose historical infrastructure conditions the rise of political movements (Comaroff 1985), or producing dissident subjectivities (Nguyen 2002). However, subjects often deploy, modify, or enact their bodies not as acts of resistance but simply as a form of pragmatic action (Lock 1998).

Modern bodies can be differentiated from premodern ones. The argument that contemporary forms of scarification express a return to tribal forms of belonging

(Maffesoli 1995) glosses significant divergences between premodern and modern practices (notably, that moderns elect to modify their bodies to signify particular social identities, in contrast to traditional societies where bodily modification is assigned). However, this argument does have the merit of pointing to how the body is treated as a social medium even in highly individualistic societies (Mascia-Lees & Sharpe 1992). Fassin shows how in premodern society the embodiment of inequality was limited to modifications of the body through ritual, a form of violence that did not significantly translate into differences in morbidity or mortality between groups at different positions on the social ladder (Fassin 1996). In modern society, inequality becomes embodied biologically, as those lower on the ladder suffer higher morbidity and mortality rates. This lends credence to the Foucaultian thesis that in modernity violence is sublimated, echoing Foucault's observation of how the spectacular nature of premodern punishment is transformed into a more insidious and pervasive ordering of bodies through institutional practices. Fassin shows how this disciplinary turn registers at the biological level and makes a convincing and important argument that in modern societies inequality is biologized (transcribed into the body) rather than ritualized (inscribed onto the body).

BLAME, RISK, AND THE VIOLENCE OF POSTMODERNITY

For moderns, risk is the primary mechanism through which social inequality is embodied and is visible in different prevalences of diseases and outcomes between different social groups. Risk, then, can be said to be a measure of social violence, capturing how power distributes unevenly down the social ladder. This echoes findings from anthropological work on AIDS that demonstrated that the HIV epidemic "tracks along social fault lines," (Farmer 1999) affecting those whose poverty and social exclusion have made them the most vulnerable to infection (Parker 2002). Marked differences in morbidity and mortality from HIV and other preventable and treatable diseases, such as tuberculosis and malaria, thus indicate a situation of structural violence (Farmer 1997). Structural violence is visible in the steep gradients of social inequality that, by producing indecent poverty in an era of increasing wealth, expose the poor to fatal diseases. The health impacts of structural violence are compounded by lack of access to effective care for the powerless (Farmer 1999). The existence of a gradient of access to biomedicine is best seen in studies of patterns of resort (Fassin 1992) and indicates that biomedicine has, by virtue of its efficacy, become an unwitting accomplice to biological inscription of social hierarchies.

Medical anthropologists have also focused on the way discourses of risk are used to label and manage particular populations, drawing on Foucault's notion of governmentality (Burchell et al. 1991) to explore how risk has become a technique for governing populations and producing particular kinds of subjects (Dean 1999, Novas & Rose 2000). Modern administration of risk involves identifying and targeting at-risk populations for preventive intervention (Lupton 1999). This practice draws its origins in the control of epidemics through the identification, isolation, and treatment of infectious cases. Although the efficacy of this strategy is established, it subjects individuals and social groups to forms of discrimination. In public health discourse and intervention, risk serves to differentiate populations variably across the social ladder, performing finely grained distinctions between social groups within populations. Risk is used to constitute specific populations—the teen drop-out (Hutson & Liddiard 1994, Bridgman 2001), the homeless (Desjarlais 1993, Lyon-Callo 2000), welfare recipients (Churchill 1995), single mothers (Coffield 2000), the poor (Newman 2001), and so on—as targets for intervention. This targeting may produce collateral damage, legitimating stereotypes and providing fodder for stigma (Hacking 2000).

The operationalization of discourses of risk into targeted interventions has the effect of refracting inequalities, producing different effects at various positions in the social spectrum. Those lower on the social ladder find themselves blamed for behavior over which they have little effective control and find themselves subject to interventions that medicalize social forms of suffering, even as they are excluded from collective forms of solidarity. Those higher on the social ladder find themselves undergoing ever more biomedical poking, prodding, and testing in a vain attempt to achieve certainty from the amorphous threat of risk of which the biomedicalization of everyday life is symptomatic (Lock 1998, Cussins 1998). Bluntly put, governmental technologies of risk blame the poor and magnify uncertainty for the rich with different embodied consequences.

Risk, by striating the social body into degrees of operability, refracts social inequalities at the level of body modification. This is most obvious in phenomena like plastic surgery where economic access is a primary determinant, but it may also be hypothesized to exist for other surgeries, such as hysterectomy and caesarian section, where rates have been demonstrated to differ markedly between localities (Fabri & Murta 2002). These differences in medical intervention may express variances in idioms of distress in groups at different positions on the social ladder (those to whom a psychological language is most available may have lower rates of biomedical body modification than those for whom distress is primarily a somatic affair) (Kirmayer 1992), different economic circumstances, or different styles of engagement with the state (Cohen 1999).

Although Foucaultian-inspired analyses have pointed out the sublimated violence that incorporates inequality in terms of epidemiological differences in survival, increasing attention is being paid to the public health impact of the proliferation of low-intensity violent conflicts around the world (McGinn 2000, Levy & Siddel 2000). The impact, in terms of mortality and physical and psychological morbidity, is devastating (De Jong 2002, Desjarlais et al. 1995, Jenkins 1998), the dark side to the biopolitical rationalization of violence. In these conflicts, civilians are the primary targets, often not just of killing but also of nonlethal violence that results in life-long debilitation (Summerfield 1998). Violence used in a manner intended to inflict lasting psychological damage (such as torture, rape, amputation, and other violent forms of degradation) is widely reported from across the world. Studies of these conflicts have detailed how a highly inegalitarian and extractive global economy fuels this kind of violence, facilitated by cheap arms exports and weakened states no longer able to enforce authority over their territories (Ellis 1999).

Despite evidence of the growing impact of violent conflict on world health, the effect of politics on population health has been most widely understood in terms of how particular policies, such as taxation, health insurance, and access to schooling, inflect disease rates. Recasting the relationship between disease and social inequality as the embodiment of social relations adds value to the core epidemiological finding by allowing affliction to be related to prevailing ideologies that inform policy, configurations of social violence, the way misfortune is conceptualized and managed, and how meaning systems influence how individuals interpret their bodily states, seek care, and fashion themselves according to prevailing moral notions. Inequality is more broadly viewed as a form of violence that can be exercised directly on the body or indirectly through risk and blame. This view allows the three epidemiological hypotheses about how inequality results in ill health to be (*a*) extended to include political processes, (*b*) sharpened to examine local social pathogenesis, and (*c*) complexified to take into account biosocial interactions. All three of these insights texture the landscape of affliction in society, focusing the question of power more centrally on the question of how therapeutic power—the power to manage misfortune—is legitimated.

THERAPEUTIC POLITICS AND LEGITIMATION

Medical systems in different cultures and at different historical moments may differ in the methods and technologies used to diagnose the causes of misfortune; the substances, objects, and practices used to alleviate it; and even the goals of therapy (Young & Leslie 1992). However, across times and places therapy retains a political dimension: Therapeutic claims must be justified and practitioners must legitimate their ability to exercise therapeutic power. These therapeutic politics mediate the impact of social inequalities on health.

Therapeutic systems texture the form affliction takes in a society and may therefore exacerbate or alleviate existing inequalities. Anthropological studies of millenarian movements have long shown that, worldwide, these movements are religions of the oppressed; similarly, possession by spirits favors women and, in some settings, effeminate men (Boddy 1994). Classic debates as to whether these therapeutic systems act as pressure valves to maintain political homeostasis and legitimate existing inequalities or, on the contrary, are sources of conflict and fission, renting communities apart (Marwick 1991), have given way to considerations of how therapeutic systems may exert indirect political effects, for example embodying forms of embodied resistance that may mature into full-fledged political movements (Anderson & Johnson 1995). Regardless of where one sides in this debate, the centrality of therapeutic systems to the political physiology of a society is uncontested. Although the actions of therapeutic systems are "infra-political," in the sense that they do not register in the arena of state power and struggles to obtain access to it, increasing attention has been paid to how the idioms of therapy and indeed therapeutic practices have crept into political life. To name a few, studies have been published of infantile citizenship and metaphors of trauma and therapy in American political life (Berlant 1991), the conflation between therapeutic experience and political power in born-again statesmen (Strandjsberg 2000), the manipulation of prophetic acquaintance to imbue politicians with an aura of infallibility (Dozon 1995), or the attribution of political longevity to occult practices (Comaroff & Comaroff 1994).

These studies indicate that the entanglement of the power to heal and the power to rule is the result not just of traffic between the symbolic domains of body and society (Douglas 1996) but also from the material intermingling of therapeutic action with the exercise of rule, as well as the proliferation of resistances to it. This entanglement occurs when the charisma of political power stems from the power to heal or the experience of being healed and when the exercise of political power is crossed with therapeutic rituals. This political/therapeutic tangle challenges Weberian notions drawn on by some scholars to argue that modernity can be characterized by a separation of powers, such that therapeutic power differentiates into a separate domain—biomedicine—from political power, with a residual interface remaining in public health and health policy (Dozon & Fassin 2001).

The therapeutic pluralism at work in the government of collective life puts the legitimation of therapeutic power firmly in the political arena (Brodwin 1997). This is most evident in the struggle for recognition waged by nonbiomedical therapeutic traditions, such as traditional African therapies on that continent or traditional Chinese medicine and its migrant reincarnations in North America (Lau 2000). Different medical traditions define and manage pathology differently; consequently, the therapeutic blend present in a given locality will impact sufferers' patterns of resort and the embodiment of inequalities (Nichter & Lock 2002). Biomedicine is often the most expensive therapy in developing countries and, as a result, is resorted to only after more accessible (whether for economic, cultural, or geograhic reasons) therapeutic options have been exhausted. Fluctuations in the availability of different therapeutic options can impact health outcomes, for instance, when public investments are made in less accessible therapies that may be more effective at an individual level but do not translate into improved health of the general population because most do not have access to them.

Although the impact of biomedicine on population health has been overshadowed by the interest in social pathways through which inequality exerts deleterious effects, differences in access to biomedical care lead to different morbidity and mortality rates for the same disease in different social groups. In industrialized settings, heart disease is underdiagnosed and undertreated in American and British women relative to men, which leads to higher morbidity and mortality rates in women as compared to men (Annandale & Hunt 2000, Ostlin et al. 2002). Similarly, cancer pain is undertreated in African Americans, which results in their suffering greater pain (Dressler 1993). Although these observations suggest gender or racial bias on the part of practitioners, clinical ethnographies advance the hypothesis that biomedical knowledge is itself "biased," not in the sense of being patently false, but rather to the extent that it is partial because it is constructed from prevailing social understandings of the body and society (Casper & Koenig 1996, Clarke & Casper 1996, Hogle 2002, Mol & Berg 1998, Simon 1999, Willems 1998). Evidence that diagnostic categories perform best in privileged groups (the articulate, white, male patient) indicate that an epistemiological bias reflects inequalities of access of certain groups to the elaboration of medical knowledge (Aronowitz 2001). For instance, if biological norms and diagnostic tests are standardized on middle-class, white populations, they may not perform accurately in groups who may differ biologically or in the way they report symptoms. Biological difference between populations should not be understood as essential but rather as differences in environment and interactions between heredity, culture, and environment (Szathmary & Farrell 1990). Vegetarians, whether they are middle-class American women or upper-caste Indian men, have lower haemoglobin values and will more often be diagnosed as anaemic.

The embodiment of inequality indexes the diverse ways in which violence translates into affliction. Examination of how the power to wound, to heal, or to prevent injury is legitimated indicates that political entanglements also unfold on an epistemological terrain, and not just in the way violence is embodied. Competing medical systems, as well as different social groups, struggle to legitimate therapeutic power, experiences of suffering, and claims for redress. These struggles refract social inequalities in myriad ways. This is not to imply a kind of epistemological war of all against all. Within society, just as collectivities have evolved political mechanisms to regulate social life, they have also evolved mechanisms to collectively manage misfortune and, in some cases, arbitrate between competing therapeutic systems. Recent anthropological study of these collective mechanisms has drawn on Foucault's notion of governmentality (Burchell et al. 1991) to develop a critical anthropology of policy, public health, and the forms the government of life has taken in industrialized countries (Petersen & Bunton 1997, Shore & Wright 997). The planetary scope of the HIV epidemic and the institutional response to it is a harbinger of how the government of life will increasingly go global, with the result that health becomes framed by mobile, issue-driven configurations of institutions—what have been called transnational advocacy networks or transnational discourse coalitions (Keck & Sikkink 1998). As the political space of health becomes an increasingly global one, anthropologists are beginning to focus on how local phenomena trace the contours of a global political apparatus of health.

GLOBALIZING THE POLITICAL SPACE OF HEALTH

In an era of accelerating and intensifying movement of capital, technology, and people, however, it is no longer possible to view political regimes for managing health and their therapeutic economies in isolation from each other, and this is having significant impacts on health. Whether or not one subscribes to the view that globalization is a new phenomenon, anthropologists have pointed out that gradients of inequality exist across national borders and will play an increasing role in shaping the health of populations (Bateman et al. 2001, Bettcher 2000). Transnational social inequalities drive migration for economic survival or therapy (Kangas 2002), as well as the movement of pharmacological agents, biologicals, and organs. The predominantly national nature of the socioeconomic data collected to explore the relationship between socioeconomic inequality and health has imposed constraints on the ability to capture the impact of migration and transnational health gradients, constraints to which ethnographic methods offer an alternative.

Much of the contemporary literature in medical anthropology addresses the relationship between health, biomedicine, and social change. Critical approaches to biomedicine have figured more prominently in studies conducted in industrialized countries than in the third world. This is not surprising because biomedicine's cultural valence is more readily visible where it is an institutional and industrial heavyweight, as seen in studies of medicalization, clinical ideologies, or micropolitical struggles (Lock & Kaufert 1998). Thus, although the role of biomedicine as a powerful cultural vector, present both in everyday life and in collective representations (Brock & Howard 1984, Lupton 1994), is by now widely accepted in anthropological scholarship on modern society, comparatively little work has investigated its corollary in the postcolonial world, still too often seen as being mired in a "traditional" therapeutic economy. Future studies of transnational health inequalities will need to pay serious attention to how transnational medical traditions, whether biomedicine or others, impact local therapeutic economies, patterns of resort, and distributions of affliction.

ETHNOGRAPHIC APPROACHES TO THE CULTURE OF INEQUALITY

A political anthropology of health offers a compelling theoretical framework for addressing the relationship between inequality and disease because it fulfils the requirement that social change and the forces that drive it be taken into account in consideration of how social inequalities are embodied. This theoretically driven approach has the additional merit of allowing a broad range of ethnographic evidence to be used to shed light on this important question and to trace the contours of social, cultural, and political formations that are too large to be captured within individual ethnographic studies. Ethnographically driven approaches offer a complementary strategy for examining the relationship between disease and inequality from the ground up. These approaches bring together a strong corpus of ethnographic studies of poverty and newer work examining situations of social inequality, structural violence, and social exclusion (Mclean et al. 2003, Pfeiffer 2002, Santana 2002).

Although this research speaks to the notion of a culture of poverty that emerged from earlier ethnographic studies and still finds resonance in today's ghettos and shantytowns (Bourgois 1996, Scheper-Hughes 1992), it differs in two important respects. First, contemporary ethnographies take pains to detail the historical dynamics that produce inequality: both wealth and poverty. While political economic approaches, drawing on Marxist and World Systems theory, have been a favored tool for capturing these historical dynamics, these studies have been careful to document how local cultural and spatial dynamics texture the way in which local actors comment on and engage with global processes. Accordingly, the cultural dimensions of poverty are no longer viewed *sui generis* but as local attempts to understand, negotiate, and even resist global political and economic processes. As a result, these studies have been sensitive to how local actors make meaning and draw on a cultural repertoire to fashion tactics in order to allow engagement with a material environment that, if not overtly hostile, offers a considerably diminished horizon of possibility. Furthermore, these studies pay serious attention to translocal and transnational phenomena that shape local worlds and possibilities for action, drawing attention to how globalization increases social inequality and, through global media, awareness of it.

This literature goes beyond ethnographies of poverty to sketch the contours of the cultural formations that emerge in settings of extreme inequality and structural violence. A range of ethnographies conducted in settings of cheek-to-jowl inequality—the urban ghettoes of inner-city America (Bourgois 1996, Broughton 2001), the bleak *cités* that ring French cities (Bourdieu 1998, Leclerc 2001), refugee camps (Malkki 1995), and rapidly growing urban metropolises in developing countries (Caldeira 1996)—have identified characteristics that are present across different geographical and social sites. Most striking has been the ethnographic rebuttal of the common-sense view that situations of distress, extreme poverty, or endemic violence are rife with psychosocial stress, social breakdown, and a feeling of emergency. This does not appear to be the case, however—indeed, these situations are remarkable for the apparent normalcy that reigns. Echoing Arendt's arguments about the banality of evil (Osiel 2001), Benjamin's notion of the "state of emergency" (Benjamin 1969), and, more recently, Agamben's theorization of the state of sovereign exception and "bare life" (Agamben 1998), anthropologists have reported situations where exceptional events—disappearances, murders, violence—are routinized. Taking up work on the culture of poverty, and drawing on Taussig's notion of a "culture of terror" (Taussig 1992), we might tentatively advance that anthropologists working in these diverse situations have been studying a culture of inequality (Lewis 1978). How do these cultures of inequality play a role in generating "unhealthy" societies?

THE SOCIAL INEQUALITY/DISEASE TRAP: A PATHOGENIC SOCIAL SPIRAL

Strikingly present across these studies is the observation that the adverse health impact of contemporary social health inequalities exacerbates those very inequalities, resulting in a spiral from which it is difficult to emerge. This is the social corollary of the "illness poverty trap" (Whitehead et al. 2001), whereby poverty produces ill health which then worsens poverty. Extensive evidence exists that new forms of social inequality erode preexisting social hierarchies. These often fulfill a public health role by assisting collectivities to weather health crises through ensuring rational distribution of resources (Sen 1981); new inequalities upset a delicate ecology of entitlements with, at times, disastrous results. This upset has already been extensively documented in colonial settings in Africa, where capitalist encroachment led to widespread famines as cash crops and indentured labor, driven by poll taxes, replaced traditional forms of agriculture (Moore & Vaughan 1994). The epidemics that raged across the continent in the interwar period have been attributed to the breakdown of indigenous public health systems—for instance the cultural systems that prevented the spread of sleeping sickness by segregating cattle from human settlements in Eastern Africa—brought about by these social changes (Lyons 1992). Migrant labor was often housed in insalubrious conditions, fulfilling the prophecy of the diseased native (Packard 1989). Even modern forms of solidarity are not immune to the impact of deepening social inequality. As the ability of states to deliver effective public health programs is compromised in an increasingly neoliberal political economy (Coburn 2000, Maskovsky 2000), the wealthier are able to maintain access to health capital—clean water, good food, medical care, salubrious living conditions—while the vulnerability of the poor increases (Bond 2000). The wealthier are thus better able to shield themselves from unhealthy environments, whereas the poor are increasingly vulnerable. Migration remains an important element of the equation because it not only contributes to erosion of existent forms of solidarity as people move further afield in search of work but also facilitates the spread of infectious diseases. These elements, and likely many others, conjugate to form a pathogenic social spiral from which it is increasingly difficult to emerge—as the poorer get sicker, and poorer, the cost of mitigating the social consequences rises, triggering a defensive reaction on the part of the rich, who do not want to shoulder the medical cost of inequality.

What is most striking about this pathogenic social spiral is the complacency that greets it. Historical studies have identified the cultural formations that conditioned the indifference of colonial elites to the plight of natives (Dozon 1991), under such terms as the sanitation syndrome (Swanson 1977) and heterophobia (Le Pape 1997). Relatively little contemporary work, particularly among international decision makers and within powerful agencies, has focused on the culture of indifference that surrounds growing evidence of a worsening "sanitary apartheid" (Bulard 2000). Exceptions include critiques of the tendency to invoke a version of cultural relativism to explain why certain health outcomes may be more acceptable to certain groups than to others (Farmer 1999). Equally criticized has been the deployment of cost-effectiveness arguments to justify inequalities in access to biomedical care. The argument that health is a human right is often used as the cornerstone for these critiques of indifference in the face of health inequalities (Kim et al. 2000, Mann et al. 1999). An important polemic, however (Irwin et al. 2002), has developed between proponents of human rights arguments, and the humanitarian appeal that underlies them, and critics of development and humanitarian intervention, who see in such appeals a commodification of suffering, a dismissal of local politics, and a disguised imperialism masking as a universal notion of human rights (Adams 1998, Butt 2002a, Cheang 1997, Malkki 1998,

Negri & Hardt 2001, Rabinow 2002). This points to the need for more empirical study of just how human rights and humanitarian intervention are operationalized in different localities and through different issues around the world (Butt 2002b, Pandolfi 2001). The issue of whether cultures of indifference and humanitarian cultures of empathy are part of a global formation that perpetuates inequality, or are simply local perversions, needs to be resolved.

MATERIALISM OF INEQUALITY: INTENSIFYING THE COMMODIFICATION OF THE BODY

Situations of extreme inequality conjugate relative deprivation with fleeting access to the world of the wealthy. Lack of access to education, capital, and other resources that would otherwise permit upward mobility in a capitalist economy limits options for survival and advancement for those who are both deprived of, and exposed to, the world of wealth. The Marxist theory of labor remains the cornerstone of theories of commodification of the body. Although debate still remains as to whether sex work represents a form of commodification, it does appear that increased inequality facilitates exchange of sex for access to economic resources (Schoepf 1998, Sobo 1995), providing increased opportunity for the spread of sexually transmitted infections such as HIV. The commodification of health was initially most visible in the increasing adoption of market mechanisms to deliver health care (Maskovsky 2000, Peterson 1998), so-called managed inequality (Rylko-Bauer & Farmer 2002). However, new markets and new biomedical technologies condition new forms of extraction (Cohen 1999), in effect intensifying the commodification of the body and its futures. The result has been a brisk trade in organs (Sharp 2001), cell lines, genetic material, biologicals, and reproduction, whether through surrogate motherhood or transnational adoption (Ragoné 1999).

Anthropologists have begun to examine the organ trade as a form of body commodification facilitated by inequality and the constitution of global markets for organs through the dissemination of biomedical technologies (Cohen 1999, Marshall & Daar 2000, Scheper-Hughes 2001). Study of illicit trade is notoriously difficult (MacGaffey & Bazenguissa-Ganga 2000, Leggett 2002), if not dangerous, explaining why other forms of body trade—such as traffic in women, children, and migrants—remain largely unexamined by anthropologists. Although only a partial view, the studies that have been conducted indicate that, whereas the driving force for such transactions is material, more affective motivations (such as the desire for emotional security, children, or status) embedded in cultural notions of value and the good life also play a role (Lock & Kaufert 1998, Sobo 1995). These studies call attention to how translocal inequalities juxtapose competing regimes of value (Appadurai 1988), establishing novel markets and economies. Simultaneously, the global dissemination of new biomedical technologies (Lock et al. 2000) works to give populations access to biomedical technologies that were previously unavailable.

The description of capital's extractive power in venous terms, as something that, via the alienation of labor, bleeds subaltern classes until they are too weak to resist the vicissitudes of life in poverty, dates to the Industrial Revolution (Marx 2000 [1873]). This metaphor persists in the political economy approach to health inequalities, an approach that insists on unmasking the bland language of epidemiology to indict policies and agencies that perpetuate and exacerbate inequalities (Navarro 2002). The political economy approach, however, has at times overlooked the accelerated and intensified mechanisms by which the very substance of life is extracted from those lower on the social ladder for the benefit of those higher up. Markets for organs and babies are the most dramatic example of just how arterial these processes of extraction have become. These phenomena are only the most lurid examples of processes that dramatically shorten life expectancy of the poor even as that of the rich increases. Biocommodities and biomarkets are often transnational in scope because the inequalities that permit them are difficult to sustain within national borders, although they clearly exist in countries, such as the United States, with sufficiently steep gradients of inequality. Study of biocommodities and biomarkets index the processes by which less-well-off individuals trade in their long-term health for short-term gain, to the benefit of the long-term health of those who are better off.

Intensified commodification is occurring throughout the biological realm, as transnational corporations claim patents over an ever-extending part of the biological realm. This, it has been argued, is nothing short of a fencing off of the intellectual commons, as seen in the reinforcement of international intellectual property law through the trade-related aspects of intellectual property rights (TRIPS) (The Panos Institute 2002, Vercellone 2002). The current struggle over expanding access to antiretroviral drugs highlights how biocommodification compromises public health, particularly in poor countries, and exacerbates health inequalities by raising the cost of treatment—and the cost of developing new treatments (Bierlich 1999, WHO/EDM 1999). The rise of biocapital essentially concentrates therapeutic options in the hands of transnational corporations, subsuming future health to the imperatives of capitalist production (Negri & Hardt 2001).

Public health in most parts of the world has been sacrificed—through structural adjustment programs and a host of other neoliberal incentives foisted on the world's poorer countries by the implementing agencies of rich donor countries—in order to create more favorable climates for investment (Braveman & Tarimo 2002, Lloyd-Sherlock 2000). The poor disproportionately suffer the consequences, resulting in the illness-poverty trap that has spiraled entire societies into demographic decline as communicable diseases spread unchecked. This finding concurs within observations that the demands of neoliberal globalization imply that the poor are dying for growth (Kim et al. 2000), just as they bled for the industrial revolution in the nineteenth century. This venous language, as strident as it may sound to some, is mild compared to the vernacular of vampire rumors and other references to the occult nature of contemporary capitalism (Ashforth 1999, Comaroff & Comaroff 1999). These authors describe arterial forms of extraction and a cannibalistic social order, where the poor sell their health to stay alive to benefit those who are better off.

This phenomenon occurs even as the care of the body, particularly in settings of high prevalence of disease, becomes ever central to maintaining life and reproduction. Although in situations of absolute poverty there is no effective access to expensive biomedical care, inequality means that even the poor will mobilize significant resources to access biomedicine (Aymé et al. 2002). Partial access to biomedicines is of particular public health concern in the case of infectious disease, where suboptimal treatment with inadequate doses or courses of antibiotics, or use of substandard antibiotics, can spread drug resistance. Drug resistant epidemics of tuberculosis have now been documented in most parts of the world (Farmer 1997). These epidemics threaten rich and poor alike, an example of a gradient-driven health effect whose consequences stretch across the socioeconomic spectrum.

CONCLUSION

Inequality, or the uneven distribution of power, is universal in any society, as witnessed by the fact that in every society misfortune is selective, affecting some but not others. The embodiment of inequality calls attention to the different forms through which violence is exercised in a given society and the ways in which the body serves as a register for, or a site of, struggle against forms of domination. The deepened inequalities that have emerged under the sign of the global (Tsing 2000) call attention to the increasing commodification of the body and its futures and to the cultures of inequality that breed indifference in the face of a pathogenic social spiral that threatens to unravel social solidarity in the face of the health threats of the new millennium. Ethnography has emerged as a key research strategy not for reciting a pious liturgy on the horrors of the forms human misery takes but for demonstrating the links between policy and everyday life and for carefully scrutinizing the legacy of those who rightfully seek to correct conditions that are all too often beyond their control.

ACKNOWLEDGMENT

The authors gratefully acknowledge the assistance of Matthew Akiyama in preparing this review.

The *Annual Review of Anthropology* is online at http://anthro.annualreviews.org

LITERATURE CITED

Adams V. 1998. Suffering the winds of Lhasa: politicized bodies, human rights, cultural difference, and humanism in Tibet. *Med. Anthropol. Q.* 12(1):74–102

Adas M. 1989. *Machines as the Measure of Men: Science, Technology, and Ideologies of Western Dominance.* Ithaca, NY: Cornell Univ. Press

Agamben G. 1998. *Homo Sacer: Sovereign Power and Bare Life*. Stanford, CA: Stanford Univ. Press

Anderson DM, Johnson DH, eds. 1995. *Revealing Prophets: Prophecy in Eastern African History*. London: James Currey

Anheier H, Kendall J. 2002. Interpersonal trust and voluntary associations: examining three approaches. *Br. J. Soc.* 53:343–62

Annandale E, Hunt K. 2000. *Gender Inequalities in Health*. London, UK: Open Univ. Press

Appadurai A, ed. 1988. *The Social Life of Things*. Cambridge, UK: Cambridge Univ. Press

Aronowitz RA. 2001. What history teaches us about symptoms. *Ann. Int. Med.* 134(9):803–8

Arnold D. 1993. Social crisis and epidemic disease in the famines of nineteenth-century India . *Soc. Hist. Med.* 6(3):383–404

Ashforth A. 1999. *Madumbo: A Man Bewitched*. Chicago, IL: The Univ. Chicago Press

Ayme M, Champagne F, Contandriopoulos AP. 2002. Economic role of solidarity and social capital in accessing modern health care services in the Ivory Coast. *Soc. Sci. Med.* 55:1929–46

Baer H. 1996. Towards a political ecology of health in medical anthropology. *Med. Anthropol. Q.* 6(4):451–54

Bateman C, Baker T, Hoornenborg E, Ericsson U. 2001. Bringing global issues to medical teaching. *Lancet* 358:1539–42

Benjamin W. 1969. Theses on the philosophy of history. In *Illuminations*, ed. H Arendt, pp. 253–64. New York: Schocken

Berlant LG. 1991. *The Queen of America Goes to Washington City: Essays on Sex and Citizenship*. Durham, NC: Duke Univ. Press

Bettcher D. 2000. Global trade and health: key linkages and future challenges. *Int. J. Public Health* 78(4):521–34

Bierlich B. 1999. Sacrifice, plants, and Western pharmaceuticals: money and health care in northern Ghana. *Med. Anthropol. Q.* 13(3):316–37

Boddy J. 1989. *Wombs and Alien Spirits: Women, Men, and the Zar Cult in Northern Sudan*. Madison, WI: Univ. Wisc. Press

Boddy J. 1994. Spirit possession revisited: beyond instrumentality. *Annu. Rev. Anthropol.* 23:407–34

Bond P. 2000. *Cities of Gold, Townships of Coal: Essays on South Africa's New Urban Crisis*. Trenton, NJ: Africa World Press

Bourdieu P. 1998. *La Misère du Monde*. Paris: Gallimard

Bourgois P. 1996. *In Search of Respect: Selling Crack in El Barrio*. Cambridge, UK: Cambridge Univ. Press

Braveman P, Tarimo E. 2002. Social inequalities in health within countries: not only an issue for affluent nations. *Soc. Sci. Med.* 54:1621–35

Bridgman R. 2001. I helped build that: a demonstration employment training program for homeless youth in Toronto, Canada. *Am. Anthropol.* 103(3):779–95

Brock DH, Howard A, eds. 1984. *The Culture of Biomedicine*. Newark, NJ: Univ. Delaware Press

Brodwin PE. 1997. Politics, practical logic, and primary health care in rural Haiti. *Med. Anthropol. Q.* 11(1):69–88

Broughton C. 2001. Work programs and welfare recipients: an ethnography of work-based welfare reform. *Berkeley J. Soc.* 45:17–41

Brunner E. 1997. Stress and the biology of inequality. *Br. Med. J.* 314(7092):1472–76

Bulard M. 2000. La nécessaire définition d'un bien public mondial. *Le Monde Dipl.* 1:8–9

Burchell G, Gordon C, Miller P, eds. 1991. *The Foucault Effect: Studies in Governmentality*. Chicago, IL: Univ. Chicago Press

Butt L. 2002a. Reply to Alec Irwin, Joyce Millen, Jim Kim, John Gershmen, Brooke G. Schoepf, and Paul Farmer. *Med. Anthropol.* 21:31–33

Butt L. 2002b. The suffering stranger: medical anthropology and international morality. *Med. Anthropol.* 21:1–24

Caldeira TP. 1996. Fortified enclaves: the new urban segregation. *Public Cult.* 8(2):303–28

Cambrosio A, Keating P. 1992. A matter of

FACS—constituting novel entities in immunology. *Med. Anthropol. Q.* 6(4):362–84

Campbell C, McLean C. 2002. Ethnic identities, social capital and health inequalities. *Soc. Sci. Med.* 55:643–57

Casper MJ, Koenig BA. 1996. Reconfiguring nature and culture: intersections of medical anthropology and technoscience studies. *Med. Anthropol. Q.* 10(4):523–36

Cattell V. 2001. Poor people, poor places, and poor health: the mediating role of social networks and social capital. *Soc. Sci. Med.* 52:1501–16

Cheang P. 1997. Posit(ion)ing human rights in the current global conjuncture. *Public Cult.* 9:233–66

Churchill N. 1995. Ending welfare as we know it: a case study in urban anthropology and public policy. *Urban Anthropol.* 24(1–2):5–35

Clarke AE, Casper MJ. 1996. From simple technology to complex arena: classification of pap smears, 1917–90. *Med. Anthropol. Q.* 10(4):601–23

Clarke PM, Gerdtham UG, Johannesson M, Bingefors K, Smith L. 2002. On the measurement of relative and absolute income-related health inequality *Soc. Sci. Med.* 55:1923–28

Coburn D. 2000. Income inequality, social cohesion and the health status of populations: the role of neoliberalism. *Soc. Sci. Med.* 51:135–46

Coffield CD. 2000. Regulating knowledge: a critical institutional ethnography of the Indiana manpower placement and comprehensive training program (Impact). *Adv. Gend. Res.* 4:55–89

Cohen L. 1999. Where it hurts: Indian material for an ethics of organ transplantation. *Daedelus* 128(4):135–65

Comaroff J. 1985. *Body of Power, Spirit of Resistance: The Culture and History of a South African People.* Chicago: The Univ. Chicago Press.

Comaroff J, Comaroff J. 1994. *Modernity and Its Malcontents: Ritual and Power in Postcolonial Africa.* Chicago: The Univ. Chicago Press

Comaroff J, Comaroff J. 1999. Alien-nation: zombies, immigrants, and millennial capitalism. *Codesria Bull.* 17:1–9

Conrad P. 1992. Medicalization and social control. *Annu. Rev. Anthropol.* 18:209–32

Cussins C. 1998. Ontological choreography: agency for women patients in an infertility clinic. In *Differences in Medicine: Unraveling Practices, Techniques and Bodies,* ed. A Mol, M Berg, pp. 261–83. Durham, NC: Duke Univ. Press

Dean M. 1999. *Governmentality: Power and rule in Modern Society.* London: Sage

De Jong J. 2002. *Trauma, War, and Violence: Public Mental Health in Socio-Cultural Context.* London, UK: Plenum

Desjarlais R. 1993. *Body and Emotion: The Aesthetics of Illness and Healing in the Nepal Himalayas.* Philadelphia, PA: Univ. Penn. Press

Desjarlais R, Eisenberg L, Good B, Kleinman A. 1995. *World Mental Health.* New York: Oxford Univ. Press

Diamond J. 1997. *Guns, Germs and Steel: The Fates of Human Societies.* New York: Norton

Donohoe M. 2003. Causes and health consequences of environmental degradation and social injustice. *Soc. Sci. Med.* 56:573–87

Douglas M. 1996. *Purity and Danger: An Analysis of Concepts of Pollution and Taboo.* London, UK: Routledge

Dozon JP. 1991. D'un tombeau l'autre. *Cah. Études Afr.* 31(1–2):135–57

Dozon JP. 1995. *La Cause des Prophètes.* Paris: Le Seuil

Dozon JP, Fassin D. 2001. *Critique de la Santé Publique: Une Approche Anthropologique.* Paris: Balland

Dressler WW. 1993. Health in the African-American community—accounting for health inequalities. *Med. Anthropol. Q.* 7(4):325–45

Elkana Y, Krastev I, Macamo E, Randeria S, eds. 2002. *Unraveling Ties: From Social Cohesion to New Practices of Connectedness.* Frankfurt, Ger.: Campus

Ellis S. 1999. *The Mask of Anarchy.* London, UK: Hurst

Elstad JI. 1998. The psycho-social perspective on social inequalities in health. *Soc. Health Ill.* 20(5):598–618

Elyachar J. 2002. Empowerment money: the world bank, non-governmental organizations, and the value of culture in Egypt. *Public Cult.* 14(3):493–513

Evans GW, Kantrowitz E. 2002. Socioeconomic status and health: the potential role of environmental risk exposure. *Annu. Rev. Public Health* 23:303–31

Evans RG, Barer ML, Marmor TR. 1994. *Why Are Some People Healthy and Others Not? The Determinants of Health of Populations.* New York: Aldine de Gruyter

Faber DR, Krieg EJ. 2002. Unequal exposure to ecological hazards: environmental injustices in the Commonwealth of Massachusetts. *Environ. Health Perspectives* 100(Suppl. 2):277–88

Fabri RH, Murta EF. 2002. Socioeconomic factors and caesarean section rates. *Int. J. Gynecol. Obstet.* 76(1):87–88

Farmer P. 1992. *AIDS and Accusation: Haiti and the Geography of Blame.* Berkeley, CA: Univ. Calif. Press

Farmer P. 1997. On suffering and structural violence: a view from below. In *Social Suffering*, ed. A Kleinman, V Das, M Lock, pp. 261–84. Berkeley, CA: Univ. Calif. Press

Farmer P. 1999. *Infections and Inequalties: The Modern Plague.* Berkeley, CA: Univ. Calif. Press

Farquhar J. 1994a. Eating Chinese medicine. *Cult. Anthropol.* 9(4):471–97

Farquhar J. 1994b. *Knowing Practice: The Clinical Encounter of Chinese Medicine.* Boulder, CO: Westview

Fassin D. 1992. *Pouvoir et Maladie en Afrique. Anthropologie Sociale de la Banlieue de Dakar.* Paris: Presses Univ. France

Fassin D. 1996. *L'Espace Politique de la Sante. Essai de Généalogie.* Paris: Presses Univ. France

Forbes A, Wainwright SP. 2001. On the methodological, theoretical and philosophical context of health inequalities research: a critique. *Soc. Sci. Med.* 53:801–16

Galea S, Karpati A, Kennedy B. 2002. Social capital and violence in the United States, 1974–1993. *Soc. Sci. Med.* 55:1373–83

Geissler PW. 1998. Worms are our life, part I. Understandings of worms and the body among the Luo of western Kenya. *Anthropol. Med.* 5:63–79

Good B. 1993. *Medicine, Rationality and Experience.* Cambridge, UK: Cambridge Univ. Press

Goodman AH, Leatherman TL, eds. 1998. *Building a New Biocultural Synthesis: Political-Economic Perspectives of Human Biology.* Ann Arbor, MI: Univ. Mich. Press

Graham H. 2002. Building an inter-disciplinary science of health inequalities: the example of life course research. *Soc. Sci. Med.* 55:2005–16

Hacking I. 2000. *The Social Construction of What?* Cambridge, MA: Harvard Univ. Press

Haraway D. 1996. *Modest-Witness@second-Millennium.Femaleman-Meets-Oncomouse: Feminism and Technoscience.* London, UK: Routledge

Hebdige D. 1979. *Subculture, the Meaning of Style.* London, UK: Methuen

Hogle LF. 2002. Claims and disclaimers: Whose expertise counts? *Med. Anthropol.* 21(3):275–306

Hutson S, Liddiard M. 1994. *Youth Homelessness: The Construction of a Social Issue.* London, UK: MacMillan

Illich I. 1977. *Medical Nemesis: The Exportation of Health.* Toronto, Can.: Bantam

Irwin A, Millen J, Kim J, Gershman J, Schoepf B, Farmer P. 2002. Suffering, moral claims, and scholarly responsibility: a response to Leslie Butt. *Med. Anthropol.* 21:25–30

Jacobs J. 1961. *The Death and Life of Great American Cities.* New York: Random House

Jenkins JH. 1998. The medical anthropology of political violence: a cultural and feminist agenda. *Med. Anthropol. Q.* 12(1):122–31

Kangas B. 2002. Therapeutic itineraries in a global world: Yemenis and their search for biomedical treatment abroad. *Med. Anthropol.* 21:35–78

Kawachi I, Kennedy BP. 2002. *The Health of Nations: Why Inequality is Harmful to Your Health.* New York: NY Press

Kawachi I, Kennedy BP, Lochner K, Prothrow-Smith D. 1997. Social capital, income inequality, and mortality. *Am. J. Public Health* 87:1491–98

Kawachi I, Kennedy BP, Wilkinson RG, eds. 1999. *Income Inequality and Health: The Society and Population Health Reader, Volume 1.* New York: New Press

Keck ME, Sikkink K. 1998. *Activists Beyond Borders: Advocacy Networks in International Politics.* Ithaca, NY/London: Cornell Univ. Press

Kelley L, ed. 2003. *Health Impacts of Globalization: Towards Global Governance.* Basingstoke/London, UK: Palgrave Macmillan

Kim JY, Millen J, Gershman J, Irwin A, eds. 2000. *Dying for Growth: Global Inequality and the Health of the Poor.* Monroe, ME: Common Courage

Kirmayer LJ. 1992. The body's insistence on meaning: metaphor as presentation and representation in illness experience. *Med. Anthropol. Q.* 6(4):323–46

Kunitz SJ. 2001. Accounts of social capital: the mixed health effects of personal communities and voluntary groups. In *Poverty, Inequality and Health*, ed. DA Leon, G Walt. Oxford, UK: Oxford Univ. Press

Latour B. 1993. *We Have Never Been Modern.* Transl. C Porter. Cambridge, MA: Harvard Univ. Press

Lau KJ. 2000. *New Age Capitalism: Making Money East of Eden.* Philadelphia, PA: Univ. Penn. Press

Leclerc A, Fassin D, Grandjean H, Kaminski M, Lang T, eds. 2001. *Inégalités Sociales et Santé.* Paris: Découverte

Leggett T. 2002. *Rainbow Vice: The Drugs and Sex Industries in the New South Africa.* London, UK: Zed Books

Le Pape M. 1997. *L'Énergie Sociale a Abidjan: Économie Politique de la Ville en Afrique Noire, 1930–1995.* Paris: Ed. Karthala

Levy BS, Sidel VW, eds. 1997. *War and Public Health.* New York: Oxford Univ. Press

Lewis IM. 1978. *The Culture of Inequality.* Amherst, MA: Univ. Mass. Press

Lewis IM. 1991. *Women's Medicine: The Zar-Bori Cult in Africa and Beyond.* Edinburgh, UK: Edinburgh Univ. Press

Lewontin R. 2000. *Triple Helix: Gene, Organism and Environment.* Cambridge, MA: Harvard Univ. Press

Lippman A. 1991. Prenatal genetic testing and screening: constructing needs and reinforcing inequities. *Am. J. Law Med.* 17:15–50

Lloyd-Sherlock P. 2000. *Healthcare Reform and Poverty in Latin America.* London, UK: Inst. Lat. Am. Stud.

Lock M. 1993. Cultivating the body: anthropology and epistemologies of bodily practice and knowledge. *Annu. Rev. Anthropol.* 22:133–55

Lock M. 1995. *Encounters with Aging: Mythologies of Menopause in Japan and North America.* Berkeley, CA: Univ. Calif. Press

Lock M. 1998. Breast cancer: reading the omens. *Anthropol. Today* 14(4):7–16

Lock M, Kaufert PA, eds. 1998. *Pragmatic Women and Body Politics.* Cambridge, UK: Cambridge Univ. Press

Lock M, Young A, Cambrosio A, eds. 2000. *Living and Working with the New Medical Technologies.* Cambridge, UK: Cambridge Univ. Press

Lomas J. 1998. Social capital and health: implications for public health and epidemiology. *Soc. Sci. Med.* 47:1181–88

Lupton D. 1994. *Medicine as Culture: Illness, Disease and the Body in Western Societies.* London, UK: Sage

Lupton D. 1999. *Risk.* New York: Routledge

Lynch JW, Kaplan GA, Salonon JT. 1997. Why do poor people behave poorly? Variations in adult health behaviour and psychosocial characteristics, by stage of the socioeconomic lifecourse. *Soc. Sci. Med.* 44:809–20

Lyon-Callo V. 2000. Medicalizing homelessness: the production of self-blame and self-governing within homeless shelters. *Med. Anthropol. Q.* 14(3):328–45

Lyons M. 1992. *The Colonial Disease: A Social History of Sleeping Sickness in Northern Zaire, 1900–1940.* Cambridge, UK: Cambridge Univ. Press

MacGaffey J, Bazenguissa-Ganga R. 2000. *Congo-Paris.* Bloomington, IN: Indiana Univ. Press

Maertens JT. 1978. *Le Dessin sur la Peau.* Paris: Aubier Montaigne

Maffesoli M. 1995. *The Time of the Tribes: The Decline of Individualism in Mass Societies.* London, UK: Sage

Malkki L. 1995. *Purity and Exile: Violence, Memory, and National Cosmology Among Hutu Refugees in Tanzania.* Chicago, IL: Univ. Chicago Press

Malkki L. 1998. Things to come: internationalism and global solidarities in the late 1990s. *Public Cult.* 10(2):431–42

Mann JM, Gruskin S, Grodin MA, Annas GJ, eds. 1999. *Health and Human Rights.* New York: Routledge

Marmot M. 1986. Social inequalities in mortality. In *Class and Health: Research and Longitudinal Data,* ed. RG Wilkinson, pp. 21–34. London, UK: Tavistock

Marshall P, Daar A. 2000. Ethical issues in the international development of human organ replacement technologies: India and the commercialization of kidney transplantation. In *Global Health Policy, Local Realities: The Fallacy of the Level Playing Field,* ed. L Whiteford, L Manderson, pp. 205–32. Boulder, CO: Lynne Rienner Publ.

Marwick M. 1991. *Witchcraft and Sorcery.* Harmondsworth, UK: Penguin

Marx K. 2000 (1873). *Capital: Volume 1.* London, UK: Penguin

Mascia-Lees FE, Sharpe P, eds. 1992. *Tattoo, Torture, Mutilation, and Adornment.* New York: State Univ. NY Press

Maskovsky J. 2000. 'Managing' the poor: neoliberalism, medicaid, HMOs and the triumph of consumerism among the poor. *Med. Anthropol.* 19:121–46

McGinn T. 2000. Reproductive health of war-affected populations: What do we know? *Int. Fam. Plan. Perspectives* 26(4):174–80

Mclean C, Campbell C, Cornish F. 2003. African-Caribbean interactions with mental health services in the UK: experiences and expectations of exclusion as (re)productive of health inequalities. *Soc. Sci. Med.* 56:657–69

Mol A, Berg M, eds. 1998. *Differences in Medicine: Unraveling Practices, Techniques and Bodies.* Durham, NC: Duke Univ. Press

Moore HL, Vaughan M. 1994. *Cutting Down Trees: Gender, Nutrition, and Agricultural Change in the Northern Province of Zambia, 1890–1990.* London, UK: Currey

Mullings L, Wali A. 2001. *Stress and Resilience: The Social Context of Reproduction in Central Harlem.* New York: Kluwer Acad./Plenum

Navarro V. 2002. *The Political Economy of Social Inequalities: Consequences for Health and Quality of Life.* Amityville, NY: Baywood

Navarro V, Shi L. 2001. The political context of social inequalities and health. *Soc. Sci. Med.* 52:481–91

Negri A, Hardt M. 2001. *Empire.* Cambridge, MA: Harvard Univ. Press

Newman KS. 2001. Hard times on 125th street: Harlem's poor confront welfare reform. *Am. Anthropol.* 103(3):762–78

Nguyen VK. 2002. Sida, ONG et la politique du témoignage en Afrique de l'Ouest. *Anthropol. Soc.* 26(1):69–87

Nichter M, Lock M. 2002. *New Horizons in Medical Anthropology.* New York: Routledge

Novas C, Rose N. 2000. Genetic risk and the birth of the somatic individual. *Econ. Soc.* 29(4):485–513

Ong A. 1987. *Spirit of Resistance and Capitalist Discipline: Factory Women in Malaysia.* Albany, NY: State Univ. NY Press

Osiel MJ. 2001. *Mass Atrocity, Ordinary Evil, and Hannah Arendt: Criminal Consciousness in Argentina's Dirty War.* New Haven, CT: Yale Univ. Press

Ostlin P, Sen G, George A. 2002. *Gender Inequalities in Health.* Cambridge, MA: Harvard Univ. Press

Packard R. 1989. *White Plague, Black Labour.* Berkeley, CA: Univ. Calif. Press

Pandolfi M. 1990. Boundaries inside the body: women's suffering in southern peasant Italy. *Cult. Med. Psychol.* 15:275–301

Pandolfi M. 2001. L'industrie humanitaire: une souveraineté mouvante et supracoloniale: réflexion sur l'expérience des Balkans. *Multitudes* 3:97–105

Parker R. 2002. The global HIV/AIDS pandemic, structural inequalities, and the politics of international health. *Am. J. Public Health* 92(3):343–46

Pearce N, Smith DG. 2003. Is social capital the key to inequalities in health? *Am. J. Public Health* 93(1):122–29

Petersen AR, Bunton R, eds. 1997. *Foucault, Health and Medicine.* London: Routledge

Peterson FA, ed. 1998. *Healthy Markets? The New Competition in Health Care.* Durham, NC: Duke Univ. Press

Pfeiffer J. 2002. African independent churches in Mozambique: healing the afflictions of inequality. *Med. Anthropol. Q.* 16(2):176–99

Popay J, Williams G, Thomas C, Gattrell A. 1998. Theorising inequalities in health: the place of lay knowledge. *Soc. Health Ill.* 20(5):619–44

Putnam RD. 1995. Bowling alone: America's declining social capital. *J. Demogr.* 6:65–78

Rabinow P. 2002. Midst anthropology's problems. *Cult. Anthropol.* 17(2):135–49

Ragoné H. 1999. The gift of life: surrogate motherhood, gamete donation, and the constructions of altruism. In *Transformative Motherhood: On Giving and Getting in a Consumer Culture*, ed. LL Layne, pp. 65–88. New York: NY Univ. Press

Richey L. 1999. Family planning and the politics of population in Tanzania: international to local discourse. *J. Mod. Afr. Stud.* 37(3):457–87

Rylko-Bauer B, Farmer P. 2002. Managed care or managed inequality? A call for critiques of market-based medicine. *Med. Anthropol. Q.* 16(4):476–502

Samuelsen H. 2001. Everyday spirits and medical interventions: ethnographic and historical notes on therapeutic conventions in Zanzibar town. *Med. Anthropol. Q.* 15(1):130–34

Santana P. 2002. Poverty, social exclusion and health in Portugal. *Soc. Sci. Med.* 55:33–45

Scheper-Hughes N. 1992. *Death Without Weeping: The Violence of Everyday Life in Brazil.* Berkeley, CA: Univ. Calif. Press

Scheper-Hughes N. 2001. Bodies for sale—whole or in parts. *Body Soc.* 7(2):1–8

Schoepf BG. 1998. Inscribing the body politic: women and AIDS in Africa. In *Pragmatic Women and Body Politics*, ed. M Lock, PA Kaufert, pp. 98–126. Cambridge, UK: Cambridge Univ. Press

Sen A. 1981. *Poverty and Famines: An Essay on Entitlement and Deprivation.* Oxford, UK: Clarendon

Sharp LA. 2001. Commodified kin: death, mourning, and competing claims on the bodies of organ donors in the United States. *Am. Anthropol.* 103(1):112–33

Sharp LA. 2002. Bodies, boundaries, and territorial disputes: investigating the murky realm of scientific. *Med. Anthropol.* 21(3):369–79

Shore C, Wright S. 1997. *Anthropology of Policy: Critical Perspectives on Governance and Power.* New York: Routledge

Simon CM. 1999. Images and image: technology and the social politics of revealing disorder in a North American hospital. *Med. Anthropol. Q.* 13(2):141–62

Sobo EJ. 1995. *Choosing Unsafe Sex: AIDS-Risk Denial Among Disadvantaged Women.* Philadelphia, PA: Univ. Penn. Press

Steinberg T. 2000. *Acts of God: The Unnatural History of Natural Disaster in America.* Oxford, UK: Oxford Univ. Press

Strandjsberg C. 2000. Kerekou, God and the ancestors: religion and the conception of political power in Benin. *Afr. Aff.* 99:395–414

Subramanian SV. 2002. The macroeconomic determinant of health. *Annu. Rev. Public Health* 23:287–302

Summerfield D. 1998. The social experience of war and some issues for the humanitarian field. In *Rethinking the Trauma of War*, ed. PJ Brackena, C Petty, pp. 9–38. London, UK: Free Assoc. Books

Swanson MW. 1977. The sanitation syndrome: bubonic plague and urban native policy in the Cape colony. *J. Afr. Hist.* 18(3):387–410

Szathmary EJE, Farrell RE. 1990. Glucose level, acculturation, and glycosylated hemoglobin—an example of biocultural interaction. *Med. Anthropol. Q.* 4(3):315–41

Taussig M. 1992. Culture of terror—space of death: Roger Casement's Putumayo report and the explanation of torture. In *Colonialism and Culture.* Ann Arbor, MI: Univ. Mich. Press

The Panos Institute. 2002. *Patents, Pills and Public Health: Can TRIPS deliver?* London, UK: Panos Inst. http://www.panos.org.uk/briefing/TRIPS_low_res.pdf

Tsing A. 2000. The global situation. *Cult. Anthropol.* 15(3):327–60

Tsing AL. 1994. *In the Realm of the Diamond Queen: Marginality in an Out-of-the-Way Place.* Princeton, NJ: Princeton Univ. Press

Turner T. 1980. The social skin. In *Not Work Alone: A Cross-Cultural Study of Activities Superfluous to Survival,* ed. J Cherfas, R Lewin, pp. 112–40. London, UK: Temple Smith

Turshen M. 1984. *The Political Ecology of Disease in Tanzania.* New Brunswick, NJ: Rutgers Univ. Press

Vercellone C. 2002. Les politiques de développement à l'heure du capitalisme cognitif. *Multitudes* 10:11–21

Wagstaff A. 2002. Poverty and health sector inequalities. *Bull. WHO* 80(2):97–105

Waitzkin H. 1981. The social origins of illness: a neglected history. *Int. J. Health Serv.* 11:77–103

Werbner P. 1999. Global pathways: working class cosmopolitans and the creation of transnational ethnic worlds. *Soc. Anthropol.* 7(1):17–35

White L. 2000. *Speaking with Vampires: Rumour and History in East and Central Africa.* Berkeley, CA: Univ. Calif. Press

Whitehead M, Dahlgren G, Evans T. 2001. Equity and health sector reforms: Can low-income countries escape the medical poverty trap? *Lancet* 358:833–36

WHO/EDM. 1999. *Globalization and Access to Drugs—Perspectives on the WTO TRIPS Agreement.* Geneva: WHO

Wilkinson R. 1996. *Unhealthy Societies: The Afflictions of Inequality.* London, UK: Routledge

Wilkinson RG, Kawachi I, Kennedy BP. 1998. Mortality, the social environment, crime and violence. *Soc. Health Ill.* 20(5):578–97

Willems D. 1998. Inhaling drugs and making worlds: the proliferation of lungs and asthmas. In *Differences in Medicine: Unraveling Practices, Techniques and Bodies,* ed. A Mol, M Berg, pp. 105–118. Durham, NC: Duke Univ. Press

Wolfson M, Kaplan G, Lynch J, Backlund E. 1999. Relation between income inequality and mortality: empirical demonstration. *Br. Med. J.* 319:953–71

Woodward A, Boffetta P. 1997. Environmental exposure, social class, and cancer risk. *IARC* 138:361–67

Wright P, Treacher A, eds. 1982. *The Problem of Medical Knowledge: Examining the Social Construction of Medicine.* Edinburgh, UK: Edinburgh Univ. Press

Young A, Leslie CM, eds. 1992. *Paths to Asian Medical Knowledge.* Cambridge, UK: Cambridge Univ. Press

Zola I. 1972. Medicine as an institution of social control. *Soc. Rev.* 20:487–504

Subject Index

CUMULATIVE INDEXES

CONTRIBUTING AUTHORS, VOLUMES 24–32

Spencer J, 29:1–24
Spindler GD,
  29:xv–xxxviii
Srinivas MN, 26:1–24
Stahl PW, 25:105–26
Stanish C, 30:41–64
Steedly MM, 28:431–54
Stewart K, 28:285–310
Stini WA, 24:397–421
Stronza A, 30:261–83
Susser I, 25:411–35

T

Tomasello M, 28:509–29
Tompkins RL,
  24:257–79
Traube EG, 25:127–51
Trostle JA, 25:253–74

U

Urciuoli B, 24:525–46

V

van der Geest S, 25:153–78
van der Veer P, 31:173–87
Van Esterik P, 31:257–78
Vigil JD, 32:225–42
Visweswaran K, 26:591–621
Viveiros de Castro E,
  25:179–200
Voland E, 27:347–74

W

Walker PL, 30:573–96
Weiss KM, 27:273–300
Wells JCK, 31:323–38
Whyte SR, 25:153–78

Wilson ML, 32:363–92
Wilson SM, 31:449–67
Wishnie M, 29:493–524
Wodak R, 28:175–99
Wolfe TC, 29:195–216
Worthman CM,
  24:593–616
Wrangham RW,
  32:363–92

Y

Yelvington KA, 30:227–60
Yoffee N, 24:281–311
Yon DA, 32:411–29

Z

Zegura SL, 31:303–21
Ziegler TE, 31:45–67

CHAPTER TITLES, VOLUMES 24–32

Overviews

Archaeology

Regional Studies

Theme I: AIDS

Theme I: Capitalism and the Reinvention of Anthropolgy

Theme I: Childhood